TRACING YOUR IRISH ANCESTORS: THE COMPLETE GUIDE
Second Edition

TRACING YOUR IRISH ANCESTORS

The Complete Guide

SECOND EDITION

John Grenham

Published in Ireland by Gill & Macmillan Ltd.
Goldenbridge, Dublin 8, Ireland

Second edition published in the USA and Canada, 1999,
by Genealogical Publishing Co., Inc.
1001 N. Calvert St., Baltimore, Md. 21202
Published by arrangement with Gill & Macmillan Ltd.

Library of Congress Catalogue Card Number 92–74687
International Standard Book Number 0–8063–1617–9

For Doireann and Eoin

CONTENTS

PART 3 ◆ A REFERENCE GUIDE

13. ROMAN CATHOLIC REGISTERS

LIST OF ILLUSTRATIONS

ACKNOWLEDGMENTS

My greatest debt is to Mr Donal Begley, former Chief Herald of Ireland; without his encouragement and endless patience this work would never have been started. I also owe a great deal to the other members and former members of staff at the Genealogical Office, in particular Colette O'Flaherty, Bernard Devaney and the late Willie Buckley, and the Deputy Chief Herald, Mr Fergus Gillespie. My former colleagues in Hibernian Research, Tom Lindert, Anne Brennan, Paul Gorry, Eileen O'Byrne and Eilis Ellis have all again generously shared their knowledge and experience, and contributed very welcome advice and suggestions. I am also grateful to the staff of the National Library, the General Register Office, the Public Record Office of Northern Ireland and the National Archives for all their help to me over the years; I am particularly indebted to Aideen Ireland of the National Archives for her help in correcting some of the mistakes in the first edition. The member centres of the Irish Family History Foundation were also of great assistance, especially Dr Chris O'Mahony of Limerick Archives, Sean Ó Suileabháin of Leitrim County Library, Brian Mitchell of Derry Inner City Trust, and Theo McMahon of Monaghan Ancestral Research, as was the late Noel Reid of the Irish Family History Society. I owe special thanks to my father, Seán Grenham, who drew the parish maps, and to Jonathan Hession, who took the photographs and helped out with rest and recreation. Needless to say, none of those who helped me has any responsibility for the errors and omissions: these are all my own.

ABBREVIATIONS

AA	Armagh Ancestry
AH	*Analecta Hibernica*
BFA	British Film Area
C of I	Church of Ireland
CCAP	Cork City Ancestral Project
CGC	Clare Genealogy Centre
CGP	Carlow Genealogy Project
CHGP	Cavan Heritage and Genealogy Centre
DA	Donegal Ancestry
DHG	Dublin Heritage Group
DLRHS	Dún Laoghaire Rathdown Heritage Society
DSHC	Dún na Sí Heritage Centre
EGFHS	East Galway Family History Society Ltd
FHP	Fingal Heritage Project
GFHSW	Galway Family History Society West Ltd
GO	Genealogical Office
GRO	General Register Office
HW	Heritage World
IA	*The Irish Ancestor*
IG	*The Irish Genealogist*
IGRS	Irish Genealogical Research Society
IMA	Irish Midlands Ancestry
IMC	Irish Manuscripts Commission
Ir.	Irish (National Library of Ireland call number prefix)
IUP	Irish University Press
J	Joly Collection pamphlet (National Library of Ireland)
JCHAS	*Journal of the Cork Historical & Archaeological Society*
JCLAHS	*Journal of the County Louth Archaeological and Historical Society*
JGAHS	*Journal of the Galway Archaeological and Historical Society*
JKAHS	*Journal of the Kerry Archaeological & Historical Society*
JKAS	*Journal of the Kildare Archaeological Society*
JNMAS	*Journal of the North Munster Archaeological Society*
JPRS	*Journal of the Parish Register Society*
JRSAI	*Journal of the Royal Society of Antiquaries of Ireland*
KAS	Kilkenny Archaeological Society
KCL	Kildare County Library
KGC	Killarney Genealogical Centre
KHGS	Kildare Heritage & Genalogical Society Co. Ltd
LA	Limerick Archives
LC	Local custody
LCL	Leitrim County Library
LDS	Latter-Day Saints
LGC	Longford Genealogical Centre

LHC	Leitrim Heritage Centre
MAR	Monaghan Ancestral Research
MHC	Mallow Heritage Centre
MHC	Meath Heritage Centre
MNFHRC	Mayo North Family History Research Centre
MSFRC	Mayo South Family Research Centre
NAI	National Archives of Ireland
NIFHS	North of Ireland Family History Society
NLI	National Library of Ireland
O'K	*O'Kief, Coshe Mang etc.* (ed. Albert Casey) NLI Ir. 94145 c 12
Ph.	Phillimore publication
Pr. pr.	Privately printed
Pos.	Positive (National Library of Ireland microfilm)
Pres.	Presbyterian
PRIA	Proceedings of the Royal Irish Academy
PRO	Public Record Office (London)
PRONI	Public Record Office of Northern Ireland
PRS	Parish Register Society Publication
RC	Roman Catholic
RCBL	Representative Church Body Library
RDKPRI	Report of the Deputy Keeper of Public Records of Ireland
RHGC	Roscommon Heritage and Genealogy Centre
RIA	Royal Irish Academy
SHGC	Sligo Heritage and Genealogical Centre
TCD	Trinity College Dublin
TGC	The Genealogy Centre, Derry
THU	Tipperary Heritage Unit
UHF	Ulster Historical Foundation
UHGGN	Ulster Historical and Genealogical Guild Newsletter
WCHC	West Cork Heritage Centre
WCL	Westmeath County Library
WH	Waterford Heritage Ltd
WHP	Wicklow Heritage Centre
WSIAHSJ	*Waterford and South East of Ireland Archaeological and Historical Society Journal*

PREFACE TO THE SECOND EDITION

The huge growth of interest in Irish local and family history since the first publication of *Tracing Your Irish Ancestors* has brought to light many new sources, and has radically changed the way in which some familiar sources can be approached. These developments are the primary reason for bringing out a second edition. Large changes have also been made in Part 3, the reference guide, with the inclusion of a listing which attempts to give a complete overview of the single most important record category, Roman Catholic parish records. This has meant the exclusion of the detailed account of Genealogical Office manuscripts, as well as the bibliography of printed family histories and the list of Church of Ireland records in Dublin repositories. The Genealogical Office material is now available in *The Genealogical Office* (Irish Manuscripts Commission, Dublin, 1998), and the Church of Ireland records are covered in the late Noel Reid's 'A Table of Church of Ireland Parochial Records' (IFHS, 1994).

The focus of the book has also been expanded somewhat — the first edition was a reflection of my own experience, which was mostly centred on Dublin. This edition tries to give a more accurate account of the holdings of the Belfast repositories and the Family History Library of the Church of Jesus Christ of the Latter-Day Saints.

INTRODUCTION

The aim of this book is to provide a comprehensive guide for anyone wishing to trace their Irish ancestors. Because the individual circumstances of each family can be so different, the areas of research which may be relevant vary widely from case to case. None the less, there are some areas which are important for the vast majority of people, and some which, though less widely relevant, can be extremely important in particular cases. This work is structured to reflect that division, with Part One examining the most basic sources, and Part Two detailing those which have a narrower application. Part Three then consists of a reference guide, to permit quick access to a range of research materials, including county-by-county source-lists, occupations and Roman Catholic records.

How the book is to be used depends very much on individual circumstances. For someone with no experience of genealogical research in Ireland, it would be best to start from this Introduction and work through Part One, leaving Parts Two and Three until the basic materials have been exhausted. Someone who has already covered parish registers, land records, census returns and the state records of births, marriages and deaths may wish to start from Part Two. Others may simply want to use the reference guide. As anyone who regularly uses Irish records will know, however, one of the pleasures of research is the constant discovery of new sources of information, and new aspects of sources long thought to be familiar. The information in this book is the product of more than eighteen years of such discovery in the course of full-time professional research, and it is quite possible that even a hard-bitten veteran will find something new in the account of the basic records given in Part One.

WHERE TO START

The first question asked by anyone embarking on ancestral research is 'What do I need to know before I start?' The answer, unhelpfully, is 'As much as possible.' Although, in the long term, the painstaking examination of original documents can provide much pleasure, in genealogy it is usually better to arrive than to travel hopefully. Theoretically, it is of course possible to start from your own birth and work back through records of births, marriages and deaths, parish records and census records. In practical terms, however, the more that can be gleaned from older family members or from family documents, the better; there is no point in combing through decades of parish records to uncover your great-grandmother's maiden name if you could find it out simply by asking Aunt Agatha. Nor does the information need to be absolutely precise. At this point, quantity is more important than quality. Later on in the research, something that seemed relatively insignificant — the name of a local parish priest, a story of a contested will, someone's unusual occupation, even a postmark — may be a vital clue enabling you to follow the family further back. In any case, whether or not such information eventually turns out to be useful, it will certainly be of interest, helping to flesh out the picture of earlier generations. For most people, the spur to starting research is curiosity about their own family, and the kind of anecdotal information provided by the family itself rarely emerges from the documents.

To enable you to use the records to their fullest, three kinds of information are vital: dates, names, and places (dates of emigration, births, marriages and deaths; names of parents, siblings, cousins, aunts, in-laws; addresses, townland names, parishes, towns, counties). Needless to say, not all of this is essential, and absolute accuracy is not vital to start out with. A general location and siblings' names can be used to uncover parents' names and addresses, and their parents' names. A precise name and a date can be used to unlock all the other records. Even the name alone, if it is sufficiently unusual, can sometimes be enough. In general, though, the single most useful piece of information is the precise locality of origin of the family. The county of origin would normally be the minimum information necessary, though in the case of a common surname (of which there are only too many), even this may not be enough. For the descendants of Irish emigrants, the locality is often one of the most difficult things to discover. There are ways of doing this, however, and the best time to do it is generally before starting research in Ireland. The Australian, American and British sources which are most useful for uncovering the locality of origin of Irish emigrants are detailed at the end of this Introduction.

The only cast-iron rule in carrying out research is that you should start from what you know, and use that to find out more. Every family's circumstances are different, and where your research will lead you depends very much on where you start from. Thus, for example, knowing where a family lived around the turn of the century will allow you to uncover a census return with the ages of the individuals, leading to birth or baptismal records giving parents' names and residence, leading on in turn to early land records, which may permit the identification of generations before the start of parish records. At each stage of such research, what the next step should be is determined by what you have found out. Each discovery is a stepping-stone to the next. Because of this, it is simply not possible to lay down a route which will serve everyone. It is possible, however, to say that there is no point in taking, say, a seventeenth-century pedigree and trying to extend it forward to connect with your family. Although there may very well be a connection, the only way to prove it is in expanding your own family information, working backwards.

WHAT YOU CAN EXPECT TO FIND

What you will uncover depends on the quality of the surviving records for the area and, again, on what you start out with. In the majority of cases, that is, for the descendants of Catholic tenant farmers, the limit is generally the starting date of the local Catholic parish records, which varies widely from place to place. It would be unusual, however, for records of such a family to go back much earlier than the 1780s, and for most people the early 1800s is more likely to be the limit. In Gaelic culture, genealogy was of crucial importance, but the collapse of that culture in the seventeenth century, and the subsequent impoverishment and oppression of the eighteenth century have left a gulf which is almost unbridgeable. This much said, exceptions immediately spring to mind. One Australian family, starting only with the name of their great-grandfather, his occupation, and the date of his departure from Ireland, uncovered enough information through parish registers and state records of deaths, marriages and births to link him incontestably to the Garveys of Mayo, for whom an established pedigree is registered in the Genealogical Office stretching back to the twelfth century. Another family, American, knowing only a general location in Ireland and a marriage that took place before emigration, discovered that marriage in the pedigree of the McDermotts of Coolavin, which is factually verified as far back as the eleventh century. Discoveries like this are rare, however, and much likelier in the case of the Anglo-Irish than for those of Gaelic or Scots Presbyterian extraction.

Whatever the outcome, genealogical research offers pleasures and insights which are unique. The desire which drives it is simple and undeniable: it is the curiosity of the child who asks, 'Where did I come from?' All history starts from here, and genealogy is the most basic form of history, tracing the continual cycle of family growth and decay, uncovering the individual strands of relationship and experience which weave together to form the great patterns of historical change. Reconstructing the details of our own family history is a way of understanding, immediately and personally, the connection of the present with the past, a way of understanding ourselves.

US SOURCES TO IDENTIFY IRISH PLACE OF ORIGIN

■ *Naturalisation Records* These may contain the date and place of birth, occupation, place of residence and the name of the ship on which the immigrant arrived. They are unlikely to give a precise place of origin in Ireland. The records are still for the most part in the courts where the naturalisation proceedings took place. Some records are now in Federal Record Centres. Indexes for the states of Maine, Massachusetts, New Hampshire and Rhode Island before 1906 are available at the National Archives, Washington.

■ *Cemetery and Burial Records* There are two kinds of potentially valuable records, gravestone inscriptions and sextons' records. These vary enormously in usefulness, but may sometimes specify the exact place of origin.

■ *Immigration Records & Passenger Lists* These are now mostly in the National Archives in Washington. Customs Passenger Lists, dating from 1820, give only the country of origin. Immigration Passenger Lists, from 1883, include details of the last place of residence. See also Chapter 7 for details of other sources.

■ *Military Records* Depending on place or branch of service, these may specify the place, or at least the county of origin. See *Guide to Genealogical Records in the National Archives* by Meredith S. Colket Jr and Frank E. Bridges (1964).

■ *Church Records* These may in some cases, particularly for the marriages of recently arrived immigrants, include details of the Irish place of origin of the persons recorded. Most Catholic records are still in the parishes. The records of other denominations may be held locally, or deposited with a variety of institutions, including public libraries, universities or diocesan archives.

■ *Vital records* Death records in particular may be of value, since they generally supply parents' names.

CANADIAN SOURCES TO IDENTIFY IRISH PLACE OF ORIGIN

■ *National and Provincial Archives* The vast bulk of information of genealogical interest can be found in the National and Provincial Archives of Canada, which are familiar with the needs of genealogical research and very helpful. The National Archives (395 Wellington Street, Ottawa ON K1A 0N3 (Tel. 613–995–5138) publish a useful 20 page booklet *Tracing Your Ancestors in Canada* which is available by post. Some of the information held in the Provincial Archives, in particular the census records, is also to be found in Ottawa, but in general the Provincial Archives have a broader range of information relating to their particular areas.

■ *Civil Records* In general the original registers of births, marriages and deaths, which have widely varying starting dates, are to be found in the offices of the Provincial Registrars General, although microfilm copies of some may also be found in Provincial Archives.

■ *Census Records* Country-wide censuses are available for 1851, 1861, 1871, 1881 and 1891. There are, however, many local returns available for earlier years which record a wide variety of information. The largest collection is in the Ottawa National Archives.

■ *Other Sources* Cemetery and burial records, gravestone inscriptions, passenger lists, Church registers and land records may all be of value. The best comprehensive guide is in Angus Baxter's *In search of your Canadian roots* (Baltimore, 1989) which gives details of a wide range of records to be found in the National and Provincial Archives.

AUSTRALIAN SOURCES TO IDENTIFY IRISH PLACE OF ORIGIN

■ *Convict Transportation Records* A database index of Dublin Castle records of those transported from Ireland to Australia was presented to Australia as part of the bicentennial celebrations of 1988. It often includes details of the conviction and place of residence. Further information on the records it covers will be found in Chapter 7. It is widely available in the Australian State Archives, in the National Archives and on the Internet at http://www.kst.dit.ie/nat-arch/. Many other classes of record, originating both in Australia and in England, also exist and can be found in most Australian repositories.

■ *Assisted Immigration Records* A detailed record was kept of those who availed of assisted passages to Australia. See the NSW State Archives *Guide to Shipping and Free Passenger Lists*.

■ *Civil Records* Australian state death records give a wealth of family detail, in most cases including precise places of origin. Marriage records also supply places of birth and parents' names.

BRITISH SOURCES TO IDENTIFY IRISH PLACE OF ORIGIN

ENGLAND AND WALES

■ *Civil Registration* of births, marriages and deaths began in 1837 and records the same details as those given in Irish records (see Chapter 1). Unfortunately, the marriage records very rarely give exact Irish addresses for parents.

■ *Census Records* Six sets of census returns are available between 1841 and 1891. Again it is rare to find a precise place of birth in Ireland recorded, though the county is sometimes given. Both census and civil records are available at the Family Record Centre, 1 Myddelton Street, London EC1R 1UW, Tel: +44 181 392 5300.

■ *Church Records* Marriage records for recent immigrants may give the place of origin in Ireland.

SCOTLAND

■ *Civil Registration* of births, marriages and deaths began in 1855, and recorded substantially more detail than in Ireland or England. In particular, birth records show a place and date of marriage, and death records supply parents' names.

■ *Census Returns* are similar to those for England and Wales. A computerised index to the 1891 census is available.

Civil and census records are available at the General Register Office (New Register House), Princes Street, Edinburgh EH1 3YT. The Scottish Record Office is next door, and holds a vast array of relevant archive material. Cecil Sinclair's *Tracing Your Scottish Ancestors: a guide to ancestry research in the Scottish Record Office* (Edinburgh 1990, Revised Edition 1997) is the standard guide.

THE CHURCH OF JESUS CHRIST OF THE LATTER-DAY SAINTS

Because of the central importance of the family in its teachings, the Church of Jesus Christ of the Latter-Day Saints, also known as the Mormon Church, places great emphasis on family history. For many decades, the Family History Library in Salt Lake City has been collecting copies of records of genealogical value as aids to its members' research. The collection is now extraordinary; its Irish section includes virtually all of the General Register Office indexes and registers, a large proportion of church records, the records of the Genealogical Office and the Registry of Deeds, and much more.

To work on these records it is not necessary to visit the Library in person. Every Mormon church has a family history section open to non-church members which can request copies of any of the microfilms from Salt Lake City — in effect providing a world-wide system of access to copies of the original records. To those for whom a research visit to Ireland is impractical, the LDS Family History Centres are almost as good.

USING THE INTERNET

Genealogy is reputed to be the second largest use of the Internet, but the speed of change means that any specific information given will probably have become obsolete in a year or so. Accordingly, only a few general pointers are offered.

First, although there is a huge amount of information available, a great deal of it is poorly organised and some is suspect. Be prepared to follow many threads without much of substance to show for it. Contrary to many researchers' expectations, very little original archive material is actually searchable online as yet, though this will certainly change. The single most useful resource at the moment is the National Archives of Ireland database index to Irish transportation records at http://www.kst.dit.ie/nat-arch/.

The most comprehensive guide to genealogy resources in general is 'Cyndi's List', an enormous and well-organised listing of virtually everything to do with online family history, at *http://www.CyndisList.com*. For specifically Irish material, the largest online guide, in which I should declare a personal interest, is part of the Irish Times site, at *http://www.irish-times.com/ancestor*.

PART 1 ◆ MAJOR SOURCES

1. CIVIL RECORDS

PART 1

State registration of non-Catholic marriages began in Ireland in 1845. All births, deaths and marriages have been registered in Ireland since 1864. In order to appreciate what precisely these records consist of, it is necessary to have some idea at least of how registration began. It was, in fact, an offshoot of the Victorian public health system, in turn based on the Poor Law, an attempt to provide some measure of relief for the most destitute. Between 1838 and 1852, 163 workhouses were built throughout the country, each at the centre of an area known as a Poor Law Union. The workhouses were normally situated in a large market town, and the Poor Law Union comprised the town and its catchment area, with the result that the unions in many cases ignored the existing boundaries of parish and county. This had consequences for research which we shall see below. In the 1850s, a large-scale public health system was created, based on the areas covered by the Poor Law Unions. Each union was divided into Dispensary Districts, with an average of six to seven districts per union, and a medical officer, normally a doctor, was given responsibility for public health in each district. When the registration of all births, deaths and marriages then began in 1864, these dispensary districts also became registrar's districts, with a registrar responsible for collecting the registrations within this district. In most cases, the medical officer for the dispensary district now also acted as the registrar for the same area, but this did not invariably happen. The superior of the registrar was the superintendent registrar, responsible for all the registers within the old Poor Law Union. The returns for the entire Poor Law Union (also known both as the Superintendent Registrar's District and, simply, the Registration District) were indexed and collated centrally, and master indexes for the entire country were produced at the General Register Office in Dublin. These are the indexes which are now used for public research.

Because of the history of the system, responsibility for registration still rests with the Department of Health. The arrangement at present is that the local health boards hold the original registers, with the General Register Office, at 8–11 Lombard St, Dublin 2, holding the master indexes to all 32 counties up to 1921, and to the 26 counties of the Republic of Ireland after that date. For Northern Ireland, from 1921, the indexes and registers are held at Oxford House, Chichester St, Belfast.

Under the original system, the local registrars forwarded their records to Dublin, where they were copied and then returned to the local office. As well as the master indexes for the entire country, the General Register Office also contains microfilms of all of these copy registers, and is the only part of the registration system which permits comprehensive public research. The indexes are available to the public on the first floor of 8 Lombard St, at a fee of £1.50 per five years searched, or £12 for a

1

general search. It is important to note that only the indexes are open to the public; to obtain the full information contained in the original register entry, it is necessary to purchase a print-out from the microfilm, at £1.50 per entry. These print-outs are supplied for information only, and have no legal standing. Full certificates, for use in obtaining passports or in testamentary transactions, cost £5.50. Limited research, covering five years of the indexes, is carried out by the staff in response to postal queries only, for the same fee, £5.50.

It is also possible to carry out research in the local registrar's offices around the country, although this is at the discretion of the local officials. In some cases, particularly for common surnames, this can be the only way to reconstruct a whole family, since the research is on the original registers, rather than indexes. Some of the local heritage centres, including Clare, Derry, Mayo and Tipperary South, now have database transcripts of these local registers. Only commissioned research is possible.

INFORMATION GIVEN

One of the peculiarities of the system of registration is that, although the local registrars were responsible for the registers themselves, the legal obligation to register births, deaths and marriages actually rested with the public, and was enforced with hefty fines. The classes of people required to carry out registration in each of the three categories is given in what follows, along with a detailed account of the information they were required to supply. It should be remembered that not all of this information is relevant to genealogical research.

BIRTHS

Persons required to register births were:
1. the parent or parents, or in the case of death or inability of the parent or parents
2. the occupier of the house or tenement in which the child was born, or
3. the nurse, or
4. any person present at the birth of the child.

The information they were required to supply was:
1. the date and place of birth;
2. the name (if any);
3. the sex;
4. the name, surname and dwelling place of the father;
5. the name, surname, maiden surname and dwelling place of the mother;
6. the rank, profession or occupation of the father.

The informant and the registrar were both required to sign each entry, which was also to include the date of registration, the residence of the informant and his or her 'qualification' (for example, 'present at birth'). Notice to the registrar of the birth was to be given within 21 days, and full details within three months. It should be noted that it was not obligatory to register a first name for the child. The very small proportion for which no first name was supplied appear in the index as, for example, 'Kelly (male)' or 'Murphy (female)'.

INDEX to BIRTHS REGISTERED in IRELAND in 1866.

General Register Office births index
(Courtesy of the National Library of Ireland)

DEATHS

Persons required to register deaths were:
1.   some person present at death; or
2.   some person in attendance during the last illness of the deceased; or
3.   the occupier of the house or tenement where the death took place; or
4.   someone else residing in the the house or tenement where the death took place; or
5.   any person present at, or having knowledge of the circumstances of, the death.

The information they were required to supply was:
1.   the date and place of death;
2.   the name and surname of the deceased;
3.   the sex of the deceased;
4.   the condition of the deceased as to marriage;
5.   the age of the deceased at last birthday;
6.   the rank, profession or occupation of the deceased;
7.   the certified cause of death, and the duration of the final illness.

Again, the informant and the registrar were both required to sign each entry, which was also to include the date of registration, the residence of the informant and his or her 'qualification' (for example, 'present at death'). Notice to the registrar of the death was to be given within 7 days, and full details within 14 days.

MARRIAGES

From 1864, any person whose marriage was to be celebrated by a Catholic clergyman was required to have the clergyman fill out a certificate containing the information detailed below, and forward it within three days of the marriage to the registrar. In practice, as had already been the case for non-Catholic marriages from 1845, the clergyman simply kept blank copies of these certificates, filled them in after the ceremony, and forwarded them to the registrar. It is still important to remember, though, that legal responsibility for the registration actually rested with the parties marrying, not the clergyman.

The information to be supplied was:
1.   the date when married;
2.   the names and surnames of each of the parties marrying;
3.   their respective ages;
4.   their condition (i.e. bachelor, spinster, widow, widower);
5.   their rank, profession or occupation;
6.   their residences at the time of marriage;
7.   the name and surname of the fathers of each of the parties;
8.   the rank, profession or occupation of the fathers of each of the parties.

The certificate, which stated where the ceremony had been performed, was signed by the clergyman, the parties marrying, and two witnesses.

GENEALOGICAL RELEVANCE

From a genealogical point of view, only the following information is of genuine interest:

■ *Births:* the name, the date of birth, the place of birth, the name, surname and dwelling place of the father, the name, surname and dwelling place of the mother, and, occasionally, the name, residence and qualification of the informant

■ *Marriages:* parish in which the marriage took place; names, ages, residences and occupations of the persons marrying; names and occupations of their fathers.

■ *Deaths:* place of death; age at death and, occasionally, the name, residence and qualification of the informant.

Of the three categories, the most useful is probably the marriage entry, both because it provides fathers' names, thus giving a direct link to the preceding generation, and because it is the easiest to identify from the indexes, as we shall see below. Birth entries are much more difficult to identify correctly from the indexes without precise information about date and place, and even with such information the high concentrations of people of the same surname within particular localities of the country can make it difficult to be sure that a particular birth registration is the relevant one. Unlike many other countries, death records in Ireland are not very useful for genealogical purposes; there was no obligation to record family information, and the 'age at death' is often very imprecise. This much said, these records can sometimes be of value. The 'person present at death' was often a family member, and the relationship is sometimes specified in the register entry. Even the age recorded may be useful, since it at least gives an idea of how old the person was thought to be by family or neighbours.

A general word of warning about civil registration is necessary: a certain proportion of all three categories simply went unregistered. It is impossible to be sure how much is not there, since the thoroughness of local registration depended very much on local conditions and on the individuals responsible; but experience in cross-checking from other sources such as parish and census records suggests that as much as 10 to 15 per cent of marriages and births simply do not appear in the registers.

RESEARCH IN THE INDEXES

In carrying out research on all three areas, a large measure of scepticism is necessary with regard to the dates of births, marriages and deaths reported by family members before 1900. This is especially true for births: the ages given in census returns, for example, are almost always inaccurate, and round figures — 50, 60, 70 — should be treated with particular caution. The true date of birth is almost always well before the one reported, sometimes by as much as fifteen years. Why this should be so is a matter for speculation, but it seems unlikely that vanity or mendacity are to blame. It would appear more probable that, up to the start of this century, very few people actually knew their precise date of birth. Since, at least after middle age, almost no one feels as old as they actually are, a guess will usually produce an underestimate. Whatever the explanation, charitable or otherwise, it is always wiser to search a range of the indexes before the reported date, rather than after.

From 1864 to 1877 the indexes consist of a single yearly volume in each category — births, marriages and deaths — covering the entire country, and recording all names in a straightforward alphabetical arrangement. The same arrangement also applies to the non-Catholic marriages registered from 1845. From 1878, the yearly volume is divided into four quarters, with each quarter covering three months and indexed separately. This means that a search for a name in, for example, the 1877 births index means looking in one place in the index, while it is necessary to check four different places in the 1878 index, one in each of the four quarters. From 1903, in the case of births only, the indexes once again cover the entire year, and only from this year also supply the mother's maiden surname. In all three categories, each index entry gives surname, first name, registration district, volume and page number. The deaths indexes also give the reported age at death. The 'volume and page number' simply make up the reference for the original register entry, necessary in order to obtain a photocopy of the full information given in that entry. The remaining three items, surname, first name and registration district, are dealt with in detail below.

Surname

The order followed in the indexes is strictly alphabetical, but it is always necessary to keep possible variants of the surname in mind. In the late nineteenth century, when a large majority of the population was illiterate, the precise spelling of their surname was a matter of indifference to most people. Thus members of the same family may be registered as, for example, Kilfoyle, Gilfoyle or Guilfoile. The question of variants is particularly important for names beginning with 'O' or 'Mac'. Until the start of the Gaelic revival at the end of the last century, these prefixes were treated as entirely optional and, in the case of the 'O's particularly, more often omitted than included. Until well into the twentieth century, for instance, almost all of the O'Briens are recorded under 'Brien' or 'Bryan'. Before starting a search in the indexes, therefore, it is essential to have as clear an idea as possible of the variants to be checked. Otherwise it may be necessary to cover the same period as many as three or four times.

First name

Among the vast majority of the population, the range of first names in use in the nineteenth century was severely limited. Apart from some localised names — 'Cornelius' in south Munster, 'Crohan' in the Caherdaniel area of the Iveragh peninsula, 'Sabina' in the east Galway/north Roscommon area — the anglicisation of the earlier Gaelic names was restrictive and unimaginative. John, Patrick, Michael, Mary and Bridget occur with almost unbelievable frequency in all parts of the country. Combined with the intensely local nature of surnames, reflecting the earlier tribal areas of the country, this can present intense difficulties when using the indexes. For example, a single quarter of 1881, from January to March, might contain twenty or more John (O')Reilly (or Riley) registrations, all in the same registration district of Co. Cavan. A further obstacle is the fact that it is very rare for more than one first name to be registered. Thus someone known to the family as

John James (O')Reilly will almost certainly appear in the index as a simple John. It is of course possible to purchase photocopies of all of the original register entries, but unless some other piece of information such as the parents' names or the townland address can be used to cross-check, it will almost certainly not be possible to identify which, if any, of the original register entries is the relevant one. This uncertainty is compounded still further by the persistent imprecision regarding ages and dates of birth, which means that over the seven or eight year period when the relevant birth could have taken place, there might be fifty or sixty births of the same name in the one county. One way to surmount the problem, if the precise district is known, is to examine the original registers themselves to build a picture of all families in which the relevant name occurs. As already mentioned, the originals are still kept in the local registrars' offices. Although the situation varies from district to district, people visiting the offices in person are usually allowed to examine the original books. The relevant addresses can be found in local telephone directories, under the Health Board. Even in the country-wide indexes, however, despite all of the problems there are a number of ways in which the births indexes can be used successfully, by narrowing the area and period to be searched with information obtained from other sources, as we shall see.

Registration District

As a result of the original arrangements for administering the system, the registration districts used were, and still are, largely identical with the old Poor Law Unions. Since these were based on natural catchment areas, normally consisting of a large market town and its rural hinterland, rather than on the already existing administrative divisions of townland, parish and county, registration districts for births, marriages and deaths cut right across these earlier boundaries, a fact which can be very significant for research. Thus, for example, Waterford registration district, centred in the town of Waterford, also takes in a large part of rural south Co. Kilkenny. The only comprehensive guide to which towns and townlands are contained in each registration district is to be found in a series of pamphlets produced in the nineteenth century by the Registrar-General's Office for the use of each of the local registrars. These are collected as *Townlands in Poor-law Unions* (repr. 1997, Higginson, Salem Ma.) copies of which can be found in the National Library (reference: Ir. 9141 b 35) or in the reading room of the National Archives. This is particularly useful when a problem arises in identifying a variant version of a townland name given in the original register entry for a marriage, birth or death. By scanning the lists of townlands in the relevant district in which the entry is recorded, it is almost always possible to identify the standard version of the name and, from this, go on to census, parish and land records. To go in the other direction, to find out what registration district a particular town or townland is in, the standard source is the *Alphabetical Index to the Towns, Townlands and Parishes of Ireland*. Three editions of this were published, based on the census returns for 1851, 1871 and 1901. In the first two, the registration district is recorded as the Poor Law Union; in the 1901 index it does not appear in the body of the work, but may be found as an appendix. Copies of these can be found on open access in the National Library, the National Archives, the General Register Office itself, or in any library. If the original townland or address of the family being researched is known, and the search narrowed to a single registration district, then at least some of the problems in picking out the relevant entry, in the births indexes particularly, can be significantly reduced.

RESEARCH TECHNIQUES

Births

As pointed out above, it is important to approach the birth indexes with as much information as possible from other sources. If the birth took place between 1864 and 1880, the family was Catholic and the relevant area is known, it may be best to try to identify a baptism from parish records first, and in many cases, if information rather than a certificate is the aim of the research, the parish record itself will be enough. If the area is known, but not the date, it may be useful to search the 1901 and 1911 census returns to obtain at least an approximate age and, hence, date of birth. If the names of siblings and the order of their birth are known, but the area and date are not, it may be necessary to search a wide range of years in the indexes, noting all births of the names which occur in the family, and then try to work out which births of the relevant names occur in the right order in the same registration district. If the name is unusual enough, of course, none of this may be necessary. In Ireland, however, few of us are lucky enough to have an ancestor called Horace Freke-Blood or Euphemia Thackaberry.

Marriages

As long as care is taken over the question of surname variants, and the names of both parties are known, research in the marriage indexes is straightforward. If two people married each other, then obviously the registration district, volume and page number references for them in the indexes have to be the same. It is simply necessary to cross-check the two names in the indexes, working back from the approximate date of birth of the eldest child if this is known, until two entries are found in which all three references correspond. Marriage records are especially important in the early years of civil registration, since they record the names of the fathers of people born *c.*1820 to *c.*1840, as well as their approximate ages, thus providing evidence which can be used to establish earlier generations in parish records. For non-Catholic families, the value of these records is even greater, since the records of non-Catholic marriages start in 1845.

Deaths

As in the case of births, it is essential to uncover as much information as possible from other sources before starting a search of the death indexes. Thus, if a date of birth is known from parish or other records, the 'age at death' given in the index along with the registration district provides at least a rough guide as to whether or not the death recorded is the relevant one. If the location of a family farm is known, the approximate date of death can often be worked out from the changes in occupier recorded in the Valuation Books of the Land Valuation Office (see Chapter 4). Similarly, if the family possessed property, the Will Calendars of the National Archives after 1858 (see Chapter 5) can be the easiest way to pinpoint the precise date of death. With such information, it is then usually a simple matter to pick out the relevant entry from the indexes. Information from a marriage entry may also sometimes be useful; along with the names of the fathers of the parties marrying, the register entry sometimes also specifies that one or both of the fathers is deceased. There is no rule about this, however. The fact that a father is recorded as, say, 'John Murphy, labourer', does not necessarily mean that he was alive at the time of the marriage. If an individual is recorded as deceased, this does at least provide an end point for any search for his death entry. As already pointed out, however, death records give no information on preceding generations, and only occasionally name a surviving family member.

LIVING RELATIVES

It is very difficult to use the records of the General Register Office to trace descendants, rather than forebears, of a particular family. As pointed out above, the birth indexes after 1902 do record the mother's maiden name, as well as the name and surname of the child, so that it can be possible to trace all the births of a particular family from that date forward. Uncovering the subsequent marriages of those children without knowing the names of their spouses is a much harder proposition, however. To take one example, the likely range of years of marriage for a Michael O'Brien born in 1905 would be 1925 to 1940; there are certainly hundreds of marriages recorded in the indexes under that name. One could, of course, purchase copies of all of the original register entries in the hope that one entry might show the relevant address and father's name, and then investigate births of that marriage, but in most cases the work involved makes the task impractical. There are, however, other ways of tracking descendants through land, census, voters' and, sometimes, parish records (Chapters 2, 3 and 4).

LATE REGISTRATIONS, ARMY RECORDS ETC.

Late Registrations

A significant proportion of all births, marriages and deaths were simply not registered, as mentioned above. When the individuals concerned, or their relatives, later needed a certificate for official purposes, it became necessary to register the event. The index references for these late registrations are included in the volume for the year in which the event took place. Thus, for example, the index reference for someone born in 1880 but whose birth was not registered until 1900 is to be found in the index for 1880. In the case of births and deaths, these references are indexed separately from the main body of the index, at the back of the volume. For marriages, late registrations are written in by hand at the relevant point in the main body of the index. Although the chances of finding a missing registration among these are quite slim, it is still necessary to include them in any thorough search of the indexes.

Maritime Records

From 1864 up to the present, the General Register Office has kept a separate 'Marine Register' of births and deaths of Irish subjects which took place at sea. From 1886 only, a printed index to this register is bound into the back of the births and deaths index for each year. For earlier registers, the indexes have to be requested from the staff in the office. No separate register was kept for marriages at sea.

Army Records

The Births, Deaths and Marriages (Army) Act of 1879 required these events to be registered with the Office of the Registrar-General in Dublin, where they affected Irish subjects serving in the British Army abroad. Separate indexes, bound into the backs of the main yearly indexes, start from 1888 and continue until 1930 for births, and 1931 for marriages and for deaths. The deaths index for 1902 also contains an index to 'Deaths of Irish Subjects pertaining to the South African War (1898–1902)'.

The Foreign Register

From 1864, the General Register Office was required to keep a separate register of births of Irish subjects abroad, where such births were notified to the relevant British consul. There is no index to this register, which is small, and is not available in the public research room. It may be requested from the staff of the office.

The Schulze Register

The General Register Office also holds the 'General Index to Baptisms and Marriages purported to have been celebrated by the Rev. J.G.F. Schulze 1806–1837'. This records 55 baptisms and *c*.14,000 marriages celebrated in Dublin by this clergyman without a licence. When some of the marriages were later challenged in court, they were held to be legal, and the volume was acquired by the Register Office. The bulk of the marriages, celebrated at the German Lutheran Church in Poolbeg St, Dublin, are for the years 1825 to 1837, and record only the names of the contracting parties.

USING CIVIL RECORDS WITH OTHER SOURCES

Some of the areas in which information from other sources may be used to simplify research in civil records have already been outlined. What follows is an expanded guide to the ways in which civil records can supplement, or be supplemented by, those other sources.

Births

Ages recorded in 1901 and 1911 census returns (see Chapter 2) can be used to narrow the range of years to be searched. If the birth registration is uncovered first, it records the precise residence of the parents, which can then lead to the relevant census returns, providing fuller information on other members of the family.

Marriages

The 1911 census records the number of years a couple have been married, the number of children born, and the number of those children still living. This information is obviously very useful in narrowing the range of years to be searched for a particular marriage. In the case of names which are common in a particular area, the fathers' names supplied in the marriage record are often the only firm evidence with which to identify the relevant baptismal record in the parish registers. Once a marriage has been located in civil records, thus showing the relevant parish, it is always worthwhile to check the church record of the same marriage. As church marriage registers were standardised from the 1860s on, they became more informative, in many cases supplying the names, addresses and occupations of both the mother and father of the parties marrying. In the case of most Dublin Catholic parishes, this information is recorded from around 1856.

Deaths

The records of the Land Valuation Office (Chapter 4) or the testamentary records of the National Archives (Chapter 5) can be used to pinpoint the year of death, thus making a successful search more likely. The place of death given, if it is not the home of the deceased person, may be the home of a relative. This can be investigated firstly through land records (Chapter 4), and then through parish and census records, and may provide further information on other branches of the family.

2. CENSUS RECORDS

1. COUNTRY-WIDE

Full government censuses were taken of the whole island in 1821, 1831, 1841, 1851, 1861, 1871, 1881, 1891, 1901 and 1911. The first four, for 1821, 1831, 1841 and 1851, were largely destroyed in 1922 in the fire at the Public Record Office; surviving fragments are detailed below. Those for 1861, 1871, 1881 and 1891 were completely destroyed earlier by order of the government. This means that the earliest surviving comprehensive returns are for 1901 and 1911. Because of this, the normal rule that census returns should not be available to the public for 100 years has been suspended in the Republic of Ireland, and the original returns for both 1901 and 1911 can be consulted in the National Archives. A full microfilm copy of the 1901 census is available at the LDS Family History Library in Salt Lake City. Indexes, published or database, are available for the 1901 returns of some counties; these are noted under the relevant county in Chapter 12. Copies of the 1901 returns for the six counties now in Northern Ireland are available at the Public Record Office of Northern Ireland.

1901 AND 1911

A. *Information Given*

Although these returns are obviously very late for most purposes, the information they contain can still be extremely useful. The 1901 returns record the following:
* name;
* relationship to the head of the household;
* religion;
* literacy;
* occupation;
* age;
* marital status;
* county of birth;
* ability to speak English or Irish.

The returns also record details of the houses, giving the number of rooms, outhouses, and windows, and the type of roof. Members of the family not present when the census was taken are not given. The same information was collected in 1911, with one important addition: married women were required to state the number of years they had been married, the number of children born alive, and the number of children still living. Unfortunately, widows were not required to give this information, although a good number obliged in any case. Only the initials, not the full names, of policemen and inmates of mental hospitals are recorded.

CENSUS OF IRELAND, 1901.

FORM A.

(Two Examples of the mode of filling up this Table are given on the other side.)

No. on Form B. 3

RETURN of the MEMBERS of this FAMILY and their VISITORS, BOARDERS, SERVANTS, &c., who slept or abode in this House on the night of SUNDAY, the 31st of MARCH, 1901.

No.	NAME and SURNAME	RELATION to Head of Family	RELIGIOUS PROFESSION	EDUCATION	AGE	SEX	RANK, PROFESSION, OR OCCUPATION	MARRIAGE	WHERE BORN	IRISH LANGUAGE	If Deaf and Dumb; Dumb only; Blind; Imbecile or Idiot; or Lunatic
1	Bernard McEnert	Head of Family	Roman Catholic	Read & Write	50	M	Farmer	Married	Co. Cavan	Irish & English	—
2	Mary McEnert	Wife	do. Catholic	Read & Write	48	F	Farmer's Wife	Married	Co. Cavan	Irish & English	—
3	Maria McEnert	Daughter	do. Catholic	Read & Write	23	F	Farmer's Daughter	Not Married	Co. Cavan	English	—
4	Ellen McEnert	Daughter	do. Catholic	Read & Write	19	F	Farmer's Daughter	Not Married	Co. Cavan	English	—
5	John McEnert	Nephew	do. Catholic	Read & Write	6	M	Scholar	Not Married	Co. Cavan	English	—
6											
7											
8											
9											
10											
11											
12											
13											
14											
15											

I hereby certify, as required by the Act 63 Vic., cap. 6, s. 6 (1), that the foregoing Return is correct, according to the best of my knowledge and belief.

Michael Gillen *(Signature of Enumerator.)*

I believe the foregoing to be a true Return.

Bernard McEnert *(Signature of Head of Family).*

Form A, 1901 Census
(Courtesy of the National Archives of Ireland)

B. Uses

(I) AGE: The most obviously useful information given in 1901 and 1911 is age; unfortunately, this is also the information which needs to be treated with the most caution. Very few of the ages given in the two sets of returns actually match precisely. In the decade between the two censuses, most people appear to have aged significantly more than ten years. Of the two, 1901 seems to be the less accurate, with widespread underestimation of age. None the less, if used with caution the returns do provide a rough guide to age which can help to narrow the range of years to be searched in earlier civil records of births, marriages and deaths, or in parish records.

(II) LOCATION: When the names of all or most of the family are known, along with the general area, but not the precise locality, it is possible to search all of the returns for that area to identify the relevant family, and thus pinpoint them. This can be particularly useful when the surname is very common: the likelihood of two families of Murphys in the same area repeating all of the children's names is slight.

(III) CROSS-CHECKING: At times, again when a name is common, it is impossible to be sure from information uncovered in civil or parish records that a particular family is the relevant one. In such cases, when details of the subsequent history of the family are known — dates of death or emigration, or siblings' names, for instance — a check of the 1901 or 1911 census for the family can provide useful circumstantial evidence. More often than not, any certainties produced will be negative, but the elimination of false trails is a vital part of any research. An illustration will show why. Peter Barry, born Co. Cork *c*.1880, parents unknown, emigrated to the US in 1897. A search of civil birth records shows four Peter Barrys recorded in the county between 1876 and 1882, with no way of distinguishing which, if any, of them is the relevant one. A search of the 1901 census returns for the addresses given in the four birth entries shows two of the four still living there. These can now be safely eliminated, and research concentrated on the other two families.

(IV) MARRIAGES: The requirement in the 1911 census for married women to supply the number of years of marriage is obviously a very useful aid when subsequently searching civil records for a marriage entry. Even in 1901, the age of the eldest child recorded can give a rough guide to the latest date at which a marriage is likely to have taken place.

(V) LIVING RELATIVES: Children recorded in 1901 and 1911 are the parents or grandparents of people now alive. The ages — generally much more accurate than those given for older members of the family — can be useful in trying to uncover later marriages in civil records. When used together with Land Valuation Office records (see Chapter 4), or the voters' lists of the National Archives, they can provide an accurate picture of the passing of property from one generation to another. Luckily the Irish attitude to land means that it is quite unusual for rural property to pass out of a family altogether.

CENSUS OF IRELAND, 1911.

Two Examples of the mode of filling up this Table are given on the other side.

FORM A.

No. on Form B. 84

RETURN of the MEMBERS of this FAMILY and their VISITORS, BOARDERS, SERVANTS, &c., who slept or abode in this house on the night of SUNDAY, the 2nd of APRIL, 1911.

NAME AND SURNAME		RELATION to Head of Family.	RELIGIOUS PROFESSION.	EDUCATION.	AGE (last Birthday) and SEX.		RANK, PROFESSION, OR OCCUPATION.	PARTICULARS AS TO MARRIAGE.				WHERE BORN.	IRISH LANGUAGE.	If Deaf and Dumb; Dumb only; Blind; Imbecile or Idiot; or Lunatic.
Christian Name.	Surname.				Ages of Males.	Ages of Females.		Whether "Married," "Widower," "Widow," or "Single."	Completed years the present Marriage has lasted.	Total Children born alive.	Children still living.			
1	2	3	4	5	6	7	8	9	10	11	12	13	14	15
Patrick	Herd	Head of Family	Roman Catholic	Read and write	68		Farmer	Widower				County Cavan	Irish and English	
Patrick	Herd	Son	Roman Catholic	Read and write	23		Farmer's Son	Single				County Cavan	English	
Alice	Herd	Daughter	Roman Catholic	Read and write		21		Single				County Cavan	English	
Mary Agnes	Herd	Daughter	Roman Catholic	Read and write		18		Single				County Cavan	English	
John	Herd	Son	Roman Catholic	Read and write	12		Scholar	Single				County Cavan	English	
James	Herd	Son	Roman Catholic	Read and write	10		Scholar	Single				Co. Cavan	English	

I hereby certify, as required by the Act 10 Edw. VII., and 1 Geo. V., cap. 11, that the foregoing Return is correct, according to the best of my knowledge and belief.

Patrick Herd *Signature of Head of Family.*

I believe the foregoing to be a true Return.

Patrick Gee Coy *Signature of Enumerator.*

Form A, 1911 Census
(Courtesy of the National Archives of Ireland)

C. Research Techniques

The basic geographical unit used in carrying out both the 1901 and 1911 censuses is the District Electoral Division, a subdivision of the county, used, as the name implies, for electoral purposes. To use the returns, ideally the relevant street or townland should be known. The 1901 *Townlands Index*, based on the census returns, supplies the name and number of the DED in which the townland is situated. County-by-county volumes, on open shelves in the National Archives reading room, go through the DEDs in numerical order, for both 1901 and 1911, giving the name and number of each of the townlands they contain. To order the returns for a specific townland, it is necessary to supply the name of the county, the number of the DED and the number of the townland, as given in these volumes. For the cities of Belfast, Cork, Dublin and Limerick separate street indexes have been compiled, and are also on open shelves in the reading room. Again, each street or part of a street is numbered, and these numbers are necessary to order specific returns. Between 1901 and 1911, some changes took place in the district electoral divisions, and their numbering is different in some cases. There is no separate townlands index for 1911, but the changes are minor, so that a DED numbered 100 in 1901 may be 103 in 1911, and can be found simply by checking the divisions above and below 100 in the 1911 volume for the county.

The returns for 1901 have been bound into large volumes, while those for 1911 are still loose and in boxes. The 1901 returns are now also available on microfilm. In each case, all the returns for a townland or street are grouped together and preceded by an enumerator's abstract which gives the details of the houses and lists the names of the heads of households. These lists can be very useful if the precise townland or street is not known, and it is necessary to search a large area, checking all households of a particular surname, though such a procedure is of course less precise than a check of each of the returns themselves. One problem which can arise in searching a large area is the difficulty of translating from the earlier geographical division of a parish, for instance, to the relevant district electoral divisions, since these latter cut across the earlier boundaries. The most straightforward, though cumbersome, way to cover a large area is to take all the townlands in a particular civil parish and check their district electoral divisions in the 1901 *Townlands Index*. The 1841 *Townlands Index*, also known as *Addenda to the 1841 Census*, and available on request from the National Archives reading room staff or in the National Library (Ir. 310 c 1), organises townlands alphabetically within civil parishes.

2. NINETEENTH-CENTURY CENSUS FRAGMENTS

1821

This census, organised by townland, civil parish, barony and county, took place on May 28th 1821, and aimed to cover the entire population. It recorded the following information:
- name;
- age;
- occupation;
- relationship to the head of the household;

Col. 1. No. of House	Col. 2. No. of Stories	Column 3. NAMES OF INHABITANTS.	Col. 4. AGE.	Column 5. OCCUPATION.	Col. 6. No. of Acres.

No. 38   Townland of *Aughalion*   in the Parish of *Castlerahan*   B:

N. B.—In Counties where Plowlands or other denominations or sub-denominations are in use, the word "Townland" ... is to be

		Eliza Fitzsimmons Daughter	15	Spinner	
8	1	Garrett Fitzsimmons	60	Farmer	12
		Cath Fitzsimmons his Wife	57	Spinner	
		Patrick Fitzsimmons his Son	32	Labourer	
		Thos Fitzsimmons Do	27	Labourer	
		John Fitzsimmons Do	23	Labourer	
		Mary Smyth	20	House Servt	
9	1	John Gilroy	39	Farmer	16
		Mary Gilroy his Wife	33	Spinner	
		Patrick Gilroy his Son	10		
		Owen Gilroy his Son	1		
		Mary Gilroy Daughter	15	Spinner	
		Mary Gilroy Do	13	Same	
		Bridget Gilroy Do	7		
		Anne Gilroy Do	5		
10	1	Peter Lynch	64	Farmer	15
		Eliza Lynch his Wife	61	Spinner	
		Hugh Lynch his Son	32	Labourer	
		James Lynch his Son	16	Labourer	
		Anne Lynch Daughter	25	Spinner	
		Mary Lynch Daughter	23	Spinner	
		John Lynch his Nephew	1		
11	1	John Flood	33	Farmer	4½
		Anne Flood his Wife	30	Spinner	
		John Flood his Son	8		
		Mary Flood Daughter	10		
		Cath Flood Do	6		
		Anne Flood Do	3		
12	1	John Smyth	55	Mason	
		Peter Smyth his Son	25	Labourer	
		James Smyth his Son	22	Labourer	
		Patk Smyth Do	15	Labourer	

1821 Census return
(Courtesy of the National Archives of Ireland)

- acreage of land-holding;
- number of storeys of house.

Almost all of the original returns were destroyed in 1922, with only a few volumes surviving for parts of Cos Cavan, Fermanagh, Galway, Meath and Offaly (King's County). These are now in the National Archives, and full details of call-numbers and areas covered will be found in Chapter 12 under the relevant county. The overall reliability of the population figures produced by the 1821 census has been questioned recently, but there is no doubt as to the genealogical value of the returns. Once again, however, the ages given need to be treated with scepticism.

1831

Again organised by townland, civil parish, barony and county, this census recorded the following:
- name;
- age;
- occupation;
- relationship to the head of the household;
- acreage of land-holding;
- religion.

Very little of this survives, with most of the remaining fragments relating to Co. Derry. Details of locations and call-numbers are in Chapter 12 under the relevant county.

1841

Unlike the two earlier censuses, the returns in 1841 were filled out by the house-holders themselves, rather than government enumerators. The information supplied was:
- name;
- age;
- occupation;
- relationship to the head of the household;
- date of marriage;
- literacy;
- absent family members;
- family members who died since 1831.

Only one set of original returns survived 1922, that for the parish of Killeshandra in Co. Cavan. There are, however, a number of transcripts of the original returns. The 1841 census was the earliest to be of use when state old age pensions were introduced in the early twentieth century, and copies of the household returns from 1841 and 1851 were sometimes used as proof of age. The forms detailing the results of searches in the original returns to establish age have survived and are found in the National Archives for areas in the Republic of Ireland, and the Public Record Office of Northern Ireland for areas now in its jurisdiction. Copies of the Northern Ireland returns are also available at the LDS Library. County-by-county indexes to the areas covered, giving the names of the individuals concerned, are found on open shelves in the reading room. A number of other miscellaneous copies, some also related to the old age pension, and mostly relating to northern counties, are detailed (though not indexed) in the pre-1901 census catalogue of the National Archives, on open shelves in the reading room. For counties with significant numbers of these copies, details will be found under the relevant county in Chapter 12. As well as these copies, there are also a number of researchers' transcripts and abstracts compiled from the original returns before their destruction, and donated to public institutions after 1922 in an attempt to replace some of the lost records. Since the researchers were usually interested in particular families, rather than whole areas, these are generally of limited value. The most significant collections are the Walsh-Kelly notebooks, which also abstract parts of the 1821, 1831 and 1851 returns and relate particularly to south Kilkenny, and the Thrift Abstracts in the National Archives. Details of dates, areas covered and locations for the Walsh-Kelly notebooks will be found under Co. Kilkenny in Chapter 12. The Thrift Abstracts are listed in detail in the National Archives pre-1901 census catalogue under 'miscellaneous copies'. Counties for which significant numbers exist are given under the relevant county in Chapter 12.

1851

This recorded the following:

- name;
- age;
- occupation;
- relationship to the head of the household;
- date of marriage;
- literacy;
- absent family members;
- family members who died since 1841;
- religion.

Most of the surviving returns relate to parishes in Co. Antrim, and details will be found in Chapter 12. The comments above on transcripts and abstracts of the 1841 census also apply to 1851.

1861, 1871, 1881, 1891

The official destruction of the returns for these years was commendably thorough. Virtually nothing survives. The only transcripts are contained in the Catholic registers of Enniscorthy (1861), and Drumcondra and Loughbraclen, Co. Meath (1871). Details appear in Chapter 12.

3. CENSUS SUBSTITUTES

Almost anything recording more than a single name can be called a census substitute, at least for genealogical purposes. What follows is a listing, chronological where possible, of the principal such substitutes. It is intended as a gloss on some of the sources given county by county under 'Census Returns and Substitutes' in Chapter 12, and as a supplement covering sources which do not fit the county-by-county format. Any material given in the source-lists of Chapter 12 which is self-explanatory is not dealt with here.

Seventeenth Century

1612–13

'Undertakers': The Historical Manuscripts Commission Report, 4 (Hastings Mss), gives lists of English and Scottish large landlords granted land in the northern counties of Cavan, Donegal and Fermanagh.

1630

Muster Rolls: These are lists of large landlords in Ulster, and the names of the able-bodied men that they could assemble to fight if the need arose. They are arranged by county, and by district within the county. The Armagh County Museum copy is available in the National Library (Pos. 206). Published lists are noted under the relevant county in Chapter 12, along with later lists in the Public Record Office of Northern Ireland.

1641

Books of Survey and Distribution: After the wars of the mid-seventeenth century, the English government needed solid information on land ownership throughout Ireland to carry out its policy of land redistribution. The Books of Survey and Distribution record ownership before the Cromwellian and Williamite confiscations, *c.*1641, and after, *c.*1666–68. The Books for Clare, Galway, Mayo and Roscommon have been published by the Irish Manuscripts Commission. For other counties manuscript copies are available at the National Library. Details will be found under the relevant counties in Chapter 12.

1654–56

The Civil Survey: This too was a record of land ownership in 1640, compiled between 1655 and 1667, and fuller than the Books of Survey and Distribution. It contains a great deal of topographical and descriptive information, as well as details of wills and deeds relating to land title. It has survived for twelve counties only, Cork, Derry, Donegal, Dublin, Kildare, Kilkenny, Limerick, Meath, Tipperary, Tyrone, Waterford and Wexford. All of these have been published by the Irish Manuscripts Commission. Details will be found under the relevant counties in Chapter 12.

1659

'Pender's Census': This was compiled by Sir William Petty, also responsible for the Civil Survey, and records the names of persons with title to land ('tituladoes'), the total numbers of English and Irish living in each townland, and the principal Irish names in each barony. Five counties, Cavan, Galway, Mayo, Tyrone and Wicklow, are not covered. The work was edited by Seamus Pender and published in 1939 (NLI I 6551 Dublin).

1662–66

Subsidy Rolls: These list the nobility, clergy and laity who paid a grant in aid to the King. They supply name and parish and, sometimes, amount paid and occupation. They relate principally to counties in Ulster.

1664–66

Hearth Money Rolls: The Hearth Tax was levied on the basis of the number of hearths in each house; these rolls list the householders' names, as well as this number. They seem to be quite comprehensive. Details of surviving lists will be found under the relevant counties in Chapter 12. For copies of the Hearth Money Rolls listed in the Public Record Office of Northern Ireland under 'T.307', an index is available on the public search room shelves.

Various Dates

Cess Tax Accounts: 'Cess' (from an abbreviation of 'assessment') was a very elastic term, which could be applied to taxes levied for a variety of reasons. In Ireland it was very often to support a military garrison. The accounts generally consist of lists of householders' names, along with amounts due.

Eighteenth and Nineteenth Centuries

1703–1838

The Convert Rolls, ed. Eileen O'Byrne, Irish Manuscripts Commission, 1981: a list of those converting from Catholicism to the Church of Ireland. The bulk of the entries date from 1760 to 1790.

1740

Protestant householders for parts of Cos Antrim, Armagh, Derry, Donegal and Tyrone. Arranged by barony and parish, it gives names only. Parts are at the Public Record Office of Northern Ireland, the Genealogical Office, the National Library and the Representative Church Body Library. Details will be found under the relevant counties in Chapter 12.

1749

Elphin Diocesan Census: arranged by townland and parish, and listing householders, their religion, the numbers, sex and religion of their children, and the numbers, sex and religion of their servants. Details of the parishes covered will be found under the relevant counties in Chapter 12.

1766

In March and April of this year, on the instructions of the government, Church of Ireland rectors were to compile complete returns of all householders in their parishes, showing their religion, and giving an account of any Catholic clergy active in their area. The result was extraordinarily inconsistent, with some rectors producing only numerical totals of population, some drawing up partial lists, and the most conscientious detailing all householders and their addresses individually. All of the original returns were lost in 1922, but extensive transcripts survive for some areas and are deposited with various institutions. The only full listing of all surviving transcripts and abstracts is in the National Archives reading room on the open shelves. However, this does not differentiate between those returns which supply names and those which merely give numerical totals. The details given under the relevant counties in Chapter 12 refer only to those parishes for which names are given.

1795–1862

Charlton Trust Fund Marriage certificates. As an encouragement to Protestant population growth, the Charlton Trust Fund offered a small marriage gratuity to members of the Protestant labouring classes. To qualify, a marriage certificate recording occupations and fathers' names and signed by the local Church of Ireland clergyman had to be submitted, and these are now in the National Archives. They are particularly useful for the years before the start of registration of non-Catholic marriages in 1845. The areas covered by the fund were mainly in Cos Meath and Longford, but a few certificates exist for parts of Cos Cavan, King's (Offaly), Louth and Westmeath, as well as Dublin city. They are indexed in NAI Accessions, Vol. 37.

1796

Spinning-Wheel Premium Entitlement Lists. As part of a government scheme to encourage the linen trade, free spinning-wheels or looms were granted to individuals planting a certain area of land with flax. The lists of those entitled to the awards, covering almost 60,000 individuals, were published in 1796, and record only the name of the individual and the civil parish in which he lived. As might be expected, the majority, over 64% of the total, were in Ulster, but some names appear from every county except Dublin and Wicklow. In the county-by-county source-lists, only those counties with significant numbers (more than 3,000 names) include a reference. A microfiche index to the lists is available in the National Archives and the Public Record Office of Northern Ireland.

1798

Persons who Suffered Losses in the 1798 Rebellion. A list of claims for compensation from the government for property destroyed by the rebels during the insurrection of 1798. Particularly useful for the property-owning classes of Cos Wexford, Carlow, Dublin, Kildare and Wicklow. NLI 94107.

1824–38

Tithe Applotment Books. See Chapter 4.

1831–1921

National School Records. In 1831, a country-wide system of primary education was established under the control of the Board of Commissioners for National Education. The most useful records produced by the system are the school registers themselves, which record the age of the pupil, religion, father's address and occupation, and general observations. Unfortunately, in the Republic of Ireland no attempt has been made to centralise these records; they remain in the custody of local schools or churches. The Public Record Office of Northern Ireland has a collection of over 1,500 registers for schools in the six counties of Northern Ireland. The administrative records of the Board of Commissioners itself are now held by the National Archives in Dublin. These include teachers' salary books, which can be very useful if an ancestor was a teacher.

1848–64

Griffith's Valuation. See Chapter 4.

1876

Landowners in Ireland: Return of owners of land of one acre and upwards . . . London: Her Majesty's Stationery Office, 1876 [reissued by the Genealogical Publishing Company, Baltimore, 1988]. This records 32,614 owners of land in Ireland in 1876, identifying them by province and county; the entries record the address of the owner, along with the extent and valuation of the property. Only a minority of the population actually owned the land they occupied, but the work is invaluable for those who did.

Various Dates

■ *Freeholders:* Freehold property is held either by fee simple, with absolute freedom to dispose of it, by fee tail, in which the disposition is restricted to a particular line of heirs, or simply by life tenure. From the early eighteenth century freeholders' lists were drawn up regularly, usually because of the right to vote which went with freehold of property over a certain value. It follows that such lists are of genealogical interest only for a small minority of the population. Details of surviving lists will be found under the relevant counties in Chapter 12.

■ *Voters' Lists and Poll Books:* Voters' lists cover a slightly larger proportion of the population than freeholders' lists, since freehold property was not the only determinant of the franchise. In particular, freemen of the various corporation towns and cities had a right to vote in some elections at least. Since membership of a trade guild carried with it admission as a freeman, and this right was hereditary, a wider range of social classes is covered. Details of surviving lists will be found under the relevant counties in Chapter 12. Poll books are the records of votes actually cast in elections.

■ *Electoral Records:* No complete collection of the electoral lists used in the elections of this century exists. This is unfortunate, since they can be of great value in tracing living relatives, listing as they do all eligible voters by townland and household. The largest single collection of surviving electoral registers is to be found in the National Archives, but even here the coverage of many areas is quite skimpy.

■ *Valuations:* Local valuations, and revaluations, of property were carried out with increasing frequency from the end of the eighteenth century, usually for electoral reasons. The best of these record all householders. Again, details are given under the relevant counties in Chapter 12.

3. CHURCH RECORDS

THE PARISH SYSTEM

After the coming of the Reformation to Ireland in the sixteenth century, the parish structures of the Catholic Church and the Church of Ireland diverged. In general, the Church of Ireland retained the older medieval parochial divisions and, as the administrative units of the state Church, these were also used for administrative purposes by the secular authorities. Thus civil parishes, the basic geographical units in early censuses, tax records and land surveys, are almost identical to Church of Ireland parishes. The Catholic Church, on the other hand, weakened by the confiscation of its assets and the restrictions on its clergy, had to create larger and less convenient parishes. In some ways, however, this weakness produced more flexibility, allowing parishes to be centred on new, growing population centres and, in the nineteenth century, permitting the creation of new parishes to accommodate this growth in population. The differences in the parish structures of the two Churches are reflected in their records. Even allowing for the fact that members of the Church of Ireland were almost always a small minority of the total population, the records of each parish are proportionately less extensive than Catholic records, covering a smaller area, and are thus relatively easy to search in detail. Catholic records, by contrast, cover the majority of the population and a much larger geographical area, and as a result can be very time consuming to search in detail. The creation of new Catholic parishes in the nineteenth century can also mean that the registers relevant to a particular area may be split between two parishes. Both Catholic and Church of Ireland parishes are organised on the diocesan basis first laid out in the Synod of Kells in the Middle Ages, and remain almost identical, although the Catholic system has amalgamated some of the small medieval dioceses.

ROMAN CATHOLIC RECORDS

DATES

Before the start of civil registration for all in 1864, virtually the only direct sources of family information for the vast majority of the population are the local parish records. However, because of the disadvantages suffered by the Catholic Church between the sixteenth and nineteenth century, record-keeping was understandably difficult, and very few registers survive from before the latter half of the eighteenth century. The earliest Catholic parish records in the country appear to be the fragments for Waterford and Galway cities dating from the 1680s, and for Wexford town dating from 1671. Generally speaking, early records tend to come from the more prosperous and anglicised areas, in particular the towns and cities of the eastern half of the island. In the poorest and most densely populated rural parishes of the West and North, those which saw most emigration, the parish registers very often do not start until the mid or late nineteenth century. However, the majority of Catholic registers begin in the first decades of the nineteenth century, and even in poor areas, if a local tradition of Gaelic scholarship survived, records were often kept from an earlier date.

The list given in Chapter 13 reflects the state of knowledge of the dates of Catholic registers at the time of writing (mid-1998). No listing can ever be absolutely definitive, however. The number of parishes covered by the local heritage centres will continue to grow, the National Library microfilming programme will carry on to completion, and no doubt there are unrecorded registers awaiting discovery in sacristies around the country.

NATURE OF THE RECORDS

Catholic registers consist mostly of baptismal and marriage records. The keeping of burial records was much less thorough than in the Church of Ireland, with fewer than half the parishes in the country having a register of burials before 1900; even where they do exist, these records are generally intermittent and patchy. For some reason, almost all Catholic burial registers are for the northern half of the island. Baptisms and marriages are recorded in either Latin or English, never in Irish. Generally, parishes in the more prosperous areas, where English was more common, tended to use English, while in Irish-speaking parishes Latin was used; there is no absolute consistency, however. The Latin presents very few problems, since only first names were translated, not surnames or placenames, and the English equivalents are almost always self-evident. The only difficulties or ambiguities are the following: *Carolus* (Charles); *Demetrius* (Jeremiah, Jerome, Darby, Dermot); *Gulielmus* (William); *Eugenius* (Owen or Eugene); *Jacobus* (James); *Ioannes* or *Joannes* (John); *Honoria* (Hannah, Nora). Apart from names, the only other Latin needing explanation is that used in recording marriage dispensations. These were necessary when the two people marrying were related, *consanguinati*, and the relationship was given in terms of degrees, with siblings first degree, first cousins second degree, and second cousins third degree. Thus a couple recorded as *consanguinati in tertio grado* are second cousins, information which can be of value in disentangling earlier generations. A less frequent Latin comment, *affinitatus*, records an earlier relationship by marriage between the families of the two parties.

Baptisms

Catholic baptismal registers almost invariably contain the following information:
- date;
- child's name;
- father's name;
- mother's maiden name;
- names of sponsors (godparents).

In addition, most registers also record the residence of the parents. A typical Latin entry in its full form would read:

> *Baptisavi Johannem, filium legitimum Michaeli Sheehan et Mariae Sullivan de Lisquill*
> *Sponsoribus, Danielus Quirk, Johanna Donoghue*

Much more often the entry is abbreviated to:

> *Bapt. Johannem, f.l. Michaeli Sheehan et Mariae Sullivan, Lisquill*
> *Sp: Daniel Quirk, Johanna Donoghue*

Translated, this is simply 'I baptised John, legitimate son of Michael Sheehan and Mary Sullivan of Lisquill, with godparents Daniel Quirk and Johanna Donoghue.' In many cases, even the abbreviations are omitted, and the entries simply consist of dates, names and places.

Marriages

The information given in marriage records is more variable, but always includes at least the following:
- date;
- names of persons marrying;
- names of witnesses.

Other information which may be supplied includes: residences (of all four people), ages, occupations, fathers' names. In some rare cases the relationships of the witnesses to the people marrying are also specified. A typical Latin entry would read:

> *In matrimonium coniunxi sunt Danielum McCarthy et Brigidam Kelliher, de Ballyboher*
> *Testimonii: Cornelius Buckley, Margarita Hennessy*

Abbreviated, the entry reads:

> *Mat. con. Danielum McCarthy et Brigidam Kelliher, Ballyboher*
> *Test. Cornelius Buckley, Margarita Hennessy*

meaning, simply, 'Daniel McCarthy and Brigid Kelliher, of Ballyboher, are joined in matrimony; witnesses, Cornelius Buckley, Margaret Hennessy.'

LOCATIONS

In the 1950s and early 1960s, the National Library carried out a project to microfilm the surviving Catholic parish registers of the entire island. Out of 1,153 sets of registers, this project covered 1,066. Among the parishes whose records it does not include are: Rathlin Island (Co. Antrim); Crossgar (Co. Down); Kilmeen, Clonfert, Fahy, Clonbern (Co. Galway); Killorglin (Co. Kerry); Lanesboro (Co. Longford); Kilmeena (Co. Mayo); Rathcore & Rathmolyon (Co. Meath); Moate (Co. Westmeath); Bray (Co. Wicklow); and the Dublin city and county parishes of Clontarf, Donnybrook, Naul, Sandyford and Santry. Almost all of these appear to have registers earlier than 1880 in local custody. In addition, the parishes of St John's (Sligo town), Cappawhite (Co. Tipperary) and Waterford city have registers held locally which are fuller than those microfilmed by the library. Not all of the microfilmed registers in the library are available to the public; permission for public research has not been granted by the Bishops of Ardagh & Clonmacnoise, Kerry, and Limerick. In the case of parishes in these dioceses, it is necessary to obtain written permission from the local parish priest before the library can allow access to the records. In addition, at the time of writing (1998) no records for the diocese of Cashel and Emly are available for research, the Archbishop having closed them in order to oblige researchers to go through the Tipperary Heritage Unit, who carry out commissioned research on indexes created in the 1970s and 1980s.

A separate microfilming project was carried out by the Public Record Office of Northern Ireland for the six counties under its jurisdiction. The results are generally identical to the National Library copies, although in some cases PRONI has used a later cut-off date. See Chapter 13 for details.

The Church of Jesus Christ of the Latter-Day Saints also has an extensive collection of Catholic parish register microfilms, made up partly of copies of some of the National Library films and partly of material microfilmed by the Church itself. Of the 1,153 parishes in the country, the LDS Library has records of 398. See Chapter 13 for details.

Apart from research in the original records, or microfilm copies, one other access route exists to the information recorded in parish registers. This is through the network of local heritage centres which has come into being throughout the country since *c.*1980. These are engaged, as part of the Irish Genealogical Project, in indexing and computerising all of the surviving parish records for the country. At the moment of writing (1998) about 75 % of all Catholic records are indexed. These records are not directly accessible to the public, but the centres do carry out commissioned research. Full details of the project and the centres will be found in Chapter 14.

RESEARCH IN CATHOLIC RECORDS

Because the records are so extensive, and there are so many parishes, the first step in any research must be to try to identify the relevant parish. In the ideal case, where a precise town or townland is known, this is relatively simple. Any of the Townland Indexes, from 1851, 1871 or 1901, will show the relevant civil parish. There are then a number of ways to uncover the corresponding Catholic parish. Lewis's *Topographical Dictionary of Ireland* (1837), available on open access at most libraries, gives an account, in alphabetical order, of all of the civil parishes of Ireland, and specifies the corresponding Catholic parish. Brian Mitchell's *Guide to Irish Parish Records* (Genealogical Publishing Co., Baltimore, 1987) contains a county-by-county alphabetical reference guide to the civil parishes of Ireland and the Catholic parishes of which they are part. The National Library 'Index of Surnames' (or 'Householders Index') includes a map of the civil parishes in each county, and a key, loosely based on Lewis, to the corresponding Catholic parishes. A guide which is less reliable, though useful if the exact position of the church is required, is *Locations of Churches in the Irish Provinces*, produced by the Church of Jesus Christ of the Latter-Day Saints (NLI Ir. 7265 i 8). For Dublin city the procedure is slightly different. Where the address is known, the relevant civil parish can be found in the street-by-street listings of the Dublin directories, Pettigrew and Oulton's *Dublin Almanac and General Register of Ireland* (yearly from 1834 to 1849) and Thom's *Irish Almanac and Official Directory* (yearly from 1844). More details of these will be found in Chapter 5. The corresponding Catholic parishes can then be found in Mitchell's *Guide*, or in James Ryan's *Tracing your Dublin Ancestors* (Flyleaf Press, 1988).

Unfortunately, in most cases a precise address is not known. How this is to be overcome depends, obviously, on what other information is known. Where a birth, death or marriage took place in the family in Ireland after the start of civil registration in 1864, state records are the first place to look. When the occupation is known, records relating to this may supply the vital link (see Chapter 11). For emigrants, the clue to the relevant area might be provided by passenger and immigration lists, naturalisation papers, burial or death records, or even the postmarks on old family letters. In general, unless the surname is quite rare, the minimum information needed to start research on parish records with any prospect of success is the county of origin. Knowing the county, the areas to be searched in the registers can then be narrowed with the help of the early and mid-nineteenth-century land records, the Tithe Books (*c.*1830) and Griffith's Valuation (*c.*1855) (see Chapter 4). The National Library 'Index of Surnames' provides a guide, on a county basis, to the surnames occurring in these records in the different civil parishes, giving at least an indication of the areas in which a particular surname was most common. The CD-ROM index to Griffith's can also be invaluable in narrowing the area of research.

Because of the creation of new Catholic parishes in the nineteenth century, the apparent starting dates of many Catholic registers can be deceptive. Quite often, earlier records for the same area can be found in the registers of what is now an adjoining parish. To take an example, the Catholic parish of Abbeyleix in Co. Laois (Queen's) has records listed in the National Library catalogue as starting in 1824. In fact, the parish was only created in that year, and before then its records will be found in Ballinakill, which has records from 1794. Where surviving records appear too late to be of interest, therefore, it is always advisable to check the surrounding parishes for earlier registers. The maps of Catholic parishes accompanying Chapter 13 are intended to simplify this task. These maps are not intended to be geographically precise; their aim is merely to show the positions of Catholic parishes relative to each other. Since the only published source of information on nineteenth-century Catholic parishes is Lewis's *Topographical Dictionary of Ireland*, which was published in 1837, and the power and public presence of the Church expanded greatly after Catholic emancipation in 1836, some caution is needed in identifying which sets of records are relevant to a particular area.

At first sight parish registers, particularly on microfilm, can appear quite daunting. The mass of spidery abbreviated Latin, complete with blots and alterations and cross-hatched with the scratches of a well-worn microfilm, can strike terror into the heart of even the most seasoned researcher. Some registers are a pleasure to use, with decade after decade of carefully laid out copper-plate handwriting; many more, unfortunately, appear to have been intended by local clergymen as their revenge on posterity. The thing to remember is that it is neither possible nor desirable to read every word on every page. The aim is to extract efficiently any relevant information, and the way to do this is by scanning the pages rather than reading them. In general, each parish takes a particular format and sticks to it. The important point is to identify this format, and where in it the relevant information is given. For most purposes, the family surname is the crucial item, so that in the baptismal example given above, the best procedure would be to scan fathers' surnames, stopping to read fully, or note, only those recording the relevant surname. For other formats, such as

1857

Richard son of Richard Adderley & Ellen his wife
Born February 28th Baptised April 19th 1857.

Andrew, son of Robert & Jeannette Rutherford
Born 13th May. Baptised 8th June 1857 —

Thomas Eld son of Thomas Heffernan of Newtown Esq & Rose his wife, Born February 18th 1857 on Received into church November 22d 1857 sober —

Sponsors { Thomas Eld
{ Thomas Heffernan & Fanny Eld.

Mary Eld daughter of Thomas Heffernan of Newtown Esq. & Rose his wife Born Novr. 10th 1857 Baptised November 22d 1857 —

Sponsors { Mary Bernard & Thomas Heffernan
{ Rose Heffernan

George Thomas son of Edward Thomas of Cookstown Parish of Drumdowna & Marianne his wife. Born Novr. 29th Baptised Decr. 20th 1857.

1858 John, son of Michael Farmer & Anne his wife Baptised March 21st 1858.

William John, son of Denis Lynch of Ballinasloe and Ellen his wife Born April 8th Baptised April 24th 1858.

Ballymodan Church of Ireland baptismal register
(Courtesy of the National Archives of Ireland)

John Maguire of Patrick and Mary Reilly
Sp. Thos McKiernan, Rose Smith

in which the family surname is given with the child's name, rather than with the father's, it is the child's surname which must be scanned. Even with very efficient scanning, however, there are registers which can only be deciphered line by line, which change format every page or two, or which are simply so huge that nothing but hours of eye strain can extract any information. The most notorious are the registers for Cork city, Clonmel, Co. Tipperary, and Clifden, Co. Galway.

In searching parish records, as for census returns and state records of births, marriages and deaths, a large measure of scepticism must be applied to all reported ages. In general, a five year span around the reported date is the minimum that can be expected to yield results, and ten years is better if time allows, with emphasis on the years before the reported date. An open mind should also be kept on surname variants — widespread illiteracy made consistency and exactness of spelling extremely rare. It is essential, especially if searching more than one parish, to keep a written note of the precise period searched; even the best memory blurs after a few hours in front of a microfilm screen, and it is perfectly, horribly, possible to have to search the same records twice. Duplication of research such as this is an endemic hazard of genealogy, since the nature of the research is such that the relevance of particular pieces of evidence often only emerges with hindsight; this is especially true of research in parish records. To take an example: a search in parish records for Ellen, daughter of John O'Brien, born c.1840. The search starts in 1842 and moves back through the baptismal registers. There are many baptisms recording different John O'Briens as father, but no Ellen recorded until 1834. If it is then necessary to check the names of her siblings, much of what has already been researched will have to be covered again. The only way to guard against having to duplicate work like this is to note all the baptisms recording John O'Brien as father, even though there is a possibility (and in many cases a probability) that none of them will ultimately turn out to have been relevant.

Apart from the obvious family information they record, Catholic parish registers may also include a wide variety of incidental information — details of famine relief, parish building accounts, marriage dispensations, local censuses, even personal letters. Anything of immediate genealogical interest is noted under the relevant county in Chapter 12.

CHURCH OF IRELAND RECORDS

DATES

Records of the Established Church, the Church of Ireland, generally start much earlier than those of the Catholic Church. From as early as 1634, local parishes were required to keep records of christenings and burials in registers supplied by the church authorities. As a result, a significant number, especially of urban parishes, have registers dating from the mid-seventeenth century. The majority, however, start in the years between 1770 and 1820; the only country-wide listing of all Church of Ireland parish records which gives full details of dates is the National Archives catalogue, a copy of which is also to be found at the National Library. In addition, the

Irish Family History Society has published *A Table of Church of Ireland Parochial Records* (ed. Noel Reid, IFHS, 1994) and the *Guide to Church Records: Public Record Office of Northern Ireland* (PRONI, 1994) gives details of PRONI's holdings.

THE NATURE OF THE RECORDS

Burials

Unlike their Catholic counterparts, the majority of Church of Ireland clergymen recorded burials as well as baptisms and marriages. These burial registers are often also of interest for families of other denominations; the sectarian divide appears to have narrowed a little after death. The information given for burials was rarely more than the name, age and townland, making definite family connections difficult to establish in most cases. However, since early burials generally record the deaths of those born well before the start of the register, they can often be the only evidence on which to base a picture of preceding generations, and are particularly valuable because of this.

Baptisms

Church of Ireland baptismal records almost always supply only
• the child's name;
• the father's name;
• the mother's Christian name;
• the name of the officiating clergyman.

Quite often the address is also given, but this is by no means as frequent as in the case of Catholic registers. The omission of the mother's maiden name can be an obstacle to further research. From about 1820, the father's occupation is supplied in many cases.

Marriages

Since the Church of Ireland was the Established Church, the only legally valid marriages, in theory at least, were those performed under its aegis. In practice, of course, *de facto* recognition was given to marriages of other denominations. None the less, the legal standing of the Church of Ireland meant that many marriages, of members of other Protestant churches in particular, are recorded in Church of Ireland registers. The information given is not extensive, however, consisting usually of the names of the parties marrying and the name of the officiating clergyman. Even addresses are not usual, unless one of the people is from another parish. More comprehensive material is included in records of marriage banns, where these exist — although it was obligatory for notification of the intention to marry to be given in church on three consecutive Sundays, written records of these are relatively rare. After 1845, when non-Catholic marriages were registered by the state, the marriage registers record all the information contained in state records, including occupations, addresses and fathers' names.

Marriage Licence Bonds

As an alternative to marriage banns, members of the Church of Ireland could take out a Marriage Licence Bond. The parties lodged a sum of money with the diocese to indemnify the Church against there being an obstacle to the marriage; in effect the system allowed the better off to purchase privacy. The original bonds were all destroyed in 1922, but the original indexes are available at the National Archives. The Dublin diocesan index was published as part of the *Index to Dublin Will and Grant Books*, RDKPRI 26, 1895 (1270–1800) and RDKPRI 30, 1899 (1800–1858). The Genealogical Office holds abstracts of Prerogative Marriage Licence Bonds from 1630 to 1858 (GO 605–607), as well as Marriages recorded in Prerogative Wills (GO 255–6). For an explanation of the Prerogative Court, see Chapter 5, Wills.

Other

As well as straightforward information on baptisms, marriages and burials, Church of Ireland parish records very often include vestry books. These contain the minutes of the vestry meetings of the local parish, which can supply detailed information on the part played by individuals in the life of the parish. These are not generally with the parish registers in the National Archives, but the Public Record Office of Northern Ireland and the Representative Church Body Library in Dublin have extensive collections.

LOCATIONS

After the Church of Ireland ceased to be the Established Church in 1869, its marriage records before 1845 and baptismal and burial records before 1870 were declared to be the property of the state, public records. Unless the local clergyman was in a position to demonstrate that he could house these records safely, he was required to deposit them in the Public Record Office. By 1922, the original registers of nearly 1,000 parishes, more than half the total for the country, were stored at the Public Record Office, and these were all destroyed in the fire at the office on June 28th of that year.

Fortunately, a large number of registers had not found their way into the office: local rectors had, in many cases, made a transcript before surrendering the originals, and local historians and genealogists using the office before 1922 had also amassed collections of extracts from the registers. All of these factors mitigated, to some extent, the loss of such a valuable collection. However, it has also meant that surviving registers, transcripts and extracts are now held in a variety of locations. The Appendix to the *28th Report of the Deputy Keeper of Public Records in Ireland* lists the Church of Ireland parish records for the entire island, giving full details of the years covered, and specifying those which were in the Public Office at the time of its destruction. No information on locations is included. A more comprehensive account is supplied by the National Archives catalogue of Church of Ireland records, available in the National Archives reading room, at the National Library, and in *A Table of Church of Ireland Parochial Records* (ed. Noel Reid, IFHS, 1994). As well as the dates of the registers, this catalogue also gives some details of locations, but only for originals, copies or transcripts held by the Archives, originals held by the the Representative Church Body Library, or originals still in local custody. The catalogue does not indicate when microfilm copies are held by the Representative Church Body Library, the Public Record Office of Northern Ireland or the National Library, simply specifying 'local custody'. This is accurate in that the originals are indeed held locally, but unhelpful to researchers.

In general, for the northern counties of Antrim, Armagh, Cavan, Derry, Donegal, Down, Fermanagh, Leitrim, Louth, Monaghan and Tyrone, surviving registers have been microfilmed by the Public Record Office of Northern Ireland and are available to the public in Belfast. The *Guide to Church Records: Public Record Office of Northern Ireland* (PRONI, 1994) gives details. For those counties which are now in the Republic of Ireland, Cavan, Donegal, Leitrim, Louth and Monaghan, copies of the Public Record Office of Northern Ireland microfilms are available to the public at the Representative Church Body Library in Dublin. For parishes further away from the border, 'local custody' is generally accurate, and it is necessary to commission the local clergyman to search his registers. The current Church of Ireland Directory will supply the relevant name and address.

The experience of 1922 has left the Church of Ireland understandably protective of its records, although the legal position remains that its early registers are state property. The National Archives has started a microfilming programme to cover the surviving registers in the Republic. However, not all the records are immediately accessible. In some cases it is necessary to obtain written permission from the local clergyman before the Archives can allow access.

PRESBYTERIAN RECORDS

DATES

In general, Presbyterian registers start much later than those of the Church of Ireland, and early records of Presbyterian baptisms, marriages and deaths are often to be found in the registers of the local Church of Ireland parish. There are exceptions, however. In areas which had a strong Presbyterian population from an early date, particularly in the north-east, some registers date from the late seventeenth and early eighteenth centuries. The only published listing remains that included in Margaret Falley's *Irish and Scotch-Irish Ancestral Research* (repr. Genealogical Publishing Co., 1988). This, however, gives a very incomplete and out of date picture of the extent and location of the records. For the six counties of Northern Ireland, and many of the adjoining counties, the *Guide to Church Records: Public Record Office of Northern Ireland* (PRONI, 1994) provides a good guide to the dates of surviving registers. The copy of the list held in the office itself includes a listing of Registers in Local Custody which covers all of Ireland, but is much less comprehensive for the south than for the north.

THE NATURE OF THE RECORDS

Presbyterian registers record the same information as that given in the registers of the Church of Ireland (see above). It should be remembered that after 1845, all non-Catholic marriages, including those of Presbyterians, were registered by the state. From that year, therefore, Presbyterian marriage registers contain all of the invaluable information given in state records.

LOCATIONS

Presbyterian registers are in three main locations: in local custody, in the Public Record Office of Northern Ireland, and at the Presbyterian Historical Society in Belfast. The Public Record Office also has microfilm copies of almost all registers in Northern Ireland which have remained in local custody, and also lists those records held by the Presbyterian Historical Society. For the rest of Ireland, almost all of the records are in local custody. It can be very difficult to locate these, since many congregations in the south have moved, amalgamated, or simply disappeared over the last sixty years. The very congregational basis of Presbyterianism further complicates matters, since it means that Presbyterian records do not cover a definite geographical area; the same town often had two or more Presbyterian churches drawing worshippers from the same community and keeping distinct records. In the early nineteenth century especially, controversy within the Church fractured the records, with seceding and non-seceding congregations in the same area often in violent opposition to each other. Apart from the PRONI listing, the only guide is *History of Congregations* (NLI Ir. 285 h 8) which gives a brief historical outline of the history of each congregation. Lewis's *Topographical Dictionary of Ireland* (1837) records the existence of Presbyterian congregations within each civil parish, and Pettigrew and Oulton's *Dublin Almanac and General Register of Ireland* of 1835 includes a list of all Presbyterian ministers in the country, along with the names and locations of their congregations. *Locations of Churches in the Irish Provinces*, produced by the Church of Jesus Christ of the Latter-Day Saints (NLI Ir. 7265 i 8), flawed as it is in many respects, can be useful in trying to identify the congregations in a particular area. A brief bibliography of histories of Presbyterianism is given under 'clergymen' in Chapter 11.

METHODIST RECORDS

Despite the hostility of many of the clergy of the Church of Ireland, the Methodist movement remained unequivocally a part of the Established Church from the date of its beginnings in 1747, when John Wesley first came to Ireland, until 1816, when the movement split. Between 1747 and 1816, therefore, records of Methodist baptisms, marriages and burials will be found in the registers of the Church of Ireland. The split in 1816 took place over the question of the authority of Methodist ministers to administer sacraments, and resulted in the 'Primitive Methodists' remaining within the Church of Ireland, and the 'Wesleyan Methodists' authorising their ministers to perform baptisms and communions. (In theory at least, up to 1844 only marriages carried out by a minister of the Church of Ireland were legally valid.) The split continued until 1878, when the Primitive Methodists united with the Wesleyan Methodists outside the Church of Ireland. What this means is that the earliest surviving registers which are specifically Methodist date from 1815/16, and relate only to the Wesleyan Methodists. The information recorded in these is identical to that given in the Church of Ireland registers.

There are a number of problems in locating Methodist records which are specific to that Church. First, the origins of Methodism, as a movement rather than a Church, gave its members a great deal of latitude in their attitude to Church membership, so that records of the baptisms, marriages and burials of Methodists may also be found in Quaker and Presbyterian registers, as well as the registers of the Church of Ireland. In addition, the ministers of the Church were preachers on a circuit, rather than administrators of a particular area, and were moved frequently from one circuit to another. Quite often the records moved with them. For the nine historic counties of Ulster, the Public Record Office of Northern Ireland has produced a county-by-county listing of the surviving registers, their dates and locations, appended to its Parish Register Index. No such listing exists for the rest of the country. Again, Pettigrew and Oulton's *Dublin Almanac and General Register of Ireland* of 1835 and subsequent years provides a list of Methodist preachers and their stations, which will give an indication of the relevant localities. The next step is then to identify the closest surviving Methodist centre and enquire of them as to surviving records. Many of the local county heritage centres also hold indexed copies of surviving Methodist records (see Chapter 14).

QUAKER RECORDS

From the time of their first arrival in Ireland in the seventeenth century, the Society of Friends (Quakers) kept rational and systematic records of the births, marriages and deaths of all of their members, and in most cases these continue without a break up to the present. Parish registers as such were not kept. Each of the local weekly meetings reported any births, marriages or deaths to a larger monthly meeting, which then entered them in a register. Monthly meetings were held in the following areas: Antrim, Ballyhagan, Carlow, Cootehill, Cork, Dublin, Edenderry, Grange, Lisburn, Limerick, Lurgan, Moate, Mountmellick, Richhill, Tipperary, Waterford, Wexford and Wicklow. For all but Antrim and Cootehill, registers have survived from an early date, and are detailed below.

The entries for births, marriages and deaths do not themselves contain information other than the names and addresses of the immediate parties involved, but the centralisation of the records, and the self-contained nature of the Quaker community, make it a relatively simple matter to establish family connections; many of the local records are given in the form of family lists in any case.

There are two main repositories for records, the libraries of the Society of Friends in Dublin and Lisburn. The LDS Library in Salt Lake City has microfilm copies of the records of the Dublin Friends' Library. As well as the records outlined below, these also hold considerable collections of letters, wills, family papers, as well as detailed accounts of the discrimination suffered by the Quakers in their early years.

BIRTHS, MARRIAGES AND BURIALS

Ballyhagan Marriages, Library of the Society of Friends, Lisburn, also NLI Pos. 4127
Bandon 1672–1713, in Casey, A. (ed.) *O'Kief, Coshe Nang*, Vol. 11, NLI Ir. 94145 c 12
Carlow, births, marriages and deaths up to 1859, Library of the Society of Friends, Dublin, also NLI Pos. 1021
Cork, births, marriages and deaths up to 1859, Library of the Society of Friends Dublin (NLI Pos. 1021), see also Cork (seventeenth to nineteenth centuries) NLI Pos. 5530

Dublin, births, marriages and deaths up to 1859, Library of the Society of Friends, Dublin, also NLI Pos. 1021 (births and marriages) and 1022 (burials)

Edenderry, births, marriages and deaths up to 1859, Library of the Society of Friends, Dublin, also NLI Pos. 1022, 1612–1814 (in the form of family lists), NLI Pos. 5531

Grange, births, marriages and deaths up to 1859, Library of the Society of Friends, Dublin, also NLI Pos. 1022

Lisburn, births, marriages and deaths up to 1859, Library of the Society of Friends, Dublin, also NLI Pos. 1022

Limerick, births, marriages and deaths up to 1859, Library of the Society of Friends, Dublin, also NLI Pos. 1022

Lurgan, births, marriages and deaths up to 1859, Library of the Society of Friends, Dublin (NLI Pos. 1022), see also Lurgan Marriage Certificates, Library of the Society of Friends, Lisburn (NLI Pos. 4126)

Moate, births, marriages and deaths up to 1859, Library of the Society of Friends, Dublin, also NLI Pos. 1022

Mountmellick, births, marriages and deaths up to 1859, Library of the Society of Friends, Dublin, also NLI Pos. 1023, also NLI Pos. 5530

Mountrath, Library of the Society of Friends, Dublin, also NLI Pos. 5530

Richhill, births, marriages and deaths up to 1859, Library of the Society of Friends, Dublin, also NLI Pos. 1023

Tipperary, births, marriages and deaths up to 1859, Library of the Society of Friends, Dublin, also NLI Pos. 1024

Waterford, births, marriages and deaths up to 1859, Library of the Society of Friends, Dublin, also NLI Pos. 1024

Wexford, births, marriages and deaths up to 1859, Library of the Society of Friends, Dublin, also NLI Pos. 1024

Wicklow, births, marriages and deaths up to 1859, Library of the Society of Friends, Dublin, also NLI Pos. 1024

Youghal, births, marriages and deaths up to 1859, Library of the Society of Friends, Dublin, also NLI Pos. 1024

Births, Marriages and Deaths throughout Ireland 1859–1949, Library of the Society of Friends, Dublin, also NLI Pos. 1024

Also:

Leinster Province, births, marriages and deaths seventeenth century, Library of the Society of Friends, Dublin (NLI Pos. 5530)

Munster Province, births, marriages and deaths 1650–1839, Library of the Society of Friends, Dublin (NLI Pos. 5531)

Ulster Province Meeting Books, 1673–1691, Library of the Society of Friends, Lisburn (NLI Pos. 3747)

Ulster Province Meetings Minute Books to 1782, Library of the Society of Friends, Lisburn (NLI Pos. 4124 & 4125)

OTHER RECORDS

1. Published

Eustace, P.B. & Goodbody, O., *Quaker Records, Dublin, Abstracts of Wills* (2 vols, 1704–1785) Irish Manuscripts Commission,1954–58
Goodbody, Olive, *Guide to Irish Quaker Records 1654–1860*, IMC, 1967, NLI Ir. 2896 g 4
Grubb, Isabel, *Quakers in Ireland*, London, 1927
Leadbetter, *Biographical Notices of the Society of Friends*, NLI J 2896
Myers, A.C., *Immigration of Irish Quakers into Pennsylvania*, NLI Ir. 2896 m 2 & 4
Wright & Petty, *History of the Quakers 1654–1700*, NLI Ir. 2896 w 1

2. Manuscript

Quaker Pedigrees, Library of the Society of Friends, Dublin, also NLI Pos. 5382, 5383, 5384, 5385
Quaker Wills and Inventories, Library of the Society of Friends, Lisburn, also NLI Pos. 4127
Manuscript records of the Quaker Library (see Guide above): Swanbrook House, Bloomfield Avenue, Donnybrook, Dublin 4. Tel. 6687157. Thurs. 11 a.m. to 1 p.m.

4. LAND RECORDS

Because of the destruction of nineteenth-century census returns, surviving land and property records from the period have acquired a somewhat unnatural importance. Two surveys cover the entire country, the Tithe Applotment Books of *c*.1823–38 and Griffith's Valuation, dating from 1848 to 1864. Both of these employ administrative divisions which are no longer in widespread use and need some explanation. The smallest division, the townland, is the one which has proved most enduring. Loosely related to the ancient Gaelic 'Bally betagh', and to other medieval land divisions such as ploughlands and 'quarters', townlands can vary enormously in size, from a single acre or less to several thousand acres. There are more than 64,000 townlands in the country. They were used as the smallest geographical unit in both Tithe Survey and Griffith's, as well as census returns, and are still in use today. Anything from 5 to 30 townlands may be grouped together to form a civil parish. These are a legacy of the Middle Ages, pre-dating the formation of counties and generally co-extensive with the parishes of the Established Church, the Church of Ireland. They are not to be confused with Catholic parishes, which are usually much larger. In turn, civil parishes are collected together in baronies. Originally related to the tribal divisions, the tuatha of Celtic Ireland, these were multiplied and subdivided over the centuries up to their standardisation in the 1500s, so that the current names represent a mixture of Gaelic, Anglo-Norman and English influences. A number of baronies, from 5 in Co. Leitrim to 22 in Co. Cork, then go to make up the modern county. Baronies and civil parishes are no longer in use as administrative units.

TITHE APPLOTMENT BOOKS

The Composition Act of 1823 specified that tithes due to the Established Church, the Church of Ireland, which had hitherto been payable in kind, should now be paid in money. As a result, it was necessary to carry out a valuation of the entire country, civil parish by civil parish, to determine how much would be payable by each land-holder. This was done over the ensuing 15 years, up to the abolition of tithes in 1838. Not surprisingly, tithes were fiercely resented by those who were not members of the Church of Ireland, and all the more because the tax was not payable on all land; the exemptions produced spectacular inequalities. In Munster, for instance, tithes were payable on potato patches, but not on grassland, with the result that the poorest had to pay most. The exemptions also mean that the Tithe Books are not comprehensive. Apart from the fact that they omit entirely anyone not in occupation of land, certain categories of land, varying from area to area, are simply passed over in silence. They are not a full list of householders. None the less, they do constitute the only country-wide survey for the period and are valuable precisely because the heaviest burden of tithes fell on the poorest, for whom few other records survive.

From a genealogical point of view, the information recorded in the Tithe Books is quite basic, consisting typically of townland name, landholder's name, area of land and tithes payable. In addition, many books also record the landlord's name and an

41   **PARISH OF** *Castlerahan*

TOWNLANDS AND LAND-LORDS.	OCCUPIERS.	1st Quality			2nd.			3rd.			4th.			A.
		A.	R.	P.	A.	R.	P.	A.	R.	P.	A.	R.	P.	
Aghlion	Forwarded	52	1	20	73	2	25	10	0	05	4	0	00	
"	Peter Lynch &c.	4	2	~	5	~	~	2	2	~	~	~	~	
"	T. B. & J. Lynch	10	~	~	17	~	~	5	~	~	~	~	~	
"	J. & P. Keogan	3	~	~	24	1	~	4	~	~	~	~	~	
"	J. Kilroy & Brady	4	~	~	12	~	~	3	~	~	7	2	~	
"	Garret Fitzsimons	3	~	~	7	~	~	1	1	15	~	~	~	
"	Jn.º Fitzsimons	4	~	~	7	~	~	~	2	15	~	~	~	
"	John Brady	~	~	1	~	~	~	~	~	~	~	~	~	
"	Luke Maginis	1	0	30	4	~	~	~	~	~	1	~	~	
"	Rich.ᵈ Glannon	1	~	~	1	~	~	~	~	~	~	~	~	
		83	1	10	150	3	25	26	1	35	12	2	~	

Tithe Applotment Book, Aghalion, Co. Cavan
(Courtesy of the National Archives of Ireland)

assessment of the economic productivity of the land; the tax was based on the average price of wheat and oats over the seven years up to 1823, and was levied at a different rate depending on the quality of the land.

An organised campaign of resistance to the payment of tithes, the so called 'Tithe War', culminated in 1831 in large-scale refusals to pay the tax. To apply for compensation for the resultant loss of income, local Church of Ireland clergymen were required to produce lists of those liable for tithes who had not paid, the 'Tithe Defaulters'. The lists can provide a fuller picture of tithe-payers than the original Tithe Book, and can be useful to cross-check against the book, especially if it dates from before 1831. Of these lists 127 survive in the NAI Chief Secretary's office, Official Papers series. They relate principally to Counties Kilkenny and Tipperary, with some coverage also of Counties Carlow, Cork, Kerry, Laois, Limerick, Louth, Meath, Offaly, Waterford and Wexford. A full list was published in *The Irish Genealogist,* Vol. 8, No. 1, 1990. County-by-county microfiche indexes have been produced by Data Tree Publishing, Suite 393, 44 Glenferrie Road, Malvern 3144, Australia. These are available at the National Library of Ireland.

Microfilm copies of the Tithe Books are available in the National Archives and the National Library. Those for the nine counties of Ulster are available in the Public Record Office of Northern Ireland.

The usefulness of the Tithe Books can vary enormously, depending on the nature of the research. Since only a name is given, with no indication of family relationships, any conclusions drawn are inevitably somewhat speculative. However, for parishes where registers do not begin until after 1850, they are often the only early records surviving. They can provide valuable circumstantial evidence, especially where a holding passed from father to son in the period between the Tithe Survey and Griffith's Valuation. The surnames in the books have been roughly indexed in the National Library 'Index of Surnames', described more fully below.

GRIFFITH'S VALUATION

In order to produce the accurate information necessary for local taxation, the Tenement Act of 1842 provided for a uniform valuation of all property in Ireland, to be based on the productive capacity of land and the potential rent of buildings. The man appointed Commissioner of Valuation was Richard Griffith, a Dublin geologist, and the results of his great survey, the Primary Valuation of Ireland, were published between 1848 and 1864. The valuation is arranged by county, barony, poor law union, civil parish and townland, and lists every land-holder and every householder in Ireland. Apart from townland address and householder's name, the particulars given are:

- name of the person from whom the property was leased ('immediate lessor');
- description of the property;
- acreage;
- valuation.

The only directly useful family information supplied is in areas where a surname was particularly common; the surveyors often adopted the Gaelic practice of using the father's first name to distinguish between individuals of the same name, so that 'John Reilly (James)' is the son of James, while 'John Reilly (Michael)' is the son of

Valuation of Tenements.

ACTS 15 & 16 VIC., CAP. 63, & 17 VIC., CAP. 8.

COUNTY OF CAVAN.

BARONY OF CASTLERAHAN.

UNION OF OLDCASTLE.

PARISH OF CASTLERAHAN.

No. and Letters of Reference to Map.		Names.		Description of Tenement.	Area.	Rateable Annual Valuation.		Total Annual Valuation of Rateable Property.
		Townlands and Occupiers.	Immediate Lessors.		A. R. P.	Land. £ s. d.	Buildings. £ s. d.	£ s. d.
		AGHALJON. (*Ord. S.* 39.)						
1	a	John Lynch,	C. T. Nesbit,	House, offices, and land,	14 2 28	6 5 0	0 10 0	6 15 0
–	b	C. T. Nesbit,	In fee,	Land,	0 3 30	0 5 0	—	0 5 0
2	a	Bryan M'Donald	C. T. Nesbit,	Herd's house & land,	19 3 22	4 0 0	1 5 0	5 5 0
–		John Fitzsimon,		Land,		4 0 0	—	4 0 0
3		John Fitzsimon,	Same,	House, offices, and land,	5 1 34	2 0 0	1 0 0	3 0 0
4		John Fitzsimon,	Same,	Land,	4 1 34	2 0 0	—	2 0 0
–	a	Rose Fitzsimon,	Same,	House,	—	—	0 10 0	0 10 0
5	a	John Fitzsimon, jun.,	Same,	House, offices, and land,	8 1 35	4 0 0	1 0 0	5 0 0
–	b	John Fitzsimon,	Same,	Land,	0 2 15	0 5 0	—	0 5 0
–	c	John Flood,	Same,	Land (*gardens*),	0 1 24	0 5 0	—	0 5 0
6	e	John Flood,	Same,	House, offices, and land,	17 2 8	8 0 0	1 15 0	9 15 0
7		Michael Cogan,	Same,	House, offices, and land,	31 0 12	10 0 0	1 5 0	14 0 0
8			Same,	Land,	7 2 16	2 15 0	—	
9	a	Peter Lynch,	Same,	House, offices, and land,	5 0 22	1 18 0	0 10 0	2 15 0
				Bog,	7 0 17	0 7 0	—	
10	b	Joseph Brady,	Same,	Ho., off., & sm. garden,	—	—	0 10 0	0 10 0
				Land,	1 1 33	0 10 0	—	0 10 0
11		Catherine Fitzsimon,	Same,	House and land,	2 0 4	0 10 0	0 5 0	0 15 0
12		Matthew Cogan,	Same,	House, office, and land,	13 0 9	4 10 0	0 10 0	5 0 0
13			Same,	Land,	11 0 24	4 0 0	—	22 5 0
14		Patrick Cogan,	Same,	House, offices, and land,	23 3 18	12 0 0	1 5 0	
15				Land,	8 2 21	4 0 0	—	
16				Land,	1 2 2	1 0 0	—	
–	a	John Lynch,	Same,	Land,	0 1 24	0 4 0	—	0 4 0
17	a	Terence & Patk. Cogan,	Same,	House, offices, and land,	38 0 30	15 0 0	1 0 0	16 0 0
–	b	Vacant,	Terence & Patk. Cogan,	House,	—	—	0 5 0	0 5 0
–	c	Vacant,	Same,	House,	—	—	0 10 0	0 10 0
18		Michael Brady,	C. T. Nesbit,	House, office, and land,	8 2 20	4 0 0	0 15 0	4 15 0
19	a	James Bennett,	Same,	House, offices, and land,	34 2 18	17 10 0	1 5 0	18 15 0
–	b	Margaret Gilroy,	James Bennett,	House,	—	—	0 10 0	0 10 0
–	c	Anne Timmon,	Same,	House,	—	—	0 5 0	0 5 0
–	d	Peter Lynch,	C. T. Nesbit,	Land,	0 0 20	0 1 0	—	0 1 0
–	c	Joseph Brady,	Same,	Land,	0 0 20	0 1 0	—	0 1 0
20		Anthony Brady,	Same,	House, offices, and land,	12 0 14	5 15 0	1 0 0	6 15 0
21		John Lynch,	Same,	House, offices, and land,	12 1 18	6 5 0	1 0 0	7 5 0
22		Edward Fitzsimons,	Same,	House, office, and land,	6 2 16	3 0 0	0 10 0	3 10 0
23	a	Michael Brady,	Same,	Herd's house and land,	14 3 13	7 10 0	0 10 0	8 0 0
–	b	Terence & Patk. Cogan,	Same,	Land,	0 1 24	0 5 0	—	0 5 0
24		Peter Brady,	Same,	Land,	7 0 31	3 0 0	—	3 0 0
25		John Brady,	Same,	Herd's house and land,	34 3 2	16 0 0	0 5 0	16 5 0
26		Patrick Brady,	Same,	House, offices, and land,	18 1 17	8 15 0	1 15 0	10 10 0
27		C. T. Nesbit,	In fee,	Land,	14 0 13	0 15 0	—	0 15 0

B

Griffith's Valuation, Castlerahan, Co. Cavan
(Courtesy of the Genealogical Office)

Michael. Copies of the valuation are widely available in major libraries and record offices, both on microfiche and in their original published form. The dates of first publication will be found under the individual counties in Chapter 12.

The valuation was never intended as a census substitute, and if the 1851 census had survived, it would have little genealogical significance. As things stand, however, it gives the only detailed guide to where in Ireland people lived in the mid-nineteenth century, and what property they possessed. In addition, because the valuation entries were subsequently revised at regular intervals, it is often possible to trace living descendants of those originally listed by Griffith. (See 'Valuation Office Records' below)

INDEXES TO GRIFFITH'S AND TITHE BOOKS

In the early 1960s, the National Library undertook a project to index the surnames occurring in Griffith's Valuation and the Tithe Books, which produced the county-by-county series known as the 'Index of Surnames' or 'Householders Index'. This records the occurrence of households of a particular surname in each of the civil parishes of a county, giving the exact number of households in the case of Griffith's, as well as providing a summary of the total numbers in each barony of the county. Since it is not a true index, providing only an indication of the presence or absence of a surname in the Tithe Books, and the numbers of the surname in Griffith's, its usefulness is limited. For names which are relatively uncommon, it can be invaluable, but is of little assistance for a county in which a particular surname is plentiful. It is most frequently used as a means of narrowing the number of parish records to be searched in a case where only the county of origin of an ancestor is known. The county volumes include outline maps of the civil parishes covered, and, a guide to the corresponding Catholic parishes. Full sets of the 'Index of Surnames' can be found at the National Library, the National Archives, the Public Record Office of Northern Ireland and the Genealogical Office.

In recent years, a number of full-name indexes to Griffith's have been produced on microfiche by All-Ireland Heritage and Andrew Morris, both in the US. These list alphabetically all the householders in the valuation, and show the townland and civil parish in which the entry is recorded. For the moment, the following areas have been covered: Cos Cork, Fermanagh, Limerick, Tipperary, Waterford, and the cities of Belfast, Cork and Dublin (All-Ireland Heritage); Cos Mayo and Wicklow (Andrew Morris). As aids to locating individual families in these counties at the time of the valuation, these are invaluable. However, they are not widely available as yet. The National Archives has copies of the indexes for Cork city and county, Dublin city and Co. Fermanagh, while the National Library has copies of all the indexes.

These indexes have now been superseded by the CD-ROM index to the entire valuation published in 1997 by Broderbund Software, in association with Heritage World of Dungannon and the Genealogical Publishing Company. The CD has the potential to be one of the most significant tools ever created for Irish genealogy, particularly for those who do not know the area of origin in Ireland, but it needs to be used with some caution — McCarthy, for instance, may be included as 'Mc Carthy', 'Mcarthy', 'M'Carthy' etc. and there are significant numbers of errors and omissions. If your ancestors do not appear where you think they should, check the originals. Despite any flaws, however, it is a very welcome resource. It is available to the public at the National Library.

129.

CASTLERAHAN BARONY

CASTLERAHAN PARISH. CASTLERAHAN BARONY, OLDCASTLE UNION,

CO. CAVAN 32.

Griffith's Valuation Year 1856 – Tithe Applotment Book
Year 1831.

Surname	G	T	Surname	G	T	Surname	G	T
Anderson	G		Cunningham	G2	T	Hanly	G2	T
Armstrong	G	T	Curran	G		Hanna	G	
			Cusack	G		Hanley		T
Balfe	G					Hartley		T
Barclay		T	Daly	G2	T	Haulton		T
Barry	G		Darcy		T	Hawthorn	G5	T
Bartley	G2	T	Darling	G		Haynes	G	
Bates	G		Dempsey	G		Heeny	G2	T
Bell	G		Dolan	G6	T	Heery	G4	T
Bennett	G3	T	Donnelly	G2	T	Henesy	G	
Blackstock		T	Dowland		T	Henway		T
Booker	G	T	Downs	G		Hourigan	G4	T
Boyd	G		Duffy	G3	T	Hughes	G3	
Boyers		T	Duigan	G		Humphries		T
Boylan	G4	T	Duignan	G2	T	Hunter	G3	T
Brady	G42	T				Hyland		T
Bray	G3	T	Evans	G2	T			
Brennan	G	T				Irwin	G2	
Briody	G		Fagan	G6	T			
Brookes	G		Farely	G	T	James		T
Brown	G		Farrell	G9	T	Johnston	G	
Browne	G		Farrelly	G15	T			
Buchanan	G	T	Finigan	G	T	Kavanagh	G	
Byres	G6		Finn		T	Keane	G	T
			Finnegan	G2	T	Keelan	G	
Caffrey	G13	T	Fitzpatrick	G3	T	Kellett	G2	
Cahill	G4	T	Fitzsimon	G9	T	Kelly	G2	
Caldwell	G3	T	Fitzsimons	G	T	Kennedy	G3	T
Callaghan	G3		Fleming	G2		Kenny	G	
Carey	G		Flood	G5	T	Keoghan	G	T
Carolin		T	Flynn	G3	T	Kerr	G	
Carr	G		Foster	G2	T	Kiernan	G	
Carroll	G		Fox	G6		Kilrian		T
Cartan	G		Freeland	G	T	Kilroy		T
Clarekin	G2	T				Kimmins		T
Clarke	G5	T	Gaffney	G2	T	King	G3	
Cobey		T	Gaghran		T			
Cochrane	G		Galaher	G		Leeson	G	
Cogan	G12		Galligan		T	Leightel	G3	
Colerigg	G2	T	Gavan	G	T	Little		T
Colgan	G4	T	Gaynor	G6	T	Lord	G	
Colingg	G		Geoghegan	G2		Lougheed	G	
Comerford		T	Gibney	G3	T	Loughlin		
Conaghty	G		Gibson	G	T	Love	G2	T
Condon		T	Gill	G		Lyddy	G	T
Connell	G4	T	Gillick	G	T	Lynch	G51	T
Connor	G	T	Gilroy	G				
Conway	G3		Glannon		T	M'Cabe	G13	T
Cooke	G	T	Goff		T	M'Cahill	G	T
Cooney	G		Gormley	G		M'Cormack	G	
Coote	G5	T	Grattan		T	M'Cutchion		T
Corrigan	G2	T	Graveny		T	M'Dermott	G	
Cosgrave	G	T	Gray		T	M'Donald	G5	T
Coyle	G	T	Griffin		T	M'Donnell	G	
Crawly	G	T	Griffith	G	T	M'Dowell	G2	
Cronin	G3	T				M'Enerny		T
Cullen	G9	T	Halpin	G3	T	M'Enroe	G14	T
Cuming	G4	T	Halton		T	M'Evoy	G	T
Cumisky	G2	T	Hamilton		T	M'Fadden	G4	T

'Index of Surnames', Co. Cavan
(Courtesy of the Genealogical Office)

VALUATION OFFICE RECORDS

The Valuation Office, set up to carry out the original Primary Valuation, is still in existence, and has two related sets of records which are potentially valuable. The first of these are the notebooks used by the original valuation surveyors, consisting of 'field books', 'house books' and 'tenure books'. All three record a map reference for the holdings they deal with, as in the published valuation. The field books then record information on the size and quality of the holding, the house books record the occupiers' names and the measurements of any buildings on their holdings, and the tenure books give the annual rent paid and the legal basis on which the holding is occupied, whether by lease or at will. The tenure books also give the year of any lease, useful to know before searching estate papers or the Registry of Deeds. As well as containing information such as this, which does not appear in the published valuation, the valuers' notebooks can also be useful in documenting any changes in occupation between the initial survey and the published results, for instance, if a family emigrated in the years immediately before publication, since they pre-date the final publication itself by several years. Unfortunately, they are not extant for all areas. The National Archives now houses those which survive for the Republic of Ireland. Those covering Northern Ireland are now to be found in the Public Record Office of Northern Ireland.

The Valuation Office itself, now situated in the Irish Life Centre, Abbey Street, Dublin 1, contains the second set of useful records. These are the 'Cancelled Land Books' and 'Current Land Books', giving details of all changes in the holdings from the time of the Primary Valuation up to the present day. Any variations in the size or status of the holding, the names of the occupier or lessor, or the valuation itself are given in the revisions carried out every few years. The books can be very useful in pinpointing a possible date of death or emigration, or in identifying a living relative. A large majority of those who were in occupation of a holding by the 1890s, when the Land Acts began to subsidise the purchase of the land by its tenant-farmers, have descendants or relatives still living in the same area. The Cancelled Land Books for Northern Ireland are now in the Public Record Office of Northern Ireland.

ESTATE RECORDS

In the eighteenth and nineteenth centuries, the vast majority of the Irish population lived as small tenant farmers on large estates owned for the most part by English or Anglo-Irish landlords. The administration of these estates inevitably produced large quantities of records — maps, tenants' lists, rentals, account books, lease books etc. Over the course of the twentieth century, as the estates have been broken up and sold off, many collections of these records have found their way into public repositories, and constitute a largely unexplored source of genealogical information.

There are, however, good reasons for their being unexplored. First, it was quite rare for a large landowner to have individual rental or lease agreements with the huge numbers of small tenants on his land. Instead, he would let a significant area to a middleman, who would then sublet to others, who might in turn rent out parts to the smallest tenants. It is very rare for estate records to document the smallest land-holders, since most of these had no right of tenure in any case, being simply tenants 'at will'.

17.

Surname		Barony	
Fitzgerald	G2		Loughtee L.
Fitzgerald	G	T	Loughtee U.
Fitzgerald		T	Tullygarvey
Fitzgerald	G2	T	Clankee
Fitzgerald	G2		Clanmahon
Fitzmaurice	G		Tullyhunco
Fitzpatrick	G25	T	Tullyhaw
Fitzpatrick	G114	T	Loughtee L.
Fitzpatrick	G24	T	Tullyhunco
Fitzpatrick	G73	T	Loughtee U.
Fitzpatrick	G30	T	Tullygarvey
Fitzpatrick	G9	T	Clankee
Fitzpatrick	G33	T	Clanmahon
Fitzpatrick	G10	T	Castlerahan
Fitzimmons		T	Tullyhunco
Fitzsimmons	G	T	Loughtee U.
Fitzsimmons	G	T	Clanmahon
Fitzsimon	G	T	Tullyhunco
Fitzsimon	G2	T	Loughtee U.
Fitzsimon	G7	T	Tullygarvey
Fitzsimon	G	T	Clankee
Fitzsimon	G		Clanmahon
Fitizsimon	G5	T	Castlerahan
Fitzsimon	G39	T	Castlerahan
Fitzsimons	G	T	Tullyhaw
Fitzsimons	G6	T	Loughtee L.
Fitzsimons	G12	T	Loughtee U.
Fitzsimons	G8	T	Tullygarvey
Fitzsimons	G7	T	Clankee
Fitzsimons	G14	T	Clanmahon
Fitzsimons	G6	T	Castlerahan
Flack		T	Tullyhunco
Flack	G2	T	Tullygarvey
Fleck	G3	T	Clankee
Flaherty		T	Loughtee L.
Flanagan	G14	T	Tullyhaw
Flanagan	G3	T	Loughtee L.
Flanagan	G		Tullyhunco
Flanagan	G10	T	Loughtee U.
Flanagan	G	T	Tullygarvey
Flanagan	G4	T	Clankee
Flanagan	G3	T	Clanmahon
Flanagan	G14	T	Castlerahan
Flanigan	G2	T	Tullyhaw
Flanigan	G		Loughtee L.
Flanigan		T	Loughtee U.
Flannagan	G		Loughtee L.
Flannery	G		Loughtee U.
Fleming	G		Tullyhaw
Fleming	G	T	Loughtee L.
Fleming	G3	T	Tullyhunco
Fleming	G8	T	Loughtee U.
Fleming	G	T	Tullygarvey
Fleming	G	T	Clankee
Fleming	G9	T	Clanmahon
Fleming	G7	T	Castlerahan
Fletcher	G		Loughtee U.
Fleuker	G	T	Clankee
Flewker	G2	T	Clankee
Flinn		T	Clankee
Flinn	G	T	Clanmahon
Flood	G	T	Tullyhaw
Flood	G8	T	Loughtee L.
Flood	G3	T	Tullyhunco

Surname		Barony	
Flood	G21	T	Loughtee U.
Flood	G18	T	Tullygarvey
Flood	G4	T	Clankee
Flood	G14	T	Clanmahon
Flood	G29	T	Castlerahan
Floody	G3	T	Tullygarvey
Floyd	G2	T	Loughtee U.
Flynn	G13	T	Tullyhaw
Flynn	G6	T	Loughtee L.
Flynn	G		Tullyhunco
Flynn	G3	T	Loughtee U.
Flynn		T	Tullygarvey
Flynn	G		Clankee
Flynn	G9	T	Clanmahon
Flynn	G20	T	Castlerahan
Foghlan	G		Tullyhaw
Folbus		T	Tullyhunco
Foley	G2		Tullygarvey
Follett	G		Loughtee U.
Fonor		T	Castlerahan
Forbes	G	T	Tullyhunco
Forbes	G	T	Clankee
Ford	G		Tullyhaw
Ford	G		Loughtee U.
Ford	G2	T	Tullygarvey
Ford	G		Clankee
Forde	G	T	Tullyhaw
Foreman	G6	T	Clankee
Forest		T	Loughtee U.
Forster		T	Loughtee U.
Forster	G10	T	Clanmahon
Forsyth	G3	T	Castlerahan
Forsythe	G3	T	Clanmahon
Fosqua		T	Tullygarvey
Foster	G	T	Tullyhaw
Foster	G6	T	Loughtee U.
Foster	G5		Tullygarvey
Foster	G9	T	Clanmahon
Foster	G3	T	Castlerahan
Fotton		T	Tullygarvey
Fottrell	G		Clankee
Fox	G2	T	Tullyhaw
Fox	G2	T	Tullyhunco
Fox		T	Loughtee U.
Fox	G4	T	Tullygarvey
Fox	G15	T	Clankee
Fox	G2	T	Clanmahon
Fox	G36	T	Castlerahan
Foy	G3	T	Loughtee L.
Foy	G2	T	Loughtee U.
Foy	G26	T	Tullygarvey
Foy	G5	T	Clankee
Foy	G	T	Clanmahon
Foy		T	Castlerahan
Foyragh		T	Tullygarvey
Frances	G	T	Clankee
Francey	G3		Clankee
Francis		T	Loughtee L.
Fraser	G3	T	Tullyhaw
Frazer	G		Tullyhaw
Frazer	G		Loughtee U.
Frazor		T	Tullyhunco
Freeland	G	T	Castlerahan
Freeman	G2	T	Tullygarvey

'Index of Surnames', Castlerahan, Co. Cavan
(Courtesy of the Genealogical Office)

A related problem is the question of access. The estate records in the two major Dublin repositories, the National Archives and the National Library, are not catalogued in detail. The only comprehensive guide is given in Richard Hayes's 'Manuscript Sources for the Study of Irish Civilization' and its supplements, copies of which can be found in the National Library and National Archives. This catalogues the records by landlord's name and by county, with entries such as 'NL Ms 3185. Rent Roll of Lord Cremorne's estate in Co. Armagh, 1797'. Hayes gives no more detail of the areas of the county covered, and it can be difficult to ascertain from the Tithe Books or Griffith's just who the landlord was; Griffith's only supplies the name of the immediate lessor. The holdings of the Public Record Office of Northern Ireland are catalogued more comprehensively, but still do not relate the papers to the precise areas covered. Again, it is necessary to know the landlord's name. In addition, it should be added that many of the collections in the National Library have still not been catalogued at all, and thus remain completely inaccessible.

The largest single collection in the National Archives is the Landed Estate Court records, also known as the Encumbered Estate Courts, which are not catalogued in Hayes. The court was set up to facilitate the sale of estates whose owners could not invest enough to make them productive, and between 1849 and 1857 oversaw the sale of more than 3,000 Irish estates. Its records contain many rentals and maps drawn up for the sales, but are so close in time to Griffith's as to make them of limited use except in very particular circumstances. The National Archives has an index to the townlands covered by the records.

There are a number of ways to overcome, or partially overcome, the obstacle of the landlord's name. With common sense, it is often possible to identify the landlord by examining Griffith's for the surrounding areas — the largest lessor is the likeliest candidate. If the immediate lessor in Griffith's is not the landlord, but a middleman, then it can be useful to try to find this middleman's own holding or residence and see who he was leasing from. Two publications may also be of value. O.H. Hussey de Burgh's *The Landowners of Ireland* provides a guide to the major landowners, the size of their holdings, and where in the country they were situated. *Landowners in Ireland: Return of owners of land of one acre and upwards . . .* (London: 1876) is comprehensive to a fault, and is organised more awkwardly, alphabetically within county.

Despite all the problems, research in estate records can be very rewarding, especially for the period before the major nineteenth-century surveys. To take one example, the rent rolls of the estate of Charles O'Hara in Cos Sligo and Leitrim, which date from *c.*1775, record a large number of leases to smaller tenants and supply the lives named in the leases, often specifying family relationships. It must be emphasised, however, that information of this quality is rare; the majority of the rentals and tenants' lists surviving only give details of major tenants.

A more detailed guide to the dates, areas covered and class of tenants recorded in the estate papers of the National Library and National Archives is in the process of preparation by the National Library, in association with the Irish Genealogical Society of Minnesota. To date, Cos Armagh, Cavan, Cork, Donegal, Fermanagh, Leitrim, Galway, Mayo, Monaghan, Roscommon, Sligo, Tyrone and Waterford have been covered, and a brief outline of the results will be found in Chapter 12 under these counties.

Part 2 ◆ Other Sources

5. WILLS

PART 1

Wills have always been an extremely important source of genealogical information on the property-owning classes in Ireland as elsewhere. They provide a clear picture of a family at a particular point in time, and can often supply enough details of a much larger network of relationships — cousins, nephews, in-laws and others — to produce quite a substantial family tree. Apart from their genealogical significance, wills can also evoke vividly the long-vanished way of life of those whose final wishes they record.

INFORMATION SUPPLIED

The minimum information to be found in a will is:
- the name, address and occupation of the testator;
- the names of the beneficiaries;
- the name(s) of the executor(s);
- the names of the witnesses;
- the date the will was made;
- the date of probate of the will.

Specific properties are usually, though not always, mentioned. The two dates, that of the will itself and of its probate, give a period during which the testator died. Up to the nineteenth century, most wills were made close to the date of death, and witnesses were normally related to the person making the will. As well as the minimum information, of course, many wills also contain much more, including at times addresses and occupations of beneficiaries, witnesses and executors, and details of family relationships, quarrels as well as affection.

TESTAMENTARY AUTHORITY BEFORE 1857

Before 1857, the Church of Ireland, as the Established Church, had charge of all testamentary affairs. Consistorial Courts in each diocese were responsible for granting probate, that is, legally authenticating a will and conferring on the executors the power to administer the estate. The courts also had the power to issue letters of administration to the next of kin or the main creditor on the estates of those who died intestate. Each court was responsible for wills and administrations in its own diocese. However, when the estate included property worth more than £5 in another diocese, responsibility for the will or administration passed to the Prerogative Court, under the authority of the Archbishop of Armagh.

CONSISTORIAL WILLS AND ADMINISTRATIONS

The wills and administration records of the Consistorial Courts were held locally in each diocese up to the abolition of the testamentary authority of the Church of Ireland in 1857. After that date, the Public Record Office began the slow process of collecting the original records, and transcribing them into Will and Grant Books. The office then indexed the wills and administration bonds, the sureties which the administrators had to produce as a guarantee that the estate would be properly administered. None of the Consistorial Courts had records of all of the wills or administrations they had dealt with. Very little earlier than the seventeenth century emerged, and the majority of the courts appear to have had serious gaps before the mid-eighteenth century.

All of the original wills and administrations in the Public Record Office were destroyed in 1922, along with almost all of the Will and Grant Books into which they had been transcribed. The only exceptions are the Will Books for Down (1850–1858) and Connor (1818–20, 1853–58), and the Grant Books for Cashel (1840–45), Derry and Raphoe (1818–21), and Ossory (1848–58).

The indexes to wills and administration bonds were not destroyed, although a number were badly damaged. These are available in the reading room of the National Archives. The wills indexes are alphabetical, and normally give the testator's address and the year of probate, as well as occasionally specifying his occupation. The administration bonds indexes are not fully alphabetical, being arranged year by year under the initial letter of the surname of the deceased person. They give the year of the bond, the full name and usually the address of the deceased, and sometimes his occupation. Some of the wills indexes have been published, and details of these will be found at the end of this chapter.

PREROGATIVE WILLS AND ADMINISTRATIONS

To recap: an estate was dealt with by the Prerogative Court, rather than a Consistorial Court, if it covered property worth more than £5 in a second diocese. In general, then, prerogative wills and administrations tend to cover the wealthier classes, merchants with dealings in more than one area, and those who lived close to diocesan borders. Up to 1816, the Prerogative Court was not housed in a single place, with hearings generally held in the residence of the presiding judge. From 1816 on, the King's Inns building in Henrietta St provided a permanent home. For this reason, the records of the court before 1816 cannot be taken as complete. After 1857, all of these records were transferred to the Public Record Office, where the original wills and grants of administration were transcribed into Prerogative Will and Grant Books, and indexed. The indexes survived 1922, but all of the original wills and grants, and almost all of the Will and Grant Books were destroyed. Details of those books which survived will be found at the end of this chapter.

The loss of the original prerogative wills is mitigated to a large extent by the project carried out in the early decades of the nineteenth century by Sir William Betham, Ulster King of Arms. As well as preparing the first index of testators, up to 1810, he also made abstracts of the family information contained in almost all of the wills before 1800. The original notebooks in which he recorded the information are now in the National Archives, and the Genealogical Office has his Sketch Pedigrees based on these abstracts and including later additions and amendments. The Public

270   WILLS AND ADMINISTRATIONS. 1871.

HORGAN Daniel.

[191]   Effects under £200.

20 March.   Letters of Administration of the personal estate of Daniel Horgan late of Great George's-street **Cork** Builder deceased who died 21 February 1870 at same place were granted at **Cork** to Michael Joseph Horgan of the South Mall in said City Solicitor the Nephew of said deceased for the benefit of Catherine Horgan Widow John Horgan the Reverend David Horgan Ellen Gillman Mary Daly and Margaret Horgan only next of kin of said deceased.

HORNE Christopher.

[67]   Effects under £100.

7 March.   Letters of Administration of the personal estate of Christopher Horne late of Ballinasloe County **Galway** Gentleman a Widower deceased who died 21 March 1867 at same place were granted at the **Principal Registry** to Patrick Horne of Ballinasloe aforesaid M.D. the only Brother of said deceased.

HORNER Isabella.

[17]   Effects under £100.

29 April.   Letters of Administration of the personal estate of Isabella Horner late of Rahaghy County **Tyrone** Widow deceased who died 13 April 1871 at same place were granted at **Armagh** to James Horner of Rahaghy (Aughnacloy) aforesaid Farmer the Son and one of the next of kin of said deceased.

HORNIDGE John Isaiah.

[79]   Effects under £450.

8 June.   Letters of Administration (with the Will annexed) of the personal estate of John Isaiah Hornidge late of the South Dublin Union Workhouse **Dublin** Master of said Workhouse a Widower deceased who died 22 April 1871 at same place were granted at the **Principal Registry** to James Seymour Longstaff of Stephen's-green Dublin Merchant and William Thomas Orpin of George's-terrace George's-avenue Blackrock County Dublin Accountant the Guardians during minority only of the Daughter and only next of kin of deceased.

HOUSTON Eliza.

[337]   Effects under £200.

22 September.   Letters of Administration of the personal estate of Eliza Houston late of Gortin County **Donegal** Spinster deceased who

Calendar of Wills and Administrations, 1871
(Courtesy of the National Archives of Ireland)

Record Office of Northern Ireland has a copy of the Genealogical Office series, without the additions and amendments, made by a successor of Betham's, Sir John Burke. Betham also made a large number of abstracts from Prerogative Grants up to 1802. The original notebooks for these are also in the National Archives. The Genealogical Office transcript copy (GO 257–260) is fully alphabetical, unlike the notebooks.

The first index to prerogative wills, up to 1810, was published in 1897 by Sir Arthur Vicars, Burke's successor as Ulster King of Arms, and can be used as a guide to Betham's abstracts and Sketch Pedigrees with the proviso that wills from the decade 1800–1810 are not covered by Betham. The manuscript index for the period from 1811 to 1857 is in the National Archives reading room. As with the consistorial administration bonds indexes, the Prerogative Grants indexes are not fully alphabetical, being arranged year by year under the initial letter of the surname of the deceased person.

Testamentary Authority after 1857

The Probate Act of 1857 did away with the testamentary authority of the Church of Ireland. Instead of the Consistorial Courts and the Prerogative Court, power to grant probate and issue letters of administration was vested in a Principal Registry in Dublin, and eleven District Registries. Rules similar to those governing the geographical jurisdiction of the ecclesiastical courts applied, with the principal registry taking the place of the Prerogative Court, as well as covering Dublin and a large area around it. Transcripts of the wills proved and administrations granted were made in the district registries, and the originals forwarded to the principal registry. Almost all of the records of the principal registry were destroyed in 1922. The few surviving Will and Grant Books are detailed below. The Will Book transcripts made by the district registries survived, however. The records of those districts covering areas now in the Republic — Ballina, Cavan, Cork, Kilkenny, Limerick, Mullingar, Tuam and Waterford — are in the National Archives. For districts now in Northern Ireland — Armagh, Belfast and Londonderry — the Will Books are in the Public Record Office of Northern Ireland.

Fortunately, from 1858 a new system of indexing and organising wills and administrations had been devised. A printed, alphabetically ordered 'Calendar of Wills and Administrations' was produced for every year, and copies of all of these have survived. For each will or administration, these record:
- the name, address and occupation of the deceased person;
- the place and date of death;
- the value of the estate;
- the name and address of the person or persons to whom probate or administration was granted.

In many cases, the relationship of the executor is also specified. This means that, despite the loss of so much original post 1857 testamentary material, some information at least is available on all wills or administrations from this period. Very often much that is of genealogical value can be gleaned from the calendars, including such information as exact dates of death, places of residence, and indications of economic status. A consolidated index covers the period between

PUBLIC RECORD OFFICE OF IRELAND.

Class.—TESTAMENTARY. *Diocese - Cork & Ross* Sub-Class.—WILLS.
District Registry - Cork.

Testator's Name.		Year of Probate.	Day.	Tray.	Number.
O'Coghlane	Donell Reige *Crookhaven*	1620	18	31	
O'Comon	Connor *Twmore*	1675			
O'Conohan	Teige *Cork*	1664			
O'Connor	Joshua *Cork*	1796			
"	Patrick	1851			
O'Crouly	Teige *Behegallane*	1683			
O'Crowly	Revᵈ Jas. Patrick *Ballinrishig*	1829			
"	Timothy P.P. *Killmocomoy*	1789			
O'Daniel	Theophilus *Cork*	1736			
O'Dea als Walsh	Beale	1649			
O'Donnell	James *Ballyeurrig*	1781			
"	Mary *Cork*	1845			
O'Donoghue	Elizabeth *Cork*	1809			

Diocesan Will Index, Cork and Ross
(Courtesy of the National Archives of Ireland)

1858 and 1877, making it unnecessary to search each yearly calendar. The calendars are on open access in the National Archives and Public Record Office of Northern Ireland reading rooms.

ABSTRACTS AND TRANSCRIPTS

As well as the original consistorial and prerogative wills and grants, and the transcripts made of them in the Will and Grant Books, a wide number of other sources exist, particularly for material before 1857. The most important of these is the collection of the National Archives itself, gathered after 1922 in an attempt to replace some at least of what had been lost. As well as original wills from private legal records and individual families, this ever expanding collection also includes pre–1922 researchers' abstracts and transcripts. It is covered by a card index in the reading room, which also gives details of those wills and grants in the surviving pre-1857 Will and Grant Books. Separate card indexes cover the Thrift, Jennings and Crossley collections of abstracts, and the records of Charitable Donations and Bequests. The Public Record Office of Northern Ireland has made similar efforts, and the copies it holds are indexed in the Pre–1858 Wills Index, part of the Subject Index in the public search room.

Inland Revenue Records

The Inland Revenue in London kept a series of annual Indexes to Irish Will Registers and Indexes to Irish Administration Registers from 1828 to 1879, which are now in the National Archives. These give the name and address of both the deceased and the executor or administrator. As well as the indexes, the Archives also hold a set of the actual Inland Revenue Irish Will Registers and Irish Administration Registers for the years 1828–39, complete apart from the Wills Register covering January to June 1834. The Will Registers are not exact transcripts of the original wills, but supply a good deal of detailed information, including the precise date of death, the principal beneficiaries and legacies, and a brief inventory of the estate. The Administration Registers are less informative, but still include details of the date of death, the administrator and the estate.

Land Commission Records

Under the provisions of the Land Purchase Acts, which subsidised the purchase of smallholdings by the tenants who occupied them, it was necessary for those wishing to sell to produce evidence of their ownership to the Irish Land Commission. As a result, over 10,000 wills were deposited with the commission, the majority from the nineteenth century, but many earlier. The National Library holds a card index to the testators. The original documents are currently in the process of being transferred to the National Archives.

The Registry of Deeds

The registration of wills was normally carried out because of a legal problem anticipated by the executor(s) in the provisions — almost certainly the exclusion of parties who would feel they had some rights over the estate. Because of this, wills at the registry cannot be taken as providing a complete picture of the family. Abstracts of all wills registered from 1708, the date of foundation of the registry, to 1832, were published in three volumes by the Irish Manuscripts Commission between 1954 and 1986. These are available on open shelves at the National Library and NAI. Although the abstracts record and index all the persons named, testators, beneficiaries and witnesses, they do not show the original provisions of the wills. These can be found in the original memorials in the registry.

The Genealogical Office

Most of the will abstracts held by the Genealogical Office are covered by the office's own index, GO Ms 429, which was published in *Analecta Hibernica*, No. 17, 1949 (NLI Ir. 941 a 10). The manuscript index has since been added to, but is still not entirely comprehensive, excluding all of the Betham material, and many of the collections relating to individual families. An outline of the major collections is included in the reference guide at the end of this chapter.

Other Sources

There are many other collections of will abstracts and transcripts in such public repositories as the National Library, the Representative Church Body Library, the Royal Irish Academy, the Public Record Office of Northern Ireland and Trinity College Library. There are no separate indexes to these testamentary collections. Where a significant group of abstracts or transcripts exists, this is noted in the reference guide which follows.

PART 2. A REFERENCE GUIDE

What follows is an attempt to provide a series of checklists and guides to the various testamentary sources. Because of the changes in testamentary jurisdiction in 1858, it is divided into two sections, dealing with records before and after that date. Section One, pre-1858, includes (1) a general checklist of surviving indexes; (2) a list of surviving Will and Grant Books; (3) a list of major collections of abstracts and transcripts, divided into (i) general collections, (ii) those relating to particular surnames, and (iii) those relating to particular diocesan jurisdictions; (4) a detailed list of surviving consistorial wills and administrations indexes, both published and in the National Archives. Section Two, post 1858, covers (1) the yearly calendars; and (2) original wills and transcripts.

SECTION ONE: PRE-1858

1. General Indexes

1. Card Indexes, NAI search room
2. Pre–1858 Wills Index, PRONI reading room
3. Indexes to Consistorial Wills and Administrations, diocese by diocese. See below for details
4. Indexes to Prerogative Wills:

    (a) Sir Arthur Vicars, *Index to the Prerogative Wills of Ireland 1536–1810* (1897)
    (b) Ms Index, 1811–1858, NAI, PRONI
5. Index to Prerogative Grants, NAI, PRONI
6. Index to Wills in the Records of the Land Commission, NLI

2. Surviving Will and Grant Books

1. Prerogative Will Books: 1664–84, 1706–08 (A–W), 1726–28 (A–W), 1728–29 (A–W), 1777 (A–L), 1813 (K–Z), 1834 (A–E) NAI, included in card index
2. Prerogative Administrations: Grants 1684–88,1748–51, 1839; Day Books, 1784–88, NAI
3. Consistorial Will Books: Connor (1818–20, 1853–58); Down (1850–58) NAI
4. Consistorial Grant Books: Cashel (1840–45); Derry & Raphoe (1812–21); Ossory (1848–58) NAI

3. Abstracts and Transcripts

(i) Gᴇɴᴇʀᴀʟ Cᴏʟʟᴇᴄᴛɪᴏɴs

1. Betham abstracts from Prerogative Wills, to *c.*1800, NAI (notebooks); GO and PRONI (Sketch Pedigrees). See Vicars above
2. Betham abstracts from Prerogative Administrations, to *c.*1800, NAI (notebooks); Genealogical Office (alphabetical listing)
3. Indexes to Irish Will Registers, 1828–79 (Inland Revenue), NAI. See Testamentary Catalogue
4. Irish Will Registers, 1828–39 (Inland Revenue), NAI. See Testamentary Catalogue
5. Indexes to Irish Administration Registers, 1828–79 (Inland Revenue), NAI. See Testamentary Catalogue
6. Irish Administration Registers, 1828–39 (Inland Revenue), NAI. See Testamentary Catalogue
7. Index to Will Abstracts at the Genealogical Office, *Analecta Hibernica*, 17, GO Ms 429
8. P.B. Phair & E. Ellis, *Abstracts of Wills at the Registry of Deeds* (1708–1832), IMC 1954–88
9. Abstracts of wills of Irish testators registered at the Prerogative Court of Canterbury 1639–98, NLI Ms 1397
10. Abstracts of miscellaneous eighteenth-century wills made by the Protestant clergy and their families, Representative Church Body Library. (For the years 1828–39, see also NLI Ms 2599.)
11. Leslie Collection, 981 wills, NLI Ms 1774. See also NLI Pos. 799
12. Ainsley Will Abstracts, GO 535 & 631
13. Wilson Collection, NLI Pos. 1990
14. Welply Collection, 1,500 wills, 100 administrations, Representative Church Body Library, indexed in *The Irish Genealogist*, 1985/86
15. Richey Collection, NLI Mss 8315–16
16. Upton Collection, Royal Irish Academy, also NLI Pos. 1997, principally families in Co. Westmeath, with some from Cos Cavan and Longford
17. MacSwiney Papers, Royal Irish Academy, mainly Cos Cork and Kerry
18. Westropp Manuscripts, Royal Irish Academy, mainly Cos Clare and Limerick

(II) BY SURNAME

Burke: GO Ms 707
Butler: Wallace Clare, *The Testamentary Records of the Butler Family*, 1932, NLI Ir.
    9292 b 11
Dawson: Almost all eighteenth-century Dawson wills, NLI Ms 5644/5
Domville: NLI Mss 9384–6
Drought: Crossley Abstracts, NAI, also GO 417/8
Gordon: GO Ms 702, abstracts of most Irish Gordon wills
Griffith: NLI Ms 8392
Greene: see NAI Card Index
Hamilton: Co. Down, PRONI T.702A
Hill: GO Ms 691–2
Kelly: GO Ms 415
Manley: NLI D.7075–86, the Manley family of Dublin and Offaly
Mathews: Prerogative wills and administrations, PRONI T.681
O'Loghlen, Co. Clare, NLI Pos. 2543
Skerrett, *The Irish Ancestor*, Vol. 5, No. 2, 1975
Young: NLI Pos. 1276

(III) BY DIOCESE

A word of warning is necessary: the identification of a collection of abstracts or
transcripts under a particular diocese does not necessarily mean that all of the wills
it covers belong to that diocese. In the case of the larger collections especially, it is
just not possible to be absolutely precise about the areas covered.

Armagh

Four Wills of old English merchants of Drogheda, 1654–1717, JCLAS, Vol. XX, 2,
    1982
Alphabetical list of the prerogative wills of residents of Co. Louth up to 1810, NLI
    Ms 7314
Index to wills of Dundalk residents, JCLAS, Vol. X, No. 2, pp. 113–15, 1942

Cashel and Emly

White, J.D. 'Extracts from original wills, formerly in the consistorial office, Cashel,
    later moved to Waterford Probate Court', *Kilkenny & South of Ire. Arch. Soc. Jnl*,
    Ser. 2, Vol. 2, Pt 2, 1859, Vol. IV, 1862

Clogher

Swanzy Collection, NAI T. 1746 (1C–53–16). Copies also at the Genealogical Office
    (GO 420, indexed in 429) and Representative Church Body Library. Abstracts
    from Clogher and Kilmore Will Books, Marriage Licence Bonds, Administrations,
    militia lists. Principal names include Beatty, Nixon, Armstrong, Young, Veitch,
    Jackson, Mee, Noble, Fiddes

Clonfert

GO 707: Numerous abstracts, mainly relating to wills mentioning Burke families

Cloyne

Welply Abstracts (4 volumes), RCBL, indexed IG, 1985/1986
Index to Will Abstracts at the Genealogical Office, *Analecta Hibernica*, 17, GO Ms
 429

Connor

Connor Will Book, 1818–20, 1853–58, NAI
Stewart-Kennedy notebooks, will abstracts, many from Down & Connor. Principal
 families include Stewart, Clarke, Cunningham, Kennedy and Wade, Trinity
 College Library & PRONI, see also NLI Pos. 4066

Cork and Ross

Welply Abstracts (4 volumes) RCBL, indexed in IG, 1985/1986
Caulfield transcripts, mainly 16th century, RCBL, see also JCHAS, 1903/1904
Notes from wills of Cork Diocese, 1660–1700, NA M. 2760

Derry

Amy Young, *300 Years in Inishowen* (NLI Ir. 9292 y 1), contains 46 Donegal wills

Down

Down Will Book, 1850–58, NAI, PRONI
Stewart-Kennedy notebooks, will abstracts, many from Down & Connor, principal
 families include Stewart, Clarke, Cunningham, Kennedy and Wade, Trinity
 College Library & PRONI

Dublin and Glendalough

Lane-Poole papers, NLI Ms 5359 (abstracts)
Abstracts of wills proved in Dublin diocesan court 1560–1710, A–E only, GO Ms
 290

Elphin

Wills & Deeds from Co. Sligo, 1605–32, NLI Ms 2164

Kildare

Betham Collection, NAI, abstracts of almost all Kildare wills up to 1827, also NLI
 Pos. 1784–5

Killaloe and Kilfenora

O'Loghlen wills from Co. Clare, NLI Pos. 2543
Wills & Administrations from Cos Clare & Limerick, Westropp manuscript, Vol. 3A
 39, RIA

Kilmore

Swanzy Collection, NAI, T. 1746 (1C–53–16), copies also at the Genealogical Office
 (GO 420, indexed in 429) and Representative Church Body Library, Abstracts
 from Clogher and Kilmore Will Books, Marriage Licence Bonds, Administrations,

militia lists, principal names include Beatty, Nixon, Armstrong, Young, Veitch, Jackson, Mee, Noble, Fiddes.

Leighlin

Carrigan Collection, NL Pos. 903 (952 wills, mainly Ossory & Leighlin), indexed in *The Irish Genealogist*, 1970
Abstracts from Ossory & Leighlin Admons, *The Irish Genealogist*, 1972

Limerick

Hayes, R., 'Some Old Limerick Wills', JNMAS, Vol. I, pp. 163–8, Vol. II, pp. 71–5
Wills & Administrations from Cos Clare & Limerick, Westropp manuscript, Vol. 3A 39, RIA

Meath

Alphabetical list of the prerogative wills of residents of Co. Louth up to 1810, NL Ms 7314
Rice, G. 'Extracts from Meath priests' wills 1658–1782', *Riocht na Midhe*, Vol. IV, No. 1, pp. 68–71, 1967

Ossory

Carrigan Collection, NL Pos. 903 (952 wills, mainly Ossory & Leighlin) indexed in *The Irish Genealogist*, 1970
Abstracts from Ossory & Leighlin Admons, *The Irish Genealogist*, 1972
T.U. Sadlier, Abstracts from Ossory Admons, 1738–1884, NAI
Calendar of Administrations, Ossory, NA T. 7425
GO 683–6, Walsh-Kelly notebooks, will abstracts, mainly from Ossory

Raphoe

Amy Young, *300 Years in Inishowen* (NLI Ir. 9292 y 1), contains 46 Donegal wills

Tuam

GO 707, numerous abstracts, mainly relating to wills mentioning Burke families 1784–1820

Waterford and Lismore

Wills relating to Waterford, *Decies* 16, 17, 19, 20, 22, 23
Jennings Collection, NAI & *Decies* (above)
166 Waterford Wills and Administrations, NLI D. 9248–9413

4. Consistorial Wills and Administration Bonds Indexes, Published and in The National Archives

DIOCESE	WILLS	ADMON BONDS
Ardagh	1695–1858 (also IA, 1970)	1697–1850
Ardfert and Aghadoe	1690–1858 (Ph. 1690–1800; O'K, Vol. 5, 1690–1858)	1782–1858 (O'K, Vol. 5, 1782–1858)
Armagh	1666–1837 (A–L) 1677–1858 (M–Y) Drogheda District 1691–1846	
Cashel and Emly	1618–1858 (Ph. 1618–1800)	1644–1858
Clogher	1661–1858	1660–1858
Clonfert	1663–1857 (IA, 1970)	1771–1857 (IA, 1970)
Cloyne	1621–1858 (Ph. 1621–1800; O'K, Vol. 8, 1547–1858)	1630–1857 (O'K Vol. 6)
Connor	1680–1846 (A–L) 1636–1857 (M–Y)	1636–1858
Cork and Ross	1548–1858 (Ph. & O'K, Vol. 8, 1548–1800; JCHAS, 1895–8, 1548–1833)	1612–1858 (O'K, Vol. 5)
Derry	1612–1858 (Ph. 1612–1858)	1698–1857
Down	1646–1858	1635–1858
Dromore	1678–1858 with Newry & Mourne, 1727–1858 (Ph.)	1742–1858 with Newry & Mourne, 1811–45 (IA, 1969, Newry & Mourne)

DIOCESE	WILLS	ADMON BONDS
Dublin and Glendalough	1536–1858 (RDKPRI, Nos 26 & 30)	1636–1858 (RDKPRI, Nos 26 & 30)
Elphin	1650–1858 (fragments) 1601–1858 (fragments) 1603–1838 (F–V) 1615–1842 (unproved, W only) (Ph. 1601–1800)	1726–1857 1765–1833
Kildare	1661–1858 (Ph. 1661–1800; JKAS, 1905, 1661–1858)	1770–1848 (JKAS, 1907, 1770–1858)
Killala and Achonry	1756–1831 (fragments)	1779–1858 (IA, 1975)
Killaloe and Kilfenora	1653–1858 (fragments) (Ph. 1653–1800)	1779–1858 (IA, 1975)
Kilmore	1682–1858 (damaged)	1728–1858
Leighlin	1642–1858 (Ph. 1642–1800)	1694–1845 (IA, 1972)
Limerick	1615–1858 (Ph. 1615–1800)	1789–1858
Meath	1572–1858 (fragments partial transcript 1635–1838) NAI	1663–1857
Ossory	1536–1858 (fragments) (Ph. 1536–1800)	1660–1857
Raphoe	1684–1858 (damaged)(Ph.)	1684–1858
Tuam	1648–1858 (damaged)	1692–1857
Waterford and Lismore	1648–1858 (damaged) (Ph. 1648–1800)	1661–1857

SECTION TWO: POST **1857**

1. Yearly Calendars of Wills & Administrations, 1858 to date

Provide: name, address & occupation of the deceased; place and exact date of death; names & addresses of grantees of probate or administration, and relationship; exact date of probate; value of the estate.

On open access in the search room of the National Archives and PRONI. The consolidated index, 1858–1877, is only in NAI.

2. Original Wills or Transcripts

(a) Card Index, NAI search room
(b) Surviving Will and Grant Books in NAI, as follows:
   (i) Principal Registry Wills, 1874, G–M
      Principal Registry Wills, 1878, A–Z
      Principal Registry Wills, 1891, G–M
      Principal Registry Wills, 1896, A–F
      Principal Registry Wills, Dublin District, 1869, G–M
      Principal Registry Wills, Dublin District, 1891, M–P
      Principal Registry Wills, Dublin District, 1901, A–F
  (ii) Principal Registry Grants, 1878, 1883, 1891, 1893
 (iii) District Registry Will Books:
      Ballina, 1865 to date
      Cavan, 1858–1909
      Cork, 1858–1932
      Kilkenny, 1858–1911
      Limerick, 1858–1899
      Mullingar, 1858–1901
      Tuam, 1858–1929,
      Waterford, 1858–1902.
(c) District Registry Will Books in the Public Record Office of Northern Ireland:
      Armagh 1858–1900 (MIC 15C)
      Belfast 1858–1900 (MIC 15C)
      Londonderry 1858–1900 (MIC 15C)

6. THE GENEALOGICAL OFFICE

The Genealogical Office is the successor to the office of Ulster King of Arms, also known simply as 'The Office of Arms', which was created in 1552 when Edward VI designated Bartholomew Butler the chief heraldic authority in Ireland, with the title of Ulster. The reasons for the choice of Ulster rather than 'Ireland' remain somewhat unclear; it seems likely that the older title of Ireland King of Arms was already in use amongst the heralds at the College of Arms in London. Whatever the reason, Ulster King of Arms acquired full jurisdiction over arms in Ireland, and retained it for almost four hundred years until 1943, when the office was renamed the Genealogical Office, and Ulster became Chief Herald of Ireland, with the same powers as his predecessor.

At the outset, the authority of Ulster was limited to those areas of the country under English authority; heraldry, as a feudal practice, was in any case quite alien to Gaelic culture. Up to the end of the seventeenth century, the functions of the office remained purely heraldic, ascertaining and recording what arms were in use, and by what right families used them. From the late seventeenth century, Ulster began to acquire other duties, as an officer of the crown intimately linked to the government. These duties were largely ceremonial, deciding and arranging precedence on state occasions, as well as introducing new peers to the Irish House of Lords, and recording peerage successions. In essence, these two areas, the heraldic and the ceremonial, remained the principal functions of the office over the succeeding three centuries, with Ulster becoming registrar of the chivalric Order of St Patrick instituted in 1783, and continuing to have responsibility for the ceremonial aspects of state occasions at the court of the viceroy.

The functioning of the office depended to an inordinate degree on the personal qualities of Ulster, and an unfortunate number of the holders of the position, in the eighteenth century especially, appear to have regarded it as a sinecure, paying little attention to the keeping of records and treating the manuscript collection as their personal property. It was only with the arrival of Sir William Betham in the early nineteenth century that the business of the office was put on a sound footing, and serious attention paid to the collection and care of manuscripts. As a consequence, although a number of the official records are much earlier, the vast majority of the office's holdings do not pre-date the nineteenth century.

In the course of carrying out its heraldic functions, the office inevitably acquired a large amount of material of genealogical interest, since the right to bear arms is strictly hereditary. None the less, the new title given to the office in 1943, the Genealogical Office, was somewhat inaccurate. Its principal function continues to be heraldic, the granting and confirmation of official achievements to individuals and corporate bodies. Up to the 1980s, the office also carried out commissioned research into family history. This service has been discontinued.

GENEALOGICAL OFFICE RECORDS

MANUSCRIPTS

The manuscripts of the Genealogical Office are numbered in a single series from 1 to 822. They are, however, of a very mixed nature, reflections of the office's changing functions over the centuries, and are best dealt with in categories based on those functions. The following account divides them into (1) Official Records, (2) Administrative Records and Reference Works, and (3) Research Material.

1. *Official Records*

A number of sets of manuscripts are direct products of the official functions of the office, and may be termed official records. On the heraldic side, the principal records are the Visitations (GO 47–9), the Funeral Entries (GO 64–79), the official grants and confirmations of arms (GO 103–111g), and the Registered Pedigrees (GO 156–182). In addition to these, four other manuscript groups reflect duties which Ulster's office acquired over the centuries. These are the Lords Entries (GO 183–188), Royal Warrants for Changes of Name (GO 26 & 149–154A), Baronets Records (GO 112–4), and Gaelic Chieftains (GO 610 & 627).

The Visitations were an attempt to carry out in Ireland heraldic visitations along the lines of those which the College of Arms had been using in England for almost a century to control the bearing of arms. The results were meagre, confined to areas close to Dublin, and almost certainly incomplete even for those areas. The following places were covered: Dublin and parts of Co. Louth, 1568–70; Drogheda and Ardee, 1570; Swords, 1572; Cork, 1574; Limerick, 1574; Dublin city, 1607; Dublin county, 1610; Wexford, 1610. They are indexed in GO 117.

The Funeral Entries, covering the period 1588–1691, make up some of the deficiencies of the Visitations. Their aim was to record the name, wife and issue of deceased nobility and gentry, along with their arms. In addition, many of the Entries include very beautiful illustrations of the arms and armorial devices used at the funeral, as well as notes on the ordering of the funeral processions and ceremonies. An index to the Entries is found in GO 386.

One of the later effects of the lack of visitations was to make it difficult for Ulster to verify from his own records that a particular family had a right to its arms. This gave rise to the practice, peculiar to Ireland, of issuing 'confirmations' of arms, which were taken as official registrations, and were dependant on an applicant being able to show that the arms in question had been in use in his family for three generations or one hundred years. The records of these confirmations, and of actual grants of arms, are found in GO 103–111g, dating from 1698, and still current. Earlier grants and confirmations are scattered through the manuscript collection; a complete index to all arms officially recorded in the office is to be found in GO 422–3. Hayes's *Manuscript Sources for the Study of Irish Civilisation* reproduces this, and includes a summary of any genealogical information.

Since the right to bear arms is hereditary, the authentication of arms required the collection of a large amount of genealogical material. This is undoubtedly the origin of the Registered Pedigrees, GO 156–182, but the series very quickly acquired a life of its own, and the majority of entries are now purely genealogical. It is particularly important for the collection of eighteenth-century pedigrees of Irish *emigrés* to France, produced in response to their need to prove membership of the nobility;

admission to such a position carried very substantial privileges, and the proofs required included the signature of Ulster. The series continues up to the present, and is indexed in GO 469, as well as Hayes's *Manuscript Sources*.

Partly as a result of difficulties concerning the status of lords who had supported James II, from 1698 one of the duties of Ulster became the keeping of an official list of Irish peers, 'Ulster's Roll'. In theory, all of those entitled to sit in the Irish House of Lords, whether by creation of a new peerage, or by succession, were obliged to inform Ulster before they could be officially introduced to the House. In practice, the vast bulk of information collected relates to successions, with the heirs supplying the date of death and place of burial, arms, marriages and issue. The series covers the period from 1698 to 1939, and is indexed in GO 470.

In order to regulate the assumption of arms and titles, after 1784 it became necessary to obtain a warrant from the King for a change of name and arms. From 1795, the Irish House of Lords made it obligatory to register such a warrant in Ulster's Office. The result is the manuscript series known officially as 'Royal Warrants for changes of name and licences for changes of name'. Most of the nineteenth-century changes came about as a result of wills, with an inheritance made conditional on a change of name. Hayes's *Manuscript Sources* indexes the series.

A similar need to regulate the improper assumption of titles produced the Baronet's records, GO 112–14. A royal warrant of 1789 for 'correcting and preventing abuses in the order of baronets' made registration of their arms and pedigrees with Ulster obligatory. The volumes are indexed in GO 470.

The records of Gaelic Chieftains in GO 610 and 627 are the consequence of a revival instituted in the 1940s by Dr Edward MacLysaght, the first Chief Herald of Ireland. He attempted to trace the senior lineal descendants in the male line of the last recorded Gaelic 'Chief of the Name', who was then officially designated as the contemporary holder of the title. The practice has met with mixed success, since the collapse of Gaelic culture in the seventeenth century left an enormous gulf to be bridged, and the chieftainships were not in any case originally passed on by primogeniture but by election within the extended kin-group. None the less, more than twenty chiefs have been designated, and the records of the research which went into establishing their right to the title are extremely interesting.

2. *Administrative Records and Reference Works*

Many of the documents now part of the general manuscript series simply derive from the paperwork necessary to run an office. These include cash books, receipts, Ulster's Diaries, letter books, day books, and records of fees due for the various functions carried out by Ulster. Of these, the most interesting from a genealogical point of view are the letter books (GO 361–378), copies of all letters sent out from the office between 1789 and 1853, and the Betham letters (GO 580–604), a collection of the letters received by Sir William Betham between *c.*1810 and 1830 and purchased by the Genealogical Office in 1943. The former are indexed volume by volume. The latter are of more potential value. The only index, however, comes in the original catalogue of the sale of the letters, dated 1936, a copy of which is to be found at the office, though not numbered among the manuscripts. The catalogue lists the letters alphabetically by addressor, and a supplementary surnames index provides a guide to the families dealt with. Another eight volumes of the series, unindexed, are to be found in the National Archives (M.744–751).

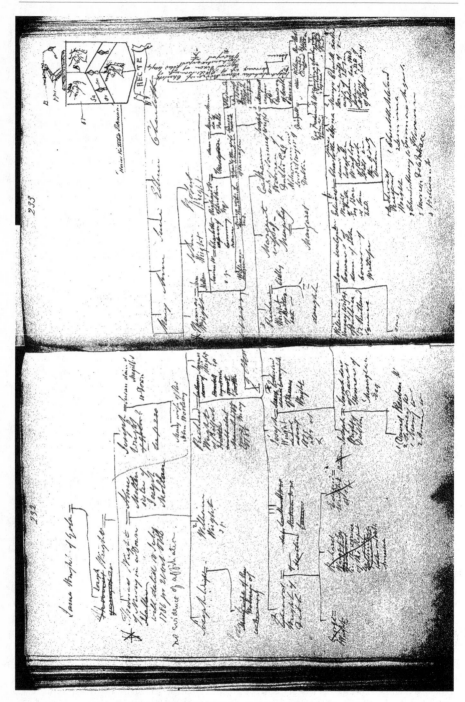

Betham's 'Sketch Pedigrees from Will Abstracts'
(Courtesy of the Genealogical Office)

As well as documents produced in the day-to-day running of the office, a large number of manuscripts also relate to the ceremonial functions performed by Ulster. These include official orders relating to changes of insignia, papers dealing with precedence and protocol, records of official functions at the viceregal court, and the records of the Order of St Patrick. There is little of genealogical interest in these.

In the course of their heraldic and genealogical work, Ulster and his officers accumulated over the years a large series of manuscripts for use as reference works. These include manuscript armories, ordinaries of arms, treatises on heraldry and precedence, a series of English Visitations, and blazons of arms of English and Scottish peers. The bulk of the material is heraldic, but there is a good deal of incidental genealogical information, particularly in the seventeenth-century ordinaries of arms.

3. Research Material

The most useful manuscripts in the Genealogical Office collection are those acquired and created to provide sources for genealogical research. The policy was begun in the early nineteenth century by Sir William Betham and continued by all of his successors, and has produced a wide range of material, much of it based on records which were destroyed in the Public Record Office in 1922. It may be divided into three broad categories: (i) Betham's own compilations; (ii) the collections of later genealogists; (iii) other records. The sheer diversity of these documents makes a complete account impractical here; what follows is a broad outline.

The greatest single work produced by Betham is the collection of abstracts of family information from prerogative wills. These are divided into a number of series: GO 223–226 ('Old Series' vols I–IV) covers wills before 1700; GO 227–254 ('New Series' vols 1–31) covers wills from 1700 to *c*.1800. The series is roughly alphabetical, with each volume containing its own index. Sir Arthur Vicars' *Index to the Prerogative Wills of Ireland 1536–1810* provides a guide to wills covered. Many of the sketch pedigrees include later amendments and additions from other sources. GO 255–6 index all of the marriage alliances recorded in the wills. Another series, GO 203–214 ('Will Pedigrees' vols I–XII) represents an unfinished attempt to re-arrange all of these sketch pedigrees into strictly alphabetical order. Betham also produced a large number of sketch pedigrees based on other sources, collected as 'Ancient Anglo-Irish Families' vols I–VI (GO 215–219), 'Milesian Families' vols I–III (GO 220–222), and the '1st series' vols I–XVI (GO 261–276) and 2nd series vols I–VII (GO 292–298). All of these are indexed in GO 470.

As well as the sketch pedigrees and the letters (covered above under 'Administrative Records'), there are two other sources in the collection which owe their origin to Betham. The first of these, genealogical and historical excerpts from the plea rolls and patent rolls from Henry III to Edward VI (GO 189–193), constitute the single most important source of information on Anglo-Norman genealogy in Ireland. Betham's transcript of Roger O'Ferrall's 'Linea Antiqua', a collation of earlier genealogies compiled in 1709, is the office's most extensive work on Gaelic, as opposed to Anglo-Irish, genealogy. This copy (in three volumes, GO 145–7, with an index to the complete work in 147) also contains Betham's inter-polations and additions, unfortunately unsourced. It records the arms of many of the Gaelic families covered, without giving any authority for them, and is the source of most of the arms illustrated in Dr Edward MacLysaght's *Irish Families*.

Pedigrees and research notes produced by later amateur and professional genealogists make up a large part of the office's manuscript collection. Among those who have contributed to these are Sir Edmund Bewley, Denis O'Callaghan Fisher, Tenison Groves, Alfred Moloney, T.U. Sadleir, Rev. H.B. Swanzy and many others. For the most part, their records concern either particular groups of families or particular geographical areas. Some of these have their own indexes, some are covered by GO 470 and 117, others have will abstracts only indexed in GO 429. As well as these, some of the results of Ulster's Office's own research in the late nineteenth and early twentieth century are classed as manuscripts, GO 800–822. These constitute no more than a fraction of the total research information produced by the office. They are indexed in Hayes's *Manuscript Sources*.

A final class of records consists of extremely diverse documents, having only their potential genealogical usefulness in common. It includes such items as freeholders' lists from different counties, extracts from parish registers, transcripts of the Dublin city roll of freemen, of returns from the 1766 census, of city directories from various periods, and much more. More detailed information will be found in the list in *The Genealogical Office* (Dublin, IMC, 1998).

ARCHIVES

As well as the manuscripts series, now closed, the Genealogical Office also has extremely extensive archive records of the commissioned research it carried out up to the 1980s. For the closing decades of the nineteenth century and the early decades of the twentieth century, these records are still largely concerned with the Anglo-Irish. Manuscripts 800–822 cover perhaps 5 per cent of this material. The remainder are sorted in roughly alphabetical order in cardboard boxes along one whole wall of the Genealogical Office strong room. It is to be hoped that the office can acquire the resources to sort and index them soon, since they contain a great deal of very valuable information.

After the creation of the Genealogical Office in 1943, the focus of the commissioned research shifted, with most work now carried out on behalf of the descendants of emigrants to Australia and North America. There are over 20,000 research files giving details of the results of this research. A continuing project to index the families concerned has so far covered over 6,000 of these; the results are on computer at the office.

RESEARCH IN GENEALOGICAL OFFICE MANUSCRIPTS

The biggest single obstacle to research in GO manuscripts is the lack of a single, comprehensive index, though this has been mitigated to some extent by the recent work of Ms V.W. McAnlis (see below). Many attempts have been made over the centuries of the office's existence to produce a complete index; the result has been a proliferation of partial indexes, each covering some of the collection, none covering it all. These are dealt with below. In addition, the policy used in the creation of manuscripts appears to have become somewhat inconsistent from the 1940s. Before then only the earliest and most heterogeneous manuscripts had been numbered in a single series, with each of the other groups simply having its own volume numbers, 'Lords Entries Vol. II' or 'Registered Pedigrees Vol. 12', for example. The laudable attempt to produce a consistent numbering system, starting at GO 1 and moving through the collection, seems to have given rise to the piecemeal addition of material which was more properly the preserve of the National Library. The subsequent transfers to the Library, and renumbering of remaining material, produced a virtual collapse of the system in the upper numbers. No manuscripts exist for many of the numbers between 600 and 800.

In recent years, Virginia Wade McAnlis has taken on the task of creating a consolidated index for Genealogical Office manuscripts, working from the microfilm copies available through the Family History Centres of the Church of Jesus Christ of the Latter-Day Saints, the Mormons. This work, in five volumes, is available from Ms McAnlis at 82 Gunn Road, Port Angeles, WA 98362–9108, USA. A copy is also available from the National Library of Ireland. It brings together the references from the indexes numbered as GO Mss 117, 148, 255–60, 386, 422–3, 470. Details of these are found below. In addition to the page references included in these indexes, Ms McAnlis also includes microfilm references for the Latter-Day Saints collection.

INDEXES

■ *GO 59:* This is a detailed calendar of manuscripts 1–58, particularly useful since many of these consist of very early heterogeneous material bound together for preservation.

■ *GO 115:* Indexes the following: Arms A–C; Grants & Confirmations, A & B; Visitations, British Families, Funeral Entries, Registered Pedigrees, vols 1–10. Only the Visitations (GO 47–49) and British Families (GO 44–46) are not indexed more fully elsewhere.

■ *GO 116:* An unfinished index.

■ *GO 117:* Duplicates much of the material indexed in GO 422, GO 470 and Hayes's *Manuscript Sources*. Only the following are not covered elsewhere: Antrim Families (GO 213), Fisher Mss (GO 280–85), Irish Arms at the College of Heralds (GO 37), Irish Coats of Arms (Fota) (GO 526), Heraldic Sketches (GO 125), Betham Letter Books (GO 362–78), Ecclesiatical Visitations (GO 198–9), Reynell Mss (GO 445).

■ *GO 148:* Index to 'Linea Antiqua'. The version at the end of GO 147, 'Linea Antiqua', vol. III, is more complete.

■ *GO 255–6:* Index to Alliances in Prerogative Wills (Betham).

■ *GO 386:* Index to the Funeral Entries.

■ *GO 422–3:* Index to arms registered at the office.

■ *GO 429:* Eustace Index to Will Abstracts at the Genealogical Office. The published version in *Analecta Hibernica*, vol. 17, is less extensive than the manuscript copy.

■ *GO 469:* Index to Registered Pedigrees. This appears to be less complete than the version included in Hayes's *Manuscript Sources*. Attached to it is a typescript copy of the index to the Genealogical Office collection of pedigree rolls.

■ *GO 470:* Index to Unregistered Pedigrees. This is the single most useful index in the office, covering the Lord's Entries, the Betham pedigrees and many of the genealogists' pedigree collections. It is divided into three separate parts, and gives the descriptive titles in use before the adoption of the single GO numbering system. The flyleaf lists the manuscripts covered.

■ *GO 476:* Numerical listing of GO manuscripts, dating from the 1950s, and now inaccurate for the higher numbers.

See also Hayes's *Manuscript Sources for the Study of Irish Civilisation*. This indexes the following: Registered Pedigrees, GO 800–822, Fisher Mss (GO 280–5).

Access

Access to the Genealogical Office collection is through the manuscript reading room of the National Library at 2 Kildare Street, the same building which houses the office itself. For the most valuable manuscripts, in general those in the lower numbers, only microfilm copies are accessible in the National Library microfilm reading room. The microfilms are as follows:

NLI Pos. 8286:	GO Mss 47, 48, 49, 64, 65
NLI Pos. 8287:	GO Mss 66, 67, 68, 69
NLI Pos. 8288:	GO Mss 70, 71, 72, 73
NLI Pos. 8289:	GO Mss 74, 75, 76, 77, 78
NLI Pos. 8290:	GO Mss 79, 103, 104, 105, 106
NLI Pos. 8290A:	GO Mss 93, 94, 95
NLI Pos. 8291:	GO Mss 107, 108, 109
NLI Pos. 8292:	GO Mss 110, 111, 111A to p. 95
NLI Pos. 8293:	GO Mss 111A from p. 96, 111B, 111C
NLI Pos. 8294:	GO Mss 111D, 111E, 111F
NLI Pos. 8295:	GO Ms 112
NLI Pos. 8295A:	GO Ms 113
NLI Pos. 8295B:	GO Ms 141
NLI Pos. 8296:	GO Mss 145, 146, 147 to p. 42
NLI Pos. 8297:	GO Mss 147 from p. 43, 148, 149, 150 to p. 319
NLI Pos. 8298:	GO Mss 150 from p. 319, 151, 152
NLI Pos. 8299:	GO Mss 153, 154
NLI Pos. 8300:	GO Mss 154A, 155, 156, 157, 158, 159 to p. 109
NLI Pos. 8301:	GO Mss 159 from p. 110, 160, 161, 162, 163, 164
NLI Pos. 8302:	GO Mss 165, 166, 167, 168
NLI Pos. 8303:	GO Mss 169, 170
NLI Pos. 8304:	GO Mss 171, 172, 173
NLI Pos. 8305:	GO Mss 174, 175
NLI Pos. 8306:	GO Ms 176

NLI Pos. 8307:	GO Mss 177, 178
NLI Pos. 8308:	GO Mss 179, 180
NLI Pos. 8309:	GO Mss 181, 182
NLI Pos. 8310:	GO Mss 182A, 183, 184
NLI Pos. 8311:	GO Mss 185, 186, 187
NLI Pos. 8312:	GO Ms 188

7. EMIGRATION

For the descendants of emigrants from Ireland wishing to trace their ancestors, it is a natural impulse to try first of all to identify emigration records in Ireland. Unfortunately, no centralised records of emigration exist. For North America in particular, where ships' passenger lists were kept, most appear to have been deposited at the port of arrival, rather than departure; in general, the authorities were more concerned with recording those entering a country than those leaving. The most comprehensive records for the US, therefore, are the Customs Passenger Lists, dating from 1820, and the Immigration Passenger Lists, from 1883, both in the National Archives in Washington. Unfortunately, the earlier lists are not very informative, giving only the country of origin of the emigrant. They have been collected by the US National Archives for the most important immigrant ports, Boston, New York, Baltimore and Philadelphia, as well as Mobile, New Bedford and New Orleans. Microfilm copies of the lists for New York and Boston are available at the National Library of Ireland. A full reference is given in the lists later in this chapter. No index to these is available, making them very difficult to use if a relatively precise date of arrival is not known.

As well as these, however, there are many less comprehensive lists, published and unpublished, which record intending and actual emigrants and ships' passengers to North America. A number of attempts have been made to systematise access to these. The most important are the *Passenger and Immigration Lists Index* (3 vols) ed. P. William Filby & Mary K. Meyer, Gale, Detroit, 1981 (NL: RR 387, p. 7), a consolidated index to a wide variety of lists relating to North American immigration from all over the world, and *The Famine Immigrants* (7 vols, indexed) Baltimore, the Genealogical Publishing Company, 1988 (NLI Ir. 942 g 12), which records more than half a million Irish arrivals in New York between 1846 and 1851. Even these, however, cover only a fraction of the material of potential value. The listings further on in this chapter organise the available materials chronologically, to allow easy reference.

For Australia and New Zealand, the situation is somewhat better. Because of the distance, very few emigrants could afford the journey themselves, and most, whether assisted free settlers or transported convicts, are therefore quite well documented. Transportation from Ireland, or for crimes committed in Ireland, lasted from 1791 to 1853, ending some fifteen years earlier than transportation from England. The only mass transportation later than 1853 was of sixty-three Fenians who were sent to Western Australia in 1868 aboard the last convict ship from England to Australia. The records of the Chief Secretary's Office, which had responsibility for the penal system, are the major Irish source of information on transportees. Not all of the relevant records have survived, particularly for the period before 1836, but what does exist can provide a wealth of information. The records were formerly housed in the State Paper Office in Dublin Castle, which is now part of the National Archives and is situated at Bishop St, Dublin 8. The principal classes of relevant records are as follows:

■ *1. Prisoners' Petitions and Cases, 1788–1836.* These consist of petitions to the Lord Lieutenant for commutation or remission of sentence, and record the crime, trial, sentence, place of origin and family circumstances.

■ *2. State Prisoners' Petitions.* These specifically concern those arrested for participation in the 1798 Rebellion, and record the same information as the main series of petitions.

■ *3. Convict Reference Files, from 1836.* These continue the earlier petitions series and may include a wide range of additional material.

■ *4. Transportation Registers, from 1836.* These record all the names of those sentenced to death or transportation, giving the name, age, date and county of trial, crime and sentence. Other details, including the name of the transport ship or the place of detention, are sometimes also given.

■ *5. Male Convict Register 1842–47.* In addition to the information supplied by the Transportation Registers, this volume also gives physical descriptions.

■ *6. Register of Convicts on Convict Ships, 1851–53.* This gives the names, dates and counties of trial of those transported to Van Dieman's Land and Western Australia for the period covered.

■ *7. Free Settlers' Papers, 1828–52.* After serving a minimum of four years, male convicts had the right to request a free passage for their wife and family. The papers contain lists of those making such a request, along with transportation details and the name and address of the wife. A number of petitions from husbands and wives, and prisoners' letters, are also included.

To celebrate the Australian Bicentenary of 1988, all of these records were microfilmed, and a computerised database of the surnames they contain was created. Copies of the microfilms and the database were presented to the Australian government and can now be found in many state archives. The National Archives in Bishop St also retains copies, and the database in particular can save a great deal of time and effort. It supplies enough details from the originals to identify the relevant record. It is available on the Internet at *http://www.kst.dit.ie/nat-arch*.

For obvious reasons, the records relating to free settlers are more scattered and less easily researched. The single most useful source for early settlers, also invaluable for convicts, is the 1828 census of New South Wales, published by the Library of Australian History in 1980. Although the precise place of origin is not recorded, the details include age, occupation, marital status, and household. For later settlers, the University of Woolongong in Australia has produced on microfiche a complete index and transcript of all information concerning immigrants of Irish origin recorded on ships' passenger lists between 1848 and 1867. The Genealogical Office has a copy of this. The later lists in particular are extremely useful, often recording the exact place of origin as well as parents' names.

Other than these, the principal records likely to be of relevance are in the Colonial Office Papers of the United Kingdom Public Record Office at Kew, class reference CO 201. This class contains a wide variety of records, including petitions for assisted passages, emigrants' lists, records of emigrants on board ship, petitions from settlers for financial assistance, and much else. A number of these have been published in David T. Hawkings' *Bound for Australia* (Sussex: Phillimore & Co., 1987).

The remainder of this chapter is an attempt to present a systematic guide to emigration records of potential genealogical interest. It is divided into (1) passenger and emigrant lists in chronological order, and (2) published works on emigration. The latter is further subdivided into works dealing with (a) North America in general, (b) localities in North America, (c) the 'Scotch-Irish' in North America, (d) Australia and New Zealand, (e) France, (f) South Africa, (g) Argentina, and (h) the West Indies.

PASSENGER AND EMIGRANT LISTS
(IN CHRONOLOGICAL ORDER)

From: —   To: North America
Date: 1538–1825
Reference: *A Bibliography of Ships' Passenger Lists*,
             London, H. Lancour & Wolfe, 1963

From: —   To: America
Date: 17th–19th centuries
Reference: *Passenger and Immigration Lists Index*
             (3 vols), ed. P. William Filby & Mary K.
             Meyer, Gale, Detroit, 1981, NLI RR 387 p 7

From: Ireland   To: New England
Date: —
Reference: *New England Passengers to America*, Baltimore,
             1986, NLI 387 p 6 (a consolidation of ships'
             passenger lists from the New England
             Historical and Genealogical Register)

From: Britain   To: North America
Date: 1600–1700
Reference: J.C. Hotten, *Original Lists of Persons*
             emigrating to America, 1600–1700,
             London, 1874 [reprint, 1968]

From: Britain & Ireland   To: America & West Indies
Date: 1727–31
Reference: 'Agreements to Serve in America and the
             West Indies', D. Galenson, *The Genealogist's*
             Magazine, Vol. 19, No. 2

From: Ireland   To: America & West Indies
Date: 1735–43
Reference: Frances McDonnell, *Emigrants from Ireland*
             to America 1735–1743, Baltimore, GPC, 1992.
             Records the names of almost 2,000 convict
             transportees.

From: Ireland   To: America
Date: 1735–54
Reference: Lockhart, A., *Emigration Ireland to North
    America, 1660–1775, New York, 1976.
    NLI Ir. 973 1 5 (indentured servants 1749–50,
    felons 1735–54)

From: Kilkenny   To: Newfoundland
Date: 1750–1844
Reference: 'Inistiogue emigrants in Newfoundland',
    in Whelan K. & Nolan W. (eds) *Kilkenny
    History and Society*, Dublin, 1990,
    pp. 205–405

From: Larne   To: Charleston, Sth Carolina
Date: 1773
Reference: Dickson, R.J., *Ulster Emigration to Colonial
    America, 1718–75*, London, 1976

From: Newry/Warrenpoint   To: New York & Philadelphia
Date: 1791–92
Reference: PRONI T. 711/1

From: Ireland   To: Philadelphia
Date: 1800–19
Reference: *Passenger Arrivals at Philadelphia Port
    1800–19*, Baltimore, 1986, NLI Ir. 970 p 12

From: Belfast, Dublin, Limerick,   To: US
    Londonderry, Newry, Sligo
Date: 1803, 1804
Reference: D.F. Begley, *Handbook on Irish Genealogy*,
    Dublin, 1984 (6th ed.) pp. 101–110, 115

From: Ulster   To: US
Date: June 1804 to March 1806
Reference: PRONI T. 521/1. Indexed in *Report of the
    Deputy Keeper of Public Records
    (Northern Ireland)* 1929

From: Ireland   To: America
Date: 1803–1806
Reference: NLI Pos. 993, PRONI T. 3262

From: Newry   To: US
Date: 1803–1831
Reference: Trainor, Brian, 'Sources for the Identification
    of Emigrants from Ireland to North America
    in the 19th Century', *Ulster Historical and*

Genealogical Guild Newsletter, Vol. 1, Nos 2 & 3
(1979), NLI Ir. 9292 u 3

From: Ireland   To: US
Date: 1811–1817
Reference: *Passengers from Ireland*, Baltimore, 1980
           (from 'The Shamrock'). See also D.F. Begley,
           Handbook on Irish Genealogy, Dublin, 1984
           (6th ed.) pp. 110–117

From: Londonderry   To: US
Date: 1815–16
Reference: PRONI T. 2964 (add.)

From: Cos Carlow & Wexford   To: Canada
Date: 1817
Reference: K. Whelan & W. Nolan (eds) *Wexford:*
           History and Society, Dublin, Geography
           Publications, 1987

From: —   To: New York
Date: 1820–65
Reference: Passenger arrivals lists, New York port,
           unindexed, NLI Pos. 3919–4580, see National
           Library, Hayes Catalogue, for details of dates

From: Ireland   To: US
Date: 1821
Reference: *Irish Genealogical Helper*, No. 6, Jan.
           1976, NLI Ir. 9291 i 3

From: (Not Given)   To: New York (Arrivals)
Date: 1820–65
Reference: NLI Pos. 3919–4520 (see Hayes
           Catalogue for details)

From: Not Given   To: Boston (Arrivals)
Date: 1820–64
Reference: NLI Pos. 5896–959
           (see Hayes Catalogue for details)

From: Ireland   To: Boston
Date: 1820–1839
Reference: NLI Special list, No. 200

From: —   To: U.S.
Date: 1821–1823
Reference: *Passengers Arriving in the U.S.*,
           1821–1823, NLI 3251 u 1

From: Ireland   To: US
Date: 1822
Reference: *Irish-American Genealogist*, 1978,
               NLI Ir. 9291 i 3

From: Londonderry   To: US
Date: 1826–90
Reference: PRONI D. 2892

From: Co. Londonderry (parishes of Aghadowey,   To: US
               Balteagh, Bovevagh, Coleraine, Dunboe,
               Drumachose, Limavady, Magilligan,
               Tamlaghfinlagan)
Date: 1833–34
Reference: See S. Martin, *Historical Gleanings from Co. Derry*,
               Dublin, 1955, NLI Ir. 94112 m 2. Also D.F. Begley,
               Handbook on Irish Genealogy, Dublin, 1984
               (6th ed.) pp. 117–20

From: Cos Antrim and Derry   To: US
Date: 1833–39
Reference: Mitchell, Brian, *Irish Emigration Lists 1833–39*,
               Baltimore, Genealogical Publishing Company,
               1989, PRONI MIC. 6

From: Newry   To: St John's,
Date: April 7, 1834   New Brunswick
Reference: Murphy, Peter, *Together in Exile*,
               Nova Scotia, 1991, pp. 272–7

From: Londonderry   To: Philadelphia
Date: 1836–1871
Reference: PRONI M-Film 14

From: Liverpool (Irish passengers)   To: Philadelphia
Date: 1840
Reference: PRONI T. 2746

From: Limerick   To: North America
Date: 1841
Reference: Passenger list for the Shemalere, dep.
               May 26, 1841, *North Munster Antiquarian
               Journal*, Vol. XXIII, 1981

From: Shillelagh, Co. Wicklow (Coolattin estate)   To: US
Date: 1842–44
Reference: NLI Ms 18,429

From: Monaghan   To: —
Date: 1843–54
Reference: Assisted emigration from the Shirley
            estate, Co. Monaghan, *Clogher Record*,
            14 (2), 1992

From: Ireland   To: US
Date: 1846–51
Reference: *The Famine Immigrants* (7 vols,
            indexed) NLI Ir. 942 g 12

From: Londonderry   To: America
Date: 1847–71
Reference: Brian Mitchell (ed.) *Irish Passenger
            Lists 1847–1871*, Baltimore,
            Genealogical Publishing Co., 1988

From: Coolattin (see above)   To: Quebec
Date: 1848
Reference: NLI Ms 18,524, see also *West Wicklow
            Historical Journal*, No. 1

From: Ahascragh, Co. Galway & Castlemaine,   To:
            Co. Kerry
Date: 1848–52
Reference: *Analecta Hibernica*, Vol. 22, 1960

From: Ireland   To: Australia
Date: 1848–1850
Reference: 'Barefoot and Pregnant: Female Orphans
            who emigrated from Irish workhouses to
            Australia', 'Familia' (*Ulster Genealogical
            Review*) Vol. II, No. 3, 1987

From: Londonderry   To: Philadelphia,
Date: 1850–65   St John, Quebec
Reference: PRONI M-Film 13

From: Co. Galway (parishes of Kilchreest,   To: US and Australia
            Killigolen, Killinane, Killora,
            Kilthomas and Isserkelly)
Date: *c.*1852–1859
Reference: GO Ms 622

From: Liverpool (Irish Passengers)   To: US
Date: Oct.–Dec. 1853
Reference: R. ffolliott, *The Irish Ancestor*, 1975, pp. 6–10

From:	Queenstown (Cobh)	To: US
Date:	May–June 1884	
Reference:	NLI Ms 20616	

From:	Armagh, Derry, Donegal, Louth, Tyrone	To: Not Given
Date:	1890–1921	
Reference:	PRONI P. 648(9) (Members of Girls' Friendly Society)	

PUBLISHED WORKS ON EMIGRATION

AUSTRALIA

Anonymous, *The Ulster Link*, NLI Ir. 994 u 1, magazine of the Northern Irish in Australia & New Zealand

Cleary, P.J.S., *Australia's Debt to Ireland's Nation-builders*, Sydney, 1933, NLI Ir. 994 c 6

Coffey & Morgan, *Irish Families in Australia and New Zealand 1788–1979*, Melbourne, 1979, NLI Ir. 942 c 14, 4 volume biographical dictionary

Costello, Con, *Botany Bay*, Cork, Mercier Press

Curry, C.H., The Irish at Eureka, Sydney, 1954, NLI Ir. 993 c 7

Donohoe, James Hugh, *The bibliography of the convict transports*, Sydney, the author, 1988, NLI 016 p 5(3)

Donohoe, H., *The convicts and exiles transported from Ireland 1791–1820*, Sydney, the author, 1992, NLI Ir. 942 p 17(3)

Fitzpatrick, David, *Home or Away? Immigrants in Colonial Australia*, Canberra, ANU, ACT

Fitzpatrick, David, *Oceans of Consolation*, Cornell University Press, 1992, personal accounts of Irish migration to Australia

Forth, G.J., *A biographical register and annotated bibliography of Anglo-Irish colonists in Australia*, Warrnambool, Deakin University, 1992, NLI Ir. 942 b 23

Grimes, Seamus, *The Irish-Australia Connection*, Irish Academic Press

Hawkings, David T., *Bound for Australia*, Sussex, Phillimore, 1987

Hogan, J., *The Irish in Australia*, Melbourne, 1888, NLI Ir. 9940

Hughes, Robert, *The Fatal Shore*, London, 1988

Kiernan, C. (ed.) *Australia and Ireland, 1788–1988*, Dublin, 1986, NLI Ir. 942 a 9

Kiernan, T.J., *The Irish in Australia*, Dublin, 1954, NLI Ir. 994 k 1

McClaughlin, Trevor, *Barefoot and Pregnant: Irish Famine Orphans in Australia*, Melbourne, GSV

McDonagh & Mandle, *Australia and Ireland, 1788–1988*, Dublin, NLI Ir. 942 a 9

McDonagh & Mandle, *Ireland & Irish-Australians*, Sydney, 1987, NLI Ir. 942 i 12

Neary, Bernard, *Irish Lives: the Irish in Western Australia*, Dublin, Lenhar Publications, 1989, NLI Ir. 92001 p 8(1)

O'Brien John (ed.) *The Irish Emigrant Experience in Australia*, Dublin, Poolbeg Press, co-editor Pauric Travers

O'Farrell, Patrick, *The Irish in Australia*, New South Wales, 1987, NLI Ir. 942 o 29

O'Farrell, Patrick, *Letters from Irish Australia*, New South Wales, New South Wales University Press, co-editor Brian Trainer, co-publisher Ulster Historical Foundation

O'Mahoney, Dr. C., *Poverty to promise: the Monteagle emigrants 1838–58*, Australia, Crossing Press, 1994, NLI Ir. 993 0 40, co-author Valerie Thompspon

Reece, Bob, *Irish Convicts*, Dept of History, University College Dublin

Reece, Bob, *Exiles from Erin: Convict Life in Ireland and Australia*, Dublin, Gill and Macmillan

Reid, Richard, *The Irish Australians*, Sydney, Society of Australian Genealogists, co-publisher Ulster Historical Foundation, co-editor Keith Johnson

Richards, Eric, *Visible Immigrants: Neglected Sources for the History of Australian Immigrants*, Canberra, ANU, co-authors Richard Reid, David Fitzpatrick

Richards, Eric, *Poor Australian Immigrants in the Nineteenth Century*, Canberra, ANU (ed.)

Robinson, P., *The Hitch and Brood of Time: Australians 1788–1828*, Oxford, 1985, NLI Ir. 993 r 5

Robson, L.L., *The Convict Settlers of Australia*, Melbourne

FRANCE

Griffin, G.T., *The Wild Geese*, NLI Ir. 920041 g 5, pen portraits

Hayes, R., *Biographical Dictionary of Irishmen in France*, Dublin, 1949, NLI Ir. 9440 h 16

Hayes, R., *Irish Swordsmen of France*, Dublin, NLI Ir. 94404 h 3

Hayes, R., *Ireland and Irishmen in the French Revolution*, Dublin, NLI Ir. 94404 h 1

Hayes, R., *Old Irish Links with France*, Dublin, NLI Ir. 944 h 11

Hennessy, M., *The Wild Geese*, London, NLI Ir. 942 h 10

Holohan, Renagh, *The Irish Chateaux — in search of descendants of the Wild Geese*, Dublin, Lilliput Press, 1989, co-author Jeremy Williams, NLI Ir. 942 h 21

Jones, P., *The Irish Brigade*, London, NLI Ir. 942 j 3

Lee, G.A., *Irish Chevaliers in the Service of France*, NLI Ir. 340 l 3

McDonnel, Hector, *The Wild Geese of the Antrim McDonnells*, Blackrock, Irish Academic Press, 1996, NLI Ir. 942 m 46

O'Callaghan, J.C., *History of the Irish Brigades*, NLI Ir. 944 o 13

O'Connell, M.J., *The Last Colonel of the Irish Brigade*, Count O'Connell, 1745–1833

Swords, L., *Irish-French Connections 1578–1978*, Paris, 1978, NLI Ir. 942 i 6

Terry, James, *Pedigrees and Papers*, NLI Ir. 9292 t 7, part of the collection of pedigrees taken to France by Terry in the early 18th century

Bordeaux

Clark de Dromentin, Patrick, *Les oies sauvages: mémoires d'une famille irlandaise réfugiée en France Nantes, Martinique, Bordeaux: 1691–1914*, Bordeaux, Presses Universitaires de Bordeaux, 1995, NLI Ir. 942 c 37

Nantes

Clark de Dromentin, Patrick, *Les oies sauvages: mémoires d'une famille irlandaise réfugiée en France Nantes, Martinique, Bordeaux: 1691–1914*, Bordeaux, Presses Universitaires de Bordeaux, 1995, NLI Ir. 942 c 37

Mathorez, J., *Les irlandais nobles ou notables a Nantes aux XVIIe et XVIIIe siecles*, NLI Ir. 941 p 20

GREAT BRITAIN

Davis, Graham, *The Irish in Britain 1815–1914*, Dublin, Gill and Macmillan
Vaughan, W.E., *A New History of Ireland, Vol. V, Ireland under the Union*, Oxford

Scotland

Devine, T.M., *Irish Immigrants and Scottish Society in the Nineteenth and Twentieth Centuries*, Glasgow, John Donald

York

Clancy, Mary, *The Emigrant Experience*, Galway Labour History Group

NEW ZEALAND

Anonymous, *The Ulster Link*, NLI Ir. 994 u 1, magazine of the Northern Irish in Australia & New Zealand
Coffey & Morgan, *Irish Families in Australia and New Zealand 1788–1979*, Melbourne, 1979, NLI Ir. 942 c 14 (4 volume biographical dictionary)

NORTH AMERICA (GENERAL)

Anonymous, 'Sources for the Identification of Emigrants from Ireland to North America in the 19th Century', *Ulster Historical and Genealogical Guild Newsletter*, 1979, Vol. 1, Nos 2 & 3
Anonymous, *The Ulster-American Connection*, New University of Ulster, NLI Ir. 942 u 3
Adams, William Forbes, *Ireland and Irish Immigration to the New World: From 1815 to the Famine*, Baltimore,
Bolton, C.K., *Scotch-Irish Pioneers*, Baltimore, 1967, NLI Ir. 973 b 5
Bradley, A.K., *History of the Irish in America*, Chartwell, 1986, NLI Ir. 942 b 19
Concannon & Cull, *Irish-American Who's Who*, NLI Ir. 942 i 13
Dickson, R.J., *Ulster Emigration to Colonial America, 1718–75*, London, 1976, NLI Ir. 3252 d 3
Doyle & Edwards, D. (eds) *America and Ireland 1776–1976*, London, NLI Ir. 973 a 5
Glasgow, M., *Scotch-Irish in Northern Ireland and the American Colonies*, New York, 1936, NLI Ir. 973 g 16
Green, E.R.R., *Essays in Scotch-Irish History*, Ulster Historical Foundation, 1989
Harris, Ruth-Ann, *The Search for Missing Friends: Vols 1–4 1831–60*, Boston, New England Historic Genealogical Society, 1995, NLI Ir. 942 s 22 (Irish immigrant advertisements placed in the *Boston Pilot*, co-editor B.E. O'Keeffe)
Holder, *Emigrants from Britain to American Plantations 1600–1700*, 9291 w 1
Knowles, Charles, *The Petition to Governor Shute in 1718: Scotch-Irish Pioneers in Ulster and America*, NLI Ir. 973614
Linden, *Irish Schoolmasters in the American Colonies, 1640–1775*, NLI Ir. 942 r 9
Lockhart, A., *Emigration: Ireland to North America, 1660–1775*, New York, 1976, NLI Ir. 973 l 5
Maguire, John, *The Irish in America*, New York, 1868, NLI Ir. 973 m 3

Marshall, W.F., *Ulster Sails West*, NLI Ir. 973 m 5, including Ulster Presbyterian ministers in America 1680–1820

McGee, *Irish Settlers in North America*, New York, 1852, NLI Ir. 970 m 1

Miller, K.A., *Exiles and Emigrants*, Oxford, 1985, NLI Ir. 942 m 26

Mitchell, Brian, *Irish Emigration Lists 1833–39*, Baltimore, 1989, Genealogical Publishing Company (Counties Antrim and Derry)

O'Brien, M.J., *Irish Settlers in America: A consolidation of articles from the journal of the American-Irish Society*, Genealogical Publishing Company, Baltimore, 1979, NLI Ir. 942 o 23

Shannon, W.V., *The American Irish*, New York, 1963, NLI Ir. 973 s 3

Shaw, J., *The Scotch-Irish in History*, Springfield, 1899, NLI Ir. 942 s 13

CANADA

Anonymous, 'The North Tipperary Settlements of Upper Canada', *Irish Family History*, 1987, Vol. 3, 21–3

Davin, N.F., *The Irishman in Canada*, Shannon, NLI Ir. 971 d 1

Elliott, B.S., *Irish Migrants in the Canadas: A New Approach*, McGill, NLI Ir. 942 e 7, Irish Protestants from Co. Tipperary especially

Fromers, V., *Irish Emigrants to Canada in Sussex Archives 1839–47*, IA, 1982, pp. 31–42

Houston, Cecil J., *Irish Emigration and Canadian Settlement: Patterns, Links and Letters*, University of Toronto Press, co-author William J. Smyth, co-publisher Ulster Historical Foundation

Leeson, F., *Irish Emigrants to Canada 1839–47*, from the Wyndham estates in Cos Clare (especially), Limerick and Tipperary

Mannion, John, *Irish Settlements in Eastern Canada*, Toronto, NLI Ir. 971 m 11

O'Driscoll & Reynolds, R. & L. (eds) *The Untold Story: the Irish in Canada* (2 vols) Toronto

New Brunswick

Cushing, J.E., *Irish Immigration to St John, New Brunswick, 1847*, St John, the New Brunswick Museum, 1979, NLI Ir. 942 c 16

Jack, D.R., *History of the City and County of St John*, St John

McDevitt, Mary Kilfoil, *We Hardly Knew Ye: St Mary's Cemetery, An Enduring Presence*, St John, New Brunswick

McGahan, Elizabeth, *The Port in the City: Saint John N.B. (1867–1911) and the Process of Integration*, University of New Brunswick, unpublished Ph. D. thesis

Murphy, Peter, *Together in Exile*, Nova Scotia, 1991, Carlingford emigrants to St John's, New Brunswick

Power, Thomas P., *The Irish in Atlantic Canada, 1780–1900*, New Brunswick, New Ireland Press, 1979

Toner, P.M., *New Ireland Remembered: historical essays on the Irish in New Brunswick*, New Brunswick, 1988

Newfoundland

Anonymous, 'Kilkennymen in Newfoundland', *Old Kilkenny Review*, 1987, 358, NLI Ir. 94139 o 3

Power, Thomas P., *The Irish in Atlantic Canada, 1780–1900*, New Brunswick, New Ireland Press, 1979

Nova Scotia

MacKenzie, A.A., *The Irish in Cape Breton*, Cape Breton, 1979, NLI Ir. 942 m 20
Power, Thomas P., *The Irish in Atlantic Canada, 1780–1900*, New Brunswick, New Ireland Press, 1979.
Punch, T.M., *Some Sons of Erin in Nova Scotia*, Halifax, 1980, NLI Ir. 971 p 10
Stewart, H.L., *The Irish in Nova Scotia*, Kentville, 1950, NLI Ir. 971 s 2

Ontario

Akenson, D.H., *The Irish in Ontario*, McGill, 1985, NLI Ir. 971 a 8
Heald, Carolyn A., *The Irish Palatines in Ontario: Religion, Ethnicity and Rural Migration*, Garanoque, Ontario, Langdale Press

Prince Edward Island

Power, Thomas P., *The Irish in Atlantic Canada, 1780–1900*, New Brunswick, New Ireland Press, 1979

Quebec

Guerin, T., *The Gael in New France*, Montreal, 1946, NLI Ir. 971 g 4
O'Gallagher, M., *St Patrick's & St Brigid's, Quebec*, Quebec, 1981, NLI Ir. 942 o 29
Redmond, P.M., *Irish Life in Rural Quebec*, Duquesne, 1983, NLI Ir. 942 r 6

USA

Anonymous, *Journal of the American-Irish Historical Society*, NLI Ir. 973 a 1
'Early Irish Emigrants to America, 1803, 1806', *The Recorder*, June 1926
Anonymous, *The Irish-American Genealogist*, 1973 to date, NLI Ir. 9291 i 3
Anonymous, *Friendly Sons of St Patrick, 1771–1892*, NLI Ir. 973 c 1
Donohoe, H., *The Irish Catholic Benevolent Union*, NLI Ir. 973 d 6
Doyle, D., *Ireland, Irishmen, and Revolutionary America*, Dublin, 1981, NLI Ir. 942 d 12
Fallows, Marjorie R., *Irish Americans: Identity and Assimilations*, New Jersey, Prentice-Hall, 1979.
Goodwin, Donn, *Look Back Upon Erin*, Milwaukee, Woodland Books
Griffin, William D., *A Portrait of the Irish in America*, Dublin, the Academic Press
Hartigan, J., *The Irish in the American Revolution*, Washington, 1908, NLI Ir. 973 h 8
Kennedy, John. F., *A Nation of Immigrants*, London, Hamish Hamilton
Meagher, T.J., *From Paddy to Studs*, Westport, 1986, NLI Ir. 942 f 8
O'Brien, M.J., *A Hidden Phase of American History*, Baltimore, 1973, NLI Ir. 9733 o 25, Irishmen in the American Revolution
O'Carroll, Ide, *Models for Movers*, Dublin, Attic Press, focuses on women emigrants
O'Dea, John, *History of the Ancient Order of Hibernians and Ladies' Auxiliary*, Notre Dame, University of Notre Dame Press, 1994, NLI Ir. 942 o 6 (3 vols)
Potter, G., *To the Golden Door*, Boston, 1960, NLI Ir. 973 p 4

Reynolds, F., *Ireland's Important & Heroic Part* . . . Chicago, n.d., NLI Ir. 973 r 3,
     Irish in the American Revolution
Ridges, J.T., *Erin's Sons in America*, New York, 1986, NLI Ir. 973 r 7, the Ancient
     Order of Hibernians
Roberts, E.F., *Ireland in America*, London, 1931, NLI Ir. 973 r 2
Werkin, E., *Enter the Irish-American*, New York, 1976, NLI Ir. 973 w 9
White, J., *Sketches from America*, London, 1870, NLI Ir. 942 w 7
Wittke, C., *The Irish in America*, Baton Rouge, 1956, NLI Ir. 973 w 2

California

Burchell, R.A., *San Francisco Irish, 1848–1880*, Manchester University Press, 1979,
     NLI Ir. 973 b 12
Prendergast, T.F., *Forgotten Pioneers: Irish Leaders in Early California*, San Francisco,
     1942, NLI Ir. 942 p 13
Quigly, H., *The Irish Race in California and on the Pacific Coast*, San Francisco, 1878,
     NLI Ir. 973 q 1

Chicago

Fanning, C. (ed.) *Mr Dooley and the Chicago Irish*, New York, 1976, NLI Ir. 973 d 10
Funchion, M.F., *The Irish in Chicago*, Chicago, 1987, NLI Ir. 970 i 15
Funchion, M.F., *Chicago's Irish Nationalists 1881–1890*, New York, 1976, NLI Ir.
     973 f 1

Cleveland

Callahan, *Irish-Americans and their Communities of Cleveland*

Connecticut

Stone, F., *Scots and Scotch-Irish in Connecticut*, University of Connecticut, 1978, NLI
     Ir. 929 p 5

Delaware

Anonymous, 'Irish Settlers in early Delaware', *Pennsylvania History*, April 1947,
     NLI Ir. 973 p 2

Kentucky

Anonymous, 'Early Irish Settlers in Kentucky', *Journal of the American-Irish
     Historical Society*, 2, 1899, 139–44, NLI Ir. 973 a 1
Anonymous, 'Irish Pioneers and Builders of Kentucky', *Journal of the American-Irish
     Historical Society*, 3, 1900, 78–88, NLI Ir. 973 a 1

Louisiana

Niehaus, E.F., *The Irish in New Orleans 1800–1860*, Baton Rouge, 1965, NLI Ir. 973
     n 3

Maryland

Anonymous, 'Irish Pioneers in Maryland', *Journal of the American-Irish Historical Society*, 14, 1915, 207–19, NLI Ir. 973 a 1

Anonymous, 'The Irish in Montgomery and Washington Counties, Maryland in 1778', *Journal of the American-Irish Historical Society*, 24, 1925, 157–61, NLI Ir. 973 a 1

Williams, H.A., *History of the Hibernian Society of Baltimore 1803–1951*, Baltimore, 1951, NLI Ir. 942 w 1

Massachusetts

Cullen, J.B., *Story of the Irish in Boston*, Boston, 1893, NLI Ir. 973 c 8

Donovan, G.F., *The Irish in Massachusetts, 1620–1775*, St Louis, 1931, NLI Ir. 9744 d 2

Gearon, M.M., *Irish Settlers in Gardner, Massachusetts*, Gardner, 1932, NLI Ir. 9744 g 1

Ryan, D.P., *Beyond the Ballot Box: Boston Irish 1845–1917*, London, 1983, NLI Ir. 973 r 4

Wood, S.G., *Ulster Scots & Blandford Scouts*, Mass., 1928, NLI Ir. 973 w 1

Michigan

Vinyard, J., *The Irish on the Urban Frontier*, New York, 1976, NLI Ir. 973 v 1, Irish in Detroit 1850–1880

Missouri

Anonymous, 'The Irish in the Early Days of St Louis', *Journal of the American-Irish Historical Society*, 9, 1910, 206–13, NLI Ir. 973 a 1

Anonymous, 'Passenger list of Ticonderoga 1850 (New Wexford, Missouri)', *The Past (Journal of the Ui Cinsealaigh Historical Society)* 12, 1978, 49–52, NLI Ir. 941382 p 1

Montana

Emmons, David A., *The Butte Irish: an American Mining Town 1875–1925*, Chicago, University of Illinois Press, 1998

New England

Anonymous, *Scotch-Irish Heritage Festival*, Winthrop, 1981, NLI Ir. 942 s 15

Anonymous, *New England Irish Guide 1987*, NLI Ir. 973 n 6

O'Brien, M.J., *Pioneer Irish in New England*, New York, 1937, NLI Ir. 974 o 6

O'Connor, Thomas H., *The Irish in New England*, Boston, New England Historic Genealogical Soc., 1985, NLI Ir. 9292 p 25(5), The Irish in New England/ Sources of Irish-American Genealogy/ The Kennedys of Massachusetts

New York

Anonymous, 'The Irish Aristocracy of Albany, 1798–1878', *New York History*, 52, 1971, 275–304

O'Brien, M.J., *In Old New York: Irish Dead in Trinity & St Paul's Churchyards*, New York, 1928, NLI Ir. 973 o 8

North Carolina

Anonymous, 'The Irish on Roanoake Island', *Irish Roots*, 3, 1993, 21

Anonymous, 'Irish Builders in North Carolina', *Journal of the American-Irish Historical Society*, 10, 1911, 258–61, NLI Ir. 973 a 1

Anonymous, 'North Carolina. Some Early MacCarthys, McGuires, [. . .]', *Journal of the American-Irish Historical Society*, 12, 1913, 161–67, NLI Ir. 973 a 1

Oregon

Anonymous, 'The Irish of Morrow County, Oregon', *Historical Quarterly*, June 1968

Pennsylvania

Anonymous, 'Irish Pioneers in Berks County, Pennsylvania', *Journal of the American-Irish Historical Society*, 27, 1928, 39–45, NLI Ir. 973 a 1

Armor, William C., *Scotch-Irish Bibliography of Pennsylvania*, Nashville, Barbee & Smith, 1896.

Cummings, H.M., *Scots Breed*, Pittsburgh, 1964, NLI Ir. 942 c 17 (Scotch-Irish in Pennsylvania)

Dunaway, W, *Scotch-Irish of Colonial Pennsylvania*, Baltimore, Genealogical Publishing Company, 1985, NLI Ir. 974 d 16

Mahony, M.E., *The Irish in Western Pennsylvania*, Pittsburgh, 1977, NLI Ir. 973 m 16

'Philadelphia Irish', *Journal of the American-Irish Historical Society*, 30, 1932, 103–17, NLI Ir. 973 a 1

Adams & O'Keeffe, E. & B.B., *Catholic Trails West: The Founding Catholic Families of Pennsylvania*, Baltimore, Genealogical Publishing Company, 1988, Vol. 1: St Joseph's Church, Philadelphia

Clark, D., *The Irish in Philadelphia*, Philadelphia, 1973, NLI Ir. 973 c 11

Clark, D., *The Irish Relations*, New Jersey, 1982, NLI Ir. 973 c 26, Irish-Americans in Philadelphia

South Carolina

Stephenson, Jean, *Scotch-Irish Migration to South Carolina*, Strasburg, Va., the author, 1971 (includes methodology on connecting families in South Carolina and Ireland using newspapers, records and other sources).

Texas

Anonymous, 'The Irish Pioneers of Texas', *Journal of the American-Irish Historical Society*, 2, 1899, 120–38, NLI Ir. 973 a 1

Anonymous, 'The Irish in Texas', *Journal of the American-Irish Historical Society*, 30, 1932, 60–70, NLI Ir. 973 a 1

Flannery, J.B., *The Irish Texans*, San Antonio, 1980, NLI Ir. 973 f 4

Oberster, W.H., *Texas Irish Empresarios and Their Colonies*, Austin, 1953, NLI Ir. 973 o 10

Virginia

Anonymous, 'Grantees of Land in Virginia', *Journal of the American-Irish Historical Society*, 13, NLI Ir. 973 a 1

Anonymous, 'Virginia's Lost Irish Colonists', *Irish Roots*, No. 4, 1994, 21–4

Anonymous, 'Early Irish Settlements in Virginia', *Journal of the American-Irish Historical Society*, 4, 1904, 30–42, NLI Ir. 973 a 1

Anonymous, 'Some Irish Settlers in Virginia', *Journal of the American-Irish Historical Society*, 2, 1899, 161–6, NLI Ir. 973 a 1

Anonymous, 'Irish Settlers on the Opequan', *Journal of the American-Irish Historical Society*, 6, 1906, 71–4, NLI Ir. 973 a 1

Chalkey, Lyman, *The Scotch-Irish Settlement in Virginia (vols 1–3)*, Baltimore, Genealogical Publishing Company, 1989, reprint, exhaustive compendium

Wisconsin

MacDonald, Grace, *History of the Irish in Wisconsin in the Nineteenth Century*, Washington, 1954, NLI Ir. 973 m 9

WEST INDIES

Anonymous, 'Documents relating to the Irish in the West Indies, with accounts of Irish Settlements, 1612–1752', *Analecta Hibernica*, Vol. 4, pp. 140–286, No. 22, 1960

Oliver, Vere L., *Caribbeana: Miscellaneous Papers Relating to the History, Topograhy, Genealogy and Antiquities of the British West Indies*, London, 1912, NLI 9729 o 1 (5 vols)

Oliver, Vere L., *Monumental Inscriptions of the British West Indies*, London, 1904

Antigua

Oliver, Vere L., *The History of the Island of Antigua*, London, 1893–94 (3 vols)

Martinique

Clark de Dromentin, Patrick, *Les oies sauvages: mémoires d'une famille irlandaise réfugiée en France Nantes, Martinique, Bordeaux: 1691–1914*, Bordeaux, Presses Universitaires de Bordeaux, 1995, NLI Ir. 942 c 37

Montserrat

Anonymous, 'How Irish is Monserrat?', *Irish Roots*, No. 1 1994, 21–3; No. 2 1994 15–17

Clancy, Mary, *The Emigrant Experience*, Galway Labour History Group

SOUTH AFRICA

Anonymous, 'The Irish Transvaal Brigades', *The Irish Sword*, 1974 (Winter)

Anonymous, 'Southern African-Irish Studies', *Southern African-Irish Studies*, 1991, Vol. 1

Anonymous, 'Irish Settlement and Identity in South Africa before 1910', *Southern African-Irish Studies*, 1991, Vol. 1

Anonymous, 'The Irish in Southern Africa, 1795–1910', *Southern African-Irish Studies*, 1991, Vol. 2

Anonymous, 'A new Era for the Irish in South Africa', *Irish Roots*, No. 4, 1994, 13

Akenson, D.H., *The Irish in South Africa, 1920–1921*, NLI Ir. 968 i 2

Akenson, D.H., *Occasional papers on the Irish in South Africa*, Grahamstown

Blake, J.Y.F., *A West Pointer with the Boers*, Boston, Irish in the Boer War

Davitt, Michael, *The Boer Fight for Freedom*, USA, Irish in the Boer War

Dickson, G.D., *Irish Settlers to the Cape (1820)*, Cape Town, NLI Ir. 968 d 7

McCracken, D.P., *The Irish Pro-Boers, 1877–1902*, Perskor, Johannesburg, Irish in the Boer War

McCracken, J.L., *New Light at the Cape of Good Hope: William Porter, the Father of Cape Liberalism*, Belfast, Ulster Historical Foundation

SOUTH AMERICA

Argentina

Bulfin, William, *Rambles in Erin*

Coghlan, Eduardo, *Los Irlandeses en Argentina*, Buenos Aires, 1987

Pyne, Peter, *The invasions of Buenos Aires, 1806–7: the Irish dimension*, Liverpool, 1996

Murray, *The Irish in Argentina*, NLI Ir. 982 m 8

Peru

Anonymous, 'Saint Patrick's Day in Peru', *Irish Roots*, No. 1, 1995, 26–7

SPAIN

Henry, Grainne, *The Irish Military Community in Spanish Flanders 1586–1621*, Dublin, 1992, NLI Ir. 942 h 23

Stradling, R.A., *The Spanish Monarchy and Irish Mercenaries: the Wild Geese in Spain 1618–68*, Dublin, 1994, NLI Ir. 94106 s 13

Walsh, Micheline, *An Exile of Ireland, Hugh O'Neill*, Dublin, 1996

McDonnel, Hector, *The Wild Geese of the Antrim McDonnells*, Blackrock, Irish Academic Press, 1996, NLI Ir. 942 m 46

8. THE REGISTRY OF DEEDS

1. THE SCOPE OF THE RECORDS

Since research in the Registry of Deeds can be very laborious and time consuming, it is prudent to be aware of the limitations of its records before starting work there. The registry was set up by the Irish Parliament in 1708 to assist in regularising the massive transfer of land ownership from the Catholic Anglo-Norman and Gaelic populations to the Protestant Anglo-Irish which had taken place over the preceding century. The registration of deeds was not obligatory; the function of the registry was simply to provide evidence of legal title in the event of a dispute. These two facts, the voluntary nature of registration and the general aim of copper fastening the Cromwellian and Williamite confiscations, determine the nature of the records held by the registry. The overwhelming majority deal with property-owning members of the Church of Ireland, and a disproportionate number of these relate to transactions which carried some risk of legal dispute. In other words, the deeds registered are generally of interest only for a minority of the population, and constitute only a fraction of the total number of property transactions carried out in the country.

The implications of these facts are worth spelling out in detail. Over the most useful period of the registry's records, the non-Catholic population of Ireland constituted, at most, 20% of the total. A large proportion of these were dissenting Presbyterians largely concentrated in the north, and suffering restrictions on their property rights similar to, though not as severe as, those imposed on Catholics; very few deeds made by dissenting Protestants are registered. Of the remaining non-Catholics, the majority were small farmers, tradesmen or artisans, usually in a position of economic dependence on those with whom they might have property transactions, and thus in no position to dispute the terms of a deed. The records of the registry therefore cover only a minority of the non-Catholic minority. There are exceptions, of course — large landlords who made and registered great numbers of leases with their smaller tenants, marriage settlements between families of relatively modest means, the business transactions of the small Catholic merchant classes, the registration of the holdings of the few surviving Catholic landowners after the relaxation of the Penal Laws in the 1780s — but these remain very definitely exceptions. And for the vast bulk of the population, the Catholic tenant farmers, the possibility of a deed being registered can almost certainly be discounted, since they owned nothing and had almost no legal rights to the property they rented.

A further limit to the scope of the records is the scant use made of the registry before the middle of the eighteenth century. It was only from about the 1750s that registration became even relatively widespread, and its major genealogical usefulness is for the century or so from then until the 1850s, when it is generally superseded by other sources.

With these limitations in mind, it should now be said that, for those who made and registered deeds, the records of the registry can often provide superb information. The propensity to register deeds appears to have run in families, and a single document can name two or three generations, as well as leading back to a chain of related records which give a picture of the family's evolving fortunes and the network of its collateral relationships.

2. REGISTRATION

Registration worked in the following way. After a deed had been signed and witnessed, one of the parties to it had a copy known as a 'memorial' made, signed it and had it witnessed by two people, at least one of whom had been a witness to the original. The memorial was then sworn before a Justice of the Peace as a faithful copy of the original and sent to the registry. Here it was transcribed into a large manuscript volume and indexed. The original memorial was retained and stored, and these are all still preserved in the vaults of the registry. For research purposes, however, the large manuscript volumes containing the transcripts of the memorials are used. Registration of a deed normally took place fairly soon after its execution, within a month or two in most cases, though delays of up to two years are quite common. If the gap between the execution and the registration of a deed is much more, this may be significant; it indicates an impending need for one of the parties to the deed or their heirs to be able to show legal proof of its execution. The most common reason for such a need would have been the death of one of the parties.

3. THE INDEXES

The indexing system used by the registry is complicated and only partial. There are two sets of indexes, one by grantor's name (i.e. the name of the party disposing of the asset), and one by the name of the townland in which the property was situated. The Grantors' Index is fully alphabetical, and is divided into a number of sets covering different initial letters and periods. Between 1708 and 1833, the Grantors' Index records only the name of the grantor, and the surname of the first grantee, along with the volume, page and deed number. No indication is given of the location of the property concerned, an omission which can make a search for references to a family with a common surname very cumbersome indeed. After 1833, the index is more comprehensive, showing the county in which the property was situated. In general, the Index is remarkably accurate, but there are some mistakes, particularly in the volume and page references. In such a case, the deed number can be used to trace the transcript; several transcribers worked simultaneously on different volumes, and the volume numbers were sometimes transposed. If, for example, Volume 380 is not the correct reference, Volumes 378–82 may contain the transcript. Within each volume the transcripts are numerically consecutive.

The Lands Index is subdivided by county, and within each county is roughly alphabetical, with townland names grouped together under their initial letter. This means that a search for deeds relating to, say, Ballyboy, Co. Roscommon, involves a search through all of the references to Co. Roscommon townlands which start with 'B'. The information given in the index is brief, recording only the surnames of two of the parties, as well as the volume, page and deed numbers. As with the Grantors' Index, the index is divided into a number of sets covering different periods. After 1828, the index further subdivides the townlands into baronies, making research a good deal more efficient. Along with the county volumes, there are separate indexes for corporation towns and cities. The subdivisions within these are somewhat eccentric, particularly in the case of Dublin, making it necessary to search even more widely than in the rural indexes. It should be pointed out that the registry does not make it possible to trace the history of all of the transactions in which a property was involved since, inevitably, some of the deeds recording the transactions have not been registered.

In general, of the registry's two sets of indexes, the Grantors' Index is the most genealogically useful, since it is strictly alphabetical and lists transactions by person rather than by property. The single greatest lack in the registry is of an index to the grantees. The social range covered, given the distribution of wealth in the country, could be enhanced greatly by the production of such an index. Microfilm copies of both the Lands Index and the Grantors' Index, amounting to more than 400 reels, are available at the National Library. Volume 1 of Margaret Falley's *Irish and Scotch-Irish Ancestral Research*, available on open shelves in the Library reading room, gives a complete breakdown of the locations and microfilm numbers of the indexes up to 1850 (pp. 71–90). The Public Record Office of Northern Ireland also has a microfilm copy of the indexes, as well as the memorial books themselves, as does the LDS Library in Salt Lake City.

4. THE NATURE OF THE RECORDS

The archaic and legalistic terminology used in deeds can often make it extremely difficult to work out what precisely the parties to a deed intended it to do. This is particularly true in cases where earlier agreements are referred to but not recited in full. However, from a genealogical point of view, the precise nature of the transaction recorded is not always vital, and with a little practice it becomes relatively easy to pare the document down to the essentials of dates, placenames and personal names. It should be kept in mind that all personal names — buyers, sellers, trustees, mortgagees, witnesses — may be important and should be noted. None the less, there are numerous cases in which the nature of the deed is of interest, and in any case some advance knowledge will speed up the process of interpretation. What follows, therefore, is an attempt to clarify some of the less familiar terms, and to describe the most common or useful documents likely to be encountered.

The most important part of most deeds, the opening, follows an almost invariable pattern. After the phrase 'A memorial of', indicating that the transcript is of a copy rather than the original, the following are stated: (1) the nature of the deed; (2) the date on which the original was made; (3) the names of the parties to the deed. It must be remembered that a number of people could constitute a single party for the purposes of a legal transaction. A typical opening would then be

> 'A memorial of an indented deed of agreement dated October 13th 1793 between John O'Hara of Oak Park, Co. Meath, farmer, and George O'Hara of Balltown, Co. Meath, farmer, his eldest son of the first part, William Coakley of Navan, Co. Meath, merchant, of the second part, and Christopher French of Navan, gentleman, of the third part, in which . . .'

Very often it is necessary to read no more than this to know that a deed is not relevant; if, for example, the research is on the O'Haras of Sligo, it is clear at a glance that the above document has no direct relevance. As happens so often in genealogy, however, the significance of information in a deed may only become clear retro-spectively, in the light of something uncovered later. When carrying out a search for a particular family, therefore, it is a good idea to note briefly the important points in all deeds examined — names, addresses and occupations — whether or not they seem immediately relevant, so that if it subsequently emerges, for example, that the O'Haras of Sligo and Meath are related, the relevant deeds can be readily identified again.

Categorising the kinds of deeds which appear in the registry can be difficult, since many of them are not what they appear to be. The most common misleading description in the opening of the memorial is the 'deed of lease and release', which may in fact be a conveyance or sale, a mortgage, a marriage settlement or a rent charge. 'Lease and Release' was a legal device whereby the obligation to record a conveyance publicly could be avoided; it was not obligatory to record a transaction to a tenant or lessee already in occupation, and it was not obligatory to record a lease for one year only. Accordingly, a lease for one year was first granted, and then the true transaction, conveyance, mortgage, marriage settlement or other, was carried out. It remained popular as a method of conveyance until 1845, when the Statute of Uses which made it possible was repealed.

Despite the difficulties created by such disguises as the 'lease and release', the underlying transactions do fall into a number of broad classes:

1. Leases

By far the most common of the records in the registry, leases could run for any term between one and 999 years, or could depend on the lives of a number of persons named in the document, or could be a mixture of the two, lasting three lives or sixty years, whichever was longer. Only leases for more than three years could be registered. The most genealogically useful information in leases is to be found in the lives they mention. The choice of lives generally rested with the lessee or grantee, and in most cases those chosen were related. Often the names and ages of the grantee's children can appear, extremely valuable for families in the eighteenth century. Leases for 900 years, or for lives renewable in perpetuity, which were much more common in Ireland than elsewhere, amounted to a permanent transfer of the property, although the grantor remained the nominal owner. As might be imagined, such leases provided a rich basis for legal disputes.

2. Marriage Settlements

Any form of pre-nuptial property agreement between the families of the prospective bride and groom was known as a 'marriage settlement' or 'marriage articles'. A variety of transactions can therefore be classed in this way. What they have in common is their aim to provide security, in particular to the women; since married women could hold no property in their own right, it was common practice for the dowry to be granted to trustees, rather than directly to the future husband, which allowed her some degree of independence. Commonly also, the family of the prospective husband, or the husband himself, granted an annuity out of the income of his land to the future wife and children if he should pre-decease them. The information given in settlements varies, but in general it should include at a minimum the names, addresses and occupations of the bride, groom and bride's father. In addition, other relatives — brothers, uncles etc. — also put in an appearance. For obvious reasons, therefore, marriage settlements are among the most useful of the records to be found in the registry. The period for which they were most commonly registered appears to have been the three decades from 1790 to 1820. In searching the Grantors' Indexes for them, it should be remembered that they are not always indicated as such, and that the formal grantor may be a member of either family, making it necessary to search under both surnames.

3. *Mortgages*

In the eighteenth and nineteenth centuries, these were very commonly used as a form of investment on the one hand, and as a way of raising short-term cash on the other. They do not generally provide a great deal of family information but, since they were an endless source of legal disputes, they form a disproportionate number of the deeds registered. It was quite common for mortgages to be passed on to third or fourth parties, each hoping to make money, and the resulting deeds can be very complicated.

4. *Bills of Discovery*

Under the Penal Laws, Catholics were not allowed to possess more than a very limited amount of land, and a Protestant who discovered a Catholic in possession of more than this amount could file a Bill of Discovery to claim it. In practice, most bills appear to have been filed by Protestant friends of Catholic landowners to pre-empt hostile discovery, and as a means of allowing them to remain in effective possession. Registered bills are not common, but they are extremely interesting, both genealogically and historically.

5. *Wills*

Only those wills likely to be contested legally, in other words those which omitted someone, almost certainly a family member who might have a legitimate claim, would have been registered. Abstracts of the personal and geographical information in all of the wills registered between 1708 and 1832 have been published in P.B. Phair and E. Ellis (eds) *Abstracts of Wills at the Registry of Deeds* (3 vols) Irish Manuscripts Commission, 1954–1988. The full provisions of the wills are only to be found in the original memorials.

6. *Rent Charges*

These were annual payments of a fixed sum payable out of the revenue from nominated lands. They were used to provide for family members in straitened circumstances, or to pay off debts or mortgages in instalments. Once made, they could be transferred to others, and were valuable assets in their own right. Depending on the terms, they can provide useful insights into family relationships and family fortunes.

Other miscellaneous classes of deeds also appear. As outlined above, the only common feature is that they record a property transaction of some description; any family information they may contain is a matter of luck.

9. NEWSPAPERS

Newspapers are one of the most enjoyable and most difficult of genealogical sources. Faced with so much of the everyday particularity of the past, it is virtually impossible to confine oneself to biographical data; again and again research is side-tracked by simple curiosity. In addition to this, the endemic imprecision of family information means that it is almost always necessary to search a wide range of dates. A sustained search for genealogical information in original newspapers is, as a result, extremely time consuming. If the efficient use of research time is a priority, newspapers are certainly not the place to start.

With this proviso in mind, it must be added that the destruction of so many Irish records in 1922 gives a disproportionate importance to Irish newspapers, and that when newspapers do produce information, it can be extremely rich. Events are reported virtually as they happen, within a few weeks at most, and the reports have an authority and accuracy which is hard to match, even making all necessary allowances for journalistic errors. Nor is it now any longer always necessary to search the original papers themselves, as we shall see.

1. INFORMATION GIVEN

There are two principal formats in which useful information appears, biographical notices and, in the early papers, advertisements. Up to the 1850s, the former consist largely of marriage announcements and obituaries; birth announcements tend to be sparse, relate only to the wealthiest classes, and often give no more than the father's name, taking the form, 'on the 12th, the lady of George Gratton Esq., of a son'. After the mid-nineteenth century, the number of birth notices rises sharply, but they remain relatively uninformative.

Marriage announcements contain a much broader range of information, from the bare minimum of the names of the two parties, to comprehensive accounts of the addresses, occupations and fathers' names. In the majority of cases, the name of the bride's father and his address are supplied in a form such as 'married on Tuesday last Michael Thomson Esq. to Miss Neville eldest daughter of James Neville of Bandon Esq.' For many eighteenth-century marriages, a newspaper announcement may be the only surviving record, particularly where the relevant Church of Ireland register has not survived.

Obituaries are by far the most numerous newspaper announcements, and cover a much broader social spectrum than either births or marriages. Again, the kind of information given can vary widely, from the barest 'died at Tullamore Mr Michael Cusack' to the most elaborate, giving occupation, exact age, and family relationships: 'died at the house of her uncle Mr Patrick Swan in George's St in the 35th year of her age Mrs Burgess, relict of Henry Burgess Esq., late of Limerick'. Precision such as this is rare, however; most announcements confine themselves to name, address, occupation and place of death. Because of the paucity of Catholic burial records, newspaper obituaries are the most comprehensive surviving records of the deaths of the majority of the Catholic middle classes. From about the 1840s, the numbers of both obituaries and marriage announcements rose sharply; unfortunately these events are by then usually more easily traceable in parish or civil records.

Advertisements, in the early newspapers especially, were more often paid announcements than true advertisements in the modern sense, and an extraordinary variety of information can be gleaned from them. The most useful types are as follows:

■ *(i) Elopements.* A husband would announce that his wife had absconded, and disclaim all responsibility for any debts she might contract. Usually his address and her maiden surname are given.

■ *(ii) Business announcements.* The most useful are those which record the place and nature of the business, which announce a change of address or ownership for the business, or which record the succession of a son to a business after his father's death.

■ *(iii) Bankruptcies.* These generally request creditors to gather at a specified time and place, and can be useful in narrowing the focus of a search for relevant transactions in the Registry of Deeds.

As well as advertisements and biographical notices, of course, newspapers also reported the news of the day, concentrating on the details of court cases with particular relish. For an ancestor who was a convict, these hold great interest, since much of the evidence was reported verbatim, and may provide vital clues for further research. However, uncovering the relevant report depends very much on knowing the date of conviction with some degree of accuracy, as well as the area in which the trial is likely to have taken place.

2. PERSONS COVERED

Apart from reports of trials, genealogical information to be found in newspapers relates to fairly well-defined social groups. First, then as now, the doings of the nobility were of general interest, and their births, marriages and deaths are extensively covered. Next in terms of coverage are the merchant and professional classes of the towns in which the newspapers were published. These would include barristers and solicitors, doctors, masters of schools, military officers and clergy, as well as the more prosperous business people. It should be remembered that, from about the 1770s, this would include the growing Catholic merchant class. Next are the farming gentry from the surrounding areas. After them come the less well-off traders, traceable largely through advertisements. Finally, the provincial papers also cover the inhabitants of neighbouring towns in these same classes, albeit sparsely at times. No information is to be found concerning anyone at or below middling farmer level, the great bulk of the population in other words. This remains true even from the third and fourth decades of the nineteenth century, when the number of announcements rose markedly, and the social classes covered broadened somewhat.

3. DATES AND AREAS

The earliest Irish newspapers were published in Dublin at the end of the seventeenth century. It was not until the mid-eighteenth century, however, that they became widespread and began to carry information of genealogical value. The period of their prime usefulness is from about this time, *c.*1750, to around the mid-nineteenth century, when other sources become more accessible and thorough. Obviously, not all areas of the country were equally well served, particularly at the start of this period. Publications tended to be concentrated in particular regions, as follows.

(i) *Dublin*

The most important eighteenth-century publications were the *Dublin Evening Post*, started in 1719, *Faulkner's Dublin Journal*, from 1725, the *Freeman's Journal*, from 1763, and the *Dublin Hibernian Journal*, from 1771. As well as carrying plentiful marriage and obituary notices relating to Dublin and surrounding areas from about the mid-century, these papers also reproduced notices which had first appeared in provincial papers, something which should be kept in mind in cases where the original local newspapers have not survived. From the early nineteenth century, a great proliferation of publications began to appear; unfortunately, the custom of publishing family notices fell into disuse in the first decades of the century, and did not resume until well into the 1820s.

(ii) *Cork*

After Dublin, Cork was the area of the country best served by newspapers, with many publications following the lead of the *Corke Journal* which began in 1753. As well as publishing notices relating specifically to Cork city and county, these papers also carried much of interest for other Munster counties, notably Co. Kerry, and, like the Dublin papers, republished notices relating to Munster which had originally appeared in other publications. An index exists to newspaper biographical notices relating to Cos Cork and Kerry between 1756 and 1827, details of which will be found below.

(iii) *Limerick/Clare*

There was a great deal of overlap between the earliest Clare newspapers, the *Clare Journal* from 1787, and the *Ennis Chronicle* from 1788, and those of Limerick, where the first publications were the *Munster Journal* (1749) and the *Limerick Chronicle*. As well as Clare and Limerick, both groups of papers had extensive coverage of Co. Tipperary, and in the case of the Limerick publications, this coverage also extended to Kerry and Galway. The Molony series of manuscripts in the Genealogical Office (see Chapter 6) includes extensive abstracts from the Clare papers. Details of a more accessible and far-ranging set of abstracts will be found below.

(iv) *Carlow/Kilkenny*

This area was covered by a single publication, *Finn's Leinster Journal*, which began in 1768. Although the advertisements are useful, early biographical notices are sparse. The earliest have been published in the *Irish Genealogist* (1987/88).

(v) Waterford

The earliest newspapers here were the *Waterford Chronicle* (1770), the *Waterford Herald* (1791), and the *Waterford Mirror* (1804). Few of the earliest issues appear to have survived. For surviving issues before 1800, the *Irish Genealogist* has published the biographical notices (1974 and 1976–80 incl.). Notices to 1821 are included with the abstracts for Clare/Limerick.

(vi) Belfast and Ulster

The single most important newspaper in this area was the *Belfast Newsletter*, which began publication in 1737. It had a wider geographical range than any of the Dublin papers, covering virtually all of east Ulster. Outside Belfast, the most significant publications were the *Londonderry Journal*, from 1772, which also covered a good area of Donegal and Tyrone, and the *Newry Journal* and *Strabane Journal*, of which very few, if any, early issues survive.

4. LOCATIONS

The best single repository for Irish newspapers is the British Library. After 1826 the library was obliged to hold a copy of all Irish publications, and from that date its collection is virtually complete. It also has an extensive, though patchy, collection before that date. Within Ireland, the largest collection is held by the National Library, though this is by no means comprehensive. Many unique copies are held in local libraries and other repositories. *The Report of the NEWSPLAN Project in Ireland* (NLI, 2nd edition 1998) lists all known hardcopy and microfilm holdings of Irish newspapers.

5. INDEXES

A number of indexes exist to the biographical material to be found in newspapers, which can greatly lighten the burden of research. Those dealing with single publications are as follows:

(i) National Library index to the *Freeman's Journal* from 1763 to 1771
(ii) National Library index to marriages and deaths in *Pue's Occurrences* and the *Dublin Gazette* 1730–1740, NLI Ms 3197
(iii) Henry Farrar's *Biographical Notices in Walker's Hibernian Magazine 1772–1812* (1889)
(iv) Card indexes to the biographical notices in the *Hibernian Chronicle* (1771–1802), and the *Cork Mercantile Chronicle* (1803–1818), held by the Irish Genealogical Research Society in London
(v) Index to biographical material in the *Belfast Newsletter* (1737–1800), held by the Linenhall Library in Belfast
(vi) Southern Education and Library Board (Northern Ireland) contains a chronological list of article references, indexed by person, subject and place. Copies available for sale. Newspapers covered: *Co. Down Spectator* 1904–1964, *Downpatrick Recorder* 1936–1986, *Mourne Observer* 1949–1980, *Newtownards Chronicle* 1871–1873, the *Northern Herald* 1833–1836, the *Northern Star* 1792–1797

(vii) As well as these, Volume 6 of Albert Casey's *O'Kief, Coshe Mang* etc. reprints the biographical notices from the *Kerry Evening Post* from 1828 to 1864, and these are included in the general index at the back of the volume. More useful than any of these, however, are two extraordinary works produced by Rosemary ffolliott, her 'Index to Biographical Notices Collected from Newspapers, Principally Relating to Cork and Kerry, 1756–1827', and 'Index to Biographical Notices in the Newspapers of Limerick, Ennis, Clonmel and Waterford, 1758–1821'. Both are in fact much more than simple indexes, transcribing and ordering alphabetically all of the notices they record. Some idea of their scope can be gleaned simply by listing the newspapers they cover. The former includes biographical notices relating to Cork and Kerry from the surviving issues of the following Cork papers: the *Cork Advertiser*, the *Cork Chronicle*, the *Cork Evening Post*, the *Cork Gazette*, the *Corke Journal*, the *Cork Mercantile Chronicle*, the *Cork Morning Intelligence*, the *Southern Reporter*, *The Constitution*, the *Hibernian Chronicle* and the *Volunteer Journal*. As well as these, it also records all notices relating to Cork and Kerry in *Finn's Leinster Journal*, the *Dublin Gazette*, the *Dublin Hibernian Journal*, *Faulkner's Dublin Journal*, the *Freeman's Journal*, the *Magazine of Magazines*, the *Limerick Chronicle* and the *Waterford Mirror*. The latter index extracts and indexes the biographical notices from the *Clonmel Herald*, the *Clonmel Gazette*, the *Clonmel Advertiser*, the *Ennis Chronicle*, the *Clare Journal*, the *Limerick Evening Post*, the *Limerick Gazette*, the *Limerick Chronicle* the *Munster Journal*, the *Waterford Chronicle* and the *Waterford Mirror*. In addition, a number of eighteenth-century Dublin newspapers are included: the *Freeman's Journal*, *Faulkner's Dublin Journal*, the *Dublin Hibernian Journal* and the *Hibernian Chronicle*, and all notices for the areas covered by the above publications are extracted, as well as notices relating to other Munster counties, and to Cos Galway, Mayo, Roscommon, Leitrim, Longford and King's (Offaly). Between the two works, then, virtually all of the surviving eighteenth-century notices for the southern half of the country are extracted, along with a large proportion of notices up to 1821/1827, and most of the entries relating to Connacht, south Leinster and Munster which were picked up and reprinted by the Dublin papers. All in all, the two works constitute a magnificent work of scholarship. Unfortunately, neither is as widely available as it should be. The National Library and Cork City Library hold manuscript copies of the Cork and Kerry index (NLI Mss 19172–5). Limerick Archives (see Chapter 14 under 'The Irish Genealogical Project') has a copy of the more extensive Limerick, Ennis, Clonmel and Waterford index. The Genealogical Office has microfiche copies of both. Unfortunately, these are not directly accessible to the public. Copies can also be found in the library of the Society of Australian Genealogists.

10. DIRECTORIES

For those areas and classes which they cover, Irish directories are an excellent source, often supplying information not readily available elsewhere. Their most obvious and practical use is to find out where precisely in the larger towns a family lived, but for members of the gentry and the professional, merchant and trading classes, they can show much more, providing indirect evidence of reversals of fortune or growing prosperity, of death and emigration. In many cases, directory entries are the only precise indication of occupation. The only classes totally excluded from all directories are, once again, the most disadvantaged, small tenant farmers, landless labourers and servants. Virtually all classes other than these are at least partly included, in some of the nineteenth-century directories in particular. One point to be kept in mind when using any directory is that every entry is at least six months out of date by the time of publication. The account which follows divides directories into (1) Dublin Directories, (2) Country-Wide Directories, and (3) Provincial Directories, supplying in each case the dates, locations and information included, followed, in the first two categories, by a chronological checklist.

1. DUBLIN DIRECTORIES

The *Gentleman's and Citizen's Almanack*, produced by John Watson, began publication in Dublin in 1736, and continued to 1844. However, the first true trade directories in Ireland were those published by Peter Wilson for Dublin city, starting in 1751 and continuing until 1837, with a break from 1754 to 1759. From the outset, these were considered as supplements to Watson's *Almanack*, and were regularly bound with it. In 1787, the two publications were put together with the *English Court Registry* and, until it ceased publication in 1837, the whole was known as the *Treble Almanack*.

Initially, the information supplied in Wilson's *Directory* consisted purely of alphabetical lists of merchants and traders, supplying name, address and occupation. In the early years these were quite scanty, but grew steadily over the decades, from less than a thousand names in the 1752 edition to almost five thousand in 1816. As well as merchants and traders, the last decades of the eighteenth century also saw the inclusion of separate lists of those who might now be termed 'The Establishment' — officers of the city guilds and of Trinity College, state officials, those involved in the administration of medicine and the law, Church of Ireland clergy etc. The range of people covered expanded markedly, if a little eccentrically, in the early nineteenth century. The most permanent addition was a new section, added in 1815, which covered the nobility and gentry. As well as this, a number of other listings of potential use to readers were added, though some appear only intermittently. Persons covered by these lists include pawnbrokers, bankers, apothecaries, police, dentists, physicians, militia officers and ships' captains.

The most significant difference between the *Treble Almanack* and Pettigrew and Oulton's *Dublin Almanac and General Register of Ireland*, which began annual publication in 1834, is the inclusion in the latter of a street-by-street listing, initially only of the inhabitants of Dublin proper, but enlarged year by year to encompass the suburbs. From 1835, this listing was supplemented by an alphabetical list of the individuals recorded. In theory at least, the combination of the two listings should now make it possible to track the movements of individuals around the city, an important feature, since changes of address were very frequent in the nineteenth century, when the common practice was to rent rather than purchase. Unfortunately, in practice the alphabetical list is much less comprehensive than the street list.

Pettigrew and Oulton also extended even further the range of persons covered. The officers of virtually every Dublin institution, club and society are recorded, as well as clergy of all denominations. Another significant difference from the earlier *Treble Almanack* which should be kept in mind is the extension of the coverage outside the Dublin area. Under the rubric 'Official Authorities of Counties and Towns' Pettigrew and Oulton record the names of many of the rural gentry and more prosperous inhabitants of the large towns in their guise as local administrators. This is particularly useful for areas which were not served by a local directory, or for which none has survived. Similarly, the officials of many of the better-known institutions and societies in the larger country towns are also recorded, as well as the more important provincial clergy.

The successor to Pettigrew and Oulton was Alexander Thom's *Irish Almanac and Official Directory*, which began in 1844 and has continued publication up to the present. As the name implies, it continued the extension of coverage outside Dublin. To take one year as an example, the 1870 edition includes, as well as the alphabetical and street listings for Dublin, alphabetical lists of the following for the entire country: army officers; attorneys, solicitors and barristers, bankers, Catholic, Church of Ireland and Presbyterian clergy, coast guard officers, doctors, MPs, magistrates, members of the Irish Privy Council, navy and marine officers, officers of counties and towns, and peers. Although Thom's is generally regarded as a Dublin directory, its usefulness goes well beyond Dublin.

As well as these annual directories, Dublin was also included in the country-wide publications of Pigot and Slater issued at intervals during the nineteenth century. The only significant difference is the arrangement of the individuals listed under their trades, making it possible to identify all of those engaged in the same occupation, important at a time when many occupations were handed down from one generation to the next. These directories are dealt with more fully below.

CHECKLIST

1751–1837: Wilson's *Directory*, from 1787, issued as part of the *Treble Almanack*
1834–1849: Pettigrew and Oulton's *Dublin Almanac and General Register of Ireland*, from 1844; Thom's *Irish Almanac and Official Directory*
See also Pigot's and Slater's country-wide directories from 1820.

The most comprehensive collections are held by the National Library and the National Archives. Copies can be requested directly at the reading room counter in the library and are on open access in the Archives.

1366

1 N.—Bessborough-avenue.
Off North-strand-road.

1 Boyd, Mrs.	8*l.*
2 Flanagan, Mr. Thomas	
3 Preest, Mr. Patrick,	9*l.*
4 M'Carthy, Mr. Patk. J. G.P.O.	7*l.*
5 Hutchin, Mrs.	7*l.*
6 Purcell, Mr. Thomas,	10*l.*
7 Conroy, Mr. John,	10*l.*
8 Hatchell, Geo. master mariner,	8*l.*
9 Harbron, Mr. Wm. J.	9*l.*
10 Bell, Mr. Peter,	9*l*
11 Keane, Alphons., photographer, and 94 North-strand,	9*l.*
12 Byrne, Mr. Joseph,	8*l.*
13 Goulding, Daniel, carpenter,	7*l.*
14 O'Kelly, Mr. Alexander,	7*l.*
15 Curtis, Mrs.	8*l*
16 O'Callaghan, Mrs.	8*l.*
Link Line	
19 Frazer, Mr. James,	7*l.*
20 Reynolds, Mr. Thomas,	6*l.*
21 Robinson, Mr. Charles,	6*l.*
22 Armstrong, Mr. Andrew,	6*l.*
Link Line.	
24 Wren, Mr. James,	6*l.*
25 Carroll, Mr. Patrick,	7*l.*
26 Byrne, Mr. Patrick,	7*l.*
27 M'Cauley, Mr. Peter,	7*l.*
28 Gregan, Mr. Hugh,	
Drumcondra Link Line Railway	
32 Tomlinson, Mr. William,	12*l.*
33 Halliday, Mr. Thomas,	9*l.*
34 Grimes, James, engineer,	9*l.*
35 Wilcocks, Mr. Joseph,	9*l.*
36 Dillon, Mr. Andrew,	9*l.*
37 Lacy, Mr. James,	9*l.*
38 Scott, Mr. William,	9*l.*
39 Lambert, Mr. Thomas	7*l.*
40 Mooney, Mr. Mathew,	7*l.*
41 Hayden, Mr. John,	7*l.*
42 Smith, Mrs.	7*l.*
43 Hendry, Mr. William,	7*l.*
44 Sweny, Mr. Herbert Sidney,	7*l.*
45 Tuites, Mr. R.	7*l.*
46 Griffith, John,	7*l.*
47 Homan, Mr. Thomas,	4*l.* 10*s.*
48 Kennedy, Mrs.	4*l.* 10*s.*
49 Murphy, Mrs.,	6*l.*
50 Holmes, Mr. William,	6*l.*
51 Langan, Mr. John	

Bethesda-place.
Upper Dorset-street.
Three small cottages

3 S.—Bishop-street.

22½ Dunne, J. fishmonger,	7*l.*
23 Tenements,	16*l.*
24 Hayden, Mrs. board & lodging,	16*l.*
here Redmond's-hill & Peter's-row inters.	
25 Kelly, James, grocer, wine and spirit dealer, & 13 Peter's-row,	58*l.*
26, 27, 27A, 28 to 39 Jacob, W. R. & Co. (limited)	
40, 41 & 42 Tonge and Taggart, *South City* foundry and iron works,	37*l.*, 17*l.*
43 to 45 Tenements,	14*l.* to 17*l.*
46 Jacob, W. R. and Co. (limited) stores,	17*l.*
..........*here Bishop-court intersects*........	
47 to 49 Tenements,	20*l.* 9*l.*
50 Jacob, W. R. and Co. stores,	30*l.*
51 Tenements,	26*l.*
52 & 53 Tenements,	21*l.*, 24*l.*
54 & 55 Tenements,	17*l.*, 16*l.*
56 Leigh, P. provision merchant,	21*l.*

Black-street.
Infirmary-road.
Twenty small houses — Artizan's Dwellings company.

3 N.—Blackhall-parade.
From Blackhall-street to King-street, Nth.
P. St. Paul.—Arran-quay W.

1 Bourke, Mr. James,	9*l.*
2 Duffy, Mrs. lodgings,	9*l.*
3 Murphy, Mrs. M.	13*l.*
4 & 5 Condron, J. horseshoer and farrier,	8*l.*
6 & 7 Chew T. C. & Co. wool merchants, with 55 and 56 Queen-street, and 27 Island-street	
8 Dardis, Mr. M.	17*l.*
9 Clarke, Joseph, watch maker,	14*l.*
10 Tenements,	14*l.*
11 Duignan, Mrs.	14*l.*

3 N.—Blackhall-place.
From Ellis's-quay to Stoneybatter.
P. St. Paul.—Arran-quay W.

KING'S, OR BLUE COAT HOSPITAL—George R. Armstrong, esq. agent and registrar; Rev. T. P. Richards, M.A. chaplain & head master
1 and 2 Menton, Denis, dairy, and 17 King-street, north, 59*l.*
3 and 4 Losty, Mr. M. J. 30*l.* 34*l.*
5 Young, Mr. William
6 and 7 Paul and Vincent, farming implement manufs. millwrights, and iron founders, chemical ma-

30 McKeever, Mr. J.	
34 Dixon, Mrs.	
35 King, Mrs. M.	
36 Kirk, Mr. B.	
37 Muldoon, Mr. T.	
38 Behan, Mr. P.	
39 Donovan, Mr. Henry,	
40 *Dublin Prison Gate Mission Laund. workroom, and dormitories—* J. C. Wilkinson, secretary.	

3 N.—Blackhall-street
From Queen-street to Blackhall-pl.
P. St. Paul.—Arran-quay W.

1 Gorman, Mrs.	
2 Hopkins, Mr. Robert,	
........*here Blackhall-parade intersec*	
3 Gordon, Samuel, wholesale manufacturer,	
4 *The National Hotel*—John We proprietor,	
5 Baird, Mrs.	
6 Clancy, Mrs. Mary,	
„ Doyle, Mr. T. M.	
„ Montgomery, Mr. James	
7 Dillon, Mr. John,	
8 Lemass, Mr. Joseph,	
9 Nurses' Training Institu Miss Tierney Superintender	
10 Mooney, Mrs.	
11 and 12 Ruins,	
13 Keogh, Mrs. J.	
14 Vacant,	
15 Tenements,	
........*here Blackhall-place interse*	
16 to 18 Fitzgerald, P. corn an stores, 10*l.*	
19 & 20 Hickey & Co. stores offi	
21 & 22 *Cairn's Memorial Home,*	
23 Correll, Mr. J.	
24 Doran, Mr. C. J.	
25 Leahy, Mr. W. J.	
26 Doheney, Mr. Joseph	
27 Eivers & Rispin, cattle sales	
„ Curtis, T. H. forage contrac	
28 Ralph, Mrs.,	
29 Hickey, Paul, & Co. cattle s corn, hay, and wool facto	
30 Scott, Mr. John F.	
31 Byrne, Mr. P. J.	
32 Cobbe, Mrs.	

3 S.—Blackpit
From New-row, South, to Gre
P. St. Nicholas Without, east sid
Luke, west.—Merchants'-qu
„ LETTER BOX, *oppo*

Thom's *Dublin Directory*, 1901
(Courtesy of the Genealogical Office)

2. COUNTRY-WIDE DIRECTORIES

Until the productions of Pigot and Co. in the early nineteenth century, very little exists which covers the entire country. Although not true directories in the sense of the Dublin publications, four works may be used in a similar way, at least as far as the country gentry are concerned. The earliest of these is George Taylor and Andrew Skinner's *Road Maps of Ireland* (1778) which prints maps of the principal routes from Dublin to the country towns, including the major country houses and the surnames of their occupants, with an alphabetical index to these surnames. The aim of William Wilson's *The Post-Chaise Companion* (1786) is similar, providing a discursive description of what might be seen on various journeys through the countryside. These descriptions include the names of the country houses and, again, their owners' surnames. There is no index. The next publications were the two editions, in 1812 and 1814, of Ambrose Leet's *Directory*. This contains an alphabetical listing of placenames — towns, villages, country houses, townlands, in an arbitrary mix — showing the county, the nearest post town and, in the case of the houses, the full name of the occupant. These names are then themselves indexed at the back of the volume.

The earliest country-wide directory covering more than the gentry was Pigot's *Commercial Directory of Ireland*, published in 1820. This goes through the towns of Ireland alphabetically, supplying the names of nobility and gentry living in or close to the town, and arranging the traders of each town according to their trade. Pigot published a subsequent edition in 1824 and his successors, Slater's, issued expanded versions in 1846, 1856, 1870, 1881 and 1894. These followed the same basic format, dividing the country into four provinces, and then dealing with towns and villages alphabetically within each province. With each edition the scope of the directory was steadily enlarged, including ever more towns and villages. 'Guide to Irish Directories', Chapter 4 of *Irish Genealogy: A Record Finder* (ed. Begley, Dublin: Heraldic Artists, 1981) includes a detailed county-by-county listing of the towns and villages covered by each edition. Otherwise, the most important differences between the various editions are as follows:

■ *1824.* Includes a country-wide alphabetical index to all the clergy, gentry and nobility listed in the entries for individual towns, omitted in subsequent issues.

■ *1846.* Includes the names of schoolteachers for the towns treated, a practice continued in following editions.

■ *1881.* This supplies the names of the principal farmers near each of the towns treated, giving the relevant parish. This feature was continued in the 1894 edition.

From 1824, separate alphabetical listings are given for the clergy, gentry and nobility of Dublin and most of the larger urban centres.

The best single collection of these directories is in the National Library, where most of the early editions are now on microfiche.

CHECKLIST

1778   George Taylor and Andrew Skinner, *Road Maps of Ireland* (reprint IUP, 1969) NLI Ir. 9141 t 1

1786   William Wilson's *The Post-Chaise Companion,* NLI J 9141 w 13

1812   Ambrose Leet, *A List of [. . .] noted places,* NLI Ir. 9141 l 10

1814   Ambrose Leet, *A Directory to the Market Towns, Villages, Gentlemen's Seats and other noted places in Ireland,* NLI Ir. 9141 l 10

1820   J. Pigot, *Commercial Directory of Ireland,* NLI Ir. 9141 c 25

1824   J. Pigot, *City of Dublin and Hibernian Provincial Directory,* NLI Ir. 9141 p 75

1846   Slater's *National Commercial Directory of Ireland,* NLI Ir. 9141 s 30

1856   Slater's *Royal National Commercial Directory of Ireland*

1870   Slater's *Royal National Commercial Directory of Ireland*

1881   Slater's *Royal National Commercial Directory of Ireland*

1894   Slater's *Royal National Commercial Directory of Ireland*

See also Dublin directories from 1834

3. PROVINCIAL DIRECTORIES

John Ferrar's *Directory of Limerick*, published in 1769, was the first directory to deal specifically with a provincial town, and the practice spread throughout Munster in the remaining decades of the eighteenth century, with Cork particularly well covered. In the nineteenth century, local directories were produced in abundance, especially in areas with a strong commercial identity, such as Belfast and the north-east and, again, Munster. The quality and coverage of these varies widely, from the street-by-street listings in Martin's 1839 *Belfast Directory* to the barest of commercial lists. A guide to the principal local directories is included in the county source-lists in Chapter 12. These lists cannot, however, be regarded as complete; many small, local publications, especially from the first half of the nineteenth century, are now quite rare, with only one or two surviving copies. Locating these can be extremely difficult. Some guides are:

James Carty, *National Library of Ireland Bibliography of Irish History 1870–1911*, Dublin, 1940.

Edward Evans, *Historical and Bibliographical Account of Almanacks, Directories etc. in Ireland from the Sixteenth Century*, Dublin, 1897.

M.E. Keen, *A Bibliography of Trade Directories of the British Isles in the Victoria and Albert Museum*, London, 1979.

PART 3 ◆ A REFERENCE GUIDE

11. OCCUPATIONS

Apothecaries

(a) GO Ms 648 Apothecaries, apprentices, journeymen and prosecutions, 1791–1829
(b) List of Licensed Apothecaries of Ireland 1872, NLI Ir. 61501 i 1
(c) Admissions to the guilds of Dublin, 1792–1837, Reports from Committees, Parliamentary Papers, 1837, Vol. 11 (ii)
(d) NLI Report on Private Collections, No. 208
(e) Records of Apothecaries Hall, Dublin, 1747–1833, NLI Pos. 929

Artists

(a) Artists of Ireland (1796), Williams, NLI Ir. 9275 w 3
(b) *Royal Hibernian Academy Exhibitors 1826–1875*, NLI Ir. 921 r 2
(c) *The Artists of Ireland*, Ann Crookshank and Knight of Glin, NLI Ir. 750 c 2
(d) Murray, Peter, *Cork artists in the 19th century*, Cork, 1991, NLI Ir. 708 c 7. (Catalogue of Crawford Gallery exhibition)

Army/Militia

(a) GO Ms 608, 1761, Militia Lists for Cos Cork, Derry, Donegal, Down, Dublin, Kerry, Limerick, Louth, Monaghan, Roscommon, Tyrone, Wicklow
(b) GO Ms 579, Army Lists 1746–1772 (Athlone, Bandon, Cork, Drogheda, Dublin, Galway, Gort, Thurles, Tullamore)
(c) Ireland's Memorial Records (Biographical notes on soldiers in Irish regiments who died in World War I) NLI Ir. 355942 i 3, see also GRO death records 1914–1918 (separate listing)
(d) British Army records:
 (i) War Office records at the Public Record Office, Kew: Regimental records; Muster Rolls; Casualties; Widows; Soldiers' Documents (pensioners). To use these, it is normally necessary to know the relevant regiment and its posting
 (ii) Registers of Royal Hospital, Kilmainham, and Chelsea Hospital. (Royal Hospital records also on microfilm at National Archives)
 (iii) Lists of fit Chelsea Hospital outpensioners, 1835, NAI, OP/1835/8. Covers almost the entire country, county by county; supplies name, pension, residence and regiment
(e) Births, Marriages and Deaths of army personnel, 1796–1880: General Register Office, St Catherine's House, London. To use these, it is normally necessary to know the relevant regiment and its posting

(f) Some published works:
   Army Lists Annual, from 1754, quarterly from 1798 (commissioned officers)
   Officers of the district corps of Ireland, 1797, NLI Ir. 355 a 10
   Officers (. . .) upon the establishment of Ireland, NLI P 91
   DAlton *English Army Lists,* NLI 355942 d 2
   Edwards, G. Hamilton, *In Search of Army Ancestry,* Phillimore, 1977, the
      standard work on tracing ancestors in the British Army
   Fowler, Simon, *Army Records for Family Historians,* PRO Readers' Guide No. 2,
      HMSO, 1998 (2nd ed.)
   King, *Officers of the district corps of Ireland, 1797,* NLI Ir. 355 a 10
   Mullan, *General & Field Officers 1740,* NLI 355942 l 4
   Mullan, *General & Field Officers 1755,* NLI LO
   Mullan, *General & Field Officers 1759,* NLI LO
   Thorpe, *The Irish Army under King James,* NLI P 11 & P 12
   White, A.S., *A Bibliography of Regimental Histories of the British Army,* NLI
      355942 w 13

Attornies and Barristers

(a) *King's Inn Admission Papers 1723–1867,* Phair & Sadlier, IMC, 1986, NLI Ir.
    340 k 1
(b) Dublin Directories, from the late eighteenth century

Bakers

(a) Admissions to the guilds of Dublin, 1792–1837, *Reports from Committees,
    Parliamentary Papers, 1837,* Vol. 11 (ii)
(b) Freemen's Rolls of the city of Dublin 1468–85 & 1575–1774 in (i) GO 490–493
    (Thrift Abstracts), (ii) Dublin City Archives (Original Registers), (iii) NLI Mss
    76–9

Aristocracy and Gentry

(a) *A Visitation of Seats and Arms of the Noblemen and Gentlemen of Great Britain
    and Ireland* (1852–3), see Hugh Montgomery-Massinberd, *Burke's Family Index*
    (Burke's, 1976) for a composite index, also covers (d), (e), (f) and (g) below
(b) Bence-Jones, Mark, *Burke's Guide to Country Houses, Vol. 1, Ireland,* Burke's
    1978, a clear guide to families who owned particular houses
(c) *Burke's Commoners of Great Britian and Ireland* (3 vols) 1837
(d) *Burke's Extinct Peerages . . .* (1831) 5 subsequent editions
(e) *Burke's Peerage and Baronetage of the United Kingdom . . .* (1826) 106 subse-
    quent editions
(f) *Burke's Landed Gentry of Great Britian and Ireland* (4 vols) subsequent editions
    1858, 1863, 1871, 1879, 1886, 1894, 1898, 1937 (Irish supplement)
(g) *Burke's Landed Gentry of Ireland,* subsequent editions 1904, 1912, 1958
(h) *Debrett's Peerage, Baronetage, Knightage and Companionage* (1852) many sub-
    sequent editions
(i) Leet, Ambrose, *A Directory to the Market Towns, Villages, Gentlemen's Seats and
    other Noted Places in Ireland,* 1812, 1814, NLI Ir. 9141 1 10, shows country
    houses and their owners

(j) Taylor and Skinner, *Road Maps of Ireland* (1778, repr. IUP 1969) NLI Ir. 9414 t 1, shows homes of gentlemen along the major routes through the country, the surnames are alphabetically indexed

(k) *The Post-Chaise Companion through Ireland* (1783) descriptions of journeys along the main coach roads, including the names of country houses and their owners' surnames, NLI

(l) Walford, E., *The County Families of the United Kingdom*, Chatto & Windus, 1877, subsequent editions annually

Barbers and Surgeons

(a) Admissions to the guilds of Dublin, 1792–1837, *Reports from Committees, Parliamentary Papers*, 1837, Vol. 11 (ii)

(b) Freemen's Rolls of the city of Dublin 1468–1485 & 1575–1774 in
  (i) GO 490–493 (Thrift Abstracts), and
  (ii) DCA (Original Registers)

Brewers

Old Kilkenny Review, 1988, p. 583

Carpenters

See 'Barbers and Surgeons' above

Cooks and Vintners

See 'Barbers and Surgeons' above

Booksellers and Printers

(a) *Dictionary of Printers & Booksellers, 1668–1775*, E.R. McC. Dix, NLI 6551 b 1, 6551 b 4

(b) *Notes On Dublin Printers in the Seventeenth Century*, T.P.C. Kirkpatrick, NLI Ir. 65510941 k 1

(c) See also under 'Dix' in NLI Author Catalogue for various provincial centres.

(d) *Irish Booksellers & English Authors*, R.C. Cole, Dublin, 1954

(e) Pollard, A.W., *A short title catalogue of books printed in England, Scotland and Ireland . . . 1475–1640*, Bibliographical Society, 1986–91, co-editor G.R. Redgrave (3 vols) Vol. 3 includes an index of printers and publishers

Board of Ordnance Employees

(Mainly concerned with the upkeep of fortifications and harbours, with some of the principal locations being Buncrana, Enniskillen, Ballincollig, Cobh, Spike Island) the *Irish Genealogist*, 1985, NLI Ir. 9291 i 2

Bricklayers

Records of the Bricklayers and Stonemasons Guild, from 1830, NAI Acc. 1097
See also 'Barbers and Surgeons' above.

Clergymen

Roman Catholic

(a) Maynooth Students 1795–1895, Hamill, NLI Ir. 37841 h 15
(b) Priests Lists (by diocese) 1735–1835, NLI Ms 1548
(c) List of priests and sureties, 1705, NLI Ms 5318

Church of Ireland

(a) List of regular clergy in Ireland, by county, with place of birth, order and residence, 1824, *Archivium Hibernicum*, Vol. 3, pp. 49–86
(b) Biographical Succession Lists
   (i) By diocese
   Ardfert & Aghadoe: *Ardfert and Aghadoe Clergy and Parishes*, 1940, Canon J.B. Leslie, NLI Ir. 274146 l 2
   Armagh: *Armagh Clergy and Parishes,* 1911, Canon Leslie, NLI Ir. 27411 l 4, *Supplement to Armagh Clergy and Parishes*, Canon Leslie, Dundalk, 1948
   Cashel & Emly: *Biographical Succession List for the Diocese of Cashel and Emly*, St John D. Seymour
   Clogher: *Clogher Clergy and Parishes*, Leslie, Canon J.B., 1908, 1927, NLI Ir. 27411 l 3
   Connor: NLI Ms 1773 (Leslie manuscript)
   Cork, Cloyne & Ross: *Biographical Succession List for the Dioceses of Cork, Cloyne, Ross*, William Meade
   Cork & Ross: *Clerical and Parochial Records of Cork, Cloyne and Ross* (3 vols) Brady, W. Maziere, London, 1864
   Derry: *Derry Clergy and Parishes*, Leslie, Canon J.B., 1937, NLI Ir. 27411 l 7
   Down: *Biographical Succession List for the Diocese of Down*, Leslie, Canon J.B., 1936, co-author V. Rev. H.B. Swanzy
   Dromore: *Biographical Succession List for the Diocese of Dromore*, Belfast, 1933, Swanzy, Rev. H.B., co-author Canon J.B. Leslie, NLI Ir. 27411 s 2
   Dublin: NLI Ms 1771 (Leslie manuscript)
   The Succession of Clergy in the Parishes of S. Bride, S. Michel le Pole and S. Stephen, Carroll, W.G., Dublin, 1884
   The Fasti of St Patrick's, Dublin, Lawler, Hugh J. (1930)
   Ferns: *Ferns Clergy and Parishes*, Leslie, Canon J.B., NLI Ir. 27413 l 3
   Leighlin: NLI Ms 1772 (Leslie manuscript)
   Ossory: *Ossory Clergy and Parishes*, Leslie, Canon J.B., NLI Ir. 27413 l 5
   Raphoe: *Raphoe Clergy and Parishes*, Leslie, Canon J.B., 1940, NLI Ir. 27413 l 8
   Ross: *Biographical Succession List for the Diocese of Ross*, Webster, Charles
   Waterford & Lismore: *Succession List of the Bishops and Clergy of the Dioceses of Waterford and Lismore*, William Remison
   Fasti Ecclesiae Hibernicae: The Succession of the Prelates and Members of the Cathedral Bodies of Ireland (Vols 1–5) Cotton, Henry, Dublin, 1847–78, NLI Ir. 2741002 c 5
   (ii) Unpublished material on all clergy not covered above in Representative Church Body Library, see also NLI Mss 1775–6 (Leslie manuscript)

(c) NLI Ms 2674. Pedigrees and families of Church of Ireland clergymen from the seventeenth to the nineteenth century
(d) Fothergill, Gerald, *A List of Emigrant Ministers to America, 1690–1811*, London, 1904
(e) Church of Ireland Directories, as follows:
    1814   *Ecclesiastical Registry*, Samuel Percy Lea
    1817   *Irish Ecclesiastical Register*
    1818   *Irish Ecclesiastical Register*
    1824   *Irish Ecclesiastical Register*
    1827   *Irish Ecclesiastical Register*
    1830   *Ecclesiastical Register*, John C. Erck
    1841   *The Churchman's Almanack and Irish Ecclesiastical Register*, John Medlicott Burns
    1842   *Irish Ecclesiastical Directory*
    1843   *The Irish Clergy List*, John Medlicott Burns
    1858   *Clerical Directory of Ireland*, Samuel B. Oldham
    1862   to date, annually: *Church of Ireland Directory*

Methodist

(a) *Minutes of the Methodist Conference*, 1757 to date, NLI Ir. 287 m 4
(b) Published works:
Crookshank, C.H., *History of Methodism in Ireland*, 1740–1860 (3 vols) Belfast, 1885–8; Vol. 4 (1860–1960) H. Lee Cole, Belfast, 1961, NLI Ir. 287 c 2
Cole, H.L., *History of Methodism in Dublin*, NLI I 287 c 4
Gallagher, W., *Preachers of Methodism*, Belfast, 1965, NLI Ir. 287 g 1
Smith, W., *History of Methodism in Ireland*, Dublin, 1830, J 2871, NLI Ir. 2871 s 2

Presbyterian

(a) Names of Presbyterian Clergymen and their congregations in Cos Antrim, Armagh, Down, Donegal, Fermanagh, Tyrone, Cork, Dublin, King's, Louth, Westmeath, Mayo, 1837. *New Plan for Education in Ireland 1838*, Part 1 pp. (27.8) 200–205
(b) Published Works:
Barkly, John M., *Fasti of the Presbyterian Church 1840–1910*, Presbyterian Historical Society
Ferguson, Rev. S., *Brief Biographical Notices of some Irish Covenanting Ministers*, (1897) particularly 18th century, NLI Ir. 285 f 1
History of Congregations, NLI Ir. 285 h 8
Irwin, C.H., *A History of Presbyterians in Dublin and the South and West of Ireland 1890*, NLI Ir. 285 i 1
Latimer, W.T., *History of the Irish Presbyterians*, Belfast, 1902, NLI Ir. 285 l 1 (early ministers especially)
McComb's Presbyterian Almanack, NLI Ir. 285 m 1
Marshall W.F., *Ulster Sails West* (including Ulster Presbyterian ministers in America 1680–1820) NLI Ir. 973 m 5
McConnell, J., *Fasti of the Irish Presbyterian Church*, Belfast, 1938, NLI Ir. 285 m 14

Reid, James Seiton, *History of the Presbyterian Church*, London, 1853, NLI Ir. 285 r 1

Smith & McIntyre, *Belfast Almanack,* 1837

Stewart, Rev, David, *The Seceders in Ireland, With Annals of Their Congregations*, Belfast, 1950.

Witherow, Thomas, *Historical and Literary Memorials of Presbyterianism in Ireland*, Belfast, 1879

(c) Belfast Directories: *Martins'*, 1835–42, NLI Ir. 9141111 [*sic*] m 4; from 1852, NLI Ir. 91411 b 3

Clockmakers

(a) National Museum Ms List of Watch & Clockmakers in Ireland, 1687–1844, NLI Pos. 204

(b) 'A List of Irish Watch and Clockmakers', Geraldine Fennell, NLI Ir. 681 f 10

Coachbuilders

Cooke, Jim, *Ireland's premier coachbuilder, John Hutton & Sons, Summerhill, Dublin 1779–1925*, Dublin 1993, NLI Ir. 670 p 33(2)

Coast Guard

(a) See Navy

(b) Database covering 1,700 coastguards and families recorded in the 1901 and 1911 censuses, Anthony Daly, 30 Gledswood Park, Clonskeagh, Dublin 14. Commissioned research only.

Convicts

(a) *Parliamentary Papers,* Vol. 22 (1824): Convictions 1814–23, Limerick City Assizes & Quarter sessions, all persons committed for trial under the Insurrection Act, 1823–24 in Cos Clare, Cork, Kerry, Kildare, Kilkenny, King's, Limerick, Tipperary.

(b) Records of the State Paper Office: Prisoners' Petitions.

(c) Prosecutions at Spring Assizes, 1842–3, *Parliamentary Papers*, 1843, Vol. 50, pp. (619) 34 ff

(d) Original Prison Registers from *c.*1845 for individual prisons, in many cases giving details of prisoners' families, unindexed, in chronological order, National Archives

Doctors

(a) Index to Biographical File of Irish Medics, T.P.C. Kirkpatrick, NLI Library Office

(b) See under Kirkpatrick in NLI Author Catalogue

(c) Local and Dublin Directories, from the late eighteenth century

(d) Medical Directories: 1846, Croly, NLI Ir. 6107 c 3; 1852–1860 (intermittent) NLI Ir. 6107 i 2; from 1872 annually, NLI Ir. 6107 i 2

(e) Addison, *Glasgow University Graduates*

(f) Doolin, W., *Dublin's Surgeon Anatomists*, NLI Ir. 610 p 4

(g) Sheppard, Julia, *Guide to the Contemporary Medical Archives Centre in the Wellcome Institute for the History of Medicine*, the Institute, 1971

Goldsmiths

(a) GO 665: Dublin Goldsmiths 1675–1810
(b) JCHAS, Ser. 2, Vol. VIII, 1902
(c) Jackson, Charles James, *English Goldsmiths*, Dover, 1964, extensive Irish listings
(d) See Silversmiths below

Linen Workers/Weavers

(a) Workers & Manufacturers in Linen, in the Stephenson Reports 1755–84, NLI Ir. 6551 Dublin
(b) 1796 Linen Board premiums for growing flax, NLI Ir. 633411 i 7
(c) 1796 Spinning-wheel premium entitlement lists (64% Ulster), All-Ireland Heritage micro-fiche index, NAI, NLI

Masons

See 'Barbers and Surgeons' above

Members of Parliament

NLI Mss 184 and 2098. See also local history source-lists under the relevant county

Merchants

(a) See 'Barbers and Surgeons' above
(b) See also local directories under county source-lists

Millers

(a) See 'Barbers and Surgeons' above
(b) Hogg, William E., *The Millers and Mills of Ireland . . . of about 1859*, Dublin 1997, NLI Ir. 620 h 2

Navy

(a) *The Navy List*, 1814, 1819, 1827–79, 1885 *et seq.*, 35905 Top floor [*sic*] (Seniority and disposition lists of all commissioned officers, masters, pursers, surgeons, chaplains, yard officers, coast guards, revenue cruisers, packets.)
(b) Records of the Public Record Office, Kew. See *Naval Records for Genealogists*, N.A.M. Rodger, HMSO, 1984
(c) *A Naval Biographical Dictionary* (1849) W.R. O'Byrne, 9235 o 1

Policemen

(a) Royal Irish Constabulary records, PRO, also on microfilm in NAI, and through LDS Family History centres. A microfiche index to the LDS copy is available from Janet Reakes, PO Box 937, Pilaba, Queensland 4655, Australia, also NLI.

(b) Dublin Metropolitan Police records, NAI & Garda Archives, Phoenix Park
(c) Annual RIC Directories, from 1840, NLI Ir. 3522 r 8
(d) Herlihy, Jim, *The Royal Irish Constabulary: a short history and geographical guide*, Dublin, Four Courts Press, 1997

Post Office Employees

(a) Pre-1922 records of the Post Office in PRONI.
(b) *Dún Laoghaire Genealogical Society Journal*, 5 (1), 1996, employees of the Irish Post Office 1784, Dublin 250 names

Plumbers

See 'Barbers and Surgeons' above

Prison Warders

General Prison Board applications for employment, NAI, Room 10, from 1847

Publicans

Excise Licences in premises valued under £10, 1832–1838, *Reports from Committees, Parliamentary Papers 1837–38*, Vol. 13 (2), pp. 558–601 & 602–607

Railway Workers

(a) (1870s to 1950s) Irish Transport Genealogical Archives, Irish Railway Record Society, Heuston Station, Dublin (open Tues. 8–10 p.m. by appointment with archivist)
(b) *Records of the Irish Transport Genealogical Museum*, Joseph Lecky, IRRS, NLI Ir. 385 L 8

Seamen

(a) 'In Pursuit of Seafaring Ancestors', Frank Murphy, *Decies* 16, NLI Ir. 9414 d 5
(b) Agreements and Crew Lists series in Public Record Office, Kew
(c) Cox, N.G., 'The Records of the Registrar General of Shipping and Seamen', *Maritime History*, Vol. 2, 1972
(d) Deceased Seamen 1887–1949, NLI 31242 d, names (and other information) for seamen whose deaths were reported to the General Register Office

Silversmiths

(a) Assay Office, registrations of goldsmiths and silversmiths from 1637. See (b) below
(b) NLI Pos. 6851 (1637–1702)
        Pos. 6785 (1704–1855, with some gaps)
        Pos. 6782 Freemen, 1637–1779
        Pos. 6784, 6788, 6851 Apprentices
(c) NA M. 465, notes and pamphlets relating to goldsmiths and silversmiths in Cork, Dublin and Galway

Smiths

See 'Barbers and Surgeons' above

Stonemasons

See 'Bricklayers' above

Teachers

(a) List of all parochial schools in Ireland, including names of teachers and other details, 1824, *Irish Education Enquiry, 1826, 2nd Report* (2 vols) NLI Ir. 372 i 6, indexed in *Schoolmasters & mistresses in Ireland*, Dingfelder, NLI Ir. 372 d 38
(b) National School Records, NAI & PRONI (National Teachers' salary books from 1831)
(c) Published Works:
Akenson, D.H., *The Irish Education Experiment*, London, 1970
Brenan, *1775–1835: Schools of Kildare & Leighlin*, NLI Ir. 37094135 b 4
Corcoran, T.S., 'Some lists of Catholic lay teachers and their illegal schools in the later Penal times', NLI Ir. 370941 c 12
ffolliott, R., 'Some schoolmasters in the diocese of Killaloe, 1808', JNMAS, Vol. XI, 1968
Linden, *Irish school-masters in the American colonies*, NLI Ir. 942 1 9
'Some Early Schools of Kilkenny', *Old Kilkenny Review*, 1960, 3
'Teachers of Cashel & Emly 1750–60', *Catholic Bulletin*, Vol. XXIX, pp. 784–8

Vintner

See 'Barbers and Surgeons' above

Watchmakers

See 'Clockmakers' above

Weavers

See 'Linen workers' above

12. COUNTY SOURCE-LISTS

The source-lists included here are intended primarily as working research tools, with references as specific as possible, and very little explanation of the records given. An outline of some of the categories used is thus necessary here.

CENSUS RETURNS AND SUBSTITUTES

Where no indication of the nature of the record is given, a description should be found in Chapter 2, Census Returns. Griffith's Valuation and the Tithe Books are dealt with in Chapter 4, Land Records. Locations are given in the text for all records mentioned, with, if possible, exact reference numbers. National Library call-numbers for published works should be found in the Local History or Local Journal sections. The absence of an LDS reference does not mean that the work is not in the library.

LOCAL HISTORY

The bibliographies given are by no means exhaustive, and the works cited vary enormously in their usefulness. A large proportion of the entries also give the National Library call-number, but the absence of such a number does not mean that the work in question is not in the library.

LOCAL JOURNALS

The journals noted are those originating in, or covering part of, the particular county. Where possible, National Library call-numbers are given. The absence of the number means that the journal started publication relatively recently and, at the time of writing, had not yet been assigned a number.

GRAVESTONE INSCRIPTIONS

Many of the largest collections of indexed transcripts of gravestone inscriptions are now held by local heritage centres. For counties where this is the case, the name of the relevant centre is supplied. Further details will be found in Chapter 15, Services. This section does not cover the transcripts published in the *Journal of the Association for the Preservation of the Memorials of the Dead*, since the records are not treated in a geographically consistent way. None the less, over the 47 years of its existence between 1888 and 1934, the journal published a huge volume of inscriptions, many of which have since been destroyed. A composite index to surnames and places for the first twenty years of publication was published in 1910; the remaining volumes have their own indexes. The references to the IGRS collection in the Genealogical Office give the number of entries recorded in each graveyard. Again, National

Library call-numbers for the local history journals or local histories will be found in the sections dealing specifically with the journals and histories.

ESTATE RECORDS

With the exception of Counties Armagh, Cavan, Cork, Donegal, Fermanagh, Leitrim, Galway, Mayo, Monaghan, Roscommon, Sligo, Tyrone and Waterford, which include a summary of relevant, catalogued records in the National Archives and National Library, the references given here cover only a fraction of the material of potential genealogical interest. A more detailed account of the nature of these records is given at the end of Chapter 4, Land Records.

PLACENAMES

References previously given here to works dealing with placenames on a county basis are now incorporated into the local history section. Material of more general use in identifying Irish placenames for the entire island is as follows:

Townlands Indexes

Produced on the basis of the returns of the 1851, 1871 and 1901 censuses, these list all the townlands in the country in strict alphabetical order. The full 1851 Townlands Index is now available online at *http://www.irish-times.com/placename /index.html*.

Addenda to the 1841 Census

Also known as the 1841 Townlands Index, this is also based on the census returns, but organises townlands on a different basis. They are grouped alphabetically within civil parishes, which are then grouped alphabetically within baronies, which are grouped by county. The organisation is very useful in tracking down variant townland spellings; once it is known that a particular townland is to be found in a particular area, but the later Townlands Indexes do not record it, the general area can be searched in the 1841 Addenda for names which are close enough to be possible variants. NLI Ir. 310 c 1.

Townlands in Poor Law Unions

Produced by the Office of the Registrar-General for use by local registration officers, this lists townlands in each Registration District, or Poor Law Union (see Chapter 1, Civil Records). It is useful in attempting to identify placenames given in civil records, NLI Ir. 9141 b 35. It has been reprinted as *Townlands and Poor Law Unions* (ed. Handran, 1997, Higginson, Salem Ma.)

Topographical Dictionary of Ireland, Samuel Lewis, 1837

This goes through civil parishes in alphabetical order, giving a brief history, an economic and social description, and the names and residences of the 'principal inhabitants'. It also records the corresponding Catholic parish, and the locations of Presbyterian congregations. The accompanying atlas is useful in determining the precise relative positions of the parishes.

Other works of general interest include Yann Goblet's *Index to Townlands in the Civil Survey 1654–6* (Irish Manuscripts Commission, 1954); *Locations of Churches in the Irish Provinces* (Church of Jesus Christ of Latter-Day Saints, 1978) NLI Ir. 7265 i 8; *The Parliamentary Gazetteer of Ireland* (1846) NLI Ir. 9141 p 30.

ANTRIM

CENSUS RETURNS AND SUBSTITUTES

1614	Carrickfergus merchants and ships' captains, *Carrickfergus and District Historical Society Journal,* Vol. 2, 1986
1630	Muster Roll of Ulster; Armagh Co. Library and PRONI D.1759/3C/1; T. 808/15164; NLI Pos. 206
1642	Muster Roll, PRONI T.3726/2
1642–1643	Muster Roll, Shankill, PRONI T.2736/1
1659	Pender's 'Census'
1666	Hearth Money Roll, NLI Pos. 207, also PRONI T/307
1666	Subsidy Roll, PRONI T/808/14889
1669	Hearth Money Roll, NLI Ms 9584, PRONI T.307
1720	Down and Antrim landed gentry, RIA 24 k 19
1734	Religious census of the barony of Cary, *The Glynns,* 1993, 1994, supplies householders' names
1740	Protestant householders in the parishes of Ahoghill, Armoy, Ballintoy, Ballymoney, Ballywillin, Billy, Drummaul, Duneane, Dunluce, Finvoy, Kilraghts, Kirkinriola, Loughguile, Ramoan, Rasharkin, Rathlin Island, PRONI T808/15258, GO 539
1766	Ahoghill parish, NAI, M.2476(1), also RCB Library and NLI Ms 4173
1766	Ballintoy parish, also GO 536 and NLI Ms 4173, PRONI T808/15264
1776	'Deputy Court Cheque Book' (votes cast) PRONI D1364/L/1
1779	Map of Glenarm, including tenants' names, *The Glynns,* No. 9, 1981
1796	Spinning-Wheel Premium List
1798	Persons who suffered losses in the 1798 rebellion, propertied classes only, NLI I 94107
1799–1800	Militia Pay Lists and Muster Rolls, PRONI T.1115/1A & B
1803	Ballintoy inhabitants, C of I registers, PRONI T.679/68–69, MIC.1/111 p
1803	Agricultural survey recording householders, occupations and agricultural possessions, covers Armoy, Ballymoney, Ballyrashane, Billy, Culfeightrin, Derrykeighan, Dunluce, Kilraghts, Loughguile, Ramoan, Rathlin Island, NAI op153/103/1–16
1820	Lisburn householders, PRONI T679/107–12
1821	Various fragments, NAI Thrift Abstracts
1823	Parishioners' list, C of I parish of Layd, Co. Antrim, PRONI T.679/359–63
1823–38	Tithe Books

1833–1839	Emigrants from Antrim, *Irish Emigration Lists 1833–39*, Baltimore, Genealogical Publishing Co., 1989
1837	House Book for Belfast, house-by-house valuation, giving house-holders' names, date not completely certain, NAI OL 70001 VO Quarto book
1837	Valuation of towns returning MPs (occupants and property values) Lisburn, *Parliamentary Papers 1837, Reports from Committees*
1841	Workhouse records: Lurgan Union 1841–1910, Larne Union 1845–78, PRONI
1851	Partial: Ahoghill — Craigs townland only; Aghagallon — 'M' to 'T' only; Ballymoney — Garryduff only; Killead — 'A' to 'C' only; Rasharkin — 'K' to 'T' only; PRONI MIC. 5A/11–26, also NAI
1856–1857	Voters, NLI ILB 324
1856	Census of united parishes of Glenavy, Camlin and Tullyrusk, Co. Antrim, taken in 1856–7, revised in 1858–9 and 1873, with Glenavy C of I registers, PRONI MIC.1/43–4, 44A, 74; C.R.1/53; T.679/1, 74
1861–1862	Griffith's Valuation
1870	Parishioners' list Carnmoney, Co. Antrim, with C of I parish registers, PRONI T.679/325–9, 332, D.852/8, 48, 85, 91, 105, 122, 125
1901	Census
1911	Census

LOCAL HISTORY

Anonymous, 'A Demographic Study of Tory Island and Rathlin Island 1841–1964', *Ulster Folk*, 17, 1971, 70–80

Anonymous, *Subject catalogue of books and other material relating to Co. Antrim*, 1969, NLI Ir. 941 p 43

Anonymous, 'Presbyterians in Glenarm', *The Glynns*, Vol. 9, 1981

Anonymous, 'Notes on the ancient deeds of Carrickfergus', JRSAI, 1893

Anonymous, 'Provisional list of pre-1900 School Registers in the Public Record Office of Northern Ireland', UHGGN, 9, pp. 60–71

Barr, W.N., *The oldest register of Derryaghy, Co. Antrim 1696–1772*, NLI Ir. 9293 b 3

Bassett, G.H., *The Book of Antrim*, 1888

Benn, George, *A History of the Town of Belfast*, London, 1877–80

Boyd, H.A., *A History of the Church of Ireland in Ramoan Parish*, 1930

Day, Angelique, *Parishes of Co. Antrim, Vol. 16 (Ordnance survey memoirs — Giant's Causeway/Ballymoney)*, Inst. of Irish Studies/RIA, Belfast, 1992, NLI Ir. 914111 o 11

Day, Angelique, *Parishes of Co. Antrim, Vol. 13 (Ordnance survey memoirs)*, Inst. of Irish Studies/RIA, Belfast, 1992, NLI Ir. 914111 o 11

Day, Angelique, *Parishes of Co. Antrim, Vol. 2 (Ordnance survey memoirs)*, Inst. of Irish Studies/RIA, Belfast, 1990, NLI Ir. 914111 o 11

Ewart, L.M., *Handbook to the dioceses of Down, Connor & Dromore*

Fulton, Eileen, *A history of the Parish of St Joseph's Hannahstown, Co. Antrim 1826–1993 Detailing the Names of the Graves (...)*, Ulster Journals Ltd, 1993

Hill, Rev. George, *Montgomery Manuscripts, 1603–1706*, Belfast, 1869

Joy, Henry, *Historical Collections relative to the town of Belfast*, Belfast, 1817

Lee, Rev. W.H.A., St *Colmanell, Aghoghill: A History of its Parish*, 1865
Liggett, Michael, *A district called Ardoyne: a brief history of a Belfast Community*, Glenravel Publications, Belfast, 1994, NLI Ir. 9411 P 41(3)
Marshall, Rev. H.C., *The Parish of Lambeg*, 1933
McSkimin, Samuel, *The History and Antiquities of the Town of Carrickfergus 1318–1839*, Belfast, 1909
Millin, S.S., *Sidelights on Belfast History*, 1932
Mullin, Julia, *A history of Dunluce Presbyterian church*, 1995, NLI Ir. 285 m 37
Observer, The Ballymena, *Old Ballymena: a history of Ballymena during the 1798 Rebellion*, 1857, republished
O'Laverty, Rev. James, *An Historical Account of the Dioceses of Down and Connor*, Dublin, 1878–89
Owen, D.J., *History of Belfast*, Belfast, 1921, NLI Ir. 94111 o 1
Reeves, William, *Ecclesiastical Antiquities of Down, Connor and Dromore*, 1847
Robinson, Philip, *Irish Historic Towns Atlas: Carrickfergus*, Dublin, RIA, 1988
Robinson, Rev. Aston, *The presbytery of Ballymena 1745–1945*, Mid-Antrim Historical group, Ballymena, 1949, NLI
Shaw, William, *Cullybackey, the Story of an Ulster Village*, 1913
Shearman, H., *Ulster*, London, 1949, NLI Ir. 91422 s 3
St John Clarke, H.J., *Thirty centuries in south-east Antrim: the Parish of Coole or Carnmoney*, Belfast, 1938, NLI Ir. 27411 c 3
Young, Robert M., *Historical Notices of Old Belfast and its Vicinity*, 1896
Young, Robert M., *The Town Book of the Corporation of Belfast, 1613–1816*, 1892 (includes freemen 1635–1796)

LOCAL JOURNALS

Carrickfergus and District Historical Society Journal, NLI Ir. 9411 c 5
Down & Connor Historical Society Magazine
East Belfast Historical Society Journal
Historic Belfast Magazine
Irish Family Links, NLI Ir. 9292 f 19
Lisburn Historical Society Journal
North Antrim Roots
North Irish Roots (Journal of the North of Ireland Family History Society)
North Belfast Historical Society Magazine, NLI Ir. 94111 n 1
South Belfast Historical Society Journal
The Glynns

DIRECTORIES

1807/8	Joseph Smith, *Belfast Directories*
1820	*Belfast Almanack*
1820	Joseph Smyth, *Directory of Belfast and its Vicinity*
1820	J. Pigot, *Commercial Directory of Ireland*
1824	J. Pigot and Co., *City of Dublin and Hibernian Provincial Directory*, NLI

1835	William T. Matier, *Belfast Directory*
1839	Mathew Martin, *Belfast Directory*, also 1841, 1842
1846	Slater, *National Commercial Directory of Ireland*, NLI
1852	James A. Henderson, *Belfast and Province of Ulster Directory*, issued also in 1854, 1856, 1858, 1861, 1863, 1865, 1868, 1870, 1877, 1880, 1884, 1887, 1890, 1894, 1900
1856	Slater, *Royal National Commercial Directory of Ireland*, NLI
1860	Hugh Adair, *Belfast Directory*
1865	R. Wynne, *Business Directory of Belfast*
1870	Slater, *Directory of Ireland*, NLI
1881	Slater, *Royal National Commercial Directory of Ireland*, NLI
1887	*Derry Almanac and Directory* (Portrush only)
1888	George Henry Bassett, *The Book of Antrim*
1894	Slater, *Royal Commercial Directory of Ireland*, NLI

GRAVESTONE INSCRIPTIONS

The Ulster Historical Foundation has transcripts for 151 graveyards in Antrim and Belfast. Heritage World has transcripts of 32 graveyards. Contact details will be found in Chapter 14. Published or publicly available transcripts are given below.

Ardclinis: Carrivemurphy, RC, *The Glynns*, Vol. 4
Blaris: Lisburn town, Carmody, V. Rev. W.P., *Lisburn Cathedral and its Past Rectors*
Carnmoney: *Carved in stone: a record of memorials in the ancient graveyard around the Church (. . .)*, NIFHS, 1994
Culfeightrin: Cross, *IA*, Vol. 2, No. 2
Culfeightrin: Bonamargy, GO
Drumbeg: C of I, Clarke, R.S.J., *Gravestone Inscriptions, Co. Down*, Vol. 3, Belfast, 1969, NLI Ir. 9295 c 1
Glynn: Glynn, Rutherford, George, *Gravestone Inscriptions, Co. Antrim*, Vol. 2, Belfast, 1990, NLI Ir. 94111 c 4
Islandmagee: Ballyprior More, Rutherford, *Gravestone Inscriptions, Co. Antrim*, Vol. 1, UHF, 1977
Islandmagee: Ballykeel, Rutherford, *Gravestone Inscriptions, Co. Antrim*, Vol. 1
Kilroot: Rutherford, *Gravestone Inscriptions, Co. Antrim*, Vol. 2, 1980
Lambeg: Lambeg North, C of I, Cassidy, William, *Inscriptions on Tombstones in Lambeg Graveyard*
Layd: Kilmore, *The Glynns*, Vol. 4
Layd: Layd, *Survey of Layde Graveyard*, Glens of Antrim Historical Soc., 1991, NLI Ir. 9295 s 2
Magheragall: Magheragall, C of I, *Family Links*, Vol. 1, Nos 2 and 3, 1981
Muckamore (Grange of): Muckamore, *Carved in stone: a record of memorials in the ancient graveyard around the Church (. . .)*, NIFHS, 1994
Raloo: Ballyvallagh, Rutherford, *Gravestone Inscriptions, Co. Antrim*, Vol. 2
Templecorran: Forthill (Ballycarry?), C of I, Rutherford, *Gravestone Inscriptions, Co. Antrim*, Vol. 2
Templepatrick: Grange of Molusk, *Mallusk Memorials*, NIFHS, 1997

Shankill: St Joseph's, Hannahstown, RC, in Fulton, *[. . .] St Joseph's, Hannahstown, [. . .],* 1993
—— Clifton Street, Clarke, R.S.J., *Gravestone Inscriptions, Belfast, Vol. 4 (Old Belfast Families and the New Burying Ground)*, UHF 1991, NLI Ir. 9295 o 1
—— Milltown, RC, Clarke, R.S.J., *Gravestone Inscriptions, Belfast,* Vol. 2, UHF, 1986
—— Friar's Bush, RC, Clarke, R.S.J., *Gravestone Inscriptions, Belfast,* Vol. 2, UHF, 1986
—— St George's interior, C of I, Clarke, R.S.J., *Gravestone Inscriptions, Belfast,* Vol. 1, UHF, 1982
—— Christ Church interior, C of I, Clarke, R.S.J., *Gravestone Inscriptions, Belfast,* Vol. 1
—— Shankill, Clarke, R.S.J., *Gravestone Inscriptions, Belfast,* Vol. 1

ARMAGH

CENSUS RETURNS AND SUBSTITUTES

1630	Muster Roll of Ulster, Armagh Co. Library and PRONI D.1759/3C/1, T. 808/15164, NLI Pos. 206
1634	Subsidy roll, NAI M. 2471, 2475
1654–1656	Civil Survey, NLI Ir. 31041 c 4
1659	Pender's 'Census'
1660	Poll Tax Returns, Co. Armagh, PRONI MIC/15A/76
1661	Books of Survey and Distribution, PRONI T370/A & D.1854/1/8
1664	Hearth Money Roll, *Archivium Hibernicum*, 1936, NLI Ms 9586, PRONI T.604
1689	Protestants attainted by James II, PRONI T808/14985, list of names only
1737	Tithe-payers, Drumcree, NLI I 920041 p 1
1738	Freeholders, NLI Pos. 206, also Armagh Co. Library
1740	Protestant householders, Creggan, Derrynoose, Loughgall, Mullagh-brack, Shankill, Tynan, NAI, also GO 539, PRONI T808/15258, LDS film 258517
1750	Volunteers & yeomanry of Markethill and district *c.*1750, see Cornascreeb in NLI Author catalogue
1753	Poll Book, NAI M. 4878, also GO 443, PRONI T808/14936, LDS film 1279237
1766	Creggan parish, NAI Parl. Ret. 657, also GO 537, PRONI T808/14936, LDS film 100173, JCLAS 8 (2)
1770	Armagh city householders, NLI Ms 7370, also PRONI T808/14977, LDS film 258621
1793–1908	Armagh Militia Records, NLI Pos. 1014, also Armagh Co. Library
1796	Catholics emigrating from Ulster to Mayo, *Seanchas Ardmhacha*, 1958, pp. 17–50, see also 'Petition of Armagh migrants in the Westport area', *Cathair na Mart*, Vol. 2, No. 1 (Appendix)
1799–1800	Militia Pay Lists and Muster Rolls, PRONI T.1115/A–C
1821–1831	Armagh Freeholders (baronies of Tiranny, Lower Fews & Upper Fews), NLI Ir. 94116 a 1, Ir. 352 p 2, also PRONI ARM 5/2/1–17
1821	Kilmore parish, PRONI T. 450

1821   Various fragments, NAI Thrift Abstracts
1823–38   Tithe Books, NAI
1834–1837   Valuation of Armagh town (heads of households), *Parliamentary Papers 1837, Reports from Committees*, Vol. II (1), Appendix G
1837   Marksmen (i.e. illiterate voters), Armagh Borough, *Parliamentary Papers 1837, Reports from Committees*, Vol. II (1), Appendix A
1839   Valuation of Co. Armagh, NLI Pos. 99, also Armagh Co. Library
1840–1855   Emigrants from Derrynoose to the US and Scotland, with parish registers, PRONI MIC.1/158
1841–1910   Lurgan Union Workhouse records, PRONI, also LDS film 259166–72
1843   Armagh voters, NAI 1842/85
1851–73   Persons entitled to vote, Armagh County Museum, D7, also LDS film 1279325
1851   Various fragments, NAI Thrift Abstracts
1864   Tynan parish *c*.1864, *The History of Charlemont Fort and Borough*, 1921
1864   Griffith's Valuation
1868   Census of the C of I parish of Shankill, Cos Armagh & Down, with the local clergymen
1871   Creggan Upper, *Archivium Hibernicum*, Vol. 3
1901   Census
1911   Census

LOCAL HISTORY

Anonymous, 'Life and Times of Fr. Edmund Murphy, Killeavy, 1680', JCLHAS, 9, 1986, 60–71

Anonymous, *Balleer School: Copy-book of letters, 1827–29*, NLI Ir. 300 p 106

Anonymous, *Armagh Road Presbyterian Church, Portadown (1868–1968)*, NLI Ir. 2741 p 25

Anonymous, *Historical sketches of various parishes*, NLI Ir. 27411 l 4 & 5

Anonymous, *Mullaghbrack from the tithepayers list of 1834*, NLI I 920041 p 1

Anonymous, *Armagh Royal School: Prizes & prizemen 1854*, NLI P 439

Anonymous, 'Provisional list of pre-1900 School Registers in the Public Record Office of Northern Ireland', UHGGN, 9, pp. 60–71

Atkinson, Edward D., *Dromore, an Ulster Diocese*, Dundalk, 1925

Bell, Rev. J. Brian A., *A History of Garmany's Grove Presbyterian Church*, Armagh, 1970

Canavan, T., *Frontier town: an illustrated history of Newry*, Belfast, Blackstaff Press, 1989

Donaldson, John, *A Historical and Statistical Account of the Barony of Upper Fews*

Galogly, John, *The History of St Patrick's Parish, Armagh*, 1880

Gwynn, A., *The medieval province of Armagh*, Dundalk, 1946, NLI Ir. 27411 g 1

Hogg, Rev. M.B., *Keady Parish: A Short History of its Church and People*, 1928

Marshall, J.J., *The History of Charlemont Fort and Borough . . .* 1921

McCorry, F.X., *Lurgan: an Irish Provincial Town*, Inglewood Press, 1993

Murray, Rev. Lawrence P., *History of the Parish of Creggan in the Seventeenth and Eighteenth Centuries*, Dundalk, 1940

Nelson, S., *History of the Parish of Creggan in Cos Armagh and Louth from 1611 to 1840*, 1974

Patterson, T., *Armagh Manor Court Rolls, 1625–7 & incidental notes on 17th century sources for Irish surnames in Co. Armagh*, Seanchas Ardmhacha, 1957, 295–322

Shearman, H., *Ulster*, London, 1949, NLI Ir. 91422 s 3

Stewart, James, *Historical Memoirs of the City of Armagh*, Dublin, 1900

Swayne, John, *The register of John Swayne, Archbishop of Armagh, and Primate of Ireland*

LOCAL JOURNALS

Craigavon Historical Society Review
Irish Family Links, NLI Ir. 9292 f 19
Mullaghbawn Historical & Folk-Lore Society, NLI Ir. 800 p 50
North Irish Roots (Journal of the North of Ireland Family History Society)
Old Newry Journal
Seanchas Ardmhacha, NLI Ir. 27411 s 4
Seanchas Dhroim Mor (Journal of the Dromore Diocesan Historical Society), NLI Ir. 94115 s 3

DIRECTORIES

1819	Thomas Bradshaw, *General Directory of Newry, Armagh, Dungannon, Portadown, Tandragee, Lurgan, Waringstown, Banbridge, Warrenpoint, Rostrevor, Kilkeel and Rathfryland*
1820	J. Pigot, *Commercial Directory of Ireland*
1824	J. Pigot and Co., *City of Dublin and Hibernian Provincial Directory*, NLI
1839	Mathew Martin, *Belfast Directory*, also 1841, 1842
1846	Slater, *National Commercial Directory of Ireland*, NLI
1852	James A. Henderson, *Belfast and Province of Ulster Directory*, issued also in 1854, 1856, 1858, 1861, 1863, 1865, 1868, 1870, 1877, 1880, 1884, 1887, 1890, 1894, 1900
1856	Slater, *Royal National Commercial Directory of Ireland*, NLI
1865	R. Wynne, *Business Directory of Belfast*
1870	Slater, *Directory of Ireland*, NLI
1881	Slater, *Royal National Commercial Directory of Ireland*, NLI
1883	S. Farrell, *County Armagh Directory and Almanac*
1888	George Henry Bassett, *The Book of Armagh*
1894	Slater, *Royal Commercial Directory of Ireland*, NLI

GRAVESTONE INSCRIPTIONS

The Ulster Historical Foundation has transcripts for 135 graveyards in Armagh. Heritage World has transcripts of 54 graveyards. Contact details will be found in Chapter 14. Published or publicly available transcripts are given below.

Armagh: Sandy Hill, *Seanchas Ardmhacha*, Vol. 11, 2, 1985
Creggan: Creggan Bane Glebe, C of I, *Seanchas Ardmhacha*, Vol. 4, 1976
Kilclooney: LDS film 1279354
Mullaghbrack: LDS film 1279384

Estate Records

Anglesea: Tenants' list, 1856, most tenants, covering areas in the civil parish of Newry, JCLAHS, 12 (2), 1950, 151–3

Charlemont: Freeholders' list, 1820, NLI Ms 3784, Rentals, 1798–1802, NLI Ms 2702, major tenants only, covering areas in the civil parishes of Eglish, Forkill, Grange, Keady, Kilclooney, Killevy, Lisnadill, Loughgall, Loughgilly, Mullaghbrack, Tartaraghan

Commissioners of Education: Rentals, 1846–54, NLI Ms 16924, all tenants, covering areas in the civil parishes of Loughgilly

Dawson: Rent rolls, 1787 (NLI Ms 3183, 3283), 1797 (NLI Ms 3185), 1812 (NLI Ms 3188), 1838–9 (NLI Ms 3189), 1846 (NLI Ms 1648), 1852–3 (NLI Ms 5674), all tenants, covering areas in the civil parish of Clonfeacle

Johnston: Rentals, 1791–1802, 1853 (with observations) NAI M. 3508, all tenants, covering areas in the civil parish of Eglish

Moore: Rentals, 1848, NAI M.2977, all tenants, covering areas in the civil parishes of Seagoe

Obins: Rent roll, 1753 (major tenants only), 1770 (all tenants) NLI Ms 4736, covering areas in the civil parish of Drumcree

[No landlord given]: Tenants' list, 1714, NLI Ms 3922, all tenants, covering areas in the civil parishes of Armagh, Clonfeacle, Derrynoose, Drumcree, Killyman, Kilmore, Tynan

CARLOW

Census Returns and Substitutes

1641	Book of Survey and Distribution, NLI Ms 971
1659	Pender's 'Census'
1669	Carlow parish housholders, JKAS, 10, 1918–2, 255–57
1767	Co. Carlow Freeholders, IG, 1980
1797	Chief Catholic inhabitants, parishes of Graiguenamanagh and Knocktopher, IA, 1978
1798	Persons who suffered losses in the 1798 rebellion, propertied classes only, NLI I 94107
1817	Emigrants from Counties Carlow and Wexford to Canada, *Wexford: History and Society*, Dublin, Geography Publications, 1987
1823–38	Tithe Books, NAI
1832–1837	Voters registered in Carlow borough, *Parliamentary Papers 1837, Reports from Committees*, Vol. II (2), 193–6
1837	Marksmen (illiterate voters) in parliamentary boroughs: Carlow, *Parliamentary Papers 1837*, Reports from Committees, Vol. II (1), Appendix A
1843	Co. Carlow voters, NAI 1843/55
1852–1853	Griffith's Valuation
1901	Census
1911	Census

LOCAL HISTORY

Anonymous, *Carlow Parliamentary Roll 1872*, NLI Ir. 94138 m 1
Brennan, M., *Schools of Kildare and Leighlin, 1775–1835*, NLI Ir. 37094135 b 4
Brophy, M., *Carlow Past and Present*, NLI Ir. 94138 b 1
Coleman, James, *Bibliography of the counties Carlow, Kilkenny and Wexford*, WSIAHSJ, ll, 1907, NLI 794105 w 1
Coyle, James, *The Antiquities of Leighlin*
Hore, H.J., *The Social State of the Southern and Eastern Counties of Ireland in the Sixteenth Century*, 1870
Mac Suibhne, Peadar, *Clonegal Parish*, Carlow, 1975
O'Toole, E., *The Place-names of Co. Carlow*, NLI Ir. 94138 o 3
O'Toole, E., *The Parish of Ballon, Co. Carlow*, 1933, NLI Ir. 94138 o 3
Ryan, J., *The history and antiquities of the County Carlow*, Dublin, 1933, NLI Ir. 94138 r 1

LOCAL JOURNALS

Carloviana, NLI Ir. 94138 c 2
Carlow Past and Present
The Carlovian

DIRECTORIES

1788	Richard Lucas, *General Directory of the Kingdom of Ireland*, NLI Pos. 3729
1820	J. Pigot, *Commercial Directory of Ireland*
1824	J. Pigot and Co., *City of Dublin and Hibernian Provincial Directory*, NLI
1839	T. Shearman, *New Commercial Directory for the cities of Waterford and Kilkenny, Towns of Clonmel, Carrick-on-Suir, New Ross and Carlow*
1840	*New Trienniel Commercial Directory for 1840, 1841, 1842* (Carlow town)
1846	Slater, *National Commercial Directory of Ireland*, NLI
1856	Slater, *Royal National Commercial Directory of Ireland*, NLI
1870	Slater, *Directory of Ireland*, NLI
1881	Slater, *Royal National Commercial Directory of Ireland*, NLI
1894	Slater, *Royal Commercial Directory of Ireland*, NLI

GRAVESTONE INSCRIPTIONS

Ballyellin: Ballyellin and Tomdarragh, *Co. Carlow Tombstone Inscriptions*, Vol. 4, NLI, Ir. 9295 c 3
Clonygoose: Borris, *Co. Carlow Tombstone Inscriptions*, Vol. 2, NLI Ir. 9295 c 3
Clonygoose: Ballycoppigan, New, *Co. Carlow Tombstone Inscriptions*, Vol. 2, NLI Ir. 9295 c 3
Clonygoose: *Co. Carlow Tombstone Inscriptions*, Vol. 2, NLI Ir. 9295 c 3
Dunleckny: Morris, Andrew, *Dunleckney Headstone Inscriptions*, GO
Kiltennell: Rathanna, RC, *Co. Carlow Tombstone Inscriptions*, Vol. 3, NLI Ir. 9295 c 3
Kiltennell: Killedmond, C of I, *Co. Carlow Tombstone Inscriptions*, Vol. 3, NLI Ir. 9295 c 3

Kiltennell: Ballinvalley and Kiltennell, *Co. Carlow Tombstone Inscriptions,* Vol. 2, NLI
    Ir. 9295 c 3
Rathvilly: Kellymount (Mountkelly), *Co. Carlow Tombstone Inscriptions,* Vol. 4, NLI
    Ir. 9295 c 3
St Mullin's: C of I, *Co. Carlow Tombstone Inscriptions,* Vol. 1, NLI Ir. 9295 c 3
St Mullin's: Ballymurphy, RC, *Co. Carlow Tombstone Inscriptions,* Vol. 3, NLI Ir. 9295
    c 3
Tullowmagimma: Linkardstown, GO
Wells: *Co. Carlow Tombstone Inscriptions,* Vol. 4, NLI Ir. 9295 c 3

CAVAN

CENSUS RETURNS AND SUBSTITUTES

1612–1613	'Survey of Undertakers Planted in Co. Cavan', *Historical Manuscripts Commission Report*, No. 4 (Hastings Mss), 1947, pp. 159–82
1630	Muster Roll of Ulster; Armagh Co. Library and PRONI D.1759/3C/1, T. 808/15164, NLI Pos. 206
1664	Hearth Money Roll, parishes of Killeshandara, Kildallan, Killenagh, Templeport, Tomregan, PRONI 184
1703–4	Tenants in Kildallan and Killeshandara, IA, 8 (2), 86–7
1761	Poll Book, PRONI T 1522
1766	Protestants in parishes of Kinawley, Lavey, Lurgan, Munterconnaught, NAI m 2476(e), also RCB Library, GO Ms 536/7, LDS film 258517, 100173
1802	Protestants in Enniskeen parish, IA, 1973
1813–21	Freeholders, NLI Ir. 94119 c 2
1814	Youthful Protestants in the parishes of Drung & Larah, IA, 1978
1821	Parishes of Annagelliff, Ballymachugh, Castlerahan, Castleterra, Crosserlough, Denn, Drumlumman, Drung, Kilbride, Kilmore, Kinawley, Larah, Lavey, Lurgan, Mullagh, Munterconnaught, NAI, LDS films 597154–8, CGHP
1823–38	Tithe Books
1833	Arms registered with the Clerk of the Peace, April, over 1,500 names, NLI ILB 04 p 12
1841	Part of Killashandra parish only, also some certified copies of census returns for use in claims for old age pensions, NAI
1843	Voters' list, NAI 1843/71
1851	'List of inhabitants of Castlerahan barony', *c.*1851, with Killinkere parish registers, NLI Pos. 5349
1851	Some certified copies of census returns for use in claims for old age pensions, NAI
1856–1857	Griffith's Valuation
1901	Census
1911	Census

LOCAL HISTORY

Anonymous, 'The Volunteer Companies of Ulster 1778–1793, III, Cavan', *The Irish Sword*, 7, 1906, 308–10

Anonymous, *Cavan County Library: Guide to Local Studies Dept.*, NLI Ir. 0179 p 6

Anonymous, 'Sources of Information on the Antiquities and History of Cavan and Leitrim: Suggestions', *Breifny*, 1920–2, NLI Ir. 794106 b 1

Anonymous, *Cavan Freeholders since 1813*, NLI Ir. 94119 c 2

Anonymous, *Parishes, baronies & denominations in each parish*, alphabetical, NLI JP 2168

Brady, J., *A short history of the parishes of the diocese of Meath, 1867–1944*, NLI Ir. 94132 b 2

Cullen, S., 'Sources for Cavan Local History', *Breifny*, 1965, 77–8, NLI Ir. 941 p 66

Farrell, Noel, *Exploring Family origins in Cavan*, Self, Longford, 1993, includes transcripts of 1901, 1911 censuses, 1838 Thoms, 1941 Electors, Griffith's for Cavan town

Gillespie, Raymond, *Cavan: Essays on the History of an Irish County*, Dublin, Irish Academic Press, 1995

Healy, John, *History of the Diocese of Meath*, Dublin, 1908

MacNamee, James J., *History of the Diocese of Ardagh*, Dublin, 1954

Monahan, Rev. J., *Records Relating to the Diocese of Ardagh and Clonmacnoise*, 1886

O'Connell, Philip, *The Diocese of Kilmore: its History and Antiquities*, Dublin, 1937

Paterson, J. (ed.) *Diocese of Meath and Kildare: an historical guide*, 1981, NLI Ir. 941 p 75

Shearman, H., *Ulster*, London, 1949, NLI Ir. 91422 s 3

Smyth, T.S., *A civic history of the town of Cavan*, Cavan, 1934, NLI Ir. 94119 s 1

LOCAL JOURNALS

Ardagh & Clonmacnoise Historical Society Journal, NLI Ir. 794105
Breifne, NLI Ir. 94119 b 2
Heart of Breifny, NLI Ir. 94119 h 1
The Drumlin: a Journal of Cavan, Leitrim and Monaghan, NLI Ir. 05 d 345

DIRECTORIES

1820	J. Pigot, *Commercial Directory of Ireland*
1824	J. Pigot and Co., *City of Dublin and Hibernian Provincial Directory*, NLI
1846	Slater, *National Commercial Directory of Ireland*, NLI
1852	James A. Henderson, *Belfast and Province of Ulster Directory*, issued also in 1854, 1856, 1858, 1861, 1863, 1865, 1868, 1870, 1877, 1880, 1884, 1887, 1890, 1894, 1900
1856	Slater, *Royal National Commercial Directory of Ireland*, NLI
1870	Slater, *Directory of Ireland*, NLI
1881	Slater, *Royal National Commercial Directory of Ireland*, NLI
1894	Slater, *Royal Commercial Directory of Ireland*, NLI

GRAVESTONE INSCRIPTIONS

Annagh: Clonosey, CHGC
—— Killoughter, CHGC
Ballintemple: Ballintemple, C of I, CHGC
—— Pottahee (Brusky?), RC, CHGC
Castlerahan: Castlerahan, C of I, *Breifne*, 1925/6, also CHGC
Castleterra: RC, CHGC
Crosserlough: Kill, *Breifne*, 1976, also CHGC
—— Crosserlough, RC, CHGC
Denn: Denn Glebe, C of I, *Breifne*, 1924
Drumgoon: Drumgoon, CHGC
Drumlane: Drumlane, *Breifne*, 1979
Drung: Magherintemple, *Breifne*, 1963
—— Drung, CHGC
Kilbride: Gallonreagh (Kilbride?) CHGC
Killinagh: Termon (Killinagh Old?) C of I, CHGC
Killinkere: Gallon, CHGC
Kilmore: Trinity Island (St Mogue's?) CHGC
Larah: CHGC
Lavey: C of I, GO, also CHGC
Lurgan: *Breifne*, 1961, also CHGC
Mullagh: Mullagh (Raffoney?) C of I, CHGC
Munterconnaught: Knockatemple, RC, *Breifne*, 1927/8, also CHGC
Scrabby: Cloone, C of I, *Seanchas Ardmhacha*, Vol. 10, No. 1, 1980–81
Templeport: Port, *Breifne*, 1971
Urney: Cavan, Church Lane, *Breifne*, 1986

ESTATE RECORDS

Annesley: Maps, with tenants' names, 1805–17, NLI Ms. 2730, coverage unclear, covering areas in the civil parishes of Annagh, Denn, Drumlumman, Drung, Kilmore, Larah, Lavey, Templeport, Urney

Commissioners of Education: Rentals, 1818–45, NLI Ms. 16920(5), 1837–42, NLI Ms. 16926, all tenants, covering areas in the civil parish of Annagelliff

Robert Craigies: Tenants' list, 1703–4, IA 1978, coverage unclear, covering areas in the civil parishes of Kildallan and Killashandra

Crofton: Rent rolls, 1792, NLI Ms. 4530, 1796–1831, NLI Ms. 8150, major tenants only, covering areas in the civil parish of Kinawley

Earl of Farnham: Rent rolls etc. 1718–90, NLI Ms. 11491, major tenants only, rentals, 1820, NLI Ms. 350; 1841–8, NLI Ms. 5012–13; 1842–3, NLI Ms. 18624, all tenants, covering areas in the civil parishes of Ballintemple, Ballymachugh, Castlerahan, Crosserlough, Denn, Drumlane, Drumlumman, Kilbride, Kildallan, Killashandra, Killinkere, Kilmore, Lurgan and Urney

Earl of Fingall: Rent rolls, 1750, NLI Ms. 8024, major tenants only, covering areas in the civil parishes of Loughan or Castlekeeran Lurgan, Mullagh, Munterconnaught

Edward Groome: Rentals, with observations, 1822, NAI M5559, all tenants, covering areas in the civil parishes of Bailieborough, Knockbride and Moybolgue

Hamilton: Rentals, with observations, 1851, NAI M5571 (1–39), all tenants, covering areas in the civil parishes of Kildallan, Killashandra and Kilmore

Hodson: Rentals, 1811–24, NLI Ms 16397–8, all tenants, covering areas in the civil parishes of Bailieborough and Knockbride

James O'Reilly: Rentals, 1815–16, NAI M.6962, all tenants, covering areas in the civil parishes of Annagelliff, Castlerahan, Crosserlough Denn and Kilbride

Lord Garvagh: Rentals, 1829–48, NAI M5535, all tenants, covering areas in the civil parishes of Drumgoon, Knockbride and Larah

Pratt: Rentals, 1837–63, NLI Ms 3021, 1837–55, NLI Ms 3284, all tenants, covering areas in the civil parish of Enniskeen

Saunderson: Rent roll, 1779, NLI Ms 13340, major tenants only, covering areas in the civil parishes of Annagelliff, Killinkere and Lavey

Tennison: Rentals, 1846–54, NLI Ms 1400–1409, all tenants, covering areas in the civil parish of Annagelliff

William Greville: Rentals, surveys etc. 1810–48, NAI M6178 (1–89), all tenants, covering areas in the civil parishes of Drumgoon and Knockbride

CLARE

CENSUS RETURNS AND SUBSTITUTES

1641	*Book of Survey and Distribution*, Dublin, Irish Manuscripts Commission, 1947, also NLI Ms 963
1659	Pender's 'Census'
1745	Voters, TCD Ms 2059
1821	Part of Ennis, NAI, see pre-1901 census catalogue
1823–38	Tithe Books
1829	Freeholders, NLI P.5556
1837	Marksmen (illiterate voters) in parliamentary boroughs: Ennis, *Parliamentary Papers 1837, Reports from Committees*, Vol. II (i), Appendix A
1843	Clare voters, NAI 1843/68
1850	Deaths in Kilrush & Ennistymon workhouses, hospitals, infirmaries, 25/3/1850–25/3/1851, *Accounts & Papers (Parliamentary Papers)* 1851, Vol. 49, pp. (484) 1 47
1855	Griffith's Valuation
1866	Kilfenora, NLI Pos. 2440
1901	Census
1911	Census

LOCAL HISTORY

Anonymous, 'Businessmen of Ennis early in the Napoleonic wars', IA, 16 (1), 1984, 6–8

Clancy, J., *Short History of the Parish of Killanena or Upper Feakle*, NLI Ir. 941 p 27

Clancy, J., 'Gleanings in 17th century Kilrush', JNMAS, 1942–3

Coffey, Thomas, *The Parish of Inchicronan (Crusheen)*, Mountshannon, Ballinakella Press, 1993

Coleman, James, 'Limerick and Clare Bibliography', *Limerick Field Club Journal*, No. 32, 1907

Dwyer, Philip, *The Diocese of Killaloe, from the Reformation to the Close of the Eighteenth Century*, Dublin, 1878

Frost, James, *The history & topography of Co. Clare from the earliest times to the beginning of the eighteenth century*, Dublin, 1893, NLI Ir. 94143 f 3

Frost, James, 'Townland Names of Co. Clare', *Limerick Field Journal*, Vols 1 & 2, 1897–1904

Gwynn, A., *A history of the diocese of Killaloe*, Dublin, 1962

Hayes McCoy, G.A., *Index to 'The Compossicion Booke of Connoght, 1585'*, Irish Manuscripts Commission, Dublin, 1945

Mac Mathúna, Seosamh, *Kilfarboy: a history of a west Clare parish*, S. Mac Mathúna, Milltown Malbay, 1976(?)

McAuliffe, E.J., *Notes on the Parishes of Kilmurry, McMahon and Killofin, Co. Clare, and Tombstone inscriptions from Kilrush*, Dublin, 1989, NLI Ir. 94143 p

Murphy, Ignatius, *A Starving People — Life and Death in West Clare 1845–1851*, Dublin, Irish Academic Press, 1995

O'Mahoney, Dr C., 'Emigration from Kilrush Workhouse, 1848–1859', *The Other Clare*, 1983

Starkie, Virginia, Indexed abtracts from Co. Clare civil records 1864–1880, Vienna, VA., 1990, LDS Film 1696528

Westropp, *Westropp Manuscripts*, RIA

White, Rev. P., *History of Clare and the Dalcassian Clans of Tipperary, Limerick and Galway*, Dublin, 1893

LOCAL JOURNALS

Dál gCais, NLI Ir. 94143 d 5

Journal of the North Munster Archaeological Society, NLI Ir. 794105 n 1

The Other Clare (Journal of the Shannon Archaeological & Historical Society) NLI Ir. 9141 p 71

DIRECTORIES

1788	Richard Lucas, *General Directory of the Kingdom of Ireland*, NLI Pos. 3729
1820	J. Pigot, *Commercial Directory of Ireland*
1824	J. Pigot and Co., *City of Dublin and Hibernian Provincial Directory*, NLI
1842	*A directory of Kilkee*, NLI Ir. 61312 k 1
1846	Slater, *National Commercial Directory of Ireland*, NLI
1856	Slater, *Royal National Commercial Directory of Ireland*, NLI
1866	George Henry Bassett, *Directory of the City and County of Limerick, and of the Principal Towns in the Cos of Tipperary and Clare*, NLI Ir. 914144 b 5
1870	Slater, *Directory of Ireland*, NLI
1881	Slater, *Royal National Commercial Directory of Ireland*, NLI
1886	Francis Guy, *Postal Directory of Munster*, NLI Ir. 91414 g 8
1893	Francis Guy, *Directory of Munster*, NLI Ir. 91414 g 8
1894	Slater, *Royal Commercial Directory of Ireland*, NLI

GRAVESTONE INSCRIPTIONS

The Clare Genealogy Centre has transcripts for 80 graveyards in the county. Contact details will be found in Chapter 14. Published or publicly available transcripts are given below.

Clooney: Clooney South, IGRS, GO
—— Killeinagh, IGRS, GO
Drumcreehy: Ballyvaghan, IGRS, GO
Inchicronan: Kilvoydan South, IGRS, GO
Kilfarboy: Kilcorcoran, IGRS, GO
—— Kildeema South, IGRS, GO
—— Kilfarboy, IGRS, GO
—— Milltown Malbay, Mullagh Road, C of I, IGRS, GO
Kilfenora: Kilfenora, Well Lane, C of I, IGRS, GO
Killaloe: Cathedral, C of I, Yearbook of St Flannan's Cathedral
Killinaboy: Coad, IGRS, GO
—— Corrofin town, Church Street, C of I, IGRS, GO
Killinaboy: Killinaboy, IGRS, GO
Kilmacrehy: Dough, IGRS, GO
Kilmurry: Killernan, IGRS, GO
—— Kilmurry town, IGRS, GO
Kilrush: Kilrush, Grace Street, C of I, IGRS, GO
Kilrush: Kilrush, Grace Street, C of I, McAuliffe, *Notes on the Parishes of Kilmurry* [. . .]
Kilshanny: Ballyalla, GO 622 pp. 79/80, GO
—— Kilshanny, IGRS, GO
Kiltenanlea: Doonass Demesne, IGRS, GO
Noughaval: Glebe, IGRS, GO
Rath: Rath, IGRS, GO

ESTATE RECORDS

Note on the **Leconfield** estate papers at the National Archives, Accession No. 1074. (Vandeleur leases, Kilrush, 1816–1929, Lord Leconfield rentals, 1846–1917, including comments on age, health, poverty, etc.) *North Munster Antiquarian Journal*, Vol. XXIII, 1981

Roxton estate rentals, Inchiquin barony, Co. Clare, 1834, NA Ms 5764
O'Callaghan-Westropp estate rentals, barony of Tulla Upper, NLI Ms 867
19th Century: **Inchiquin** Papers, NLI Mss 14, 355 ff. (Dromoland especially).

CORK

CENSUS RETURNS AND SUBSTITUTES

1500–1650   The Pipe Roll of Cloyne. *JCHAS*, 1918
1641   Book of Survey and Distribution, Proprietors in 1641, grantees in 1666–8, NLI Ms 966–7

1641	Survey of Houses in Cork city, listing tenants and possessors, NAI Quit Rent Office Papers
1654	Civil Survey, *Civil Survey*, Vol. VI
1659	Pender's 'Census'
1662–67	Subsidy rolls, Extracts for Condons and Clangibbons baronies, NAI M.4968, M.2636
1700–52	Freemen of Cork city, NAI M. 4693
1753	Householders, St Nicholas parish, Cork city, also later years, NAI MFCI 23, 24, 25, M 6047
1766	Aghabulloge, Aghada, Ardagh, Ballintemple, Ballyhay, Ballynoe, Carrigdownane, Carrigrohanebeg, Castlelyons, Castletownroche, Churchtown, Clenor, Clondrohid, Clondulane, Clonfert, Clonmeen, Clonmult, Clonpriest, Cloyne, Coole, Farahy, Garrycloyne, Glanworth, Grenagh, Ightermurragh, Imphrick, Inishcarra, Kildorrery, Kilmahon, Kilnamartry, Kilshannig, Kilworth, Knockmourne, Lisgoold, Litter, Macroney, Macroom, Magourney, Mallow, Marshalstown, Matehy, Middleton, Mogeely, Mourneabbey, Roskeen, Shandrum, St Nathlash, Templemolaga, Whitechurch, Youghal, NAI M5036a; Rathbarry, Ringrone, NAI; *Parl. Ret.*, 773, 774 Dunbulloge, *JCHAS*, Vol. 51; Kilmichael, Vol. 26
1783	Freemen & freeholders, Cork city, NLI P 2054
1793	Householders in the parish of St Anne's, Shandon, also includes householders of additional houses built up to 1853, *JCHAS*, Vol. 47, pp. 87–111
1814	Jurors, Co. Cork, NAI M2637, Grove-White Abstracts
1817	Freemen, Cork city, NLI P 722
1823–38	Tithe Books
1830	House-owners, St Mary's Shandon, *JCHAS*, Vol. 49
1830–1837	Registered householders, Cork city (alphabetical), *Parliamentary Papers 1837, Reports from Committees*, 1837/8, Vol. 13 (2), pp. 554–7
1832–1837	Voters, Cork city, *Parliamentary Papers 1837, Reports from Committees*, 1837/8, Vol. 13 (1), pp. 320/1
1834	Protestant parishioners, Bandon town (Ballymodan only), NLI Ms 675
1834–1837	Valuation of Bandonbridge, Kinsale, Youghal towns (£5 householders), *Parliamentary Papers 1837, Reports from Committees*, Vol. II (1), Appendix G
1834	Protestant families Magourney parish, with the C of I Registers, NAI M 5118
1837	Marksmen (i.e. illiterate voters), Bandonbridge, Kinsale, Youghal Boroughs, *Parliamentary Papers 1837, Reports from Committees*, 1837, Vol. II (1), Appendix A
1837	Lists of waste and poor Cork city parishes, *Parliamentary Papers 1837, Reports from Committees*, 1837/8, Vol. 13 (1), pp. 324–34
1842	Cork voters, West 1842/26, East 1842/23
1843–1850	Records of Easter and Christmas dues, Catholic parish of Ballyclogh, includes names of parishioners, with children, NLI Pos. 5717, NLI Pos. 5717
1851	Extensive extracts for Kilcrumper, Leitrim and Kilworth parishes, NAI M4685

1851–1853 Griffith's Valuation
1901 Census
1911 Census

LOCAL HISTORY

Anonymous, *Newmarket Court (1725–1994)*, Duhallow Heritage Project, Newmarket, 1994, NLI Ir. 720 n 10

Barry, E., *Barrymore: the records of the Barrys of Co. Cork*, NLI Ir. 9292 b 19

Bennett, G., *The history of Bandon & the principal towns of the West Riding of Cork*, Cork, 1869, NLI Ir. 94145 b 1

Bowen, Elizabeth, *Bowen's Court*, London, 1944, NLI Ir. 9292 b 18

Brady, W. Maziere, *Clerical and Parochial Records of Cork, Cloyne and Ross* (3 vols), London, 1864

Cadigan, Tim, *Tracing your Cork Ancestors*, Dublin, Flyleaf Press, 1998

Caulfield, R., *Council Book of the Corporation of Kinsale*, Guildford, 1879

Caulfield, R., *Council Book of the Corporation of Youghal (1610–1659, 1666–87 and 1690–1800)*, Guildford, 1878

Cole, Rev. J.H., *Church and Parish Records of the United Dioceses of Cork, Cloyne and Ross*, Cork, 1903

Collins, J.T., *Co. Cork families 1630–35*, JCHAS, No. 204, 1961

Cusack, Mary F., *A History of the City and County of Cork*, Dublin, 1875

Darling, John, *St Multose Church Kinsale*, Cork, 1895

Dennehy, The Ven. Archdeacon, *History of Queenstown*, Cork, 1923

Ellis, Éilis, *Emigrants from Ireland 1847–52*, Baltimore, GPC, 1977, NLI Ir. 325 e 5

Gibson, C.B., *The history of the county and city of Cork*, London, 1861, NLI J 94145

Grove-White, Col. James, *History of Kilbryne, Doneraile, Cork*, Cork

Grove-White, Col. James, *Historical and Topographical Notes etc. on Buttevant, Castletownroche, Doneraile, Mallow and places in their vicinity*, Cork, 1905–16

Holland, Rev. W., *History of West Cork and the Diocese of Ross*, Skibbereen, 1949

Hore, H.J., *The Social State of the Southern and Eastern Counties of Ireland in the Sixteenth Century*, 1870

MacSwiney, *Unpublished manuscripts*

O'Flanagan & Buttimer (eds), *Cork History and Society*, Dublin, Geography Publications, 1994, NLI Ir. 94145 c 25

O'Murchadha, D., *Family Names of Co. Cork*, Glendale Press, Dublin, 1985

O'Sullivan, Florence, *The History of Kinsale*, Dublin, 1916

Power, V. Rev. P., *Waterford and Lismore: A Compendious History of the Dioceses*, Cork, 1937

Quinlan, P., *Old Mitchelstown and the Kingston family*, NLI Ir. 941 p 66

Reedy, Rev. Donal A., *The Diocese of Kerry*, Killarney

Smith, Charles, *The ancient and present state of the county and city of Cork*, Dublin, 1750, see JCHAS 1893–4

Tucky, Francis, *The County and City of Cork Remembered*

West, W., *Directory & picture of Cork*, 1810, NLI J 914145

Williams, R. Allan, *The Berehaven Copper Mines, Allihies, Co. Cork*, Northern Mine Research Soc., Sheffield, 1991, NLI Ir. 621 w 5

Windele, J., *Cork: historical & descriptive notices . . . to the middle of the 19th century*, Cork, 1910, NLI Ir. 94145 w 3

LOCAL JOURNALS

Bandon Historical Journal, NLI Ir. 794105 c 1
Journal of the Cork Historical & Archaeological Society, NLI Ir. 794105 c 1
Kinsale Historical Journal, NLI Ir. 95145 k 5
Seanchas Chairbre, NLI Ir. 94145 s 6
Seanchas Duthala (Duhallow magazine), NLI Ir. 94145 s 3

DIRECTORIES

1787	Richard Lucas, *Cork Directory*, NLI Journal of the Cork Hist. & Arch. Soc., 1967
1788	Richard Lucas, *General Directory of the Kingdom of Ireland*, NLI Pos. 3729
1797	John Nixon, *Cork Almanack*, NLI Pos. 3985
1809	Holden, *Triennal Directory*
1810	William West, *Directory of Cork*, NLI Pos. 3985
1812	John Connor, *Cork Directory*, also 1817, 1826, 1828, NLI Pos. 3985
1820	J. Pigot, *Commercial Directory of Ireland*
1824	J. Pigot and Co., *City of Dublin and Hibernian Provincial Directory*, NLI
1846	Slater, *National Commercial Directory of Ireland*, NLI
1856	Slater, *Royal National Commercial Directory of Ireland*, NLI
1870	Slater, *Directory of Ireland*, NLI
1875	Francis Guy, *City and County Cork Almanack and Directory*, NLI Ir. 91414 g 9
1881	Slater, *Royal National Commercial Directory of Ireland*, NLI
1886	Francis Guy, *Postal Directory of Munster*, NLI Ir. 91414 g 8
1889	Francis Guy, *City and County Cork Almanack and Directory*, annually from this year
1894	Slater, *Royal Commercial Directory of Ireland*, NLI

GRAVESTONE INSCRIPTIONS

Aghadown: Glebe, C of I, IGRS, GO
Aghinagh: Caum, *JCHAS*, No. 216, 1967, also *O'K*, Vol. 8
—— Ballaghboy IGRS, GO, also Cork County Library
Ballyclogh: Village of Ballyclogh, Main St, *O'K*, Vol. 8
Ballycurrany: Ballycurrany West, *JCHAS*, No. 237, 1978
—— Ballydesmond, *O'K*, Vol. 6
—— Ballyhoolahan East, *O'K*, Vol. 6
Ballymartle: Mill-land, C of I, *JCHAS*, 235, 1989
Ballymodan: Clogheenavodig (Kilbeg?), WCHC
Ballymodan: Knockanreagh, RC?, WCHC
Ballymodan: Knockaveale, St Peter's, *Droichead na Banndan Community Cooperative Society Ltd.*, Bandon, 1986
—— Ballynakilla, Castletown Berehaven, IGRS, GO
—— Ballynamona, *O'K*, Vol. 11

Ballynoe: *Ballynoe Cemetery, a guide and brief history*, Ballynoe, Co. Cork, Ballynoe
    Cemetery Committee, 1993, NLI, Ir. 9295 p 3(1)
Ballyvourney: Glebe, C of I, *O'K*, Vol. 6
Brinny: C of I, WCHC
Buttevant: Templemary, *O'K*, Vol. 11
Caheragh: Caheragh, RC, IGRS, GO
—— Cappyaughna, RC, IGRS, GO
Carrigrohanebeg: *JCHAS*, No. 218, 1968
—— Castle-land (Buttevant?), C of I, *O'K*, Vol. 11
Castlemagner: *O'K*, Vol. 6
Churchtown: Village of Churchtown, Georges St, *O'K*, Vol. 11
Clondrohid: *O'K*, Vol. 6
—— Clonfert, *O'K*, Vol. 6
Clonfert: Newmarket, Main Street, C of I, *O'K*, Vol. 6
Clonmeen: Clonmeen North, C of I, *O'K*, Vol. 7
Clonmult: Ballyeightragh, *JCHAS*, No. 223/4/5, 1976/7
—— Cloonaghlin West (Killaconenagh?), Cork County Library
—— Cooranuller, C of I, IGRS, GO
Creagh: Skibbereen IGRS, GO
Cullen: Cullen, *O'K*, Vol. 6
—— Curradonohoe, Bere Island, IGRS, GO
Dangandonovan: Kilcounty, *JCHAS*, No. 229, 1974
Desertmore: Kilcrea, *JCHAS*, No. 219, 1969
Doneraile: Oldcourt (Donraile), *O'K*, Vol. 11
Drishane: Millstreet, *O'K*, Vol. 6
—— Dromtariff, *O'K*, Vol. 6
Dromtarriff: Garraveasoge or Dromagh, *O'K*, Vol. 8
Dunderrow: Horsehill More North, *JCHAS*, No. 224, 1971
Fermoy: Carringnagroghera, *The Irish Sword*, Nos 51/3 1977/9 (Military only)
—— Inchigeelagh interior, *O'K*, Vol. 6
—— Inchigeelagh New, *O'K*, Vol. 6
Inchigeelagh: Glebe, C of I, *O'K*, Vol. 6
Kilbrin: Castlecor Demesne (Kilbrin?), *O'K*, Vol. 8
Kilbrogan: Kilbrogan, RC, C of I, *Droichead na Banndan Community Cooperative
    Society Ltd*, Bandon, 1986
Kilcaskan: Adrigole, C of I, IGRS, GO, also Cork County Library
Kilcatherine: Gortgarriff, IGRS, GO
Kilcoe: IGRS, GO
Kilcorney: *O'K*, Vol. 7
—— Kilcrea Friary, *JCHAS*, No. 226, 1972
Kilgrogan: *O'K*, Vol. 11
Killaconenagh: Clanlaurence, Cork County Library
Killeagh: Town of Killeagh, Main Street, C of I, *JCHAS*, No. 226, 1972
Kilmeen: Glebe (Boherbue?), C of I, *O'K*, Vol. 6
Kilmocomoge: Bantry (St Finbarr's) IGRS, GO
Kilmonoge: Coolnagaug (Kilmonoge?), *JCHAS*, 251, 1987
Kilnaglory: Kilnaglory, *JCHAS*, No. 220, 1969
Kilnamanagh: Cloan (Kilnamanagh?), Cork County Library
Kilnamartry: Glebe, *O'K*, Vol. 6

Kinsale: Kinsale, Church Street, C of I, McCarthy, M., *Kinsale inscriptions* (C of I), Kinsale, the author
—— Kishkeam, *O'K,* Vol. 6
Liscarroll: Village of Liscarroll, Main Street, *O'K,* Vol. 11
Lisgoold: Lisgoold East, C of I, *JCHAS,* No. 237, 1978
Macloneigh: *O'K,* Vol. 8
Macroom: Castle Street, C of I, *O'K,* Vol. 8
Magourney: Coachford, *O'K,* Vol. 11
—— Mallow, Main Street, C of I, *O'K*
Mallow: Mallow, Main Street, RC, *O'K,* Vol. 8
Middleton: Middleton, RC, *The cemetery, Church of Our Lady of the Most Holy Rosary [. . .],* Middleton, Canon B. Troy, 1994, NLI, Ir. 9295 t 1, Vol. 8
—— Millstreet (Old), *O'K,* Vol. 6
Mourneabbey: Kilquane (Mourneabbey?), *O'K,* Vol. 11
        Nohaval Lower, *O'K,* Vol. 8
Nohavaldaly: Knocknagree, *O'K,* Vol. 6
Rathgoggan: Charleville, Main Street, C of I, *O'K,* Vol. 11
—— Rodeen, IGRS, GO
—— Rossmackowen, Cork County Library
Shandrum: Dromina, *O'K,* Vol. 11
St Finbar's: Curraghconway, C of I, Robinson, A.C., *St Finbarr's Cathedral,* 1897
St Peter's: Duncan Street, *JCHAS,* 252, 198
Timoleague: Castle Lower, C of I, GO
Tisaxon: Tisaxon Beg, *JCHAS,* No. 222, 1970
Titeskin: *JCHAS,* No. 221, 1970
Tullylease: Tullylease, *O'K,* Vol. 8
Youghal: Nelson Place, *The Handbook for Youghal,* 1896/1973

ESTATE RECORDS

Lord Arden: NLI Ms 8652, Rentals 1824–1830, all tenants, covering townlands in the civil parishes of Bregoge, Buttevant, Castlemagner, Clonfert, Dromtarriff, and Dungourney.
Earl of Bantry: NLI Ms 3273, Rentals, 1829, all tenants, covering townlands in the civil parishes of Kilcaskan, Kilcatherine and Killaconenagh
(Barrymore barony): 'Tenant Farmers on the Barrymore Estate', JCHAS, Vol. 51, pp. 31–40
Bennett: Rental of the Bennett estate 1770 (mainly Cork city and surrounding areas) NLI Pos. 288
Sir John Benn-Walsh: Donnelly, J.S., 'The journals of Sir John Benn-Walsh relating to the management of his Irish estates (1823–64)', JCHAS, Vol. LXXXI, 1975
Bishop of Cork: NA M6087, Rentals 1807–1831, major tenants only, townlands in the civil parishes of Aghadown, Ardfield, Fanlobbus, Kilbrogan, Kilmocomoge, Kilsillagh, Ross, St Finbarr's, Skull.
Boyle/Cavendish: NLI Mss 6136–6898, The Lismore Papers, Rentals, valuations, lease books, account books for the estates of the Earls of Cork and the Dukes of Devonshire, 1570–1870, generally covering only major tenants; a detailed listing is given in NLI Special List 15, covering townlands in the civil parishes

of Ahern, Ardagh, Ballymodan, Ballynoe, Brinny, Clonmult, Clonpriest, Ightermurragh, Kilbrogan, Killeagh, Killowen, Kinneigh, Knockmourne, Lismore, Mogeely, Murragh, St Finbarr's, Youghal,

Richard Cox: NA Gordon Presentation 214; rentals 1839, major tenants only, townlands in the civil parishes of Aghinagh, Clondrohid, Desertserges, Fanlobbus, Kilcaskan, Kilmeen, Kilmichael, Kilnamartery, Macloneigh.

Earbery estates: NLI Ms 7403, Rentals 1788–1815 (principally major tenants), NLI Ms 5257, full tenants' list, 1800, townlands in the civil parishes of Aghabulloge, Clondrohid, Donoghmore, Kilmurry.

Robert Hodges Eyre: NLI Mss 3273, 3274, Rentals, 1833 and 1835, of the Bere Island estate, all tenants, civil parish of Killaconenagh.

James Graham: NA M2329, Rentals c.1763, major tenants only, covering townlands in the civil parish of Killathy.

Rev. Edmund Lombard: NLI Ms 2985, Rentals, 1795, major tenants only, covering townlands in the civil parishes of Kilmacdonagh and Kilshannig

Newenham?: NLI Ms 4123, Rentals, c.1825, all tenants, covering townlands in the civil parishes of Kilcrumper, Kilworth, Leitrim, Macroney.

Richard Neville: NLI Ms 3733, Rentals of lands in Cos Cork, Kildare and Waterford, principally major tenants, covering townlands in the civil parishes of Aglishdrinagh and Cooliney.

O'Murchadha, D. 'Diary of Gen. **Richard O'Donovan** 1819–23', JCHAS, 1986, (Lands in West Cork).

Perceval, Lord Egmont: Rentals, 1688–1750, major tenants only, NLI Pos. 1355 (1688), NLI Pos. 4674 (1701–12, 1713–14), NLI Pos. 4675 (1714–19), NLI Pos. 4676 (1720–24, 1725–27), NLI Pos. 4677 (1728–33), NLI Pos. 4678 (1734–38), NLI Pos. 4679 (1739–41, 1742–46), NLI Pos. 4680 (1747–50), covering townlands in the civil parishes of Aglishdrinagh, Ballyclogh, Bregoge, Brigown, Britway, Buttevant, Castlemagner, Churchtown, Clonfert, Cullin, Dromtarriff, Hackmys, Imphrick, Kilbrin, Kilbrogan, Kilbroney, Kilcaskan, Kilgrogan, Kilmichael, Kilroe, Liscarroll, Rathbarry.

George Putland: NLI Mss 1814–1827, eleven rentals of land in Cos Cork, Carlow, Kilkenny, Tipperary and Wicklow, principally major tenants, covering townlands in the civil parishes of Garrycloyne, Matehy and Templeusque.

Thomas Ronayne: NLI Ms 1721, Rentals 1755–1777, major tenants only, covering townlands in the civil parishes of Carrigaline, Clonmel, Killanully, Kilquane, Middleton and Templerobin.

Shuldam: NLI Ms 3025, estate map 1801–1803, with some tenants' names given, covering townlands in the civil parishes of Dreenagh, Fanlobbus, Iveleary and Kilmichael.

(No landlord given): NLI Ms 13018, Rental, c.1835–7, major tenants only, covering townlands in the civil parishes of Castlelyons, Gortroe, Knockmourne and Rathcormack.

(No landlord given): NLI Ms 3273, Rentals, 1821, covering all tenants, townlands in the civil parish of Kilmocomoge.

DERRY

Census returns and substitutes

1618	Survey of Derry city & county, TCD Ms 864 (F.I.9.)
1620–1622	Muster Roll, PRONI T510/2
1630	Muster Roll of Ulster, Armagh Co. Library and PRONI D.1759/3C/2, NLI Pos. 206
1654–1656	Civil Survey, Civil Survey, Vol. III (NLI I 6551 Dublin)
1659	Pender's 'Census'
1661	Books of Survey and Distribution, PRONI D.1854/1/23 & T370/C
1663	Hearth Money Roll, PRONI T307, also NLI Ms 9584 (indexed in Ms 9585)
1740	Protestant householders, Aghadowey, Aghanloo, Artrea, Ballinderry, Ballyaghran, Ballynascreen, Ballyrashane, Ballyscullion, Ballywillin, Balteagh, Banagher, Bovevagh, Clondermot, Coleraine, Cumber Lower, Cumber Upper, Derryloran, Desertlyn, Desertmartin, Desertoghill, Drumachose, Dunboe, Dungiven, Errigal, Faughanvale, Kilcronaghan, Killelagh, Killowen, Kilrea, Lissan, Macosquin, Maghera, Magherafelt, Tamlaght, Tamlaght Finlagan, Tamlaght O'Crilly, Templemore, Termoneeny, PRONI T808/15258, also GO 539, LDS films 100182, 1279327, Magherafelt, NAI M2809
1766	Artrea, Desertlyn, Magherafelt, NAI Parl. Ret. 650, 659, 674, Boveagh, Comber, Drumachose, Inch NAI 2476, Protestants in Ballynascreen, Banagher, Donaghedy, Dungiven, Leck, NAI M2476 Desertmartin (all) RCB M23, also PRONI T808/15264–7
1775	Arboe parish census, with C of I registers, PRONI T.679/111, 115–119, D.1278
1796	Census of Garvagh 1st Presbyterian congregation, also 1840, 1850, PRONI, MIC.1P/257
1796	Spinning-Wheel Premium List
1797–1804	Yeomanry muster rolls, PRONI T1021/3, also LDS film 993910
1803	Faughanvale Local census, with C of I registers, PRONI MIC1/7B, also the Genealogy Centre (database) and UHGGN 1 (10), 1984, pp. 324–32
1808–1813	Freeholders, NAI M.6199
1813	Freeholders (A–L), PRONI T2123
1823–38	Tithe Books
1829	Census of Protestants, Chapel of the Woods parish, PRONI T308
1830	Census of Drumachose parish, with C of I Registers, PRONI T.679/3, 394, 396–7, 416–7
1831	Aghadowey, Aghanloo, Agivey, Arboe, Artrea, Ballinderry, Balteagh, Banagher, Ballyaughran, Ballymoney, Ballynascreen, Ballyrashane, Ballyscullion, Ballywillin, Boveagh, Clondermot, Coleraine, Cumber, Desertlyn, Derryloran, Desertmartin, Desertoghill, Drumachose, Dunboe, Dungiven, Errigal, Faughanvale, Kilcrea, Kilcunaghan, Killeagh, Killowen, Lissane, Maghera, Magherafelt, Macosquin, Tamlaght, Tamlaght Finlagan, Tamlaght O'Crilly, Tamlaghtard, Templemore, Termoneny, Killdollagh (Glendermot), NAI, PRONI MIC5A/6–9, the Genealogy Centre (database)

1831–2	*First Valuation of the City of Derry, parish of Templemore*, (1832), LDS fiche 6342808, also NAI
1832	Voters Londonderry city, PRONI T1048/1–4
1833–1834	Emigrants to the US, *Historical gleanings from Co. Derry and some from Co. Fermanagh*, Dublin, 1955
1833–1839	Emigrants list, originals in PRONI, MIC.6, *Irish Emigration Lists 1833–39*, Baltimore, Genealogical Publishing Co., 1989
1837	Marksmen (illiterate voters) in parliamentary boroughs: Londonderry and Coleraine, *Parliamentary Papers 1837, Reports from Committees*, Vol. II (i), Appendix A
1837	Aldermen, Burgesses and Freemen of Coleraine, *Parliamentary Papers 1837, Reports from Committees*, Vol. II (2), Appendix B
1840	Freeholders, PRONI D834/1
1842–99	Magherafelt Workhouse records, PRONI, also LDS film 259179–80
1858–1859	Griffith's Valuation
1868	Voters' list, PRONI D1935/6, NLI JP 733
1888	Ballinascreen local census, with C of I registers, PRONI T.679/45, 206–208, 227
1901	Census
1911	Census

LOCAL HISTORY

Anonymous, *A Register of Trees for Co. Londonderry, 1768 1911*, PRONI, Belfast, 1984

Anonymous, 'Provisional list of pre-1900 School Registers in the Public Record Office of Northern Ireland', UHGGN, 9, pp. 60–71

Bernard, Nicholas (ed.), *The Whole Proceedings of the Siege of Drogheda [&] Londonderry*, Dublin, 1736

Boyle, E.M.F-G., *Records of the town of Limavady, 1609–1808*, Londonderry, 1912, NLI Ir. 94112 b 2

Carson, W.R.H., *A bibliography of printed material relating to the county & county borough of Londonderry*, 1969, NLI Ir. 914112 c 8

Colby, Col., *Ordnance Survey Memoir of the county of Londonderry*, Dublin, 1837

Ewart, L.M., *Handbook to the dioceses of Down, Connor & Dromore*

Ferguson, Rev. S., *Some items of Historic Interest about Waterside*, Londonderry, 1902

Graham, Rev. John, *Derriana, a History of the Siege of Derry and the Defence of Enniskillen in 1688 and 1689, with Biographical Notes*, 1823, NLI J94112

Henry, Samuel, *The Story of St Patrick's Church, Coleraine*, n.d.

Hughes, Samuel, *City on the Foyle*, Londonderry, 1984

Innes, R., *Natural History of Magiligan Parish in 1725*

Kernohan, J.W., *The County of Londonderry in Three Centuries*, Belfast, 1921

King, R.G.S., *A particular of the houses and families in Londonderry, 15/5/1628*, NLI Ir. 94112 l 1

Martin, Samuel, *Historical gleanings from Co. Derry, and some from Co. Fermanagh*, Dublin, 1955, NLI Ir. 94112 m 2

Mirchell, Brian, *Derry — Sources for Family History*, Derry, the Genealogy Centre, 1992

Mirchell, Brian, *Derry, A City Invincible*, Eglinton, 1990

Moody, T.W., *The Londonderry plantation, 1609–41*, Belfast, 1939, NLI Ir. 94112 m 2
Mullin, T.H., *Ballyrashane*, 1969
Mullin, T.H., *Ulster's Historic City, Derry, Londonderry*, Coleraine, 1986
Mullin, T.H., *Aghadowey*, NLI Ir. 94112 m 8
Mullin, Julia, *The Presbytery of Limavady*, Limavady, 1989
Munn A. M., *Note on the placenames (...) of Derry*, NL Ir. 92942 m 18
O'Laverty, Rev. James, *An Historical Account of the Dioceses of Down and Connor*,
    Dublin, 1878–89
Phillips, Sir Thomas, *Londonderry and the London Companies*, PRONI, Belfast, 1928
Reeves, William, *Ecclesiastical Antiquities of Down, Connor and Dromore*, 1847
Shearman, H., *Ulster*, London, 1949, NLI Ir. 91422 s 3
Simpson, Robert, *The Annals of Derry*, Londonderry, 1847
Witherow, Thomas, *Derry and Enniskillen, in the year 1689*, 1873, 1885
Witherow, Thomas, *A True Relation of the Twenty Week Siege . . .* , London, 1649

LOCAL JOURNALS

Benbradagh (Dungiven parish magazine)
Derriana
Down & Connor Historical Society Magazine
Irish Family Links, NLI Ir. 9292 f 19
North Irish Roots (Journal of the North of Ireland Family History Society)
Seanchas Ardmhacha, NLI Ir. 27411 s 4
South Derry Historical Society Journal

DIRECTORIES

1820	J. Pigot, *Commercial Directory of Ireland*
1824	J. Pigot and Co., *City of Dublin and Hibernian Provincial Directory*, NLI
1835	William T.Matier, *Belfast Directory*
1839	Mathew Martin, *Belfast Directory*, also 1841, 1842
1846	Slater, *National Commercial Directory of Ireland*, NLI
1852	James A. Henderson, *Belfast and Province of Ulster Directory*, issued also in 1854, 1856, 1858, 1861, 1863, 1865, 1868, 1870, 1877, 1880, 1884, 1887, 1890, 1894, 1900
1856	Slater, *Royal National Commercial Directory of Ireland*, NLI
1865	R. Wynne, *Business Directory of Belfast*
1870	Slater, *Directory of Ireland*, NLI
1881	Slater, *Royal National Commercial Directory of Ireland*, NLI
1887	*Derry Almanac and Directory*
1888	George Henry Bassett, *The Book of Antrim* (Portglenone only)
1894	Slater, *Royal Commercial Directory of Ireland*, NLI

GRAVESTONE INSCRIPTIONS

The Ulster Historical Foundation has transcripts for 76 graveyards in Derry. Heritage World has transcripts of 42 graveyards. Contact details will be found in Chapter 14. Published or publicly available transcripts are given below.

Aghanloo: Rathfad (Aghanloo Old?), *Irish Family Links* 1985 2 (3)
—— Derramore, Presbyterian, *Irish Family Links*, 2 (4), 1985
—— Drumbane, C of I, *Irish Family Links*, 1985 2 (3)
Artrea: Ballyeglish Old, *South Derry Historical Society Journal*, 1981/2
Ballinderry: Ballinderry, Methodist, *South Derry Historical Society Journal*, 1982/3
Balteagh: Lislane, Presbyterian, *Irish Family Links*, 2 (4), 1985
Carrick: Largy, Presbyterian, *Irish Family Links*, 2 (5), 1985
Coleraine: Coleraine, Church Street, C of I, Henry, [. . .] *St Patrick's Church, Coleraine*, n.d.
Drumachose: Limavady, First Presbyterian, *Irish Family Links*, 2 (5), 1985
—— Rathbrady More, Presbyterian, *Irish Family Links*, 2 (5), 1985
—— Limavady, Myroe, Presbyterian, *Irish Family Links*, 2 (5), 1985
—— Limavady, RC, *Irish Family Links*, 2 (5), 1985
—— Drummond (Drumachose Old?), *Irish Family Links*, 2 (4), 1985
Magherafelt: Magherafelt, Castledawson Street, C of I, *South Derry Historical Society Journal*, 1980/1
Magilligan: Tamlaght, RC, *Irish Family Links*, 2 (5), 1985
—— Magilligan, Presbyterian, *Irish Family Links*, 2 (5), 1985
Tamlaght Finlagan: Ballykelly town, *Irish Family Links*
—— Oghill, RC, *Irish Family Links*, 2 (5), 1985
—— Ballykelly town, Presbyterian, *Irish Family Links*
Templemore: Creggan, McMahon, Kevin, *Guide to Creggan Church and Graveyard*, Creggan, 1988, Creggan Historical Society
Templemore: Derry, Glendermot, C of I, NAI *[Unpublished]*

ESTATE RECORDS

Desertmartin Estate Rentals, *Derriana*, 1981–2, tenants' lists, Magherafelt & Ballinderry parishes (Aghaskin, Ballyheifer, Ballylifford, Ballymilligan) 1752–1930, *South Derry Historical Society Journal* 1 (2).

DONEGAL

CENSUS RETURNS AND SUBSTITUTES

1612–1613	'Survey of Undertakers Planted in Co. Donegal', *Historical Manuscripts, Commission Report*, No. 4 (Hastings Mss), 1947 pp. 159–82
1630	Muster Roll of Ulster, Armagh Co. Library and PRONI D.1759/3C/1, T. 808/15164, NLI Pos. 206
1641	Book of Survey and Distribution, NLI Ms 968
1654	Civil Survey, *Civil Survey*, Vol. III, NLI I 6551 Dublin
1659	Pender's 'Census'
1665	Hearth Money Roll, PRONI T.307/D, also GO 538, NLI Ms 9583

1669	Subsidy Roll, covering baronies of Kilmacrenan, Raphoe, Tirhugh, Taughboyne, PRONI T 307, also LDS film 2 58502
1740	Protestant Householders: parishes of Clonmany, Culdaff, Desertegny, Donagh, Fawne, Moville, Templemore, GO 539, LDS film 100182
1761–75	Freeholders, PRONI T.808/14999, also GO 442, NLI P.975, LDS film 100181
1766	Diocesan census, Donoghmore parish, NA m 207/8, Protestants in Leck and Raphoe, NA M2476
1770	Freeholders entitled to vote, NLI Mss 787–8
1782	Persons in Culdaff, *300 Years in Inishowen*, Amy Young
1796	Spinning-Wheel Premium List
1796	Clondevaddock local census, with C of I registers, PRONI MIC.1/164
1799	Protestant Householders, Templecrone parish, IA, 1984
1802	Protestants in part of Culdaff parish, *300 Years in Inishowen*
1823–38	Tithe Books
1857	Griffith's Valuation
1860–1867	Emigrants to North America from Inver, with Church of Ireland registers, PRONI MIC.1/158
1901	Census
1911	Census

LOCAL HISTORY

Anonymous, 'A Demographic Study of Tory Island and Rathlin Island 1841–1964', *Ulster Folk*, 17, 1971, 70–80

Anonymous, 'Kinship and Land Tenure on Tory Island', *Ulster Folk*, 12, 1966, 1–17

Anonymous, *Historical notes of Raphoe, Finn Valley, Lifford and Twin towns*, Knights of Columbanus, Stranorlar, 1991

Aalen, F.H., *Gola: the life and last days of an island community*, Mercier Press, Cork, 1969

Allingham, Hugh, *Ballyshannon: its history and antiquities (with some account of the surrounding neighbourhood)*, Londonderry, 1879

Beattie, Seán, *The book of Inistrahull*, Lighthouse, Carndonagh, 1992

Briody, Liam, *Glenties and Iniskeel*, Donegal Democrat, Ballyshannon, 1986

Campbell, Patrick, *Memories of Dungloe* [the author], New Jersey, 1993

Conaghan, Charles, *History and antiquities of Killybegs*, Donegal Democrat, Ballyshannon, 1975

Conaghan, Pat, *Bygones: New Horizons on the History of Killybegs*, Killybegs, 1989

Doherty, William J., *Inis-Owen and Tirconnel: being some account of the antiquities… of Donegal*, Dublin, 1895, NLI Ir. 94113 d 1

Doherty, William J., *The abbey of Fahan in Inishowen, Co. Donegal*, P. Traynor, Dublin, 1881

Duffy, Godfrey F., *A guide to tracing your Donegal ancestors*, Flyleaf Press, Dublin, 1996, NLI Ir. 941 D 9

Duffy, J. (ed.), *A Clogher Record Album: a diocesan history*, NLI Ir. 94114 c 3

Egan, Bernard, *Drumhome*, Donegal Democrat, Ballyshannon, 1986

Farrell, Noel, *Exploring Family origins in Letterkenny*, Self, Longford, 1997, includes transcripts of 1901, 1911 censuses, 1838 Thoms, 1941 Electors, Griffith's

Farrell, Noel, *Exploring Family origins in Ballybofey/Stranorlar & Killygordon*, Self, Longford, 1994, includes transcripts of 1901, 1911 censuses, 1838 Thoms, 1941 Electors, Griffith's

Fleming, Sam, *Letterkenny: past and present*, Donegal Denocrat, Ballyshannon, 197–

Gallagher, Barney, Arranmore Links: the families of Arranmore, Dublin, Aiden Gallagher, 1986, NLI Ir. 94109 g 18

Harkin, William, *Scenery and Antiquities of North West Donegal*, 1893

Hill, Rev. George, *Facts from Gweedore*, Dublin, 1854

Lucas, Leslie W., *More about Mevagh*, Appletree Press, Belfast, 1982

Lucas, Leslie W., *Mevagh Down the Years*, Belfast, 1983

MacDonagh, J.C.T., 'Bibliography of Co. Donegal', *Donegal Historical Society Journal, 1947–50*, pp. 217–30

Maguire, V. Rev. Canon, *The History of the Diocese of Raphoe*, Dublin

Maguire, Edward, *Letterkenny past and present*, McKinney & O'Callaghan, Letterkenny, 192–

Maguire, Edward, *Ballyshannon past and present*, Stepless, Bundoran, 193–

Manning, Aidan, *Glencolumbkille 3000 B.C.–1985 A.D.*, Donegal Democrat, Ballyshannon, 1985

McClintock, May, *After the battering ram: the trail of the dispossessed from Derryveagh, 1861*, An Taisce, Letterkenny, 1991

McCreadie, John, *Glenwar & Oughterlin*, Foyle Press, Carndonagh, 198–

McGarrigle, Joe, *Donegal Past and present*, McGarrigle family, Donegal, 1995, NLI Ir. 94113 m 11

Mullin, T.H., *The kirk and lands of Convoy since the Scottish settlement*, Belfast Newsletter, Belfast, 1960

Nolan, W., *Donegal history & society*, Geography Publications, Dublin, 1995, NLI Ir. 94113 d 12

O'Carroll, Declan, *Rockhill House, Letterkenny, Co. Donegal: a history*, Donegal Democrat, Ballyshannon, 1984

O'Donnell, Vincent, *Ardaghey Church and people*, St Naul's Church, Ardaghey, 1995, NLI

Patterson, W.J., *Rossnowlagh remembered*, Donegal Democrat, Ballyshannon, 1992

Shearman, H., *Ulster*, London, 1949, NLI Ir. 91422 s 3

Swan, H.P., *The Book of Inishowen*, Buncrana, 1938

Young, Amy, *300 Years in Inishowen*, 1929, NLI Ir. 9292 y 1

LOCAL JOURNALS

Journal of the Donegal Historical Society, NLI Ir. 94113 d 3
Clogher Record, NLI Ir. 94114 c 2
Donegal Annual

DIRECTORIES

1824	J. Pigot and Co., *City of Dublin and Hibernian Provincial Directory*, NLI
1839	*Directory of the Towns of Sligo, Enniskillen, Ballyshannon, Donegal [...]*
1846	Slater, *National Commercial Directory of Ireland*, NLI

1852	James A. Henderson, *Belfast and Province of Ulster Directory*, issued also in 1854, 1856, 1858, 1861, 1863, 1865, 1868, 1870, 1877, 1880, 1884, 1887, 1890, 1894, 1900
1856	Slater, *Royal National Commercial Directory of Ireland*, NLI
1870	Slater, *Directory of Ireland*, NLI
1881	Slater, *Royal National Commercial Directory of Ireland*, NLI
1887	*Derry Almanac and Directory*
1894	Slater, *Royal Commercial Directory of Ireland*, NLI

GRAVESTONE INSCRIPTIONS

Aghanunshin: Kiltoy, DA
—— Killydonnell, DA
Aughnish: Tullyaughnish, DA
Fahan Lower: Buncrana town, C of I, HW
Gartan: Churchtown (Gartan?), DA
Inishmacsaint: Ballyshannon town (Assaroe?), RC, DA
—— Finner: O Gallachair, *Where Erne and Drowes Meet the Sea*
Inver: Cranny Lower (Old Inver?), C of I, DA
—— Cranny Lower (Old Inver?), C of I, IGRS Collection, GO
Kilbarron: Ballyshannon, Church Lane, C of I, *Donegal Annual*, Vol. 12, No. 2
Killaghtee: Beaugreen Glebe (Old Killaghtee?), IGRS Collection, GO, also DA
Killybegs Lower: Kilrean Upper, IGRS Collection, GO
Killybegs Upper: St Catherine's, DA
Kilmacrenan: Kilmacrenan town, DA
Leck: Leck, DA
Muff: Muff, Sacred Heart, RC, HW
Taughboyne: St Johnstown town, Presbyterian, HW
Tullaghobegly: Magheragallan, DA
—— Ballintemple (Tullaghobegly?), *Tulach eaglaoich inné agus inniú*, Vol. 8

ESTATE RECORDS

Andrew Ferguson: Maps, with names, 1790, NLI Ms 5023, major tenants only, Rentals, 1838–42. NLI Ms. 8410 (2), all tenants, Tenants' list, 1840, NLI Ms 8410 (3), all tenants, covering areas in the civil parish of Donagh

Connolly: Rent rolls, 1724–1831, NLI Ms 17302, major tenants only, Rent rolls, 1772–93, NAI M. 6917 (1–17), major tenants only, Rent rolls, 1848, NAI M. 6917 (18), major tenants only, covering areas in the civil parishes of Drumhome, Glencolumbkille, Inishkeel, Inishmacsaint, Kilbarron, Kilcar, Killybegs Upper and Killymard

Connolly: Rent rolls, 1782–6, NLI Ms 17302, major tenants only, covering areas in the civil parishes of Donaghmore and Urney

William Forward: Valuation and survey, 1727, NLI Ms 4247, major tenants only, maps, with tenants, 1727, NLI Ms 2614, all tenants, covering areas in the civil parishes of Allsaints and Burt

Hart: Rentals, 1757–67, NLI Ms 7885, all tenants, covering areas in the civil parishes of Clonca and Muff

Leslie: Rentals, 1819–37, NLI Ms 5811–2, all tenants, covering areas in the civil parish of Templecarn

Leslie: Valuation, with names and observations, 1833, NLI Ms 5813, all tenants, Rental, 1846, NLI Ms 5813, all tenants, covering areas in the civil parish of Templecarn

Maxwell: Valuation, with names, 1807, NLI Ms 5357, all tenants, covering areas in the civil parishes of Clonleigh and Fahan Upper

Stewart: Rentals, 1813–53, NAI BR DON 21/1/1–3, all tenants, covering areas in the civil parishes of Clondahorky, Clonmany, Raymunterdoney and Tullyfern

Stuart-Murray: Rentals, 1842–50, NLI Ms 5465–70, all tenants, Rentals, 1849, NLI Ms 3084, all tenants, Rentals, 1851–9, NLI Ms 5472–67, 5892–96, covering areas in the civil parishes of Inishkeel, Kilcar, Killaghtee, Killea, Killybegs Lower and Killymard

Sir Charles Styles: Valuation and survey, 1773, NLI Ms 402, major tenants only, covering areas in the civil parish of Kilteevoge

Lord Wicklow: Rent roll, with leaseholders, 1780, NLI Ms 9582, major tenants only, covering areas in the civil parishes of Allsaints, Burt, Raymoghy and Taughboyne

[No landlord given]: Visiting book, with observations, 1842–3, NLI Ms 7938, coverage unclear, covering areas in the civil parish of Inishkeel

DOWN

CENSUS RETURNS AND SUBSTITUTES

1642–1643	Muster Roll, PRONI T.563/1
1642	Muster Roll, Donaghadee, PRONI T.3726/1
1659	Pender's 'Census'
1661	Books of Survey and Distribution, PRONI T.370/A & D.1854/1/18
1663	Subsidy Roll, NAI M. 2745, also NLI Pos. 206, PRONI T.307, LDS film 1279356
1669	Newry & Mourne Poll Tax Returns, PRONI T1046
1708	Householders in Downpatrick town, *The City of Downe*, R.E. Parkinson
1720	Down and Antrim landed gentry, RIA 24 k 19
1722–1970	Records of Southwell Charity School Downpatrick, PRONI D/2664
1740	Protestant Householders (Partial), PRONI T.808/15258
1766	Kilbroney, Seapatrick, Inch, Shankill, NLI Ms 4173
1777	Freeholders Register, PRONI DOW 5/3/1 & 2
1780	Freeholders Register, PRONI DOW 5/3/1 & 2
1789	'Deputy Court Cheque Book' (votes cast), PRONI D.654/A3/1B
1790	Freeholders Lecale barony, *c.*1790, PRONI T.393/1
1795	Freeholders Register, PRONI DOW 5/3/1 & 2
1796	Spinning-Wheel Premium List
1798	Persons who suffered losses in the 1798 rebellion, propertied classes only, NLI I 94107
1799–1800	Militia Pay Lists and Muster Rolls, PRONI T.1115/4A C
1813–1821	Freeholders, PRONI T.761/19
1815–1846	Downpatrick electors, NLI Ms 7235
1821	Some extracts, NAI Thrift Abstracts

1823–38	Tithe Books
1824	Freeholders, PRONI T.761/20
1837	Valuation of Newry town (heads of households), *Parliamentary Papers 1837, Reports from Committees*, Vol. II (1), Appendix G
1837	Marksmen (illiterate voters) in parliamentary boroughs: Newry and Downpatrick, *Parliamentary Papers 1837, Reports from Committees*, Vol. II (i), Appendix A
1841–1861	Religious censuses: Aghaderg, RCB Library, Ms 65
1851	Some extracts, NAI Thrift Abstracts
1851	Presbyterians only: Loughinisland, *Family Links*, Vol. 1, Nos 5 & 7, 1982/83
1852	Poll Book (votes cast), incomplete, PRONI D.671/02/5 6, D.671/02/7 8, LDS film 993158
1861	Loughinisland, Presbyterians only, *Family Links*, Vol. 1, Nos 5 & 7, 1982/83
1863–1864	Griffith's Valuation
1868	Census of the C of I parish of Shankill, Cos Armagh & Down, local clergyman
1873	Census of the congregation of the Church of Ireland parish of Knockbreda, Co. Down, also 1875, with C of I registers
1901	Census
1911	Census

LOCAL HISTORY

Anonymous, *Donaghadee: a local history list*, NLI Ir. 9411 s 12

Anonymous, *Clandeboye: a reading guide*, NLI Ir. 914115 p 15

Anonymous, *Killyleagh & Crossegar: a local history list*, NLI Ir. 914115 p 15

Anonymous, 'Provisional list of pre-1900 School Registers in the Public Record Office of Northern Ireland', UHGGN, 9, pp. 60–71

Atkinson, Edward D., *Dromore, an Ulster Diocese*, Dundalk, 1925

Atkinson, Edward D., *An Ulster Parish: Being a History of Donaghcloney*, 1898

Barry, J., *Hillsborough: a parish in the Ulster Plantation*, 1982

Canavan, T., *Frontier town: an illustrated history of Newry*, Belfast, Blackstaff Press, 1989

Carr, P., *The most unpretending of places: a history of Dundonald*, Belfast, White Row Press, 1987

Cowan, J. Davison, *An Ancient Parish, Past and Present: being the Parish of Donaghmore, County Down*, London, 1914, NLI Ir. 94115 c 1

Crossle, Francis, *Local Jottings of Newry Collected and Transcribed*, Vols 1–34, Newry, 1890–1910

Ewart, L.M., *Handbook to the dioceses of Down, Connor & Dromore*

Haddock, Josiah, *A Parish Miscellany, Donaghcloney*

Hill, Rev. George, *Montgomery Manuscripts, 1603–1706*, Belfast, 1869

Irwin, David, *Tide and Times in the 'Port: a narrative history of the Co. Down village of Groomsport*, Groomsport, Groomsport Presbyterian Church, 1993

James W.V., *Strangford: The Forgotten Past of Strangford Village*, Belfast, the *Northern Whig*, 1994

Keenan, Padraic, *Historical Sketch of the Parish of Clonduff*, Newry, 1941
Keenan, Padraic, *'Clonallon Parish; its Annals and Antiquities'*, NLI, JCLAHS, Vol. X
Knox, Alexander, *History of the County Down*, Dublin, 1875
Linn, Capt. Richard, *A history of Banbridge*, Belfast, 1935
McCavery, T., *Newtown: a history of Newtownards*, Belfast, White Row Press, 1994
McCullough, S., *Ballynahinch, Centre of Down*, Ballynahinch, Chamber of Commerce, 1968
O'Laverty, Rev. James, *An Historical Account of the Dioceses of Down and Connor*, Dublin, 1878–89
Parkinson, Edward, *The City of Down from its earliest days*, Belfast, 1928
Pilson, A., *Downpatrick & its Parish Church*, 1852, NLI P 1938
Pooler, L.A., *Down and its Parishes*, 1907
Reeves, William, *Ecclesiastical Antiquities of Down, Connor and Dromore*, 1847
Reside, S.W., *St Mary's Church, Newry: its History*, 1933
Shearman, H., *Ulster*, London, 1949, NLI Ir. 91422 s 3
Smith, Charles, *The Ancient and Present State of the County of Down*, Dublin, 1744, NLI I 94115 h 2
Wilson, A.M., *Saint Patrick's Town*, Isabella Press, 1995
Smith, K., Bangor Reading List, *Journal of the Bangor Historical Society*

LOCAL JOURNALS

12 Miles of Mourne: journal of the Mourne Local Studies Group, NLI Ir. 94115 T 1
Craigavon Historical Society Review
Down & Connor Historical Society Magazine
Irish Family Links, NLI Ir. 9292 f 19
Journal of the Bangor Historical Society
Lecale Miscellany
Lisburn Historical Society Journal
North Irish Roots (Journal of the North of Ireland Family History Society)
Old Newry Journal
Saintfield Heritage
Seanchas Dhroim Mor (Journal of the Dromore Diocesan Historical Society), NLI Ir. 94115 s 3

DIRECTORIES

1819	Thomas Bradshaw, *General Directory of Newry, Armagh, Dungannon, Portadown, Tandragee, Lurgan, Waringstown, Banbridge, Warrenpoint, Rostrevor, Kilkeel and Rathfryland*
1820	Joseph Smyth, *Directory of Belfast and its Vicinity*
1820	J. Pigot, *Commercial Directory of Ireland*
1824	J. Pigot and Co., *City of Dublin and Hibernian Provincial Directory*, NLI
1835	William T. Matier, *Belfast Directory*
1839	Mathew Martin, *Belfast Directory*, also 1841, 1842
1846	Slater, *National Commercial Directory of Ireland*, NLI
1852	James A. Henderson, *Belfast and Province of Ulster Directory*

1854	James A. Henderson, *Belfast and Province of Ulster Directory*, issued also in 1854, 1856, 1858, 1861, 1863, 1865, 1868, 1870, 1877, 1880, 1884, 1887, 1890, 1894, 1900
1856	Slater, *Royal National Commercial Directory of Ireland*, NLI
1865	R. Wynne, *Business Directory of Belfast*
1870	Slater, *Directory of Ireland*, NLI
1881	Slater, *Royal National Commercial Directory of Ireland*, NLI
1883	Farrell, *County Armagh Directory and Almanac* (Newry)
1888	George Henry Bassett, *The Book of Antrim* (Lisburn & Dromara)
1888	George Henry Bassett, *The Book of Armagh* (Donaghcloney, Moira, Waringstown)
1894	Slater, *Royal Commercial Directory of Ireland*, NLI

GRAVESTONE INSCRIPTIONS

The Ulster Historical Foundation has transcripts for 128 graveyards in Down. Heritage World has transcripts of 56 graveyards. Contact details will be found in Chapter 14. Published or publicly available transcripts are given below, ordered by civil parish.

Gravestone Inscriptions, Co. Down
Vols 1–20, R.S.J. Clarke, 1966–81, NLI Ir. 9295 c 1

Annaclone: Ballydown, Pres., Vol. 20
Annahilt: Cargacreevy, Pres., Vol. 18
—— Cargygary (Loughaghery), Pres., Vol. 18
—— Glebe (Annahilt), C of I, Vol. 18
Ardglass: Ardglass town, C of I, Vol. 8
Ardkeen: Ardkeen, Vol. 13
—— Kirkistown, C of I, Vol. 13
—— Ballycran Beg, RC (1 inscription), Vol. 13
—— Lisbane, RC, Vol. 13
Ardquin: Ardquin, C of I, Vol. 13
Ballee: Church Ballee, C of I, Vol. 8
—— Church Ballee, Pres., (N.S.)/ Unitarian, Vol. 8
Ballyculter: Ballyculter Upper, C of I, Vol. 8
—— Strangford Lower, C of I, Vol. 8
Ballykinler: Ballykinler Upper, RC, Vol. 16
—— Ballykinler Upper, RC, Vol. 9
Ballyphilip: Portaferry town (Ballyphilip), Vol. 13
—— Ballygalget, RC, Vol. 13
Ballytrustan: Ballytrustan, RC, Vol. 13

Ballywalter: Whitechurch, Vol. 15
—— Bangor: Castle Park, Bangor, 1 inscription, Vol. 17
—— Conlig town, Pres., Vol. 17
—— Groomsport, Pres., Vol. 17
—— Groomsport, C of I, Vol. 17
—— Ballyleidy (Clandeboye House), Family graveyard, Vol. 17
—— Bangor Church, C of I interior, Vol. 17
—— Bangor Abbey, Vol. 17
—— Ballygilbert Church, Pres., (1 inscription), Vol. 17
—— Copeland Island, Vol. 16
—— Bangor, Pres. (1st), Vol. 17
Blaris: Maze, Pres., Vol. 18
—— Blaris, Vol. 5
—— Eglantine, C of I, Vol. 18
—— Eglantine, C of I, Vol. 18
Bright: Bright, C of I/Mixed, Vol. 8
Castleboy: Cloghy/Clough, Pres., Vol. 14
Comber: Comber, the Square, C of I, Vol. 5
—— Gransha, Pres., Vol. 1
—— Moneyreagh, Pres., N.S. (Unitarian), Vol. 1

Donaghadee: Templepatrick, Vol. 14
—— Ballymacruise (Millisle), Pres., Vol. 16
—— Ballycopeland, Pres., Vol. 16
—— Donaghadee, Church Lane, C of I, Vol. 16
—— Ballyrawer, C of I, Vol. 14
Donaghcloney: Donaghcloney, Vol. 19
—— Waringstown town, C of I, Vol. 19
Down: Downpatrick, Church Lane, C of I, Vol. 7
—— Downpatrick, Fountain Street, Pres., Vol. 7
—— Downpatrick, Stream Street, RC, Vol. 7
—— Downpatrick, Stream Street, Unitarian (N.S. Pres.), Vol. 7
—— Downpatrick, English Street, C of I, Vol. 7
Dromara: Finnis, RC, Vol. 19
—— Drumgavlin, Magherahamlet, Vol. 9
—— Dromara, C of I, Vol. 19
—— Drumgavlin, Magherahamlet Pres., Vol. 9
Dromore: Dromore, Church Street, C of I, Vol. 19
—— Drumlough, Vol. 19
Drumbeg: Drennan, Pres. (Baileysmill), Vol. 2
—— Drumbeg, C of I, Vol. 3
Drumbo: Ballycarn, Pres., Vol. 1
Knockbreckan, Pres., (reformed), Vol. 1
—— Edenderry House, Dunlop family, Vol. 3
—— Carrickmaddyroe, Pres., Vol. 2
—— Drumbo, Pres., Vol. 4
—— Carryduff, Pres., Vol. 1
—— Ballelessan, C of I, Vol. 1
—— Legacurry, Pres., Vol. 2
—— Ballelessan, C of I, Vol. 18
—— Carryduff, Pres., Vol. 18
Dundonald: Dundonald town, C of I, Vol. 2
Dunsfort: Dunsfort, C of I, Vol. 8
—— Dunsfort, St Mary's, RC, Vol. 8
Garvaghy: Fedany (Garvaghy?), C of I, Vol. 19
—— Kilkinamurry, Pres., Vol. 19
—— Ballooly, Vol. 19
Greyabbey: Rosemount, Grey Abbey grounds and graveyard, Vol. 12

Hillsborough: Hillsborough, Main Street, C of I, Vol. 18
—— Ballykeel, Edenagonnell (Annahilt), Pres., Vol. 18
—Corcreeny, Moravian, Vol. 18
—Corcreeny, C of I, Vol. 19
—Hillsborough, Park Street, Quaker, Vol. 18
—Reilly's Trench, RC, Vol. 18
—Corcreeny, C of I, Vol. 18
Holywood: Holywood, Old Church Lane, Priory? Vol. 4
Inch: Inch, C of I, Vol. 7
Inishargy: Balliggan, C of I, Vol. 14
—Kircubbin, Pres., Vol. 12
—Inishargy, Old, Vol. 14
Kilclief: Kilclief, C of I, Vol. 8
—Kilclief, St Malachy's, RC, Vol. 8
Kilkeel: Kilkeel, Bridge Street, Vol. 10
—Mourne Abbey, 1 inscription only, Vol. 10
—Glasdrumman, RC, Vol. 10
—Moneydorragh More, C of I (Kilhorne), Vol. 10
—Kilkeel, Newry Street, C of I, Vol. 10
Kilkeel, Greencastle Street, Pres., (Mourne), Vol. 10
—Ballymartin, RC, Vol. 10
—Ballymageogh, RC, Vol. 10
—— Kilkeel, Newcastle Street, Moravian, Vol. 10
Killaney: Carrickmaddyroe, Pres. (Boardmills), Vol. 2
—— Killaney, C of I, Vol. 2
Killinchy: Ballygowan (Killinchy?), Pres., Vol. 5
—— Killinakin, 2 inscriptions only, Vol. 6
—— Ballymacashen, Pres. (reformed), Vol. 6
—— Ravara, Unitarian, Vol. 5
—— Killinchy, C of I, Vol. 5
—— Balloo, Pres., Vol. 6
—— Drumreagh (Kilcarn?), RC, Vol. 5
Killyleagh: Killyleagh, Church Hill Street, C of I, Vol. 6
—— Killyleagh, the Plantation, Pres., Vol. 7
—— Toy and Kirkland, Killaresy graveyard, Vol. 6
—— Killyleagh Old, Vol. 6
—— Tullymacnous, 1 inscription, Vol. 6

Kilmegan: Moneylane (Kilmegan?), C of I, Vol. 9
—— Aghalasnafin, RC, Vol. 9
Kilmood: Kilmood and Ballybunden, C of I, Vol. 5
—— Ballyministragh, Pres., Vol. 5
Kilmore: Barmaghery, 1 inscription only, Vol. 1
—— Carnacully (Kilmore?), C of I, Vol. 3
—— Drumaghlis, Pres. (Kilmore), Vol. 3
—— Rademan, Pres. N.S. (Unitarian), Vol. 3
Lambeg: Lisnatrunk, Pres. (Hillhall), Vol. 1
Loughinisland: Tievenadarragh, mixed, Vol. 9
—— Seaforde town, C of I, Vol. 9
—— Clough town, Pres., Vol. 9
—— Clough town, Unitarian, Vol. 9
—— Drumaroad, RC, Vol. 9
Magheradrool: Ballynahinch, C of I, Vol. 9
—— Ballynahinch, Windmill Street, Pres., Vol. 9
—— Ballynahinch, Dromore Street, Pres., Vol. 9
Magheralin: Ballymakeonan (Magheralin?), Vol. 19
Magherally: Magherally, C of I, Vol. 20
—— Magherally, Pres., Vol. 20
Moira: Moira (Clare), Vol. 18
—— Moira, Pres. (N.S.), Vol. 18
—— Lurganville, RC, Vol. 18
—— Moira, Pres., Vol. 18

Newtownards: Ballyblack, Pres., Vol. 12
—— Milecross, RC (Killysuggan), Vol. 5
Movilla, Vol. 11
—— Newtownards Chuch interior, C of I, Vol. 11
—— Newtownards Priory, Vol. 11
Rathmullan: Rathmulland Upper, C of I, Vol. 9
—— Rossglass, RC, Vol. 8
—— Killough, Palatine Square, C of I, Vol. 8
Saintfield: Saintfield town, Pres., Vol. 3
—— Saintfield town, C of I, Vol. 3
—— Saintfield, Cow Market, Pres., Vol. 3
Saul: Saul, C of I, Vol. 7
—— Ballysugagh (Saul?), RC, Vol. 8
Seapatrick: Banbridge, Scarva Street, Vol. 20
—— Kilpike (Seapatrick?), Vol. 20
Slanes: Slanes, Vol. 14
St Andrew's alias Ballyhalbert: Ballyesborough, C of I, Vol. 15
—— Ballyhemlin, Pres., (N.S.)/ Unitarian, Vol. 14
—— Ballyhalbert, Vol. 15
—— Glastry, Pres., Vol. 15
Tullylish: Tullylish, C of I, Vol. 20
—— Moyallon, Quaker, Vol. 20
—— Laurencetown. Vol. 20
—— Clare, Vol. 19
Tullynakill: Tullynakill, C of I, Vol. 1

ESTATE RECORDS

Anglesea: Tenants on the Anglesea estate, 1856, *JCLAHS*, 12 (2), 1950, 151–3, covering areas in the civil parish of Newry
Chichester Fortescue: Rental, ?1817–1817, NAI, M3610, covering areas in the civil parishes of Donaghcloney, Magherally, Seapatrick, Donaghadee

DUBLIN

CENSUS RETURNS AND SUBSTITUTES

1568	Herald's Visitation of Dublin, GO 46, also NLI Pos. 957
1610	Herald's Visitation of Dublin county, GO 48, also NLI Pos. 957
1621	St John's parish Cess lists, also for years 1640, 1687, *JPRS*, Appendix to Vol. 1, 1906, LDS film 82407

1634	Book of Survey and Distribution, NLI Ms 964
1652	Inhabitants of the baronies of Newcastle & Uppercross, NAI M. 2467
1654–56	Civil Survey, *Civil Survey*, Vol. VII
1659	Pender's 'Census'
1663–8	Subsidy roll for Co. Dublin, NAI NA M. 2468
1664	Persons with 6 hearths or upwards, Dublin city, *Report of the Deputy Keeper of the Public Records*, No. 57, p. 560
1667–1810	Assessments for the parish of St Bride's, TCD M. 2063
1680–86	Index only to an applotment book for Dublin city, NAI M. 4979
1680	Pipe water accounts, IG, 1987, also 1703–4, IG 1994
1711–1835	Annual Cess Applotment books of St Michan's parish, RCB Library
1766	Crumlin, RCB Library, also in GO 537, Castleknock, RCB Ms 37, Taney, NAI M2478, LDS film 258517
1730–1740	Index to marriages and deaths in *Pue's Occurrences* and *The Dublin Gazette*, NLI Ms 3197
1756	Inhabitants of St Michael's parish, *The Irish Builder*, Vol. 33, pp. 170/1
1761	Dublin city voting freemen and freeholders, NLI I 6511 Dubl
1767	Freeholders, NAI M. 4910–2
1778–1782	Catholic Merchants, Traders & Manufacturers of Dublin, *Reportorium Novum*, 2(2), 1960, p. 298, 323
1791–1831	Register of children at Baggot St school (Incorporated Soc. for Promoting Protestant Schools), NLI Pos. 2884
1791–1957	Register of Admissions to Pleasant's Female Orphan Asylum, including places of birth and families, NLI Ms 1555, see also Mss 1556 & 1558
1793–1810	Census of Protestants in Castleknock, GO 495, LDS film 100225
1798	Persons who suffered losses in the 1798 rebellion, propertied classes only, NLI I 94107
1798–1831	Register of children at Santry school (Incorporated Soc. for Promoting Protestant Schools), NLI Pos. 2884
1800–16	Card index to biographical notices in Faulkner's Dublin Journal, NLI
1805–39	Register of children at Kevin St school (Incorporated Soc. for Promoting Protestant Schools), NLI Pos. 2884
1806	Voters Lists, by occupation, NLI Ir. 94133 d 13
1820	Freemen voters, NLI P 734
1821	Some extracts, NAI Thrift Abstracts
1823–38	Tithe Books
1830	Freeholders, NLI Ms 11, 847
1831	Householders in St Bride's parish, NLI P. 1994
1834–35	Returns of those liable for paving tax, Inquiry into the impeachment of Alderman Richard Smith (formerly in State Paper Office), NAI
1835	Alphabetical list of voters with addresses and occupations, NLI Ir. 94133 d 12
1835–37	Dublin county freeholders & leaseholders, NLI Ms 9363
1840–1938	Admissions and Discharge registers for Dublin city workhouses (North and South Union), NAI
1841	Some extracts, NAI Thrift Abstracts
1843	Voters, NAI 1843/52
1844–50	Householders, St Peter's parish, RCBL P45/15/1, 2

1848–51	Griffith's Valuation
1851	Index only to heads of households, by street and parish, NAI Cen 1851/18/1
1864	City of Dublin Voters List, by district and street, NLI Ir. 94133 d 16
1865–1866	Voters, NLI Ir. 94133 d 15
1878	Voters, South Dock Ward only, NLI ILB 324 d
1901	Census
1911	Census

LOCAL HISTORY

Anonymous, *Alphabetical list of the constituency of the University of Dublin*, Dublin, 1865, NLI Ir. 37841 t 2 & 1832: JP 1375, also LO

Anonymous, *Dublin in Books: A reading list from the stock of Dublin Public Libraries*, Dublin, 1982, NLI Ir. 01 p 9

Anonymous, *Dublin corporation meetings, lists of freemen, aldermen, bailiffs etc.*, NLI

Anonymous, *Alphabetical list of the constituency of the University of Dublin*, Dublin, 1865. NLI Ir. 37841 t 2 & 1832: JP 1375, also LO

Anonymous, *Gilbert Library: Dublin and Irish Collections*, Dublin, NLI Ir. 02 p 50

Anonymous, *Parish Guide to the Archdiocese of Dublin* (1958), NLI Ir. 27413 d 3

Anonymous, *St Peter's Parochial Male & Female Boarding Schools, Sunday, Daily & Infant Schools: Reports 1850 60*, NLI P. 439

Anonymous, *Stephen's Green Club, list of members, 1882*, 1882, NLI Ir. 367 s 12

Aalen, F.H., *Dublin city and county: From prehistory to present*, Geography Publications, Dublin, 1992, NLI Ir. 94133 d 48

Adams, B.N., *History and Description of Santry and Cloghran Parishes*, Dublin, 1883

Appleyard, D.S., *Green Fields Gone Forever*, NLI Ir. 94133 a 5

Ball, F.E., *A history of the county of Dublin, Vol. 1–6*, Dublin, 1902–20, NLI Ir. 94133 b 1
   1. Monkstown, Kill-of-the Grange, Dalkey, Killiney, Tully, Stillorgan, Kilmacud
   2. Donnybrook, Booterstown, St Bartholomew, St Mark, Taney, St Peter, Rathfarnham
   3. Tallaght, Cruagh, Whitechurch, Kilgobbin, Kiltiernan, Rathmichael, Old Connaught, Saggart, Rathcoole, Newcastle
   4. Clonsilla, Leixlip, Lucan, Aderrig, Kilmactalway, Kilbride, Kilmahuddrick, Esker, Palmerstown, Ballyfermot, Clondalkin, Drimnagh, Crumlin, St Catherine, St Nicholas Without, St James, St Jude, Chapelizod
   5. Howth
   6. Castleknock, Mulhuddert, Cloghran, Ward, St Margaret's, Finglas, Glasnevin, Grangegorman, St George, Clonturk

Black, A & C., *Guide to Dublin & Co. Wicklow*, 1888

Blacker, Rev. Beaver H., *Sketches of the Parishes of Booterstown and Donnybrook*, Dublin, 1860–74

Clarke, Mary, *Sources for Genealogical Research in Dublin Corporation Archives*, IG, 1987

Costello, Peter, Dublin Churches, Dublin, 1989, NLI Ir. 720 c 23

Craig, Maurice, *Dublin 1660–1800*, Dublin, 1952

Cullen, L.N., *Princes and Pirates: the Dublin Chamber of Commerce 1783–1983*, NLI Ir. 94133 c 17

Donnelly, N., *State of RC Chapels in Dublin 1749*, NLI I 2820941 p 10

Donnelly, N., *Series of short histories of Dublin parishes*, NLI Ir. 27413 d 1

Doolin, W., *Dublin's Surgeon Anatomists*, NLI Ir. 610 p 4

Gilbert, Sir John T., *A History of the City of Dublin*, Dublin, 1885–9

Harris, Walter, *The History and Antiquities of the city of Dublin*, Dublin, 1776

Harrison, W., *Dublin Houses/or Memorable Dublin Houses*, Dublin, 1890, NLI Ir. 94133 h 5

Keane, Rory, *Ardgillan Castle and the Taylor Family*, Ardgillan Castle, Balbriggan, Co. Dublin, 1995, NLI Ir. 94133 a 8

Kingston, Rev. John, *The Parish of Fairview*, Dundalk, 1953

Le Fanu, T.P., *The Huguenot Churches of Dublin and their Ministries*, 1905. NLI P. 2274

MacGiolla Phadraig, Brian, *History of Terenure*, Dublin, 1954

MacSorley, Catherine M., *The Story of Our Parish: St Peter's Dublin*, Dublin, 1917

Maxwell, Constantia, *Dublin under the Georges, 1714–1830*, London, 1956, NLI Ir. 94133 h 5

McCready, C.T., *Dublin street names, dated and explained*, Dublin, 1892, NLI Ir. 92941 m 1 (& LO)

Monks, W., *Lusk, a Short History*, NLI Ir. 9141 p 85

Mulhall, Mary, *A History of Lucan*, Lucan, 1991

O'Broin, Liam, *Traditions of Drimnagh*, NLI, JRSAI

O'Driscoll, J., *Cnucha: a history of Castleknock & district*, NLI Ir. 94133 o 9

The O'Rahilly, *Placenames of Dublin*, NLI Ir. 92942 o 2

O'Sullivan, Peter, *Newcastle Lyons, A Parish of the Pale*, Geography Publications, Dublin, 1986

Refaussé, Raymond, *Historic Dublin Guilds*, Dublin, Dublin Public Libraries, 1993

Shepherd, E., *Behind the Scenes: the story of Whitechurch district*, NLI Ir. 94133 s 8

Warburton, John, *History of the City of Dublin*, London, 1818

LOCAL JOURNALS

Dublin Historical Record (Journal of the Old Dublin Society), NLI Ir. 94133 d 23

Dún Laoghaire Genealogical Society Journal

Reportorium Novum, NLI Ir. 27413 r 3

DIRECTORIES

1751	Peter Wilson, *An Alphabetical List of Names and Places of Abode of the Merchants and Traders of the City of Dublin*, NLI
1820	J. Pigot, *Commercial Directory of Ireland*
1824	J. Pigot and Co., *City of Dublin and Hibernian Provincial Directory*, NLI
1834	Pettigrew and Oulton, *Dublin Almanack and General Register of Ireland*, NLI
1844	Alexander Thom, *Irish Almanack and Official Directory*, NLI
1846	Slater, *National Commercial Directory of Ireland*, NLI

1850	Henry Shaw, *New City Pictorial Directory of Dublin city*, NLI Ir. 914133 n 1
1856	Slater, *Royal National Commercial Directory of Ireland*, NLI
1870	Slater, *Directory of Ireland*, NLI
1881	Slater, *Royal National Commercial Directory of Ireland*, NLI
1894	Slater, *Royal Commercial Directory of Ireland*, NLI

GRAVESTONE INSCRIPTIONS

MDDCC = *Memorials of the Dead: Dublin City and County,* Volumes 1–6 (Dublin 1988–93), compiled and edited by Dr Michael T.S. Egan, NAI open shelves

MDSD = *Memorials of the Dead: South Dublin* (Dublin, 1990), compiled and edited by Brian Cantwell, NAI open shelves

Dublin County

Aderrig: MDSD

Baldoyle: Grange, MDDCC, Vol. 4, also IGRS Collection (3 entries), GO

Ballyboghil: MDDCC, Vol. 6

Ballymadun: MDDCC, Vol. 5

Balrothery: Balbriggan, George's Street, C of I, MDDCC, Vol. 6

—— Balrothery town, C of I, MDDCC, Vol. 6

—— Bremore, MDDCC, Vol. 6

—— Balrothery Union, MDDCC, Vol. 6

Balscaddan: Tobertown (Balscaddan Old), MDDCC, Vol. 6

—— Balscaddan New, MDDCC, Vol. 6

Booterstown: Church interior, RC, MDSD

Castleknock: Abbotstown, MDDCC, Vol. 3, also IGRS Collection (29 entries), and GO 622, p. 82

Chapelizod: C of I, IG, Vol. 5, No. 4, 1977

Cloghran: C of I, *History and Description of Santry and Cloghran Parishes,* B.N. Adams, Dublin, 1883

—— Cloghran-hidart, MDDCC, Vol. 4

—— Cloghran, MDDCC, Vol. 4

Clondalkin: Mount St Joseph, MDDCC, Vol. 2

Clonmethan: Glebe (Clonmethan), C of I, MDDCC, Vol. 5

Cruagh: MDDCC, Vol. 4

Crumlin: C of I, IG, Vol. 7, No. 2, 1988 Mount Argus interior, RC, MDSD

Dalkey: Dalkey, MDSD, also IG, Vol. 5 No. 2, 1975

Donabate: Kilcrea, MDSD

Donnybrook: Irishtown (St Mathew's), C of I, MDDCC, Vol. 2

—— Merrion, MDDCC, Vol. 2

—— St Bartholomew's interior, C of I, MDSD

—— Church of the Sacred Heart interior, RC, MDSD

—— Sandymount: Star of the Sea, RC interior, MDSD

Drimnagh: Bluebell, MDDCC, Vol. 3

Garristown: Garristown, C of I, MDDCC, Vol. 5

Grallagh: Grallagh, MDDCC, Vol. 5

Hollywood: Hollywood Great, MDDCC, Vol. 5

—— Damastown, MDDCC, Vol. 5

Kilbride: Kilbride, IG, Vol. 6, No. 3, 1982

—— Kilbride, MDDCC, Vol. 2

Kilgobbin: Kilgobbin, MDDCC, Vol. 2

—— Kilgobbin New, MDDCC, Vol. 3

Kill: Kill of the Grange, IG, Vol. 4, No. 5, 1972

—— *Deansgrange. Memorial Inscriptions of Deansgrange Cemetery, Blackrock, Co. Dublin,* Dun Laoghaire Genealogical Society, 1993, NLI Ir. 9295 d

Killeek: Killeek, MDDCC, Vol. 5

Killiney: Killiney, IG, Vol. 4, No. 6, 1973
—— Killiney, MDSD
—— Ballybrack, RC interior, MDSD
Killossery: MDDCC, Vol. 5
Kilmactalway: MDDCC, Vol. 2
—— IG, Vol. 6, No. 3, 1982
—— Loughtown Lower, MDDCC, Vol. 2
Kilmahuddrick: Kilmahuddrick,
    MDDCC, Vol. 2
Kilsallaghan: Castlefarm (Kilsallaghan),
    C of I, MDDCC, Vol. 4
—— Corrstown (Chapelmidway),
    MDDCC, Vol. 5
Kiltiernan: Kiltiernan, MDDCC, Vol. 2,
    also MDSD
—— Glencullen, RC, MDSD
Lucan: Lucan and Pettycannon
    (St Mary's), RC, MDDCC, Vol. 2,
    also IG, Vol. 5, No. 6, 1976
Monkstown: York Road interior,
    Presbyterian, MDSD
—— St Paul's Glenageary, C of I
    interior, MDSD
—— Northumberland Avenue interior,
    Methodist, MDSD
—— Mariner's Church interior, C of I,
    MDSD
—— Christ Church Kingstown interior,
    C of I, MDSD
—— Monkstown, IG, Vol. 4, Nos 3, 4,
    1970/1
—— Monkstown interior, C of I, MDSD
Mulhuddart: Buzzardstown
    (Mulhuddart), MDDCC, Vol. 4,
    also GO Ms 622, p. 96, GO
Naul: C of I, MDDCC, Vol. 5
Newcastle: Colmanstown, MDDCC, Vol. 3
—— Glebe, C of I, MDDCC, Vol. 2
—— Esker, Old, MDDCC, Vol. 2
—— Newcastle, RC, MDDCC, Vol. 2
Oldconnaught: St James's interior, C of
    I, MDSD
—— Little Bray, RC, IGRS Collection
    (54 inscriptions), GO
—— Little Bray, RC, Memorials of the
    Dead, North-East Wicklow (1)
—— Oldconnaught, MDSD

Palmerstown: Palmerstown (Oldtown),
    IG, Vol. 5, No. 8, 1978
—— Palmerstown (Oldtown),
    MDDCC, Vol. 4
Rathcoole: Rathcoole, C of I, MDDCC,
    Vol. 2
—— Rathcoole, C of I, IG, Vol. 6, No. 4,
    1983
Rathfarnham: Rathfarnham, IG, 1987
—— Rathfarnham interior, RC, MDSD
Rathmichael: Rathmichael interior, C
    of I, MDSD
Saggart: Newtown Upper, MDDCC,
    Vol. 3
—— Saggart New, MDDCC, Vol. 3
Santry: Adams [. . .] *Santry and Cloghran
    [. . .],* History and Description of
    Santry and Cloghran Parishes
St Peter's: Adelaide Road, Presbyterian,
    MDSD
—— Rathmines interior, RC, MDSD
Stillorgan: Stillorgan South, C of I,
    MDSD
Swords: Swords Glebe, C of I, *'In Fond
    Remembrance': Headstone
    Inscriptions No. 2, St Columba's
    Graveyard,* Fingal Heritage Group,
    1990, GO
Swords: Swords, St Colmcille's RC,
    *'Rest in Peace': Fingall Cemeteries,
    No. 1, St Colmcille's, Swords,* Fingal
    Heritage Group, 1990, GO
Tallaght: Templeogue, MDDCC, Vol. 2
—— Tallaght, C of I, IG, Vol. 4, No.1,
    1968
Taney: Dundrum, Churchtown Road,
    Ball, *The Parish of Taney*
—— Dundrum interior, RC, MDSD
Tully: Laughanstown, IGRS Collection
    (50 inscriptions), GO
—— Laughanstown, MDSD
Ward: Ward Lower, MDDCC, Vol. 4
Westpalstown: Westpalstown, MDDCC,
    Vol. 5
Whitechurch: Whitechurch New,
    MDDCC, Vol. 4
—— Whitechurch, MDDCC, Vol. 3,
    also IG, 1990

Dublin City

St Andrew's: St Andrew's Street, C of I, MDSD

—— St Andrew's (Coffin plates), IG, Vol. 5, No. 1, 1974

St Anne's: Dawson Street, C of I, MDSD

St Bride's: Peter Street, French Protestant, MDSD

St Catherine's: Thomas Street, C of I, *Memorial Inscriptions from St Catherine's Church and Graveyard*, S. Murphy, Dublin, 1987

St James: Military Road, *Bully's Acre and Royal Hospital Kilmainham graveyards: history and inscriptions*, S. Murphy, Dublin, 1989, Bully's Acre and Royal Hospital Kilmainham graveyards: history and inscriptions

—— Goldenbridge North, MDDCC, Vol. 1

—— Royal Hospital, *Bully's Acre and Royal Hospital Kilmainham graveyards: history and inscriptions*, S. Murphy, Dublin, 1989, Bully's Acre and Royal Hospital Kilmainham graveyards: history and inscriptions

—— James' Street, C of I, open shelves, National Archives of Ireland

St John's: SS Michael's & John's, RC (coffin plates), IG, Vol. 5, No. 3, 1976

St Michael's: Merchant's Quay interior, RC, MDSD

St Nicholas Without: St Nicholas interior, RC, MDSD

—— St Patrick's Cathedral, A. Leeper, *Historical Handbook to the monuments, inscriptions [. . .] of St Patrick's*, Dublin, 1891

St Paul's: St Paul's, C of I, *JRSAI*, Vol. 104, 1974, also IGRS Collection (6 inscriptions), GO

St Peter's: Harrington Street interior, RC, MDSD

—— Kevin Street Lower, C of I, MDSD

—— Merrion Row, French Protestant, MDDCC, Vol. 2

FERMANAGH

CENSUS RETURNS AND SUBSTITUTES

1612–1613	'Survey of Undertakers Planted in Co. Fermanagh', *Historical Manuscripts Commission Report*, No. 4 (Hastings Mss), 1947, pp. 159–82
1630	Muster Roll of Ulster, Armagh Co. Library and PRONI D.1759/3C/1, T/934, NLI Pos. 206
1631	Muster Roll, *History of Enniskillen*
1659	Pender's 'Census'
1660	Poll Tax Returns, PRONI MIC/15A/80
1661	Books of Survey and Distribution, PRONI T.370/B & D.1854/1/20
1662	Subsidy roll, Enniskillen town, NLI Ms 9583, also PRONI T.808/15068
1665–6	Hearth Money Roll, NLI Ms 9583 and PRONI T.808/15066, Lurg barony, *Clogher Record*, 1957
1747	Poll Book (votes cast), PRONI T.808/15063
1766	Boho, Derryvullen, Devenish, Kinawley, Rossory, NAI m. 2476(d)
1770	Freeholders, NLI Ms 787 8, also GO 443
1785	Male Protestants aged over 17 — Trory, Magheracloone, Errigal Trough, LDS film 258517
1788	Poll Book (votes cast), PRONI T.808/15075, T.543, T.1385, LDS films 100181, 1279356

1794–99	Militia Pay Lists and Muster Rolls, PRONI T.1115/5A–C
1796	Spinning-Wheel Premium List
1796–1802	Freeholders, PRONI D.1096/90
1797	Yeomanry Muster Rolls, PRONI T.1021/3
1821	Parishes of Derryvullan and Aghalurcher (part only), NAI & PRONI
1823–38	Tithe Books
1832	Enniskillen registered voters, *Parliamentary Papers* 1837, *Reports from Committees*, Vol. 13 (2), pp. 554 7
1837	Freeholders, *Parliamentary Papers 1837, Reports from Committees*, Vol. 11 (1), pp. (39) 7 21
1841	Certified copies of census returns for use in claims for old age pensions, NAI & PRONI, LDS film 258357
1842	Voters, NAI 1842/ii4
1845	Workhouse records Irvinestown (1845–1918) and Enniskillen (1845–1913), PRONI, also LDS films 259187–90 and 25914–53 respectively
1851	Clonee townland only, NAI CEN 1851/13/1
1851–2	Galloon parish, PRONI D.2098
1861	Boho parish, Protestants only, *c.*1861, NAI T.3723
1862	Griffith's Valuation
1874	Census of Devenish C of I parish, Local custody
1901	Census, *Fermanagh: 1901 census index*, Largy Books, Alberta, 1993
1911	Census

LOCAL HISTORY

Anonymous, 'Provisional list of pre-1900 School Registers in the Public Record Office of Northern Ireland', UHGGN, 9, pp. 60–71

Belmore, Earl of, *Parliamentary Memoirs of Fermanagh and Tyrone 1613 1885*, Dublin, 1887

Bradshaw, W.H., *Enniskillen Long Ago: an Historic Sketch of the Parish . . .* , 1878

Duffy, J. (ed.) *A Clogher Record Album: a diocesan history*, NLI Ir. 94114 c 3

Dundas, W.H., *Enniskillen parish and town*, Dundalk, 1913, NLI Ir. 94118 d 2

Graham, Rev. John, *Derriana, a History of the Siege of Derry and the Defence of Enniskillen in 1688 and 1689, with Biographical Notes*, 1823, NLI J94112

King, Sir Charles (ed.) *Henry's 'Upper Lough Erne in 1739'*, Dublin, 1892

MacKenna, J.E., *Devenish, its history, antiquities and traditions*, 1897

Maguire, Thomas, *Fermanagh: its Native Chiefs and Clans*, S.D. Montgomery, 1954

Martin, Samuel, *Historical gleanings from Co. Derry, and some from Co. Fermanagh*, Dublin, 1955, NLI Ir. 94112 m 2

O'Connell, Philip, *The Diocese of Kilmore: its History and Antiquities*, Dublin, 1937

Shearman, H., *Ulster*, London, 1949, NLI Ir. 91422 s 3

Steele, W.B., *The parish of Devenish*, 1937

Trimble, W.C., *The history of Enniskillen*, Enniskillen, 1921, NLI Ir. 94118 t 1

Witherow, Thomas, *Derry and Enniskillen, in the year 1689*, 1873, 1885

LOCAL JOURNALS

Clogher Record, NLI Ir. 94114 c 2
North Irish Roots (Journal of the North of Ireland Family History Society)
Irish Family Links, NLI Ir. 9292 f 19

DIRECTORIES

1824	J. Pigot and Co., *City of Dublin and Hibernian Provincial Directory,* NLI
1839	*Directory of the Towns of Sligo, Enniskillen, Ballyshannon, Donegal [. . .]*
1846	Slater, *National Commercial Directory of Ireland,* NLI
1852	James A. Henderson, *Belfast and Province of Ulster Directory,* issued also in 1854, 1856, 1858, 1861, 1863, 1865, 1868, 1870, 1877, 1880, 1884, 1887, 1890, 1894, 1900
1856	Slater, *Royal National Commercial Directory of Ireland,* NLI
1870	Slater, *Directory of Ireland,* NLI
1881	Slater, *Royal National Commercial Directory of Ireland,* NLI
1887	*Derry Almanac and Directory* (Enniskillen)
1894	Slater, *Royal Commercial Directory of Ireland,* NLI

GRAVESTONE INSCRIPTIONS

Heritage World has transcripts for 46 graveyards in Fermanagh. Contact details will be found in Chapter 14. Published or publicly available transcripts are given below, ordered by civil parish.

Aghavea: Aghavea, C of I, *Clogher Record,* Vol. 4, Nos 1, 2, 1960/1
Cleenish: Templenaffrin, *Clogher Record,* Vol. 2, No. 1, 1957
Clones: Rosslea, St Tierney's, RC, *Clogher Record,* 1982–84
Derryvullan: Monea, C of I, Steele, W.B., *The parish of Devenish,* 1937
Devenish: St Molaise's and Devenish Abbey, MacKenna, J.E, *Devenish, its history, antiquities and traditions,* 1897
Drummully: *Clogher Record,* Vol. 1, No. 2, 1954
Enniskillen: St Macartin's, C of I, Dundas, W.H., *Enniskillen parish and town,* Dundalk, 1913
Galloon: Galloon, *Clogher Record,* Vol. 10, No. 2, 1980
Galloon: Donagh, *Clogher Record,* Vol. 1, No. 3, 1955

ESTATE RECORDS

Balfour family: Tenants' list, 1735, NLI Mss 10259, 10305, major tenants only, Rentals, 1735–89, NLI Ms 10259, major tenants only, Rentals, 1818–22, NLI Ms 10260, all tenants, covering areas in the civil parishes of Aghalurcher and Kinawley
Commissioners of Education: Rentals, 1832–51, NLI Ms 17956, all tenants, covering areas in the civil parishes of Cleenish and Killesher
Hassard family: Rentals, 1810–20, NAI M3136, major tenants only, covering areas in the civil parish of Enniskillen

J.C. Broomfield: Rentals, 1810–20, NAI M.3563, all tenants, covering areas in the civil parish of Belleek

GALWAY

CENSUS RETURNS AND SUBSTITUTES

1640	Irish Papist Proprietors, Galway town, *History of the town and county of Galway to 1820*, Hardiman, Galway, 1958
1641–1703	Book of Survey and Distribution, NLI Ms 969
1657	English Protestant Proprietors, Galway town, *History of the town and county of Galway to 1820*, Galway, 1958
1727	A Galway election list, *JGAHS*, 1976
1749	Ahascra, Athleague, Ballynakill, Drimatemple, Dunamon, Kilbegnet, Killian, Killosolan, NAI MFS 6, LDS film 101781
1791	Survey of Loughrea town (occupiers), *JGAHS*, Vol. 24, No. 3
1794	Catholic Freemen of Galway town, *JGAHS*, Vol. 9, No. 1
1798	Convicted Rebels from Galway, *JGAHS*, Vol. 23, No. 1
1798	Persons who suffered losses in the 1798 rebellion, propertied classes only, NLI I 94107
1806–1810	Catholic householders, Killalaghten; In the Catholic parish registers of Cappataggle, NLI Pos. 2431
1821	Parishes of Aran, Athenry, Kilcomeen, Kiltallagh, Killimore, Kilconickny, Kilreekill. NAI CEN 1821/18–25, LDS film 597734, also Loughrea (fragments), GO Ms 622, pp. 53 ff
1823–38	Tithe Books
1827	Protestants in Aughrim parish, NA M 5359
1834	List of parishioners, Kinvara and Killina, NL Pos. 2442, also GFHSW
1837	Valuation of towns returning MPs (occupants and property values): Galway. *Parliamentary Papers 1837, Reports from Committees*, Vol. II (i), Appendix G
1841	Fragments, for Loughrea town, NAI M 150(2), also GO 622, pp. 53 ff
1848–1852	Ahascra assisted passages, *AH*, Vol. 22, 1960
1850–1859	Emigrants to Australia and the US from the parish of Kilchreest, with some from the parishes of Killogilleen, Killinane, Killora, Kilthomas and Isertkelly, GO Ms 622
1851	Fragments, for Loughrea town, NAI M 150
1855	Griffith's Valuation
1901	Census
1911	Census

LOCAL HISTORY

Anonymous, 'The Ethnography of the Aran Islands', PRIA, 3rd Ser., Vol. 2, 1891–3, 827–9

Anonymous, 'The Ethnography of Carna and Mweenish in the Parish of Moyruss', PRIA, 3rd Ser., Vol. 6, 1900–2, 503–34

Anonymous, *Portrait of a Parish: Ballynakill, Connemara*, Irish Countrywomen's Association

Berry, J.F., *The Story of St Nicholas' Church*, Galway, 1912, NLI Ir. 7265 b 5

Cronin, Denis, *A Galway gentleman in the age of improvement: Robert French of Monivea, 1716–76*, Irish Academic Press, Blackrock, Co. Dublin, 1995, NLI Ir. 94124 c 12

D'Alton, E., *History of the Archdiocese of Tuam*, Dublin, 1928, NLI Ir. 27412 d 1

Dwyer, Philip, *The Diocese of Killaloe, from the Reformation to the Close of the Eighteenth Century*, Dublin, 1878

Egan, Patrick K., *The parish of Ballinasloe, its history from the earliest times to the present day*, Dublin, 1960

Ellis, Éilis, *Emigrants from Ireland 1847–52*, Baltimore, GPC, 1977, NLI Ir. 325 e 5

Fahey, J., *The History and Antiquities of the Diocese of Kilmacduagh*, Dublin, 1893

Goaley, M., *History of Annaghdown*, NLI Ir. 274 p 31

Hardiman, James, *History of the town and county of Galway . . . to 1820*, Galway, 1958

Hayes McCoy, G.A., *Index to 'The Compossicion Booke of Connoght, 1585'*, Irish Manuscripts Commission, Dublin, 1945

Kavanagh, M., *A Bibliography of the Co. Galway*, NLI Ir. RR 01524

Knox, H.T., *Notes on the Early History of the Dioceses of Tuam, Killala and Achonry*, Dublin, 1904

MacLochlainn, T., *The Parish of Laurencetown & Kiltormer*, 1981, NLI Ir. 94124 m 5

MacLochlainn, T., *A Historical Survey of the Parish of Ahascra, Caltra & Castleblakeney*, 1979, NLI Ir. 9141 p 79

MacLochlainn, T., *The Parish of Aughrim & Kilconnell*, 1980, NLI Ir. 94124 m 4

MacLochlainn, T., *A Short history of the Parish of Killure, Fohenagh and Kilgerrill*, Galway, 1975

Naughton, M., *The History of St Francis' Parish, Galway*, 1984, NLI Ir. 27412 n 1

O'Neill, T.P., *The Tribes & Other Galway Families, 1484–1984*, NLI Ir. 927, p 5

O'Sullivan, M.D., *Old Galway: the history of a Norman colony in Ireland*

Regan, D., *Abbeyknockmoy, a time to remember*, Abbeyknockmoy Community Council, Co. Galway, 1996, NLI Ir. 94124 a 4

Regan, Carol, *Moylough, a people's heritage*, Moylough Community Council, Moylough, 1993, NLI Ir. 94124 p 5(4)

Rynne, Etienne, *Athenry: a medieval Irish town*, Athenry Historical Society, Athenry, 1992, NLI Ir. 941 p 132(1)

White, Rev. P., *History of Clare and the Dalcassian Clans of Tipperary, Limerick and Galway*, Dublin, 1893

LOCAL JOURNALS

Galway Roots: Journal of the Galway Family History Society West
Journal of the Galway Archaeological and Historical Society, NLI Ir. 794105 g 1

DIRECTORIES

1820	J. Pigot, *Commercial Directory of Ireland*
1824	J. Pigot and Co., *City of Dublin and Hibernian Provincial Directory*, NLI
1846	Slater, *National Commercial Directory of Ireland*, NLI
1856	Slater, *Royal National Commercial Directory of Ireland*, NLI

1870   Slater, *Directory of Ireland*, NLI
1881   Slater, *Royal National Commercial Directory of Ireland*, NLI
1894   Slater, *Royal Commercial Directory of Ireland*, NLI

GRAVESTONE INSCRIPTIONS

Galway Family History Society West Ltd has transcripts for 61 graveyards mainly in the west of the county. Contact details will be found in Chapter 14. Published or publicly available transcripts are given below.

Addergoole: Carrowntomush: IGRS Collection: GO
Claregalway: Claregalway (Abbey?), IGRS Collection (172 inscriptions), GO
Drumacoo: Drumacoo, IGRS Collection, GO
Kilmacduagh: Lisnagyreeny, *IA*, NLI Ir. 9205 i 3, Vol. VII, No.1, 1975
St Nicholas: St Nicholas' Church, C of I, Higgins, Jim, *Monuments of St Nicholas Collegiate Church [. . .]*, Galway, Rock Crow's Press, 1992, NLI Ir. 9295 m 2
St Nicholas: Galway, Forthill Road, RC, *Forthill graveyard*, Galway, GFHSW, 1992, NLI Ir. 941 p 118 (4)

ESTATE RECORDS

Bellew estate wages book, 1679–1775, NLI Ms 9200
Col John Browne: NLI Pos. 940, Account of the sales of the estates of Col. John Browne in Cos Galway and Mayo, compiled in 1778, giving names of major tenants and purchasers 1698–1704, and those occupying the estates in 1778, covering townlands in the civil parishes of Ballynakill, Cong, Kilcummin, Killannin, Omey, Ross.
Lord Clanmorris: NLI Ms 3279, Estate rental, 1833, all tenants, covering townlands in the civil parish of Claregalway
Dillon, Barons Clonbrock: NLI Ms 19501, tenants' ledger 1801–6, indexed; NLI Mss 19585–19608 (24 vols), rentals and accounts, 1827–1840, all tenants; NLI Mss 22008, 22009, maps of the Co. Galway estates, with full valuation of all tenants' holdings; NLI Mss 19609–19616, Rentals and accounts, 1840–44, all tenants, covering townlands in the civil parishes of Ahascragh, Aughrim, Fohanagh, Kilcoona, Killaan, Killallaghtan, Killosolan, Kilteskil.
Francis Blake Knox: NLI Ms 3077, Rental, 1845–66, covering townlands in the civil parishes of Annaghdown, Kilmacduagh, Kilmoylan.
French family: NLI Ms 4920, rent ledger, Monivea estate, 1767–77, major tenants only, NLI Ms 4929, estate accounts and wages book, 1811/12, all tenants, with index, NLI Ms 4930, accounts and wages book, 1830–33, covering townlands in the civil parishes of Abbeyknockmoy, Athenry, Cargin, Claregalway, Monivea, Moylough, Oranmore.
Lieut Edward Hodson: NLI Ms 2356, Rent rolls and tenants' accounts, 1797–1824, indexed, covering townlands in the civil parish of Kiltormer.
Richard St George, Mansergh St George: NLI Pos. 5483 (a) Rental of Headford town (all tenants), (b) estate rentals (major tenants only), both 1775, covering townlands in the civil parishes of Cargin, Donaghpatrick, Kilcoona, Kilkilvery, Killursa

George Shee: NA M3105–3120, Yearly rentals of the estate in and around Dunmore, 1837–1859, all tenants, covering townlands in the civil parishes of Addergoole, Boyounagh, Clonbern, Dunmore.

Trench: NLI Ms 2577, Estate rental, 1840–50, covering townlands in the civil parishes of Ballymacaward, Kilbeacanty, Killaan, Killimordaly.

Theobold Wolfe: NLI Ms 3876, Estate maps with names of major tenants, 1760, indexed, covering townlands in the civil parishes of Kilmallinoge and Tiranascragh.

(No Landlord Given): NLI 21 g 76 (14) and 21 g 76 (26), Maps of Cloonfane and Carogher townlands in Dunmore parish, with tenants' names, mid-nineteenth century.

(No Landlord Given): NLI Ms 4633, Survey of occupiers, townlands of Ballinasoora, Streamsfort, Fortlands, Woodlands, parish of Killimordaly, 1851

(No Landlord Given): NLI Mss 2277–2280, Rentals, 1854–85, townlands of Ballyargadaun, Leitrim More, Kylebrack, Knockash in the civil parishes of Leitrim and Kilteskil.

KERRY

Census Returns and Substitutes

1586	Survey of the estates of the Earl of Desmond recording leaseholders, NAI M.5037
1641	Book of Survey and Distribution, NLI Ms 970
1654	Civil Survey, Vol. IV, Dysert, Killury, Rathroe, *Civil Survey*, Vol. IV (NLI I 6551 Dublin)
1659	Pender's 'Census'
1799	Petition of 300 prominent Catholics of Co. Kerry, *The Dublin Evening Post*, June 9, 1799
1821	Some extracts for Tralee and Annagh, NAI Thrift Abstracts
1821	Parish of Kilcummin, Royal Irish Academy, McSwiney papers, parcel f, No. 3, LDS film 596419
1823–38	Tithe Books, NAI
1834–1835	Householders, parishes of Dunquin, Dunurlin, Ferriter, Killemlagh, Kilmalkedar, Kilquane, Marhin, Prior, *JKAHS*, 1974–5
1835	Tralee Voters, *JKAHS*, No. 19, 1986
1847–1851	Assisted passages Castlemaine estate, Kiltallagh parish, *AH*, Vol. 22, 1960
1901	Census, King's, *County Kerry, Past and Present* (1931) appears to have an index to the entire county
1911	Census

Local History

Anonymous, *A span across time: Finuge, a folk history*, Finuge Heritage Society
Allman, J., *Causeway, location, lore and legend*, Naas, 1983
Barrington, T.J., *Discovering Kerry*, Dublin, 1976
Barr, V.A., *Houses of Co. Kerry*, Clare, Ballinakella Press, 1994

Brady, W. Maziere, *The McGellycuddy Papers*, London, 1867

Cusack, Mary F., *History of the kingdom of Kerry*, London, 1871

Denny, H.A., *A Handbook of Co. Kerry Family History etc.*, 1923, NLI Ir. 9291 d 1

Donovan, T.M., *A Popular History of East Kerry*, 1931

Hickson, Mary, *Selections from Old Kerry Records, Historical and Genealogical*, London, 1872–4

Hore, H.J., *The Social State of the Southern and Eastern Counties of Ireland in the Sixteenth Century*, 1870

Keane, L., *Knocknagoshel: then and now*, Kerry County Library, 1985

King, Jeremiah, *County Kerry, Past and Present*, 1931, NLI I 94146

Lansdowne, H., *Glanarought and the Petty Fitzmaurices*, 1937, NLI Ir. 94146 l 1

MacLysaght, Edward, *The Kenmare Manuscripts*, Irish Manuscripts Commission, Dublin, 1947

MacSwiney, *Unpublished manuscripts*

McMoran, R., *Tralee, a short history and guide to Tralee and environs*, 1980

Mould, D.C. Pochin, *Valentia: portrait of an island*, Dublin, 1978

O'Connor, T., *Ardfert in times past*, Foilseachain Breanainn, Ardfert, 1990, NLI Ir. 94146 oo 11

Reedy, Rev. Donal A., *The Diocese of Kerry*, Killarney

Smith, Charles, *The Ancient and Present State of the County of Kerry*, Dublin, 1756

Windele, J., *Unpublished manuscripts*, NLI Pos. 5479

LOCAL JOURNALS

Journal of the Kerry Archaeological & Historical Society, NLI Ir. 794105 k 1

Kenmare Literary and Historical Society Journal

DIRECTORIES

1824	J. Pigot and Co., *City of Dublin and Hibernian Provincial Directory*, NLI
1846	Slater, *National Commercial Directory of Ireland*, NLI
1856	Slater, *Royal National Commercial Directory of Ireland*, NLI
1870	Slater, *Directory of Ireland*, NLI
1881	Slater, *Royal National Commercial Directory of Ireland*, NLI
1886	Francis Guy, *Postal Directory of Munster*, NLI Ir. 91414 g 8
1893	Francis Guy, *Directory of Munster*, NLI Ir. 91414 g 8
1894	Slater, *Royal Commercial Directory of Ireland*, NLI

GRAVESTONE INSCRIPTIONS

The situation with transcripts compiled by the Kerry Genealogical Society and Finuge Heritage Society is unclear. They may be available through Killarney Library, Rock Road, Killarney.

Aghadoe: Parkavonear (Fossa?), O'K, Vol. 6

Aghadoe: Knoppoge (Aghadoe?), C of I, O'K, Vol. 6

Aghavallen: Rusheen, C of I, Kerry Genealogical Society

Aglish: C of I, O'K, Vol. 6
Ardfert: Ardfert town, C of I, O'K, Vol. 8
Ballincuslane: Cordal East, O'K, Vol. 6
Ballincuslane: Kilmurry, O'K, Vol. 6
Ballymacelligott: C of I, O'K, Vol. 8
—— Ballymacelligot, O'K, Vol. 11
Ballynahaglish: Spa, O'K, Vol. 11
Brosna: O'K, Vol. 6
Caher: Caherciveen (Killevanoge), IGRS Collection, Go
Caher: Caherciveen, Marian Place, IGRS Collection, GO, also Finuge Heritage
    Society
Castleisland: Church Lane, C of I, O'K, Vol. 6
—— Kilbannivane, O'K, Vol. 6
—— Meenbannivane (Dysert?), O'K, Vol. 6
Clogherbrien: Clogherbrien, O'K, Vol. 8
Currans: Ardcrone, O'K, Vol. 6
Dingle: Raheenyhooig, IGRS Collection, GO
Duagh: Islandboy (Duagh?), O'K, Vol. 11
Dysert: Kilsarkan East, O'K, Vol. 6
Finuge: Finuge Heritage Society, also Kerry Genealogical Society
Kilcummin: Glebe, O'K, Vol. 6
—— Gneevegullia, O'K, Vol. 6
Kilcummin: Kilquane, O'K, Vol. 6
Killarney: Muckross, O'K, Vol. 6
—— Killarney (new), O'K, Vol. 6
Killeentierna: C of I, O'K, Vol. 6
Killehenny: (Ballybunion?), O'K, Vol. 11
Killorglin: O'K, Vol. 11
—— Dromavally (Killorglin?), O'K, Vol. 8
Kilnanare: Kilnanare, O'K, Vol. 6
Listowel: Listowel, O'K, Vol. 11
Molahiffe: Castlefarm (Molahiff?), O'K, Vol. 6
Murher: Murher, Kerry Genealogical Society
Nohaval: Ballyregan, O'K, Vol. 8
—— Nohaval, O'K, Vol. 11
O'Brennan: O'K, Vol. 11
—— Crag, O'K, Vol. 8
Tralee: Tralee, Nelson Street, C of I, O'K, Vol. 8
—— Tralee, Brewery Road, O'K, Vol. 8
—— Tralee, Castle Street Lower, C of I, O'K, Vol. 8

ESTATE RECORDS

Browne, Earls of Kenmare: assorted rentals, maps and estate accounts for areas
    around Kenmare and in the barony of Dunkerron, from 1620 to 1864 in
    McLysaght, E., The **Kenmare** Manuscripts, Dublin, 1942, see also O'Kief
    Coshe Nang etc., Vols 6, 7, 9.
The **Orpen** estates: G. Lyne, 'Land Tenure in Tuosist and Kenmare' [1696–1775],
    Kerry Arch. & Hist. Soc. Jnl, 1976/78/79

Thomas **Sandes**: Rental of the estate 1792–1828, covering parts of the parishes of Aghavallin, Kilnaughtin, Murher, NL Ms 1792

KILDARE

CENSUS RETURNS AND SUBSTITUTES

1641	Book of Survey and Distribution, also NLI Ms 971, *JKAS*, Vol. X, 1922–8
1654	Civil Survey, Vol. VIII, *Civil Survey*, Vol. VIII
1659	Pender's 'Census'
1766	Catholic householders in Kilrush, *Collections relating to Kildare and Leighlin*, Rev. M. Comerford, 1883
1766	Ballycommon, parish of Clonaghlis, *JKAS*, 7 (4), 1913, 274–6
1798	Persons who suffered losses in the 1798 rebellion, propertied classes only, NLI I 94107
1823–38	Tithe Books
1831	Kilcullen, Protestant returns only, NAI, also GO Ms 622, pp. 53 ff., NAI M 150(2)
1837	Voters, NLI Ms 1398
1840	Castledermot & Moone, NLI Pos. 3511
1843	Voters, NAI 1843/53
1 851	Griffith's Valuation
1901	Census
1911	Census

LOCAL HISTORY

Anonymous, *Some Authorities for Kildare County History*, *JKAS*, No. 10, 1922 8, 155 60

Anonymous, Journal of Michael Carey, Athy, Co. Kildare (manuscipt), NLI Ms 25299 (Letters, leases, social commentary 1840–59)

Andrews, J.H., *Irish Historic Towns Atlas: Kildare*, RIA, Dublin, 1989

Brennan, M., *Schools of Kildare and Leighlin, 1775–1835*, NLI Ir. 37094135 b 4

Carville, Geraldine, *Monasterevin, Valley of Roses*, Moore Abbey, 1989

Comerford, Rev. M., *Collections relating to Kildare and Leighlin*, 1883

Costello, Con, *Kildare: Saints, Soldiers & Horses*, Naas, 1991

Costello, Con, *Looking Back, Aspects of History, Co. Kildare*, Naas, 1988

Coyle, James, *The Antiquities of Leighlin*

Doohan, Tony, *A History of Celbridge*, n.d.

Dunlop, Robert, *Waters under the Bridge*, Brannockstown, 1988, NLI Ir. 9292 p 29(3)

Hore, H.J., *The Social State of the Southern and Eastern Counties of Ireland in the Sixteenth Century*, 1870

Kavanagh, M., *A Bibliography of the History of the County Kindare in Printed Books*, Newbridge, Kildare Co. Library, 1976

Leadbeater, Mary, *The Annals of Ballitore*, London, 1862, NLI Ir. 92 1 8

Mac Suibhne, Peadar, *Rathangan*, 1975

Naas Local History Group, *Nas na Riogh: . . . an illustrated history of Naas*, Naas, 1990

Nelson, Gerald, *A History of Leixlip*, Kildare Co. Library, 1990

Ó Conchubhair, Seamus, *A History of Kilcock and Newtown*, 1987

Ó Muineog, Micheal, *Kilcock GAA, A History*, 1989

Paterson, J. (ed.), *Diocese of Meath and Kildare: an historical guide*, 1981, NLI Ir. 941 p 75

Raymond, B., *The Story of Kilkenny, Kildare, Offaly and Leix*, 1931, NLI I 9141 p 1

Reid, J.N.S., *Church of St Michael & All Angels*, Clane, 1983

LOCAL JOURNALS

Journal of the Kildare Archaeological Society, NLI Ir. 794106 k 2

Reportorium Novum, NLI Ir. 27413 r 3

DIRECTORIES

1788	Richard Lucas, *General Directory of the Kingdom of Ireland*, NLI Pos. 3729
1824	J. Pigot and Co., *City of Dublin and Hibernian Provincial Directory*, NLI
1846	Slater, *National Commercial Directory of Ireland*, NLI
1856	Slater, *Royal National Commercial Directory of Ireland*, NLI
1870	Slater, *Directory of Ireland*, NLI
1881	Slater, *Royal National Commercial Directory of Ireland*, NLI
1894	Slater, *Royal Commercial Directory of Ireland*, NLI

GRAVESTONE INSCRIPTIONS

Ardkill: Ballyshannon, GO Ms 622, p. 108, GO

Ballaghmoon: Ballaghmoon, KCL

Ballynafagh: Ballynafagh, C of I, KCL

Belan: Belan, KCL

Castledermot: Knockbane, IGRS Collection, GO

—— Castledermot town, C of I, KCL, also C of I, IGRS Collection, GO

—— Ballyhade, KCL

—— St James, KCL

—— Franciscan Friary, KCL

—— Prumplestown, KCL

Clane: Clane town, C of I, KCL

Donadea: Donadea South, C of I, KCL

Dunmanoge: KCL

Dunmanoge: Maganey Upper, RC, GO Ms 622, p. 108, GO

—— Castleroe Rath, KCL

—— Levistown, KCL

Dunmurraghill: Dunmurraghill, KCL

Fontstown: Fontstown Lower, GO Ms 622, p. 148/9, GO

Graney: Knockpatrick, KCL

Harristown: Harristown Lower, GO Ms 622, 126/7, GO

Kilcock: Kilcock, Church Lane, C of I, KCL

Kilcullen: Old Kilcullen, *Co. Carlow Tombstone Inscriptions*, Vol. 3, NLI Ir. 9295 c 3
—— Kineagh, KCL
Kildare: Church and Friary Lane, C of I, GO
Kilkea: Kilkea Lower, KCL
Killelan: Killelan, KCL
—— Killeen Cormac, KCL, also IGRS Collection, GO
Kilteel: JKAS, 1981/2, NLI Ir. 794106 k 2
Moone: KCL
—— Moone Abbey, KCL
Narraghmore: Moyleabbey, KCL
—— Mullamast, KCL
St Michael's: Athy, GO Ms. 622, 89, GO
Straffan: Barberstown, JKAS, 1977/8
Taghadoe: C of I, KCL
Tankardstown: Levistown, KCL
Timahoe: Timahoe East, KCL
Timolin: C of I, IGRS Collection, GO
—— Ballitore, Quaker, KCL
—— Timolin, C of I, KCL

KILKENNY

CENSUS RETURNS AND SUBSTITUTES

1641	Book of Survey and Distribution, NLI Ms 975
1650–1800	Dunnamaggan, *Old Kilkenny Review*, 1992, 958
1654	Civil Survey, Vol. VI, Kilkenny City, *Civil Survey*, Vol. VI (NLI I 6551 Dublin)
1659	Pender's 'Census'
1664	Hearth Money Rolls, parishes of Agherney, Aghavillar, Bellaghtobin, Belline, Burnchurch, Callan, Castleinch, Clone, Coolaghmore, Coolcashin, Danganmore, Derrinahinch, Dunkitt, Earlstown, Eyverk, Fartagh, Inishnagg & Stonecarthy, Jerpoint, Kells, Kilbeacon & Killahy, Kilcolm, Kilferagh, Kilkredy, Killamery, Killaloe, Killree, Kilmoganny, Kiltackaholme, Knocktopher & Kilkerchill, Muckalee & Lismatigue, Outrath, Ratbach, Rathpatrick, Tullaghanbrogue, Tullaghmaine, Urlingford, IG, 1974–5
1684–1769	Registers of Kilkenny College, NLI Pos. 4545
1702	Partial parishioners lists, St Mary's and St Canice's parishes, Kilkenny city, NAI List 63 (Priim 8, 11, 15, 16)
1715	Protestant males between 16 and 60 in St John's parish, Kilkenny city, NAI
1750–1844	Inistiogue emigrants in Newfoundland, *Kilkenny History and Society*, Dublin, Geography Publications, 1990
1766	Portnascully, Catholic householders, GO 683–4, also LDS film 100158
1775	Landowners, GO 443
1785–1879	Kilkenny city deeds, *Old Kilkenny Review*, Vol. 2, No. 4

1797	Chief Catholic inhabitants, Parishes of Graiguenamanagh and Knocktopher, IA, 1978
1809–1819	Freeholders, NLI Ms 14181
1811–1858	Registers & Accounts of St Kieran's College, NLI Pos. 973
1821	Extracts only for Pollrone, IA 1976, 1977, Extracts from the 1821 census, parishes of Aglish, Clonmore, Fiddown, Kilmacow, Polerone, Rathkyran, Whitechurch, GO 684 (Walsh-Kelly notebooks), also IG Vol. 5, 1978
1823–38	Tithe Books.
1831	Extracts from the 1831 census, parishes of Aglish, Clonmore, Kilmacow, Polerone, Rathkyran, Tybroghney, GO 684 (Walsh-Kelly notebooks)
1841	Townlands of Aglish and Portnahully only, *IA*, 1977
1841	Extracts from the 1841 census, parishes of Aglish and Rathkyran, GO 684 (Walsh-Kelly notebooks)
1842	Voters, NAI 1842/79
1849–1850	Griffith's Valuation, NLI
1851	Parish of Aglish, IA, 1977, also GO 684 (Walsh-Kelly notebooks)
1901	Census
1911	Census

LOCAL HISTORY

Anonymous, Kilkenny Corporation: Catalogue of Deeds, NLI Ir. 94139 k 2

Alsworth, W.J., *History of Thomastown and District*, 1953, NLI JP, 1996

Brennan, M., *Schools of Kildare and Leighlin, 1775–1835*, NLI Ir. 37094135 b 4

Brennan, T.A., *A History of the Brennans of Idaugh in Co. Kilkenny*, New York, 1979, NLI Ir. 9292 b 45

Burtchaell, G., *MPs for the County and City of Kilkenny 1295–1888*, Dublin, 1888

Carrigan, Rev. William, *The History and Antiquities of the Diocese of Ossory*, Dublin, 1905

Coleman, James, *Bibliography of the counties Carlow, Kilkenny and Wexford*, WSIAHSJ, II, 1907, NLI 794105 w 1

Coyle, James, *The Antiquities of Leighlin*

Egan, P.M., *Illustrated Guide to the City & County of Kilkenny*, NLI Ir. 914139 e 2

Fitzmaurice, S.A., *Castleharris*, NLI, *Old Kilkenny Review*, 1979

Healy, William, *History & antiquities of Kilkenny county & city*, Kilkenny, 1893, NLI Ir. 94139 h 1

Hogan, John, *Kilkenny, the Ancient City of Ossory*, Kilkenny, 1884

Hore, H.J., *The Social State of the Southern and Eastern Counties of Ireland in the Sixteenth Century*, 1870

Kenealy, M., *The Parish of Aharney and the Marum Family*, NLI, *Old Kilkenny Review*, 1976, Ir. 94139 o 3

Nolan, W., *Fassidinin: Land, Settlement and Society in South East Ireland, 1600–1850*, 1979, NLI Ir. 94139 n 1

O'Kelly, O., *The Placenames of the Co. Kilkenny*, 1985, Ir. 92942 o 15

Phelan, M., *Callan Doctors*, NLI, *Old Kilkenny Review*, 1980, Ir. 94139 o 3

Prim, J.G.A., 'Documents connected with the city of Kilkenny militia in the 17th and 18th centuries', *Kilkenny & SE Ire. Arch. Soc. Jnl*, 1854 5, 231 74

Prim, J.G.A., *The History (. . .) of St Canice, Kilkenny*, 1857
Raymond, B., *The Story of Kilkenny, Kildare, Offaly and Leix*, 1931, NLI I 9141 p 1
Silverman, M., *In the Vally of the Nore: Social History of Thomastown, Co. Kilkenny 1843–1983*, Dublin, Geography Publications, 1986
Whelan, Kevin, *Kilkenny History and Society*, Geography Publications, Dublin, 1990

LOCAL JOURNALS

Deenside
Journal of the Butler Society, NLI Ir. 9292 b 28
Kilkenny & South-East of Ireland Archaeological Society Journal, NLI J 7914 (to 1890), Ir. 794105 r 1 (after 1890)
Old Kilkenny Review, NLI Ir. 94139 o 3
Transactions of the Ossory Archaeological Society, NLI Ir. 794105 0 1

DIRECTORIES

1788	Richard Lucas, *General Directory of the Kingdom of Ireland*, NLI Pos. 3729
1820	J. Pigot, *Commercial Directory of Ireland*
1824	J. Pigot and Co., *City of Dublin and Hibernian Provincial Directory*, NLI
1839	T. Shearman, *New Commercial Directory for the cities of Waterford and Kilkenny, Towns of Clonmel, Carrick-on-Suir, New Ross and Carlow*
1846	Slater, *National Commercial Directory of Ireland*, NLI
1856	Slater, *Royal National Commercial Directory of Ireland*, NLI
1870	Slater, *Directory of Ireland*, NLI
1881	Slater, *Royal National Commercial Directory of Ireland*, NLI
1884	George Henry Bassett, *Kilkenny City and County Guide and Directory*
1885	George Henry Bassett, *Wexford County Guide and Directory*
1894	Slater, *Royal Commercial Directory of Ireland*, NLI

GRAVESTONE INSCRIPTIONS

Ballygurrim: Jamestown, IGRS Collection (16), GO
Ballytarsney: IGRS Collection (24), GO
Blackrath: Maddockstown, IGRS Collection (60), GO
Castlecomer: Dysert, IGRS Collection (13), GO
Castleinch or Inchyolaghan: IGRS Collection (30), GO
Clara: Churchclara, IGRS Collection (56), GO
Clashacrow: Clashacrow, IGRS Collection (57), GO
Clonmore: IGRS Collection (30), GO
Danesfort: GO Ms 622, p. 147, GO
—— Annamult, IGRS Collection (7), GO
Dunkitt: IGRS Collection (113), GO
—— Killaspy, IGRS Collection (3), GO
Dunmore: Dunmore, C of I, IGRS Collection (33), GO
Fiddown: Fiddown, C of I, GO Ms 622, p. 150

Freshford: Freshford, Kilkenny Street, C of I, IGRS Collection (148), GO
Gaulskill: Ballynamorahan, C of I, IGRS Collection (39), GO
—— Gaulskill Old, IGRS Collection (39), GO
Inistioge: Cappagh, IGRS Collection (173), GO
Jerpointchurch: Kilvinoge, IGRS Collection (10), GO
Kells: Glebe, IGRS Collection (16), GO
—— St Kieran's, IGRS Collection (76), GO
Kilbeacon: Garrandarragh, C of I, IGRS Collection (42), GO
—— Garrandarragh, RC, IGRS Collection (42), GO
Kilbride: Kilbride, IGRS Collection (13), GO
Kilcolumb: Rathinure, IGRS Collection (53), GO
Kilferagh: IGRS Collection (3), GO
—— Sheastown, IGRS Collection (3), GO
Killahy: Killahy, IGRS Collection (13), GO
Kilmacow: Kilmacow, C of I, IGRS Collection (119), GO
Kilmademoge: Kilmademoge, IGRS Collection (6), GO
Kilree: Kilree, IGRS Collection (73), GO
Knocktopher: Kilcurl (Anglesea), IGRS Collection (5), GO
—— Knocktopher town, *Kilkenny Gravestone Inscriptions: 1 Knocktopher*, Kilkenny,
     1988, KAS
—— Sheepstown, IGRS Collection (4), GO
Muckalee: Muckalee, IGRS Collection (23 inscriptions), GO
Odagh: Threecastles, IGRS Collection (66), GO
Outrath: Outrath, IGRS Collection (86), GO
Portnascully: Portnascully, IGRS Collection (52), GO
Rathcoole: Johnswell, IGRS Collection (197), GO
—— Carrigeen, IGRS Collection (22), GO
Rosbercon: Rosbercon town, C of I, Cantwell, Brian, *Memorials of the Dead*, West
     Wexford (9), Dublin, 1985, NLI Ir. 9295 c 2
—— Rosbercon, RC, Cantwell, Brian, *Memorials of the Dead, West Wexford (9)*,
     Dublin, 1985, NLI Ir. 9295 c 2
St Canice: St Canice's interior, RC, IGRS Collection (45), GO
—— St Canice's Cathedral, Prim, J.G.A., *The History (. . .) of St Canice, Kilkenny*,
     1857
—— Kilkenny, the Colonnade, C of I, IGRS Collection (502), GO
St John's: Kilkenny, John Street Lower, C of I, IGRS Collection (116), GO
—— Radestown North, IGRS Collection (27), GO
—— Kilkenny, Dublin Road, RC, IGRS Collection (611), GO
St Martin's: Templemartin, IGRS Collection (51), GO
St Mary's: Kilkenny, St Mary's Lane, C of I, *Old Kilkenny Review*, 1979/1980/1981
St Maul's: Kilkenny, Green's Bridge Street, IGRS Collection (18), GO
St Patrick's: Kilkenny, Patrick Street Upper, IGRS Collection (280), GO
Stonecarthy: Stonecarthy East, IGRS Collection (22), GO
Tiscoffin: Freynestown, C of I, IGRS Collection (18), GO
Treadingstown: Ballyredding, IGRS Collection (7), GO
Tubbrid: Tubbrid, IGRS Collection (3), GO
—— Tullaghanbrogue: Grove, IGRS Collection (119), GO
Tullamaine: Tullamaine (Ashbrook), IGRS Collection (34), GO
Ullid: Ullid, IGRS Collection (15), GO

LAOIS

CENSUS RETURNS AND SUBSTITUTES

1641	Book of Survey and Distribution, NLI Ms 972
1659	Pender's 'Census'
1664	Hearth Money Roll, NAI Thrift Abstracts 3737
1668–69	Hearth Money Roll, Baronies of Maryborough and Clandonagh (Upper Ossory), NAI Thrift Abstracts 3737
1758–75	Freeholders, *JKAS*, Vol. VIII, pp. 309–27
1766	Lea parish RCB Library, also LDS film 258517
1821	Mountrath, NAI m 6225(1)–(5)
1823–38	Tithe Books
1832–40	Owners and occupiers, Lea parish, NLI Ms 4723/4
1844	Register of Arms, baronies of Clandonagh (Upper Ossory), Maryborough, Cullenagh, 433 names, NAI
1847	Voters, NLI ILB O4 P12
1851–1852	Griffith's Valuation
1901	Census
1911	Census

LOCAL HISTORY

Anonymous, *Abbeyleix*, 1953, NLI Ir. 94137 s 1

Brennan, M., *Schools of Kildare and Leighlin, 1775–1835*, NLI Ir. 37094135 b 4

Carrigan, Rev. William, *The History and Antiquities of the Diocese of Ossory*, Dublin, 1905

Coyle, James, *The Antiquities of Leighlin*

Dwyer, Philip, *The Diocese of Killaloe, from the Reformation to the Close of the Eighteenth Century*, Dublin, 1878

Feehan, J., *The Landscape of Slieve Bloom: a study of the natural & human heritage*, 1979, NLI Ir. 91413 f 4

Meehan, Patrick, *Members of Parliament for Laois and Offaly 1801–1918*, 1983, NLI Ir. 328 m 6

O'Byrne, *History of Queen's County*, 1856, NLI Ir. 94137 o 2

O'Hanlon, John, *History of the Queen's County*, Dublin, 1907–14, NLI Ir. 94137 o 3, GO

O'Shea, *Aspects of Local History*, 1977, NLI Ir. 941 p 36

Paterson, J. (ed.), *Diocese of Meath and Kildare: an historical guide*, 1981, NLI Ir. 941 p 75

Raymond, B., *The Story of Kilkenny, Kildare, Offaly and Leix*, 1931, NLI I 9141 p 1

LOCAL JOURNALS

Laois Heritage: Bulletin of the Laois Heritage Society, NLI Ir. 9413705 1 1

DIRECTORIES

1788	Richard Lucas, *General Directory of the Kingdom of Ireland*, NLI Pos. 3729
1824	J. Pigot and Co., *City of Dublin and Hibernian Provincial Directory*, NLI
1846	Slater, *National Commercial Directory of Ireland*, NLI
1856	Slater, *Royal National Commercial Directory of Ireland*, NLI
1870	Slater, *Directory of Ireland*, NLI
1881	Slater, *Royal National Commercial Directory of Ireland*, NLI
1894	Slater, *Royal Commercial Directory of Ireland*, NLI

GRAVESTONE INSCRIPTIONS

Irish Midlands Ancestry has transcripts for a large number of graveyards in the county. Contact details will be found in Chapter 14. Published or publicly available transcripts are given below.

Castlebrack: Campbell, Rosaleen, *Tombstone Inscriptions of Castlebrack*, Castlebrack, 1990, NLI, Ir. 9295 p 2(3)
Kyle: KCL
Rathdowney: Errill, O'Dea, Kieran, *Errill Cemetery*, Kilkenny, 1994, Errill Tidy Towns Committee

LEITRIM

CENSUS RETURNS AND SUBSTITUTES

1600–1868	Roll of all the gentlemen, NLI P 2179
1659	Pender's 'Census'
1726–27	Protestant Householders, Edgeworth papers, NAI M1501, Annaduff, Kiltogher, Kiltubbrid, Fenagh, Mohill
1791	Freeholders, GO 665, also LDS film 100213
1792	Protestants in the barony of Mohill, IA, Vol. 16, No. 1
1807	Freeholders Mohill barony, NLI Ms 9628
1820	Voting freeholders, NLI Ms 3830
1821	Parish of Carrigallen, NLI Pos. 4646
1823–38	Tithe Books
1839	Workhouse records Mohill (1839–83), Manorhamilton (1839–81) and Carrick-on-Shannon (1843–82) unions, LCL
1852	Voters, Oughteragh, Cloonclare, Cloonlogher, *Breifne*, Vol. 5, No. 20
1856	Griffith's Valuation
1861	Catholic Householders, Mohill parish, LHC
1901	Census
1911	Census

LOCAL HISTORY

Anonymous, *Sources of Information on the Antiquities and history of Cavan and Leitrim: Suggestions*, NLI Breifny, 1920–2, Ir. 794106 b 1

Anonymous, *Kiltubbrid*, 1984, NLI Ir. 397 k 4

Clancy, *Ballinaglera Parish, Co. Leitrim: aspects of its history and traditions*, 1980, NLI Ir. 94121 c 2

Farrell, Noel, *Exploring Family origins in Carrick-on-Shannon*, Longford Leader, Longford, 1994, includes transcripts of 1901, 1911 censuses, 1838 Thoms, 1941 Electors, Griffith's

Freeman, T.W., *The Town & District of Carrick on Shannon*, 1949, NLI P. 1916

Hayes McCoy, G.A., *Index to 'The Compossicion Booke of Connoght, 1585'*, Irish Manuscripts Commission, Dublin, 1945

Logan, P.L., *Outeragh, My Native Parish*, 1963, NLI Ir. 941 p 74

MacNamee, James J., *History of the Diocese of Ardagh*, Dublin, 1954

McNiffe, L., *Short History of the Barony of Rosclogher, 1840–60*, 'Breifny', 1983–4

Monahan, Rev. J., *Records Relating to the Diocese of Ardagh and Clonmacnoise*, 1886

O'Flynn, T., *History of Leitrim*, Dublin, 1937

O'Connell, Philip, *The Diocese of Kilmore: its History and Antiquities*, Dublin, 1937

LOCAL JOURNALS

Ardagh & Clonmacnoise Historical Society Journal, NLI Ir. 794105

Breifne NLI Ir. 94119 b 2

Breifny NLI Ir. 794106 b 1

The Drumlin: a Journal of Cavan, Leitrim and Monaghan, NLI Ir. 05 d 345

DIRECTORIES

1824	J. Pigot and Co., *City of Dublin and Hibernian Provincial Directory*, NLI
1846	Slater, *National Commercial Directory of Ireland*, NLI
1856	Slater, *Royal National Commercial Directory of Ireland*, NLI
1870	Slater, *Directory of Ireland*, NLI
1881	Slater, *Royal National Commercial Directory of Ireland*, NLI
1894	Slater, *Royal Commercial Directory of Ireland*, NLI

GRAVESTONE INSCRIPTIONS

Leitrim Heritage Centre/Leitrim County Library have transcripts for 105 graveyards in the county. Contact details will be found in Chapter 14. Published or publicly available transcripts are given below.

Kiltubbrid: Church & Graveyard, C of I, RCBL

ESTATE RECORDS

Earl of **Bessborough**: NA M3374, rental, 1805, major tenants only; NA M3370, valuation of estate, 1813, all tenants; NA M3383, tenants with leases, 1813; NA M3384, rental, 1813, all tenants, covering townlands in the civil parishes of Fenagh and Kiltubbrid.

Clements: NLI Mss 3816–3827, Rentals of the Woodford estate, 1812–1828, all tenants, covering townlands in the civil parish of Carrigallen; NLI Mss 12805–7, 3828, rental, 1812–1824 (with gaps) of Bohey townland in Cloone civil parish.

Sir Humphrey **Crofton**: NLI Ms 4531. Rental, March 1833, with tenants' names in alphabetical order, covering townlands in the civil parishes of Cloone, Kitoghert, Mohill, Oughteragh.

William **Johnson**: NLI Ms 9465, Rental of the Drumkeeran estate, 1845–56, all tenants, covering townlands in the civil parish of Inishmagrath

King: NLI Ms 4170, Rent roll and estate accounts, 1801–1818, major tenants only, covering townlands in the civil parishes of Fenagh and Kiltubbrid

Earl of **Leitrim**: NLI Ms 12787, rental and accounts 1837–42, all tenants; NLI Mss 5728–33, rentals 1838–65, all tenants; NLI Mss 5803–5, rentals 1842–55, all tenants; NLI Mss 12810–12, rentals 1844–8, all tenants; NLI Mss 179, 180, rentals 1844 & 1854, all tenants, covering townlands in the civil parishes of Carrigallen, Cloone, Clooneclare, Inishmagrath, Killasnet, Kiltoghert, Mohill.

Viscount **Newcomen**: NA M2797, Rental, 1822, mainly larger tenants, covering townlands in the civil parish of Drumlease.

Francis **O'Beirne**: NLI Ms 8647 (14), Rental, 1850, mainly large tenants, covering townlands in the civil parishes of Cloone, Drumlease, Kiltoghert.

Charles Manners **St George**: NLI Mss 4001–22, Annual accounts and rentals, covering townlands in the civil parish of Kiltoghert.

Nicholas Loftus **Tottenham**: NLI Ms 9837, 26 maps, with major tenants only, covering townlands in the civil parishes of Clooneclare, Inishmagrath, Rossinver.

Ponsonby **Tottenham**: NLI Ms 10162, printed rental, 1802, mainly larger tenants, covering townlands in the civil parishes of Clooneclare and Rossinver

Owen **Wynne**: NLI Mss 5780–5782, rentals and expense books, 1737–68, major tenants only; NLI Mss 5830–1, rent ledgers 1738–53, 1768–73, major tenants only, indexed; NLI Mss 3311–3, a rental and two rent ledgers, yearly from 1798 to 1825, with all tenants, covering townlands in the civil parishes of Clooneclare, Cloonlogher, Killanummery, Killasnet, Rossinver.

LIMERICK

CENSUS RETURNS AND SUBSTITUTES

1569	Freeholders, NLI Pos. 1700
1570	Freeholders & Gentlemen, *JNMAS*, 1964
1586	Survey of leaseholders on the Desmond estates, NAI M.5037
1641	Book of Survey and Distribution, NLI Ms 973
1654–1656	Civil Survey, Vol. IV, *Civil Survey*, Vol. IV (NLI I 6551 Dublin)
1659	Pender's 'Census'

1660	Rental of lands in Limerick City and County, NLI Ms 9091
1664	Hearth Money Rolls, Askeaton, *JNMAS*, 1965
1673	Valuation of part of Limerick city (estates of the Earls of Roscommon and Orrery) with occupiers' names and valuation, NLI Pos. 792
1715–94	Limerick City Freemen, PRO, also LDS film 477000
1746–1836	Freemen, Limerick, also NLI Pos. 5526, *JNMAS*, 1944–5
1761	Freeholders, Limerick city (16092) and county (16093), NLI Ms 16092, Ms 16093
1766	Abington, Cahircomey, Cahirelly, Carrigparson, Clonkeen, Kilkellane, Tuogh, NAI Parl. Ret. 681/684; Protestants only, Croagh, Kilscannel, Nantinan and Rathkeale, IA, 1977
1776	Freeholders entitled to vote, NAI M 1321–2
1776	Voters, NAI M.4878
1793–1821	Two Lists of People Resident in the Area of Newcastle in 1793 and 1821, *IA*, Vol. 16, No. 1 (1984)
1798	Rebel Prisoners in Limerick Jail, *JNMAS*, Vol. 10 (1), 1966
1813	Chief inhabitants of the parishes of St Mary's and St John's, Limerick, *IA*, Vol. 17, No. 2, 1985
1816–28	Freeholders, GO 623, also LDS film 100224
1821	Some extracts, NAI Thrift Absracts
1821	Fragments only, Kilfinane district, *JNMAS*, 1975
1823–38	Tithe Books, NAI
1829	Freeholders, GO 623
1835	Housholders, Parish of Templebredin, *JNMAS*, 1975
1835–39	List of inhabitants of Limerick taking water (Waterworks accounts), NLI Pos. 3451
1840	Freeholders, Barony of Coshlea, NLI Ms 9452
1843	Voters, NAI 1843/66
1846	Survey of Households in connection with famine relief, Loughill, Foynes, Shanagolden areas, NLI Ms 582
1851–1852	Griffith's Valuation
1851	Some extracts, NAI Thrift Absracts
1870	Rate Book for Clanwilliam barony, NAI M 2434
1901	Census
1911	Census

LOCAL HISTORY

Anonymous, *Atlas of the parishes of Cashel & Emly*
Anonymous, *Cromwellian Settlement of Co. Limerick*, NLI, *Limerick Field Journal*, Vols 1–8, 1897–1908, Ir 794205 l 1
Cronin, Patrick, *The auld town: a chronicle of Askeaton*, Askeaton Civic Trust, Limerick, 1995, NLI Ir. 94144 c
Dowd, Rev. James, *Limerick and its Sieges*, Limerick, 1896
Dowd, Rev. James, *St Mary's Cathedral Limerick*, Limerick, 1936
Dunraven, Countess of, *Memorials of Adare*, Oxford, 1865
Dwyer, Philip, *The Diocese of Killaloe, from the Reformation to the Close of the Eighteenth Century*, Dublin, 1878

Ferrar, John, *The History of Limerick, Ecclesiastical, Civil and Military, from the earliest records to the year 1787*, Limerick, 1787

Ferrar, John, *A History of the City of Limerick*, Limerick, 1767

Fitzgerald, P., *The history, topography and antiquities of the city and county of Limerick*, Dublin, 1826–7

Hamilton, G.F., *Records of Ballingarry*, Limerick, 1930. NLI Ir. 94144 h 2

Hayes, R., *The German Colony in County Limerick*, *JNMAS*, 1937

Lee, Rev. Dr C., 'Statistics from Knockainy and Patrickswell parishes, 1819–1940', JCHAS, Vol. 47, No. 165

Lenihan, Maurice, *Limerick, its history and antiquities*, Dublin, 1866, NLI Ir. 94144 l 1

MacCaffrey, James, *The Black Book of Limerick*, 1907

Meredyth, Francis, *Descriptive and Historic Guide, St Mary's Cathedral*, Limerick, 1887

Nash, Roisín, *A bibliography of Limerick*, Limerick, 1962

Seymour, St John D., *The Diocese of Emly*, Dublin, 1913

Westropp, *Westropp Manuscripts*, RIA

White, Rev. P., *History of Clare and the Dalcassian Clans of Tipperary, Limerick and Galway*, Dublin, 1893

LOCAL JOURNALS

Journal of the North Munster Archaeological Society, NLI Ir. 794105 n 1

Limerick Field Journal, NLI Ir. 794205 l 1

Lough Gur Historical Society Journal

Old Limerick Journal, NLI Ir. 94144 o 2

DIRECTORIES

1769	John Ferrar, *Directory of Limerick*
1788	Richard Lucas, *General Directory of the Kingdom of Ireland*, NLI Pos. 3729
1809	Holden, *Triennal Directory*
1820	J. Pigot, *Commercial Directory of Ireland*
1824	J. Pigot and Co., *City of Dublin and Hibernian Provincial Directory*, NLI
1846	Slater, *National Commercial Directory of Ireland*, NLI
1856	Slater, *Royal National Commercial Directory of Ireland*, NLI
1866	George Henry Bassett, *Directory of the City and County of Limerick, and of the Principal Towns in the Cos of Tipperary and Clare*, NLI Ir. 914144 b 5
1870	Slater, *Directory of Ireland*, NLI
1879	George Henry Bassett, *Limerick Directory*
1881	Slater, *Royal National Commercial Directory of Ireland*, NLI
1886	Francis Guy, *Postal Directory of Munster*, NLI Ir. 91414 g 8
1889	George Henry Bassett, *The Book of Tipperary* (Ballylooby)
1893	Francis Guy, *Directory of Munster*, NLI Ir. 91414 g 8
1894	Slater, *Royal Commercial Directory of Ireland*, NLI

GRAVESTONE INSCRIPTIONS

Abbeyfeale: Main Street, RC, *O'K,* Vol. II
Ardcanny: Mellion, *IA*, Vol. 9, No. 1, 1977
Ardpatrick: Fleming, John, *Reflections (. . .) on Ardpatrick,* 1979
Askeaton: C of I, IGRS, GO
Athlacca: Athlacca South, C of I, Seoighe, Mainchin, Dromin, Athlacca, 1978
Ballingarry: Hamilton, G.F., *Records of Ballingarry,* Limerick, 1930, NLI, Ir. 94144 h 2
Bruree: Howardstown North, Seoighe, Mainchin, *Brú Rí: Records of the Bruree District,* 1973
—— Ballynoe, C of I, Seoighe, Mainchin, *Brú Rí: Records of the Bruree District,* 1973
Dromin: Dromin South, Seoighe, Mainchin, Dromin, Athlacca, 1978
Grange: Grange Lower, *IA*, NLI, Ir. 9205 i 3
Kilbeheny: Churchquarter, C of I, *IG*
Killeedy: Mountcollins, Casey, Albert, *O'K*, Vol. II
Knockainy: Loughgur, *Lough Gur Historical Society Journal,* 1 (1985) 51–61
—— Patrickswell, RC, *Lough Gur Historical Society Journal,* 2 (1986) 71–9
Nantinan: Nantinan, C of I, *IA*, NLI, Ir. 9205 i 3
Rathkeale: Rathkeale, Church Street, C of I, *IA*, NLI, Ir. 9205 i 3, Vol. 14, No. 2, 1982
Stradbally: Stradbally North, Shannon Lodge, C of I, IGRS, GO
Tankardstown: Tankardstown Sough, Seoighe, Mainchin, *Brú Rí: Records of the Bruree District,* 1973

ESTATE RECORDS

Description of the estate of John **Sadleir** in Limerick & Tipperary, NLI JP 3439

LONGFORD

CENSUS RETURNS AND SUBSTITUTES

1641	Book of Survey and Distribution, NLI Ms 965
1659	Pender's 'Census'
1726–7	Protestant householders, Abbeylara, Abbeyshrule, Ardagh, Clonbroney, Clongesh, Kilcommock, Killashee, Rathreagh, Shrule, Taghshiny (Longford); Rathsapick, Russagh (Westmeath); list compiled for the distribution of religious books, NAI M1502
1729	Presbyterian exodus from Co. Longford, *Breifny*, 1977–8
1740	Protestants, Shrule & Rathreagh (Longford), Rathaspick (Westmeath), RCBL, GS 2/7/3/25
1747–1806	Freeholders, Registration book, NAI M 2745
1790	Freeholders *c*.1790, NAI M 2486 8, also NLI Pos. 1897
1795–1862	Charlton Marriage Certificates, NAI M2800, indexed in Accessions, Vol. 37
1796	Spinning-Wheel Premium List
1800–1835	Freeholders, GO 444, also LDS 100181
1823–38	Tithe Books
1828–1836	Freeholders' certificates, NAI M.2781

1854	Griffith's Valuation, indexed in *Co. Longford Survivors of the Great Famine*, Leahy, Longford, 1996
1901	Census, full index in Greahy, *Co. Longford and its People*, Dublin, Flyleaf Press, 1990
1911	Census

LOCAL HISTORY

Brady, G., *In Search of Longford Roots*, Offaly Historical Society, 1987, NLI Ir. 94136 t 1

Brady, J., *A short history of the parishes of the diocese of Meath, 1867–1944*, NLI Ir. 94132 b 2

Butler, H.T & H.E., *The Black Book of Edgeworthstown 1585 1817*, 1927

Cobbe, D., *75 Years of the Longford Leader*, 1972, NLI ILB 07

Devaney, O., *Killoe: History of a Co. Longford Parish*, 1981, NLI Ir. 9413 d 1

Farrell, James, P., *History of the county of Longford*, Dublin, 1891, NLI Ir. 94131 f 2

Farrell, Noel, *Exploring Family origins in Longford*, Self, Longford, 1991

Gillespie, Raymond, *Longford: Essays in County History*, Lilliput Press, Dublin, 1991, Dublin City Library (1) 941.812

Healy, John, *History of the Diocese of Meath*, Dublin, 1908

Leahy, David, *Co. Longford and its People*, Flyleaf Press, Dublin, 1990

Leahy, David, *Co. Longford Survivors of the Great Famine: index to Griffith's for Co. Longford*, Longford, Derryvrin Press, 1996

MacNamee, James J., *History of the Diocese of Ardagh*, Dublin, 1954

McGiveny, J., *Placenames of the Co. Longford*, Longford, 1908

Monahan, Rev. J., *Records Relating to the Diocese of Ardagh and Clonmacnoise*, 1886

Murray, C., Bibliography of the Co. Longford, Longford, 1961, LDS film 1279275

Murtagh, H., *Irish Midland Studies*, 1980, NLI Ir. 941 m 58

Paterson, J. (ed.), *Diocese of Meath and Kildare: an historical guide*, 1981, NLI Ir. 941 p 75

Stafford, R.W., *St Patrick's Church of Ireland Granard: Notes of Genealogical & Historical Interest*, 1983, NLI Ir. 914131 s 3

LOCAL JOURNALS

Ardagh & Clonmacnoise Historical Society Journal, NLI Ir. 794105

Teathbha, NLI Ir. 94131 t 1

DIRECTORIES

1824	J. Pigot and Co., *City of Dublin and Hibernian Provincial Directory*, NLI
1846	Slater, *National Commercial Directory of Ireland*, NLI
1856	Slater, *Royal National Commercial Directory of Ireland*, NLI
1870	Slater, *Directory of Ireland*, NLI
1881	Slater, *Royal National Commercial Directory of Ireland*, NLI
1894	Slater, *Royal Commercial Directory of Ireland*, NLI

GRAVESTONE INSCRIPTIONS

Ballymacormick: RC, Farrell, *Exploring Family origins in Longford*, Longford, 1991
—— Ballinamore, Farrell, *Exploring Family origins in Longford*, Longford, 1991
Granard: Granard, The Hill, C of I, Stafford, R.W., St *Patrick's Church of Ireland Granard: Notes of Genealogical & Historical Interest*, 1983, NLI Ir. 914131 s 3
Templemichael: Longford town, Pres., Farrell, *Exploring Family origins in Longford*, Longford, 1991
Templemichael: Longford, Church Street, C of I, Farrell, *Exploring Family origins in Longford*, Longford, 1991

ESTATE RECORDS

Adair estate, Clonbroney parish, 1738–67, NL Ms 3859
Aldborough estate rentals, 1846, NA M. 2971
Newcomen estates, maps of estates to be sold, July 20, 1827, NLI map room

LOUTH

CENSUS RETURNS AND SUBSTITUTES

1600	Gentlemen of Co. Louth, *JCLAHS*, Vol. 4, No. 4, 1919/20
1641	Book of Survey and Distribution, NLI Ms 974
1659	Pender's 'Census'
1663	Hearth Money Roll, *JCLAHS*, Vol. 6, Nos 2 & 4, Vol. 7, No. 3
1666	Hearth Money Roll, Dunleer parish, IG, 1969
1683	Louth brewers and retailers, *JCLAHS*, Vol. 3, No. 3
1683	Drogheda merchants, *JCLAHS*, Vol. 3, No. 3
1739–41	Corn census of Co. Louth, *JCLAHS*, Vol. 11, No. 4, pp. 254–86
1756	Commissions of Array, giving lists of Protestants who took the oath, NLI Pos. 4011
1760	Ardee parish, also PRONI, *IG*, 1961
1766	Ardee, Ballymakenny, Beaulieu, Carlingford, Charlestown, Clonkeehan, Darver, Drumiskan, Kildermock, Kileshiel, Louth, Mapastown, Philipstown, Shanlis, Smarmore, Stickallen, Tallonstown, Termonfeckin, NAI M2476 (b); Creggan, NAI Parl. Ret. 657 and *History of the Parish of Creggan* . . . Nelson
1782–92	Cess payers, parishes of Cappoge, Drumcar, Dysart, Monasterboice, Mullary, *JCLAHS*, Vol. 9, No. 1
1791	Landholders, Dromiskin parish, *History of Kilsaran Union of Parishes*, 1908
1796	Spinning-Wheel Premium List
1798	Drogheda voters' list, *JCLAHS*, Vol. XX, 1984
1801	Tithe applotment Stabannon & Roodstown, *History of Kilsaran Union of Parishes*, 1908
1802	Drogheda voters, *JCLAHS*, Vol. XX, 1984
1802	Carlingford, Protestants only, *JCLAHS*, Vol. 16, No. 3
1816	Grand Jurors, NLI Ir. 6551, Dundalk
1823–38	Tithe Books

1834	Tallanstown parish, *JCLAHS*, Vol. 14
1837	Valuation of towns returning MPs (occupants and property values), Drogheda, Dundalk, *Parliamentary Papers 1837, Reports from Committees*, Vol. II (i), Appendix G
1837	Marksmen (illiterate voters) in parliamentary boroughs, Drogheda, Dundalk, *Parliamentary Papers 1837, Reports from Committees*, Vol. II (i), Appendix A
1842	Voters, NAI 1842/70
1852	Mosstown and Phillipstown, *JCLAHS*, 1975
1852	Voting electors, NLI Ms 1660
1854	Griffith's Valuation.
1865	Parliamentary voters, NLI P. 2491
1901	Census
1911	Census

LOCAL HISTORY

Anonymous, *Notes on the Volunteers, Militia & Yeomanry, and Orangemen of Co. Louth*, JCLAHS, Vol. XVIII, 4, 1976

Anonymous, *A copy of the book of the corporation of Atherdee [Ardee] (manuscript)*, NLI Ms 31778

Anonymous, *Henderson's Post Office Directory of Meath & Louth*, 1861

Anonymous, *Families at Mosstown & Phillipstown in 1852*, JCLAHS, Vol. XVIII, 3, 1975

Anonymous, *Cromwellian & Restoration settlements in the parish of Dundalk*, JCLAHS, Vol. XIX, 1, 1977

Anonymous, *Old Title Deeds of Co. Louth: Dundalk 1718, 1856*, JCLAHS, Vol. XX, 1, 1981

Bernard, Nicholas (ed.), *The Whole Proceedings of the Siege of Drogheda [&] Londonderry*, Dublin, 1736

Conlon, L., *The Heritage of Collon*, 1984, NLI Ir. 94132 c 5

D'Alton, John, *The history of Drogheda*, Dublin, 1844, Ir. 94132 d 1

Duffner, P., *Drogheda: the Low Lane Church 1300–1979*, Ir. 94132 d 7

ICA, *A Local History Guide to Summerhill and Surrounding Areas*, NLI Ir. 94132 i 1

L'Estrange, G., *Notes and Jottings concerning the parish of Charlestown Union*, 1912, NLI Ir. 94132 l 2

Leslie, Canon J.B., *History of Kilsaran Union of Parishes*, 1908, NLI Ir. 94132 l 1

Murphy, Peter, *Together in Exile*, Nova Scotia, 1991

Murray, Rev. Lawrence P., *History of the Parish of Creggan in the Seventeenth and Eighteenth Centuries*, Dundalk, 1940

Nelson, S., *History of the Parish of Creggan in Cos Armagh and Louth from 1611 to 1840*, 1974

O'Neill, C.P., *History of Dromiskin*, 1984, NLI Ir. 94132 o 4

Redmond, B., *The Story of Louth*, 1931, NLI Ir. 9141 p 1

Tempest, H.S., *Descriptive and Historical Guide to Dundalk and District*, 1916, NLI Ir. 94132 t 1

LOCAL JOURNALS

Journal of the County Louth Archaeological and Historical Society, NLI Ir. 794105 L 2
Journal of the Old Drogheda Society, NLI Ir. 94132 0 3
Seanchas Ardmhacha, NLI Ir. 27411 s 4

DIRECTORIES

1820	J. Pigot, *Commercial Directory of Ireland*
1824	J. Pigot and Co., *City of Dublin and Hibernian Provincial Directory*, NLI
1830	McCabe, *Drogheda Directory*, NLI Pos. 3986
1846	Slater, *National Commercial Directory of Ireland*, NLI
1856	Slater, *Royal National Commercial Directory of Ireland*, NLI
1870	Slater, *Directory of Ireland*, NLI
1881	Slater, *Royal National Commercial Directory of Ireland*, NLI
1886	George Henry Basset, *Louth County Guide and Directory*
1894	Slater, *Royal Commercial Directory of Ireland*, NLI

GRAVESTONE INSCRIPTIONS

Ardee: Ardee, Market Street, C of I, *IG*, 3 (1), 1956
Ballymakenny: C of I, *Seanchas Ardmhacha*, 1983/4
Ballymascanlan: C of I, *JCLAS*, Vol. 17, No. 4, 1972
—— Faughart Upper, HW
Beaulieu: C of I, *JCLAS*, Vol. 20, No. 1
Carlingford: Church Lane, C of I, *JCLAS*, Vol. 19, No. 2, 1978
Castletown: Ross, Noel, *Tombstone Inscriptions in Castletown Graveyard, Dundalk*, Old Dundalk Society, Dundalk, 1992, NLI Ir. 9295 p1(1)
Charlestown: C of I, L'Estrange, G., *Notes and Jottings concerning the parish of Charlestown Union*, 1912, NLI Ir. 94132 1 2
Clonkeen: Churchtown, C of I, L'Estrange, G., *Notes and Jottings concerning the parish of Charlestown Union*, 1912, NLI Ir. 94132 1 2
Clonmore: C of I, *JCLAS*, Vol. 20, No. 2
Collon: Church Street, LDS Family history library, 941.825/k29c
Darver: C of I, Cavan Heritage and Genealogy Centre, also *Breifne*, 1922
Dromin: LDS Family history library, 941.825/k29c
Drumshallon: *JCLAS*, Vol. 19, No. 3, 1979
Dunany: *JCLAS*, Vol. 20, No. 3, 1983
Dundalk: Seatown, *Tempest's Annual*, 1967, 1971/2
Dunleer: Main Street, C of I, *JCLAS*, Vol. 22, No. 4, 1992
Dysart: *JCLAS*, Vol. 19, No. 3, 1979
Faughart: Dungooly, *Tombstone Inscriptions from Fochart*, Dundalk, 1968, Dundalgan press, also Mac Iomhair, D., *Urnai*, Dundalk, 1969
Gernonstown: Castlebellingham, Leslie, Canon J.B., *History of Kilsaran Union of Parishes*, 1908, NLI Ir. 94132 1 1
Kildemock: Drakestown, *JCLAS*, Vol. 13, No. 1
—— Millockstown, Leslie, Canon J.B., *History of Kilsaran Union of Parishes*, 1908, NLI Ir. 94132 1 1

—— Kilsaran, Leslie, Canon J.B., *History of Kilsaran Union of Parishes*, 1908, NLI Ir. 94132 l 1

Louth: Priorstate, *JCLAS*, Vol. 19, No. 4, 1980

—— Grange, *JCLAS*, Vol. 19, No. 3, 1979

Mansfieldstown: Mansfieldstown, Leslie, Canon J.B., *History of Kilsaran Union of Parishes*, 1908, NLI Ir. 94132 l 1

Mayne: Glebe East, *JCLAS*, Vol. 20, No. 4, 1984

Monasterboice: King, Philip, *Monasterboice heritage: a centenary celebration [. . .]*, Monasterboice, 1994, NLI Ir. 94132 k 1, Philip King

Mosstown: Mosstown North, LDS Family history library, 941.825/k29c

Port: *JCLAS*, 21 (2), 1986, 208–18

Rathdrumin: Glebe, C of I, *JCLAS*, Vol. 19, No. 1, 1970

Salterstown: *JCLAS*, Vol. 20, No. 3, 1983

Shanlis: *JCLAS*, Vol. 22, No. 1, 1989

Smarmore: *JCLAS*, Vol. 22, No. 1, 1989

Stabannan: C of I, Leslie, Canon J.B., *History of Kilsaran Union of Parishes*, 1908, NLI Ir. 94132 l 1

Stickillin: *JCLAS*, Vol. 22, No. 1, 1989

Tullyallen: RC, *Seanchas Ardmhacha*, Vol. 7, No. 2, 1977

Tullyallen: Newtownstalaban, *JCLAS*, Vol. 17, No. 2, 1970

ESTATE RECORDS

Anglesea: Tenants' list for Anglesea estate, Carlingford parish, 1810, *JCLAHS*, 12 (2), 1950, 136–43, covering areas in the civil parish of Carlingford

Anglesea: Tenants on the Anglesea estate, 1856, *JCLAHS*, 12 (2), 1950, 143–51, covering areas in the civil parish of Carlingford

Details of the **Anglesea** estate papers in PRONI, JCLAS, Vol.17, 1, 1973 (see also JCLAS 12, 2)

Balfour: Tenants, Ardee parish, 1838, *JCLAHS*, 12 (3), 1951, 188–90, covering areas in the civil parish of Ardee

Drumgooter: A Tenant Farm in the 18th & 19th Centuries (from a rent roll of the estate of Sir John **Bellew**), JCLAS, Vol. 20, 4, 1984, Rathdrumin cvil parish

Caraher: Cardistown, tenants on potato land, 1810–17, *JCLAHS*, 165 (3), 1967, 177–83, covering areas in the civil parish of Clonkeen

Clanbrassil: Tenants on two Clanbrassil estate maps of Dundalk, 1782–8, *JCLAHS*, 15 (1), 1961, 39–87, covering areas in the civil parish of Dundalk

John Foster: Rental and Accounts of Collon Estate, 1779–81, *JCLAHS*, 10 (3), 1943, 222–9, covering areas in the civil parish of Collon

McClintock: Tenants on the McClintock estate, Drumcar & Kilsaran, 1852, *JCLAHS*, 16 (4), 1968, 230–32, covering areas in the civil parishes of Drumcar and Kilsaran

Papers from the **Roden** estate, **Clanbrassel** estate map, 1785, JCLAS, Vol. 20, 1 1981

Trench estate rentals, Drogheda, NLI Ms 2576

[No Landlord given]: Families (all) in the townlands of Mosstown and Philipstown, 1852, *JCLAHS*, 18 (3), 1975, 232–7, covering areas in the civil parish of Mosstown

[No Landlord given]: 'Tenants in Culver House Park Drogheda', 30 tenants, with maps, 1809, *JCLAHS*, 11 (3), 1947, 206–8, covering areas in the civil parish of St Peter's

Tenants of Omeath, 1865, JCLAHS, Vol. XVII, 1, 1973

MAYO

CENSUS RETURNS AND SUBSTITUTES

1600–1700	Mayo landowners in the 17th century, *JRSAI*, 1965, 153–62
1693	List of those outlawed after the Williamite wars, in some cases addresses and family relationships are specified, *AH*, 22, 1–240
1716	Ballinrobe Protestant freeholders requesting the building of walls, 70 names, *JGAHS*, 7, 1911/2, 168–170
1783	Ballinrobe householders, *AH*, Vol. 14
1786	Petition for a postal service between Westport and Castlebar, 70 inhabitants of Westport listed, *Cathair Na Mart (Journal of the Westport Historical Society)*, 16, 1996
1796	Catholics Emigrating from Ulster to Mayo, *Seanchas Ardmhacha*, 1958, pp. 17–50, see also 'Petition of Armagh migrants in the Westport area', *Cathair na Mart*, Vol. 2, No. 1 (Appendix)
1798	Persons who suffered losses in the 1798 rebellion, propertied classes only, NLI I 94107
1818	Tithe Collectors' account book, parishes of Kilfian and Moygawnagh, NAI M. 6085
1820	Protestants in Killala, NAI MFCI 32
1823–38	Tithe Books
1823	Defendants at Westport Petty sessions, NLI Ms. 14902
1825	Petition to have the River Moy dredged (100 names, Ballina), NAI OP 974/131
1831	750 names to a petition for poor relief in Coolcarney (Kilgarvan and Attymass), NAI OP 9974/116
1832–39	Freeholders, alphabetical listing showing residence and valuation, NAI OP 1839/138
1832	Protestants in Foxford, NLI Ms 8295
1833	Defendants at Mayo Lent Assizes, alphabetical list, giving crime, *Claremorris in History*, Mayo, Mayo Fam. Hist. Soc., 1987
1836	Defendants at Mayo Summer Assizes, *Claremorris in History*, Mayo, Mayo Fam. Hist. Soc., 1987
1839	Crossmolina parishioners, 170 names of nominators of Tithe apploters, NAI OP/1839/77
1841	Some extracts only, for Newport, NAI Thrift Abstracts
1842	Freeholders (excludes the baronies of Erris and Tirawley), NAI OP/1842/71
1845	Defendants at Mayo Summer Assizes (Notebook of Justice Jackson), NAI M55249
1845	Clare Island tenants, *South Mayo Family History Research Journal*, 7, 1994, 46–7

1850	Voters' lists, *South Mayo Family History Research Journal*, 1996, 27–41
1856–57	Voters' registers, Costello barony (NAI M.3447), Clanmorris barony (NAI M.3448), Tirawley barony (NAI M.2782), Kilmaine barony (NAI M.2783), Gallen barony (NAI M.2784)
1856–57	Griffith's Valuation
1901	Census (index for Achill, William G. Masterson, *Achill parish: Census Index*, Indianapolis, 1994, Ir. 94123 m 21)
1911	Census

LOCAL HISTORY

Anonymous, 'The Ethnography of Inishbofin and Inishark', PRIA, 3rd Ser., Vol. 3, 1893–6, 360–80

Anonymous, *Crossmolina Parish: An Historical Survey*, NLI Ir. 94123 c 5

Anonymous, *Achill, 15th report of the mission/ report of Achill Orphan Refuges*, 1849, NLI Ir. 266 a 8

Anonymous, *St Muiredach's College, Ballina, Roll 1906 1979*, NLI Ir. 259 m 2/ Ir. 37941 s 18

Anonymous, *Claremorris in History*, Mayo Fam. Hist. Soc., Mayo, 1987, none specified

Hayes McCoy, G.A., *Index to 'The Compossicion Booke of Connoght, 1585'*, Irish Manuscripts Commission, Dublin, 1945

Kingston, Rev. John, *Achill Island, the deserted village at Slievemore: a study . . .* , Bob Kingston, Achill Island, 1990, NLI Ir. 720 k 6

Knox, H.T., *The history of Mayo to the close of the 16th century*, Dublin, 1908, NLI Ir. 94123 k 2 (& LO)

Knox, H.T., *Notes on the Early History of the Dioceses of Tuam, Killala and Achonry*, Dublin, 1904

MacHale (ed.), *The Parishes in the Diocese of Killala*, NLI Ir. 27414 m 6

McDonald, Theresa, *Achill 5000 B.C. to 1900 A.D.: archaeology, history, folklore*, IAS Publications, 1992, NLI Ir. 94123 m 12

McDonnell, T., *Diocese of Killala*, NLI Ir. 94123 m 7

McGrath, Fiona, *Emigration and landscape: the case of Achill Island*, TCD Dept of Geography, Dublin, 1991, NLI Ir. 900 p 10 (3)

O'Hara, B., *Killasser: a history*, 1981, NLI Ir. 94123 o 6

O'Sullivan, W. (ed.), *The Strafford Inquisition of Co. Mayo*, NLI Ir. 94123 o 4

Walsh, Marie, *An Irish country childhood: memories of a bygone age*, Smith Gryphon, London, 1995, NLI Ir. 92 w 242

LOCAL JOURNALS

Cathair na Mart (Journal of the Westport Historical Society), NLI Ir. 94123 c 4
North Mayo Historical & Archaeological Journal, NLI Ir. 94123 n 4
South Mayo Family History Research Journal

DIRECTORIES

1824	J. Pigot and Co., *City of Dublin and Hibernian Provincial Directory*, NLI
1846	Slater, *National Commercial Directory of Ireland*, NLI
1856	Slater, *Royal National Commercial Directory of Ireland*, NLI
1870	Slater, *Directory of Ireland*, NLI
1881	Slater, *Royal National Commercial Directory of Ireland*, NLI
1894	Slater, *Royal Commercial Directory of Ireland*, NLI

GRAVESTONE INSCRIPTIONS

Mayo South Family Research Centre has transcripts for 142 graveyards, mainly in the south of the county. Mayo North Family History Research also has a large number of transcripts. Galway Family History Society has transcripts for Inishbofin and Sligo Heritage and Genealogy Centre has transcripts for the parish of Kilmoremoy. Contact details will be found in Chapter 14.

ESTATE RECORDS

Lord Altamont: NAI M5788(2), Rental of the Westport estate, 1787, principally major tenants. The section on Westport town is published in *Cathair na Mart*, Vol. 2, No. 1, along with a rent roll for the town from 1815, covering townlands in the civil parishes of Aghagower, Burriscarra, Burrishoole, Kilbelfad, Kilbride, Kilconduff, Kildacomoge, Kilfian, Kildeer, Kilmaclasser, Kilmeena, Moygownagh, Oughaval

Earl of Arran: NLI Ms 14087, leases on the Mayo estate, 1720–1869, mentioning lives in the leases. NLI Ms 14086, valuation survey of the Mayo estates, 1850–52, all tenants, covering townlands in the civil parishes of Addergoole, Ardagh, Ballysakeery, Crossmolina, Kilbelfad, Kilcummin, Kilfian, Killala, Kilmoremoy.

Col John Browne: NLI Pos. 940, account of the sales of the estates of Col. John Browne in Cos Galway and Mayo, compiled in 1778, giving names of major tenants and purchasers 1698–1704, and those occupying the estates in 1778, covering townlands in the civil parishes of Addergoole, Aghagower, Aglish, Ballintober, Ballyhean, Ballyovey, Ballysakeery, Breaghwy, Burrishoole, Cong, Crossmolina, Drum, Islandeady, Kilcommon, Kilgeever, Killeadan, Kilmaclasser, Kilmainemore, Kilmeena, Manulla, Moygownagh, Oughaval, Robeen, Tonaghty, Turlough.

Lord Clanmorris: NLI Ms 3279. Rental, 1833, all tenants, covering townlands in the civil parishes of Kilcommon, Kilmainemore, Mayo, Robeen, Rosslee, Tonaghty, Toomour.

Domville: NLI Ms 11816, Rentals, 1833–36, 1843, 1847, 1851, all tenants, covering townlands in the civil parishes of Killasser, Manulla, Robeen.

Henry Knox: NAI 5630 (1), Rental, early nineteenth century, all tenants, covering townlands in the civil parishes of Crossmolina, Doonfeeny, Kilfian, Kilmoremoy.

Thomas Medlicott: NLI Ms 5736 (3), Tithe Applotment Book, Achill, NLI Mss 5736 (2), 5821, Rent rolls, showing lives in leases, 1774, 1776, major tenants only, covering townlands in the civil parishes of Achill, Aghagower, Burrishoole, Kilcommon, Kilmeena, Kilmore.

Sir Neal O'Donel: NLI Ms 5738 & 5744, leaseholders on the estates, 1775–1859, 1828, giving lives mentioned in leases, mainly major tenants; NLI Ms 5736, Rental, 1788, major tenants only; NLI Ms 5281, Rental, 1805, major tenants only; NLI Ms 5743, Rental, 1810, major tenants only; NLI Ms 5281, Rental, 1828, major tenants only, covering townlands in the civil parishes of Achill, Aghagower, Burrishoole, Cong, Kilcommon, Kilgeever, Kilmore, Kilmaclasser.

Sir Samuel O'Malley: NAI M1457 (published in *Cathair na Mart*, Vol. 6, No. 1), valuation of the Mayo estates, 1845, all tenants, covering townlands in the civil parishes of Aglish, Kilgeever, Kilmeena

MEATH

CENSUS RETURNS AND SUBSTITUTES

1641	Book of Survey and Distribution, NLI Ms 974
1654–1656	Civil Survey, Vol. III, *Civil Survey*, Vol. III (NLI I 6551 Dublin)
1659	Pender's 'Census'
1663	Hearth Money Roll, *JCLAHS*, Vol. 6, Nos 2 & 4, Vol. 7, No. 3
1710	Voters in Kells, PRONI T. 3163, NLI. Headford papers
1766	Ardbraccan, Protestants only, GO 537, also RCB Library
1770	Freeholders, NLI Ms 787–8, also LDS film 100181
1781	Voters, NAI M4910–12
1792	Hearth tax collectors account and collection books, parishes of Colp, Donore, Duleek, Kilshalvan, NL Ms 26735; Ardcath, Ardmulchan, Ballymagarvy, Brownstown, Clonalvy, Danestown, Fennor, Kentstown, Knockcommon, Rathfeigh, NL Ms 26736; Athlumney, Danestown, Dowdstown, Dunsany, Kilcarn, Killeen, Macetown, Mounttown, Tara, Trevet, NL Ms 26737; St Mary's Drogheda, NL Ms 26739, NLI Ms 26735
1793	Hearth tax collectors account and collection books, parishes of Ardagh, Dowth, Gernonstown, Killary, Mitchelstown, Siddan, Slane, Stackallan, NL Ms 26738, NLI Ms 26738
1795–1862	Charlton Marriage Certificates, NAI, List 37, M2800, indexed in Accessions, Vol. 37
1796	Spinning-Wheel Premium List
1797–1801	Tithe Valuations Athboy, NAI MFCI 53, 54
1798	Drogheda voters' list, *JCLAHS*, Vol. XX, 1984
1802–06	Protestants in the parishes of Agher, Ardagh, Clonard, Clongill, Drumconrath, Duleek, Emlagh, Julianstown, Kentstown, Kilbeg, Kilmainhamwood, Kilskyre, Laracor, Moynalty, Navan, Robertstown, Raddenstown, Rathcore, Rathkenny, Rathmolyon, Ratoath, Skryne, Straffordstown, Stamullin, Tara, Trevet, Templekeeran, *The Irish Ancestor*, 1973
1802	Drogheda Voters, *JCLAHS*, Vol. XX, 1984
1813	Protestant children at Ardbraccan school, IA, 1973
1815	Voters, PRONI T3163, also NLI, Headford papers

1816	Grand Jurors, NLI Ir. 6551, Dundalk
1821	Parishes of Ardbraccan, Ardsallagh, Balrathboyne, Bective, Churchtown, Clonmacduff, Donaghmore, Donaghpatrick, Kilcooly, Liscartan, Martry, Moymet, Navan, Newtownclonbun, Rathkenny, Rataine, Trim, Trimblestown, Tullaghanoge, NAI
1823–38	Tithe Books
1830	Census of landowners in Julianstown, Moorchurch, Stamullen and Clonalvey, *Riocht na Midhe* 3 (4), 1966, 354–8
1833	Protestant Cess payers, parishes of Colpe and Kilshalvan, *Riocht na Midhe*, 4 (3), 1969, 61–2
1837	Valuation of towns returning MPs (occupants and property values), Drogheda, Dundalk, *Parliamentary Papers 1837, Reports from Committees*, Vol. II (i), Appendix G
1837	Marksmen (illiterate voters) in parliamentary boroughs, Drogheda, Dundalk, *Parliamentary Papers 1837, Reports from Committees*, Vol. II (i), Appendix A
1843	Voters, NLI Ms 1660
1850	Register of land occupiers, with particulars of land and families, in the Unions of Kells and Oldcastle, NLI Ms 5774
1852	Voting electors, NLI Ms 1660
1855	Griffith's Valuation, NLI
1865	Parliamentary voters, NLI P. 2491
1871	Drumcondra and Loughbrackan, NLI Pos. 4184
1901	Census
1911	Census

LOCAL HISTORY

Anonymous, *Henderson's Post Office Directory of Meath & Louth*, 1861

Anonymous, *Notes on the Volunteers, Militia & Yeomanry, and Orangemen of Co. Louth*, NLI, JCLAHS, Vol. XVIII, 4, 1976

Anonymous, *Parish Guide to Meath*, 1968, NLI Ir. 270 p 2

Bernard, Nicholas (ed.), *The Whole Proceedings of the Siege of Drogheda [&] Londonderry*, Dublin, 1736

Brady, J., *A short history of the parishes of the diocese of Meath, 1867–1944*, NLI Ir. 94132 b 2

Carty, Mary Rose, *History of Killeen Castle*, Dunsany, 1991

Cogan, A., *The ecclesiastical history of the diocese of Meath*, Dublin, 1874

Cogan, J., *Ratoath*, NLI Ir. 9141 p 84

Coogan, Tony, *Charlesfort: the story of a Meath estate and its people 1668–1968*, the author, Kells, 1991, NLI Ir. 94132 9 2(2)

Coogan, O., *A short history of south-east Meath*, 1979

Coogan, O., *Dunshaughlin, Culmullen and Knockmark*, 1988

Connell, P., *Changing Forces Shaping a Nineteenth Century town: A Case Study of Navan*, Maynooth, 1978

D'Alton, John, *The history of Drogheda*, Dublin, 1844, NLI Ir. 94132 d 1

D'Alton, John, *Antiquities of the County of Meath*, Dublin, 1833

Duffner, P., *Drogheda: the Low Lane Church 1300–1979*, NLI Ir. 94132 d 7

Fitzsimons, J., *The Parish of Kilbeg*, 1974

French, Noel, *Navan by the Boyne*

French, Noel, *Trim Traces and Places*

French, Noel, *Bellinter House*, Trymme Press, Trim, Co. Meath, 1993, NLI Ir. 941 p 124(3)

French, Noel, *Athboy, a short history*

French, Noel, *Nobber, a step back in time*

French, Noel, *Tracing Your Ancestors in Co. Meath*, Trymme Press, 1993

French, Noel, *A short history of Rathmore and Athboy*, s.n., s., 1995, NLI Ir. 94132 f

Healy, John, *History of the Diocese of Meath*, Dublin, 1908

Kieron, J.S., *An Outline History of the Parish of St Mary's Abbey*, 1980, NLI Ir. 91413 p 12

MacLochlainn, T., *The Parish of Laurencetown & Kiltormer*, 1981, NLI Ir. 94124 m 5

McCullen, J., *The Call of St Mary's*, 1984, NLI Ir. 27413 m 8

Paterson, J. (ed.), *Diocese of Meath and Kildare: an historical guide*, 1981, NLI Ir. 941 p 75

Redmond, B., *The Story of Louth*, 1931, NLI Ir. 9141 p 1

Sims, A., *Irish Historic Towns Atlas: Kells*, Royal Irish Academy, Dublin, 1991

LOCAL JOURNALS

Annala Dhamhliag: The annals of Duleek, NLI Ir. 94132 a 1

Riocht na Midhe, NLI Ir. 94132 r 1

DIRECTORIES

1824	J. Pigot and Co., *City of Dublin and Hibernian Provincial Directory*, NLI
1846	Slater, *National Commercial Directory of Ireland*, NLI
1856	Slater, *Royal National Commercial Directory of Ireland*, NLI
1870	Slater, *Directory of Ireland*, NLI
1881	Slater, *Royal National Commercial Directory of Ireland*, NLI
1894	Slater, *Royal Commercial Directory of Ireland*, NLI

GRAVESTONE INSCRIPTIONS

Agher: C of I, *IA*, Vol. 10, No. 2, 1978

Agher: C of I, GO, IGRS Collection

Ardmulchan: French, Noel, *Monumental Inscriptions from Some Graveyards in Co. Meath*, Typescript, 1990, NAI open shelves

Ardsallagh: French, Noel, *Monumental Inscriptions from Some Graveyards in Co. Meath*, Typescript, 1990, NAI open shelves

Athboy: Church Lane, C of I, *IA*, Vol. 12, Nos 1 and 2, 1981

Athlumney: IGRS Collection, GO

Balfeaghan: IGRS Collection, GO

Ballygarth: IGRS Collection, GO

Balrathboyne: Cortown, IGRS Collection, GO

Balsoon: *IA*, Vol. 7, No. 2, 1976

Bective: Clady, GO

Castlejordan: C of I, IGRS Collection, GO

Churchtown: IGRS Collection (59), GO

Clonard: Tircroghan, IGRS Collection (4), GO

Colp: Mornington town, RC, *Journal of the Old Drogheda Society*, 1989

—— Stagreenan, *Journal of the Old Drogheda Society* 1977,

—— Colp West, C of I, LDS Family History Library

Danestown: Danestown, *Riocht na Midhe*, Vol. 5, No. 4, 1974

Diamor: Clonabreaney, *Riocht na Midhe*, Vol. 6, No. 2, 1976

Donaghmore: Donaghmore, RC, French, Noel, *Monumental Inscriptions from Some Graveyards in Co. Meath*, Typescript, 1990, NAI open shelves

Dowdstown: French, Noel, *Monumental Inscriptions from Some Graveyards in Co. Meath*, Typescript, 1990, NAI open shelves

Drumlargan: *IA*, Vol. 12, Nos 1 & 2, 1980

Duleek: Church Lane, C of I, *IG*, Vol. 3, No. 12, 1967

Dunboyne: Dunboyne, GO, IGRS Collection, also *IA*, Vol. 11, Nos 1 & 2, 1979

Dunboyne: Dunboyne, *IA*, Vol. 11, Nos 1 & 2, 1979

Dunmoe: French, Noel, *Monumental Inscriptions from Some Graveyards in Co. Meath*, Typescript, 1990, NAI open shelves

Gallow: Gallow, IGRS Collection (39), GO

Gernonstown: French, Noel, *Monumental Inscriptions from Some Graveyards in Co. Meath*, Typescript, 1990, NAI open shelves

Girley: Girley, French, Noel, *Monumental Inscriptions from Some Graveyards in Co. Meath*, Typescript, 1990, NAI open shelves

Kells: Headford Place, *IG*, Vol. 3, No. 11, 1966

Kilbride: Baytown, *Riocht na Midhe*, Vol. 6, No. 3, 1977

Kilcarn: French, Noel, *Monumental Inscriptions from Some Graveyards in Co. Meath*, Typescript, 1990, NAI open shelves

Kilcooly: Kiltoome (Kilcooly?), IGRS Collection (8), GO

Kildalkey: IGRS Collection (117), GO

Killaconnigan: Killaconnigan, IGRS Collection (100), GO

Killeen: Killeen, *Riocht na Midhe*, Vol. 4, No. 3, 1970

Kilmore: Arodstown, *Riocht na Midhe*, Vol. 6, No. 1, 1975

—— Kilmore, C of I, *Riocht na Midhe*, Vol. 6, No. 1, 1975

Laracor: Moy, *IA*, Vol. 6, No. 2, 1974

—— Summerhill Demesne, LDS Family History Library

Loughan or Castlekeeran: IGRS Collection (39), GO

Loughcrew: C of I, *IA*, Vol. 9, No. 2, 1977

Macetown: IGRS Collection (7), GO

Martry: Allenstown Demesne, French, Noel, *Monumental Inscriptions from Some Graveyards in Co. Meath*, Typescript, 1990, NAI open shelves

Moymet: IGRS Collection (54), GO

Moynalty: Hermitage, French, Noel, *Monumental Inscriptions from Some Graveyards in Co. Meath*, Typescript, 1990, NAI open shelves

Navan: Church Hill, C of I, MF CI 45, NAI

Oldcastle: *Riocht na Midhe*, Vol. 4, No. 2, 1968

Rataine: GO

Rathfeigh: IGRS Collection (42), GO

Rathkenny: C of I, French, Noel, *Monumental Inscriptions from Some Graveyards in Co. Meath*, Typescript, 1990, NAI open shelves

Rathmore: RC, *IA*, Vol. 7, No. 2, 1975

Rathmore: Moyagher Lower, *IA*, Vol. 8, No. 1, 1976

Ratoath: Main Street, C of I, French, Noel, *Monumental Inscriptions from Some Graveyards in Co. Meath*, Typescript, 1990, NAI open shelves

Scurlockstown: IGRS Collection (17), GO

Skreen: French, Noel, *Monumental Inscriptions from Some Graveyards in Co. Meath*, Typescript, 1990, NAI open shelves

St Mary's: Drogheda, New Road, C of I, *Journal of the Old Drogheda Society*, 1986

Stackallan: French, Noel, *Monumental Inscriptions from Some Graveyards in Co. Meath*, Typescript, 1990, NAI open shelves

Tara: Castleboy, C of I, Meath Heritage Centre

Trim: Tremblestown, RC, French, Noel, *Monumental Inscriptions from Some Graveyards in Co. Meath*, Typescript, 1990, NAI open shelves

Trim: Maudlin, IGRS Collection (3), GO

Tullaghanoge: French, Noel, *Monumental Inscriptions from Some Graveyards in Co. Meath*, Typescript, 1990, NAI open shelves

ESTATE RECORDS

Balfour: Balfour tenants in the townlands of Belustran, Cloughmacow, Doe and Hurtle, 1838, JCLAHS, 12 (3), 1951, 190, Nobber civil parish.

Newcomen estates: maps of estates to be sold, July 20, 1827, NLI map room

Reynell family rent books 1834–48, NLI Ms 5990

William Barlow **Smythe**, Collinstown, Farm a/c book, NLI Ms 7909

Trench estate rentals, Drogheda, NLI Ms 2576

Wellesley: Tenants of the Wellesley estate at Dangan, Ballymaglossan, Moyare, Mornington and Trim, 1816, *Riocht na Midhe*, 4 (4), 1967, 10–25, Ballymaglassan, Colp, Laracor, Rathmore and Trim civil parishes

MONAGHAN

CENSUS RETURNS AND SUBSTITUTES

	Medieval Clones families, *Clogher Record*, 1959
1630	Muster Roll of Ulster, Armagh Co. Library, PRONI D.1759/3C/1, T. 808/15164, NLI Pos. 206
1641	Index to the rebels of 1641 in the Co. Monaghan depositions, *Clogher Record*, 15 (2), 1995, 89
1659	Pender's 'Census'
1663–65	Hearth Money Roll, *History of Monaghan for two hundred years 1660–1860*, Dundalk, 1921
1738	Some Clones Inhabitants, *Clogher Record*, Vol. 2, No. 3, 1959
1777	Some Protestant Inhabitants of Carrickmacross, *Clogher Record*, Vol. 6, No. 1, 1966
1785	Male Protestants aged over 17, Magheracloone & Errigal Trough, LDS film 258517

1796	Spinning-Wheel Premium List
1821	Some abstracts only, see *Clogher Record*, 1991, NAI Thrift Abstracts
1823	Some Church of Ireland members in the Aghadrumsee area, *Clogher Record*, 15 (1), 1994
1823–38	Tithe Books
1824	Protestant householders, Aghabog parish, RCBL D1/1/1
1832	Donagh parish Co. Monaghan (with C. of I records), PRONI MIC.1/127
1841	Some abstracts only, NAI Thrift Abstracts
1842–9	Workhouse records, Castleblayney Union, MAR
1843	Magistrates, landed proprietors, 'etc.', NLI Ms 12,767
1847	Poor Law Rate Book, Castleblayney, *Clogher Record*, Vol. 5, No. 1, 1963
1851	Some abstracts only, NAI Thrift Abstracts
1858–1860	Griffith's Valuation
1901	Census
1911	Census

LOCAL HISTORY

Anonymous, *Monaghan Election Petition 1826: minutes of evidence*, NLI Ir. 32341 m 52
Anonymous, *Old Monaghan 1775–1995*, Monaghan, Clogher Historical Society, 1995
Carville, G., *Parish of Clontibret*, NLI Ir. 941 p 74
Cotter, Canon J.B.D., *A Short History of Donagh Parish*, Enniskillen, 1966
Duffy, J. (ed.), *A Clogher Record Album: a diocesan history*, NLI Ir. 94114 c 3
Gilsenan, M., *Hills of Magheracloone 1884, 1984*, 1985, NLI Ir. 94117 g 1
Haslett, A., *Historical Sketch of Ballyalbany Presbyterian Church*, Belfast, n.d.
Leslie, Seymour, *Of Glaslough in Oriel*, 1912
Livingstone, Peadar, *The Monaghan Story*, Enniskillen, 1980
Marshall, J.J., *History of the Town & District of Clogher, Co. Tyrone, parish of Errigal Keerogue, Tyrone, & Errigal Truagh in the Co. of Monaghan*, 1930, NLI I 94114
McCluskey, Seamus, *Emyvale Sweet Emyvale*, Monaghan, 1985
McIvor, John, *Extracts from a Ballybay Scrapbook*, Monaghan, 1974
McKenna, J.E., *Parochial Records*, Enniskillen, 1920
Mulligan, E., *The Replay: A Parish History: Kilmore & Drumsnat*, Monaghan, 1984, NLI Ir. 94117 m 10
Na Braithre Criostai Mhuineachain, *Monaghan Memories*, Monaghan, 1984
O Mordha, P., *The Story of the GAA in Currin and an outline of Parish History*, Monaghan, 1986
O'Donnell, Vincent, *Ardaghey Church and people*, St Naul's Church, Ardaghey, 1995, NLI
Rushe, D.C., *Monaghan in the 18th century*, Dublin & Dundalk, 1916
Rushe, D.C., *Historical Sketches of Monaghan*, Dundalk, 1895.
Shearman, H., *Ulster*, London, 1949, NLI Ir. 91422 s 3

LOCAL JOURNALS

Clann MacKenna Journal
Clogher Record, NLI Ir. 94114 c 2
Macalla
The Drumlin: a Journal of Cavan, Leitrim and Monaghan, NLI Ir. 05 d 345

DIRECTORIES

1824	J. Pigot and Co., *City of Dublin and Hibernian Provincial Directory*, NLI
1846	Slater, *National Commercial Directory of Ireland*, NLI
1852	James A. Henderson, *Belfast and Province of Ulster Directory*, issued also in 1854, 1856, 1858, 1861, 1863, 1865, 1868, 1870, 1877, 1880, 1884, 1887, 1890, 1894, 1900
1856	Slater, *Royal National Commercial Directory of Ireland*, NLI
1865	R. Wynne, *Business Directory of Belfast*
1870	Slater, *Directory of Ireland*, NLI
1881	Slater, *Royal National Commercial Directory of Ireland*, NLI
1894	Slater, *Royal Commercial Directory of Ireland*, NLI
1897	Gillespie's *Co. Monaghan Alamanack and Directory*

GRAVESTONE INSCRIPTIONS

Aghabog: Crover (Aghabog?), C of I, *Clogher Record*, 1982
Clones: Abbey Lane, *Clogher Record*, 1982–84
Clones: The Diamond, C of I, *Clogher Record*, Vol. 13, No. 1, 1988
Clontibret: Annayalla, RC, *Clogher Record*, Vol. 7, No. 2, 1974
Clontibret: Gallagh, C of I, MAR
Clontibret: Clontibret, Pres., MAR
Donagh: Glaslough town, C of I, *Clogher Record*, Vol. 9, No. 3, 1978
Donagh: Donagh, *Clogher Record*, Vol. 2, No. 1, 1957
Drumsnat: Mullanacross, C of I, *Clogher Record*, Vol. 6, No. 1, 1966
Ematris: Rockcorry town, C of I, *Clogher Record*, Vol. 6, No. 1, 1966
Ematris: Edergoole, MAR
Errigal Trough: Attiduff, St Jospeh's, RC, HW
Killanny: Aghafad, C of I, *Clogher Record*, Vol. 6, No. 1, 1966
Killeevan: Drumswords, *Clogher Record*, 1985
Killeevan: Killeevan Glebe, *Clogher Record*, 1982
Killeevan: Killyfuddy, RC, HW
Kilmore: Kilnahaltar (Kilmore?), C of I, *Clogher Record*, 1983, 1985
Monaghan: Aghananimy, RC, MAR
Monaghan: Rackwallace, *Clogher Record*, Vol. 4, No. 3, 1962
Tedavnet: Drumdesco (Urbeshanny?), RC, MAR
Tehallan: Templetate, C of I, GO

ESTATE RECORDS

Anketell estate rentals 1784–89, *Clogher Record*, Vol. XI, No. 3
Balfour rentals of 1632 & 1636, *Clogher Record*, 1985
Earl of Bath: NLI Pos. 5894, Rentals, 1784–1809, major tenants only, covering townlands in the civil parishes of Donaghmoyne, Iniskeen, Magheracloone and Magheross.
Crofton: NLI Ms 4530, Rental, 1792, all tenants; NLI Ms 8150, Rentals 1769–1851, some full, some major tenants only; NLI Ms 20783, Rentals 1853, 1854, 1859,

all tenants, covering townlands in the civil parish of Aghnamullen, Errigal Trough and Tednavnet.

Earl of Dartry (later Viscount Cremorne): NLI Ms 3181, Maps with tenants' names, 1779; NLI Ms 3282, Rental, 1780, major tenants only; NLI Ms 3184 Rental 1790, major tenants only; NLI Ms 1696, Leaseholders; NLI Ms 3674, Rental, 1796–7, major tentants only; NLI Mss 3186–7, Rental, 1800–1, major tenants only; NLI 3189, Rental, 1838, all tenants; NLI Ms 1648, Rental 1846, all tenants; NLI Ms 1698, Valuation, 1841–2, all tenants, covering townlands in the civil parishes of Aghabog, Aghnamullen, Donagh, Ematris, Errigal Trough, Killeevan, Kilmore, Monaghan, Tyholland.

James **Forster:** Five Rent Rolls, 1803–08, 1812–24, covering areas in the parishes Aghabog, Killeevan, Tydavnet, Tyholland, MAR

Kane: Rentals and Reports for the Kane estates, Errigal Truagh, 1764, also 1801, 1819–21, *Clogher Record*, 13 (3), 1990, Errigal Trough civil parish

Kane: Rentals 1840–1; Account Books, 1842–4; Arrears, 1848, 1849, 1852; Rent Receipts, 1851–2, covering townlands in the parish of Tydavnet. MAR

Ker: Landholders, Newbliss, 1790–*c.*1830, Killeevan civil parish, *Clogher Record*, 1985

Leslie: NLI 5783, Rentals 1751–66, major tenants only & leases; Donagh civil parish NLI 5809 Rent rolls, 1751–1780, NLI, Ms 13710 (part 3); 5809, coverage unclear, Glaslough and Emy estates, Donagh civil parish; NLI Ms 5813, Rental, 1839–40, all tenants, covering townlands in the civil parishes of Aghabog, Drummully, Drumsnat, Errigal Trough, Kilmore,

Edward Mayne: NAI M.7036 (18 & 19), Rental, 1848 and 1853, all tenants.

Murray-Ker: Full rentals, 1840–3 (NA BR Mon 8/1), and 1853–4 (NA BR Mon 9/1), covering townlands in the civil parishes of Aghabog, Aghnamullen and Killeevan.

Rossmore estate: Maps with tenants' names, *c.*1820–1852, Monaghan town and surrounding areas, MAR

Edward **Smyth:** NAI 7069, Rental, n.d., all tenants, covering townlands in the civil parishes of Ballybay and Clontibret.

Weymouth estate, Magheross, Survey, major tenants only, MAR

Wingfield estate: Rentals and arrears, 1852, county and town of Monaghan, MAR

OFFALY

Census returns and substitutes

1641	Book of Survey and Distribution, NLI Ms 972
1659	Pender's 'Census'
1766	Ballycommon, also GO 537, *JKAS*, Vol. VII
1770	Voters, NLI Ms 2050
1773–1907	Register of tenants who planted trees: Geashill 1793–1907, Eglish 1809–37, JKAS, 15 (3), 1973/4, 310–18
1802	Protestants in the parishes of Ballyboggan, Ballyboy, Castlejordan, Clonmacnoise, Drumcullin, Eglish, Gallen, Killoughey, Lynally, Rynagh, Tullamore, *IA*, 1973
1821	Parishes of Aghacon, Birr, Ettagh, Kilcolman, Kinnitty, Letterluna, Roscomroe, Roscrea, Seirkieran, NAI CEN 1821/26–34
1823–38	Tithe Books, NAI

1824	Catholic householders, Lusmagh parish, in Roman Catholic parish registers, NLI
1830	Contributors to new Catholic church in Lusmagh, in Roman Catholic parish registers, NLI
1835	Tubber parish, NLI Pos. 1994
1840	Eglish and Drumcullin parishes, in Roman Catholic parish registers, NLI Pos. 4175
1852	Assisted passages from Kilconouse, Kinnitty parish, *AH*, Vol. 22, 1960
1854	Griffith's Valuation
1901	Census, database version in IMA
1911	Census

LOCAL HISTORY

Anonymous, *Ferbane Parish & its Churches*, NLI Ir. 91413 f 4

Brady, J., *A short history of the parishes of the diocese of Meath, 1867–1944*, NLI Ir. 94132 b 2

Byrne, M., *Durrow and its History*, NLI Ir. 9141 p 71

Byrne, M., *Sources for Offaly History*, 1977, NLI Ir. 94136 b 1

Byrne, M., *Towards a History of Kilclonfert*, NLI Ir. 94136 t 1

Byrne, M., *Tullamore Catholic parish: a Historical Survey*

Carrigan, Rev. William, *The History and Antiquities of the Diocese of Ossory*, Dublin, 1905

Cooke, William Antisell, *History of Birr*, Dublin, 1875

Dwyer, Philip, *The Diocese of Killaloe, from the Reformation to the Close of the Eighteenth Century*, Dublin, 1878

Feehan, J., *The Landscape of Slieve Bloom: a study of the natural & human heritage*, 1979, NLI Ir. 91413 f 4

Finney, C.W., *Monasteroris Parish, 8th May 1778–8th May 1978*, NLI Ir. 200 p 23

Gleeson, John, *History of the Ely O'Carroll Territory or Ancient Ormond*, 1915, NLI Ir. 94142 g 1

Healy, John, *History of the Diocese of Meath*, Dublin, 1908.

Meehan, Patrick, *Members of Parliament for Laois and Offaly 1801–1918*, 1983, NLI Ir. 328 m 6

Monahan, Rev. J., *Records Relating to the Diocese of Ardagh and Clonmacnoise*, 1886

Paterson, J. (ed.), *Diocese of Meath and Kildare: an historical guide*, 1981, NLI Ir. 941 p 75

Raymond, B., *The Story of Kilkenny, Kildare, Offaly and Leix*, 1931, NLI I 9141 p 1

LOCAL JOURNALS

Ardagh & Clonmacnoise Historical Society Journal, NLI Ir. 794105

DIRECTORIES

1824	J. Pigot and Co., *City of Dublin and Hibernian Provincial Directory*, NLI
1846	Slater, *National Commercial Directory of Ireland*, NLI

1856   Slater, *Royal National Commercial Directory of Ireland*, NLI
1870   Slater, *Directory of Ireland*, NLI
1881   Slater, *Royal National Commercial Directory of Ireland*, NLI
1894   Slater, *Royal Commercial Directory of Ireland*, NLI

GRAVESTONE INSCRIPTIONS

Irish Midlands Ancestry has transcripts for a large number of graveyards in the county. Contact details will be found in Chapter 14.

Ballykean: Stranure (Cloneygowan?), C of I, GO, Ms 622, p. 182
Kilclonfert: Kilclonfert, Byrne, M., *Towards a History of Kilclonfert*, NLI, Ir. 94136 t 1
Lusmagh: *Offaly Tombstone Inscriptions, Vol. 3*, Tullamore, Offaly Historical Society
Monasteroris: *Offaly Tombstone Inscriptions, Vol. 2*, Tullamore, Offaly Historical
    Society
Rahan: Rahan Demesne, C of I, *Offaly Tombstone Inscriptions, Vol. 1*, Tullamore,
    Offaly Historical Society

ESTATE RECORDS

Earl of Charleville: Tullamore tenants, ?1763–1763, LDS Family History Library,
    941.5 A1, Kilbride civil parish
[No Landlord given]: Rental & maps, ?1855–1855, NAI, M601, Killoughy parish,
    Ballyfarrell & Derrymore townlands, Killoughy civil parish
[No Landlord given]: Rentals, 1840–50, NLI, Ms 4337 Clonsast parish, 7
    townlands, 154 tenants, Clonsast civil parish

ROSCOMMON
CENSUS RETURNS AND SUBSTITUTES

1659   Pender's 'Census'
1749   Aughrim, Ardcarn, Ballintober, Ballynakill, Baslick, Boyle, Bumlin,
            Cam, Clontuskert, Cloocraff, Cloonfinlough, Cloonygormican, Creeve,
            Drimatemple, Dunamon, Dysart, Estersnow, Elphin, Fuerty, Kilbride,
            Kilbryan, Kilcolagh, Kilcooley, Kilcorkey, Kilgefin, Kilglass, Kilkeevin,
            Killinvoy, Killuken, Kilumnod, Kilmacallen, Kilmacumsy, Kilmore,
            Kilronan, Kiltoom, Kiltrustan, Kilnamagh, Lisonuffy, Ogulla, Oran,
            Rahara, Roscommon, St John's, St Peter's Athlone, Shankill, Taghboy,
            Termonbarry, Tibohine, Tisrara, Tumna, NAI MFS 6
1780   Freeholders, GO 442, also LDS film 100181
1790–1799   Freeholders C. 30 lists, NLI Ms 10130
1813   Freeholders, NLI ILB 324
1821   Some extracts, NAI Thrift Abstracts
1823–38   Tithe Books
1830–47   Detailed account of the fate of Ballykilcline townland, Kilglass parish,
            Scally, Robert, *The End of Hidden Ireland*, Oxford, Oxford University
            Press, 1997

1837	Marksmen (i.e. illiterate voters), Athlone Borough, *Parliamentary Papers 1837, Reports from Committees*, Vol. II (1), Appendix A
1841	Some extracts, NAI Thrift Abstracts
1843	Workhouse records Carrick-on-Shannon union 1843–82, LCL
1848	Male Catholic inhabitants of the parish of Boyle, NLI Pos. 4692
1851	Some extracts, NAI Thrift Abstracts
1857–58	Griffith's Valuation
1861	Athlone voters, WCL, also LDS film 1279285
1901	Census
1911	Census

LOCAL HISTORY

Anonymous, *Athlone: Materials from printed sources relating to the history of Athlone and surrounding areas, 1699, 1899*, NLI Mss 1543–7

Beckett, Rev. M., *Facts and Fictions of Local History*, 1929

Burke, Francis, *Lough Cé and its annals: North Roscommon and the diocese of Elphin in times of old*, Dublin, 1895, NLI Ir. 27412 b 1

Clarke, Desmond, 'Athlone, a bibliographical study', *An Leabhar*, No. 10, 1952, 138–9

Egan, Patrick K., *The parish of Ballinasloe, its history from the earliest times to the present day*, Dublin, 1960

Gacquin, W., *Roscommon before the Famine — the parishes of Kiltoom and Cam*, Dublin, Irish Academic Press, 1996

Hayes McCoy, G.A., *Index to 'The Compossicion Booke of Connoght, 1585'*, Irish Manuscripts Commission, Dublin, 1945

Keaney, Marion, *Athlone bridging the centuries*, Westmeath County Council, Mullingar, 1991, NLI Ir. 94131 a 2

Knox, H.T., *Notes on the Early History of the Dioceses of Tuam, Killala and Achonry*, Dublin, 1904

MacNamee, James J., *History of the Diocese of Ardagh*, Dublin, 1954

Monahan, Rev. J., *Records Relating to the Diocese of Ardagh and Clonmacnoise*, 1886

Moran, James A., *Stepping on stones: Roscommon Mid West, the Suck lowlands, the Ballinturly-Correal valley*, James Moran, Cartur, Co. Roscommon, 1993, NLI Ir. 94125 m 10

Murtagh, H., *Irish Historic Towns Atlas: Athlone*, RIA, Dublin, 1994, NLI ILB 941 p (13) 3

Murtagh, H., *Athlone besieged*, Temple Printing Co., Athlone, 1991, NLI Ir. 94107 p 21(1)

O'Brien, Brendan, *Athlone Workhouse and the Famine*, Old Athlone Society, Athlone, 1995, NLI Ir. 300 p 207(8)

Stokes, George T., *Athlone, the Shannon & Lough Ree*, Dublin & Athlone, 1897, NLI Ir. 91413 s 1

LOCAL JOURNALS

Journal of the Old Athlone Society, NLI Ir. 94131 o 1
Journal of the Roscommon Historical and Archaeological Society, NLI Ir. 94125 r 5

DIRECTORIES

1824   J. Pigot and Co., *City of Dublin and Hibernian Provincial Directory*, NLI
1846   Slater, *National Commercial Directory of Ireland*, NLI
1856   Slater, *Royal National Commercial Directory of Ireland*, NLI
1870   Slater, *Directory of Ireland*, NLI
1881   Slater, *Royal National Commercial Directory of Ireland*, NLI
1894   Slater, *Royal Commercial Directory of Ireland*, NLI

GRAVESTONE INSCRIPTIONS

Aughrim: RHGC
Bumlin: Killinordin, RHGC
Cam: IGRS Collection (138 inscriptions), GO, also Gacquin, William, *Tombstone inscriptions Cam Old Cemetery*, Cam Cemetery Committee, Cam, 1992, NLI Ir. 941 p 120(1)
Cloonfinlough: Ballintemple, RHGC
Cloontuskert: IGRS Collection, GO
Dysart: RHGC, also IGRS Collection (103 inscriptions), GO
Elphin: Elphin Cathedral, C of I, GO, Ms 622, p. 151, GO
Fuerty: RHGC
Kiltrustan: RHGC
Lissonuffy: RHGC
Roscommon: Hill St., C of I, GO, Ms 622, p. 170, GO, also RHGC
St Peter's: Athlone, King Street, C of I, Pos. 5309 (with parish registers), NLI
Taghboy: Jamestown?, GO, Ms 622, p. 170, GO
Taghmaconnell: C of I, IGRS Collection (71 inscriptions), GO
Tisrara: Mount Talbot (Tisrara?), C of I, IGRS Collection (144 inscriptions), GO
Tisrara: Carrowntemple, Higgins, Jim, *The Tisrara medieval church Carrowntemple [. . .]*, Tisrara Heritage [. . .] Committee, Four Roads, 1995, NLI Ir. 7941 h 25

ESTATE RECORDS

Frances Boswell: NLI Pos. 4937, Rent ledger, *c.*1760–86, major tenants only, covering townlands in the civil parish of Kilronan
John Browne: NLI 16 1 14(8), map of Carronaskeagh, Cloonfinlough parish, May 1811, with tenants' names
Baron Clonbrock: NLI Ms 19501, Tenants' ledger, 1801–06, indexed, covering townlands in the civil parish of Taughmaconnell.
Edward Crofton: NLI Ms 19672, Rent roll, May 1778, major tenants only, covering townlands in the civil parishes of Baslick, Estersnow, Kilbryan, Kilgefin, Killinvoy, Killumod, Kilmeane, Kiltrustan, Ogulla.
Sir Humphrey Crofton: NLI Ms 4531, Rental, March 1833, tenants' names alphabetically, covering townlands in the civil parish of Tumna.
Sir Thomas Dundas: NLI Mss 2787, 2788, Rentals, 1792, 1804, major tenants only, covering townlands in the civil parishes of Boyle, Estersnow, Kilnamanagh, Tumna.

Walker Evans: NLI Ms 10152, Leases, *c.*1790, covering townlands in the civil parish of Creeve

Gen'l (?) Gunning: NLI Ms 10152. Rental, 1792, major tenants only, covering townlands in the civil parishes of Athleague, Fuerty, Kilcooley

King: NLI Ms 4170, Rent rolls and accounts, 1801–1818, major tenants only, covering townlands in the civil parishes of Creeve, Elphin, Kilmore

Francis Blake Knox: NLI Ms 3077, Rentals, 1845–66, covering townlands in the civil parishes of Cloonfinlough, Rahara.

Lord Lorton: NLI Mss 3104/5, Lease Books, 1740–1900, including many leases to small tenants, with lives mentioned in the leases, covering townlands in the civil parishes of Ardcarn, Aughrim, Boyle, Creeve, Elphin, Estersnow, Kilbryan, Kilnamanagh.

Charles Manners St George: NLI Mss 4001–22, Accounts and rentals (annual), 1842–6, 50–55, 61–71, covering townlands in the civil parishes of Ardcarn, Killukin, Killumod

Rev. Rodney Ormsby: NLI Ms 10152, Leases *c.*1803, Grange townland.

Pakenham-Mahon: NLI Ms 10152, Rent roll, 1725, major tenants only; NLI Ms 10152, rent roll, 1765–68, major tenants only; NLI Ms 2597, rent ledger, 1795–1804, indexed; NLI Mss 5501–3, rent ledgers, 1803–18, 1824–36, part indexed; NLI Ms 9473, tenants of Maurice Mahon, *c.*1817; NLI Ms 9471, rentals and accounts, 1846–54, covering townlands in the civil parishes of Bumlin, Cloonfinlough, Elphin, Kilgefin, Kilglass, Kilnamanagh, Kiltrustan, Lisonuffy, Shankill, also NLI Ms 9472, rent ledger 1840–48, Kilmacumsy parish.

Sandford: NLI 10,152, Rental (major tenants only), 1718; NLI Ms 10,152, Leases, *c.*1750; NLI Ms 10,152, Lands to be settled on the marriage of Henry Sandford, with tenants' names, 1750; NLI Mss 4281–9, Annual Rentals, 1835–45, covering townlands in the civil parishes of Ballintober, Baslick, Kilkeevin, Boyle, Kiltullagh, Tibohine

Thomas Tenison: NLI Ms 5101, Rental & Accounts, 1836–40, covering townlands in the civil parishes of Ardcarn, Kilronan

(No Landlord Given): NLI Ms 24880, List of tenants, Moore parish, 1834

SLIGO

Census Returns and Substitutes

1659	Pender's 'Census'
1664	Hearth Money Roll, *Hearth Money Roll, Co. Sligo*, 1967
1749	Parishes of Aghanagh, Ahamlish, Ballynakill, Ballysumaghan, Drumcliff, Drumcolumb, Killadoon, Kilmacallan, Kilmactranny, Kilross, Shancough, Sligo, Tawnagh, NAI MFS 6
1790	Voters, NLI Ms 2169
1795–6	Freeholders, NLI MS 3136
1798	Persons who suffered losses in the 1798 rebellion, propertied classes only, NLI I 94107
1823–38	Tithe Books
1832–1837	Voters registered in Sligo borough, *Parliamentary Papers 1837, Reports from Committees*, Vol. II (2), 193–6

1852	Sligo electors, NLI MS 3064
1858	Griffith's Valuation
1901	Census
1911	Census

LOCAL HISTORY

Anonymous, *Petition by Sligo Protestants, 1813*, 1813, NLI P. 504

Farry, M., *Killoran and Coolaney: a local history*, 1985, NLI Ir. 94122 f 1

Finn, J., *Gurteen, Co. Sligo, its history, antiquities and traditions*, 1981, NLI Ir. 94122 p 1

Hayes McCoy, G.A., *Index to 'The Compossicion Booke of Connoght, 1585'*, Irish Manuscripts Commission, Dublin, 1945

Knox, H.T., *Notes on the Early History of the Dioceses of Tuam, Killala and Achonry*, Dublin, 1904

MacHale (ed.), *The Parishes in the Diocese of Killala*, NLI Ir. 27414 m 6

MacNamee, James J., *History of the Diocese of Ardagh*, Dublin, 1954

McDonagh, J.C., *History of Ballymote and the Parish of Emlaghfad*, 1936, NLI Ir. 94122 m 8 Ir. 94122 m 1

McDonnell, T., *Diocese of Killala*, NLI Ir. 94123 m 7

McGuinn, J., *Curry*, 1984

McTernan, J.C., *Historic Sligo*, 1965, NLI Ir. 94122 m 4

O'Connell, Philip, *The Diocese of Kilmore: its History and Antiquities*, Dublin, 1937

O'Rourke, T., *History and Antiquities of the Parishes of Ballysadare and Kilvarn*, 1878, NLI Ir. 94122

Wood Martin, W.G., *Sligo and the Enniskilleners, from 1688–91*, Dublin, 1882

Wood Martin, W.G., *History of Sligo*, NLI Ir. 94122 w 1

DIRECTORIES

1820	J. Pigot, *Commercial Directory of Ireland*
1824	J. Pigot and Co., *City of Dublin and Hibernian Provincial Directory*, NLI
1839	*Directory of the Towns of Sligo, Enniskillen, Ballyshannon, Donegal [. . .]*
1846	Slater, *National Commercial Directory of Ireland*, NLI
1856	Slater, *Royal National Commercial Directory of Ireland*, NLI
1870	Slater, *Directory of Ireland*, NLI
1881	Slater, *Royal National Commercial Directory of Ireland*, NLI
1889	*Sligo Independent County Directory*
1894	Slater, *Royal Commercial Directory of Ireland*, NLI

GRAVESTONE INSCRIPTIONS

Sligo Heritage and Genealogy Centre has transcripts for 146 graveyards in the county. Contact details will be found in Chapter 14. Published or publicly available transcripts are given below.

Calry C of I, IGRS Collection, GO

ESTATE RECORDS

Francis Boswell: NLI Pos. 4937, Rental, *c.*1760–1786, major tenants only, covering townlands in the civil parishes of Ahamlish, Drumrat.

Cooper family: NLI Mss 3050–3060, eleven volumes of rentals and rent ledgers, 1775–1872, major tenants only; NLI Ms 3076, rental 1809/10, major tenants only; NLI Mss 9753–57, rentals and accounts, major tenants only, covering townlands in the civil parishes of Achonry, Ahamlish, Ballysadare, Ballysumaghan, Drumcolumb, Drumcliff, Killery, Killaspugbrone, Kilmacallan, Kilmorgan, Kilross, Tawnagh, Templeboy.

Sir Malby Crofton: NAI M938X, rental, 1853, with all tenants; NAI M940X, leases on the estate, including many small tenants, and mentioning lives in the leases, covering townlands in the civil parishes of Dromard, Templeboy.

Sir Thomas Dundas: NLI Mss 2787, 2788, rentals, 1792, 1804, major tenants only, covering townlands in the civil parishes of Aghanagh, Drumrat, Emlaghfad, Kilcolman, Kilfree, Kilglass, Kilmacallan, Kilmacteigue, Kilmactranny, Kilmoremoy, Kilshalvey, Skreen.

Lord Lorton: NLI Mss 3104, 3105, lease books, 1740–1900, including many leases to small tenants, with lives mentioned in leases, covering townlands in the civil parishes of Aghanagh, Drumcolumb, Kilfree, Killaraght, Kilmacallan, Kilshalvey, Toomour.

Charles O'Hara the younger: NLI Pos. 1923, Rent roll. *c.*1775, all tenants, giving lives named in leases, covering townlands in the civil parishes of Achonry, Ballysadare, Killoran, Kilvarnet.

The Earl of Strafford (and others): NLI Ms 10223. Estate rentals, 1682 and 1684, major tenants only, includes a large part of Sligo town, covering townlands in the civil parishes of Ahamlish, Ballysadare, Ballysumaghan, Calry, Cloonoghill, Dromard, Drumcliff, Kilfree, Killoran, Killaspugbrone, Kilmacallan, Kilmacowen, Kilmacteigue, Kilross, St John's, Skreen, Templeboy, Toomour.

Owen Wynne: NLI Mss 5780–5782, rentals and expense books, 1737–68, major tenants only; NLI Mss 5830–1, rent ledgers 1738–53, 1768–73, major tenants only, indexed; NLI Mss 3311–3, a rental and two rent ledgers, yearly from 1798 to 1825, with all tenants, covering townlands in the civil parishes of Ahamlish, Ballysadare, Calry, Drumcliff, Killoran, St John's, Tawnagh, Templeboy.

TIPPERARY

CENSUS RETURNS AND SUBSTITUTES

1595	Freeholders, NLI Pos. 1700
1641	Book of Survey and Distribution, NLI Ms 977
1641–1663	Proprietors of Fethard, *IG*, Vol. 6, No. 1, 1980
1653	Names of soldiers & adventurers who received land in the county under the Cromwellian settlement, *The Cromwellian Settlement of Ireland*, Dublin, 1922
1654	Civil Survey, Vols 1 & 11, *Civil Survey*, Vols 1 & 11, (NLII 6551 Dublin)
1659	Pender's 'Census'
1666–68	Three Hearth Money Rolls, *Tipperary's Families*, Dublin, 1911

1703	Minister's money account, Clonmel, *AH*, 34
1750	Catholics in the parishes of Barnane, Bourney, Corbally, Killavanoge, Killea, Rathnaveoge, Roscrea, Templeree, Templetouhy, IG, 1973
1766	Ballingarry, Uskeane, GO 536; Athassel, Ballintemple, Ballycahill, Ballygriffin, Boytonreth, Brickendown, Bruis, Clerihan, Clonbeg, Cloneen, Clonoulty, Clonbolloge, Clonpet, Colman, Cordangan, Corrogue, Cullen, Dangandargan, Drum, Dustrileague, Erry, Fethard, Gaile, Grean, Horeabbey, NAI, Parl. Ret. 682–701
1776	Voters, NAI M.4910 12
1776	Freeholders, NAI M.1321–2, also GO 442
1799	Census of Carrick on Suir, NLI Pos. 28
1813	Valuation of Roscrea, NAI MFCI 3
1821	Clonmel NAI m 242(2), Modreeny (extracts only), GO 572
1823–38	Tithe Books
1828	Clonmel, houses & occupiers, *Parliamentary Papers 1837, Reports from Committees*, Vol. 11 (2)
1832–37	Registered voters, Clonmel and Cashel boroughs, *Parliamentary Papers 1837, Reports from Committees*, Vol. II (2)
1835	Census of Newport and Birdhill, NLI Pos. 1561
1835	Parish of Templebredin, *JNMAS*, 1975
1837	Protestant parishioners, Clogheen union, 1837, 1877, 1880, *IA*, Vol. 17, No. 1, 1985
1851	Griffith's Valuation
1864–70	Protestants in the parishes of Shanrahan and Tullagherton, IA, 16 (2), 1984, 61–7
1901	Census
1911	Census

LOCAL HISTORY

Anonymous, 'Emigration from the Workhouse of Nenagh Union, Co. Tipperary, 1849–1860', *IA*, 17 (1), 1985

Anonymous, *Atlas of the parishes of Cashel & Emly*

Burke, William P., *History of Clonmel*, Waterford, 1907, NLI Ir. 94142 b 1

Coffey, G., *Evicted Tipperary*, NLI Ir. 330 p 22

Fitzgerald, S., *Cappawhite and Doon*, NLI Ir. 9141 p 43

Flynn, Paul, *The book of the Galtees and the golden vale: a border history of Tipperary, Limerick and Cork*, Dublin, 1926, NLI Ir. 94142 f 2

Gleeson, John, *Cashel of the Kings*, Dublin, 1927

Gleeson, John, *History of the Ely O'Carroll Territory or Ancient Ormond*, 1915, NLI Ir. 94142 g 1

Gorman (ed.), *Records of Moycarkey and Two Mile Borris*, 1955, NLI Ir. 94142 g 4

Gwynn, A., *A history of the diocese of Killaloe*, Dublin, 1962

Hayes, W.J., *Tipperary Remembers*, 1976, NLI Ir. 914142 H 9

Hemphill, W.D., *Clonmel and the surrounding country*, 1860

Kenny, M., *Glankeen of Borrisoleigh: a Tipperary Parish*, 1944, NLI Ir. 94142 k 2

McIlroy, M., *Gleanings from Garrymore*, n.d.

Murphy, Nancy, *Tracing Northwest Tipperary Roots*, Nenagh, 1982

Neely, W.S., *Kilcooley: land and parish in Tipperary*, 1983, NLI Ir. 94142 n 1

Nolan, W., *Tipperary: History and Society*, Dublin, 1985

Power, V. Rev. P., *Waterford and Lismore: A Compendious History of the Dioceses*, Cork, 1937

Pyke, D., *Parish Priests and Churches of St Mary's, Clonmel*, 1984, NLI Ir. 274 p 40

Ryan, C.A., *Tipperary Artillery, 1793–1889*, 1890, NLI Ir. 355942 t 1

Seymour, St John D., *The Diocese of Emly*, Dublin, 1913

Sheehan, E.H., *Nenagh and its Neighbourhood*, n.d.

Watson, Col. S.J., *A Dinner of Herbs: a history of Old St Mary's church, Clonmel*, Clonmel, 1988

White, James (ed.), *My Clonmel Scrap Book*, n.d.

White, Rev. P., *History of Clare and the Dalcassian Clans of Tipperary, Limerick and Galway*, Dublin, 1893

LOCAL JOURNALS

Clonmel Historical and Archaeological Society Journal, NLI Ir. 94142 c 2

Cois Deirge, NLI Ir. 94142 c 4

Eile (Journal of the Roscrea Heritage Society), NLI Ir. 94142 e 1

Journal of the North Munster Archaeological Society, NLI Ir. 794105 n 1

DIRECTORIES

1788	Richard Lucas, *General Directory of the Kingdom of Ireland*, NLI Pos. 3729
1820	J. Pigot, *Commercial Directory of Ireland*
1824	J. Pigot and Co., *City of Dublin and Hibernian Provincial Directory*, NLI
1839	T. Shearman, *New Commercial Directory for the cities of Waterford and Kilkenny, towns of Clonmel, Carrick-on-Suir, New Ross and Carlow*
1846	Slater, *National Commercial Directory of Ireland*, NLI
1856	Slater, *Royal National Commercial Directory of Ireland*, NLI
1866	George Henry Bassett, *Directory of the City and County of Limerick, and of the Principal Towns in the Cos. of Tipperary and Clare*, NLI Ir. 914144 b 5
1870	Slater, *Directory of Ireland*, NLI
1881	Slater, *Royal National Commercial Directory of Ireland*, NLI
1886	Francis Guy, *Postal Directory of Munster*, NLI Ir. 91414 g 8
1889	George Henry Bassett, *The Book of Tipperary*
1889	Francis Guy, *City and County Cork Almanack and Directory*
1894	Slater, *Royal Commercial Directory of Ireland*, NLI

GRAVESTONE INSCRIPTIONS

Ballyclerahan: IGRS Collection (145 inscriptions)

Holycross: C of I, GO, Ms 622 P. 176/7

Kilmore: *IG*, Vol. 2, No. 10, 1953

Kiltinan: GO, Ms 622, P. 144

Knigh: open shelves, NAI
Twomileborris: Littleton, GO, Ms 622, p. 171
Uskane: *IG*, Vol. 3, No. 2, 1957

ESTATE RECORDS

Description of the estate of John **Sadleir** in Limerick & Tipperary, NLI JP 3439
Newcomen estates, maps of estates to be sold, July 20, 1827, NLI map room

TYRONE

CENSUS RETURNS AND SUBSTITUTES

1612–1613	Survey of Undertakers Planted in Co. Tyrone, *Historical Manuscripts Commission Report*, No. 4 (Hastings Mss), 1947, pp. 159–82
1630	Muster Roll of Ulster, Armagh Co. Library and PRONI D.1759/3C/1, T. 808/15164, NLI Pos. 206
1631	Muster Roll, Co. Tyrone, PRONI T.934
1654–56	Civil Survey, *Civil Survey*, Vol. III (NLI I 6551 Dublin)
1661	Books of Survey and Distribution, PRONI T.370/C & D.1854/1/23
1664	Hearth Money Roll, NL Mss 9583/4, also PRONI T.283/D/2, Clogher diocese in *Clogher Record* (1965), Dungannon barony in *Seanchas Ardmhacha* (1971)
1665	Subsidy roll, PRONI T.283/D/1, also NLI Pos. 206
1666	Hearth Money Roll, PRONI T.307
1699	Protestants in the parishes of Drumragh, Bodoney and Cappagh, GO Sources Box 6
1740	Protestants, Derryloran and Kildress, PRONI T.808/15258, RCB Library, LDS film 1279327
1766	Aghaloo, Artrea, Carnteel, Clonfeacle, Derryloran, Donaghendry, Drumglass, Dungannon, Kildress, Tullyniskan, Errigal Keerogue, Kildress, PRONI T.808/15264 7, also NAI, Parliamentary returns 648–66, LDS film 258517
1775	Arboe, with Arboe Church of Ireland registers, PRONI T.679/111, 115–119, D.1278
1795–98	Voters' List, Dungannon barony, PRONI TYR5/3/1
1796	Spinning-Wheel Premium List
1821	Some extracts, Aghaloo, NAI Thrift Abstracts
1823–38	Tithe Books
1830	Census of the C of I parish of Donaghenry, Co. Tyrone, *c*.1830, PRONI C.R.1/38
1832	Census of rural deanery of Derryloran, 1832, PRONI T.2574
1834	Valuation of Dungannon, *Parliamentary Papers 1837, Reports from Committees*, Vol. II (i), Appendix G
1834	Clonoe (Coalisland), NLI Pos. 5579
1842	Voters, NAI 1842/77
1842	Workhouse records Clogher (1842–9), Irvinestown (1845–1918), Enniskillen (1845–1913) and Strabane (1861–83) unions, PRONI,

also LDS films 259162–3, 259187–90, 25914–53 and 259164–5 respectively

1851	Griffith's Valuation
1851–2	Clogherny C of I parishioners, PRONI DIO 4.32C/9/4/2
1866	Parishioners' list, C of I parish of Termonmaguirk, Local custody
1901	Census, *Tyrone: 1901 census index*, Largy Books, Alberta, 1995
1911	Census

LOCAL HISTORY

Anonymous, *Ardtrea Parish Ordnance Survey Memoir 1833–36*, NLI Ir. 914112 o 6

Anonymous, *Drumquin . . . A Collection of Writings and Photographs of the Past*, NLI Ir. 91411 p 10

Anonymous, *Tyrone Almanac & Directory 1872*, NLI Ir. 914114 t 2

Anonymous, 'Provisional list of pre-1900 School Registers in the Public Record Office of Northern Ireland', UHGGN, 9, pp. 60–71

Belmore, Earl of, *Parliamentary Memoirs of Fermanagh and Tyrone 1613–1885*, Dublin, 1887

Donnelly, T.P., *A History of the Parish of Ardstraw West and Castlederg*, 1978, NLI Ir. 94114 d 6

Duffy, J. (ed.), *A Clogher Record Album; a diocesan history*, NLI Ir. 94114 c 3

Hutchison, W.R., *Tyrone precinct: a history of the plantation settlement of Dungannon and Mountjoy to modern times*, Belfast, 1951

Johnson, *Methodism in Omagh . . . over two centuries*, NLI Ir. 27411 p 5

Marshall, J.J., *History of the Town & District of Clogher, Co. Tyrone, parish of Errigal Keerogue, Tyrone, & Errigal Truagh in the Co. of Monaghan*, 1930, NLI I 94114

Marshall, J.J., *Vestry Records of the Church of St John, parish of Aghalow*

McEvoy, J., *County of Tyrone*, 1802

O'Daly, B., *Material for a history of the parish of Kilskeery*, Clogher Record, 1953/4/5

Rutherford, J., *Donagheady: Presbyterian Churches & Parish*, 1953, NLI Ir. 285 r 7

Shearman, H., *Ulster*, London, 1949, NLI Ir. 91422 s 3

LOCAL JOURNALS

Clogher Record, NLI Ir. 94114 c 2
Derriana
Dúchas Néill: Journal of the O'Neill Country Society
North Irish Roots (Journal of the North of Ireland Family History Society)
Irish Family Links, NLI Ir. 9292 f 19
Seanchas Ardmhacha, NLI Ir. 27411 s 4

DIRECTORIES

1819	Thomas Bradshaw, *General Directory of Newry, Armagh, Dungannon, Portadown, Tandragee, Lurgan, Waringstown, Banbridge, Warrenpoint, Rostrevor, Kilkeel and Rathfryland*
1820	J. Pigot, *Commercial Directory of Ireland*

1824	J. Pigot and Co., *City of Dublin and Hibernian Provincial Directory*, NLI
1839	Mathew Martin, *Belfast Directory*, also 1841, 1842
1846	Slater, *National Commercial Directory of Ireland*, NLI
1852	James A. Henderson, *Belfast and Province of Ulster Directory*, issued also in 1854, 1856, 1858, 1861, 1863, 1865, 1868, 1870, 1877, 1880, 1884, 1887, 1890, 1894, 1900
1856	Slater, *Royal National Commercial Directory of Ireland*, NLI
1865	R. Wynne, *Business Directory of Belfast*
1870	Slater, *Directory of Ireland*, NLI
1881	Slater, *Royal National Commercial Directory of Ireland*, NLI
1882	*Omagh Almanac*
1887	*Derry Almanac and Directory*, annually from this year
1888	George Henry Bassett, *The Book of Armagh* (Moy)
1891	*Omagh Almanac*
1894	Slater, *Royal Commercial Directory of Ireland*, NLI

GRAVESTONE INSCRIPTIONS

Heritage World has transcripts of 112 graveyards in Tyrone. The Ulster Historical Foundation has transcripts for 53 graveyards. Contact details will be found in Chapter 14. Published or publicly available transcripts are given below.

Carnteel: Pres., Johnstone, John, *Clogher Cathedral Graveyard*, 1972
Donacavey: *Clogher Record*, Vol. 7, No.2, 1970
Drumglass: Dungannon, Old Drumglass, RC, *Seanchas Ardmhacha*, Vol. 7, No. 2, 1974
Kilskeery: C of I, *Clogher Record*, Vol. 8, No. 1, 1973
Leckpatrick: Todd, Sheelagh, *Register of gravestones in Leckpatrick Old Burial Ground*, 1991, NLI Ir. 9295 p 1(4)

ESTATE RECORDS

Alexander MacKenzie: Rentals, 1825, NLI Ms 18980, all tenants, covering areas in the civil parish of Drumglass

Charlemont: Rentals, 1798–1802, NLI Ms 2702, major tenants only, covering areas in the civil parishes of Clonfeacle and Donaghmore

Leslie: Rental, 1846, NLI Ms 5813, all tenants, valuation, with names and observations, 1833; NLI Ms 5813, all tenants, covering areas in the civil parishes of Carnteel and Errigal Keerogue

Lindsay: Rentals, 1745–61, NLI Ms 5204, all tenants; Rentals, 1778–1817, NLI Ms 5205, all tenants; Survey, 1800 NLI Ms 2584, major tenants only; Rentals, 1808–17, NLI Ms 5206, all tenants; Rentals, 1836–48, NLI Ms 5208, all tenants, covering areas in the civil parishes of Artrea, Derryloran, Desertcreat and Donaghenry

Maxwell: Valuation, with names, 1807, NLI Ms 5379, all tenants; Survey and valuation, 1830, NLI Ms 5380, all tenants, covering areas in the civil parish of Urney

Powerscourt: Rentals, 1809, NLI Ms 19191, all tenants; Rentals, 1835, 1838, NLI Ms 19192, all tenants, covering areas in the civil parish of Clonfeacle

Stewart: Survey, with tenants' names, 1730, NLI Ms 8734 (1), major tenants only, covering areas in the civil parishes of Carnteel, Clonfeacle and Killeeshil
Stewart: Survey with tenants' names, 1767, NLI Ms 9627, major tenants only, covering areas in the civil parish of Derryloran
Stewart: Rentals, 1786–8, NLI Ms 766, all tenants, covering areas in the civil parishes of Artrea, Carnteel, Clonfeacle, Derryloran, Desertcreat, Donaghenry, Donaghmore, Kildress, Killeeshil and Pomeroy

WATERFORD

CENSUS RETURNS AND SUBSTITUTES

1542–1650	Freemen of Waterford, *IG*, Vol. 5, No. 5, 1978
1641	Houses and tenants, Waterford city, *JCHAS*, Vol. 51, 1946, also NAI, Quit Rent Office Papers
1641	Book of Survey and Distribution, NLI Ms 970
1659	Pender's 'Census'
1662	Subsidy Roll of Co. Waterford, *AH*, 30, 1982, 47–96
1663	Inhabitants of Waterford City, including occupations, *JCHAS*, Vol. 51
1664–66	Civil Survey, *Civil Survey*, Vol. VI
1700	Members of some Waterford Guilds, WSIAHSJ 7, 1901, 61–5
1766	Killoteran householders, NAI Parl. Ret, 1413, GO 684, LDS film 100158
1772	Hearth Money Rolls, for parts of Co. Waterford only, *WSIAHSJ*, Vol. XV, 1912
1775	Gentry of Co. Waterford, *WSIAHSJ*, Vol. XVI, No. 1, 1913
1778	Inhabitants of Waterford city, *Freeman's Journal*, 29 Oct. 1778, 5 Nov. 1778
1792	Leading Catholics of Waterford, *IA*, Vol. 8, No. 11
1792	Rent & arrears due to Waterford corporation, 1, NLI P 3000
1807	Waterford city voters, *IA*, Vol. 8, No. 11
1821	Townland of Callaghane, parish of Ballygunner, *Decies* 16, extracts from Waterford city, *IG* 1968/9, typescript index to Waterford city extracts by Thomas Veale, NAI open access
1823–38	Tithe Books
1839	Waterford city Polling List, *IG*, 8 (2), 1991, 275–89
1843	Voters, NAI 1843/65
1847	Principal fishermen, Ring. J. Alcock, *Facts from the Fisheries*, 1847
1848–1851	Griffith's Valuation
1901	Census
1911	Census

LOCAL HISTORY

Anonymous, *Abbeyside reference archive*, Abbeyside reference committee, Abbeyside, 1995, NLI
Anonymous, *Waterford Historical Society Proceedings*, NLI ILB 94141
Butler, M., *The Barony of Gaultiere*, n.d.
Cuffe, Major O.T., *Records of the Waterford Militia 1584–1885*, 1885, NLI 355942

Downey, Edmund, *The story of Waterford to the middle of the 18th century*, Kilkenny, 1891, NLI Ir. 94191

Fitzpatrick, Thomas, *Waterford during the Civil War, 1641–53*, 1912

Hore, H.J., *The Social State of the Southern and Eastern Counties of Ireland in the Sixteenth Century*, 1870

Nolan. W. (ed.), *Waterford History and Society*, Dublin, Geography Publications, 1986, NLI Ir. 94141 w 6

Ochille, F., *The Holy City of Ardmore, Co. Waterford*, Youghal, n.d.

Power, V. Rev. P., *Waterford and Lismore: A Compendious History of the Dioceses*, Cork, 1937

Power, V. Rev. P., *History of the County of Waterford*, Waterford, 1933

Power, V. Rev. P., *Placenames of Decies* (1907)

Pyke, D., *Parish Priests and Churches of St Mary's, Clonmel*, 1984, NLI Ir. 274 p 40

Ryland, R.H., *The history, topography and antiquities of the county and city of Waterford*, London, 1824, NLI Ir. 9141 r 1

Smith, Charles, *The ancient and present state of the county and city of Waterford . . .* Dublin, 1774, NLI J Ir. 94141 s 1

Watson, Col. S.J., *A Dinner of Herbs: a history of Old St Mary's church, Clonmel*, Clonmel, 1988

LOCAL JOURNALS

Decies, NLI Ir. 9414 d 5

Journal of the Waterford & South-East of Ireland Archaeological Society, NLI Ir. 794105 w 1

DIRECTORIES

1788	Richard Lucas, *General Directory of the Kingdom of Ireland*, NLI Pos. 3729
1809	Holden, *Triennal Directory*
1820	J. Pigot, *Commercial Directory of Ireland*
1824	J. Pigot and Co., *City of Dublin and Hibernian Provincial Directory*, NLI
1839	T. Shearman, *New Commercial Directory for the cities of Waterford and Kilkenny, Towns of Clonmel, Carrick-on-Suir, New Ross and Carlow*
1839	T.S. Harvey, *Waterford Directory*
1846	Slater, *National Commercial Directory of Ireland*, NLI
1856	Slater, *Royal National Commercial Directory of Ireland*, NLI
1866	T.S. Harvey, *Waterford Almanac and Directory*
1869	Newenham Harvey, *Waterford Directory*
1870	Slater, *Directory of Ireland*, NLI
1881	Slater, *Royal National Commercial Directory of Ireland*, NLI
1884	George Henry Bassett, *Kilkenny City and County Guide and Directory*
1886	Francis Guy, *Postal Directory of Munster*, NLI Ir. 91414 g 8
1889	George Henry Bassett, *The Book of Tipperary*
1894	Slater, *Royal Commercial Directory of Ireland*, NLI

GRAVESTONE INSCRIPTIONS

Affane: Affane Hunter, C of I, *IG*, Vol. 2, No. 9, 1952
Ballygunner: Ballygunnertemple, IGRS Collection (56), GO
Ballynakill: C of I, IGRS Collection (40), GO
Ballynakill: Ballynakill House, IGRS Collection (16), GO
Clashmore: Clashmore town, C of I, *IG*, Vol. 2, No. 8, 1950
Clonagam: Portlaw, C of I, IGRS Collection (7), GO
Corbally: Corbally Beg, RC, IGRS Collection (153), GO
Crooke: IGRS Collection (138), GO
Crooke: RC, IGRS Collection (4), GO
Drumcannon: IGRS Collection (86), GO
Dunhill: IGRS Collection (23), GO
Dysert: Churchtown, C of I, *Decies*, No. 25, 1984
Faithlegg: Coolbunnia (Faithlegg?), RC, IGRS Collection (166), GO
Guilcagh: C of I, IGRS Collection (11), GO
Islandikane: Islandikane South, IGRS Collection (9), GO
Kilbarry: IGRS Collection (48), GO
Kilburne: Knockeen, IGRS Collection (6), GO
Kill St Lawrence: IGRS Collection (170), GO
Kill St Nicholas: Passage, 1 inscription, IGRS Collection, GO
Killea: Commons (Killea Old?), RC, IGRS Collection (94), GO
Killea: Dunmore East, C of I, IGRS Collection (123), GO
Killoteran: C of I, IGRS Collection (31), GO
Kilmeadan: Coolfin (Kilmeadan?), IGRS Collection (122), GO
Lisnakill: IGRS Collection (35), GO
Mothel: C of I, *Decies*, Nos 38, 39, 40, 41, 42
Newcastle: Ardeenloun East (Newcastle?), IGRS Collection (38), GO
Rathgormuck: *Decies*, No. 37
Reisk: IGRS Collection (86), GO
Stradbally: Faha Chapel of Ease, *Decies*, No. 17, 1981
Stradbally: *Decies*, No. 16, 1981
Trinity Without: Waterford, Chapel Lane, RC (Ballybricken), Power, V. Rev. P., *Catholic Records of Waterford and Lismore*, 1916
Whitechurch: Ballykennedy (Whitechurch?), C of I, *IA*, NLI, Ir. 9205 i 3, Vol. 5, No. 1, 1973

ESTATE RECORDS

[No Landlord given]: Rentals, 1849, *Decies,* No. 27, 1984, all tenants, covering areas in the civil parishes of Lismore and Mocollop
Anne Power: Rental, 1853, NAI M.1830, all tenants, covering areas in the civil parish of Dysert
Bellew: Tenants' list, 1760, WSIAHSJ, Vol. XIX, No. 4, 1911, all tenants, covering areas in the civil parish of Dungarvan
Charles Manners St George: Rentals and accounts, 1842–71, NLI Mss 4001–22, all tenants, covering areas in the civil parishes of Affane, Fews and Whitechurch
Chearnley family: Rental, 1752, NLI Ms 8811, major tenants only, covering areas in the civil parishes of Lismore and Mocollop

Crown Lands: Rental, 1784, NAI, M.3199, all tenants, covering areas in the civil parishes of Crooke, Faithlegg and Kill St Nicholas

Francis Sargeant: Rentals, 1798, NLI Ms 10,072, all tenants, covering areas in the civil parish of Clashmore

George Lane Fox: Tenants' list, 1857, *Decies,* No. 26, 1984, all tenants, covering areas in the civil parish of Kilbarry

James Fox: Rental, 1745–73, NLI Pos. 4065, major tenants only, covering areas in the civil parishes of Drumcannon and Kilbarry

John Mansfield: Rent ledger, 1783–94, NLI Ms 9633, major tenants only, covering areas in the civil parishes of Clashmore, Clonea, Dungarvan, Kilmolash, Lisgenan or Grange, Modelligo and Rathgormuck

Lord Middleton: Estate survey, 1784, NLI Ms 9977, coverage unclear, covering areas in the civil parish of Kilronan

Newport-Bolton family: Rental, 1840–76, NLI Ms 8488, all tenants, covering areas in the civil parishes of Drumcannon and Kilmacomb

Osborne Family: Rentals, 1850, NAI D. 6057, all tenants; Rentals, 1863–77, NAI M. 3052, all tenants, covering areas in the civil parishes of Clashmore, Colligan, Dungarvan, Kilbarrymeaden, Kilgobnet, Killaloan, Kilronan, Kilrossanty, Monksland, Rathgormuck, Ringagonagh, St Mary's Clonmel, Stradbally, Whitechurch

Patrick Cunningham: LEC Rental, 1869, NAI M.1834, coverage unclear, covering areas in the civil parish of Fenoagh

Richard Dawson: Rental, 1781–1901, NLI Ms 3148, major tenants only, covering areas in the civil parishes of Colligan, Dungarvan, Fews, Kilgobnet, Kilrossanty, Lismore and Mocollop, Modelligo and Templemichael

WESTMEATH

CENSUS RETURNS AND SUBSTITUTES

1640	Irish Proprietors in Moate and District, in *Moate, Co. Westmeath: a history of the town and district,* Cox, 1981
1641	Book of Survey and Distribution, NLI Ms 965
1659	Pender's 'Census'
1666	Hearth Money Roll of Mullingar, *Franciscan College Journal,* 1950
1726–7	Protestant householders, Abbeylara, Abbeyshrule, Ardagh, Clonbroney, Clongesh, Kilcommock, Killashee, Rathreagh, Shrule, Taghshiny (Longford), Rathsapick, Russagh (Westmeath), list compiled for the distribution of religious books, NAI M1502
1731	Protestants, Shrule & Rathreagh (Longford), Rathaspick (Westmeath), RCBL GS 2/7/3/25
1749	St Peter's Athlone, NAI MFS 6
1761–88	Freeholders, NLI Mss 787/8
1763	Poll Book, GO 443
1766	Russagh, LDS film 258517
1802–1803	Protestants in the parishes of Ballyloughloe, Castletown Delvin, Clonarney, Drumraney, Enniscoffey, Kilbridepass, Killalon, Kilcleagh, Killough, Killua, Killucan, Leney, Moyliscar, Rathconnell, *IA,* 1973

1823–38	Tithe Books
1832	Voters, *IG*, Vol. 5, Nos 2 & 6, Vol. 6, No. 1 (1975, 1979, 1980)
1835	Tubber parish, NLI Pos. 1994
1837	Marksmen (i.e. illiterate voters), Athlone Borough, *Parliamentary Papers 1837, Reports from Committees*, Vol. II (1), Appendix A
1854	Griffith's Valuation
1855	Partial census of Streete parish *c.*1855, NLI Pos. 4236
1861	Athlone Voters, WCL, also LDS film 1279285
1863–1871	Census for the united parish of Rathaspick and Russagh, Co. Westmeath, PRONI T.2786
1901	Census
1911	Census

LOCAL HISTORY

Anonymous, *Westmeath Local Studies; a guide to sources*, NLI Ir. 94131 k 1

Anonymous, *Irish Midland Studies*, 1980, NLI Ir. 941 m 58

Anonymous, *Athlone: Materials from printed sources relating to the history of Athlone and surrounding areas, 1699–1899*, NLI Mss 1543–7

Anonymous, *Genealogies of the grand jurors of Co. Westmeath, 1727–1853*, NLI Ir. 94131 g 1

Brady, J., *A short history of the parishes of the diocese of Meath, 1867–1944*, NLI Ir. 94132 b 2

Clarke, M.V., *Register of the priory of the Blessed Virgin Mary at Tristernagh*, IMC, NLI Ir. 271 c 22

Clarke, Desmond, *Athlone, a bibliographical study*, An Leabhar, No. 10, 1952, 138–9

Cox, Liam, *Moate, Co. Westmeath: a history of the town and district*, Athlone, 1981, NLI Ir. 994131 c 2

Egan, O., *Tyrellspass, Past and Present*, 1986, NLI Ir. 271 c 22

Grouden, Breda, *The contribution of the Clibborn family to Moate town and district*, Moate Historical Society, Moate, 1990, NLI Ir. 941 P 108(4)

Healy, John, *History of the Diocese of Meath*, Dublin, 1908.

Keaney, Marion, *Sources for Westmeath Studies*, Mullingar, 1982, NLI Ir. 94131 k 1

Keaney, Marion, *Athlone bridging the centuries*, Westmeath County Council, Mullingar, 1991, NLI Ir. 94131 a 2

MacNamee, James J., *History of the Diocese of Ardagh*, Dublin, 1954

Monahan, Rev. J., *Records Relating to the Diocese of Ardagh and Clonmacnoise*, 1886

Murtagh, H., *Athlone besieged*, Temple Printing Co., Athlone, 1991, NLI Ir. 94107 p 21(1)

Murtagh, H., *Irish Historic Towns Atlas: Athlone*, RIA, Dublin, 1994, NLI ILB 941 p (13) 3

O'Brien, Brendan, *Athlone Workhouse and the Famine*, Old Athlone Society, Athlone, 1995, NLI Ir. 300 p 207(8)

O'Brien, Gearóid, *St Mary's Parish Atlone, a history*, St Mel's Trust, Longford, 1989, NLI Ir. 27412

Paterson, J. (ed.), *Diocese of Meath and Kildare: an historical guide*, 1981, NLI Ir. 941 p 75

Sheehan, J., *Westmeath as others saw it . . . A.D. 900 to the present*, 1982, NLI Ir. 94131 s 5

Stokes, George T., *Athlone, the Shannon & Lough Ree*, Dublin & Athlone, 1897, NLI
    Ir. 91413 s 1
Upton, *Upton Papers, RIA*, NLI Pos. 1997
Woods, James, *Annals of Westmeath*, Dublin, 1907, NLI Ir. 94131 w 1

LOCAL JOURNALS

Ardagh & Clonmacnoise Historical Society Journal, NLI Ir. 794105
Journal of the Old Athlone Society, NLI Ir. 94131 o 1
Riocht na Midhe, NLI Ir. 94132 r 1

DIRECTORIES

1820	J. Pigot, *Commercial Directory of Ireland*
1824	J. Pigot and Co., *City of Dublin and Hibernian Provincial Directory*, NLI
1846	Slater, *National Commercial Directory of Ireland*, NLI
1856	Slater, *Royal National Commercial Directory of Ireland*, NLI
1870	Slater, *Directory of Ireland*, NLI
1881	Slater, *Royal National Commercial Directory of Ireland*, NLI
1894	Slater, *Royal Commercial Directory of Ireland*, NLI

GRAVESTONE INSCRIPTIONS

Ballyloughloe, Labaun (Mount Temple?), C of I, *IA*, Vol. 4, No. 2, 1972
Carrick, GO, Ms 622, p. 171
Foyran, Castletown (Finnea), GO, Ms 622, p. 107
Kilcleagh, Killomenaghan, Cox, Liam, *Moate, Co. Westmeath: a history of the town
    and district*, 1981, National Library of Ireland, Ir. 994131 c 2, Athlone
Kilcleagh, Moate, Main Street, C of I, Cox, Liam, *Moate, Co. Westmeath: a history of
    the town and district*, Athlone, 1981, NLI Ir. 994131 c 2
     Moate, Main Street, Quaker, Cox, Liam, *Moate, Co. Westmeath: a history of the
    town and district*, Athlone, 1981, NLI Ir. 994131 c 2
Killua, French, Noel, *Monumental Inscriptions from Some Graveyards in Co. Meath*,
    Typescript, 1990, NAI open shelves
Mullingar, Church Street, C of I, DSHC
St Mary's, Athlone, Church Street, C of I, Pos. 5309 (with parish registers), NLI,
    Athlone, Abbey ruins, Ryan, Hazel A., *Athlone Abbey Graveyard Inscriptions*,
    Longford Westmeath joint library committee, Mullingar, 1987, NLI Ir. 9295 p 2(1)
Stonehall, C of I, GO, Ms 622, p. 183
Street, Barradrum (Street?), C of I, *Riocht na Midhe*, Vol. 4, No. 3, 1969

WEXFORD

CENSUS RETURNS AND SUBSTITUTES

1618	Herald's Visitation of Co. Wexford, GO, 48, also NLI Pos. 957
1641	Book of Survey and Distribution, NLI Ms 975

1654–56	Civil Survey, Vol. IX, *Civil Survey*, Vol. IX (NLI I 6551 Dublin)
1659	Pender's 'Census'
1665–1839	Free Burgesses of New Ross, *Proceedings of the Royal Society of Antiquaries of Ireland*, Ser. 5, Vol 1, pt 1 (1890) pp. 298, 309
1766	Edermine, Protestants only, GO, 537, LDS film 258517, Ballynaslaney, NAI. M2476
1776	Freemen of Wexford, *IG*, 5, Nos 1, 3, 4, 1973
1789	Protestant householders in the parish of Ferns, *IA*, Vol. 13, No. 2, 1981
1792	Some Protestant householders in the parishes of Ballycanew and Killisk, *IA*, Vol. 13, No. 2, 1981
1798	Protestants murdered in the 1798 rebellion, *Memorials of the Dead Co. Wexford & Wicklow supplementary volume with amendments and indices*, Dublin, 1986, Vol. 10, p. 432
1798	Persons who suffered losses in the 1798 rebellion, propertied classes only, NLI I 94107
1817	Emigrants from counties Carlow and Wexford to Canada, *Wexford: History and Society*, Dublin, Geography Publications, 1987
1823–38	Tithe Books
1842	Voters, NAI 1842/82
1853	Griffith's Valuation
1861	Catholics in Enniscorthy parish, with Catholic records, NLI
1867	Marshallstown, *IG*, 1985
1901	Census
1911	Census

LOCAL HISTORY

Anonymous, *Shapland Carew Papers & maps*, IMC, NLI Ir. 399041 c 5

Anonymous, *Owners of Land of one acre and upwards, Co. Wexford*, n.d., NLI I 6551
    1877, Wexford Independent

Brennan, M., *Schools of Kildare and Leighlin, 1775–1835*, NLI Ir. 37094135 b 4

Coghlan, P.J., *A directory for the Co. of Wexford . . . townlands, gentlemen's seats & noted places*, 1867, NLI Ir. 914138

Coyle, James, *The Antiquities of Leighlin*

Doyle, Martin, *Notes and Gleanings Relating to the County of Wexford*, Dublin, 1868

Doyle, Lynn, *Ballygullion, County Wexford*, 1945

Flood, W.H. Grattan, *History of the Diocese of Ferns*, Waterford, 1916

Flood, W.H. Grattan, *History of Enniscorthy, County Wexford*, 1898

Griffiths, George, *The chronicles of the county of Wexford to 1877*, Enniscorthy, 1877,
    NLI Ir. 94138 g 1

Hennessy, Patrick, *Davidstown, Courtnacuddy — A Wexford Parish*, Enniscorthy,
    1986

Hay, Edward, *History of the Insurrection of County Wexford in 1798*, Dublin, 1803

Hore, P.H., *History of the town and County of Wexford*, London, 1900–11, NLI Ir.
    94138 h 2

Hore, H.J., *The Social State of the Southern and Eastern Counties of Ireland in the Sixteenth Century*, 1870

Jeffrey, W.H., *The Castles of Co. Wexford*, Wexford, Old Wexford Society, 1979

Kinsella, A., *The Waveswept Shore — A history of the Courtown district*, Wexford, 1982

Kirk, Francis J., *Some Notable Conversions in the Co. of Wexford*, 1901

Mac Suibhne, Peadar, *Clonegal Parish*, Carlow, 1975

Whelan, Kevin (ed.), *Wexford History and Society*, Dublin, Geography Publications, 1987

Whelan, Kevin, *Tintern Abbey, Co. Wexford: Cistecians and Colcloughs — 8 centuries of occupation*, Friends of Tintern, Saltmills, Co. Wexford, 1990, NLI Ir. 700 p 77 (5)

LOCAL JOURNALS

Journal of the Old Wexford Society, NLI Ir. 94138 o 5
The Past (Journal of the Ui Cinsealaigh Historical Society), NLI Ir. 941382 p 1

DIRECTORIES

1788	Richard Lucas, *General Directory of the Kingdom of Ireland*, NLI Pos. 3729
1820	J. Pigot, *Commercial Directory of Ireland*
1824	J. Pigot and Co., *City of Dublin and Hibernian Provincial Directory*, NLI
1839	T. Shearman, *New Commercial Directory for the cities of Waterford and Kilkenny, Towns of Clonmel, Carrick-on-Suir, New Ross and Carlow*
1846	Slater, *National Commercial Directory of Ireland*, NLI
1856	Slater, *Royal National Commercial Directory of Ireland*, NLI
1870	Slater, *Directory of Ireland*, NLI
1872	George Griffith, *County Wexford Almanac*
1881	Slater, *Royal National Commercial Directory of Ireland*, NLI
1885	George Henry Bassett, *Wexford County Guide and Directory*
1894	Slater, *Royal Commercial Directory of Ireland*, NLI

GRAVESTONE INSCRIPTIONS

Memorials of the Dead, Brian J. Cantwell, Co. Wexford (complete), Vols V to IX, Master Index, Vol. X, Ir. 9295 c 2 & National Archives search room

ESTATE RECORDS

Alcock estate tenants, Clonmore, 1820, NL Ms 10169

Baron **Farnham** estate rent books for Bunclody, 1775–1820, NLI Mss 787–8

Farnham: Tenants and Tradesmen from Baron Farnham's Estate of Newtownbarry, 1774, *Irish Family History Society Newsletter*, 10, 1993, 5–7

Co. Wexford rent lists, 18th century, NL Ms 1782

WICKLOW

CENSUS RETURNS AND SUBSTITUTES

1641	Book of Survey and Distribution, NLI Ms 969
1669	Hearth Money Roll, NAI m 4909, also GO 667
1745	Poll Book, PRONI 2659
1766	Parishes of Drumkay, Dunganstown, Kilpoole (?Kilcoole), Rathdrum, Rathnew, GO 537, also Wicklow Heritage Centre and LDS film 258517
1798	Persons who suffered losses in the 1798 rebellion, propertied classes only, NLI I 94107
1823–38	Tithe Books, NAI
1842–48	Emigrants' list, Shilelagh, see also *West Wicklow Historical Journal*, No. 1 *et seq.* NLI Mss 18,429, 18,524
1852–53	Griffith's Valuation
1901	Census
1911	Census

LOCAL HISTORY

Black, A & C., *Guide to Dublin & Co. Wicklow*, 1888

Bland, F.E., *The Story of Crinken 1840–1940*, Bray, 1940

Brennan, M., *Schools of Kildare and Leighlin, 1775–1835*, NLI Ir. 37094135 b 4

Brien, C., *In the Land of Brien: a short history of the Catholic Church and other institutions in Bray and district from earliest times*, Bray, 1984

Chavasse, C., *Baltinglass and its Abbey*, Baltinglass, 1962

Coleman, James, *Bibliography of the counties Carlow, Kilkenny and Wexford*, WSIAHSJ, ll, 1907, NLI 794105 w 1

de Lion, C., *The vale of Avoca*, Dublin, 1967/91

Doran, A.L., *Bray and environs*, Bray, 1903

Earl, L., *The Battle of Baltinglass*, London, 1952

Eustace, E.A.R., *Short history of Ardoyne Parish*, Carlow, 1967

Flynn, A., *History of Bray*, Bray, 1986

Flynn, A., *Famous Links with Bray*, Bray, 1985

Forde, F., *Maritime Arklow*, Arklow, 1988

Garner, W., *Bray: architectural heritage*, Dublin, 1980

Hannigan, Ken & Nolan, W., *Wicklow History and Society*, Geography Publications, Dublin, 1994, Dublin City Library (1) 941.84

Hore, H.J., *The Social State of the Southern and Eastern Counties of Ireland in the Sixteenth Century*, 1870

MacEiteagain, E., *Ballynagran: an historical perspective*, Wicklow, 1994

Mansfield, C., *The Aravon Story*, Dublin, 1975

Martin, C., *The Woodcarvers of Bray 1887–1914*, Bray, 1985

Martin, C., *A drink from Broderick's well*, Dublin, 1980

Morris, J., *The story of the Arklow lifeboats*, Coventry, 1987

Murphy, H., *The Kynoch era in Arklow 1895–1918*, Arklow, 1977

Power, P.J., *The Arklow calendar, a chronicle of events from earliest times to 1900 A.D.*, 1981, Arklow

Price, Liam, *The Place-names of Co. Wicklow*, Dublin 1945–58, Ir. 92942 p 3

Rees, J., *Arklow — last stronghold of sail: Arklow ships 1850–1985*, Arklow, 1985
Taylor, R.M., *St Mary's Church Blessington, 1683–1970*, Greystones, 1970

LOCAL JOURNALS

Ashford and District Historical Journal, NLI Ir. 94134.a
Bray Historical Record, NLI Ir. 94134 o 3
Glendalough: (. . .) Journal of the Glendalough Historical and Folklore Society
Imaal: *Journal of the St Kevin's Local Studies Group*
Journal of the Arklow Historical Society, NLI Ir. 94134 a
Journal of the Cualann Historical Society, NLI Ir. 94134 b
Journal of the Greystones Historical & Archaeological Society, NLI Ir. 94134 g V.1
Journal of the West Wicklow Historical Society, NLI Ir. 94134 w 5
Report of the Old Bray Society, NLI Ir. 94134 o 3
Reportorium Novum, NLI Ir. 27413 r 3
Roundwood and District History and Folklore Journal, NLI Ir. 94134 r 1
Wicklow Historical Society Journal
Wicklow Journal

DIRECTORIES

1788	Richard Lucas, *General Directory of the Kingdom of Ireland*, NLI Pos. 3729
1824	J. Pigot and Co., *City of Dublin and Hibernian Provincial Directory*, NLI
1846	Slater, *National Commercial Directory of Ireland*, NLI
1856	Slater, *Royal National Commercial Directory of Ireland*, NLI
1870	Slater, *Directory of Ireland*, NLI
1881	Slater, *Royal National Commercial Directory of Ireland*, NLI
1894	Slater, *Royal Commercial Directory of Ireland*, NLI

GRAVESTONE INSCRIPTIONS

Memorials of the Dead, Brian J. Cantwell, Co. Wicklow (complete), Vols I to IV, Master Index, Vol. X, Ir. 9295 c 2 & National Archives search room

13. ROMAN CATHOLIC REGISTERS

What follows is a listing of all copies of Roman Catholic parish registers, microfilm and database transcript, to be found at present (1998) in the National Library of Ireland, the Public Record Office of Northern Ireland, the LDS Family History Library and local heritage centres, as well as those which have been published. The aim is to assist research by providing an overview of the dates and locations of records available, in any sense, to the public. For this reason, and because such an undertaking is beyond the scope of the present work, no attempt has been made to list the dates of the originals held in local custody. Considerations of space also made it impossible to include in the tables the conditions of access to the records, if any; these are detailed in Chapter 3 Church Records and Chapter 14 Libraries etc.

The tables relate the parish or church to the parish maps; it should be borne in mind that these maps can only be approximate, to be used primarily in identifying which parishes adjoin each other. The spelling of parish names is inexact. For many parishes, several names or variant versions have been used. This is reflected in the tables and maps. In a few cases, parishes are listed in the tables but not on the maps, where the sources used for the maps and tables disagreed. The general location of these parishes is indicated by their numerical position in the table. For example, Roundwood in County Wicklow is omitted from the map but included as part of Wicklow 10 (Glendalough) in the table to give an idea of its location.

ANTRIM

DOWN & CONNOR DIOCESE

1	Aghagallon & Ballinderry	15	Cushendun
2	Ahoghill	16	Derriaghy
3	Antrim	17	Duneane
4	Armoy	18	Dunloy
5	Ballintoy	19	Glenavy
6	Ballyclare	20	Glenarm
7	Ballymoney	21	Greencastle
8	Belfast city	22	Kirkinriola
9	Blaris	23	Larne
10	Braid & Glenravel	24	Loughguile
11	Carnlough	25	Portglenone
12	Carrickfergus	26	Portrush & Bushmills
13	Culfeightrin	27	Ramoan
14	Cushendall	28	Randalstown
		29	Rasharkin

Rathlin Island

North Channel

Co. Derry

Lough Neagh

Belfast Lough

Co. Armagh

Co. Down

Map	Church	Baptisms	Marriages	Burials	Location	Reference
			ANTRIM			
1	Aghagallon	1828–1900	1828–1900		UHF	
		Apr. 1, 1828– Dec. 20, 1880	May 25, 1828– Nov. 8, 1880	Mar. 29, 1828– July 5, 1848; May 25, 1872– Dec. 22, 1880	NLI	Pos. 5467
		1828–1889	1828–1889	1828–1848; 1873–1881	PRONI	MIC.1D/6.6 3
2	Ahoghill	1833–1881	1833–1881	1833–1847 (patchy)	PRONI	MIC.1D/68
		1864–1900	1866–1900		UHF	
		1833–1863; Jan. 10, 1864– Dec. 25, 1880	1833–1863 Apr. 3, 1864– Dec. 25, 1880	1833–1863	NLI	Pos. 5472
3	Antrim	Jan. 19, 1874 –Dec. 3, 1880			NLI	Pos. 5472
		1873–1881			PRONI	MIC.1D/68
		1873–1900	1873–1900		UHF	
4	Armoy	Apr. 23, 1848– Mar. 10, 1872; Oct. 12, 1873– Dec. 23 1880	May 18, 1848– Jan. 7, 1872; Nov. 29, 1973– Oct. 24, 1880		NLI	Pos. 5473
		1873–1900	1873–1900		UHF	
		1848–1880	1848–1882		PRONI	MIC.1D/69
5	Ballintoy	1872–1900	1872–1900		UHF	
		1872–1882	1872–1882		PRONI	MIC.1D/69
		Apr. 14, 1872– Nov. 6, 1880	May 20, 1872– Mar. 27, 1879		NLI	Pos. 5473
6	Ballyclare	1869–1881	1870–1872		PRONI	MIC.1D/63
		1869–1900	1870–1900		UHF	
		July 4, 1869– Dec. 25, 1880 (original and transcript)	Feb. 26, 1870– Dec. 29, 1880 (original and transcript)		NLI	Pos. 5467
7	Ballymoney	1853–1882 Mar. 9, 1853– Oct. 15, 1880	1853–1879 Apr. 1853– June 30, 1879		PRONI NLI	MIC.1D/69A Pos. 5473
		1853–1900	1853–1900	1879–1887	UHF	
9	Blaris	1840–	1840–		LC	
10	Braid	Sept. 1878– Dec. 22, 1880	Nov. 2, 1878– Dec. 25, 1880		NLI	Pos. 5473
		1878–1881	1878–1881		PRONI	MIC.1D/69A
10	Glenravel	1825–1856; 1864–1881	1825–1841; 1864–1869; 1878–1882	1825–1841; 1864–1869	PRONI	MIC.1D/70
		1825–1900	1873–1900		UHF	
		June 25, 1825– 1832; July 3, 1825– Sept. 30, 1856; July 8, 1832–Sept. 13, 1841; Feb. 15, 1864–July 21, 1878; Oct. 10, 1878–Dec. 24, 1880	June 25, 1825– 1832 (also a transcript); July 8, 1832– Sept. 13, 1841; Nov. 19, 1864– Jan. 11, 1869; Oct. 20, 1878– Nov. 25, 1880	June 25, 1825–1832; July 8, 1832– Sept. 13, 1841;	NLI	Pos. 5474

→

			ANTRIM			
MAP	CHURCH	BAPTISMS	MARRIAGES	BURIALS	LOCATION	REFERENCE
11	Carnlough	1857–1869 1872–1900 (Glenarriffe)	1869–1900		UHF	
		Aug. 4, 1869– Dec. 18, 1880	Aug. 15, 1869– Oct. 21, 1880		NLI	Pos. 5474
		1825–1880	1869–1882		PRONI	MIC.1D/70–71
12	Carrickfergus	1820–1900	1821–1900		UHF	
		Aug. 15, 1821– Nov. 23, 1828; Dec. 14, 1828– Feb. 9, 1841; Mar. 8, 1852– May 12, 1872	Sept. 21, 1821– Nov. 9, 1828; Dec. 28, 1828– Oct. 1, 1840; Apr. 11, 1852– June 3, 1872		NLI	Pos. 5472
		1852–1872	1852–1872		PRONI	MIC.1D/68, 90
13	Culfeightrin	July 3, 1825– Apr. 7, 1834 (also a transcript); Dec. 20, 1834– Dec. 26, 1838; May 1839–Feb. 5, 1847; 1845–Apr. 17, 1848; May 7, 1848– May 15. 1867	Nov. 1834–Dec. 1838 Jan. 1, 1839–June 9, 1844; Aug. 3, 1845– Mar. 6, 1848; June 2. 1848–Feb. 27, 1867; June 18, 1867– Nov. 14, 1880		NLI	Pos. 5472; Pos. 5473
		1825–1881	1834–1880		PRONI	MIC.1D/68, 69A
		1848–1900	1894–1900		UHF	
14	Cushendall (Layde)	1858–1900	1860–1900		UHF	
		Apr. 8, 1838–Mar. 31, 1844; Jan. 12, 1858–July 4, 1871; Apr. 23, 1871– Nov. 28, 1880	July 1, 1837–May 26, 1844; Mar. 25, 1860– Mar. 15, 1872; Apr. 27, 1872– Nov. 14, 1880		NLI	Pos. 5472
		1838–1844; 1858–1881	1837–1844; 1860–1881		PRONI	MIC.1D/68
15	Cushendun	1848–1852; 1862–1881	1848–1852; 1862–1881	1845–1852	PRONI	MIC.1D/59A–B
		1834–1900	1845–1900		UHF	
		Apr. 1848–Feb. 24, 1852; June 8, 1862– Nov. 11, 1880	May 1, 1848–Feb. 24, 1852; June 15, 1862–Sept. 28, 1880		NLI	Pos. 5473
16	Derriaghy, Hannastown and Rock	Oct. 7, 1877– Dec. 30, 1880	Oct. 13, 1877– Nov. 7, 1880		NLI	Pos. 5467
		1877–1880 1848–1900	1877–1880 1848–1900		PRONI UHF	MIC.1D/63
17	Dunean	1834–1861	1835–1861		PRONI	MIC.1D/70
		May 16, 1834– June 1844; June 4, 1844– Apr. 13, 1847; Sept. 26, 1847– Feb. 3, 1861	May 16, 1835– May 2, 1844; June 14, 1844– Feb. 20, 1847; Oct. 10, 1847– Dec. 29, 1880		NLI	Pos. 5474
		1834–1900	1834–1900		UHF	
18	Dunloy	1860–1900	1877–1900	1877–1900	UHF	
		1840–1881	1877–1881	1877–1881	PRONI	MIC.1D/71

→

Map	Church	Baptisms	Marriages	Burials	Location	Reference
			ANTRIM			
18	Dunloy (*cont.*)	June 17, 1860–Dec. 26, 1876; Apr. 25, 1877–Nov. 21, 1880	June 4, 1877–Nov. 23, 1880	Apr. 26, 1877–Dec. 24, 1880	NLI	Pos. 5475
19	Glenavy and Killead	1849–1900	1848–1900		UHF	
		1849–1881	1848–1883		PRONI	MIC.1D/63
		May 30, 1849–Dec. 31, 1880	Mar. 25, 1848–Dec. 31, 1880		NLI	Pos. 5467
20	Glenarm	Dec. 18, 1825–Mar. 6, 1859; June 7, 1857–Dec. 8, 1862 (transcript); June 6, 1865–Dec., 26, 1880 (transcript)	Oct. 6, 1825–Mar. 6, 1859; May 3, 1859–Dec. 30, 1880	Jan 24, 1831–May 15, 1838	NLI	Pos. 5475
		1865–1880	1825–1880	1831–1838	PRONI	MIC.1D/71
		1836–1900	1859–1900		UHF	
21	Greencastle (Whitehouse)	1854–1881	1854–1881		PRONI	MIC.1D/71
		1854–1900	1854–1900		UHF	
		Mar. 21, 1854–Dec. 25, 1880	Apr. 3, 1854–Oct. 21, 1880		NLI	Pos. 5475
22	Kirkinriola	1848–1881	1840–1842; 1847–1882		PRONI	MIC.1D/69A
		1848–1900	1847–1900	1852–1900	UHF	
		1848–Dec. 25, 1880; Jan. 30, 1866 –Dec. 25, 1880 (transcript)	Jan. 22, 1847–Nov. 27, 1880; Jan 10, 1840–July 28, 1842; Dec. 28, 1847–Nov. 27, 1880 (transcripts)		NLI	Pos. 5473
23	Larne	Aug. 15, 1821–Nov. 23, 1828; Dec. 14, 1828–Feb. 9, 1841; Mar. 8, 1852–May 12, 1872	Sept. 21, 1821–Nov. 9, 1828; Dec. 28, 1828–Oct. 1, 1840; Apr. 11, 1852–June 3, 1872		NLI	Pos. 5472
		1821–1883	1821–1883		PRONI	MIC.1D/68, 90
		1820–1900	1821–1900		UHF	
23	Larne: St Mac Nissi	1828–1900	1828–1900		UHF	
24	Loughguile	May 13, 1845–June 1, 1868; June 21, 1868–Nov. 1, 1869; Nov. 10, 1869–Dec. 20, 1880	May 4, 1845–May 14, 1868; June 5, 1868–Nov. 2, 1869		NLI	Pos. 5473
		1845–1881	1845–1869		PRONI	MIC.1D/69A
		1825–1900	1825–1900		UHF	
25	Portglenone	1864–1900	1864–1900		UHF	
		1864–1881	1864–1882		PRONI	MIC.1D/71
		Jan. 14, 1864–Nov. 28, 1880	Feb 13, 1864–Sept. 30, 1880		NLI	Pos. 5475

→

Map	Church	Baptisms	ANTRIM			Location	Reference
			Marriages	Burials			
26	Portrush	July 7, 1844– Dec. 23, 1880	May, 14, 1848– Nov. 4, 1880 (also a transcript)			NLI	Pos. 5476
		1844–1881	1848–1889			PRONI	MIC.1D/72
27	Ramoan	Oct. 21, 1838– Dec. 14, 1880	Oct. 13,1838– Sept. 16, 1880			NLI	Pos. 5476
		1838–1900	1838–1900			UHF	
		1838–1881	1838–1883			PRONI	MIC.1D/72
28	Randalstown (Drumaul)	Oct. 5, 1825–May 25, 1832; May, 27, 1832– Aug. 1835; Aug. 30, 1835–Aug. 14, 1842; Aug. 23, 1842–Sept. 5, 1854; Aug. 1855– Jan. 1, 1868; Sept. 5, 1871–May 18, 1873; Jan. 2, 1866–Jan. 1, 1868; Feb. 2, 1872– Dec. 26, 1880	Apr. 21, 1835– Oct. 23, 1842; Oct. 30, 1842– May 13, 1854; May 16, 1858– Nov. 14, 1867 (fragmented); 1871–July 4, 1873; Oct. 13, 1872– Nov. 11, 1880	Apr. 21, 1835– Oct. 23, 1842		NLI	Pos. 5474 to 1842; Pos. 5475 to 1880
		1825–1881	1825–1884	1837–1848		PRONI	MIC.1D/70–71
		1825–1900	1825–1900			UHF	
29	Rasharkin	1848–1881	1848–1881			PRONI	MIC.1D/72
		Aug. 16, 1848– Nov. 13, 1880	July 20, 1848– Dec. 4, 1880			NLI	Pos. 5476
		1847–1900	1847–1900			UHF	
–	Rathlin Island	1856–1880	1857–1880			PRONI	MIC.1D/92
		No registers microfilmed				NLI	

ARMAGH DIOCESE
1 Armagh
2 Ballymacnab
3 Ballymore &
  Mullaghbhrac
4 Clonfeacle (Moy)
5 Creggan Lr
6 Creggan Upr
7 Derrynoose
8 Drumcree
9 Dungannon
10 Egish
11 Faughart
12 Forkhill
13 Killeavy Lr
14 Killeavy Upr
15 Kilmore
16 Loughgall
18 Loughgilly
19 Tynan

DROMORE DIOCESE
20 Magheralin
21 Newry
22 Seagoe
23 Shankill (Lurgan)

ARMAGH

Map	Church	Baptisms	Armagh Marriages	Burials	Location	Reference
1	Armagh	July 15, 1796– Oct. 29, 1810; Nov. 1810–Nov. 3, 1835; Nov. 3, 1835– Dec. 7, 1843; Dec. 6, 1843–May 8, 1861; May 12, 1861–May 17, 1870; May 15, 1870– Dec. 30, 1880	Jan. 4, 1802– May 13, 1803; Jan. 2, 1817– Nov. 11, 1835; Nov. 17, 1835– Dec. 25, 1880		NLI	Pos. 5590; Baptisms from 1843 Pos. 5591
		1796–1880	1802–1803; 1806–1810; 1816–1881		PRONI	MIC.1D/41–42
		1796–1900	1802–1809; 1816–1823; 1835–1900		AA	
2	Ballymacnab	Jan. 6, 1844–Aug. 21, 1870; Aug. 20, 1870–Dec. 24, 1880	Jan. 16, 1844– Dec. 16, 1880		NLI	Pos. 5586
		1844–1881	1844–1880		PRONI	MIC.1D/37–38
		1820–1900	1844–1900		AA	
3	Ballymore and Mullabrack	1798–1802; 1831–1900	1831–1900		AA	
		1843–1856; 1859–1880	1843–1856; 1859–1880		LDS	BFA 0926031
		1843–1865; 1859–1880	1843–1865; 1859–1880		PRONI	MIC.1D/37
		Oct. 9, 1843–May 27, 1853; Oct. 7, 1853–Nov. 20, 1856; June 5, 1859– Dec. 12, 1880	Oct. 21, 1843–Oct. 16, 1853; Oct. 16, 1853– Nov. 23, 1856; July 24, 1859–Nov. 12, 1880		NLI	Pos. 5586
4	Clonfeacle	See Tyrone 6				
5	Creggan Lower	See NLI			LDS	BFA 0926034
		1845–1900	1845–1900		AA	
		1845–1880	1845–1881		PRONI	MIC.1D/40
		Feb. 14, 1845– Dec. 30, 1880	Feb. 13, 1845– Nov. 27, 1880		NLI	Pos. 5589
6	Creggan Upper	1796–1803; 1812–1900	1796–1803; 1812–1900		AA	
		1796–1803; 1812–1829; 1845–1881	1796–1803; 1812–1829; 1845–1881		PRONI	MIC.1D/43
		Aug. 5, 1796–Jan. 19, 1803; Sept, 23, 1812–Mar. 28, 1822; Apr. 2, 1822–May 29, 1829; May 26, 1845–May 31, 1871 Jan. 2, 1870– Dec. 28, 1880	Aug. 8, 1796–Feb. 16, 1803; Dec. 18, 1812–Mar 22, 1822; Apr. 8, 1822–July 24, 1829; May 8, 1845–Mar. 1, 1870; May 13, 1871– Nov. 26, 1880		NLI	Pos. 5592
7	Derrynoose	Feb. 1, 1835–Jan. 29, 1837; Dec. 1846– Jan. 28, 1866; Feb. 1, 1866–Dec. 30, 1880	July 17, 1846–Jan. 31–1875; Feb. 8, 1875–Dec. 9, 1880	July 22, 1846– Apr. 1851	NLI	Pos. 5589
		1835–1837; 1846–1881	1846–1881	1846–1851	PRONI	MIC.1D/40

→

		ARMAGH				
MAP	**CHURCH**	**BAPTISMS**	**MARRIAGES**	**BURIALS**	**LOCATION**	**REFERENCE**
7	Derrynoose (*cont.*)	1814–1819; 1823–1830; 1832–1837; 1846–1900	1808–1814; 1823–1833; 1846–1900	1823–1851	AA	
		See NLI			LDS	BFA 1279356 item 1
8	Drumcree	1844–1899	1844–1900	1863–1900	AA	
		1844–1881 (some gaps)	1844–1881 (some gaps|)	1863–1880	PRONI	MIC.1D/37; C.R.2/8
		Jan. 1, 1844–June 30, 1864; June 17, 1864–Dec. 31, 1880	Feb. 9, 1844–Nov. 23, 1863; July 23, 1864 –Nov. 27, 1880	May 26–Dec. 22, 1863; June 24, 1864–Dec. 30, 1880	NLI	Pos. 5586
9	Dungannon	See Tyrone 13				
10	Eglish	1862–1881	1862–1882		PRONI	MIC.1D/36
		1862–1900	1862–1900		AA	
		Jan. 21, 1862–Nov. 4, 1880	Jan. 27, 1862–Nov. 5, 1880		NLI	Pos. 5585
		1862–1900	1862–1900	1877–1900	HW	
11	Faughart	See Louth 10				
12	Forkhill	Jan. 1, 1845–Apr. 29, 1879	Jan. 12, 1844–Dec. 29, 1880		LDS	BFA 0926041 items 1–2
		Jan. 1, 1845–Apr. 29, 1879	Jan. 12, 1844–Dec. 29, 1880		NLI	Pos. 5587
		1845–1879	1844–1878		PRONI	MIC.1D/38
		1845–1900	1844–1900		AA	
13, 14	Dromintee	1853–1900	1853–1877; 1883–1884; 1887–1900		AA	
		1853–1879	1853–1877		PRONI	MIC.1D/41
		June 7, 1853–Aug. 31, 1879	Nov. 8, 1853–Dec. 13, 1877		NLI	Pos. 5590
13	Killeavy Lower	1835–1881	1835–1862; 1868–1869; 1874–1878	1858–1862	PRONI	MIC.1D/39
		Jan. 4, 1835–Jan. 27, 1860; Jan. 1, 1860–Dec. 29, 1880	1835–1862 ; 1874–1878	1858–1862	LDS	BFA 0926042
		1835–1900	1835–1852; 1868–1900		AA	
		Jan. 4, 1835–Jan. 27, 1860; Jan. 1, 1860–Dec. 29, 1880	Jan. 6, 1835–Jan. 26, 1860; Jan. 15, 1860–Dec. 29, 1862; May 21, 1874 –Nov. 29, 1878	Aug. 1858–Jan. 30, 1860; Jan. 9, 1860–Dec. 24, 1862	NLI	Pos. 5588
14	Killeavy Upper	1832–1880	1832–1882		PRONI	MIC.1D/39
		See NLI			LDS	BFA 0926042
		1832–1900	1832–1900		AA	
		Oct. 22, 1832–Oct. 31, 1868; Nov. 7, 1868–Dec. 31, 1880	Nov. 4, 1832–Oct. 13, 1868; Dec. 30, 1868–Dec. 29, 1880		NLI	Pos. 5588
15	Kilmore	Jan. 7, 1845–Dec. 19, 1880	Jan. 3, 1845–Dec. 31, 1880		NLI	Pos. 5587

→

Map	Church	ARMAGH			Location	Reference
		Baptisms	Marriages	Burials		
15	Kilmore (*cont.*)	1845–1900	1845–1900		AA	
		1845–1881	1845–1881		PRONI	MIC.1D/38
16	Loughgall and Tartaraghan	Jan. 1835–Aug. 29, 1852; Oct. 8, 1854–May 2, 1858; July 12–Dec. 27, 1857; Sept. 18, 1859–Dec. 28, 1880	Aug. 20, 1833–Jan. 5, 1854; Feb. 8, 1860–Nov. 22, 1880		NLI	Pos. 5587
		1835–1881	1833–1880		PRONI	MIC.1D/38
		1834–1900	1833–1900		AA	
18	Loughgilly	1825–1900	1825–1900		AA	
		May 17, 1825–Dec. 31, 1844; Feb. 4, 1849–Dec. 19, 1880	Feb. 12, 1825–Nov. 29, 1844; Feb. 18, 1849–Dec. 20, 1880		NLI	Pos. 5587
		1825–1844; 1849–1881	1825–1844; 1849–1881		PRONI	MIC.1D/38
19	Tynan	1822–1900	1822–1834; 1836 1888–1900		AA	
		1822–1834; 1838–1842; 1845–1884 1845–1877	1822–1834		PRONI	MIC.1D/40
		1822–1880 (gaps)	1822–1877 (gaps)		LDS	BFA 09799710 items 6–8
		June 2, 1822–Aug. 11, 1834; Aug. 12, 1838–July 25, 1842; May 17, 1845–Sept. 2, 1880	June 6, 1822–Oct. 26, 1834; June 22, 1845–Oct. 18, 1877		NLI	Pos. 5589
20	Magheralin	See Down 38				
21	Newry	See Down 39				
22	Seagoe	1836–1880	1836–1880	1837–1880	LDS	BFA 0926088 items 1–4
		Sept. 1836–Feb. 25, 1870; Mar. 3, 1870–Dec. 26, 1880	Oct. 16, 1836–Feb. 5, 1860; Feb. 10, 1860–Nov. 18, 1880	Apr. 13, 1837–Jan. 27, 1860; Feb. 16, 1860–Dec. 5, 1880	NLI	Pos. 5498
		1836–1881	1836–1881	1837–1880	PRONI	MIC.1D/23–24
		1836–1900	1836–1900		AA	
23	Shankill	1822–1880 (gaps)	1866–1880	1866–1880	LDS	BFA 0926089
		Sept. 13, 1822–Dec. 30, 1865 (modern transcript with gaps); Jan. 1, 1866–Dec 31, 1880	Jan. 19, 1866–Dec. 28, 1880	Jan. 5, 1866–Dec. 27, 1880	NLI	Pos. 5498
		1822–1881	1866–1881	1866–1881	PRONI	MIC.1D/23
		1822–1900	1822–1900	1825–1900	AA	

BELFAST CITY

Map	Church	Baptisms	Marriages	Burials	Location	Reference
Down 4	Ballymacarrett	Oct. 11, 1841–Oct. 7, 1865; Nov. 5, 1865–Dec. 29, 1880	Oct. 8, 1841–May 7, 1865; Oct. 12, 1865–Dec. 30, 1880		NLI	Pos. 5469
		1841–1888	1841–1888		PRONI	MIC.1D/65
Antrim 8	Holy Cross	Sept. 20, 1868–Dec. 31, 1880	Sept. 12, 1868–Dec. 25, 1880		NLI	Pos. 5469
		1834–1900	1868–1900		UHF	
		1868–1881	1868–1881		PRONI	MIC.1D/65
Antrim 8	Holy Family	1869–1900	1895–1900		UHF	
Antrim 8	Holy Rosary	1888–1900	1894–1900		UHF	
Antrim 8	Sacred Heart	1849–1900	1890–1900		UHF	
Antrim 8	St Brigid's	1886–1900	1891–1900		UHF	
Antrim 8	St Joseph's	Dec. 22, 1872–Dec. 27, 1880	Sept. 24, 1872–Dec. 1, 1880		NLI	Pos. 5471
		1872–1881	1872–1881		PRONI	MIC.1D/67
			1872–1900		UHF	
Antrim 8	St Malachy's	1858–1881	1858–1881		PRONI	MIC.1D/64
		1858–1900	1858–1900		UHF	
		May 10, 1858–Dec. 28, 1880	June 9, 1858–Dec. 26, 1880		NLI	Pos. 5468
		Jan. 1, 1870–Dec. 28, 1880 (transcript)	(many pages mutilated)			
Antrim 8	St Mathew's	1841–1900	1841–1900		UHF	
Antrim 8	St Patrick's	Apr. 5, 1798–Oct. 20, 1811; Jan. 23, 1814–Aug. 18, 1841; Aug. 18, 1841–July 15, 1853; July 14, 1853–July 17, 1867; Aug. 10, 1875–June 7, 1880	Apr. 19, 1798–June 18, 1812; Jan. 29, 1814–Aug. 17, 1841; Aug. 17, 1841–July 28, 1853; July 25, 1853–July 2, 1867		NLI	Pos. 5470, 5471
		1798–1811; 1814–1867; 1875–1880	1798–1812; 1814–1867		PRONI	MIC.1D/66–67
		1794–1900	1798–1900		UHF	
Antrim 8	St Paul's	1887–1900	1887–1900		UHF	
		1887–	1887–		LC	
Antrim 8	St Peter's	1866–1881	1866–1881		PRONI	MIC.1D/64–65
		1866–1900	1866–1900		UHF	
		Oct. 31, 1866–May 8, 1871; May 14, 1871–Feb. 17, 1875; Feb. 22, 1875–Aug. 2, 1879; Aug. 2, 1879–Dec. 29, 1880	Oct. 22, 1866–Dec. 29, 1880		NLI	Pos. 5468; Pos. 5469
Antrim 8	St Vincent de Paul	1894–1900	1896–1900		UHF	
Antrim 8	Union Workhouse	1884–1900			UHF	
Antrim 8	St Mary's	1867–1900	1867–1900		UHF	
		1867–1881	1867–1881		PRONI	MIC.1D/67
		Feb. 18, 1867–Sept. 21, 1876; Sept. 22, 1876–Dec. 31, 1880	Feb. 18, 1867–Dec. 27, 1880		NLI	Pos. 5471

CARLOW

KILDARE & LEIGHLIN DIOCESE

1 Bagenalstown
2 Ballon & Rathoe
3 Borris
4 Carlow
5 Clonegall
6 Clonmore
7 Graiguenamanagh
8 Hacketstown
9 Leighlinbridge
10 Myshall
11 Rathvilly
12 St Mullin's
13 Tinryland
14 Tullow

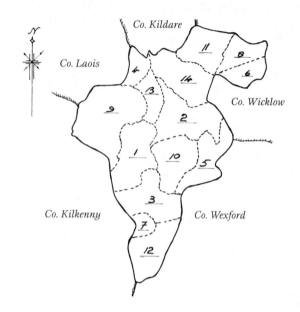

			CARLOW			
Map	**Church**	**Baptisms**	**Marriages**	**Burials**	**Location**	**Reference**
1	Bagenalstown (Dunleckney)	Jan. 1, 1820–June 27, 1841; July 1, 1841–Dec. 25, 1857; Jan. 3, 1858–Nov. 27, 1880	Jan. 8, 1820–June 26, 1841; July 8, 1841–Nov. 28, 1857; Jan. 19, 1858–Nov. 27, 1880		NLI	Pos. 4195
		See NLI			LDS	BFA 0926113
		1820–1899	1820–1899		CGP	
2	Ballon and Rathoe	1782–1896 Jan. 2, 1785–Sept. 10, 1795; July 2, 1816–Dec. 26, 1830; Jan. 9, 1820–Feb. 14, 1825 (not a duplicate); Jan. 6, 1831–Dec. 27, 1867	Not specified Aug. 10, 1782–Dec. 10, 1795; Jan. 8, 1820–Dec. 14, 1825; Aug. 10, 1816–Nov. 26, 1880	Aug. 9, 1825–Dec. 6, 1834; Jan. 15, 1861 –Dec. 28, 1871	CGP NLI Pos. 4189	
3	Borris	See NLI			LDS	BFA 0926107
		May 2, 1782–Dec. 23, 1813; Feb. 2, 1825–Mar. 15, 1840; Mar. 22, 1840–Dec. 30, 1855; Jan. 1, 1856–Dec. 30, 1876; Jan. 7, 1877–Dec. 25, 1880	Jan. 26, 1782–Dec. 4, 1813; Feb. 8, 1825–Mar. 3, 1840; Apr. 28, 1840–Nov. 23, 1868; Feb. 2, 1869–Nov. 27, 1880		NLI	Pos. 4196
4	Carlow	See NLI			LDS	BFA 0926119 items 1–2
		1774–1900	1769–1899		CGP	⟶

			CARLOW			
MAP	CHURCH	BAPTISMS	MARRIAGES	BURIALS	LOCATION	REFERENCE
4	Carlow (*cont.*)	June 15, 1774–Sept. 4, 1775; Feb. 5, 1777–July 31, 1782; Nov. 15, 1787–Jan. 14, 1789; Dec. 7, 1793–Dec. 17, 1793; Jan. 19, 1794–Dec. 17, 1795; Jan. 1, 1799–May 9, 1804; Jan. 10, 1806–Apr. 15, 1806; Jan. 2, 1807–Feb. 5, 1807; Jan. 1, 1809–May 8, 1809; Jan. 5, 1811–Jan. 12, 1811; Jan. 1, 1820–Aug. 19, 1834; Aug. 22, 1834–June 29, 1845; Jan. 1, 1845–Apr. 19, 1856; Apr. 22, 1856–Dec. 28, 1880 Indexed 1834–49	Nov. 8, 1769–Aug. 20, 1786; 1791 (some); 1794 (some); Jan. 1, 1820–June 17, 1845; Jan. 22, 1845–Apr. 14, 1856; May 10, 1856–Nov. 22, 1880		NLI	Pos. 4193
5	Clonegal	See NLI			LDS	BFA 0926110
		1833–1899	1833–1899		CGP	
		Jan. 7, 1833–Nov. 27, 1842; Nov. 27, 1842–Dec. 5, 1852; Dec. 5, 1852–Mar. 29, 1868; Apr. 2, 1868–Apr. 30, 1871 (all transcripts); June 5, 1871–Nov. 16, 1880 (original)	Feb. 14, 1833–May 20, 1871; May 25, 1871–Nov. 16, 1880		NLI	Pos. 4197
6	Clonmore	1820–1900	1813–1826; 1834–1900		WHC	
		Nov. 23, 1819–Apr. 9, 1833; Apr. 7, 1833–Feb. 26, 1860; Mar. 4, 1860–Dec. 11, 1880	Feb. 10, 1813–Feb. 19, 1833; May 4, 1833–Feb. 19, 1860; May 16, 1860 –Dec. 11, 1880		NLI	Pos. 4198
		1819–1899	1819–1899		CGP	
7	Graignamanagh	See Kilkenny 32				
8	Hacketstown	1815–20 (a few entries) Aug. 29, 1820–Apr. 20, 1823; July 10, 1826–Sept. 7, 1826; Oct. 14, 1827–Mar. 23, 1877; Jan. 4, 1862–Mar. 23, 1878; Mar. 10, 1878–Dec. 26, 1879	Aug. 31, 1820–Dec. 1, 1827; Mar. 3, 1829–Nov. 28, 1863; Nov. 20, 1861 –Sept. 25, 1870; Feb. 2, 1877–Aug. 1, 1878; May 9, 1878–Nov. 25, 1880		NLI	Pos. 4191
		See NLI			LDS	BFA 0926115 item 1
		1827–1899	1828–1899		CGP	
9	Leighlinbridge	Jan. 1, 1783–Oct. 22, 1786; Dec. 1, 1819–June 26, 1827; July 6, 1827–Nov. 16, 1844; Nov. 17, 1844–Sept. 29, 1867; Jan. 2, 1859–Dec. 26, 1880	Feb. 9, 1783–Jan. 14, 1788; Jan. 12, 1820–Feb. 27, 1827; July 12, 1827–Nov. 22, 1880		NLI	Pos. 4195
		1783–1900	1783–1899	1898–1899	CGP	
		See NLI			LDS	BFA 1363869
10	Myshall	Feb. 11, 1822–May 3, 1846; Oct. 25, 1846–Dec. 25, 1880	Sept. 17, 1822–Jan. 30, 1845 (pages missing and mutilated); Feb. 17, 1846–Nov. 27, 1880		NLI	Pos. 4198
		See NLI			LDS	BFA 0926123
11	Rathvilly	1792–1887	1799–1884		WHC	
		1797–1899	1800–1899		CGP	→

Map	Church	Baptisms	CARLOW Marriages	Burials	Location	Reference
11	Rathvilly *(cont.)*	Oct. 19, 1797–Jan. 15, 1813; June 29, 1813–Apr. 25, 1842; Apr. 25, 1842–Dec. 12, 1880	Oct. 5, 1800–Feb. 13, 1812; June 29, 1813–Nov. 27, 1880		NLI	Pos. 4189
12	St Mullin's	May 8, 1796–Sept. 28, 1800; Feb. 1, 1801–Apr. 16, 1807; Sept. 4, 1807–Mar. 3, 1810; Jan. 19, 1812–Apr. 16, 1814; Feb. 8, 1816–Mar. (?) 25, 1816; Jan. 6, 1820–July 30, 1832; Aug. 10, 1832–Nov. 30, 1871; Jan. 4, 1872–Dec. 30, 1880	June 20, 1796–Feb. 5, 1807; Jan. 8, 1808–May 20, 1809; Jan. 24, 1820–June 10, 1832; Oct. 25, 1807–Mar. (?) 8, 1813; Aug. 10, 1832–Nov. 30, 1871; Feb. 6, 1872–Nov. 25, 1880		NLI	Pos. 4196
13	Tinryland	1813–1899	1813–1899	1898–1899	CGP	
		Mar. 28, 1813–May 24, 1833; June 2, 1833–Dec. 20, 1857; Jan. 6, 1858–Nov. 27, 1880	June 20, 1813–Feb. 28, 1843; Apr. 25, 1843–Nov. 26, 1857; Jan. 21, 1858–Nov. 27, 1880		NLI	Pos. 4192
14	Tullow	Aug. 13, 1763–Jan. 10, 1781; Jan. 19, 1798–Jan. 1, 1802; June 5, 1807–July 4, 1831 (?); Aug. 23, 1830–Apr. 18, 1858; Apr. 22, 1858–Oct. 9, 1876; Oct. 10, 1876–Dec. 21, 1880	May 5, 7, 1775–Feb. 20 1776 (2 entries for 1777); Jan. 18, 1799–Feb. 27, 1800; June 19, 1807–May 20, 1830 (transcript, many gaps); Nov. (?) 20, 1830–Feb. 20, 1860; Apr. 30, 1860–Nov. 18, 1880		NLI	Pos. 4194
		1748–1899	1748–1899		CGP	

CAVAN

Co. Fermanagh

Co. Monaghan

Co. Leitrim

Co. Meath

Co. Longford

Co. Westmeath

ARDAGH & CLONMACNOISE DIOCESE
1 Drumlumman North
2 Drumlumman South
3 Scrabby

MEATH DIOCESE
4 Carnaross
5 Kilbride
6 Kingscourt

KILMORE DIOCESE
7 Annagh
8 Ballintemple
9 Castlerahan
10 Castleterra
11 Corlough
12 Crosserlough
13 Denn
14 Drumgoon (Cootehill)
15 Drumlane (Staghall)
16 Drung (see Kilsherdony)
17 Drumreilly
18 Glangevlin
19 Kildallon (Ballyconnell)
20 Killan (Bailieboro)
21 Killeshandra
22 Killinagh
23 Killinkere

24 Kilmainhamwood & Moybologue
25 Kilmore
26 Kilawley (Swanlinbar)
27 Knockbride
28 Kilsherdony
29 Laragh
30 Lavey
31 Lurgan (Virginia)
32 Mullagh
33 Templeport
34 Urney & Annegeliff

Map	Church	Baptisms	Cavan Marriages	Burials	Location	Reference
1	Drumlumman North (Mullahoran)	1859–1902	1859–1902	1859–1875; 1925–1937	LDS	BFA 1279229 item 10
		Jan. 21, 1859–Dec. 26, 1880	Jan. 31, 1859–Dec. 6, 1880	Feb. 7, 1859–Feb. 26, 1875	NLI	Pos. 4237
		1859–1899	1837–1899	1837–1899	CHGC	
2	Drumlumman South	1837–1899	1837–1899	1837–1899	CHGC	
		See NLI			LDS	BFA 1279229 item 7
		Nov. 13, 1837–Aug. 3, 1873; May 5, 1875–Dec. 5, 1880	Dec, 2, 1837–June 18, 1873; Feb. 27, 1876–Nov. 30, 1880	Dec. 21, 1837–Sept. 17, 1869; Feb 16, 1876–Dec. 18, 1880	NLI	Pos. 4236
3	Scrabby	See Longford 17				
4	Carnaross	See Meath 10				
5	Kilbride and Mountnugent	Jan. 1, 1832–Jan., 27, 1864; Jan. 13, 1864–Nov. 27, 1880	Jan. 1, 1832–Nov. 22, 1863; Feb. 4, 1864–Nov. 27, 1880		NLI	Pos. 4172
		See NLI			LDS	BFA 0926174
		1832–1899			CHGC	
		1830–1891	1830–1892	1906–1993	DSHC	
6	Enniskeen (Kingscourt)	Oct. 16, 1838–Aug. 13, 1854; Jan. 1 1864–Dec. 31, 1880	Aug. 15, 1838–May 27, 1861	Sept. 1846–May 30, 1858	NLI	Pos. 4183
		See NLI			LDS	BFA 0926175
7	Annagh	Nov. 12, 1845–Oct. 25, 1864 (Anna East); Jan. 1849–Sept. 1875 (Anna West); Oct. 3, 1875–Dec. 29, 1880	July 1847–Dec. 1880 (Anna East);Nov. 1864–Aug. 1899 (Anna West)		NLI	Pos. 7505, 5342
		1875–1881			PRONI	MIC.1D/75
		1845–1899	1847–1899	1849–1899	CHGC	
8	Ballintemple	Oct. 16, 1862–Dec. 26, 1880	Oct. 20, 1862–Nov. 20, 1880	NLI	Pos. 5343	
		1862–1881	1862–1881		PRONI	MIC.1D/76
9	Castlerahan and Munterconnaught	Feb. 6, 1752–July 1771; Feb. 3, 1773–Nov. 4, 1776; Nov. 6, 1814–Aug. 16, 1820; Oct. 26, 1828–May 2, 1841; Aug. 1854–Feb. 17, 1879	Sept. 5, 1751–June 8, 1771; Feb. 4, 1773–Feb. 26, 1775; Nov. 20, 1814–June 7, 1820; May 17, 1832–Nov. 27, 1841; Aug. 7, 1855–Nov. 26, 1878	Sept. 1751–June 1758; Dec. 1761–July 1769; Feb. 1773–Oct. 1775; Dec. 1814–Oct. 1820; May 26, 1832–Oct. 24, 1841	NLI	Pos. 5348
		1752–1771; 1773–1776; 1814–1820; 1828–1841; 1854–1879	1751–1771; 1773–1775; 1814–1820; 1832–1841; 1855–1878	1751–1758; 1761–1769; 1773–1775; 1814–1820; 1832–1841	PRONI	MIC.1D/81
		1752–1899	1751–1899	1751–1899	CHGC	
10	Castleterra	June 26, 1763–June 12, 1809; Apr. 19, 1862–Dec. 26, 1880; Oct. 28, 1808–June 11, 1809	June 12, 1763–Apr. 29, 1793		NLI	Pos. 5350, 6430

⟶

Map	Church	Baptisms	Marriages	Burials	Location	Reference
		CAVAN				
10	Castleterra *(cont.)*	1763–1809 1862–1881	1763–1793 1808–1809		PRONI	MIC.1D/ 83–84
		1763–1899	1763–1899		CHGC	
11	Corlough	1877–1899	1877–1899		CHGC	
		See NLI			LDS	BFA 0926129 item 3
		1877–1881	1877–1882	1877–1881	PRONI	MIC.1D/79
		Feb. 12, 1877–Dec. 16, 1880	Feb. 12, 1877–Oct. 21, 1880	Feb. 16, 1877– Dec. 19, 1880	NLI	Pos. 5346
12	Crosserlough	See NLI			LDS	BFA 0926130
		1843–1881	1843–1881	1843–1876	PRONI	MIC.1D/77
		Oct. 1843–Feb. 17, 1876; Dec. 1866–Dec. 13, 1880; Apr. 2, 1876– Aug. 6, 1880	Dec. 1866–Dec. 13, 1880; Oct. 10, 1868– Nov. 27, 1880	Dec. 1866–Dec. 13, 1880	NLI	Pos. 5344
		1843–1899	1843–1899	1843–1899	CHGC	
13	Denn	Oct. 19, 1856–Jan.16, 1874 (transcript-many gaps)	Oct. 20, 1856–Oct. 28, 1858		NLI	Pos. 5350
		1856–1874 (gaps)	1856–1858		PRONI	MIC.1D/83
		1856–1899	1856–1899		CHGC	
14	Drumgoon	Feb. 22, 1829–July 25, 1872; Oct. 1, 1872–Sept. 12, 1879			NLI	Pos. 5348
		1829–1879	1829–1872		PRONI	MIC.1D/81
15	Drumlane	1835–1899	1835–1899		CHGC	
		1836–1881	1870–1880		PRONI	MIC.1D/75
		Jan. 1836–Nov. 20, 1867 (out of order); Jan. 6, 1868–Dec. 12, 1880	Sept. 1, 1870–Dec. 8, 1880		NLI	Pos. 5342
16	Drung	1847–1883 No records microfilmed			PRONI NLI	C.R.2/10
17	Drumreilly Lower	See Leitrim 17				
18	Glangevlin	1867–1899	1867–1899		CHGC	
		Mar. 2, 1867–Dec. 29, 1880	Jan. 28. 1867–Nov. 15, 1880		NLI	Pos. 5345
		1867–1881 See NLI	1867–1881		PRONI LDS	MIC.1D/78 BFA 0979703 item 5
19	Kildallen	1867–1899	1867–1899		CHGC	
		Apr. 15, 1867–Dec. 31, 1880	Jan. 1, 1867–Dec. 9, 1880		NLI	Pos. 5345
		1867–1881	1867–1881		PRONI	MIC.1D/78
		See NLI			LDS	BFA 0979703 item 2
20	Killanne	See NLI			LDS	BFA 0926132 item 2
		Jan. 28, 1835–Nov. 20, 1849; Jan. 13, 1868– Nov. 19, 1880	Jan. 12, 1835–Feb. 12 1850; Jan. 28. 1868– Sept. 22, 1880		NLI	Pos. 5349
		1835–1849; 1868–1880	1835.–1850; 1868–1880		PRONI	MIC.1D./82

──────▶

Map	Church	Baptisms	Cavan Marriages	Burials	Location	Reference
21	Killeshandra	Jan. 4, 1835–Oct. 14, 1840; Dec. 24, 1840–Aug. 24, 1844; Mar. 15, 1845–July 17, 1852; Aug. 1, 1853–Oct. 15, 1868 Oct. 3, 1868–Dec. 31, 1880	Jan. 7, 1835–Sept. 1, 1840; Aug. 19, 1849–May 20, 1852; Aug. 1, 1853–Oct. 15, 1868; Sept. 28, 1868 –Nov. 15, 1880		NLI	Pos. 5345/6
		See NLI			LDS	BFA 099703 item 7
		1835–1880	1835–1840; 1849–1881		PRONI	MIC.1D/ 78–79
		1835–1899	1835–1899	1835–1899	CHGC	
22	Killinagh	Apr. 1, 1869–Dec. 31, 1880	June 28, 1869–Nov. 28, 1880	Feb. 21, 1875–Dec, 27, 1880	NLI	Pos. 5350
		1869–1881	1869–1881	1875–1881	PRONI	MIC.1D/83
		1867–1899	1867–1899	1875–1899	CHGC	
23	Killinkere and Mullagh	May 27, 1766–Oct. 19, 1790; Jan. 1, 1842–Apr. 11, 1862; Mar. 5, 1864–Dec. 12, 1880	Dec. 23, 1766–Aug. 29, 1789; Jan. 22, 1842–Nov. 32, 1861; June 4, 1864–Nov. 19, 1880		NLI	Pos. 5349
		1766–1790; 1842–1861; 1864–1880	1766–1789; 1842–1861; 1864–1880		PRONI	MIC.1D/82
		1766–1899	1766–1899		CHGC	
24	Kilmainham-wood and Moybologue	See Meath 2				
25	Kilmore	1859–1881	1859–1881	1859–1881	PRONI	MIC.1D/76
		May 1, 1859–Dec. 31, 1880	May 1, 1859–Dec. 31, 1880	May 1, 1859–Dec. 31, 1880	NLI	Pos. 5343
26	Kinawly	See Fermanagh 19				
27	Knockbride	May 15, 1835–Aug. 19, 1860; Sept. 7, 1860–May 20, 1879	Jan. 15, 1835–Aug. 20, 1860; Sept. 12, 1860–Jan. 25, 1877	Jan. 11, 1835–1860; Sept. 10, 1860–Mar. 6, 1875	NLI	Pos. 5349
		1835–1879	1835–1879	1835–1875	PRONI	MIC.1D/82
		See NLI			LDS	BFA 0926133 item 3
28	Kilsherdany	June 26, 1803–Nov. 26, 1814; Nov. 19, 1826–Apr. 29, 1849; Oct. 4, 1855–Jan. 10, 1860	July 10 1803–Jan. 18, 1814; Jan. 12–May 20, 1835; 1843–Apr. 29, 1849; Oct. 1, 1855–Aug. 16, 1857		NLI	Pos. 5342
		1803–1814; 1826–1849; 1855–1860	1803–1814; 1835; 1843–1849; 1855–1857		PRONI	MIC.1D/48
29	Laragh	1876–1899	1876–1899		CHGC	
		May 2, 1876–Dec. 1, 1880			NLI	Pos. 5342
		1876–1881			PRONI	MIC.1D/75
30	Lavey	1867–1881			PRONI	MIC.1D/75
		Jan. 12, 1867–Sept. 19, 1880			NLI	Pos. 5342
		1867–1899	1867–1899		CHGC	
31	Lurgan	1755–1899	1755–1899		CHGC	
		See NLI			LDS	BFA 0926134
		1755–1795 (gaps); 1821–1881	1855– 1770; 1773–1780; 1821–1875	1821–1855	PRONI	MIC.1D/ 80–81

Map	Church	Baptisms	Marriages	Burials	Location	Reference
		CAVAN				
31	Lurgan *(cont.)*	Jan. 6, 1755–Aug. 1, 1795 (very patchy); Nov. 1, 1821–Sept. 30, 1840; Oct. 10, 1840–Dec. 31, 1875; Jan. 4, 1876–Dec. 24, 1880	Feb. 1755–Aug. 29, 1770; Jan. 14, 1773–Sept. 6, 1780; Nov. 21, 1821– Sept. 23, 1840; Oct. 10, 1840–Nov. 27, 1875	Nov. 12, 1821– Oct. 5, 1840; Oct. 1, 1840–Mar. 30, 1855	NLI	Pos. 5347
32	Mullagh	1760–1790; 1842–1872	1766–1789; 1842–1872	1842–1857	PRONI	MIC.1D/80, 82
		June 29, 1842–Feb. 18, 1872	June 29, 1842 Feb. 18, 1872	Sept. 29, 1842– Feb. 3, 1857	NLI	Pos. 5347
33	Templeport	1836–1899	1836–1899	1827–1845	CHGC	
		Sept. 4, 1836–July 14, 1870; July 26, 1870– Dec. 24, 1880	Nov. 18, 1836–July 4, 1870; Sept. 15, 1870– Oct. 16, 1880	Feb. 26, 1827– Dec. 1845; July 26, 1870–Dec. 16, 1880	NLI	Pos. 5345
		1836–1880	1836–1882	1827–1845; 1870–1880	PRONI	MIC.1D/78
		See NLI			LDS	BFA 0979703 item 6
		1836–1899	1836–1899	1836–1899	Cavan County Library	
34	Urney	July 6, 1812–Dec. 12, 1829; Dec. 1829–July 24, 1859; Jan. 1, 1860–Dec. 30, 1880	July 19, 1812–Feb. 23, 1830; Feb. 23, 1830–Aug. 3, 1859; Sept. 14, 1859– Nov. 27, 1880		NLI	Pos. 5342/3
		1812–1881	1812–1880		PRONI	MIC.1D/ 75–76
		1812–1899	1812–1899		CHGC	

CLARE

GALWAY DIOCESE
1 Beagh
2 Ennistymon (Kilmanaheen & Cloony)
3 Glanaragh (Ballyvaughan)
4 Kilcronin & Kilconry
5 Kilfenora
6 Kilshanny
7 Liscannor (Kilmacrehy)
8 Lisdoonvarna
9 New Quay (Glanamanagh)

KILLALOE DIOCESE
10 Broadford
11 Carrigaholt
12 Clarecastle
13 Clondegad
14 Clonrush (Mountshannon)
15 Corofin
16 Crusheen
17 Donnass & Truagh
18 Doora & Kilraghtis
19 Dysart
20 Ennis
21 Feakle
22 Inagh
23 Inch & Kilmaley

Co. Tipperary
Liscannor Bay
Atlantic Ocean
Loop Head
Shannon Estuary
Co. Limerick

24 Kilballyowen
25 Kildysart
26 Kilfarboy (Milltownmalbay)
27 Kilfidane
28 Kilkee
29 Kilkeedy
30 Killaloe
31 Killanena (Flagmount)
32 Killard
33 Killimer
34 Kilmacduane
35 Kilmihil
36 Kilmurry-Ibrickane
37 Kilmurry-McMahon

38 Kilnoe & Tuamgraney
39 Kilrush (St Senan's)
40 Newmarket
41 O'Callaghan's Mills
42 Ogonneloe
43 Quin & Clooney
44 Scarriff & Moyne
45 Sixmilebridge
46 Tulla

LIMERICK DIOCESE
47 Cratloe
48 Parteen & Meelick

MAP	CHURCH	BAPTISMS	CLARE MARRIAGES	BURIALS	LOCATION	REFERENCE
1	Beagh	See Galway 31				
2	Ennistymon (Kilmanaheen)	Jan. 15, 1870–Sept. 8, 1880			NLI	Pos. 2440
		1823–1900	Not specified		CGC	
		~~See NLI~~			LDS	BFA 0926067
3	Glanaragh (Bally-vaughan)	Sept. 1, 1854–July 29, 1876; Aug. 18, 1876–Dec. 31, 1880			NLI	Pos. 2440
		1854–1900	Not specified		CGC	
4	Kilcronin (Carron)	1854–1900	Not specified		CGC	
		See NLI			LDS	BFA 0926063
		Oct. 26, 1853–Dec. 25, 1880	Nov. 24, 1856–June 22, 1880		NLI	Pos. 2440
5	Kilfenora	June 1, 1836–May 15, 1847; Sept. 3, 1854–Sept. 12, 1876; Oct. 8, 1876–Dec. 27, 1880	Dec. 2, 1865–Nov. 26, 1880		NLI	Pos. 2440
		See NLI			LDS	BFA 0926065
		1836–1900	Not specified		CGC	
6	Kilshanny	1869–1900	Not specified		CGC	
		No records microfilmed			NLI	
7	Liscannor	1843–1900	Not specified		CGC	
		June 15, 1843–July 4, 1854; July 3, 1854–Feb. 27, 1873	Feb. 17, 1866–Oct. 4, 1880 (transcript); May 25, 1873–Oct. 4, 1880		NLI	Pos. 2440
8	Lisdoonvarna	June 1, 1854–Nov. 19, 1876	Jan. 12, 1860–Nov. 23, 1880		NLI	Pos. 2440
		1854–1900	Not specified		CGC	
9	New Quay	1836–1900	Not specified		CGC	
		1847–1880	1848–1863		LDS	BFA 0979691 item 1
		Oct. 4, 1847–Aug. 31, 1854 (transcript); Oct. 3, 1854–Dec. 30, 1880	Feb. 5, 1848–Apr. 20, 1863 (transcript)		NLI	Pos. 2441
10	Broadford	1845–1900	Not specified		CGC	
		1844–1880	1844–1880		LDS	BFA 0979694 item 3
		Jan. 19, 1844–Dec. 19, 1880	Feb. 10, 1844–Nov. 27, 1880		NLI	Pos. 2476
11	Carrigaholt	Feb. 8, 1853–Mar. 17, 1878; Feb. 19, 1878–Dec. 15, 1880	Jan. 12, 1852–Mar. 17, 1878; Mar. 5, 1878–Nov. 15, 1880		NLI	Pos. 2485
		1853–1900	Not specified		CGC	
		See NLI			LDS	BFA 0926099
12	Killone (Clarecastle)	1834–1900	Not specified		CGC	
		Jan. 25, 1863–July 21, 1880 (Killone); Dec. 10, 1853–Dec. 15, 1880 (Clarecastle)	Feb. 17, 1853–Dec. 15, 1880 (Killone); Jan. 21, 1854–Nov. 19, 1880 (Clarecastle)		NLI	Pos. 2471

⟶

Map	Church	Baptisms	CLARE Marriages	Burials	Location	Reference
12	Killone *(cont.)*	1853–1880	1854–1880		LDS	BFA 0979693 items 1–2
13	Clondegad (Kilchrist)	Oct. 2, 1846–Dec. 29, 1880	Nov. 1, 1846–June 20, 1880		NLI	Pos. 2471
		1846–1900	Not specified		CGC	
		Oct. 2, 1846–Dec. 29, 1880	Nov. 1, 1846–June 20, 1880		LDS	BFA 0926092
14	Clonrush (Mount-shannon)	1846–1900	Not specified		CGC	
		See NLI			LDS	BFA 0926093 item 1
		July 1846–Mar. 3, 1880	Jan. 22, 1846–Feb. 10, 1880		NLI	Pos. 2476
15	Corofin (Rath)	Apr. 4, 1819–Dec. 25, 1836; Feb. 16, 1837–Nov. 15, 1862; Oct. 31, 1862–Dec, 23, 1880	Jan. 27, 1818–Feb. 25, 1844; Feb. 27, 1859–Nov. 26, 1862; Nov. 10, 1862–June 27, 1880		NLI	Pos. 2474 (B. to 1862); remainder 2475
		1819–1900	Not specified		CGC	
16	Crusheen	Feb. 1860–Dec. 29, 1880			NLI	Pos. 2472
		1860–1900	Not specified		CGC	
		Feb. 1860–Dec. 29, 1880			LDS	BFA 0926093 item 2
17	Doonass and Truagh	1851–1880	1851–1880		LDS	BFA 0979694 item 2
		1851–1900	Not specified		CGC	
		July 27, 1851–Dec. 12, 1880	Sept. 6, 1851–Nov. 29, 1880		NLI	Pos. 2476
18	Doora and Kilraghtis	Mar. 1, 1821–Jan. 23, 1863; Mar. 1862–Dec. 23, 1880	Jan. 10, 1823–Dec. 5, 1880		NLI	Pos. 2472 (B. to 1862); remainder 2474
		1821–1900	Not specified		CGC	
19	Dysart (Ruan)	Aug. 18, 1845–Dec. 23, 1880	July 2, 1846–June 23, 1880		NLI	Pos. 2473
		1845–1900	Not specified		CGC	
20	Ennis (Drumclift)	1841–1900	Not specified		CGC	
		Mar. 19, 1841–Oct. 1, 1879	Apr. 3, 1837–Dec. 1, 1880		NLI	Pos. 2472
21	Feakle	Apr. 22, 1860–Dec. 25, 1880	Sept. 21, 1860–Aug. 17, 1880		NLI	Pos. 2476
		1860–1900	Not specified		CGC	
		1842–1861; 1860–1880	1842–1861; 1860–1880		LDS	BFA 0979696 items 5, 7; 0979694 it 5
22	Inagh and Kilnamona	Feb. 23, 1850–Oct. 1, 1865 (indexed); Oct. 6, 1865–Dec. 25, 1880	Apr. 14, 1850–July 26, 1865 (indexed); Oct. 9, 1865–July 29, 1880		NLI	Pos. 2472
		1850–1900	Not specified		CGC	
23	Inch and Kilmaley	See NLI			LDS	BFA 0926094
		Sept. 23, 1828–Dec. 31, 1880			NLI	Pos. 2474
		1829–1900	Not specified		CGC	$\longrightarrow$

Map	Church	Baptisms	CLARE Marriages	Burials	Location	Reference
24	Kilballyowen	See Carrigaholt				
25	Kildysart	July 1829–Nov. 1866 (indexed transcript, with parish history); Nov. 14, 1866–Dec. 28, 1880	Jan. 1867–Dec. 22, 1880		NLI	Pos. 2475
		1829–1900	Not specified		CGC	
26	Kilfarboy (Milltown-malbay)	Nov. 16, 1831–July 8, 1855; May 1, 1855–Dec. 1, 1858; Dec. 4, 1858–Dec. 31, 1880	Nov. 24, 1856–Dec. 1, 1858; Feb. 9, 1859–Nov. 27, 1880		NLI	Pos. 2486
		1831–1900	Not specified		CGC	
27	Kilfiddane	1868–1900	Not specified		CGC	
		Aug. 15, 1868–Dec. 20, 1880	Jan. 8, 1869–Feb. 10, 1880		NLI	Pos. 2485
28	Kilkee	Mar. 3, 1869–Dec. 12, 1880			NLI	Pos. 2485
		See NLI			LDS	BFA 0926100
		1836–1900	Not specified		CGC	
29	Killkeady	1833–1900	Not specified		CGC	
		Feb. 1833–1840 (transcript); 1840–1855 (transcript); 1855–1866 (transcript); Dec. 24, 1870–Dec. 31, 1880	Feb. 20. 1871–July 24, 1880		NLI	Pos. 2473
30	Killaloe	May 24, 1828–June 19, 1844; June 23, 1844–Jan. 21, 1855; Feb. 1, 1855–Dec. 8, 1880	Feb. 26, 1829–Sept. 7, 1880		NLI	Pos. 2477
		1828–1900	Not specified		CGC	
31	Caher Feakle (Flagmount, Killanena)	Feb. 16, 1842–Mar. 27, 1861; Mar. 25, 1861–Jan. 28, 1873; Feb. 4, 1873–Dec. 26, 1880	Jan. 16, 1842–Feb. 12, 1861; Nov. 15, 1862–July 28, 1880		NLI	Pos. 2487
		1842–1900	Not specified		CGC	
32	Killard	May 13, 1855–Dec. 29, 1880 (transcript)	Feb. 12, 1867–Oct. 31, 1880		NLI	Pos. 2487
		1855–1880	1867–1880		LDS	BFA 0979696 items 2–3
		1855–1900	Not specified		CGC	
33	Killimer (Knockera)	Jan. 23, 1859–Dec. 30, 1880	Feb. 10, 1859–Nov. 23, 1880		NLI	Pos. 2485
		1859–1900	Not specified		CGC	
34	Kilmacduane	Jan. 17, 1854–Dec. 30, 1880	May 1, 1853–Nov. 29, 1867		NLI	Pos. 2485
		1854–1900	Not specified		CGC	
35	Kilmihil	Mar. 20, 1849–Jan. 12, 1870 (indexed); Jan. 1, 1870–Dec. 29, 1880	Jan. 20,1849–Sept. 19, 1869 (indexed); Apr. 8, 1869–Nov. 13, 1880		NLI	Pos. 2485
		1849–1900	Not specified		CGC	
36	Kilmurry-Ibricken	Apr. 25, 1839–Apr. 12, 1876; Jan. 1, 1876–Dec. 26, 1880 (transcript)	Apr. 13, 1839–Aug. 14, 1852; Sept. 1855–Aug. 2, 1863; Feb. 11, 1863–Oct. 15, 1876; Feb. 5, 1876–Nov. 27, 1880		NLI	Pos. 2486
		1839–1900	Not specified		CGC	
		See NLI			LDS	BFA 0926101
37	Kilmurry McMahon	Nov. 1, 1845–Dec. 19, 1880	Sept. 20, 1837–Oct. 16, 1880	Nov. 5, 1844–Apr. 1848	NLI	Pos. 2485
		1842–1900	Not specified		CGC	⟶

Map	Church	Baptisms	CLARE Marriages	Burials	Location	Reference
38	Kilnoe	Nov. 1, 1832–Dec. 31, 1880	Nov. 2, 1832–July 4, 1880		NLI	Pos. 2477
		1832–1900	Not specified		CGC	
39	Kilrush (St Senan's)	1827–1880	1829–1880		LDS	BFA 0979696 item 4
		1827–1900	Not specified		CGC	
		Aug. 1, 1827–Dec. 8, 1831; Jan. 14, 1833–Sept. 29, 1863; Oct. 1, 1863–Dec. 31, 1880	Jan. 7, 1829–Dec. 6, 1880		NLI	Pos. 2487
40	Newmarket-on-Fergus	Apr. 29, 1828–Feb. 25, 1866	1828–Aug. 13, 1865		NLI	Pos. 2471–2
		1828–1900	Not specified		CGC	
		See NLI			LDS	BFA 0926095 item 2
41	O'Callaghan's Mills	Jan. 4, 1835–Dec. 31, 1880	Jan. 14, 1835–Nov. 14, 1880		NLI	Pos. 2476
		1835–1900	Not specified		CGC	
		1835–1880	1835–1880		LDS	BFA 0979694 item 6
42	Ogonnelloe	1832–1900	Not specified		CGC	
		1832–1869	1857–1869		LDS	BFA 0979694 item 1
		Mar. 29, 1832–Feb. 25, 1869 (transcript)	Feb. 9, 1857–Feb. 9, 1869 (transcript)		NLI	Pos. 2476
43	Quin	Jan. 4, 1816–Mar. 1, 1855; Jan. 1855–Dec. 31, 1880	Jan. 29, 1833–Feb. 14, 1855; Jan. 10, 1855–June 26, 1880		NLI	Pos. 2473
		See NLI			LDS	BFA 0926096
		1815–1900	Not specified		CGC	
44	Scarriff	1852–1900	Not specified		CGC	
		May 5, 1852–Mar. 24, 1872; Mar. 24, 1872–Dec. 31, 1880	Nov. 22, 1852–Apr. 20, 1872; Apr. 20, 1872–June 15, 1880		NLI	Pos. 2476
		See NLI			LDS	BFA 0926097
45	Sixmilebridge	Dec. 15, 1828–Aug. 28, 1839; Jan. 28, 1840–Dec. 23, 1864; Jan. 6, 1865–Dec. 26, 1880	Jan. 25, 1829–July 29, 1839; May 1840–Nov. 26, 1864; Feb. 12, 1865–Oct. 12, 1880		NLI	Pos. 2474
		1828–1900	Not specified		CGC	
46	Tulla	Jan. 1819–Mar. 28, 1846; Apr. 21, 1846–Dec. 28, 1861 (indexed); Jan. 1, 1862–Dec. 29, 1880 (indexed)	Jan. 1, 1819–Feb. 24, 1846; Apr. 20, 1846–Nov. 30, 1861 (indexed); Jan. 21, 1862–Oct. 21, 1880		NLI	Pos. 2471
		1819–1880	1819–1880		LDS	BFA 0979693 item 4
		1819–1900	Not specified		CGC	
47	Cratloe	1802–1900	Not specified		CGC	
		Nov. 26, 1802–Dec. 30, 1856; Jan. 16, 1857–Nov. 19, 1877	Jan. 15, 1822–Dec. 10, 1856; Feb. 3, 1857–Sept. 8, 1877		NLI	Pos. 2410/11
48	Parteen	See Limerick	Not specified		CGC	→

CORK SOUTHWEST

CORK & ROSS DIOCESE

1 Ardfield & Rathberry
2 Aughadown
3 Ballinhassig
4 Bandon
5 Bantry
6 Lislee (Barryroe)
7 Caheragh
8 Castlehaven
9 Clonakilty
10 Clonthead
11 Coucey's Country
12 Drimoleague
13 Dunmanway
14 Enniskeane & Desertserges
15 Goleen
16 Innishannon
17 Kilbritain
18 Kilmacabea
19 Kilmeen & Castleventry
20 Kinsale
21 Muintervarra
22 Murragh
23 Rath and the Islands
24 Rosseletteri (Rosscarbery)
25 Skibbereen

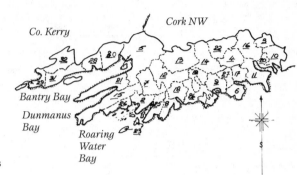

26 Schull
27 Timoleague

KERRY DIOCESE
28 Adrigole
29 Allihies
30 Conane & Glengarriff
31 Castletownbere
32 Eyeries

			CORK SOUTHWEST			
Map	Church	Baptisms	Marriages	Burials	Location	Reference
1	Ardfield and Rathberry	Jan. 1, 1801–April 5, 1837 (1802 missing); April 7, 1832–Dec. 27, 1876	May, 1800–July 2, 1837 (1812–1816 missing) May 17, 1832–May 30, 1880		NLI	Pos. 4771
2	Aughadown	June 1822–Oct. 12, 1838; Oct. 20, 1838–Jan. 28, 1864; Jan. 1, 1865–Dec. 31, 1880	Oct.15, 1822–Feb. 28, 1865		NLI	Pos. 4775
3	Ballinhassig	March 8, 1821–Dec. 24, 1874; Mountain parish: Oct. 10, 1858–Dec. 20, 1877; Jan. 9, 1875–Dec. 20, 1880	July 15, 1821–Sept. 29, 1877; Feb. 6, 1875–Nov. 23, 1880		NLI	Pos. 4795; from 1875 on Pos. 4796
4	Bandon	Jan. 5, 1794–Dec. 30, 1803; Jan. 2, 1804–Oct. 25, 1811; Jan. 1, 1814–Dec. 31, 1822; Jan. 1, 1823–Dec. 30, 1835; Jan. 1, 1836–Jan. 27, 1855 Jan. 7, 1855–Dec. 30, 1880	July 29, 1794–Dec. 1, 1803 (some entries for 1790 also); Jan. 10, 1804–Sept. 25, 1811; Jan. 9, 1814–March 7, 1848; Jan. 9, 1848–Nov. 27, 1880		NLI	Pos. 4793; baptisms from 1823, marriages from 1848 on Pos. 4794
5	Bantry	1788, 1791–2 (parts); Nov. 1794–July 1799 (parts); Jan. 1808–May 1809; 1812–1814 (parts); July 1822–June 11, 1824; March 31, 1823–Dec. 31, 1866; Jan. 1, 1867–Sept. 28, 1875; Oct. 1, 1875–Dec. 28, 1880	May 7, 1788–May 28, 1823; May, 1823–Dec. 5, 1857; Jan. 7, 1872–Nov. 5, 1880		NLI	Pos. 4802; baptisms from 1875, marriages from 1872 on Pos. 4803

⟶

| Map | Church | Baptisms | CORK SOUTHWEST | Burials | Location | Reference |
			Marriages			
6	Barryroe (Lislee)	Aug. 1, 1804–Oct. 1, 1836 (Transcript made in 1873); June 23, 1835–Aug. 27, 1873;	Nov. 12, 1771–Aug 31, 1873 (Transcript made in 1873); Feb. 13, 1836–March 16, 1873 (Original)		NLI	Pos. 4776; baptism and marriage from 1835 on Pos. 4777
7	Caheragh	June 10, 1818–Sept. 1858; Oct. 1858–Dec. 27, 1880	June 23, 1818–Aug. 25, 1858; Nov. 27, 1858–Dec. 4, 1880		NLI	Pos. 4799
8	Castlehaven	Oct.14, 1842–Dec. 30, 1880			NLI	Pos. 4774
9	Clonakilty	Aug. 3, 1809–March, 1827; Jan. 1, 1827–Dec. 31, 1873	Jan. 8, 1811–Nov. 17, 1880		NLI	Pos. 4772
10	Ballymartle	Nov. 20, 1841–Dec. 12, 1859	Aug. 28, 1841–Jan 12, 1860		NLI	Pos. 4801
10	Clountead (Ballingarry)	April 27, 1836–Dec. 27, 1878	April 21, 1836–Nov. 30, 1878		NLI	Pos. 4801
10	Clountead, Ballingarry and Ballymartle	Jan. 1, 1879–Dec. 26, 1880 1809–1835; 1836–1880	Jan. 30, 1879–Oct. 30, 1880		NLI LC	Pos. 4801
11	Courcey's Country (Ringrone)	Sept. 16, 1819–Nov. 19, 1854; Jan. 6, 1855–Dec. 24, 1880	Sept. 30, 1819–June 12, 1857; Jan. 20, 1856–Nov. 16, 1880		NLI	Pos. 4802
12	Drimoleague	July 20, 1817–Oct. 20, 1846; Oct. 25, 1846–June 12, 1876; June 4, 1876–Dec. 26, 1880	July 20, 1817–Nov. 14, 1863; Dec. 8, 1876–Dec. 10, 1880 (1878 missing)		NLI	Pos. 4801
13	Dunmanway	June 21, 1818–April 24, 1838; July 1, 1837–Dec. 29, 1880	June 21, 1818–Nov. 27, 1880		NLI	Pos. 4805
14	Desertserges	June 14, 1817–May 28, 1855; June 11, 1855–Dec. 17, 1880	(with Enniskeane) Sept. 29, 1813–Sept. 26, 1880		NLI	Pos. 4798
14	Enniskeane	Nov. 24, 1813–July 1837; Aug. 1, 1837–Dec. 30, 1880	(with Desertserges) Sept. 29, 1813–Sept. 26, 1880		NLI	Pos. 4798
15	Goleen (Schull West)	Jan. 1, 1827–Feb. 24, 1864; Nov. 15, 1863–Dec. 20, 1880	Jan. 25, 1827–Feb. 9, 1864 (with gaps); Apr. 9, 1864–Apr. 27, 1880		NLI	Pos. 4800
16	Innishannon	Aug. 20, 1825–Dec. 29, 1846; Jan. 4, 1847–Nov. 30, 1880	Aug. 16, 1825–Oct. 9, 1880		NLI	Pos. 4797
17	Kilbrittain	Aug. 1810–Sept. 8, 1814; July 9, 1811–Feb. 1848; Mar. 29, 1850–Mar. 30, 1851; April 6, 1852–April 23, 1863; April 16–1863–Dec. 28, 1880	Aug. 1810–Sept. 8, 1814; Aug. 2, 1810–June 7, 1863 (with Rathulareen); Nov. 7, 1863–Sept. 12, 1880		NLI	Pos. 4796
18	Kilmacabea	June 9, 1832–Dec. 24, 1880	July 10, 1832–Feb. 28, 1865; May 28, 1865–Sept. 14, 1880		NLI	Pos. 4771
19	Kilmeen and Castleventry	Aug. 1821–Feb. 13, 1858; Feb. 19, 1858–Dec. 31, 1880			NLI	Pos. 4772

→

Map	Church	Baptisms	CORK SOUTHWEST Marriages	Burials	Location	Reference
			Marriages			
20	Kinsale	Jan. 20, 1805–July 20, 1806; Jan. 1, 1815–Sept. 4, 1821; Sept. 3, 1817– Dec. 28, 1829; Aug. 29, 1828–May 2, 1859; May 16, 1859–Dec. 23, 1880	Aug. 31, 1828–April 26, 1859; May 16, 1859– Dec. 23, 1880		NLI	Pos. 4800; baptisms and marriages from 1859 on Pos. 4801
21	Muintervarra	May 5, 1820–Feb. 16, 1856; Mar. 2, 1856– Dec. 24, 1880	Feb. 4, 1819–Sept. 30, 1880		NLI	Pos. 4799
22	Murragh	Jan. 1834–Dec. 29, 1864; Jan. 7, 1865–Nov. 27, 1880	Jan. 26, 1834–Oct. 8, 1864;		NLI	Pos. 4796
23	Rath and The Islands Dec. 28, 1880	July 21, 1818–Sept. 15, 1851; Oct. 4, 1851– 25, 1880	Jan. 31, 1819–Aug. 18, 1851; Feb. 5, 1852–Nov.		NLI	Pos. 4773; baptisms and marriages from 1853 on Pos. 4774
24	Roscarberry	Nov. 13, 1814–Dec. 28, 1880	Jan. 12, 1820–Oct. 20, 1880		NLI	Pos. 4773
25	Skibbereen	Mar. 27, 1814–Dec. 31, 1826; Jan. 6, 1827–Dec. 31, 1864; Jan. 1, 1865– Oct. 16, 1880	Nov. 3, 1837–Oct.16, 1880		NLI	Pos. 4774; baptisms from 1865, marriages from 1837 on Pos. 4775
26	Schull East	Oct. 24, 1807–Sept. 30, 1815; Jan. 1816–Dec. 27, 1839; Jan. 1, 1840–Dec. 31, 1870; Jan. 1, 1871– Dec. 27, 1880	Feb. 1809–Nov. 5, 1815; Jan 21, 1816–Nov. 25, 1832; Jan. 31, 1833–Sept. 17, 1870; Feb. 4, 1871– Dec. 21, 1880		NLI	Pos. 4804; baptisms and marriages from 1871 on Pos. 4805
27	Timoleague	Nov. 1842–Dec. 24, 1880	Apr. 6, 1843–Feb. 10, 1880		NLI	Pos. 4773
28	Adrigole	Jan. 1, 1830–Dec. 9, 1849; Aug. 12 1855– Jan. 20 1879	Jan. 1831–Oct. 26, 1849; Sept. 1, 1855–Aug. 10, 1878		NLI	Pos. 4287
29	Allihies	1822–	1823–		Published	O'Dwyer, Riobárd, *Who Were My Ancestors? Family Trees of Allihies Parish,* K.K. Publishing 1988. NLI Ir. 9292 0 60
		Oct. 6, 1822–June 10, 1860; Sept. 10, 1859– Dec. 29, 1874; Jan. 1, 1875–Dec. 26, 1880	Jan. 1823–Feb. 27, 1826 Jan. 10, 1832–Feb. 12, 1861; Jan. 8, 1860–Feb. 13, 1872; Oct. 7, 1871– Aug. 20, 1880		NLI	Pos. 4286
30	Bonane and Glengarriff	July 22, 1846–Dec. 25, 1856; Jan. 3, 1857–Dec. 21, 1877; Jan. 9 1878– Dec. 26, 1880	July 18, 1847–Nov. 29, 1856; Feb. 1, 1857–Feb. 9, 1875; Feb. 2 1876– Feb. 10 1880		NLI	Pos. 4288
31	Castletown- bere	1819–	1819–		Published	O'Dwyer, Riobárd, *Who Were My Ancestors? Family Trees of Castletownbere Parish,* K.K. Publishing 1989. NLI Ir. 9292 0 62
		May 4, 1854–Dec. 28, 1859; Jan. 1, 1859– Sept. 22, 1878	July 1819–Feb. 5, 1859; Jan. 8, 1858–Nov. 20, 1880		NLI	Pas. 4284
32	Eyeries	1843–	1824–		Published	O'Dwyer, Riobárd, *Who Were My Ancestors? Family Trees of Eyeries Parish,* K.K. Publishing 1976. NLI Ir. 9292 0 61
		April 1843–March 25, 1873; Jan. 5, 1873– Dec. 31, 1880	Feb. 1824–Feb. 23, 1873; Feb. 6 1873–Aug. 28, 1880		NLI	Pos. 4286

CORK EAST

CLOYNE DIOCESE

1 Aghada
2 Annakissy
3 Ballymacoda
4 Blarney
5 Carrigtohill
6 Castlelyons
7 Castletownroche
8 Cloyne
9 Cobh
10 Conna
11 Doneraile
12 Fermoy
13 Glanworth &
   Ballindangan
14 Gloutane
15 Imogeela
16 Kildorrerry
17 Lisgoold
18 Mallow
19 Lisgoold
20 Mallow
21 Middleton
22 Mitchelstown
23 Rathcormac
24 Youghal

*Co.
Tipperary*

Cork NW

Co. Waterford

Cork SW

Youghal Bay

*Cork
Harbour*

CORK & ROSS
DIOCESE
25 Carrigaline
26 Cork city:
   Blackrock
   St Finbarr (South)
   St Mary
   St Patrick
   SS Peter & Paul
27 Douglas

28 Glanmire
29 Glouthaune
30 Monkstown
31 Passage West
32 Tracton Abbey
33 Watergrasshill

WATERFORD &
LISMORE DIOCESE
34 Lismore

| MAP | CHURCH | CORK EAST | | | | |
		BAPTISMS	MARRIAGES	BURIALS	LOCATION	REFERENCE
1	Aghada	Jan. 1, 1815–March 26, 1837; March 12, 1838–Nov. 26, 1880	May 11, 1838–Nov. 26, 1880		NLI	Pos. 4990
		1792–1895	1785–1819		MHC	
2	Annakissy	1805–1895	1805–1895		MHC	
		June 16, 1806–Dec. 28, 1829; Jan. 3, 1830–Dec. 26, 1880	July 28, 1805–Nov. 19, 1835; Jan. 21–June 4, 1837; July 9, 1837–Nov. 27, 1880		NLI	Pos. 5001
3	Ballymacoda and Ladysbridge	1835–1899	1835–1899		MHC	
		Nov. 10, 1835–Aug. 28, 1880	Sept. 22, 1835–Nov. 11, 1879		NLI	Pos. 4991
4	Blarney	Aug. 12, 1791–June 6, 1792; Feb. 2, 1821–Dec. 19, 1825; Oct. 29, 1826–May 25, 1845; June 1, 1845–Dec. 22, 1880	Sept. 24, 1778–March 2, 1813; Feb. 15, 1821–Nov. 26, 1825; Dec. 17, 1826–Aug. 26, 1849; Jan. 11, 1848–Nov. 8, 1880		NLI	Pos. 5006; marriages from 1848 on Pos. 5007
		1878–1899	1791–1899		MHC	
5	Carrigtohill	1817–1900	1817–1900		MHC	
		Dec. 2, 1817–July 18, 1873; July 19, 1873–Nov. 5, 1880	Nov. 22, 1817–Oct. 13, 1878		NLI	Pos. 4989
6	Castlelyons	Aug. 12, 1791–Dec. 28, 1828; Jan. 3, 1830–Dec. 22, 1880	Jan. 17, 1830–Nov. 19, 1880		NLI	Pos. 4994

MAP	CHURCH	BAPTISMS	CORK EAST MARRIAGES	BURIALS	LOCATION	REFERENCE
7	Castletown-roche	Aug. 25, 1811–Dec. 29, 1834; Jan. 2, 1835–Dec. 27, 1866	Sept. 19, 1811–Oct. 18, 1845; Nov. 29, 1845–Oct. 13, 1880		NLI	Pos. 4995; baptisms from 1835, marriages from 1845, Pos. 4996
8	Cloyne	Sept. 2, 1791–Nov. 4, 1793; Oct. 5, 1803–July 30, 1812; Jan. 2, 1821–Dec. 29, 1831; July 1, 1833–Dec. 29, 1878	Feb. 3, 1786–Feb. 17, 1801; April 14, 1801–Dec. 2, 1820; Jan. 11, 1821–Nov. 26, 1831; Jan. 10, 1832–May 18, 1880		NLI	Pos. 4989 baptisms; Pos. 4990 marriages
9	Cobh	1812–Dec. 31, 1820; Jan, 22, 1821–May 24, 1827; June 5, 1827–May, 1842; August 1842–May 31, 1863; June 4, 1863–Dec. 30, 1877; Jan. 3, 1878 –Dec. 19, 1880			NLI	Pos. 4986; baptisms from 1821, marriages from 1812 on Pos. 4987
10	Conna	1834–1895	1834–1895		MHC	
		Sept. 1834–Sept. 1844 (some gaps); Dec. 16, 1845–Dec. 26, 1880	Oct.30, 1845–Nov.13, 1880		NLI	Pos. 4996
11	Doneraile	April 16, 1815–Sept. 17, 1836; Dec. 21, 1836–May 12, 1867; March 1, 1866–Dec. 28, 1880	Jan. 26, 1815–May 14, 1867; March 4, 1866–Dec. 2, 1880		NLI	Pos. 5000
		1815–1900	1815–1900		MHC	
12	Fermoy	Jan. 1, 1828–Aug. 27, 1848; Jan. 4, 1849–Dec, 27, 1880; Workhouse: April 28, 1854–Sept. 17, 1880	May 18, 1828–Dec. 21, 1880		NLI	Pos. 4993 baptisms; Pos. 4994 marriages
13	Glanworth and Ballindangan	1836–1899	1836–1899		MHC	
		Jan. 1, 1836–Dec. 12, 1880; Ballindangan Sept. 1870–Dec. 29, 1880	Glanworth only: Jan 12, 1836–Oct. 19, 1880		NLI	Pos. 4996
14	Kilpadder	Feb. 12, 1858–Nov. 20, 1869			NLI	Pos. 5008
14	Kilshannig	Apr. 10, 1842–June 23, 1850			NLI	Pos. 5008
14	Glountane	May 20, 1829–Aug., 1844; May 16, 1847–Dec. 21, 1880			NLI	Pos. 5008
		1829–1895	1858–1895		MHC	
15	Imogeela	Feb. 1, 1833–Dec. 19, 1880	Sept. 22, 1833–Sept. 6, 1879		NLI	Pos. 4991
		1835–1895	1835–1895		MHC	
16	Kildorrery	May, 15, 1824–Sept. 30, 1853	Jan. 25, 1803–Aug. 15, 1880		NLI	Pos. 4994
		1824–1899	1803–1896		MHC	
17	Killeagh	1829–1895	1829–1895		MHC	
		March 29, 1829–Sept. 30, 1880	Nov. 1, 1822–July 10, 1880		NLI	Pos. 4992
18	Kilworth	Sept. 19, 1829–Oct. 9, 1876	Oct. 3, 1829–Dec. 16, 1880		NLI	Pos. 4996

→

MAP	CHURCH	BAPTISMS	CORK EAST MARRIAGES	BURIALS	LOCATION	REFERENCE
19	Killeagh	1807–1899	1821–1899		MHC	
		July 13. 1807–July 26, 1821; July 31, 1821–April 29, 1853; May 8, 1853–Dec. 31, 1880	Oct. 16, 1821–Nov. 13, 1880		NLI	Pos. 4991
20	Kilworth	Jan. 1–July 17, 1809; June 28, 1817–Feb. 19, 1818; Aug. 27, 1820–June 23, 1828; Jan. 2, 1825–July 31, 1828; Jan. 2, 1825–Dec. 28, 1828; April 13, 1832–Feb. 11, 1835; Feb. 4, 1835–Dec. 14, 1840; Jan. 4, 1841–June 8, 1853; Aug. 8, 1847–Dec 29, 1880	April 17. 1757–Nov. 22, 1823; Oct. 6, 1805–Sept. 6, 1820; April, 30, 1832–Jan. 31, 1841; Feb. 2, 1844–Oct. 17, 1880		NLI	Pos. 4997; baptisms from 1847, marriages from 1844 on Pos. 4998
		1809–1900	1757–1900		MHC	
21	Middleton	Sept. 24, 1819–Dec. 29, 1863; Jan 3, 1864–Dec. 30, 1880;	Oct. 31, 1819–April 21, 1864; Jan. 16, 1864–Dec. 31, 1880		NLI	Pos. 4986
		1819–1899	1819–1899		MHC	
22	Mitchelstown	Jan. 1, 1792–July 13, 1801; Sept. 11, 1814–Aug. 1833; Sept. 12, 1833–Nov. 1845; July 6, 1845–Dec. 26, 1880	Jan. 7, 1822–Nov. 27, 1845; July 13, 1845–Nov. 1, 1880		NLI	Pos. 4992; from 1845, Pos. 4993
		1815–1899	1792–1899		MHC	
23	Rathcormack	Jan.10, 1792–March, 1850; March 4, 1850–June 7, 1866; June 12, 1866–Dec. 28, 1880	Jan. 7, 1829–June 2, 1866		NLI	Pos. 4995
24	Youghal	Sept. 15, 1803–Mar. 2, 1830; Feb. 1, 1830–Aug. 1846; Sept. 4, 1846–Aug. 21, 1875; Sept. 1, 1875–Nov. 30, 1880	Feb. 16, 1830–June 29, 1862; June 7, 1866–Nov. 27, 1880		NLI	Pos. 4988; marriages from 1866 on Pos. 4989
25	Carrigaline	Jan. 1, 1826–Dec. 19, 1880	Jan. 23, 1826–Nov. 18, 1880		NLI	Pos. 4790
		1826–1880	1826–1880		Published	Thompson, Francis, *Families of the Catholic Parish of Carrigaline-Crosshaven* 1986, LDS BFA 144105
26	Cork city: Blackrock	1848–1899	1848–1899		CCAP	Catholic Parish of Carrigaline-
		July 10, 1810–May 31, 1811; Feb. 5, 1832–Aug. 15, 1837; Feb. 3, 1839–June 17, 1839; Jan. 6, 1841–Aug. 16, 1847; Jan. 13, 1848–Dec. 5, 1880	Sept. 16, 1810–May 18, 1811; Feb 7, 1832–Aug. 15, 1837; Feb. 13, 1841 –Oct. 9, 1847; Jan. 18, 1848–Nov. 2, 1880		NLI	Pos. 4791
	St Finbarr's (South)	Aug. 10, 1756–Sept. 7, 1757; July 5, 1760–Sept. 17, 1763; Mar. 22, 1772–July 30, 1777; Jan. 15, 1789–Dec. 30, 1802; Jan 1, 1803–June 10, 1810; June 21, 1810–Dec. 1834; Jan. 3, 1835–Dec. 19,	Banns 1753–1774 (many gaps) Apr. 22, 1775–Sept. 3, 1789; Jan. 7, 1789–June 20, 1810; June 21, 1810–Jan. 14, 1860; Jan. 1, 1860–Dec. 2, 1877; Jan. 8, 1878–Nov. 27, 1880		NLI	B. 1776–1856, Pos. 4778; B. 1857–1880, Pos. 4779; M. 1775–1810, Pos. 4779; M. 1810–1880 Pos. 4780

MAP	CHURCH	BAPTISMS	CORK EAST MARRIAGES	BURIALS	LOCATION	REFERENCE
	St Finbarr's (South) (*cont.*)	1856; Jan. 12, 1857–May 24, 1874; May 20, 1874–Jan. 6, 1878; Jan. 7, 1878–Dec. 31, 1880				
		1756–1900	1756–1900		CCAP	
	St Mary's	July 10, 1748–May 8, 1764; Mar. 3, 1765–Dec. 31, 1772; Jan. 1, 1773–Nov. 25, 1788 (uneven); Aug. 3, 1780–1783; Jan 17, 1781–Dec. 1785; July 5, 1784–Dec. 31, 1788; Jan. 16, 1786–May 26, 1786; Jan. 18, 1789–Dec. 30, 1802; Jan. 9, 1803–Dec. 1807; Aug. 27, 1806–Jan. 30, 1807; Jan. 1808–Mar. 26, 1834; Mar. 1831–1834 (odd pages); Nov. 30, 1833–Oct. 6, 1853; 1846–1853 (odd pages) Nov. 10, 1852–July 4, 1869; June 21, 1869–Oct. 25, 1878; Oct. 27, 1878–Dec. 31, 1880	July 10, 1748–May 30, 1764; April 16, 1765–Nov. 19, 1788; Jan. 7, 1789–Dec. 26, 1812; Jan. 7, 1813–Nov. 25, 1845; Mar. 1831–1834 (odd pages); Jan. 14, 1845–Dec. 30, 1880; 1846–1853 (odd pages)		NLI	B.1748–1764, Pos. 4780; B. 1773–1807, Pos. 4781; B. 1789–1834, Pos. 4782; B. 1833–1859, Pos. 4783; B. 1869–1880, Pos. 4784; M. 1748 –1788, Pos 4784; M. 1789–1880, Pos. 4785
		1748–1899	1748–1899		CCAP	
	St Patrick's	Oct. 7, 1831–Jan. 3, 1851; Nov. 30, 1836–Mar. 27, 1872; April 1, 1872–Dec. 29, 1880	July 16, 1832–June 29, 1851 (very few for 1831–34); Nov. 19, 1836–Dec. 20, 1880		NLI	Pos. 4788
		1831–1899	1831–1899		CCAP	
	SS Peter and Paul's	April 24, 1766–Oct. 22, 1766; Nov. 14, 1780–Jan. 21, 1798; Jan. 21, 1798–Sept. 23, 1803; Jan. 1, 1809–June 17, 1811; April 1834–May 31, 1840; Jan. 15, 1837–Dec. 30, 1855; Feb. 1, 1856–Sept. 13, 1870; Mar. 3, 1870–Dec. 25, 1880	April 30 1766–Sept. 18, 1776; Oct. 22, 1780–Oct. 6, 1803; Jan. 22, 1809–Aug. 23, 1810; July 22, 1814–Aug. 30, 1817; May 5, 1834–May 30, 1840 (some pages for 1825 and 1827); Jan. 17, 1838–Dec. 3, 1853; Jan. 3, 1856–Sept. 13, 1870; Sept. 17, 1870–Nov. 27, 1880		NLI	Pos. 4785; B. from 1798, M. from 1780, on Pos. 4786; B. from 1870, M. from 1856 on Pos. 4887
27	Douglas	Nov. 15,1812–Aug. 30, 1851; Sept. 27, 1851–Dec. 23, 1867; Feb. 26, 1867–Dec. 17, 1880	Nov. 25, 1812–July 25, 1851; Aug. 23, 1851–Mar. 3, 1867; Mar. 2, 1867–Nov. 13, 1880		NLI	Pos. 4790
28	Glanmire	May 10. 1818–Oct. 12, 1828; Oct. 13, 1828–Dec. 31, 1841	May 29, 1818–Oct. 6, 1828; Nov. 11, 1828–Dec. 1841; Feb. 11, 1871–Oct. 2, 1880		NLI	Pos. 4789; marriages from 1871 on Pos. 4790
		1818–1828;	1818–1828;		LC	
		1828–1841;	1828–1841;			
		1842–1871; to date	1842–1871; to date			
29	Glounthane	Aug. 20, 1864–Dec. 25, 1880	Oct. 8, 1864–Nov. 25, 1880		NLI	Pos. 4789
30	Monkstown	May 2, 1875–Dec. 26, 1880	June 5, 1875–Nov. 29, 1880		NLI	Pos. 4791
31	Passage West	Apr. 5, 1795–May 15, 1832; July 3, 1813–Sept. 29, 1816; May 1, 1832–	Aug. 23, 1813–Sept. 21, 1816; May 1, 1832–Aug. 26, 1844; Sept. 12, 1844–		NLI	Pos. 4791, 4792

→

Map	Church	Baptisms	CORK EAST Marriages	Burials	Location	Reference
31	Passage West (*cont.*)	Sept. 14, 1844; Sept. 4, 1844–Feb. 12, 1865; Mar. 6, 1859–Dec. 30, 1880	Feb. 12, 1865; Mar. 1, 1859–Oct. 19, 1880			
32	Tracton Abbey	Dec. 12, 1802–Dec. 25, 1853; Jan. 24, 1853– Dec. 10, 1880	June 6, 1840–Feb. 10, 1880		NLI	Pos. 4789
33	Watergrasshill	Jan. 5, 1836–Dec. 24, 1855; Jan. 21, 1856– Dec. 21, 1880			NLI	Pos. 4790
34	Lismore	See Waterford 18				

CORK NORTHWEST

CLOYNE DIOCESE
1 Aghabullogue
2 Aghinagh
3 Ballyclough
4 Ballylea
5 Ballyvourney
6 Banteer (Clonmeen)
7 Buttevant
8 Castlemagner
9 Charleville
10 Clondrohid
11 Donaghmore
12 Freemount (Milford)
13 Glountane
14 Grenagh
15 Inniscarra
16 Kanturk
17 Kilnamartyra
18 Liscarroll
19 Macroom
20 Mourneabbey
21 Newmarket
22 Rock & Meelin
23 Shandrum

CORK & ROSS DIOCESE
24 Ballincollig
25 Iveleary
26 Kilmichael
27 Kilmurray
28 Ovens

KERRY DIOCESE
29 Ballydesmond
30 Boherbue
31 Dromtariffe
32 Millstreet
33 Rathmore

LIMERICK DIOCESE
34 Ballyagran
35 Kilmallock

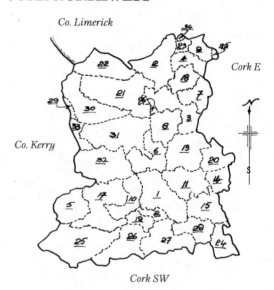

Map	Church	Baptisms	CORK NORTHWEST Marriages	Burials	Location	Reference
			CORK NORTHWEST			
1	Aghabulloge	1820–1895 Jan. 4, 1820–April 13, 1856; Jan. 5, 1856–Dec. 19, 1880	1820–1895 Jan. 5, 1820–Nov. 20, 1880		MHC NLI	Pos. 5007
2	Aghinagh	1848–1895 April 3, 1848–Dec. 12, 1880	1848–1895		MHC NLI	Pos. 5007
3	Ballyclough	1807–1896 Aug. 15, 1807–Dec. 30, 1818; Jan. 3 1819–Dec. 14, 1845; Jan. 4, 1846–July 15, 1880	1805–1896 Jan. 19, 1805–Dec. 2, 1827; Feb. 3, 1828–Aug. 18, 1867		MHC NLI	Pos. 5009 baptisms to 1845; Pos. 5010
4	Ballyhea	1809–1899 Jan. 12, 1809–July 24, 1873; Nov. 12, 1871–Dec. 2, 1880	1811–1899 June 23, 1811–July 20–1873; Nov. 8, 1871–July 18, 1880		MHC NLI	Pos. 4992
5	Ballyvourney	1810–1868 (Vol. 11) April 11, 1825–Dec. 29, 1829 1810–1868 (gaps) 1810–1895	1871–1895		Published NLI LDS MHC	O'K Pos. 5007 BFA 823808
6	Banteer	1828–1899 Jan. 1, 1847–Dec. 24, 1880	1828–1899 Feb. 2, 1847–Dec. 9, 1880		MHC NLI	Pos. 5011
7	Buttevant	July 1, 1814–Dec. 27, 1879 1814–1895	July 23, 1814–Sept. 14, 1880 1814–1895		NLI MHC	Pos. 4998
8	Castlemagner	1817–1900 May 7, 1832–Dec. 26, 1880	1817–1900 May 8, 1832–Oct. 12, 1880		MHC NLI	Pos. 5009
9	Charleville	May 2, 1827–Dec. 31, 1880	Aug. 10, 1774–Nov. 15, 1792; Nov. 23, 1794–July 3, 1822; June 3, 1827–Dec. 9, 1880		NLI	Pos. 5001; from 1827, Pos. 5002
10	Clondrohid	1807–1895 1807–1822; April 11, 1822–Oct. 22, 1843; June 2, 1844–Dec. 30, 1880	1807–1895 Apr. 21, 1822–June 1, 1847; Jan. 18, 1848–Nov. 21, 1880		MHC NLI	Pos. 5002; from 1844, Pos. 5003
11	Donaghmore	April 1, 1803–Dec. 13, 1815; Oct. 1, 1815–April 3, 1828; April 6, 1828–Oct. 21, 1834; Oct, 23, 1834–Sept. 17, 1875; Jan. 1, 1870–July 8, 1880	Jan. 18, 1790–Feb. 3, 1828; Feb. 7, 1828–Jan. 7, 1835; Oct. 23, 1834–Sept. 17, 1875; Feb. 13, 1870–July 8, 1880		NLI	Pos. 5003 baptisms to 1828; Pos. 5004 remainder
12	Freemount	Sept. 10, 1827–March 22, 1840; July 15–Dec. 28, 1843; Jan. 10, 1858–Dec. 18, 1880 1827–1895	Oct. 15, 1827–Oct 2, 1880 1827–1895		NLI MHC	Pos. 5008
13	Glountane	May 20, 1829–Aug., 1844; May 16, 1847–Dec. 21, 1880 1829–1895	1858–1895		NLI MHC	Pos. 5008

Map	Church	Baptisms	CORK NORTHWEST Marriages	Burials	Location	Reference
			Marriages	**Burials**		
14	Grenagh	1840–1900	1840–1900		MHC	
		April 3, 1840–Dec. 31, 1880	April 26, 1840–Sept. 25, 1880		NLI	Pos. 5002
15	Inniscarra	1814–1895	1814–1900		MHC	
		July 3, 1814–Sept. 29, 1844; Jan 1, 1845–Dec. 31, 1879	Aug. 7, 1814–June 1, 1871; July 15, 1871–Nov. 25, 1880		NLI	Pos. 5005 baptism to 1844; Pos. 5006 remainder
16	Kanturk	July 28, 1822–Oct. 16, 1849; Sept. 21, 1849–Dec. 26, 1880; Workhouse: Sept. 1, 1844–Aug. 18, 1867	Feb. 20, 1824–Jan. 19, 1850; Sept. 29, 1849–Dec. 26, 1880		NLI	Pos. 5008
		1822–1899	1824–1899		MHC	
17	Kilnamartyra	Jan. 30, 1803–Dec. 16, 1820; Jan. 16, 1821–Dec. 11, 1880	Jan. 8, 1803–June, 4, 1833; Sept. 1839–Feb.10, 1880		NLI	Pos. 5003
		1803–1894	1803–1895		MHC	
18	Liscarroll	March 1, 1812–Oct. 14, 1837; Nov. 24, 1833–Dec. 19, 1880	Feb. 14, 1813–Oct.15, 1837; July 6, 1831–Oct. 28, 1880		NLI	Pos. 4999
		1812–1895	1813–1895		MHC	
19	Macroom	April 11–18, 1803; Sept. 28, 1805–April 7, 1814; Jan. 5, 1814–June 30, 1823; July 1, 1823–Oct. 26, 1843; Dec. 21, 1843–Dec. 31, 1880	Jan. 20, 1808–Aug. 14, 1813; Sept. 19, 1813–Nov. 7, 1880		NLI	Pos. 5004 baptisms to 1823; Pos. 5005 remainder
			1864–1866 (Vol. 14); 1831–1947 (Vol. 14)		Published	O'K
20	Mourneabbey	1830–1899	1829–1899		MHC	
		June 1, 1829–Dec. 29, 1880	Oct. 22, 1829–Sept. 24, 1880		NLI	Pos. 4999
21	Newmarket	1833–1899	1822–1899		MHC	
		Nov. 17, 1821–Dec. 24, 1833; July 8, 1833–Oct. 8, 1865; March 13, 1866–Dec. 30, 1880	Jan. 10, 1822–Sept. 16, 1865; March 9, 1866–Aug. 21, 1880		NLI	Pos. 5010 baptisms; Pos. 5011 marriages
22	Rock and Meelin	1865–1899	1865–1899		MHC	
		March 17, 1866–Dec. 26, 1880	April 14, 1866–March 1, 1880		NLI	Pos. 5009
23	Shandrum	1829–1895	1829–1895		MHC	
		March 1, 1829–Dec. 26, 1880			NLI	Pos. 5001
24	Ballincollig	Jan. 16, 1820–March 19, 1828; Aug. 26, 1828–Dec. 30, 1857; Jan. 3, 1858–Dec. 24, 1880	Jan. 12, 1825–Feb. 19, 1828; Aug. 28, 1828–Nov. 28, 1857; Oct. 25, 1873–Aug. 29, 1880		NLI	Pos. 4791
25	Iveleary	1816–1863 (Vol. 7); 1853–1900 (Vol. 9)	1816–1899 (Vol. 7)		Published	O'K
		Nov. 1, 1816–Aug. 29, 1843; Sept. 3, 1843–Dec. 30, 1880	Nov. 20, 1816–May 9, 1880		NLI	Pos. 4794 baptisms to 1843; remainder on Pos. 4795

Map	Church	CORK NORTHWEST BAPTISMS	MARRIAGES	BURIALS	Location	Reference
25	Iveleary (*cont.*)	1816–1875	1816–1880		LDS	BFA 0883696 item 1; 0883784 item 3
26	Kilmichael	Oct. 6, 1819–Feb. 23, 1847; Mar. 10, 1847–Dec. 23, 1880	Jan. 9, 1819–Feb. 12, 1850; Jan. 23, 1851–Aug. 7, 1880		NLI	Pos. 4797; marriage from 1851 on Pos. 4798
27	Kilmurry	June 2, 1786–Feb. 1812; Feb. 22, 1812–Dec. 20, 1825; Jan. 8, 1826–Dec. 30, 1838; Dec. 14, 1838–June 29, 1872; July 2, 1872–Dec. 31, 1880	1803–1805 (fragmented); Feb. 22, 1812–Nov. 24, 1825; Jan 8, 1826–Dec. 1, 1838; Jan. 30, 1839–Nov. 13, 1880		NLI	Pos. 4803
28	Ovens	Sept. 24, 1816–May 24, 1825; Sept. 11, 1825–Sept. 8, 1833; Oct. 27, 1834–Dec. 30, 1877	Sept. 24, 1816–May 24, 1825; Sept. 22, 1825–Aug. 27, 1833; Oct. 25, 1834–Feb. 14, 1837; Jan. 22, 1839–Nov. 13, 1877		NLI	Pos. 4795
29	Ballydesmond	1888–1900 (Vol. 14)	1888–1900 (Vol. 11)		Published	O'K
30	Boherbue	1833–1875	1863–1880		LDS	BFA 0883696 item 12; 0883884 item 4 B. to 1865, Pos. 4265; remainder 4266
		July 22, 1833–Dec. 7, 1860; Feb. 8, 1863–Dec. 29, 1873; Jan. 6, 1873–Dec. 24, 1880	March 22, 1863–Nov. 25, 1880		NLI	
		1833–1864 (Vol. 2); 1863–1900 (Vol. 11)	1863–1870 (Vol. 3); 1863–1900 (Vol. 11); 1903–1947 (Vol. 14)		Published	O'K
31	Dromtarriffe	Feb. 6, 1832–July 26, 1851; Aug. 1, 1851–Dec. 26, 1880	Jan. 25, 1832–July 17, 1852; Jan. 25, 1852–July 27, 1880		NLI	Pos. 4264
		1832–1840 (Vol. 4); 1841–1848 (Vol. 3); 1851–1865 (Vol. 4); 1865–1900 (Vol. 6)	1832–1865 (Vol. 2); 1865–1900 (Vol. 14)		Published	O'K
		1832–1875	1832–1880		LDS	BFA 0883884 item 5; 0883696 13
		1832–1884	1832–1884		KGC	
32	Millstreet	1822–1823; 1853–1875	1855–1880		LDS	BFA 0883884 item 6; 08836972
		Dec. 4, 1853–July 14, 1865; July 23, 1865–Dec. 31, 1878; Jan. 12, 1873–Dec. 21, 1880	Jan. 14, 1855–Nov. 6, 1880		NLI	Pos. 4267
		1822–1823 (Vol. 11); 1859–1900 (Vol. 11); 1860–1862 (Vol. 11)	1855–1870 (Vol. 2); 1870–1900 (Vol. 11)		Published	O'K
33	Rathmore	See Kerry 37				
34	Ballyagran	See Limerick West 7				
35	Kilmallock	See Limerick East 31				

DERRY

ARMAGH DIOCESE
1 Arboe
2 Ballinderry
3 Cookstown
    (Desertcreight)
4 Magherafelt
5 Moneymore
6 Lissan

DERRY DIOCESE
7 Ballinascreen
8 Ballyscullion (Bellaghy)
9 Banagher
10 Coleraine (Killowen)
11 Cumber Uppr
12 Desertmartin
13 Dungiven
14 Errigal (Garvagh)
15 Faughanvale
16 Glendermot
17 Greenlough
18 Kilrea
19 Limavady
20 Magilligan
21 Maghera
22 St Eugene's (Derry city)

23 Templemore (Derry city)
24 Termoneeny

DOWN & CONNOR
DIOCESE
25 Ballymoney
10 Coleraine

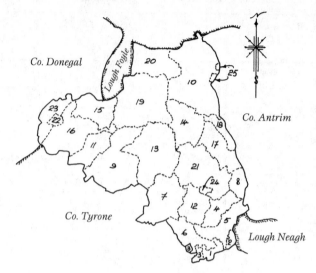

Map	Church	Baptisms	Marriages	Burials	Location	Reference
			DERRY			
1	Arboe	1827–1900	1827–1900		HW	
		1827–1880	1827–1881		PRONI	MIC.1D/34
		Nov. 9, 1827–Dec. 30, 1860; Jan. 1, 1861–Dec. 10, 1880	Nov. 12, 1827–Dec. 12, 1861; Jan. 5, 1862–Dec. 27, 1880		NLI	Pos. 5583
		See NLI			LDS	BFA 0926029
2	Ballinderry	See Tyrone 4				
3	Cookstown (Desertcreight)	See Tyrone 10				
4	Magherafelt		1830–1900	1858	TGC	
		1834–1880	1834–1881		PRONI	MIC.1D/30–31
		Jan. 4, 1834–July 26, 1857; Jan. 10, 1858–Dec. 26, 1880	Jan. 2, 1834–Apr. 21, 1857; Feb. 10, 1858–Dec. 16, 1880		NLI	Pos. 5579
5	Moneymore (Ardtrea and Desertlin)	1832–1834; 1838–1843; 1854–1939	1830–1843; 1854–1837 (gaps)		PRONI	MIC.1D/35
		See NLI			LDS	BFA 0926030
		1832–1900	1830–1900		HW	
		July 1, 1832–Mar. 28, 1834; Jan. 20, 1838–Feb. 16, 1843; Nov. 1, 1854–Feb. 21, 1869; Jan. 18, 1864–June 14, 1880	Apr. 14, 1830–July 12 , 1843; Nov. 12, 1854–Feb. 6, 1869		NLI	Pos. 5584

$\longrightarrow$

MAP	CHURCH	BAPTISMS	DERRY MARRIAGES	BURIALS	LOCATION	REFERENCE
6	Lissan	1822–1830; 1839–1900			TGC	
		July 22, 1823–Dec. 30, 1880	Sept. 1, 1839–Nov. 20, 1880		NLI	Pos. 5585
		1822–1900	1822–1900		HW	
		1839–1881	1839–1880		PRONI	MIC.1D/36
7	Ballinascreen	Nov. 20, 1825–Feb. 21, 1834; June 5, 1836–May 31, 1863; June 1, 1863–Dec. 28, 1880	Nov. 29, 1825–Feb. 11, 1834; Apr. 3, 1834–May 17, 1863; June 3, 1863–Oct. 17, 1880		NLI	Pos. 5764
		1836; 1846–1881	1834–1885	1831–1832; 1848–1851	PRONI	MIC.1D/59
		1836; 1846–1900	1834–1900	1882–1884	TGC	
8	Ballyscullion	1844–1900	1844–1900		TGC	
		Sept. 8, 1844–Dec. 22, 1880	Sept. 14, 1844–Nov. 2, 1880		NLI	Pos. 5763
		1844–1881	1844–1883		PRONI	MIC.1D/58
9	Banagher	1848–1878 (incomplete)	1857–1878 (incomplete)		PRONI	MIC.1D/59
		1848–1900	1850–1878; 1884–1900		TGC	
		Jan. 16, 1848–July 21, 1878 (incomplete)	Dec. 24, 1851–Jan. 6, 1878		NLI	Pos. 5764
10	Coleraine	1843–1900	1864–1900		TGC	
		Aug. 4, 1843–Aug. 2, 1863; Aug. 29, 1863–Dec. 13, 1880			NLI	Pos. 5767
		1843–1880			PRONI	MIC.1D/62
11	Cumber Upper	1853–1854; 1863–1900	1863–1900		TGC	
		May 18, 1863–Dec. 27, 1880	Sept. 20, 1863–Dec. 28, 1880		NLI	Pos. 5762
		1863–1881	1863–1882		PRONI	MIC.1D/57
12	Desertmartin and Kilcronaghan	Nov. 1, 1848–Dec. 19, 1880	Nov. 13, 1848–Nov, 27, 1880	Nov. 11, 1848–Dec. 6, 1880	NLI	Pos. 5765
		1848–1881	1848–1880	1848–1882	PRONI	MIC.1D/60
		1848–1900	1848–1900	1848–1900	TGC	
13	Dungiven	July 4, 1847–May 4 1853; Sept. 7, 1863–Dec. 26, 1880	Sept. 29, 1864–Dec. 26, 1880	Mar. 4, 1870–Dec. 31, 1871	NLI	Pos. 5764
		1825–1834; 1847–1900	1825–1834; 1864–1900	1825–1832; 1870–1871	TGC	
		1825–1834; 1847–1881	1825–1834; 1864–1882	1825–1832; 1870–1871	PRONI	MIC.1D/59
14	Errigal	1846–1900	1872–1900		TGC	
		1846–1881	1873–1880		PRONI	MIC.1D/59
		Apr. 26, 1846–Dec. 15, 1880	Feb. 25, 1873–Dec. 23, 1880		NLI	Pos. 5764
15	Faughanvale	Nov. 4, 1860–Nov. 2, 1880	Sept. 1863–Dec. 25, 1880		NLI	Pos. 5762
		1863–1881	1860–1880		PRONI	MIC.1D/57
		1863–1900	1860–1900		TGC	
16	Glendermot (Waterside)	1864–1900	1864–1900		TGC	→

MAP	CHURCH	BAPTISMS	DERRY MARRIAGES	BURIALS	LOCATION	REFERENCE
16	Glendermot (*cont.*)	Jan. 6, 1864–Nov. 29, 1874; Dec. 1, 1874–Dec. 26, 1880	Jan. 7, 1864–Nov. 30, 1880		NLI	Pos. 5761
		1864–1881	1864–1880		PRONI	MIC.1D/56
17	Greenlough	Oct. 5, 1846–Dec. 29, 1880	June 14, 1846–Dec. 25, 1880	June 21, 1846–Aug. 18, 1870	NLI	Pos. 5763
		1845–1900	1846–1900		TGC	
		1846–1881	1846–1882	1846–1870	PRONI	MIC.1D/58
18	Kilrea	Aug. 23, 1846–Dec. 26, 1860; Jan. 1861–Aug. 1865	Aug. 23, 1846–Dec. 26, 1860; Jan. 1861–Mar. 12, 1877	Aug. 23, 1846–Dec. 26, 1860; Jan. 1861–Mar. 12, 1877	NLI	Pos. 5763 and Pos. 5764
		1846–1865	1846–1877	1846–1877	PRONI	MIC.1D/58–59
		1846–1865; 1874–1900	1846–1900	1846–1877	TGC	
19	Limavady	1855–1900	1856–1900	1859–1900	TGC	
		Dec, 1855–Dec. 25, 1962; Jan. 12, 1862–Dec. 26, 1880; Jan. 3, 1862–June 9, 1879 (Ballykelly)	Apr. 9, 1856–Dec. 18, 1861; Apr. 20, 1862–Dec. 23, 1880	May 2, 1859–Dec. 10, 1869	NLI	Pos. 5761
		1855–1880	1856–1881	1859–1869	PRONI	MIC.1D/56
20	Magilligan (Tamlaghtard)	Sept. 13, 1863–Dec. 24, 1880	Oct. 29, 1863–Nov. 16, 1880	Sept. 28, 1863–Jan. 2, 1880	NLI	Pos. 5761
		1833–1900	1833–1900	1863–1880	TGC	
		1863–1881	1863–1881	1863–1880	PRONI	MIC.1D/56
21	Maghera and Killylough	Mar. 17, 1841–Oct. 18, 1857; Oct. 25, 1857–Dec. 28, 1880	May 13, 1841–May 11, 1853; Oct. 25, 1857–Nov. 16, 1880	May 18, 1848–Sept. 7, 1857; Oct. 29, 1857–Sept. 15, 1880	NLI	Pos. 5763
		1841–1900	1841–1900	1848–1888	TGC	
		1841–1881	1841–1853; 1857–1882	1848–1880; 1887–1888	PRONI	MIC.1D/58
22	Derry city: St Eugene's Cathedral	1873–1881			PRONI	MIC.1D/57
		June 11, 1873–Dec. 30, 1880			NLI	Pos. 5762
		1873–1900	1873–1900		TGC	
23	Derry city: St Columb's (Templemore)	Oct. 12, 1823–Sept. 10, 1826; Sept. 3, 1836–Dec. 1851 (3 sections); Jan. 1, 1852–Apr. 17, 1863; Jan. 1, 1864–July 23, 1880	Nov. 28, 1823–Sept. 6, 1826; Mar. 28, 1835–July 20, 1836; Jan. 4, 1841–Nov. 6, 1851 (transcript); Apr. 6, (1854?)–Dec. 30, 1863 (fragmented)	Apr. 19, 1863–Dec. 30, 1863	NLI	Pos. 5762
		1823–1826; 1836–1881	1823–1826; 1835–1836; 1841–1863	1863	PRONI	MIC.1D/57
		1823–1826; 1833–1900	1823–1826; 1835–1837; 1841–1900		TGC	
24	Termoneeny	Sept. 27, 1837–Aug. 1839; June 22, 1852–Aug. 15, 1865; Oct. 27, 1867–Aug. 18, 1871; Nov. 27, 1871–Dec. 30, 1880	Sept. 27, 1837–Aug. 1839; Apr. 19, 1852–Aug. 15, 1865; Jan. 12, 1868–Feb. 12, 1871; Dec. 7, 1873–Dec. 28, 1880	Sept. 27, 1837–Aug. 1839	NLI	Pos. 5763
		1837–1839; 1852–1865; 1867–1900	1837–1839; 1852–1900	1837–1839; 1868–1900	TGC	
		1837–1839; 1852–1865; 1867–1881	1837–1839; 1852–1865; 1868–1871; 1873–1880	1837–1839	PRONI	MIC.1D/58
25	Ballymoney	See Antrim 7				

DONEGAL

CLOGHER DIOCESE
1 Carn (Pettigo)
2 Inishmacsaint

DERRY DIOCESE
3 Burt
4 Clonea
5 Clonleigh
6 Clonmany
7 Culduff
8 Desertegney
9 Donagh
10 Donaghmore
11 Iskaheen (MovilleUppr)
12 Moville Lr
13 Urney

RAPHOE DIOCESE
14 All Saints
15 Annagry
16 Ardara
17 Aughnish
18 Clondahorky
19 Clondavaddog
20 Conwal & Leck
21 Drumhilm
22 Glencolumkille

23 Gortahork (Raymunterdoney)
24 Gweedore
25 Inishkeel (Glenties)
26 Inver
27 Kilbarron
28 Kilcar
29 Killaghtee
30 Killybegs
31 Killygarvan

32 Killymard
33 Kilmacrennan
34 Kilteevogue
35 Lettermacaward (Dungloe)
36 Mevagh
37 Raphoe
38 Stranorlar
39 Tawnawily
40 Termon & Gartan

DONEGAL

Map	Church	Baptisms	Marriages	Burials	Location	Reference
1	Carn	See Fermanagh 3			NLI	Pos. 5569
2	Innismacsaint	See Fermanagh 11			NLI	
3	Burt and Inch	Nov. 20, 1859–Sept. 26, 1880	Jan. 7, 1856–Sept. 30, 1880	Apr. 21, 1860–July 9, 1866	NLI	Pos. 5766
		1859–1880	1856–1880	1860–1866	PRONI	MIC.1D/55
		1859–1900	1850; 1856–1900	1860–1866; 1898–1899	TGC	
4	Clonca	Nov. 2, 1856–Dec. 8, 1880; May 5, 1868–Dec. 26, 1880	Apr. 22, 1870–Dec. 26, 1880; Jan. 14, 1877–Dec. 6, 1880		NLI	Pos. 5765
		1856–1881	1870–1885		PRONI	MIC.1D/54
		1856–1900	1870–1900		TGC	
5	Clonleigh	1773–1795; 1836–1837; 1853–1900	1778–1779; 1781; 1785; 1791; 1842–1900		TGC	
		Apr. 1, 1773–Feb 22, 1795; Jan. 10, 1836–May 18, 1837; Mar. 3, 1853–Sept. 7, 1879; Mar. 12, 1853–Mar. 25, 1870; May 1, 1864–Dec. 31, 1880	Aug. 1788–Sept. 14, 1781 [sic]; 1843–1879; Nov. 14, 1853–Apr. 20, 1870; Sept. 16, 1879–Nov. 13, 1880		NLI	Pos. 5766
		1773–1795; 1836–1837; 1853–1880	1778–1781; 1843–1881		PRONI	MIC.1D/61
6	Clonmany	1852–1900	1852–1900		TGC	
		1852–1881			PRONI	MIC.1D/54
		Jan. 12, 1852–Dec. 30, 1880			NLI	Pos. 5765 →

MAP	CHURCH	BAPTISMS	DONEGAL MARRIAGES	BURIALS	LOCATION	REFERENCE
7	Culdaff	1838–1841; 1847–1880	1849–1880		PRONI	MIC.1D/55
		1838–1900	1838–1843; 1848–1900		TGC	
		Jan. 3, 1838–Nov. 6, 1841; June 7, 1847–Dec. 13, 1880	Jan. 14, 1849–Dec. 19, 1880		NLI	Pos. 5766
8	Desertegney	1864–1881	1871–1872		PRONI	MIC.1D/54
		1864–1900	1871–1900		TGC	
		Dec. 3, 1864–Dec. 21, 1880	Nov. 9, 1871–Dec. 30, 1880		NLI	Pos. 5765
9	Donagh (Carndonagh)	Jan. 23, 1847–Oct. 16, 1873; Nov. 23, 1873–Dec. 26, 1880	Jan. 12, 1849–Sept. 11, 1873; Nov. 23, 1873–Nov, 7, 1880		NLI	Pos. 5765
		1847–1881	1849–1881		PRONI	MIC.1D/54
		1846–1900	1846–1900	1846–1851	TGC	
10	Donaghmore	1840–1900	1846–1900		TGC	
		1840–1880	1846–1883		PRONI	MIC.1D/62
		Nov. 16, 1840–Dec. 20, 1863; Jan. 1, 1864–Dec. 18, 1880	Apr. 16, 1846–Nov. 28, 1863; Jan. 1, 1864–Nov. 14, 1880		NLI	Pos. 5767
11	Iskaheen	1858–1900			TGC	
		1858–1880			PRONI	MIC.1D/55
		Sept. 19, 1858–Dec. 26, 1880			NLI	Pos. 5766
		1858–1923	1858–1921		LDS	BFA 1279235 items 17–20
12	Moville	Nov. 7, 1847–Dec. 28, 1880	Nov. 4, 1847–Dec. 12, 1880	Nov. 2, 1847–July 23, 1854	NLI	Pos. 5762
		1847–1880	1847–1880	1847–1854	PRONI	MIC.1D/55
		1847–1900	1847–1900	1847–1854	TGC	
13	Urney	See Tyrone 40				
14	All Saints	Dec. 10, 1843–Mar. 25, 1870; Dec. 1, 1856–Dec. 13, 1880; Mar. 22, 1857–Dec. 25, 1880; Apr. 30, 1870–Nov. 7, 1880	Nov. 30, 1843–Mar. 20, 1870		NLI	Pos. 4598
		1884–1911	1886–1921		LDS	BFA 1279235 items 7–10
		1843–1886	1843–1886		TGC	
		1843–1881	1843–1870		PRONI	MIC.1D/85
15	Annagry	1868–			LC	
16	Ardara	1867–1912	1856–1921		LDS	BFA 1279234 items 7–10 and others
		Jan. 6, 1869–Nov. 18, 1877; Jan. 3, 1878–Dec. 31, 1880	May 13, 1867–Apr. 2, 1875		NLI	Pos. 4599
		1869–1880	1867–1875		PRONI	MIC.1D/86
17	Aughnish	See NLI			LDS	BFA 1279234 items 27–29
		Nov. 24, 1873–Dec. 18, 1880	Dec. 18, 1873–Dec. 12, 1880		NLI	Pos. 4598
		1873–1899	1873–1899		DA	
		1873–1881	1873–1881		PRONI	MIC.1D/85

			DONEGAL			
MAP	CHURCH	BAPTISMS	MARRIAGES	BURIALS	LOCATION	REFERENCE
18	Clondahorkey	1877–1913	1877–1920		LDS	BFA 1279235 items 1–3
		1856–1899	1856–1899		DA	
		Oct. 7, 1877–Dec. 28, 1880	Jan. 28, 1879–Nov. 2, 1880		NLI	Pos. 4599
		1877–1881	1877–1882		PRONI	MIC.1D/86
19	Clondavadoc	1847–1899	1847–1899	1847–1899	DA	
		1847–1871	1847–1869	1847–1869	PRONI	MIC.1D/87
		Feb. 21, 1847–Jan. 29, 1871	Feb. 24, 1847–July 12, 1869	Feb. 21, 1847–Feb. 5, 1869	NLI	Pos. 4600
		See NLI			LDS	BFA 1279236 item 2
20	Conwal and Leck	1874–1881	1877–1881		PRONI	MIC.1D/85
		1853–1899	1853–1899		DA	
		May 15, 1853–Mar. 13, 1862; Sept. 1854–Jan. 4, 1855;May 26, 1856–Dec. 30, 1862; Mar. 29, 1868–Dec. 31, 1880; Oct. 11, 1874–Dec. 26, 1880	May 15, 1853–Mar. 13, 1862; Jan. 8, 1857–Nov. 22, 1863; Feb. 1, 1877–Nov. 27, 1880		NLI	Pos. 4598
		1851–1950	1854–1962		LDS	BFA 1279236 items 22–26 and others
21	Drumholm	June 17, 1866–Dec. 28, 1880	Aug. 12, 1866–Sept. 28, 1880		NLI	Pos. 4599
		1866–1881	1866–1881		PRONI	MIC.1D/86
		1866–1912	1866–1947		LDS	BFA 1279237 items 10–11
22	Glencolmkille	No records microfilmed			NLI	
		No records microfilmed			PRONI	
		1879–1949	1879–1949		LDS	BFA 1279235 items 6, 11
23	Gortahork	Nov. 11, 1849–Apr. 14, 1861; Nov. 23, 1871–Dec. 26, 1880	Aug. 20, 1861–Dec. 3, 1880	Nov. 2, 1849–Aug. 6, 1869	NLI	Pos. 4600
		1849–1861; 1871–1880	1861–1880	1849–1869	PRONI	MIC.1D/87
		1856–1896; 1887–1959	1856–1880; 1900–1939		LDS	BFA 1279234 items 4, 5
24	Tullaghobegley West (Gweedore)	Jan. 6, 1868–Mar. 17, 1871; May 11, 1873–Dec. 29, 1880			NLI	Pos. 4600
		1868–1935	1866–1943		LDS	BFA 1279234 items 8–13 and others
		1868–1871; 1873–1881			PRONI	MIC.1D/87
25	Glenties	Nov. 30, 1866–Nov. 6, 1880			NLI	Pos. 4599
25	Inniskeel	Oct. 11, 1866–Dec. 29, 1880			NLI	Pos. 4599
		1866–1881			PRONI	MIC.1D/86
		1866–1917	1866–1923		LDS	BFA 1279237, items 4–7 and others

Map	Church	Baptisms	DONEGAL Marriages	Burials	Location	Reference
26	Inver	Jan. 30, 1861–Dec. 25, 1880	Feb. 3, 1861–June 27, 1867; Nov 26, 1875–Dec. 27, 1880		NLI	Pos. 4599
		1861–1881	1861–1867; 1875–1881		PRONI	MIC.1D/86
		See NLI			LDS	BFA 0926210
		1861–1877	1861–1899		DA	
27	Kilbarron	Nov. 19, 1854–Jan. 4, 1858; Jan. 1, 1858–Oct. 11, 1866; Oct. 14, 1866–Dec. 8, 1880	Jan. 7, 1858–Nov. 20, 1880		NLI	Pos. 4601
		1854–1881	1858–1881		PRONI	MIC.1D/88
28	Kilcar	1848–1911	1901–1921	1906–1958	LDS	BFA 1279236 items 4–7
		Jan. 4, 1848–Dec. 29, 1880			NLI	Pos. 4599
		1848–1881			PRONI	MIC.1D/86
29	Killaghtee	1845–1847; 1850–1853; 1857–1881	1857–1881		PRONI	MIC.1D/88
		1857–1886	1857–1886		LDS	BFA 1279234 item 6
		Jan. 12, 1845–Apr. 18, 1847; Oct. 10, 1850–Oct. 9, 1853; July 26, 1857–Nov. 24, 1880	Sept. 20, 1857–Nov. 7, 1880		NLI	Pos. 4601
30	Killybegs	1850–1881			PRONI	MIC.1D/88
		1850–1911	1850–1914		LDS	BFA 1279234 items 24–26
		Oct. 12, 1850–Dec. 29, 1880			NLI	Pos. 4601
31	Killygarvan	Oct. 11, 1868–Dec. 26, 1880	Feb. 2, 1873–Jan. 15, 1879		NLI	Pos. 4598
		1868–1880	1873–1879		PRONI	MIC.1D/85
		1859–1899	1872–1899		DA	
32	Killymard	Sept. 20, 1874–Dec. 25, 1880			LDS	
		1874–1881			PRONI	MIC.1D/86
		Sept. 20, 1874–Dec. 25, 1880			NLI	4599 Pos.
33	Kilmacrennan	1862–1912	1863–1973		LDS	BFA 1279235 items 24–28
		Nov. 2, 1862–Sept. 26, 1880			NLI	Pos. 4598
		1862–1880			PRONI	MIC.1D/85
		1862–1899	1877–1899		DA	
34	Kilteevogue	1855–1910	1855–1913		LDS	BFA 1279234 items 22–23 and others
		1855–1862; 1870–1880	1855–1862; 1870–1882		PRONI	MIC.1D/85
		Dec. 2, 1855–Apr. 8, 1862; Apr. 1, 1870–Dec. 8, 1880	Nov. 8, 1855–Mar. 23, 1862; May 5, 1870–Dec. 1880		NLI	Pos. 4598

→

MAP	CHURCH	BAPTISMS	DONEGAL MARRIAGES	BURIALS	LOCATION	REFERENCE
35	Dungloe	1876–1921	1878–1921		LDS	BFA 1279236 items 14–19 and others
		1876–1881			PRONI	MIC.1D/87
		Nov. 1, 1876–Dec. 31, 1880			NLI	Pos. 4600
36	Mevagh	1853–1859; 1871–1927	1878–1921		LDS	BFA 1279234 items 11–16
		Jan. 1, 1871–July 28, 1878 (transcript)			NLI	Pos. 4600
		1871–1878			PRONI	MIC.1D/87
37	Raphoe	Feb. 13, 1876–Dec. 11, 1880	Feb. 10, 1876–Nov. 7, 1880		NLI	Pos. 4598
		1876–1949	1876–1936 (gaps)		LDS	BFA 1279235 items 14–16
		1876–1881	1876–1881		PRONI	MIC.1D/85
		1876–1899	1876–1899		DA	
38	Stranorlar	No records microfilmed			NLI	
		1877–1899	1877–1899		DA	
		1860 earliest			LC	
		1877–1926	1877–1921	1905–1935	LDS	BFA 1279235 items 21–3
39	Tawnawilly	1872–1932	1873–1911		LDS	BFA 1279234 items 17–19 and others
		Dec. 12, 1872–Dec. 30, 1880	Jan. 9, 1873–Oct. 2, 1880		NLI	Pos. 4599
		1872–1881	1873–1882		PRONI	MIC.1D/86
40	Termon and Gartan	1882–1949	1880–1928		LDS	BFA 1279237 items 8–9
		1862 earliest			LC	

DOWN

DOWN &
CONNOR
DIOCESE

1 Ardkeen
2 Ballyculler
3 Ballygalget
4 Ballymacarrett
5 Ballyphilip
6 Bangor
7 Blaris (Lisburn)
8 Bright
9 Carrickmannon
10 Downpatrick
11 Drumaroad
12 Dundrum & Tyrella
13 Dunsford
14 Holywood
15 Kilclief & Strangford
16 Kilcoo

17 Kilkeel
18 Kilmegan (see also Drumaroad)
19 Kilmore (Crossgar)
20 Loughlinisland
21 Maghera & Bryansford
22 Mourne Lower
23 Newtownards
24 Saul

DROMORE
DIOCESE
25 Aghaderg
26 Annaclone
27 Ballynahinch
28 Banbridge
29 Clonallon
30 Clonduff

31 Donaghmore
32 Dromara
33 Dromore & Garvaghy
34 Drumgath
35 Dromgooland Lr
36 Drumgooland Uppr
37 Kilbroney
38 Magheralin
39 Newry
40 Tullyish

Strangford Lough
Belfast Lough
Co. Antrim
North Channel
Co. Armagh
Dundrum Bay
Irish Sea
Co. Louth
Carlingford Lough

Map	Church	Baptisms	DOWN Marriages	Burials	Location	Reference
1	Ardkeen	Jan. 11, 1828–Nov. 26, 1838; June 2, 1852–Dec. 22, 1880	Jan. 13, 1828–June 3, 1839; June 9, 1852–Dec. 24, 1880		NLI	Pos. 5478
		1828–1838; 1852–1882	1828–1839; 1852–1889		PRONI	MIC.1D/74
2	Ballyculter	1844–1864; 1870–1881	1843–1882		PRONI	MIC.1D/73
		Jan. 17, 1844–May 21, 1864; Nov. 19, 1870–Dec. 1, 1880 (transcript)	Aug. 27, 1843–Apr. 15, 1880		NLI	Pos. 5477
3	Ballygalget	Jan. 11, 1828–Apr. 18, 1835; June 18, 1852–Feb. 20, 1853 (transcript); June 2, 1852–Feb. 28, 1864; Nov. 10, 1866–Dec. 19, 1880	June 9, 1852–Sept. 5, 1866; Mar. 4, 1867–Oct. 20, 1880		NLI	Pos. 5478
		1828–1899	1852–1899	1894–1899	UHF	
		1828–1835; 1852–1864; 1866–1881	1852–1882		PRONI	MIC.1D/74
4	Ballymacarrett	See Belfast city				
5	Ballyphilip and Portaferry	1843–1881	1843–1881	1843–1881 (partial)	PRONI	MIC.1D/74
		Mar. 20, 1843–Dec. 31, 1880 (transcript)	Mar. 20, 1843–Dec. 31, 1880 (transcript)		NLI	Pos. 5478
		1843–1900	1843–1900		UHF	
6	Bangor	1855–			LC	
7	Blaris	1840–	1840–		LC	
8	Bright, Rossglass and Killough	1856–1900	1856–1900	1877–1900	UHF	
		1856–1881	1856–1881		PRONI	MIC.1D/74
		Nov. 10, 1856–Nov. 26, 1880 (also a transcript)	Nov. 22, 1856–Sept. 17, 1880		NLI	Pos. 5478
9	Carrick-mannon and Saintfield	1837–1900	1845–1900		UHF	
		1837–1881	1845–1883		PRONI	MIC.1D/63
		Oct. 1, 1837–Dec. 4, 1880	Oct. 18, 1845–Nov. 17, 1880		NLI	Pos. 5467
10	Downpatrick	1851–1900	1852–1900		UHF	
		1851–1882	1853–1882	1851–1882	PRONI	MIC.1D/74
		Oct. 6, 1851–Dec. 29, 1880	Feb. 16, 1853–Nov. 8, 1880	Aug. 22, 1851–Dec. 31, 1880	NLI	Pos. 5478
11	Drumaroad	1853–1900	1853–1900		UHF	
		Jan. 20, 1853–Oct. 24, 1880	May 22, 1853–Nov. 3, 1880		NLI	Pos. 5476
		1853–1881	1853–1880		PRONI	MIC.1D/72
12	Tyrella (Dundrum)	Apr. 21, 1854–Dec. 26, 1880	July 10, 1854–Dec. 5, 1880		NLI	Pos. 5476
		1854–1900	1855–1900		UHF	
		1854–1881	1854–1881		PRONI	MIC.1D/72
13	Dunsford	1880–1900			UHF	
		1845–1881	1845–1880	1848–1868	PRONI	MIC.1D/72
		April 1845;	April 1845;	Feb. 22, 1848–Feb. 28, 1868	NLI	Pos. 5476

MAP	CHURCH	BAPTISMS	DOWN MARRIAGES	BURIALS	LOCATION	REFERENCE
13	Dunsford (*cont.*)	Feb. 27, 1848–Dec. 19, 1880	Feb. 28, 1848–Nov. 24, 1880			
14	Holywood	Nov. 18, 1866–Dec. 25, 1880	May 3, 1867–Nov. 4, 1880		NLI	Pos. 5471
		1866–1880	1867–1883		PRONI	MIC.1D/67
		1866–1900	1867–1900		UHF	
15	Kilclief and Strangford	1898–1900	1898–1900		UHF	
		1866–1881	1865–1881		PRONI	MIC.1D/72
		Jan. 14, 1866–July 26, 1867; Oct. 9, 1870–Nov. 19, 1880	Nov. 25, 1865–Oct. 26, 1868; Jan. 8, 1871–Jan. 13, 1881		NLI	Pos. 5476
16	Kilcoo	1832–1880			PRONI	MIC.1D/72
		Oct. 22, 1832–Dec. 1, 1880			NLI	Pos. 5476
		1832–1899	1899		UHF	
17	Kilkeel	July 1839–Sept. 12, 1877; May 26, 1845–Dec. 27, 1880 (transcript); May 3, 1857–Aug. 9, 1878	May 9, 1838–Apr. 18, 1876; Oct. 30, 1867–Apr. 19, 1869		NLI	Pos. 5477
		1839–1881	1839–1876		PRONI	MIC.1D/73
		1837–1900	1839–1900		UHF	
18	Castlewellan (Kilmegan)	1859–1881			PRONI	MIC.1D/73
		1859–1899	1859–1899	1866–1868	UHF	
		Nov. 18, 1859–Dec. 25, 1880	Nov. 18, 1859–Dec. 25, 1880		NLI	Pos. 5477
19	Kilmore	1837–1900	1896–1900		UHF	
20	Loughinisland	1806–1900	1805–1900	1730–1900	UHF	
		1806–1852	1805–1852	1805–1852	PRONI	MIC.1D/73
		1806–Oct. 24, 1852	Nov. 1, 1805–Oct. 23,	Nov. 10, 1805–Oct. 5, 1852 (some pages missing)	NLI	Pos. 5477
21	Bryansford and Newcastle (Maghera)	Feb. 24, 1845–Dec. 30 1880	Mar. 25, 1845–Dec. 28, 1880	Apr. 18, 1860–Nov. 8, 1880	NLI	Pos. 5477
		1845–1881	1845–1885	1860–1882	PRONI	MIC.1D/73
		1845–1900	1845–1900	1860–1900	UHF	
22	Mourne Lower	1842–1881	1839–1880		PRONI	MIC.1D/74
		Aug.. 28, 1842–Dec. 18, 1867; Jan. 11, 1868–Dec. 14, 1880	Sept. 11, 1839–Nov. 21, 1866; Aug. 25, 1867–Oct. 10, 1880		NLI	Pos. 5478
		1842–1900	1839–1900		UHF	
23	Newtownards	1856–1900	1855–1900		UHF	
		June 17, 1864–Dec. 23, 1880			NLI	Pos. 5467
		1864–1881			PRONI	MIC.1D/63
24	Saul	1785–1900	1785–1900		UHF	
		May 17, 1868–Dec. 10, 1880	May 1, 1868–Dec. 21, 1880		NLI	Pos. 5478
		1868–1880	1868–1881		PRONI	MIC.1D/74

MAP	CHURCH	BAPTISMS	DOWN MARRIAGES	BURIALS	LOCATION	REFERENCE
25	Aghaderg	1840–1876	1839–1876	1843–1875	UHF	
		1816–1876	1816–1876	1816–1876	PRONI	MIC.1D/29
		Jan. 5, 1816–Aug. 20, 1840; Sept. 11, 1840– Aug. 25, 1876	Feb. 1, 1816–Sept. 5, 1839; Oct. 4, 1839– Aug. 17, 1876	Sept. 22, 1838– Nov. 1840; Jan. 30. 1843– Aug. 9, 1876	NLI	Pos. 5504
26	Annaghlone	1834–1900	1836–1900		UHF	
		Sept. 21, 1834–Mar. 4, 1851; Mar. 29, 1851– Nov. 15, 1880	May 22, 1851–Nov. 18, 1880	Apr. 13, 1851– Nov. 28, 1880	NLI	Pos. 5499
		See NLI			LDS	BFA 0926074 items 1–2
		1834–1881	1851–1881	1851–1882	PRONI	MIC.1D/24
27	Ballynahinch and Dunmore	May 1, 1827–July 1, 1836; Apr. 14, 1836–July 28, 1864; July 1, 1863– Dec. 31, 1880	Mar. 3, 1829–July 25, 1864		NLI	Pos. 5500
		See NLI			LDS	BFA 0926075 items 1–2
		1827–1881	1829–1864		PRONI	MIC.1D/25
		1827–1900	1826–1900		UHF	
28	Seapatrick (Banbridge)	See NLI			LDS	BFA 0926076
		1843–1881	1850–1882	1833–1880	PRONI	MIC.1D/26
		1843–1900	1850–1900	1850–1900	UHF	
		Jan. 24, 1843–Dec. 14, 1880	July 10, 1850–Oct. 4, 1880	July 31, 1850– Dec. 16, 1880	NLI	Pos. 5501
29	Clonallon	1826–1900	1826–1900		UHF	
		Nov. 28, 1826–Nov. 17, 1838; Nov. 19, 1838– Jan. 9, 1869	Nov. 23, 1826–Dec. 30, 1880		NLI	Pos. 5497
		See NLI			LDS	BFA 0926077 items 1–2
		1826–1869	1826–1882		PRONI	MIC.1D/22
30	Clonduff	Sept. 15, 1850–Dec. 26, 1880	Aug. 4, 1850–Dec. 30, 1880	July 3, 1850– Dec. 6, 1880	NLI	Pos. 5504
		1850–1880	1850–1880	1850–1881	PRONI	MIC.1D/29
		See NLI			LDS	BFA 0926078
		1850–1900	1850–1900		UHF	
31	Donoughmore	May 30, 1835–July 22, 1874; Sept. 30, 1871– Dec. 20, 1880	Sept. 2, 1825–Sept. 25, 1880	Oct. 17, 1840– 1871	NLI	Pos. 5497
		1835–1880	1825–1882	1840–1871	PRONI	MIC.1D/22
		See NLI			LDS	BFA 0926079
			1828–1900		UHF	
32	Dromara	1844–1900	1844–1900		UHF	
		Jan. 14, 1844–Dec. 19, 1880	Jan. 14, 1844–Dec. 18, 1880	Jan. 10, 1844– Sept. 12, 1880	NLI	Pos. 5499
		1844–1880	1844–1880	1844–1880	PRONI	MIC.1D/24; C.R.2/3
		See NLI			LDS	BFA 0926080

⟶

MAP	CHURCH	BAPTISMS	DOWN MARRIAGES	BURIALS	LOCATION	REFERENCE
33	Dromore	1823–1900	1821–1900		UHF	
		1823–1881	1821–1882	1821–1882	PRONI	MIC.1D/29
		1823–1881			LDS	
		Mar. 3, 1823–Jan. 17, 1845; Jan. 1, 1845–Dec. 30, 1880	Sept. 8, 1821–Dec. 31, 1844; Feb. 4, 1845–Nov. 17, 1880	Nov. 9, 1821–Jan. 5, 1845; Nov. 15, 1847–Dec. 27, 1880	NLI	Pos. 5504
34	Drumgath	Apr. 13, 1829–Dec. 10, 1880	July 6, 1837–Nov. 14, 1880	June 5, 1837–Nov. 24, 1880	NLI	Pos. 5499
		See NLI			LDS	BFA 0926084 items 1–2
		1829–1881	1837–1880	1837–1880	PRONI	MIC.1D/24
35	Drumgooland Lower	Mar. 24, 1832–Dec. 3, 1880	Apr. 27, 1832–Nov. 18, 1880	Mar. 11, 1832–Nov. 14, 1880	NLI	Pos. 5497
		1832–1881	1832–1881	1832–1881	PRONI	MIC.1D/22
		See NLI			LDS	BFA 0926083
		1832–1900	1886–1900		UHF	
36	Drumgooland Upper	May, 26, 1827–Dec. 28, 1880	Aug. 9, 1827–Dec. 28, 1880	May 6, 1828–Nov. 2, 1880	NLI	Pos. 5497
		1827–1880	1827–1880	1828–1881	PRONI	MIC.1D/22
		1817–1946	1827–		LDS	BFA 0990108 item 4; 0994208 item 1
		1827–1900	1827–1900		UHF	
37	Kilbroney	Jan. 1, 1808–Jan. 22, 1843; Jan. 2, 1843–Dec. 19, 1880	Jan. 29, 1808–Dec. 6, 1853; Mar. 22, 1848–Dec. 30, 1880	Jan. 1, 1808–Jan. 7, 1843; Jan. 4, 1843–Dec. 30, 1880	NLI	Pos. 5499
		1808–1900	1848–1900		UHF	
		1808–1881	1808–1881	1808–1881	PRONI	MIC.1D/24–25
		See NLI			LDS	BFA 0990108 item 4; 0926085 items 1–3
38	Magheralin	1815–1816; Jan. 1, 1817–Dec. 20, 1845; Dec. 6, 1845–June 4, 1871; July 17, 1871–Dec. 9, 1880	1815–1816; Jan. 5, 1817–Dec. 27 1845; Dec. 26, 1845–May 12, 1871; July 10, 1871–Dec. 18, 1880	Jan. 1, 1817–Oct. 4, 1845; Jan. 10, 1846–May 11, 1871; Oct. 3, 1871–Dec. 6, 1880	NLI	Pos. 5501
		1815–1900	1814–1900		UHF	
		See NLI			LDS	BFA 0926086
		1815–1881	1815–1882	1815–1880	PRONI	MIC.1D/26
39	Newry	See Armagh			LDS	BFA 0926087 items 1–3
40	Tullyish	Jan. 1, 1833–Apr. 14, 1844; May 7, 1844–Aug. 13, 1844; Apr. 26, 1846–Feb. 5, 1856 (Clare and Gilford); Jan. 21, 1843–Dec. 31, 1880	Jan. 10, 1833–Apr. 8, 1844; Feb. 4, 1845–Dec. 31, 1880; Apr. 26, 1846–Nov. 25, 1853 (Clare and Gilford)	Jan. 18, 1833–Apr. 17, 1844; May 1, 1844–Dec. 30, 1880; Apr. 26, 1846–Nov. 25, 1853 (Clare and Gilford)	NLI	Pos. 5500
		1833–1881	1833–1881	1833–1881	PRONI	MIC.1D/25
		1853–1900	1853–1900	1853–1900	UHF	
		See NLI			LDS	BFA 0926090 items 1–3

DUBLIN

DUBLIN DIOCESE
1. Artane, Coolock, Clontarf, Santry
2. Balbriggan (Balrothery)
3. Baldoyle, Howth, Kilbarrack, Kinsealy
4. Blanchardstown (Castleknock)
5. Booterstown (Blackrock)
6. Clondalkin, Lucan & Palmerstown
7. Donabate & Portrane
8. Donnybrook & Irishtown (Haddington Road)
9. Finglas & St Margaret's
10. Garristown, Rolleston & Ballymadun
11. Kingstown
12. Lusk
13. Maynooth & Leixlip
14. Rathfarnham
15. Rush
16. Saggart
17. Sandyford
18. Skerries
19. Swords

DUBLIN CITY
Aughrim St
Berkeley Road
Cabra
Cabinteely
Chapelizod
Coolock
Dalkey
Donnybrook
Dundrum
Fairview
Harrington St
Rathgar
Rathmines
St Agatha's
St Andrew's
St Audeon's
St Catherine's
St James's
St Laurence O'Toole
St Mary's (Pro-Cathedral)
SS Michael & John
St Michan's
St Nicholas's
St Paul's
Sandymount
Terenure

Co. Meath

Lambay Island

Co. Kildare

Dublin City

Irish Sea

Co. Wicklow

Map	Church	Baptisms	DUBLIN Marriages	Burials	Location	Reference
1	Artane, Coolock, Clontarf, Santry	1771–1899	1771–1899		FHP	
		1774–	1774–		LC	
2	Balbriggan	Oct. 27, 1816–Dec. 29, 1856; Jan. 1, 1856–Dec. 26, 1880	Feb. 12, 1817–Nov. 25, 1856; Jan. 12, 1856–Oct. 25, 1880		NLI	Pos. 6617
		1770–1899	1796–1899		FHP	
2	Naul	1832–1899	1836–1899		FHP	
		No registers microfilmed			NLI	
3	Malahide	No registers microfilmed			NLI	
		1856–			LC	
		1856–1900			FHP	
3	Baldoyle	1784–1899	1784–1899		FHP	
		Dec. 24, 1784–Dec. 26, 1800; Aug. 6, 1806–Aug. 31, 1831; Aug. 26, 1831–Dec. 28, 1853; Jan. 6, 1854–Dec. 25, 1880	Jan. 9, 1785–Dec. 1, 1800; Aug. 5, 1806–Nov. 16, 1815; May 13, 1818–Nov. 25, 1824; Jan. 1, 1826–July 13, 1831; Sept. 2, 1831–Dec. 30, 1856; Jan. 6, 1857–Nov. 14, 1880		NLI	Pos. 6618
4	Blanchards-town	1771–1878	1771–1899		FHP	

Map	Church	Baptisms	DUBLIN Marriages	Burials	Location	Reference
4	Blanchards-town (*cont.*)	Dec. 3, 1774–Dec. 8, 1824; Jan. 5, 1824–Dec. 28, 1856; Apr. 25, 1852–Dec. 26, 1880	Jan. 1775–Nov. 7, 1824; Aug. 8, 1824–Nov. 11, 1856; Jan. 18, 1857–Nov. 25, 1880		NLI	Pos. 6613, 6617
5	Blackrock	1854–1900			DLRHS	
		No registers microfilmed			NLI	
		1850–	1922–		LC	
5	Booterstown	Oct. 13, 1755–Dec.. 20, 1790; Jan. 1, 1791–Oct. 20, 1816; Jan. 3 1817–Dec. 29, 1845; Jan. 4, 1846–July 2, 1854; July 2, 1854–Mar. 7, 1902	June 4, 1756–Dec. 20, 1794; Jan. 1, 1791–Sept. 31, [*sic*] 1816; Oct. 5, 1816–Dec.. 26, 1845; Jan. 11, 1846–Feb. 11, 1856; Jan. 13, 1856–Oct. 34, 1899		NLI	Pos. 9084 (b); 9085 (m)
		1755–1900	1755–1900		DLRHS	
6	Clondalkin	May 3, 1778–Apr. 6, 1800; June 21, 1812–May 20, 1822; Dec. 25, 1823–July 24, 1826; Jan. 1837; Aug. 6, 1809–Feb. 20, 1813; June 3, 1813–June 23, 1818; June 1, 1822–Aug. 15, 1830; Dec. 25, 1830–Aug. 25, 1833; Jan. 4, 1834–Mar. 22, 1837; July 9, 1848; Apr. 22, 1849–May 26, 1850; Jan. 6, 1851–Aug. 29, 1852; Transcript 1809–1852; June 5, 1853–Mar. 30, 1856; Apr. 6, 1856–Oct. 24, 1880	June 11, 1778–Feb. 24, 1800; Aug. 23, 1812–Feb. 19, 1822; Aug. 3, 1835–Aug. 28, 1842; Apr. 20, 1856–Nov. 28, 1880		NLI	Pos. 6612
		1778–1896	1778–1900		DHG	
6	Lucan	1818–1901	1818–1900		DHG	
		Sept. 1818–July 1834; Aug. 23, 1835–Aug. 28, 1842; Feb. 4, 1849–Jan. 26, 1862	Sept. 5, 1818–July 13, 1835; Jan. 11, 1831–Nov. 22, 1834; Aug. 3, 1835–Sept. 18, 1842; Feb. 18, 1849–Nov. 1861		NLI	Pos. 6612
6	Palmerstown	1798–1862	1838–1858		DHG	
		Aug. 26, 1798–Dec. 31, 1799; Sept. 3, 1837–Apr. 24, 1864	Sept. 24, 1837–Sept. 27, 1857		NLI	Pos. 64
7	Donabate	Nov. 3, 1760–Dec. 27, 1807; July 4, 1824–Oct. 5, 1869; Feb. 28, 1869–Oct. 17, 1880	Feb. 1, 1761–June 6, 1805; Feb. 9, 1865–Nov. 29, 1880		NLI	Pos. 6618
		1760–1899	1761–1899		FHP	
8	Haddington Road	No registers microfilmed			NLI	
		1798–1876	1812–1876		DHG	
9	Finglas and St Margaret's	1812–1899	1812–1899		FHP	
		Mar. 4, 1788–July 31, 1788; Dec. 6, 1784–Oct. 16,1823; Nov. 5, 1823–Nov. 18, 1827; Jan. 6, 1828–Nov. 27, 1828; Dec. 7, 1828–May 30, 1841; June 1, 1841–Feb. 20, 1854; Jan. 3, 1854–Dec. 12, 1880	Nov. 20, 1757–July 11, 1760; Dec. 12, 1784–July 17, 1794; Oct. 11, 1821–Aug. 10, 1823; Nov. 5, 1823–Nov. 18, 1827; Jan. 6,1828–Nov. 27, 1828; Jan. 8, 1829–June 1, 1841; June 1, 1841–Feb. 20, 1854; Jan. 24, 1854–Nov. 24, 1880		NLI	Pos. 6613

→

MAP	CHURCH	BAPTISMS	DUBLIN MARRIAGES	BURIALS	LOCATION	REFERENCE
10	Garristown and Rolestown	1857–1899	1857–1899		FHP	
		Jan. 4, 1857–Dec. 27, 1874; Jan. 1, 1875–Nov. 25, 1880	July 27, 1857–Oct. 29, 1880		NLI	Pos. 6617
11	Ballybrack	1841–1900	1860–1900		DLRHS	
		1841–	1860–		LC	
		No registers microfilmed			NLI	
11	Cabinteely	No registers microfilmed			NLI	
		1862–1900			DLRHS	
		1859–	1859–		LC	
11	Dalkey	1861–1900			DLRHS	
		No registers microfilmed			NLI	
		1861–	1894–		LC	
11	Glasthule	No registers microfilmed			NLI	
		1865–			LC	
		1865–1900			DLRHS	
11	Kingstown	1755–1900	1755–1900		DLRHS	
		1769–	1769–		LC	
		Dec. 4, 1768–July 31, 1861 (Indexed); Aug. 9, 1861–Mar. 22, 1914 (Indexed)	Jan. 27 1769–Mar. 27 1932 (Indexed to 1861)		NLI	Pos. 9071 (B. to 1861); Pos. 9072 (B. to 1914); Pos. 9073 (M)
		1790–1859	1790–1859		WHC	
11	Monkstown	1865–	1881–		LC	
		1855–1900	1865–1900		DLRHS	
		No registers microfilmed			NLI	
12	Lusk	Sept. 1757–Aug. 6, 1801; Mar. 11, 1802–Dec. 27, 1835 (early years very faint); Aug. 3, 1856–Dec. 21, 1880	Nov. 20, 1757–Jan. 12, 1801 (poor condition); Mar. 11, 1802–Dec. 27, 1835 (early years very faint); Mar. 6, 1856–Nov. 22, 1880		NLI	Pos. 6616
		1701–1900	1701–1900		FHP	
13	Maynooth	See Kildare 24	1806–1899		KHGS	
		Aug. 24, 1814–Sept. 10, 1827; Sept. 15, 1827–Feb. 1, 1857; Jan. 4, 1857–Dec. 24, 1880	Jan. 12, 1806–Aug. 27, 1827; Sept. 16, 1827–Nov. 24, 1856		NLI	Pos. 6615
16	Newcastle-Lyons	No records microfilmed			NLI	
		1773–	1773–		LC	
14	Boherna-breena	No registers microfilmed			NLI	
		1868–1901			DHG	
		1868–			LDS	
14	Rathfarnham	Jan. 1, 1777–May, 1781; May 1781–Nov. 14, 1781; Nov. 18, 1781–Dec. 1, 1788; Sept. 18, 1807–Jan.	Feb. 5, 1777–May 19, 1781; May 26, 1781–Nov. 18, 1781 Sept. 22, 1807–Jan. 9, 1832; Jan. 23,	Newscuttings, Parochial notes	NLI	Pos. 64

→

MAP	CHURCH	BAPTISMS	DUBLIN MARRIAGES	BURIALS	LOCATION	REFERENCE
14	Rathfarnham (*cont.*)	15, 1832; Jan. 22, 1832– Feb. 1, 1852; Jan. 1, 1852 –Feb. 7, 1857; Jan. 7, 1861 –Oct. 2, 1864; Oct. 9, 1864–Mar. 24, 1878; Mar. 31, 1878–June 27, 1917	1832–Jan. 8, 1852; Jan. 5, 1852 –Nov. 21, 1858; Nov. 19, 1862–Nov. 3, 1864; Nov. 12, 1864–Mar. 4, 1877; Feb. 12, 1878– July 24, 1933			
		1777–1864	1777–1864		DHG	
		1777–	1777–		LC	
15	Rush	July 12, 1785–Dec. 27, 1828; Mar. 13, 1829–Dec. 27, 1856; Dec. 31, 1856– Dec. 28, 1880	Sept. 22, 1785–Dec. 27, 1796; July 14, 1799–Apr. 28, 1810; Aug. 16, 1813– Dec. 3, 1828; 1829–Sept. 29, 1856; Jan. 1, 1857– Nov. 27, 1880		NLI	Pos. 6617
		1785–1826	1785–1826		FHP	
16	Saggart	Oct. 4, 1832–Feb. 1862; May 13, 1878; Jan. 12, 1862–Dec. 26, 1880	May 21, 1832–Aug. 14, 1878		NLI	Pos. 6483
		1832–1899	1832–1878		DHG	
17	Sandyford	No registers microfilmed			NLI	
		1823–1900	1823–1856		DHG	
		1823–	1823–		LC	
18	Holmpatrick (Skerries)	Oct. 12, 1751–Dec. 31, 1781; Jan. 6, 1872–June 23, 1814; July 12, 1814– Dec. 23, 1853; Jan. 1, 1854–Dec. 23, 1880	June 22, 1751–Nov. 17, 1781; Jan. 10, 1782–July 5, 1814 (poorly filmed); Aug. 15, 1814–Mar. 25, 1856; Apr. 24, 1856– Nov. 6, 1880		NLI	Pos. 6614
		1751–1899	1751–1899		FHP	
19	Swords	1763–1899	1751–1899		FHP	
		Dec. 26, 1763–July 7, 1777; June 2, 1802–Nov. 29, 1819; Dec. 3, 1819- Sept. 15, 1828; Sept. 15, 1828–Dec. 4, 1845; Dec. 2, 1845–Mar. 23, 1856 (Indexed); Mar. 28, 1858 –Dec. 21, 1880	Oct. 3, 1763–June 7, 1777; June 24, 1802–Nov. 25, 1819; Dec. 26, 1819– Dec. 15, 1828; Jan. 19, 1829–Dec. 3, 1845; Jan. 12, 1846–Nov. 26, 1856; Feb. 2, 1857–Nov. 7, 1880		NLI	Pos. 6616

DUBLIN CITY

		BAPTISMS	MARRIAGES	BURIALS	LOCATION	REFERENCE
	Aughrim St	1888–	1888–		LC	
		No registers microfilmed			NLI	
	Berkeley Road	1890–	1890–		LC	
		No registers microfilmed			NLI	
	Cabra	1909–	1856–		LC	
		No registers microfilmed			NLI	
	Chapelizod	1846–	1846–		LC	
		No registers microfilmed			NLI	
		1850–1900			DHG	

→

Map Church	Baptisms	DUBLIN CITY Marriages	Burials	Location	Reference
Coolock	1879–	1879–		LC	
Donnybrook	1865– No registers microfilmed	1865–		LC NLI	
Dundrum	1854–1900 No registers microfilmed	1865–1900		DLRHS NLI	
Fairview	June 18, 1879–Dec. 23, 1880	June 10, 1879–Nov. 27, 1880		NLI	Pos. 6609
Harrington St.	1865– No registers microfilmed			LC NLI	
Rathgar	No records microfilmed 1874–	1874–		NLI LC	
Rathmines	1823– No registers microfilmed	1823–		LC NLI	
St Agatha's	Dec. 15, 1852–Dec. 31, 1800; Dec. 29, 1879–Dec. 31, 1880	Jan. 7, 1853–Dec. 16, 1880		NLI	Pos. 6611
	1852–1900	1853–1900		DHG	
St Andrew's	1742–1900	1742–1900		DHG	
	Jan. 1, 1741/2–July 21, 1752; July 18, 1750–June 27, 1773; Sept. 26, 1751–June 1776; Feb. 22, 1777–Sept. 18, 1787; Oct. 1772–Sept. 18, 1790; Aug. 31, 1779–Mar. 3, 1789; Apr. 12, 1789–May 11, 1793; Aug. 4, 1790–Jan. 14, 1801; Jan. 9, 1792–Nov. 28, 1793; May 18, 1793–Jan. 28, 1799; Feb. 4, 1799–Aug. 27, 1801; Mar. 24–Apr. 2, 1802; Jan. 2, 1801–July 19, 1810; June 24, 1810–Dec. 9, 1812; Jan. 14, 1811–July 22, 1822; June 3, 1810–Jan. 29, 1832; Jan. 30, 1832–Dec. 30, 1846; Jan. 3, 1847–Mar. 14, 1858; Mar. 15, 1858–July 30 1861; Aug. 2, 1861–Mar. 19, 1865; Mar. 19, 1865–Aug. 6, 1869; Aug. 6, 1869–June 9, 1873; June 9, 1873–Dec. 24, 1877; Dec. 14, 1877–Apr. 23, 1880; Apr. 23, 1880–Dec. 31, 1880	Jan. 24, 1741/2–July 21, 1751; Oct. 7, 1751–June 20, 1773; June 1756–Oct. 17, 1756; Mar. 17, 1759–May 27, 1776; June 11, 1792–May 3, 1793; July 26, 1773–Dec. 18, 1778; July 7, 1776–Oct. 6, 1777; Apr. 12, 1789–May 12, 1793; Sept. 8, 1790–Jan. 14, 1801; June 9, 1793–Feb. 3, 1799; Feb. 4, 1799–Oct. 21, 1801; Apr. 8, 1804–Aug. 12, 1804; Jan. 23, 1801–July 15, 1810; Apr. 27, 1810–July 29, 1838; Aug. 4, 1838–Feb. 16, 1858; Jan. 3, 1858–Oct. 2, 1870; Oct. 2, 1870–Dec. 29, 1880		NLI	Pos.6605–6610
St Audoen's	Dec. 1778–Dec. 1799; June 22, 1800–Aug. 19, 1825; Sept. 22, 1825–July 14, 1833; July 1833–Sept. 19, 1856 (poor condition); June 11, 1878–Dec. 31, 1880	Feb. 8, 1747–Aug. 13, 1785; Jan. 1800–Aug. 30, 1825; Oct. 3, 1825–June 14, 1833; Aug. 4, 1833–June 21, 1859; Oct. 14, 1856–Dec. 12, 1880		NLI	Pos. 6778
St Catherine's	May 4, 1740–Dec. 31, 1749; Jan. 4, 1750–Aug. 14, 1765; Feb. 2, 1761–	May 4, 1740–Dec. 31, 1749; Jan. 22, 1750–Aug. 18, 1765; June 24, 1765–		NLI	Pos.7138–7141

→

		DUBLIN CITY			
MAP CHURCH	BAPTISMS	MARRIAGES	BURIALS	LOCATION	REFERENCE
St Catherine's (*cont.*)	Oct. 14, 1766; June 24, 1765–Mar. 30, 1781; Apr. 2, 1781–Feb. 27, 1794; Dec.10, 1797; Nov. 23, 1799–Dec. 29, 1805; Feb. 2, 1806–Nov. 30 1819; Mar. 1, 1820–Dec. 28, 1820; June 19, 1821–Jan. 1823; June 2, 1823–June 21, 1824; Nov. 23, 1799–Dec.1810; Jan. 12, 1811–Sept. 5, 1821; Jan. 1, 1823 –Mar. 30, 1828; Jan. 1, 1822–Dec. 30 1851; Apr. 7, 1834–Jan. 2, 1852; Jan. 2, 1852–Dec. 30, 1856 (barely legible); Jan. 2, 1857–June 24, 1862; June 27, 1862–July 23, 1866; June 13, 1871–Dec. 29, 1875; Dec. 31, 1875–Oct. 29, 1880; Nov. 2, 1880–Dec. 31, 1880	Sept. 30, 1776; Oct. 5, 1776–Dec. 27, 1792; Feb. 4, 1794–July 10, 1794; 1799 (a few entries); Jan. 5, 1800–Nov. 1818; Jan. 16, 1811–Aug. 21, 1821; Nov. 26, 1823–Feb. 17, 1828; Jan. 6, 1822–Nov. 29, 1851 (some gaps); Oct. 28, 1849–May 4, 1863 (John's Lane); Jan. 16, 1852–Nov. 16, 1856; Jan. 1, 1857–Sept. 21, 1873; Sept. 22, 1873– Dec. 8, 1880			
St James's	1803–1882	1806–1896		DHG	
	Sept. 25, 1752–Sept. 2, 1798; Oct. 7, 1752–June 1755; Mar. 10–Sept. 28, 1760; Jan. 8, 1761–Sept. 11, 1774; Feb. 12–Oct. 4, 1775; Oct. 17, 1776; Sept. 24–Nov. 26, 1778; Jan.10, 1779–Oct. 10, 1784; Apr. 11, 1785–Aug. 30, 1798/9; Apr. 16, 1800–Aug. 1840; Jan. 1803–Dec. 1824; Apr. 8–May 27, 1816; Jan. 1 –Oct. 30, 1817; Jan. 1, 1818–Sept. 14, 1819; May 27, 1823; Mar. 17–Nov. 26, 1824; Jan. 10–Dec. 22, 1825; Jan. 1826–Dec. 23, 1832; Feb. 8–May 16, 1830; Feb. 15, 1832–Dec. 9, 1843; Dec. 26, 1843– Jun 14, 1847; Jan.–Nov. 21, 1833; June 14, 1847– Dec. 29, 1856; July 27, 1856–Mar. 10. 1863; Jan. 1, 1857–Dec. 29, 1859; Jan. 16–Aug. 16, 1860; Jan. 1, 1868–Feb. 4, 1869; Oct. 7, 1875–Dec. 26, 1880; Mar. 12, 1863–Sept. 10, 1868; Jan. 31, 1869– Oct. 7, 1875 Many of the registers are poorly legible, with large numbers of entries out of chronological order.	1754–1755; Oct. 8, 1804–Dec. 13, 1833; 1856–1858; Mar. 4, 1832–Nov. 26, 1856; June 3, 1859–May, 1868; Aug. 23, 1868–Dec. 29, 1880 Many entries are not in chronological order.		NLI	Pos. 7228– 7232
St Laurence O'Toole's	July 20, 1853–June 4, 1875; June 7, 1875– Dec. 31, 1880	June 19, 1856–Dec. 26, 1880		NLI	Pos. 6611
St Mary's (Pro-Cathedral)				NLI	
	1734–	1734–		LC	Pos. 9148-67
	1741–1900 (Indexed 1810-39)	1741–1900		NLI	

→

	DUBLIN CITY				
Map Church	**Baptisms**	**Marriages**	**Burials**	**Location**	**Reference**
SS Michael and John's	Jan. 1, 1768–Jan. 1857; Mar. 2, 1856–Dec. 30, 1880; Indexed 1876–1880	Jan. 8, 1784–Dec. 1851; Jan. 11, 1852–Nov 28, 1880; Indexed *c.*1743–1842		NLI	Pos. 7358–7360
	1743–1833	1742–1900		DHG	
St Michan's	Feb. 25, 1726–July 19, 1730; June 1730–Jan. 1734; Jan. 1735–Dec. 1739; Sept. 20, 1739–Oct. 9, 1744; June 9, 1755–Sept. 1763; Oct. 11, 1744 –Mar. 8, 1768; Sept. 1770; Aug. 8, 1795–Aug. 23, 1823; Sept. 2, 1823–June 13, 1854; May 28, 1830–July 14, 1842; Sept. 1, 1842–June 14, 1850; May 22, 1850–July 1854; July 9,. 1854–Nov. 11, 1861; Nov. 11, 1861–July 5, 1865; July 5, 1865–Dec. 7, 1869; Nov. 2, 1868–Nov. 20, 1869; Nov. 10, 1869–Apr. 12, 1873 indexed; Apr. 6, 1873–Mar. 19, 1877 indexed; Feb. 27, 1877–Dec. 29, 1880 indexed; Jan. 3, 1881–Feb. 11, 1884 indexed; Feb. 13, 1884–Jan. 30, 1888 indexed	Feb. 25, 1726–July 19, 1730; June 1730–Jan. 1734; Jan. 1735–Dec. 1739; Dec. 18, 1739–Sept. 25, 1744; Oct. 1744–May 29, 1763; Mar. 18, 1756–Oct. 26, 1763; Aug. 16, 1795–Aug. 23, 1823; Sept. 2, 1823–Mar. 17, 1856; Mar. 31, 1856–Sept. 11, 1870 indexed; Sept. 12, 1870–Jan. 28, 1884 indexed		NLI	Pos. 8829–8831
St Nicholas's (Without)	Jan. 3, 1742–Aug. 21, 1752; Jan. 11, 1767–Dec. 26, 1801; Aug. 15, 1772 –Nov. 26, 1780; Dec. 1, 1782–Jan. 2, 1785; Mar. 22, 1788–Sept. 20, 1790; 1781–1794 (scraps); 1823 (3 pages only); Nov. 21, 1824–Aug. 12, 1853; Aug. 13, 1838–Aug. 12, 1853; Aug. 15, 1853–Dec. 30, 1857; Jan. 3, 1858–Feb. 3, 1860; Feb. 3, 1860–Mar. 19, 1862 (indexed); Mar. 19, 1862–Apr. 15, 1864 (indexed); Apr. 18, 1864 –Nov. 7, 1866 (indexed); Nov. 9, 1866–Aug. 5, 1870 (indexed); Aug. 8, 1870–Mar. 10, 1874 (indexed); Mar. 9, 1874–May 27, 1878 (indexed); Apr. 1, 1878–Dec. 31, 1880 (indexed)	Sept. 29, 1767–Dec. 13, 1801; Dec. 21, 1783–Dec. 22, 1796; Mar.–Oct. 1791; Jan.–Feb. 1793; Jan. 2, 1802–Aug. 16, 1828; Jan. 1, 1807–June 1, 1807; Nov. 20, 1814; 1824–1827; 1822–July 29, 1866; Sept. 14, 1856–Sept. 13, 1865; Sept. 17, 1865–Aug. 8, 1880; Aug. 8–Dec. 24, 1880	Apr. 7, 1829–May 2, 1856; Dec. 3, 1857–May 22, 1905	NLI	Pos. 7267–7270; 7275; 7277; 7368
St Paul's	1731–1882 (indexed)	1731–1889 (indexed)		NLI	Pos. 8828–8838
	1731–1898	1732–1900		FHP	
Sandymount	1865–	1865–		LC	
	No registers microfilmed			NLI	
Terenure	1870–	1894–		LC	
	No registers microfilmed			NLI	

FERMANAGH

CLOGHER DIOCESE
1 Aghavea
2 Aughalurcher
   (Lisnaskea)
3 Carn (Pettigo)
4 Cleenish
5 Clones
6 Derrygonnelly
7 Drumully
8 Enniskillen
9 Galloon
10 Garrison
11 Inishmacsaint
12 Irvinestown
13 Magherculmany
14 Roslea
15 Tempo

KILMORE DIOCESE
16 Drumlane
17 Kildallan
18 Killesher
19 Kinawley
20 Knockninny

Map	Church	Baptisms	FERMANAGH Marriages	Burials	Location	Reference
1	Aghavea	Mar. 31, 1862–Dec. 26, 1880	May 11, 1866–June 15, 1880		NLI	Pos. 5572
		1862–1882	1866–1881;			
			1896–1897		PRONI	MIC.1D/15
2	Aughalurcher	See NLI			LDS	BFA 979704 item 6
		Oct. 19, 1835–Dec. 28, 1880			NLI	Pos. 5569
		1835–1883			PRONI	MIC.1D/12; CR.2/12
3	Carn	Mar. 19, 1851–Oct. 28, 1877; Nov. 18, 1877–Dec. 30, 1880	Jan. 9, 1836–Nov. 23, 1880		NLI	Pos. 5569
		See NLI			LDS	BFA 0926049 item 1
		1851–1881	1836–1881		PRONI	MIC.1D/12–13
4	Cleenish	See NLI			LDS	BFA 979705 items 1–4
		Dec. 28, 1835–Sept. 8, 1839; Feb 8, 1859–Jan. 25, 1868; Apr. 8, 1866–Dec. 3, 1880	Apr. 8, 1866–Nov. 14, 1880		NLI	Pos. 5571
		1835–1839; 1859–1881	1866–1881		PRONI	MIC.1D/14
5	Clones	See Monaghan 7			PRONI	
6	Derrygonnelly	Feb. 12, 1853–Aug. 1879; Arranged chronologically by letter			NLI	Pos. 5567
		1853–1879			PRONI	MIC.1D/10
		See NLI			LDS	BFA 926050

Map	Church	Baptisms	FERMANAGH Marriages	Burials	Location	Reference
7	Drumully	See Monaghan 11				
8	Enniskillen	1838–Sept. 27, 1868; Sept. 30, 1868– Dec. 26, 1880	Feb. 10, 1818– Dec. 26, 1880		NLI	Pos. 5567 to 1868; remainder on Pos. 5568
		1838–1881	1817–1880		PRONI	MIC.1D/10–11
9	Galloon	1853–1859;				
		1863–1881	1847–1879		PRONI	MIC.1D/15
		Jan. 1, 1853–Feb. 27, 1859; June 14, 1863– Dec. 30, 1880	May 10, 1847–July 24, 1879		NLI	Pos. 5572
10	Garrison	See NLI			LDS	BFA 979704 item 3–5
		July 12, 1860–Apr. 14, 1874; Oct. 31, 1871–Dec. 23, 1880	Jan. 12, 1860–May 19, 1873; Oct. 2, 1871–Oct. 4, 1880		NLI	Pos. 5569
		1860–1881	1860–1880		PRONI	MIC.1D/12
11	Innismacsaint	July 25, 1848–Nov. 22, 1880	Sept. 5, 1847–Oct. 21, 1880		NLI	Pos. 5569
		1847–1880	1847–1880		PRONI	MIC.1D/12
		See NLI			LDS	BFA 979704 item 6
12	Irvinestown	1846–1881	1851–1882		PRONI	MIC.1D/14
		Nov. 29, 1846–July 3, 1874; Aug. 18, 1874– Dec. 21, 1880	Dec. 22, 1851–Aug. 28, 1874; Aug. 7, 1874– Aug. 7, 1880		NLI	Pos. 5571
		See NLI			LDS	BFA 979705 items 7–10
13	Maghera- culmany	1836–1881	1837–1881		PRONI	MIC.1D/14; C.R.2/1
		Aug. 24, 1836–Jan. 11, 1857; Mar. 22, 1857–Dec. 26, 1869; Jan. 2, 1870– Dec. 29, 1880	Nov. 13, 1837–Nov. 1, 1844; Apr. 24, 1857–Dec. 6, 1869; Nov. 12, 1844– Apr. 13, 1857; Jan. 15, 1870–Dec. 27, 1880		NLI	Pos. 5571
		See NLI			LDS	BFA 979705 items 11–14
14	Roslea	Jan. 6, 1862–Dec. 26, 1880	Jan. 19, 1862–Nov. 26, 1880		NLI	Pos. 5577
		1862–1881	1862–1881		PRONI	MIC.1D/20
		See NLI			LDS	BFA 0926057
15	Tempo	Nov. 1, 1845–Oct. 13, 1870; Aug. 2, 1871–Dec. 18, 1880	Oct. 11, 1845–Nov. 23, 1870; Jan. 3, 1871– Nov. 8, 1880		NLI	Pos. 5570
16	Drumlane	See Cavan 15				
17	Glangevlin	See Cavan 18				
17	Kildallen	See Cavan 19				
18	Killesher	1855–1881	1855–1881	1855–1881	PRONI	MIC.1D/78
		See NLI			LDS	BFA 0926133 item 1
		Sept. 2, 1855–Dec. 16, 1880	Sept. 2, 1855–Dec. 16, 1880	Sept. 2, 1855– Dec. 16, 1880	NLI	Pos. 5345

→

Map	Church	Baptisms	FERMANAGH Marriages	Burials	Location	Reference
			FERMANAGH			
19	Kinnally	1835–1899	1835–1899	1852–1857	CHGC	
		1835–1881	1835–1857	1853–1857	PRONI	MIC.1D/79
		Dec. 11, 1835–Mar. 28, 1853; Apr. 5, 1853–Mar. 7, 1857; Mar. 16, 1857–Dec. 17, 1880	Dec. 3, 1835–Apr. 29, 1853; Apr. 5, 1853–Mar. 7, 1857	Apr. 5, 1853–Mar. 7, 1857	NLI	Pos. 5346
20	Knockninny	May 21, 1855–Nov. 27, 1870	Jan. 1855–Nov. 24, 1870		NLI	Pos. 5349
		1855–1870	1855–1870		PRONI	MIC.1D/78
		See NLI			LDS	BFA 979703 item 1

GALWAY EAST

CLONFERT DIOCESE
1 Abbeygormican & Killoran
2 Aughrim & Kilconnell
3 Ballymacaward & Cloonkeenkerril
4 Ballinakill
5 Ballinasloe (Creagh & Kilcloony)
6 Clonfert
7 Clontuskert
8 Duniry & Ballinakill
9 Fahy & Kilquain
10 Fohenagh & Kilgerill
11 Kilconickney
12 Kilcooley & Leitrim
13 Killallaghten
14 Killimorbologue
15 Killimordaly (Kiltullagh)
16 Kilmalinogue (Portumna)
17 Killeenadeema
18 Kiltormer
19 Loughrea
20 New Inn
21 Tynagh
22 Woodford

ELPHIN DIOCESE
23 Ahascragh
24 Athleague & Fuerty
25 Dysart & Tisrara
26 Glinsk & Kilbegnet
27 Killian & Cilleroran
28 Oran (Cloverhill)

GALWAY DIOCESE
29 Ardrahan
30 Ballindereen (Kilcolgan)
31 Beagh
32 Claregalway
33 Clarenbridge (Kilcornan)
34 Craughwell

35 Gort (Kilmacduagh)
36 Kilbeacanty
37 Kilchreest
38 Oranmore (Kilcameen & Ballymacourty)
39 Peterswell (Kilthomas)
40 Kinvarra

KILLALOE DIOCESE
41 Mountshannon (Clonrush)

TUAM DIOCESE
42 Abbeyknockmoy
43 Addergoole & Kisleevy
44 Annaghdown

45 Athenry
46 Boyounagh
47 Donaghpatrick & Kilcloona
48 Dunmore
49 Kilconly & Kilbannon
50 Kilkerrin & Clonberne
51 Killascobe
52 Killererin
53 Killursa & Killower
54 Kilmeen
55 Kilmoylan & Cummer
56 Lackagh
57 Mounbellew (Moylough)
58 Tuam

Map	Church	Baptisms	GALWAY EAST Marriages	Burials	Location	Reference
1	Mullagh (Abbey-gormican)	Feb. 11, 1859–Dec. 24, 1880; 1846–1885 (incomplete); Jan. 3, 1863 –Sept. 13, 1880	Apr. 26, 1863–Oct. 22, 1880; 1846–1885 (incomplete); Jan. 3, 1863 –Sept. 13, 1880		NLI	Pos. 2434
		1863–1903	1846–1920		LDS	BFA 1279218 items 7–9
		1863–1900			EGFHS	
2	Aughrim	Mar. 27, 1828–Dec. 28, 1880			NLI	Pos. 2431
		1828–1901	1828–1921	1892–1901	LDS	BFA 1279215 items 9–12
		1828–1900	1829–1897	1825–1830	EGFHS	
3	Ballymacward and Clonkeen -kerrill	Oct. 1, 1841– Nov. 15, 1843; May, 2, 1855–Feb. 15, 1874; May 12, 1855– Dec. 30, 1880			NLI	Pos. 2431
		1856–1890	1885–1900		EGFHS	
		1855–1901	1885–1902		LDS	BFA 1279226 items 26–28
4, 8	Ballinakill (Duniry)	Apr. 15, 1839–Oct. 22, 1851; Feb. 5, 1859–Dec. 24, 1880; Nov. 20, 1858– Dec. 26, 1859			NLI	Pos. 2434
		1839–1900	1870–1900		EGFHS	
		1839–1851; 1858–1859 1859–1880; 1890–1902	1891–1903		LDS	BFA 0979689 items 12, 14; 1279216 22/
5	Ballinasloe	1820–1900	1853–1902		LDS	BFA 1279217 items 9–17
		1820–1900	1820–1900	1825–1830	EGFHS	
		Sept. 23, 1820–July 27, 1832; July 19, 1832–Feb. 21, 1841; June 7, 1841– June 14, 1847; July 6, 1847 –May, 30, 1862; June 6, 1862–Dec. 31, 1880	Sept. 23, 1820–July 27, 1832; July 19, 1832– Feb. 21, 1841	Sept. 23, 1820– July 27, 1832; July 19, 1832– Feb. 21, 1841	NLI	Pos. 2432
6	Clonfert	No records microfilmed			NLI	
		1884–1900			EGFHS	
		1893–1901	1894–1904		LDS	BFA 1279215 items 13–14
7	Clontuskert	1827–1901	1827–1901		LDS	BFA 1279215 items 1–2
		1827–1900	1853–1875		EGFHS	
		Oct. 2, 1827–Dec. 20, 1880 (modern transcript); Oct. 2, 1827–Oct. 4, 1868; Mar. 2, 1870–Dec. 5, 1880	Oct. 2, 1827–Oct. 4, 1868; Mar. 2, 1870– Dec. 5, 1880	Oct. 2, 1827– Oct. 4, 1868;	NLI	Pos. 2431
9	Fahy and Kilquain	1873–1900	1876–1900		EGFHS	
		No records microfilmed			NLI	
		1893–1903	1894–908		LDS	BFA 1279216 items 24–25

→

MAP	CHURCH	BAPTISMS	GALWAY EAST MARRIAGES	BURIALS	LOCATION	REFERENCE
10	Fohenagh	1827–1877; 1889–1902	1827–1877; 1890–1905		LDS	BFA 1279215 4–8; 0926058
		1828–1900	1828–1885		EGFHS	
		Aug. 1, 1827–Apr. 4, 1877	Aug. 1, 1827–Apr. 4, 1877	Aug. 1, 1827–Apr. 4, 1877	NLI	Pos. 2431
11	Carabane (Kilconickny)	1831–1878	1834–1877		EGFHS	
		July 14, 1831–Mar. 6, 1878	July 24, 1831–Jan. 29, 1878		NLI	Pos. 2434
		1831–1902	1832–1912		LDS	BFA 0979689 item 15; 1279216 15–17
12	Leitrim	See NLI			LDS	BFA 1279215 items 15–16
		1815–1840; 1846–1929	1816–1830; 1842–1850; 1887–1900	1816–1830; 1847–1887	EGFHS	
		May 22, 1815–Aug. 3, 1819; Oct. 13, 1819–Dec. 28, 1822; Jan. 4, 1823–June 1, 1829; Sept 30, 1850–Dec. 17, 1880	May 22, 1815–Aug. 3, 1819; Oct. 13, 1819–Dec. 28, 1822; Jan. 4, 1823–June 1, 1829; Dec. 9, 1846–Nov. 28, 1880	May 22, 1815–Aug. 3, 1819; Oct. 13, 1819–Dec. 28, 1822; Jan. 4, 1823–June 1, 1829; Dec. 16, 1846–Sept. 18, 1880	NLI	Pos. 2434
13	Cappataggle (Killalaghtan)	Jan. 6, 1809–Mar. 10, 1814; Jan. 1, 1814–May 29, 1827; Sept. 23, 1827–June 24, 1844; June 26, 1844–Sept. 15, 1869	Jan. 6, 1809–Mar. 10, 1814; Jan. 1, 1814–May 29, 1827; Sept. 23, 1827–June 24, 1844; Nov. 1, 1831–June 25, 1844; July 18, 1844–July 30, 1863	Jan. 6, 1809–Mar. 10, 1814; Jan. 1, 1814–May 29, 1827; Sept. 23, 1827–June 24, 1844; June 26, 1844–Sept. 15, 1869	NLI	Pos. 2431
		1809–1844; 1844–1917	1831–1844; 1844–1865	1827–1844; 1844–1869	LDS	BFA 1279215 items 31–3; 1279216 1–2
		1799–1900	1806–1863; 1893–1900	1806–1849	EGFHS	
14	Killimorbologe and Tiranascragh	Oct. 8, 1831–Dec. 29, 1846; Jan. 1, 1847–Sept. 10, 1879	Nov. 7, 1831–July 27, 1880		NLI	Pos. 2433
		1831–1891	1831–1841;			
			1851–1897		EGFHS	
		1831–1901	1831–1902		LDS	BFA 1279215 items 3–8
15	Kiltullagh (Killimoredaly)	1844–1881	1826–1883	1830–1841	EGFHS	
		June 25, 1844–Jan. 15, 1854; Dec. 21, 1862–Oct. 12, 1872	Jan. 30, 1830–Aug. 4, 1880	Sept. 5, 1830–May 23, 1837	NLI	Pos. 243434
		1844–1901	1826–1902	1830–1841	LDS	BFA 1279216 items 10–14
16	Portumna	Oct. 6, 1830–Feb 1, 1878; Feb 22, 1878–Dec. 24, 1880	Oct. 27, 1830–Nov. 1, 1876; Feb. 6, 1878–Oct. 14, 1880		NLI	Pos. 2433
		1830–1891	1832–1864		EGFHS	
		1830–1891	1830–1890		LDS	BFA 1279216 items 20–21

→

Map	Church	Baptisms	GALWAY EAST Marriages	Burials	Location	Reference
17	Killeenadeema	May 1, 1836–Dec. 12, 1880	Apr. 24, 1836–Oct. 2, 1880		NLI	Pos. 2434
		1836–1900	1836–1900		EGFHS	
		1836–1932	1837–1915		LDS	BFA 1279216 items 18–19
18	Laurencetown (Kiltormer)	Mar. 12, 1834–July 15, 1860; May 22, 1862–Dec. 20, 1880	Feb. 9, 1834–May 20, 1860; Sept. 30, 1860–Sept. 28, 1873		NLI	Pos. 2433
		1834–1897	1834–1892		EGFHS	
		1834–1903	1834–1926	1834–1836	LDS	BFA 1279217 items 24–27
19	Loughrea	1810–1901	1810–1901	1817–1826	LDS	BFA 1279216/7 items 29–32; 1–8
		1810–1900	1786–1900	1817–1826	EGFHS	
		Apr. 29, 1827–Dec. 27, 1848; Jan. 1, 1849–July 27, 1863; July 21, 1863–Aug. 8, 1871; July 21, 1868–Dec. 21, 1880	May, 12, 1827–Nov. 24, 1880; July 21, 1868–Dec. 21, 1880		NLI	Pos. 2435
20	New Inn	Oct. 17, 1827–Apr. 23, 1840; Aug. 11, 1841–Dec. 5, 1880	Oct. 28, 1827–May 15, 1842; July 29, 1839–Nov. 15, 1880		NLI	Pos. 2431
		1827–1900	1827–1900		EGFHS	
		1827–1903	1827–1908	1893–1930	LDS	BFA 1279216 items 3–9
21	Tynagh	May 1, 1816–Dec. 31, 1842; Sept. 25, 1846–Dec. 31, 1880	May 22, 1809–Dec. 10, 1842; Sept. 26, 1846–Feb. 10, 1863		NLI	Pos. 2433
		1816–1842; 1846–1864; 1874–1900	1809–1842; 1846–1864		EGFHS	
22	Woodford	Apr. 20, 1821–Nov. 25, 1843; Mar. 6, 1851–Aug. 4, 1861; Apr. 22, 1865–Sept. 13, 1868; Feb. 20, 1869–Oct. 16, 1880	Apr. 22, 1821–Nov. 25, 1843; Mar. 1, 1851–July 23, 1861; July 27, 1865–Feb. 9, 1869; Feb. 18, 1871–Feb. 19, 1880		NLI	Pos. 2433
		1821–1900	1821–1900		EGFHS	
		1821–1860; 1865–1908	1821–1866; 1881–1889		LDS	BFA 1279217/8, 18, 19–21, 1–6
23	Ahascragh and Killosolan	See NLI			LDS	BFA 09899751 items 1–2
		Jan. 10, 1840–May 6, 1880; Aug. 15, 1870–Dec. 31, 1880 (Ahascragh only)	Jan. 29, 1866–Nov. 26, 1880 (Ahascragh only)		NLI	Pos. 4616, 4617
		1840–1899	1866–1899		RHGC	
24	Athleague	See Roscommon 7				
25	Dysart	See Roscommon 11				
26	Kilbegnet	Sept. 5, 1836–Jan. 28, 1846; Nov. 2, 1846 (?)–June 22, 1848; Mar. 15, 1849–Sept. 23, 1866; Oct. 6, 1866–Dec. 26, 1880	Nov. 1, 1836–Apr. 24, 1865; July 6, 1865–Nov. 1, 1880	Sept. 14, 1836–Sept. 20, 1839	NLI	Pos. 4620
		1836–1900	1836–1900	1836–1839	RHGC	
27	Killian	1804–1900	1804–1900	1844–1859	RHGC	

→

Map	Church	Baptisms	GALWAY EAST Marriages	Burials	Location	Reference
27	Killian (*cont.*)	Apr. 22, 1804–July 26, 1833; Oct. 19, 1844–Dec. 29, 1863; Dec. 13, 1859–Mar. 23, 1861; May 12, 1860–Nov. 21, 1880 (Newbridge); Jan. 14, 1864–Nov. 21, 1879	Apr. 21, 1804–Feb. 28, 1843; Oct. 13, 1844–Mar. 31, 1863; Jan. 16, 1860–Oct. 5, 1865 (Newbridge); Jan. 24, 1864–Nov. 18, 1880	Oct. 21, 1844–Dec. 5, 1859	NLI	Pos. 4613, 4614
		1804–1900	1844–1900		EGFHS	
		See NLI			LDS	BFA 0989748 items 1–3
28	Oran	See Roscommon 25				
29	Ardrahan	See NLI			LDS	BFA 0926062
		1839–1900	1845–1900	1878	GFHSW	
		May 30, 1839–Mar. 22, 1846; Nov. 18, 1866–Nov. 15, 1880	Mar. 26, 1845–Feb. 20, 1850; Feb. 3, 1867–Sept. 13, 1887		NLI	Pos. 2442
30	Ballindereen	Nov. 12, 1854–July 21, 1881	Jan. 29, 1871–Sept. 6, 1884		NLI	Pos. 2442
		1854–1881	1871–1884		LDS	BFA 0979691 item 10
		1854–1900	1871–1900		GFHSW	
31	Beagh	Feb. 5, 1851–June 25, 1851; Jan. 14, 1855–Apr. 3, 1881	Mar. 1849–Feb. 23, 1850; May 19. 1860–Oct. 18, 1881		NLI	Pos. 2442
		1855–1900			EGFHS	
		See NLI			LDS	BFA 0979692 items 1–2
32	Claregalway	Nov. 11, 1849–Dec. 29, 1880	Nov. 12, 1849–Nov. 23, 1880	Nov. 11, 1849–Nov. 1876	NLI	Pos. 2429
		1849–1902	1849–1908	1849–1876	GFHSW	
33	Clarenbridge	1854–1900	1837–1900		GFHSW	
		Aug. 7, 1854–Mar. 29, 1881	June 13, 1837–Feb. 18, 1882		NLI	Pos. 2442
		See NLI	See NLI		LDS	BFA 0979690 item 1
34	Craughwell	1847–1894	1847–1858; 1869–1876	1847–1850	EGFHS	
		See NLI			LDS	BFA 0979692 item 8
		Nov. 20, 1847–Mar. 28, 1881	July 6, 1856–Nov. 25, 1876		NLI	Pos. 2442
35	Gort	Feb. 14, 1848–Feb. 13, 1862; July 17, 1854–Dec. 28, 1872; Feb. 18, 1862–Feb. 17, 1863; Jan. 5, 1873–Mar. 2, 1881	Dec. 6, 1853–Feb. 20, 1862; Feb. 23, 1862–Feb. 17, 1863		NLI	B. to 1872, M. to 1862: Pos. 2441; remainder 2442
		See NLI			LDS	BFA 0979691 item 3
		1848–1880			EGFHS	
36	Kilbeacanty	Aug. 6, 1854–Jan. 7, 1881			NLI	Pos. 2442
		1855–1900	1881–1900		EGFHS	
		See NLI			LDS	BFA 0979692 item 3 →

Map	Church	Baptisms	GALWAY EAST Marriages	Burials	Location	Reference
37	Kilchreest	1855–1900	1865–1897		EGFHS	
		Feb. 1, 1855–June 25, 1881	Feb. 2, 1865–Feb. 23, 1886		NLI	Pos. 2442
		See NLI			LDS	BFA 0926064
38	Oranmore	Mar. 11, 1833–Apr. 29, 1839; May. 25, 1833–Dec. 28, 1843; Dec. 28, 1843–Dec. 25, 1880	May 2, 1833–July 18, 1838; Aug. 24, 1843–Nov. 8, 1880	Jan. 7, 1833–Dec. 24, 1837	NLI	Pos. 2438
		1833–1900	1833–1900	1848–1900	GFHSW	
		See NLI			LDS	BFA 0979690 item 1
39	Peterswell	1854–1900	1856–1900		EGFHS	
		Jan. 27, 1854–Jan. 15, 1881	Jan. 28, 1856–July 24, 1886		NLI	Pos. 2442
		See NLI			LDS	BFA 0979692 item 4
40	Kinvara	1831–1853			LDS	BFA 0926068
		June 28, 1831–May 15, 1837; June 23, 1843–Aug. 29, 1853; July 31, 1854–Sept. 29, 1867; Oct. 11, 1867–Mar. 27, 1881	July 9, 1831–May 13, 1837; June 26, 1843–Aug. 12, 1853; Nov. 17, 1867–Jan. 18, 1881	List of the inhabitants showing Christmas dues 1834, Easter dues 1835, and remembrance masses July 27, 1835–May 13, 1837. Also list of certificates issued 1844–1855	NLI	B. and M. to 1853: Pos. 2442; remainder 2443
		1831–1900	1831–1900		GFHSW	
41	Mountshannon (Clonrush)	See Clare 14				
42	Abbeyknock-moy	1828–	1828–		LC	
		1821–1832; 1837–1858; 1841–1854; 1894–1915	1837–1844; 1894–1901	1847–1848	LDS	BFA1279210 items 9–14
		1821–1900	1844–1900	1847–1848	GFHSW	
		No records microfilmed			NLI	
43	Addergoole and Liskeevy	1858–1900	1859–1900		GFHSW	
		Aug. 7,1858–Nov. 18, 1877; Jan. 8, 1878–Dec. 31, 1880	Jan. 10, 1859–Dec. 11, 1880		NLI	Pos. 4210
		1858–1891; 1878–1918	1859–1884		LDS	BFA 1279208 items 1–2
44	Annaghdown	Sept. 1834–Sept. 12, 1869; Feb. 2, 1875–Jan. 4, 1880	Mar.15, 1834–Nov. 29, 1868; Feb. 6, 1875–June 12, 1880		NLI	Pos. 4219
		1834–1900	1834–1900		GFHSW	
		1834–1909 (gaps)	1834–1909 (gaps)		LDS	BFA 1279206 items 1–2
45	Athenry	1858–1900	1858–1900		GFHSW	
		Aug. 3, 1858–Sept. 21, 1878; 1858–1919	Aug. 15, 1858–Oct. 1, 1878; 1858–1901		NLI	Pos. 4219

→

Map	Church	Baptisms	GALWAY EAST Marriages	Burials	Location	Reference
45	Athenry (*cont.*)				LDS	BFA 1279207 items 6–7; 1279209 4–5
46	Templetoher (Williamstown)	1856–1900	1859–1872	1858–1870	EGFHS	
		1856–1900	1858–1889		LDS	BFA 1279259 items 11, 12
		Aug. 25, 1858–Jan. 25, 1872	Sept. 11, 1858–Feb. 11, 1872		NLI	Pos. 4213
46	Boyounagh	1859–1908			LDS	BFA 1279211 item 9
		1838–1900	1838–1865		EGFHS	
		Oct. 5, 1838–June 11, 1858; Dec. 11, 1859–Oct. 25, 1863; Oct. 8, 1865–Dec. 26, 1880	Oct. 9, 1838–July 17, 1865		NLI	Pos. 4211
47	Donaghpatrick	1857–1901	1857–1905		LDS	BFA 1279206 item 12
		1844–1900	1844–1900		GFHSW	
		Apr. 8, 1844–June 30, 1844; Nov. 12, 1849–June 9, 1861; Aug. 1, 1863–Dec. 27, 1880	Apr. 8, 1844–Dec. 6, 1846; Dec. 8, 1849–June 15, 1861; Sept. 12, 1863–Nov. 18, 1880		NLI	Pos. 4219
48	Dunmore	1833–1860;				
		1877–1910	1833–1860		LDS	BFA 1279210 items 4–8
		Mar. 2, 1833–Mar. 1, 1846; Dec. 12, 1853–Oct. 21, 1859 (two sections 1856–59); Dec. 14, 1847–Jan. 20, 1854; Sept. 16, 1877–Dec. 30, 1880	Mar. 17, 1833–Sept. 6, 1860; Jan. 13, 1861–Sept. 9, 1877		NLI	Pos. 4211
		1833–1900	1833–1900		GFHSW	
49	Kilconly	1872–1913			LDS	BFA 1279214 item 4
		1872–1900	1872–1900		GFHSW	
		Mar 3, 1872–Dec. 29, 1880			NLI	Pos. 4212
50	Kilkerrin and Clonberne	No records microfilmed			NLI	
		1892–1900	1884–1893		EGFHS	
		1892–1903	1893–1935	1920–1926	LDS	BFA 1279213 items 8–9
51	Killascobe	July 13, 1867–Dec. 24, 1880	May 7, 1807–July 20, 1819; Nov. 25, 1825–June 8, 1847; July 25, 1849–Dec. 15, 1880		NLI	Pos. 4220
		1806–1902	1806–1902		LDS	BFA 1279259 item 13
52	Killereran	1870–1900	1851–1879; 1888–1900		LDS	BFA 1279214 items 1–2
		1870–1900	1851–1900		GFHSW	
		June 12, 1870–Dec. 26, 1880	Feb. 26, 1851–Aug. 8, 1858; Oct. 24, 1870–July 1, 1879		NLI	Pos. 4220

→

Map	Church	Baptisms	GALWAY EAST Marriages	Burials	Location	Reference
53	Killursa and Killower	No records microfilmed			NLI	
		1880–1912	1880–1916		LDS	BFA 1279207 items 13–14
		1880–1916	1880–1920		GFHSW	
54	Kilmeen	See Leitrim (12)				
55	Kilmoylan	1835–1900	1813–1900		GFHSW	
		1835–1906	1813–1894	1835–1868	LDS	BFA 1279207 items 1–5
		Dec. 18, 1835–Aug. 5, 1860; Aug. 4, 1872–July 9, 1879	Oct. 14, 1813–July 20, 1872; Aug. 1, 1871–Nov. 26, 1880		NLI	Pos. 4220
56	Lackagh	1842–1900	1841–1900	1858–1876	GFHSW	
		July 1842–Sept. 24, 1847; Apr. 1, 1848–Sept. 25, 1853; Sept. 5, 1853–Dec. 26, 1880	Sept. 10, 1841–Dec. 20, 1847; Sept. 25, 1853–Mar 1. 1880		NLI	Pos. 4220
		See NLI			LDS	BFA 0976227 items 2–3
57	Moylough	1848–1903	1848–1903		LDS	BFA 1279210 items 4–8
		Jan. 16, 1848–Oct. 28, 1863; Sept. 20, 1860–July 1870; Jan. 11, 1871–Dec. 8, 1880; Jan. 2, 1873–Dec. 31, 1880	Nov. 20, 1848–Sept. 29, 1863; Dec. 17, 1860–Dec. 7, 1870; Jan. 12, 1871–Oct. 23, 1880; Feb. 17, 1873–Oct. 18, 1880		NLI	Pos. 4220
		1848–1900	1837–1900		EGFHS	
58	Tuam	Mar. 3, 1790–July 2, 1804; Oct. 14, 1811–Oct. 5,1829; Nov. 1, 1829–Apr. 12, 1845; May 1, 1845–Oct. 1, 1857; Oct. 3, 1858–July 13, 1873	Jan. 26, 1799 (?)–Mar 6, 1832; Oct. 17, 1832–Dec. 26, 1880		NLI	Pos. 4221, 4222
		1790–1900	1790–1900		GFHSW	
		1790–1929	1795–1901		LDS	BFA 1279208/9 items 7–15; 1

GALWAY WEST

GALWAY DIOCESE
1. Castlegar
2. Galway City
   (St Nicholas)
3. Killanin (see also
   Oughterard)
4. Moycullen
5. Oranmore (Kilcameen
   & Ballynacourty)
6. Oughterard (Kilcummin)
7. Rahoon
8. Rosmuck (see also
   Oughterard)
9. Salthill
10. Spiddal

TUAM DIOCESE
11. Aran Islands
12. Ballinakill
13. Clifden (Omey &
    Ballindoon)
14. Cong
15. Clonbur (Ross)(see also Leenane)
16. Killeen (Lettermullen & Carraroe)
17. Leenane (Kilbride)
18. Moyrus
19. Roundstone (see also Moyne)

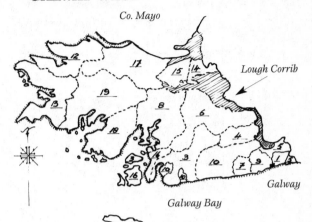

			GALWAY WEST			
MAP	**CHURCH**	**BAPTISMS**	**MARRIAGES**	**BURIALS**	**LOCATION**	**REFERENCE**
1	Castlegar	See NLI			LDS	BFA 0979690 item 2
		1827–1908	1827–1912	1828–1908	GFHSW	
		Mar. 8, 1827–Dec. 31, 1841; Jan. 2, 1842–July 31, 1863; Nov. 3, 1864–Nov. 21, 1880	Mar. 8, 1827–Dec. 15, 1841; Jan. 8, 1842–Oct. 24, 1864; Nov. 3, 1864–Nov. 21, 1880	Mar. 25, 1827–Oct. 28, 1841; Jan. 9, 1842–July 31, 1864; Nov. 13, 1864–Nov. 14, 1880	NLI	Pos. 2438
2	Galway city: St Nicholas	Apr. 21, 1690–Dec. 28, 1690; Mar 31, 1723–Mar. 10, 1726			NLI	Pos. 2436
		See NLI			LDS	BFA 0926070
2	Galway city: St Nicholas East	Nov. 15, 1810–Dec. 30, 1821; Oct. 1, 1831–Dec. 1858	Jan. 7, 1789–Nov. 29, 1824; Oct. 17, 1831–Dec. 23, 1858	Sept. 1, 1788–Dec. 17, 1809; Oct. 16, 1831–Dec. 26, 1858	NLI	Pos. 2436 & 2437
		1810–1900	1789–1858	1789–1858	GFHSW	
		See NLI			LDS	BFA 0926070
2	Galway city: St Nicholas North	Apr. 5, 1818–Mar. 30, 1835; Apr. 7, 1835–Oct. 28, 1867	Apr. 12, 1818–Aug. 22, 1868	Apr. 5, 1818–Mar. 31, 1861; 1866–8 (2 pages only)	NLI	Pos. 2436 & 2437
		See NLI			LDS	BFA 0926070
		1818–1867	1818–1868	1818–1868	GFHSW	→

Map	Church	Baptisms	GALWAY WEST Marriages	Burials	Location	Reference
2	Galway city: St Nicholas North & East	Feb. 2, 1859–Dec. 26, 1880	Feb. 3, 1859–Nov. 30, 1880	Feb. 20, 1859–Dec. 31, 1880	NLI	Pos. 2437
		1859–1900	1859–1900	1859–1900	GFHSW	
		See NLI			LDS	BFA 0926070
2	Galway city: St Nicholas South and West	1805–1821 (2 pages only); Feb. 27, 1814–Dec. 13, 1826; Oct. 16, 1822–Aug. 20, 1866; Aug 13, 1828–Oct. 13, 1845; Jan. 6, 1846–Apr. 12, 1853; Nov. 14, 1859–Nov. 16, 1868; Nov. 2, 1872–Dec. 23, 1880	1809–1821 (3 pages only); Mar. 12, 1814–Dec. 26, 1826; Feb. 13, 1822–Sept. 29, 1859; Aug. 13, 1828–Oct. 13, 1845; Jan. 9, 1846–Jan. 31, 1852; Nov. 4, 1859–Oct. 8, 1868; Nov. 9, 1872–Dec. 31, 1880	1811–1869 (5 pages only); Mar. 5, 1814–Nov. 16, 1826; Aug. 15, 1847–July 3, 1859; Aug. 13, 1828–Oct. 13, 1845; Feb. 7, 1846–Dec. 21, 1851; Nov. 8, 1859–Sept. 8, 1868; Nov. 25, 1872–Dec. 5, 1880	NLI	Pos. 2436
		See NLI			LDS	BFA 0926070
		1814–1900	1809–1900	1810–1900	GFHSW	
3	Killanin	Jan. 1, 1875–Dec. 26, 1880	Jan. 26, 1875–Dec. 6, 1880		NLI	Pos. 2439
		1834–1900	1875–1900	1881–1888	GFHSW	
		See NLI			LDS	BFA 0926228 item 2
4	Moycullen	Jan. 2, 1786–Mar. 9, 1823; Jan. 4, 1837–May 3, 1841; Oct. 6, 1843–Oct. 3, 1848; Nov. 4, 1848–Dec. 26, 1880	Jan. 8, 1786–Jan. 13, 1823; Oct. 1, 1843–Oct. 3, 1848; Feb. 18, 1849–Nov. 16, 1880	Jan. 4, 1786–Mar. 13, 1823; Nov. 1848–Dec. 21, 1880	NLI	Pos. 2441
		See NLI			LDS	BFA 0926071
		1793–1812	1793–1812		Published	Analecta Hibernica, No. 14, pp. 126–134
		1848–1900	1849–1900	1848–1900	GFHSW	
5	Oranmore	See East Galway				
6	Oughterard	1809–1821; 1827–1880	1809–1816; 1827–1880	1827–1874	LDS	BFA 0979690 item 3
		1809–1900	1809–1900	1827–1874	GFHSW	
		June 27, 1809–Aug. 18, 1821; Mar. 9, 1827–Dec. 30, 1880	July 27, 1809–Feb. 23, 1816; Mar. 20, 1827–Dec. 28, 1880	Mar. 8, 1827–Feb. 4, 1874	NLI	Pos. 2438
7	Rahoon	See NLI			LDS	BFA 0926069
		1806–1913	1806–1913	1806–1913	GFHSW	
		Jan. 3, 1819–Dec. 31, 1832; Jan. 1, 1833–Jan. 28, 1845; Apr. 17, 1845–Mar. 25, 1877	Jan. 3, 1819–Dec. 27, 1832	Jan. 3, 1819–July 23, 1826; 2 pages for 1830	NLI	Pos. 2437
8	Rosmuck	1840–1900		1863	GFHSW	
		Aug. 11, 1840–Dec. 27, 1880			NLI	Pos. 2439
9	Salthill	No records microfilmed			NLI	

→

MAP	CHURCH	BAPTISMS	GALWAY WEST MARRIAGES	BURIALS	LOCATION	REFERENCE
10	Spiddal	Feb. 7, 1861–Mar. 25, 1873; Apr. 13, 1873–Dec. 25, 1880	Apr. 29, 1873–Nov. 3, 1880	Apr. 22, 1873–Dec. 8, 1880	NLI	Pos. 2438
		1861–1900	1873–1900	1873–1900	GFHSW	
		See NLI			LDS	BFA 0979690 item 4
11	Aran Islands	1872–1900	1872–1900		GFHSW	
		1872–1905	1872–1905		LDS	BFA 1279214 item 8
		Nov. 7, 1874–Dec. 23, 1880	Feb. 20, 1872–Dec. 21, 1880		NLI	Pos. 4219
12	Ballinakill	July 23, 1869–Dec. 26, 1880; May 14, 1876–Dec. 26, 1880 (separate register)	July 25, 1869–Dec. 5, 1880; Jan. 12, 1875–Nov. 17, 1880 (separate register)		NLI	Pos. 4218
		1869–1903	1870–1903		LDS	BFA 1279212 items 17–19
		1869–1900	1869–1900		GFHSW	
13	Omey	1838–1900 (Clifden)	1838–1900 (Clifden)	1869–1877	GFHSW	
		1864–1900 (Ballyconneely); 1881–1900 (Omey/Ballindoon) Jan. 7, 1838–Oct. 7, 1855; July 1856–Oct. 26, 1874; Oct. 2, 1864–Aug. 7 1880 (Ballyconneely)	1864–1900 (Ballyconeely) 1885–1900 (Omey/Ballindoon) Sept. 15, 1839–May 6, 1855 (various groups of entries for different dates); Aug. 19, 1858–Feb. 27, 1874 (various groups of entries for different dates); Oct. 29, 1864–Dec. 18, 1873; June 26, 1874–Dec. 14, 1880		NLI	Pos. 4218
		1838–1924	1839–1938	1869–1872	LDS	BFA 1279213 items 1–7; 1279213 1;
14	Cong	See Mayo 44				
15	Ross	1853–1919	1883–1903		LDS	BFA 1279259 items 6–10
		1853–1900	1883–1900		GFHSW	
		Dec. 25, 1853–Apr. 29, 1871; Jan. 10, 1873–Dec. 19, 1880			NLI	Pos. 4216
16	Lettermullin	1861–1900	1853–1895		LDS	BFA 127921 items 11–13
		Aug. 17, 1853–May 16, 1880; Aug. 18, 1872–Nov. 21, 1880 (Killeen)	July 18, 1853–Nov. 1, 1880		NLI	Pos. 4218
		1853–1900	1853–1900		GFHSW	
17	Leenane (Kilbride)	See NLI			LDS	BFA 0926221 item 2
		1853–1900	1853–1900		MSFRC	
		Ross			LC	
		Dec. 11, 1853–Nov. 12, 1880 (transcript)			NLI	Pos. 4214

→

Map	Church	Baptisms	GALWAY WEST Marriages	Burials	Location	Reference
18	Moyrus	1852–1903	1852–1903		LDS	BFA 1279212 items 8–10
		1853–1900	1854–1900		GFHSW	
		Dec. 8, 1853–Sept. 20, 1873; Oct. 18, 1874– Nov. 7, 1880	Sept. 9, 1852–Sept. 6, 1874; Nov. 1, 1874– Nov. 20, 1880		NLI	Pos. 4218
19	Roundstone	1872–1910	1872–1900		LDS	BFA 1279212 items 8–10
		1872–1900	1872–1900		GFHSW	
		Aug. 3, 1872–Dec. 26, 1880	Aug., 4, 1872–Dec. 19, 1880		NLI	Pos. 4218

KERRY

KERRY DIOCESE
1 Abbeydorney
2 Annascaul
   (Ballyvoher)
3 Ardfert
4 Ballybunion &
   Ballydonohoe
5 Ballyferriter
6 Ballyheigue
7 Ballylongford
8 Ballymacelligot
9 Boherbue
10 Bonane
11 Brosna
12 Caherciveen
13 Caherdaniel
14 Castlegregory
15 Castleisland
16 Castlemaine
17 Causeway
18 Dingle
19 Dromad (Waterville)
20 Duagh
21 Firies
22 Fossa
23 Glenbeigh
24 Glenflesk
25 Kenmare
26 Kilcummin
27 Kilgarvan
28 Killarney
29 Killeentierna
30 Killorglin
31 Knocknagoshel
32 Listowel
33 Lixnaw

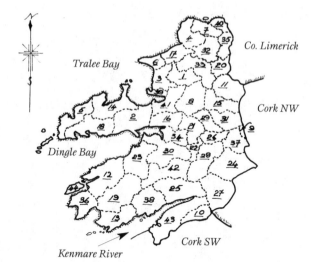

34 Milltown
35 Moyvane
36 Prior (Ballinskelligs)
37 Rathmore
38 Sneem
39 Spa
40 Tarbert
41 Tralee
42 Tuogh
43 Tuosist
44 Valencia

Map	Church	Baptisms	KERRY Marriages	Burials	Location	Reference
1	Abbeydorney	Oct. 2, 1835–Sept. 10, 1844; Feb. 27, 1851–Sept. 6, 1859; Nov. 7, 1880–Dec. 6, 1880	Jan. 24, 1837–July 20, 1859; Nov. 2, 1859–Nov. 10, 1880		NLI	Pos. 4274
		1835–1900	1835–1900		KGC	
2	Ballyvohir (Annascaul)	1829–1834; 1837–1839; 1851–1899	1829–1899		KGC	
		Apr. 2, 1829–Mar. 12, 1834; Mar. 23, 1837–Mar. 19, 1839; Oct. 2, 1851–Dec. 26, 1880 (transcript)	May 1, 1829–June 3, 1835; May–Oct. 1837; Sept. 1855–Nov. 14, 1880 (transcript)		NLI	Pos. 4274
3	Ardfert	1818–1839; 1839–1846 (Vol. 8)	1825–1843 (Vol. 8)		Published	O'K
		1818–1846	1825–1846		LDS	BFA 0883784 item 6; 0883740 item 3
		1859–1900	1860–1900		KGC	
		Mar. 1819–Nov. 1819; July–Sept. 1824; Feb. 8, 1835–Oct. 2, 1846; Oct. 1, 1859–Dec. 20, 1874; Dec. 24, 1984–Dec. 26, 1880	Feb. 15, 1825–Jan. 25, 1826; Jan. 10, 1835–Feb. 24, 1846; Nov. 4, 1859–Nov. 30, 1880		NLI	Pos. 4272
4	Ballybunion	1831–1900	1860–1900		KGC	
		Nov. 1, 1831–Jan. 4, 1870; Jan. 2, 1870–Dec. 27, 1880	Feb. 7, 1837–Nov. 13, 1869; Jan. 15, 1870–Nov. 21, 1880		NLI	Pos. 4280
5	Ballyferriter (Kilmelchidar)	Jan. 14, 1807–Jan. 19, 1808; Jan. 1, 1808–June 29, 1828; July 1, 1828–July 30, 1871; Aug. 24, 1871–Dec. 19, 1880	Jan. 1808–Aug. 5, 1808; Feb. 5, 1808–May 31, 1828; July 24, 1828–Nov. 1880		NLI	Pos. 4274 to 1828; remainder 4275
6	Ballyheigue	Dec. 1, 1857–Dec. 17, 1880	Jan. 13, 1858–Feb. 10, 1880		NLI	Pos. 4273
		1867–1900	1857–1900		KGC	
7	Ballylongford	1823–1900	1823–1900		KGC	
		Mar. 20, 1823–May 12, 1838 (very fragmented); Oct. 1869–Dec. 31, 1880	June 1826–Jan. 1827; Feb. 1828–Aug. 1828; Jan. 1832–Nov. 1837 (very fragmented)		NLI	Pos. 4284
8	Ballymacelligot	Oct. 4, 1868–Dec. 19, 1880	Nov. 14, 1868–July 30, 1880		NLI	Pos. 4273
		1868–1900	1859–1900		KGC	
9	Boherbue	See Cork Northwest 30				
10	Bonane and Glengarriff,	July 22, 1846–Dec. 25, 1856; Jan. 3, 1857–Dec. 21, 1877; Jan. 9, 1878–Dec. 26, 1880	July 18, 1847–Nov. 29, 1856; Feb. 1, 1857–Feb. 9, 1875; Feb. 2 1876–Feb. 10 1880		NLI	Pos. 4288
11	Brosna	Mar. 15, 1868–May 14, 1878			NLI	Pos. 4283
		1866–1875			LDS	BFA 1238660 item 3
		1866–1900 (Vol. 8)	1872–1900 (Vol. 8)		Published	O'K
		1866–1900	1880–1900		KGC	
12	Cahirciveen	Nov. 11, 1846–June 24, 1863 (some pages mutilated); Apr. 16, 1863–Jan. 18, 1879 (transcript)			NLI	Pos. 4285

→

Map	Church	Baptisms	KERRY Marriages	Burials	Location	Reference
12	Cahirciveen (*cont.*)		1863–1900	1863–1900		KGC
13	Cahirdaniel	Feb. 1831–July 29, 1867 (mutilated)	May 1831–Feb. 18, 1868 (many pages mutilated)		NLI	B., Pos. 4287; M. 4288
		1831–1893	1831–1893		KGC	
14	Castlegregory (Killiny)	Dec. 7, 1828–Dec. 31, 1864; Jan. 3,165–June 16, 1879	Feb. 28, 1829–Nov. 13, 1864; Jan. 18, 1865–Sept. 11, 1880		NLI	Pos. 4275 to 1864; remainder 4276
		1828–1899	1829–1899		KGC	
15	Castleisland	1823–1858 (Vol. 6); 1859–1869 (Vol. 4); 1870–1872 (Vol. 6)	1822–1891 (Vol. 7); 1878–1900 (Vol. 7)		Published	O'K
		1829–1913	1825–1918		LDS	BFA 1279379
		Apr. 1823–Dec. 29, 1859; Jan. 1, 1859–Aug. 29, 1869; Feb. 15, 1870–Dec. 18, 1880	Oct. 10, 1822–Aug. 10, 1858; Feb. 8, 1859–May 6, 1880		NLI	M. and B. to 1869, Pos. 4276; remainder 4277
		1823–1899	1823–1899		KGC	
16	Castlemaine (Keel)	Feb. 5, 1804–July 8, 1813; Jan. 9, 1815–Oct. 1817; Apr. 7, 1818–June 30, 1834; July 6, 1834–Mar. 1845; Feb. 29, 1845–Nov. 1, 1880	Feb. 4, 1804–Mar. 15, 1818; May 1818–June 18, 1834; Aug. 28, 1834–Feb. 4, 1845; Apr. 9, 1845–July 31, 1880		NLI	Pos. 4273
17	Causeway (Killury)	Dec. 10, 1782–July 1786; Nov. 4, 1806–Nov. 29, 1819; July 18, 1820–Apr. 29, 1835; Sept. 4, 1831–June 29, 1845; Aug. 31, 1845–Apr. 20, 1858; May 8, 1858–Dec. 25, 1880	Feb. 13, 1809–Feb. 16, 1836 (many pages illegible)		NLI	Pos. 4278, 4279
		1782–1900	1782–1900		KGC	
		1782–1900	1809–1900		KGC	
18	Dingle	Feb. 25, 1825–Apr. 20, 1837; Sept. 30, 1837–Dec. 6, 1859; Jan. 1, 1860–Sept. 15, 1869; Sept. 11, 1869–Jan. 12, 1880	May 1, 1821–Dec. 30, 1859; Jan. 28, 1860–Oct. 13, 1880		NLI	Pos. 4277 to 1859; remainder 4278
		1824–1899	1860–1900		KGC	
19	Dromod	Feb. 1850–Aug. 5, 1867; Apr. 13, 1867–Dec. 31, 1880	Jan. 29, 1850–Mar. 5, 1867; Apr. 13, 1867–Dec. 31, 1880		NLI	Pos. 4288
20	Duagh	Jan. 1, 1819–Dec. 2, 1833; Dec. 2, 1833–Nov. 27, 1852; 1853–Sept. 28, 1871 (some early pages missing); Oct. 1, 1871–Dec. 27, 1880	Jan. 24, 1832–Nov. 10, 1833; Jan. 26, 1834–Aug. 14, 1852; 1853–June 18, 1871 (some early pages missing); Jan. 18, 1872–Oct. 19, 1880	May 9, 1844–Dec. 6, 1846	NLI	Pos. 4282
		1819–1906	1827–1911		KGC	
21	Firies (Molahiff)	1872–1900 (Vol. 8)	1881–1900 (Vol. 8)		Published	O'K
		1830–1894	1830–1894		KGC	
		Jan. 1, 1830–Sept. 22, 1872 (very poor condition); Sept. 29, 1859 –June 8, 1871 (Aglis); Jan. 20, 1871–Aug. 10, 1872; Oct. 1872–Oct. 23, 1880 (damaged)	Jan. 13, 1830–Mar. 13, 1872 (very poor condition)		NLI	Pos. 4267

→

Map	Church	Baptisms	KERRY Marriages	Burials	Location	Reference
22	Fossa	1857–1900			KGC	
		Jan. 11, 1857–Dec. 17, 1880	Jan. 21, 1858–Sept. 26, 1880		NLI	Pos. 4265
23	Glenbeigh	Mar. 17, 1830–Aug. 1837 (fragmented); June 21, 1841–Mar. 25, 1870 (fragmented, pages missing); Apr. 9, 1870–Dec. 30, 1880	Mar. 1830–Feb. 1835 (fragmented)		NLI	Pos. 4285
		1825–1837; 1885–1900	1829–1837; 1843–1898		KGC	
24	Glenflesk	1820–1873 1820–1875	1831–1848; 1852–1873 1831–1880 (gaps)		KGC LDS	BFA 0883747 items 2,19
		Sept. 1821–Mar. 12, 1873	Feb. 13, 1831–Feb. 25, 1873		NLI	Pos.4266
		1820–1832 (Vol. 7); 1832–1862 (Vol. 7); 1862–1894 (Vol. 8)	1831–1900 (Vol. 6)		Published	O'K
25	Kenmare (Templenoe)	Jan. 1, 1819–Dec. 24, 1838; Jan. 2, 1839–Dec. 30, 1858; Jan. 2, 1859–Dec. 19, 1870; Jan. 1, 1871 –Aug. 1, 1876; Aug. 6, 1876–Feb. 16, 1879	Jan. 26, 1819–Mar. 2, 1824; Jan. 17, 1826–June 30, 1838; Jan. 23, 1839–Nov. 27, 1858; Jan. 9, 1859–Oct. 24, 1880		NLI	Pos. 4289
		1819–1846; 1848–1876; 1887–1900	1819–1900		KGC	
26	Kilcummin	Jan. 10, 1821–Aug. 31, 1859; Feb. 8, 1873–May 11, 1880	Jan. 31, 1823–Sept. 23, 1859; Feb. 8, 1873–May 11, 1880		NLI	Pos. 4265
		1821–1900 (Vol. 5)	1823–1859 (Vol. 5);		Published	O'K
		1821–1900	1873–1900 (Vol. 5)		KGC	
		1821–1875	1823–1859; 1873–1900		LDS	
		1873–1880	1823–1859			BFA 0883784 item 5, 0883740 item 5
27	Kilgarvan	1841–1895	1818–1895		KGC	
		Apr. 15, 1818–Aug. 23, 1846; Aug. 10, 1846–Nov. 30, 1853; Dec. 2, 1863–Dec. 31, 1880	Nov. 4, 1818–Aug. 1, 1846; Sept. 23, 1846–Apr. 16, 1864; Sept. 6, 1864–May, 1880		NLI	Pos. 4290
28	Killarney	Aug. 5, 1792–June 24, 1803; June 27, 1803–July 12, 1809; July 16, 1809–Sept. 5, 1816; Sept. 3, 1816–Apr. 15, 1824; Apr. 16, 1824–Jan. 17, 1830; Jan. 3, 1830–Mar. 24, 1839; Mar. 24, 1839–Feb. 26, 1854; Mar. 1, 1854–Dec. 29, 1857; Jan. 1, 1858 –Feb. 19, 1865; Feb. 19, 1865–Feb. 24, 1874; Feb. 26, 1874–Dec. 25, 1880	Aug. 15, 1792–June 27, 1803; June 29, 1803–July 18, 1809; July 16, 1809–Sept. 1,1816; Sept. 2, 1816–May 23, 1824; June 11, 1824–Jan. 28, 1830; Feb. 1, 1830–Feb. 12, 1839; Feb. 11, 1839–Feb. 28, 1854; May 6, 1854–May 24, 1857; Jan. 7, 1858–Nov. 9, 1880		NLI	Pos. 4262 to 1830; B. to 1865 M. to 1857, 4263; remainder 4264
		1785–1839	1792–1880		LDS	BFA 0883697 items 4,5; 0883851 1

→

MAP	CHURCH	BAPTISMS	KERRY MARRIAGES	BURIALS	LOCATION	REFERENCE
28	Killarney (*cont.*)	1786–1900 1785–1803 (Vol. 5); 1803–1833 (Vol. 6); 1833–1840 (Vol. 7); 1840–1865 (Vol. 8); 1865–1900 (Vol. 14)	1796–1900 1792–1839 (Vol. 5); 1839–1890 (Vol. 7); 1891–1900 (Vol. 7)		KGC Published	O'K
29	Killeentierna	June 14, 1801–Dec. 24, 1809; July 24, 1823–Nov. 14, 1880	June 12, 1803–Feb. 28, 1828; Jan. 8, 1830–July 10, 1880 (transcript)		NLI	Pos. 4272
		1801–1875	1803–1880		LDS	BFA 0883740 item 4, 0883818 item 18
		1801–1809 (Vols 4 & 6); 1823–1870 (Vols 4 & 6); 1871–1900 (Vol. 6) 1801–1809; 1823–1920	1803–1900 (Vol. 6) 1803–1812; 1815–1828; 1830–1860; 1864–1884		Published KGC	O'K
30	Killorglin	1798–1802; 1806–1851; 1881–1917 No records microfilmed	1798–1802; 1806–1850; 1884–1946		KGC NLI	
31	Knocknagoshel	1866–1900 No records microfilmed			KGC NLI	
32	Listowel	1802–1906	1837–1906		KGC	
		Aug. 3, 1802–June 7, 1826; Oct. 1, 1826–Dec. 29, 1833; Jan. 9, 1837–May 29, 1838; Nov. 5, 1842–May 20, 1843; Sept. 7, 1843–Feb. 11, 1844; Mar. 12, 1846–July 11, 1846; May 18, 1850–Jan. 26, 1851; Mar. 2, 1852–May 26, 1853; May 31, 1855–July 10, 1855; Jan. 5–July 10, 1841; May 26, 1856–Dec. 26, 1880	Jan. 8, 1837–May 26, 1828; Nov. 10, 1842–Feb. 28, 1842; Sept. 2, 1843–Feb. 12, 1844; Mar. 9, 1846–July 10, 1846; June 25, 1850–Jan. 1851; Feb. 6, 1851–May 5, 1853; June 7, 1855–May 30, 1855; June 18, 1855–Nov. 21, 1880		NLI	Pos. 4281
33	Lixnaw	Aug. 4, 1810–Mar 27, 1843; Apr. 2, 1843–Feb. 20, 1845; June 4, 1848–Dec. 25, 1875; Feb. 14, 1876–Dec. 1, 1880	Jan. 15, 1810–June 6, 1852; Aug. 17, 1856–Nov. 27, 1875; Jan. 17, 1876–Dec. 1, 1880		NLI	B. to 1849 Pos. 4281; remainder 4282
		1810–1901	1810–1900		KGC	
34	Milltown	1825–1859; 1886–1895	1821–1829; 1841–1861; 1887–1894		KGC	
		Oct. 9, 1825–Sept. 20, 1840; Oct. 1, 1841–Aug. 21, 1859	Oct. 7, 1821–Nov. 1832; Oct. 17, 1841–June 6, 1861		NLI	Pos. 4266
35	Moyvane	1830–1917	1831–1917		KGC	
		July 21, 1855–Oct. 7, 1877	Oct. 4, 1855–Nov. 27, 1880		NLI	Pos. 4283
36	Prior	1851–1900 No records microfilmed	1853–1900		KGC NLI	

Map	Church	Baptisms	Kerry Marriages	Burials	Location	Reference
37	Rathmore	1837–1900	1839–1874		KGC	
		1837–1846 (Vol. 1); 1846–1874 (Vol. 1); 1875–1900 (Vol. 5)	1839–1874 (Vol. 1); 1875–1900 (Vol. 5)		Published	O'K
		1837–1875	1839–1880		LDS	BFA 0883875 item 11, 0883698 item 2
		Sept. 19, 1837–March 14, 1841; Jan. 14, 1844–Dec. 20, 1874	Jan. 26, 1839–May 3, 1874		NLI	Pos. 4268
38	Sneem	Aug. 17, 1845–Nov. 26, 1848; Nov. 1, 1857–Dec. 25, 1880	Feb. 2, 1858–Nov. 27, 1880		NLI	Pos. 4288
		1833–1848; 1857–1900	1858–1868; 1882–1900		KGC	
39	Ballynahaglish (Spa)	Nov. 11, 1866–Dec. 31, 1880	Jan. 27, 1867–Nov. 11, 1880		NLI	Pos. 4274
40	Tarbert (Kilnaughten)	1859–1900	1859–1900		KGC	
		Oct. 1, 1859–Dec. 26, 1880	July 26, 1859–May 29, 1880		NLI	Pos. 4280
41	Tralee	Jan. 1, 1772–Feb. 24, 1795; Mar. 1, 1795–Dec. 28, 1813; Jan. 14, 1818–July 30, 1832; Aug. 1, 1832–July 30, 1843; Aug. 1, 1843–June 22, 1856; June 24, 1856–Dec. 22, 1867; Jan. 1, 1868–June 4, 1874	May 1, 1832–Nov. 26, 1853; Nov. 18, 1853–June 21, 1856; June 24, 1856–Feb. 1, 1876		NLI	B. to 1845, Pos. 4269; B. to 1874, M. to 1832, 4270; remainder 4271
		1772–1900	1875–1900		KGC	
42	Tuogh (Beaufort)	1844–1880	1846–1896		KGC	
		Mar. 10, 1844–Jan. (?), 1880	Jan. 7, 1843–Feb. 25, 1879		NLI	Pos. 4265
43	Tuosist	Apr. 22, 1844–May 26, 1880 (some pages missing)			NLI	Pos. 4287
44	Valentia	1825–1864; 1867–1902	1827–1855		KGC	
		Mar. 7, 1825–July 5, 1864; May 15, 1867–Dec. 14, 1880	Feb. 5, 1827–April 1856		NLI	Pos. 4287

KILDARE

KILDARE & LEIGHLIN
DIOCESE
1 Allen & Milltown
2 Baltinglass
3 Ballyna (Johnstown)
4 Caragh (Downings)
5 Carbury
6 Carlow
7 Clane
8 Conbulloge
9 Curragh Camp
10 Kilcock
11 Kildare & Rathangan
12 Kill
13 Monasterevin
14 Naas & Eadestown
15 Newbridge
16 Robertstown
17 Suncroft (Curragh)

DUBLIN DIOCESE
18 Athy
19 Ballymore Eustace
20 Blessington
21 Castledermot
22 Celbridge
23 Kilcullen
24 Maynooth & Leixlip
25 Narraghmore

Map	Church	Baptisms	Kildare Marriages	Burials	Location	Reference
1	Allen and Milltown	1820–1899	1820–1899		KHGS	
		Oct. 15, 1820–Oct. 31, 1852	Oct. 17, 1820–Oct. 26, 1876		NLI	Pos. 4206
2	Baltinglass	See Wicklow 17				
3	Ballyna	1785–1899	1797–1899		KHGS	
		Oct. 17, 1785–Oct. 27, 1801; Nov. 6, 1801–July 17, 1803; Aug. 24, 1807–Oct. 21, 1811; Jan. 15, 1815–Feb. 22, 1815; Feb. 1, 1818–Apr. 12, 1829; Feb. 1, 1818–Dec. 21, 1865 (1818–1829 duplicate entries); Jan. 27, 1866–Dec. 23, 1880	Nov. 5, 1797–May 23, 1799; Nov. 13, 1801–Jan. 31, 1802; Oct. 1, 1807–Oct. 26, 1811; Jan. 25, 1815–Feb. 7, 1815; Apr. 7, 1817–Aug. 21, 1830; Mar. 23, 1818–Nov. 15, 1880 (1818–1830 duplicate entries)		NLI	Pos. 4206
4	Caragh	June 19, 1849–Aug. 12, 1866; Aug. 6, 1849–July 4, 1875; June 17, 1866–Apr. 19, 1874 (transcript)	Feb. 7, 1850–Nov. 23, 1859; Feb. 7, 1850–June 30, 1875 (transcript)		NLI	Pos. 4206
		1849–1899	1850–1899		KHGS	
5	Carbury and Dunforth	Oct. 1, 1821–May 22, 1850; June 9, 1850–Dec. 5, 1880	Nov. 2, 1821–Oct. 27, 1850; Oct. 6, 1850–Nov. 14, 1880	Feb. 18, 1869–June 9, 1879	NLI	Pos. 4206
6	Carlow	See Carlow 4				

			KILDARE			
MAP	**CHURCH**	**BAPTISMS**	**MARRIAGES**	**BURIALS**	**LOCATION**	**REFERENCE**
7	Clane (Rathcoffey)	1821–1899	1821–1899		KHGS	
		Mar. 17, 1785–Sept. 4, 1785; Feb. 1, 1786–July 3, 1786; Dec. 8, 1788–Apr. 8, 1789; Feb. 28, 1825–Feb. 28, 1827; Sept. 6, 1829–May 31, 1840; June 2, 1840–Dec. 26, 1880	Apr. 10, 1825–June 2, 1828; Nov. 15, 1829–June 5, 1840; July 19, 1840–Nov. 23, 1880		NLI	Pos. 4206
8	Clonbulloge	See Offaly 6				
9	Curragh Camp	1855–1899	1855–1899	1877–1890	KHGS	
		Aug. 5, 1855–July 9, 1871; Nov. 12, 1871–Dec. 19, 1880	Sept. 15, 1855–Jan. 15, 1871; Dec. 3, 1871–Sept. 13, 1880		NLI	Pos. 4207
10	Kilcock	July 6, 1771–Dec. 4, 1786; Aug. 14, 1816–Dec. 23, 1826; Oct. 9, 1831–June 28, 1834; July 8, 1834–Dec. 19, 1880	Jan. 28, 1770–May 28, 1787; Feb. 27, 1791–May 1, 1791; Aug. 7, 1816–Sept. 29, 1822; July 8, 1834–Nov. 16, 1880		NLI	Pos. 4207
		1770–1791	1770–1791		LDS	BFA 0926117 item 1
		1771–1899	1770–1899	1889–1897	KHGS	
11	Kildare and Rathangan	Nov. 1, 1815–Dec. 31, 1837; Jan. 6, 1838–Mar. 28, 1864; Apr. 3, 1864–Nov. 28, 1880	Nov. 1, 1815–Nov. 30, 1837; Jan. 17, 1838–Feb. 7, 1864; Apr. 18, 1864–Nov. 28, 1880		NLI	Pos. 4208
		1815–1899	1815–1899		KHGS	
12	Kill	Nov. 9, 1840–June 30, 1872; June 23, 1872–Dec. 19, 1880	Feb. 27, 1843–Apr. 8, 1872		NLI	Pos. 4208
		See NLI			LDS	BFA 0926115 item 2
		1813–1899	1813–1899		KHGS	
13	Monasterevan	1819–1899	1819–1900		KHGS	
		Jan. 1, 1819–Feb. 22, 1835; Mar. 28, 1829–Aug. 15, 1835; Jan. 4, 1835–June 24, 1855; June 29, 1855–Dec. 26, 1880	Sept. 11, 1819–Feb. 26, 1835; Jan. 15, 1835–July 17, 1855; July 10, 1855–Nov. 25, 1880		NLI	Pos. 4203
14	Naas	Mar. 1, 1813–Jan. 24, 1865; Feb. 5, 1865–Dec. 28, 1880	Feb. 28, 1813–Aug. 15, 1877; June 5, 1876–Oct. 26, 1880	Mar. 14, 1861–Dec. 30, 1868	NLI	Pos. 4208
		1813–1899	1813–1899		KHGS	
15	Newbridge	Aug. 2, 1786–Jan. 18, 1795; Jan. 14, 1820–Aug. 18, 1832; Jan. 1, 1834–Oct. 1, 1846; Oct. 23, 1836 –Dec. 31, 1843; Sept. 20, 1846–Aug. 5, 1860 (index to 1861); Mar. 4, 1849–Sept. 22, 1861; Oct. 5, 1861–Nov. 24, 1867; May 12, 1867–Dec. 27, 1880	Aug. 6, 1786–Jan. 20, 1795; Jan. 17, 1820–Aug. 15, 1846; Oct. 25, 1849–Sept. 25, 1861; Sept. 21, 1846–Sept. 25, 1862; Oct. 1, 1861–Nov. 24, 1880		NLI	Pos. 4209
		1786–1899	1786–1899	1889–1894	KHGS	
11	Rathangan	1880–1899	1880–1899	1888–1892	KHGS	
		No records microfilmed			NLI	

→

Map	Church	Baptisms	KERRY Marriages	Burials	Location	Reference
16	Robertstown	No records microfilmed			NLI	
17	Suncroft	Mar. 29, 1805–Dec. 26, 1880	May 15, 1805–July 29, 1880		NLI	Pos. 4209
		1805–1899	1889–1899	1888–1892	KHGS	
18	Athy	1753–1899	1753–1899		KHGS	
		Dec. 7, 1779–Mar. 21, 1797; Sept. 11, 1803–Aug. 21, 1807; Aug. 23, 1807–Nov. 26, 1816; Dec. 10, 1821–Mar. 5, 1837; Mar. 17, 1837–Aug. 14, 1853; Aug. 21, 1853–Apr. 7, 1873; Apr. 9, 1873–Dec. 31, 1880	Jan. 14, 1780–Feb. 12, 1797; Sept. 21, 1803–Feb. 2, 1810; Feb. 9, 1812–June 25, 1812; July 17, 1815–Mar. 7, 1816; June 24, 1822–Jan. 25, 1837; Apr. 6, 1837–Nov. 22, 1853; Jan. 10, 1854–Nov. 26, 1880		NLI	Pos. 6479/80
19	Ballymore Eustace	1779–1899	1779–1899		KHGS	
		1779–1900	1779–1900		WHC	
		Mar. 8, 1779–Apr. 27, 1792; Jan. 10, 1787–Mar. 1, 1790; May 3, 1792–Apr. 6, 1796; Jan. 5, 1797–Oct. 28, 1830; Apr. 23, 1826–Dec. 26, 1838; Jan.1, 1839 –Apr. 27, 1854; May 7, 1854–Dec. 31, 1880	Oct. 18, 1779–Nov. 27, 1794; Feb. 21, 1787–June 11, 1796; May 15, 1797–July 19, 1830; Apr. 22, 1826–Dec. 1, 1838; Jan. 27, 1839–Nov. 26, 1863; Jan. 25, 1864–Oct. 25, 1880		NLI	Pos. 6481
20	Blessington	See Wicklow 5				
21	Castledermot	1789–1899	1789–1899		KHGS	
		Nov. 5, 1789–Feb. 3, 1821; 1822–Oct. 18, 1829; 1829–Nov. 9, 1842; Dec. 4, 1842–Dec. 10, 1856 (index 1854–80); Jan. 18, 1857–Dec. 26, 1880	Nov. 5, 1789–Feb. 3, 1821; May, 1822–Dec. 14, 1829; Jan. 18, 1830–Nov. 2, 1842; Jan. 10, 1843–Dec. 27, 1856; Feb. 15, 1857–Dec. 19, 1880		NLI	Pos. 6480/81
22	Celbridge	Jan. 4. 1857–Dec. 19, 1880			NLI	Pos. 6613
23	Kilcullen	Oct. 22, 1777–Sept. 1, 1818; Apr. 25, 1829–Sept. 13, 1840; Jan. 11, 1857–Dec. 14, 1880	May 11, 1786–Nov. 20, 1806; Apr. 24, 1810–Oct. 27, 1816; May 11, 1829–Nov. 14, 1831; Apr. 11, 1836–June 23, 1840; Jan. 25, 1857–Nov. 26, 1880		NLI	Pos. 6484
		1777–1899	1786–1899		KHGS	
24	Maynooth	1814–1899	1806–1899		KHGS	
		Aug. 24, 1814–Sept. 10, 1827; Sept. 15, 1827–Feb. 1, 1857; Jan. 4, 1857–Dec. 24, 1880	Jan. 12, 1806–Aug. 27, 1827; Sept. 16, 1827–Nov. 24, 1856		NLI	Pos. 6615
25	Crookstown and Kilmeade	Apr. 28, 1837–Aug. 17, 1840; Aug. 1840–Aug. 7, 1843; Apr. 28, 1843–July 7, 1846; Aug. 9, 1849–May 5, 1853; May 5, 1853 –Mar. 17, 1856	July 1, 1837–Aug. 8, 1840; July 1, 1842–July 25, 1846; Jan. 16, 1853–Feb. 5, 1856		NLI	Pos. 6485
25	Narraghmore	Apr. 27, 1827–Apr. 26, 1837; Mar. 23, 1856–Dec. 30, 1880; Feb. 8, 1868–Dec. 27, 1880	Oct. 26, 1827–June 11, 1837; Apr. 3, 1856–Nov. 23, 1880		NLI	Pos. 6485

KILKENNY

OSSORY DIOCESE
1 Aughaviller
2 Ballyhale
3 Ballyragget
4 Callan
5 Castlecomer
6 Clara (see Gowran)
7 Clough
8 Conahy
9 Danesfort
10 Dunamaggan
11 Freshford
12 Galmoy
13 Glanmore
14 Gowran
15 Inistioge
16 Johnstown
17 Kilkenny city:
   St Canice's
   St John's
   St Mary's
   St Patrick's
18 Kilmacow
19 Kilmanagh
20 Lisdowney
21 Mooncoin
22 Muckalee

23 Mullinavat
24 Rosbercon
25 Slieverue
26 Templeorum
27 Thomastown
28 Tullaherin
29 Tullaroan

30 Urlingford
31 Windgap

KILDARE & LEIGHLIN
DIOCESE
32 Graiguenamanagh
33 Paulstown

N

Co. Laois

Co. Carlow

Co. Tipperary

Co. Wexford

Co. Waterford

			KILKENNY			
MAP	CHURCH	BAPTISMS	MARRIAGES	BURIALS	LOCATION	REFERENCE
1	Aughaviller	Oct. 22, 1847–Dec. 14, 1880	Feb. 24, 1848–Nov. 2, 1880		NLI	Pos. 5022
2	Ballyhale	Aug. 26, 1823–Apr. 4, 1876			NLI	Pos. 5021
		1823–1900 (?)			KAS	
3	Ballyragget	Aug. 31, 1856–Dec. 31, 1880	Apr. 10, 1856–Nov. 18, 1880		NLI	Pos. 5017
		1801–1805; 1856–1911			KAS	
		See NLI			LDS	BFA 0979702 item 4
4	Callan	1821–1880	1821–1880		LDS	BFA 0926189
		Jan. 27, 1821–Oct. 29, 1844; Nov. 14, 1844–June 11, 1875; Nov. 28, 1871–Dec. 28, 1880	Jan. 28, 1821–Oct. 16, 1844; Nov. 4, 1844–Feb. 15, 1874; Jan. 28, 1871–Nov. 25, 1880		NLI	Pos. 5025
5	Castlecomer	1812–1880 (gaps)	1831–1880		LDS	BFA 0926190; 0979702 items 1–3

→

MAP	CHURCH	BAPTISMS	KILKENNY MARRIAGES	BURIALS	LOCATION	REFERENCE
5	Castlecomer (*cont.*)	Jan. 1, 1812–Oct. 2, 1818; Dec. 24, 1828–June 3, 1847; Apr. 12, 1847–Dec. 7, 1880	Aug. 13, 1831–June 6, 1847; July 15, 1847–Nov. 24, 1880		NLI	Pos. 5019
		1812–1818; 1828–1911	1812–1818; 1828–1911		KAS	
6	Clara	1779–1890	1778–1876		KAS	
		No records microfilmed			NLI	
6	Pitt	July 8, 1855–Dec. 31, 1880	Aug. 13, 1855–Oct. 14, 1880		NLI	Pos. 5028
7	Clough	1812–1880 (gaps)	1831–1880		LDS	BFA 0926190; 0979702 items 1–3
		1832–1856; 1858–1911	1830–1911		KAS	
		Jan. 1, 1812–Oct. 2, 1818; Dec. 24, 1828–June 3, 1847; Jan. 3, 1858–Nov. 21, 1880	Aug. 13, 1831–June 6, 1847; Aug. 3, 1859–Nov. 11, 1880		NLI	Pos. 5017
8	Conahy	1832–1911 1832–1880	1832–1876; 1876–1911		KAS	
			1832–1880		LDS	BFA 0926191 items 2–3
		June 2, 1832–Dec. 22, 1876; Jan. 8, 1877–Dec. 28, 1880	June 17, 1832–Nov. 22, 1880		NLI	Pos. 5016
9	Danesfort	1819–1869 (many gaps)	1819–1869 (many gaps)		NLI	Pos. 5025
		See NLI			LDS	BFA 0926193
10	Dunamaggan	1844–1900	1844–1900		KAS	
		Sept. 25, 1826–June 7, 1840; Apr. 25, 1843–May 12, 1845; May 17, 1844–Dec. 20, 1880	Oct. 20, 1826–June 16, 1842; Feb. 25, 1843–Apr. 29, 1844; Feb. 24, 1870–Nov. 25, 1880		NLI	Pos. 5022
11	Freshford	1773–1880 (gaps)	1775–1800 (gaps)		LDS	BFA 0926192 items 1–7
		1772–1797; 1800–1911	1775–1779; 1799–1911		KAS	
		Jan. 12, 1773–Aug. 31, 1797; Mar. 27, 1800–Feb. 9, 1825; Jan. 2,1825–Dec. 28, 1847; Jan. 2, 1848–Jan. 3, 1878; Jan. 5, 1878–Dec. 25, 1880	Aug. 13, 1775–Nov. 11, 1779; Feb. 1, 1801–Nov. 28, 1877; Jan. 7, 1878–Nov. 24, 1880		NLI	Pos. 5015
12	Galmoy	Sept. 10, 1805–May 2, 1807; June 6, 1861–Dec. 15, 1880	Sept. 16, 1861–Jan. 29, 1880		NLI	Pos. 5017, 6955
		1805–1807; 1861–1880	Sept. 16, 1861–Jan. 29, 1880		LDS	BFA 0979701 item 4–5
13	Glenmore	Mar. 28, 1831–Dec. 11, 1880	Jan. 17, 1831–Aug. 31, 1880		NLI	Pos. 5022
14	Gowran	1809–1880	1810–1879		LDS	BFA 0926194 items 1–5
		1809–1911	1819–1911		KAS	
		Jan. 1, 1809–July 20, 1828; July 1. 1828–May 4, 1852; May 8, 1852–Dec. 20, 1880	Jan. 11, 1810–Nov. 28, 1828; July 17, 1828–Apr. 28, 1852; July 1, 1852–Feb. 24, 1879		NLI	Pos. 5026, 5027

Map	Church	Baptisms	KILKENNY Marriages	Burials	Location	Reference
15	Inistioge	1811–1911	1811–1911		KAS	
		Dec. 2, 1810–Feb. 2, 1829; Feb. 3, 1829–Dec. 22, 1876; Oct. 20, 1840– Feb. 4, 1877	Jan. 22, 1827–Oct. 9, 1876; Oct. 27, 1840– Feb. 1, 1877		NLI	Pos. 5021, 5022
16	Johnstown	Aug. 16, 1814–Jan. 26, 1845; Mar. 1, 1845– Dec. 18, 1880	Feb. 2, 1851–Nov. 13, 1880		NLI	Pos. 5012
		1815–1880	1851–1880		LDS	BFA 0979700 item 2
17	Kilkenny city: St Canice's	1768–1810	1768–1810	1777–1779	LDS	BFA 0926195
		Apr. 6, 1768–Jan. 15, 1785; Jan. 18, 1785–Dec. 30, 1810; Jan. 7,1811– Dec. 22, 1844; Jan. 3, 1845–Dec. 30, 1880	June 12, 1768–Nov. 27, 1810; Jan. 10, 1811–Nov. 26, 1844; Jan. 7, 1845– Nov. 24, 1880		NLI	Pos. 5029, 5030
17	Kilkenny city: St John's	Jan. 1809–July 8, 1830; Feb. 1, 1842–Feb. 17, 1877	June 24, 1809–July 5, 1830; Apr. 11, 1842– May 30, 1872		NLI	Pos. 5030
		1789–1900	1789–1900		KAS	
17	Kilkenny city: St Mary's	1754–1910	1754–1910	1754–1786	KAS	
		1754–1833	1754–1858	1754–1787	LDS	BFA 0926196 items 1–3; 0926197 1–5
		Jan. 1, 1754–Aug. 23, 1782; Aug. 6, 1784–Dec. 1810; Oct. 5, 1762–Aug. 21, 1766; Feb. 4, 1811– Oct. 7, 1816; Oct. 12, 1816–May 7, 1833; May 2, 1833–Oct. 13, 1858; Oct. 28, 1858–Dec. 27, 1880	Jan. 1754–Sept. 3, 1809; Oct. 23, 1762–Apr. 26, 1766; Jan. 9, 1798–Aug. 27, 1799; Jan. 24, 1801– Feb. 7, 1842; Feb. 4, 1811 –Oct. 7, 1816; Nov. 3, 1816–Oct. 13, 1858; Nov. 8, 1858–Nov. 18, 1880		NLI	Pos. 5028, 5029
17	Kilkenny city: St Patrick's	Aug. 11, 1800–Mar. 31, 1867; Apr. 2, 1867–Dec. 31, 1880	July 19, 1801–Jan. 26, 1868		NLI	Pos. 5027, 5028
17	Kilkenny city: Workhouse	Apr. 30, 1876–Dec. 6, 1880			NLI	Pos. 5030
18	Kilmacow	July 2, 1858–Dec. 31, 1880	Aug. 9, 1858–Nov. 18, 1880	June 30, 1858– Dec. 24, 1880	NLI	Pos. 5023, 5024
		See NLI			LDS	BFA 0926198
19	Ballycallan (Kilmanagh)	1820–1911	1820–1911		KAS	
		See NLI			LDS	BFA 0926187
		May 26, 1845–Dec. 30, 1880	July 22, 1845–Nov. 25, 1880		NLI	Pos. 5027
20	Lisdowney	1817–1880	1771–1778; 1828–1880		LDS	BFA 0979701 items 1–3; 0926199 1–3
		May 26, 1817–Oct. 2, 1853; Apr. 15, 1854–Aug. 20, 1877; Oct. 30, 1853– Dec. 29, 1880	Sept. 12, 1771–Apr. 28, 1778; Nov. 26, 1828– Aug. 13, 1853; Nov. 17, 1853–Oct. 27, 1880		NLI	Pos. 5017

MAP	CHURCH	BAPTISMS	KILKENNY MARRIAGES	BURIALS	LOCATION	REFERENCE
21	Mooncoin and Carrigeen	Sept. 12, 1779–Nov. 19, 1780; Oct. 21, 1781–Feb. 7, 1782; Feb. 8, 1782–Oct. 14, 1797; Dec. 3, 1797–Feb. 13, 1816; Feb. 20, 1816–Dec. 29, 1836; Jan. 5, 1837–Dec. 29, 1878	Jan. 26, 1772–Mar. 4, 1783; Jan. 16, 1789–Feb. 21, 1814; Feb. 21, 1816–Sept. 27, 1836; Jan. 16, 1837–May 12, 1879		NLI	Pos. 5018
22	Muckalee	1801–1806; 1840–1911 Oct. 30, 1801–Sept. 1806 (very damaged); June 15, 1840–Jan. 8, 1854; May 1, 1853–Dec. 28, 1857; Jan. 5, 1858–Jan. 28, 1873; May 12, 1871–Jan. 28, 1873; Aug. 3, 1873–Dec. 5, 1880 1801–6; 1840–1880	1809–1911 Apr. 19, 1809–June 25, 1853; Apr. 28, 1853–Nov. 28, 1857; Jan. 28, 1858–Feb. 19, 1873 1809–1873		KAS NLI LDS	Pos. 5026 BFA 0926200 items 1–5
23	Mullinavat	See NLI Feb. 21, 1843–Dec. 15, 1880	May 18, 1843–Mar 1, 1880		LDS NLI	BFA 0926201 Pos. 5021
24	Rosbercon (Tullagher)	1817–1819; 1825–1910 Apr. 6, 1817–June 28, 1819; Jan. 26–Mar. 17, 1825; Jan. 6, 1830–July 12, 1840; July 12, 1840–Dec. 29, 1877; Feb. 1, 1834–Dec. 31, 1877	1830–1910 Jan. 27, 1835–Nov. 3, 1877		KAS NLI	 Pos. 5020, 5021
25	Slieverue	Nov. 26, 1766–Apr. 14, 1778; Feb. 27, 1781–June 25, 1799; Apr. 1777–Sept. 18, 1801; Oct. 4, 1801–Dec. 31, 1836; Dec. 26, 1836–Dec. 26, 1880	Feb. 2, 1766–May 23, 1778; May 26, 1791–July 9, 1801; Oct. 1, 1801–Nov. 25, 1836; Jan. 1837–Nov. 16, 1880	Dec. 1766–Feb. 21, 1778	NLI	Pos. 5031
26	Templeorum and Owning	Oct. 7, 1803–June 21, 1815; Sept. 15, 1815–May 8, 1846; May 10, 1846–1851; 1851 –1854 (many large gaps); Jan. 31, 1851 –Dec. 27, 1864; Jan. 3, 1865–Dec. 29, 1880	Aug. 5, 1815–Nov. 29, 1849; Nov. 25, 1851–Oct. 24, 1864; Jan. 19, 1851–Nov. 22, 1864; Jan. 30, 1865–Nov. 6, 1880	Sept. 12, 1803–March 1806; Apr. 29, 1808–June 17, 1815	NLI	Pos. 5019, 5020
27	Thomastown	1782–1911 1782–1880 June 23, 1782–Sept. 27, 1809; Jan. 9, 1810–Mar. 28, 1834; Mar. 17, 1834–Dec. 23, 1880	1785; 1810–1911 1786–1880 (gaps) Jan. 1786–Aug. 10, 1806; May 27, 1810–Aug. 8, 1833; Aug. 7, 1833–Nov. 22, 1880		KAS LDS NLI	 BFA 0926202 Pos. 5024
28	Tullaherin	See Thomastown				
29	Tullaroan	Mar. 5, 1843–Apr. 15, 1876 See NLI	Apr. 27, 1843–Feb. 7, 1880		NLI LDS	Pos. 5026 BFA 0926204

⟶

Map	Church	Baptisms	KILKENNY Marriages	Burials	Location	Reference
30	Urlingford	May 5, 1805–Feb. 15, 1844; May 5, 1805–July 11, 1823 (transcript); Feb. 16, 1844–Oct. 18, 1857; Feb. 15, 1846–Dec. 3, 1870; Aug. 21, 1869–Dec. 26, 1880; Dec. 16, 1870–Dec. 18, 1880	May 9, 1805–Nov. 7, 1843; Aug. 5, 1843–Sept. 1870; Feb. 20, 1871 –July 20, 1880		NLI	Pos. 5016
31	Windgap	Aug. 18, 1822–Feb. 27, 1852 (transcript); Mar. 10, 1852–Dec. 27, 1869 (transcript); Jan. 5, 1870 –Dec. 10, 1880	Sept. 14, 1822–Mar. 1, 1880 (transcript)		NLI	Pos. 5023
		1822–1889	1822–1880		LDS	BFA 0926205
32	Graig-namanagh	Apr. 22, 1838–Dec. 27, 1868; Jan. 1, 1869 –Dec. 24, 1880	July 5, 1818–Nov. 26, 1868; Jan. 17, 1869 –Nov. 3, 1880		NLI	Pos. 4198
33	Paulstown	July 9, 1824–Apr. 19, 1846; May 20, 1852–May 30, 1869; June 3, 1855–Mar. 4, 1860; Mar. 11, 1860–May 1, 1870; Jan. 2, 1870–Dec. 12, 1880	Jan. 21, 1824–Nov. 28, 1840; Jan. 21, 1841–Feb. 11, 1861; Jan. 22, 1861 –Nov. 25, 1869; Feb. 28, 1870–Nov. 27, 1880		NLI	Pos. 4198
		1824–1880 (gaps)	1824–1880 (gaps)		LDS	BFA 0926124

LAOIS

DUBLIN DIOCESE
1 Athy

KILDARE & LEIGHLIN DIOCESE
2 Abbeyleix
3 Arles
4 Ballinakill
5 Ballyadams
6 Ballyfin (Cappinrush)
7 Clonaslee
8 Doonane
9 Emo
10 Graigue (Killeshin)
11 Leighlinbridge
12 Mountmellick
13 Mountrath
14 Portarlington
15 Portlaoise
16 Raheen
17 Rosenalis
18 Stradbally

KILLALOE DIOCESE
19 Roscrea

OSSORY DIOCESE
20 Aghaboe
21 Ballyragget

22 Borris-in-Ossory
23 Camross
24 Castletown
25 Durrow

26 Galmoy
27 Lisdowney
28 Rathdowney

Map	Church	Baptisms	LAOIS Marriages	Burials	Location	Reference
1	Athy	See Kildare				
2	Abbeyleix and Ballyroan	1824–1899	1824–1899		IMA	
		June 6, 1824–Aug. 23, 1830; Jan. 19, 1838–Dec. (?) 26, 1849; Apr. 6, 1850– Jan. 5, 1879; Jan. 6, 1878– Dec.5, 1880; Index 1850–1878	July 2, 1824–July 28, 1830; Jan. 30, 1838–Nov. 22, 1880		NLI	Pos. 4199
3	Arles	1821–1899	1821–1899	1821–1856	IMA	
		1821–1856 (arranged by townland, possibly some missing);	1821–1856 (arranged by townland, possibly some missing)	(arranged by townland, possibly some missing);	NLI	Pos. 4190
		Mar. 20, 1831–Jan. 22, 1843; Jan. 6, 1843–Aug. 15, 1861; Jan. 1, 1849– Dec. 27, 1858 (not a duplicate); Jan. 9, 1859 –Dec. 26, 1880	Sept. 28, 1831–Feb. 27 1843; Aug. 30, 1843– July 24, 1861; June 19, 1850–Nov. 25, 1858 (not a duplicate); Jan. 17, 1859–Nov. 24, 1880			
4	Ballynakill	1794–1899	1800–1899	1794–1815	IMA	
		Oct. 14, 1794–Mar. 19, 1815; Jan. 16, 1820– May 26, 1820; Nov. 4, 1820–Sept. 19, 1872; Sept. 29, 1872–June 11, 1876; Apr. 1, 1877– Nov. 3, 1880	Oct. 27, 1794–Feb. 7, 1815; Jan. 15, 1820– July 7, 1820; Nov. 3, 1820–Nov. 25, 1875; May 22, 1877–Nov. 3, 1880		NLI	Pos. 4200
5	Ballyadams	Jan. 3, 1820–Feb. 28, 1847; Feb. 9, 1845–June 14, 1874 (transcript); June 14, 1874–Dec. 20, 1880	Jan. 12, 1820–Nov. 24, 1853; Mar. 3, 1845 –Apr. 25, 1874 (transcript)		NLI	Pos. 4200
6	Cappinrush	1862–1899	1862–1899		IMA	
		Oct. 20, 1824–Aug. 3, 1862; July 6, 1862–Dec. 26, 1880	Aug. 1, 1819–July 27, 1862; July 24, 1862–Oct. 19, 1880		NLI	Pos. 4201
7	Clonaslee	Jan. 15, 1849–Dec. 20, 1880	Feb. 20, 1849–Oct. 14, 1880		NLI	Pos. 4202
		1849–1906	1849–1899	1892–1970	IMA	
8	Mayo and Doonane	1843–1899	1843–1899		IMA	
		See NLI			LDS	BFA 0926112
		June 21, 1843–Sept. 17, 1877; Sept. 24, 1877– Dec. 12, 1880	May 1843–Sept. 2, 1877; Feb. 14, 1878–Nov. 27, 1880		NLI	Pos. 4190
9	Emo	July 4, 1875–Dec. 19, 1880	Apr. 26, 1875–Nov. 25, 1880		NLI	Pos. 4203
		1875–1899	1843–1899		IMA	
10	Killeshin	1783–1899	1783–1899	1898–1899	CGP	
		Nov. 23, 1819–Oct. 16, 1843; Feb. 12, 1840– June 2, 1844; Aug. 16, 1846–Aug. 5, 1849; Oct. 10, 1846–Dec. 28, 1856; Jan. 4, 1857–Dec. 19, 1880	Jan. 20, 1822–Nov. 24, 1846; Jan. 26, 1840–May 19, 1844; Nov. 27, 1846– Aug. 5, 1849; Nov. 27, 1846–Nov. 27, 1856; Jan. 27, 1857–Nov. 21, 1880		NLI	Pos. 4190
11	Leighlinbridge	See Carlow				→

MAP	CHURCH	BAPTISMS	LAOIS MARRIAGES	BURIALS	LOCATION	REFERENCE
12	Mountmellick	Jan. 1, 1814–Dec. 23, 1837; Aug. 6, 1837–May 27, 1860; 1837–1859 (alphabetical transcript); Apr. 19, 1860–Dec. 26, 1880; Feb. 26, 1864–Feb. 4, 1879; 1860–1886 (alphabetical transcript)	Feb. 2, 1814–Apr. 27, 1843; July 7, 1843–Nov. 21, 1872; Jan. 19, 1873–Aug. 29, 1880		NLI	Pos. 4204
		1814–1899	1814–1899	1890–1948	IMA	
		1814–1886	1814–1880		LDS	BFA 0926121
13	Mountrath	Oct. 12, 1823–Apr. 21, 1867; May 13, 1867–Dec. 26, 1880	Oct. 12, 1823–Apr. 21, 1867; May 13, 1867–Dec. 26, 1880		NLI	Pos. 4201
		1823–1902	1827–1899	1882–1899	IMA	
		See NLI			LDS	BFA 0926122
14	Portarlington	1820–1899	1820–1899	1904–1960	IMA	
		Jan. 1, 1820–Nov. 22, 1846 (indexed); Nov. 25, 1846–Feb. 27, 1876 (indexed); Mar. 5, 1876–Dec. 26, 1880 (indexed)	Nov. 24, 1822–July 16, 1845; July 21, 1845–June 21, 1876; Jan. 14, 1876–Nov. 27, 1880		NLI	Pos. 4205
15	Portlaoise (Maryborough)	May 14, 1826–Feb. 4, 1838; Feb. 4, 1838–Nov. 16, 1851; 1845–1873 (alphabetical transcript); Apr. 28, 1873–Dec. 27, 1880	Apr. 27, 1826–Jan. 30, 1838; Feb. 14, 1838–Jan. 8, 1855; 1850–1940 (alphabetical transcript); Jan. 10, 1858–Nov. 25, 1880		NLI	Pos. 4201
		1826–1909	1828–1899	1876–1916	IMA	
16	Raheen	1819–1899	1819–1899	1884–1925	IMA	
		Apr. 5, 1819–Dec. 19, 1880; Jan. 1, 1843–Aug. 27, 1875; Feb. 4, 1844–Sept. 10, 1875	Jan. 20, 1820–Sept. 30, 1880; Nov. 30, 1866–May 30, 1868; Aug. 15, 1844–Feb. 13, 1855; July 4, 1860–May 24, 1866; Jan. 20, 1870–Jan. 10, 1875		NLI	Pos. 4202, 4205
17	Rosenallis	1766–1901	1765–1899	1921–1987	IMA	
		Oct. 21, 1765–Jan. 19, 1777; Feb. 1, 1782–Aug. 13, 1782; Aug. 3, 1823–Dec. 27, 1879	Oct 12, 1765–June 10, 1777; Feb. 7, 1782–June 10, 1782; July 1823–July 24, 1859; Jan. 18, 1865–Oct. 26, 1880	Oct 14, 1824–Sept 21, 1827	NLI	Pas. 4205
18	Stradbally	1820–1899	1820–1899	1893–1983	IMA	
		Jan. 2, 1820–May 18, 1855; Jan. 26, 1851–Dec. 26, 1880	Jan. 20, 1820–June 24, 1849; Feb. 24, 1851–Nov. 4, 1880		NLI	Pos. 4202
19	Roscrea	See Tipperary North 34				
20	Aghaboe	1795–1899	1794–1899		IMA	
		1795–1825 (some large gaps); June 18, 1826–Dec. 19, 1850; Jan. 28, 1849–Dec. 12, 1880	July 4, 1794–Feb. 1807; Nov. 1, 1816–Aug.10, 1824; Aug. 2, 1825–Aug. 4, 1846		NLI	Pos 5012
		See NLI	June 25, 1850–May 20, 1880		LDS	BFA 0979700
21	Ballyragget	See Kilkenny 3				

			LAOIS			
MAP	CHURCH	BAPTISMS	MARRIAGES	BURIALS	LOCATION	REFERENCE
22	Borris–in–Ossory	See NLI			LDS	BFA 0926188
		May 4, 1840–Mar. 12, 1878; Nov. 17, 1855–Nov. 25, 1879	July 20, 1840–Sept. 23, 1880; Nov. 17, 1855–Nov. 25, 1879		NLI	Pos. 5014
23	Camross	1816–1899	1820–1899		IMA	
		May 12, 1816–Sept. 1, 1829; Mar. 12, 1821–Dec. 27, 1829; May 1818–Oct. 6, 1820; July 12, 1823–Mar. 18, 1830; Oct. 14, 1838–Sept. 11, 1865 (many pages missing 1838–50); Oct. 8, 1865–Dec. 26, 1880	Jan. 21, 1820–Mar. 1830; Aug. 18, 1839–Feb. 8, 1842; Aug. 30, 1846–1851; Aug. 9, 1855–Sept. 17, 1865; Oct. 26, 1865–, Nov. 25, 1880		NLI	Pos. 5014
24	Castletown (Offerlane)	May 8, 1782–Sept. 8, 1816; May 4, 1831–May 27, 1880	Sept. 21, 1784–May 9, 1816; Feb. 9, 1831–Feb. 11, 1855; Sept. 17, 1857 –May 4, 1880		NLI	Pos. 5018
		1784–1900	1784–1900		IMA	
25	Durrow	Jan. 1, 1789–Mar. 30, 1792; Jan. 2, 1801–Feb. 28, 1805 (also a transcript); June 9, 1811–Jan. 27, 1820; May 19, 1822-Feb. 18, 1827; May 26, 1832–Feb. 15, 1857; Mar. 8, 1857–Dec. 28, 1880	July 29, 1811–Mar. 27, 1820; May 23, 1822–Sept. 18, 1827; July 17, 1832– May 28, 1860; June 9, 1861–Nov. 18, 1880		NLI	Pos. 5013
		1789–1900	1811–1899		IMA	
26	Galmoy	See Kilkenny 12				
27	Lisdowney	See Kilkenny 20				
28	Rathdowney	1763–1900			IMA	
		July 13, 1763–Nov. 28, 1781; Sept. 14, 1782–July 20, 1789; May 6, 1790–Nov. 20, 1791; Apr. 14–Sept. 1, 1810; June 2, 1839–Jan. 29, 1840; Apr. 26, 1840–Dec. 31, 1880	May 18, 1769–Nov. 7, 1781; Sept. 7, 1782–July 15, 1789; Sept. 15, 1789–Nov. 22, 1791; Jan. 14–May 3, 1808; Oct 6, 1839–Mar. 3, 1840; May 27, 1840–Nov. 9, 1880		NLI	Pos. 5013, 5014.

LEITRIM

ARDAGH &
CLONMACNOISE
DIOCESE
1 Aughavas
2 Annaduff
3 Bornacoola
4 Cloone-
    Conmaicne
5 Drumshanbo
    (Murhan)
6 Fenagh
7 Gorleteragh
8 Killenummery &
    Killery
9 Kiltoghert
10 Kiltubbred
11 Mohill-
    Manachain

KILMORE
DIOCESE
12 Ballinaglera
13 Ballymeehan
14 Carrigallen
15 Clooneclare
16 Drumlease
    (Drumahair)
17 Drumreilly Lr
18 Drumreilly
    Uppr (Corlough)
19 Glenade
20 Inishmagrath
21 Killargue
22 Killasnet
23 Kinlough
24 Oughteragh
    (Ballinamore)

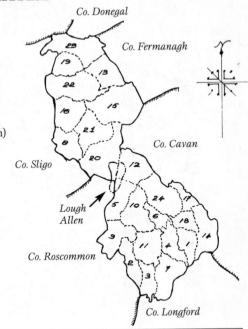

			LEITRIM			
MAP	CHURCH	BAPTISMS	MARRIAGES	BURIALS	LOCATION	REFERENCE
1	Aughavas	1845–1900	1845–1900	1845–1900	LHC	
		May 19, 1845–Feb. 4, 1876; Jan. 1, 1876–Dec. 23, 1880	Aug. 28, 1845–July 4, 1879; Jan. 10, 1876–Nov. 14, 1880	May 11, 1845 –July 2, 1880; May 5, 1876–Nov. 18, 1880	NLI	Pos. 4240
		1845–1968	1845–1920	1845–1899	LDS	BFA 1279224 items 15–17
2	Annaduff	Feb. 29, 1849–Dec. 31, 1880	Feb. 12, 1849–Feb. 10, 1880	Feb. 5, 1849–Dec. 21, 1880	NLI	Pos. 4236
		1849–1900	1849–1900	1849–1900	LHC	
		1849–1984	1849–1983	1849–1886; 1930–1984	LDS	BFA 1279224 items 18–20; 1279225 1–3
3	Bornacoola	Jan. 4, 1871–Dec. 31, 1880	June 13, 1836–Sept. 28, 1837; May 9, 1850–Nov. 1, 1880		NLI	Pos. 4234
		1824–1897	1824–1838; 1850–1897	1833–1892	LDS	BFA 1279224 items 13–14
		1824–1837; 1850–1900	1824–1900	1824–1900	LHC	
4	Cloone–Conmaicne	Feb. 1, 1820–Mar. 12, 1820; Jan. 1, 1834–May 27, 1834; Nov. 13, 1834 –Oct, 4, 1849; Jan. 6, 1850 –Nov. 20, 1880	Jan, 6, 1823–Jan. 6, 1839; Jan. 12, 1843–Feb. 14, 1879	Jan. 6, 1823–Feb. 17, 1845; Jan. 13, 1850–Feb. 25, 1878	NLI	Pos. 4241
		1823–1900	1823–1900	1823–1878	LHC	
		1820–1927	1823–1921	1850–1878;	LDS	BFA ⟶

Map	Church	Baptisms	LEITRIM Marriages	Burials	Location	Reference
4	Cloone–Conmaicne (*cont.*)			1919–1921		1279223 items 12–14
5	Drumshanbo (Murhan)	May 18, 1861–Dec. 21, 1880	June 10, 1868–Nov. 20, 1880		NLI	Pos. 4240
		1861–1895			LDS	BFA 1279223 item 8
		1861–1900	1867–1900		LHC	
6	Fenagh	June 5, 1825–Oct. 13, 1829; Nov. 24, 1834–Apr. 12, 1843; June 5, 1843–Nov. 4, 1852; Nov. 22, 1852–Dec. 9, 1880 (indexed)	Oct. 4, 1826–Feb. 18, 1832; June 15, 1835–Mar. 22, 1842; Jan. 17, 1844–Feb. 9, 1880	June, 1825–Feb 21, 1834–Nov. 24, 1834–Dec. 21, 1841	NLI	Pos. 4239
		1825–1900	1826–1900	1825–1865	LHC	
		1825–1829; 1843–1849;	1825–1899	1825–1894	LDS	BFA 1279223 items 1–3
7	Gortletteragh	1830–1840; 1848–1895	1826–1835; 1852–1895	1826–1839 (gaps); 1851–1869	LDS	BFA 1279224 items 4–6
		Apr. 4, 1830–Aug. 1, 1840; July 16, 1848–Mar. 6, 1874; Mar. 30, 1874–Dec. 31, 1880	Jan. 6, 1826–Sept. 12, 1827; Feb. 16, 1830–Apr. 30, 1835; May 22, 1848–Feb. 17, 1874 (disordered)	Jan. 10, 1826–Sept. 15, 1826; Mar. 29, 1830–Feb. 17, 1831; Mar. 9, 1839–July 29, 1839; Aug. 1, 1851–July 29, 1869	NLI	Pos. 4238
		1830–1900; 1841–1900 [*sic*]	1826–1834; 1834; 1849–1900	1826–1838; 1872–1898	LHC	
8	Killenummery	1828–1900	1827–1900	1829–1900	LHC	
		1828–1920	1828–1883; 1908–1910; 1922–1923	1838–1846	LDS	BFA 1279223 items 6–7
		1828–1899	1827–1899		SHGC	
		May 8, 1828–Aug. 7, 1846; Nov. 1, 1848–Dec. 30, 1880	June 22, 1827–Aug. 16, 1846; Nov. 10, 1848–Dec. 28, 1880	May 18, 1838–Apr. 15, 1846	NLI	Pos. 4241
9	Kiltoghart	1826–1900	1832–1900	1832–1900	LHC	
		1826–1891	1841–1891	1841–1879	LDS	BFA 1279223 items 4–5
		Aug. 16, 1826–Apr. 23, 1854; May 7, 1854–Dec. 30, 1880; (Gowel) Mar. 4, 1866–Dec. 26, 1880	July 19, 1832–May 3, 1854; July 30, 1854–Nov. 24, 1880; (Gowel) May 13, 1866–Feb. 29, 1876	Aug. 10, 1832–Apr. 10, 1854; May 31, 1854–Aug. 11, 1874; (Gowel) Apr. 11, 1866–Sept. 10, 1877	NLI	Pos. 4240
10	Kiltubrid	1841–1900	1841–1900	1847–1900	LHC	
		Jan. 6, 1841–Apr. 27, 1874	Jan. 7, 1841–May 22, 1873	Jan. 15, 1847–May 1, 1873	NLI	Pos. 4234
		1841–1874; 1880–1924	1841–1873; 1883–1922 1883–1922	1847–1873	LDS	BFA 1279223 items 9–11
11	Mohill	1836–1900	1836–1900	1836–1900	LHC	
		Aug. 4, 1836–May 7, 1854; June 11, 1854–Dec. 23, 1880 including workhouse baptisms, 1846–55	July 14, 1836–May 18, 1854; Aug. 28, 1854–July 19, 1879	July 3, 1836–May 9, 1854; May 22, 1854; –July 27, 1879	NLI	Pos. 4239

→

Map	Church	Baptisms	LEITRIM Marriages	Burials	Location	Reference
11	Mohill (*cont.*)	1836–1905	1836–1905; 1910–1916	1836–1883	LDS	BFA 1279224 items 1–3
12	Ballinaglera	No records microfilmed			NLI	
		1883–1900	1887–1900		LHC	
13	Ballymeehan (Rossinver)	1851–1875 very poor condition	1844–1870 very poor condition		PRONI	MIC.1D/83
		1851–1900	1844–1869; 1875–1900		LHC	
		Aug. 17, 1851–Jan. 29, 1875 (many gaps)	Aug. 28, 1844–Sept. 8, 1870		NLI	Pos. 5350
14	Carrigallen	1829–1900	1841–1900	1841–1860	LHC	
		1829–1891 (gaps)	1841–1890 (gaps)	1841–1860	PRONI	MIC.1D/7, 83
		Nov. 2, 1829–Feb. 7, 1830; Dec. 30, 1838– Dec. 12, 1880 (many pages missing)	Jan. 27, 1841–Apr. 24, 1848; 1854–Dec. 10, 1875 (some pages missing)	Mar. 12, 1842– June 25, 1860	NLI	Pos. 5350
15	Clooneclare	1841–1900	1850–1900		LHC	
		Apr. 29, 1841–Dec. 1885	Nov. 12, 1850–Sept. 9, 1884		NLI	Pos. 7505
16	Drumlease	Aug. 21, 1859–Apr. 12, 1879	Sept. 15, 1859–Oct. 31, 1880		NLI	Pos. 5344
		1859–1900	1859–1900		LHC	
		1859–1879	1859–1881		PRONI	MIC.1D/77
17	Drumreilly Lower	Mar. 4, 1867–Dec. 26, 1880			NLI	Pos. 5345
		1867–1880			PRONI	MIC.1D/78
		1867–1900	1893–1900		LHC	
		See NLI			LDS	BFA 0926129 item 4
18	Drumreilly Upper	1878–1900	1870–1900		LHC	
		No records microfilmed			NLI	
19	Glenade	1867–1900	1866–1900		LHC	
		Nov. 10, 1867–Dec. 16, 1880	Nov. 10, 1867–June 15, 1880		NLI	Pos. 5344
		1867–1881	1873–1880		PRONI	MIC.1D/77
		1867–1899	1866–1899		SHGC	
20	Innismagrath	Jan. 1835–July 1839; 1834	1830–1839	1833–1839	NLI	Pos. 7505
		1834–1900; 1881–1900 [*sic*]	1834–1900; 1881–1900 [*sic*]	1834–1900; 1881–1900 [*sic*]	NLI	
21	Killargue	1853–1900	1852–1900		LHC	
		1852–1881	1852–1881		PRONI	MIC.1D/77
		Sept. 26, 1852–Dec. 26, 1880	Nov. 2, 1852–Feb. 4, 1880		NLI	Pos. 5344
22	Killasnet	1852–1900; 1879–1897 [*sic*]	1852–1900; 1879–1897 [*sic*]	1852–1866	LHC	
		Mar. 28, 1852–Apr. 1868; Feb. 23, 1868–Jan. 31,	Mar. 28, 1852–Apr. 1868; Jan. 30, 1868–	Mar. 28, 1852– Apr. 1868	NLI	Pos. 5350

MAP	CHURCH	BAPTISMS	LEITRIM MARRIAGES	BURIALS	LOCATION	REFERENCE
22	Killasnet (*cont.*)	1869; Nov. 29, 1878–Nov. 23, 1880	May 21, 1871; Nov. 11, 1878–Nov. 15, 1880			
		1852–1871; 1878–1881	1852–1869; 1878–1881		PRONI	MIC.1D/83
23	Kinlough	1835–1881	1840–1881		PRONI	MIC.1D/77
		1835–1900	1840–1900	1867–1900	LHC	
		July 12, 1835–Mar. 1860; Apr. 8, 1860–Dec. 24, 1880	Nov. 26, 1840–Dec. 16, 1880		NLI	Pos. 5344
24	Oughteragh	1841–1900	1841–1900		LHC	
		Nov. 9, 1869–Dec. 28, 1880; May 26, 1871–Dec. 16, 1880	Jan. 17, 1870–Nov. 20, 1880		NLI	Pos. 5346/7
		1869–1881	1787–1881		PRONI	MIC.1D/79–80

LIMERICK EAST

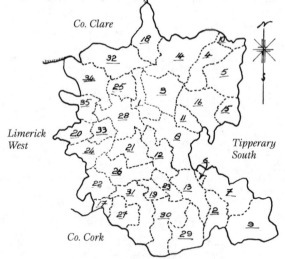

CASHEL & EMLY DIOCESE
1   Ballybricken
2   Ballylanders
3   Caherconlish
4   Cappamore
5   Doon
6   Emly
7   Galbally
8   Hospital
9   Kilbehenny
10 Kilcommon
11 Kilteely
12 Knockaney
13 Knocklong
14 Murroe & Boher
15 Oola
16 Pallasgreen

CLOYNE DIOCESE
17 Charleville

KILLALOE DIOCESE
18 Castleconnell

LIMERICK DIOCESE
19 Ardpatrick (see Kilfinane)
20 Banogue (see Croom)
21 Bruff
22 Bruree & Rockhill
23 Bulgaden
24 Croom
25 Donaghmore
26 Domin & Athlacca
27 Effin
28 Fedamore

29 Glenroe & Ballyorgan
30 Kilfinane
31 Kilmallock
32 Limerick city:
         St John's
         St Mary's
         St Michael's
         St Munchin's
         St Patrick's
33 Manister (see Fedamore)
34 Mungret & Crecora
35 Patrickswell & Ballybrown

MAP	CHURCH	BAPTISMS	LIMERICK EAST MARRIAGES	BURIALS	LOCATION	REFERENCE
1	Ballybricken and Bohermore	1801–1841	1801–1841	1801–1841 (scraps)	LDS	BFA 1279253 item 2
		1800–1900	1801–1900		THU	
		1800–1900	1805–1900		LA	
		Nov. 9, 1800–July 25, 1841; Aug. 2, 1841–Dec. 26, 1880	Aug. 10, 1805–Oct. 27, 1841; Nov. 6, 1841–Oct. 23, 1880		NLI	Pos. 2509
2	Ballylanders	1849–1900	1857–1900		LA	
		1842–1899	1841–1900		THU	
		Mar. 6, 1849–Dec. 25, 1877	Jan. 3, 1857–Nov. 25, 1877 (modern transcript)		NLI	Pos. 2500
3	Caherconlish	1841–1900	1841–1900		THU	
		Jan. 19, 1841–Dec. 30, 1880	Feb. 6, 1841–Oct. 8, 1880		NLI	Pos. 2508
		1841–1900	1841–1900		LA	
4	Cappamore	1845–1900	1843–1900		LA	
		1842–1900	1843–1900		THU	
		Apr. 4, 1845–Dec. 31, 1880	Feb. 25, 1845–Nov. 14. 1880		NLI	Pos. 2508
5	Doon and Castletown	1824–1900	1839–1900		LA	
		1824–1900	1839–1900		THU	
		Mar. 25, 1824–Dec. 27, 1874	Jan. 20, 1839–Feb. 17, 1874		NLI	Pos. 2497
6	Emly	1810–1899	1809–1898		THU	
		July 31, 1810–May 4, 1839; May 10, 1839–Dec. 24, 1880	Apr. 27, 1809–Oct. 20, 1838; Jan. 26, 1839–Nov. 25, 1880		NLI	Pos. 2500
7	Galbally and Aherlow	1810–1900	1809–1900		THU	
		Mar. 9, 1810–June 23, 1828 (July 1820–1821 missing); Dec. 1828 –June 1871	Oct. 1809–Aug. 34, 1880 (Mar. 1820–July 1821 missing)		NLI	Pos. 2499
		1810–1900	1809–1900		LA	
8	Hospital	1810–1900	1812–1900		LA	
		Jan. 11, 1810–Jan. 10, 1842; Jan. 20, 1842–Dec. 29, 1880	Feb. 10, 1812–Jan. 16, 1842; Jan. 22, 1842–Nov. 6, 1880		NLI	Pos. 2507
		1810–1899	1812–1899		THU	
9	Kilbehenny	1824–1899	1825–1899		THU	
		Dec. 17, 1824–Apr. 30, 1843; May 4, 1843 –Jan 23, 1870	Jan. 30, 1825–Feb. 28, 1843; May 1, 1843–Jan. 20, 1870		NLI	Pos. 2500
10	Kilcommon	See Tipperary North (9)				
11	Kilteely and Drumkeen	1810–1899	1815–1899		THU	
		1815–1900	1832–1900		LA	
		Dec. 3, 1815–Apr. 5, 1829; Sept. 3, 1832–Dec. 20, 1880	Nov. 14, 1832–Nov. 17, 1880		NLI	Pos. 2506

⟶

Map	Church	Baptisms	Marriages	Burials	Location	Reference
			LIMERICK EAST			
12	Knockany and Patrickswell	1808–1900	1808–1900		LA	
		1808–1899	1808–1899		THU	
		Mar. 14, 1808–Nov. 24, 1821; Dec. 3, 1921–Nov. 22, 1841; May 3, 1841–Dec. 22, 1880	Apr. 25, 1808–Oct. 21, 1821; Jan. 20, 1822–Feb. 23, 1841; May 3, 1841–Oct. 188, 1880	June 1, 1819–Mar. 29, 1821	NLI	Pos. 2505
13	Knocklong and Glenbrohane	1809–1900	1809–1900		LA	
		1809–1899	1809–1899		THU	
		Apr. 26, 1809–June 5, 1819; Sept. 14, 1823–June 11, 1830; Jan. 30, 1832–July 30, 1854; Nov. 30, 1854–Jan. 15, 1878	Apr. 12, 1809–Oct. 17, 1819; Jan. 28, 1824–Oct. 1, 1831; Jan. 7, 1832–Feb. 4, 1854; Aug. 20, 1854–Jan. 15, 1878		NLI	Pos. 2509
14	Murroe, Boher and Abington	June 15, 1814–Nov. 3, 1845; Nov. 3, 1845–Dec. 25, 1880	Nov. 29, 1815–Nov. 2, 1845; Nov. 16, 1845–Sept. 1, 1880		NLI	Pos. 2508
		1814–1900	1815–1900		LA	
		1814–1899	1815–1899		THU	
15	Oola (Solohead)	Oct. 18, 1809–Feb. 27, 1823; Mar. 2, 1823–Apr. 30, 1828; Feb. 25, 1837–Jan.23, 1854; Feb. 12, 1854–Dec. 31, 1880	Jan. 7, 1810–Nov. 24, 1828; Oct. 14, 1832–Jan. 30, 1854; Feb. 7, 1854–Nov. 27, 1880		NLI	Pos. 2498 to 1828; remainder on Pos. 2499
		1809–1900	1810–1900		THU	
		1809–1880	1810–1880		LA	
16	Pallasgreen and Templebredin	1811–1900	1811–1900		LA	
		1811–1899	1811–1899		THU	
		Jan. 2, 1811–Dec. 29, 1833; Jan. 1, 1934–Oct. 13, 1861; Oct. 20, 1861–Dec. 26, 1880	Jan. 9, 1811–Jan. 29, 1838; Feb. 8, 1838–Oct. 13, 1861; Oct. 26, 1861–Dec. 11, 1880		NLI	Pos. 2498
17	Charleville	See Cork Northwest (9)				
18	Castleconnell	1850–1900	1863–1900		LA	
		Feb. 5, 1850–Jan. 10, 1864; Aug. 10, 1863–Dec. 31, 1880	Aug. 10, 1863–Nov. 27, 1880		NLI	Pos. 2477
19	Ardpatrick	1861–1900	1861–1900		LA	
		No records microfilmed			NLI	
20	Banogue	1861–1900	1861–1900		LA	
		Sept. 21, 1861–Dec. 21, 1880	Oct. 6, 1861–Apr. 27, 1880		NLI	Pos. 2427
21	Bruff, Grange and Gilnogra	Jan. 6, 1808–July 30, 1827; Aug. 10, 1827–Nov. 10, 1845; Nov. 2, 1845–Dec. 23, 1880	Jan. 27, 1808–July 8, 1827; Sept. 20, 1827–Oct. 22, 1845; Nov. 17, 1845–Nov. 23, 1880		NLI	B & 1827 Pos. 2428; remainder 2429
		1781–1900	1781–1900		LA	
22	Bruree	1826–1900	1826–1900		LA	
		Jan. 6, 1842–Mar. 11, 1868; Mar. 22, 1868–Dec. 23, 1880	July (?)28, 1861–Oct. 13, 1880		NLI	Pos. 2428

→

			LIMERICK EAST			
MAP	**CHURCH**	**BAPTISMS**	**MARRIAGES**	**BURIALS**	**LOCATION**	**REFERENCE**
23	Bulgaden	Mar. 22, 1812–Sept. 27, 1832; Oct. 6, 1832–Jan. 5, 1854; Jan. 23, 1854–Dec. 31, 1880	June 4, 1812–Jan. 27, 1833; Feb. 5, 1833–Nov. 30, 1853; Feb. 2, 1854–Nov. 27, 1880		NLI	Pos. 2428
		1812–1900	1812–1900		LA	
24	Croom	1828–1900	1770–1900		LA	
		Oct. 29, 1828–Oct. 30, 1844; Oct. 4, 1844–Dec. 30, 1880	Dec. 1770–July 23, 1794; Aug. 23, 1807 –Feb. 26, 1810; May 6, 1806–Mar. 3, 1829; May 2, 1829–Sept. 28, 1844; Sept. 29, 1844– Nov. 27, 1880	Dec. 1770– July 23, 1794	NLI	Pos. 2427
25	Donaghmore (Cahirnorry)	Jan. 3, 1830–Jan. 2, 1840; Jan. 4, 1840–Dec. 15, 1880	July 12, 1827–Dec. 2, 1843; Jan. 11, 1844– Nov. 8, 1880		NLI	Pos. 2419
		1830–1900	1827–1900		LA	
26	Dromin	1817–1900	1817–1900		LA	
		May 19, 1817–Sept. 19, 1837; Mar. 21, 1849– Dec. 16, 1880	June 23, 1817–Dec. 1, 1837; Mar. 21, 1849– Nov. 14, 1880		NLI	Pos. 2426
27	Effin and Gamenderk	Mar. 1843–Dec. 31, 1880	Apr. 24, 1843–Nov. 1880		NLI	Pos. 2427
		1843–1900	1843–1900		LA	
28	Fedamore	1806–1900	1806–1900		LA	
		Oct. 29, 1806–July 16, 1813; Jan. 1, 1814–Jan. 29, 1822; July 30, 1854– Dec. 25, 1880 Jan. 4, 1826–May 31, 1833 (Manister); June 2, 1833–Dec. 26, 1880 (Manister)	Jan. 9, 1814–Nov. 26, 1825; Aug. 1854–Dec. 27, 1880; Oct. 29, 1806– July 16, 1813; Jan. 7, 1826–June 12, 1833 (Manister); June 20, 1833–Aug. 6, 1880 (Manister)		NLI	Pos. 2409, 2429, 2430
29	Glenroe	June 27, 1853–Dec. 26, 1880	Aug. 2, 1853–Mar. 19, 1880		NLI	Pos. 2428
		1853–1900	1853–1900		LA	
30	Kilfinane	June 1832–July 30, 1856; Aug. 14, 1856–Apr. 22, 1859; Mar. 23,1859– Mar. 8, 1880; July 1, 1861–Dec. 28, 1880 (Ardpatrick)	Aug. 20. 1832–July 39, 1856; Sept. 5, 1856–Mar. 8, 1859; May 4, 1859– Aug. 18, 1880; Aug. 18, 1861–Sept. 13, 1880 (Ardpatrick)		NLI	Pos. 2429; B & M 1861– 1880, 2423
		1832–1900	1832–1900		LA	
31	Kilmallock	Oct. 22, 1837–Dec. 19, 1880	Nov. 2, 1837–Nov. 24, 1880		NLI	Pos. 2427
		1837–1900	1837–1900		LA	
		1855–1900	1855–1900		LA	
32	Parteen	1831–1900	Not specified		CGC	
		Sept. 26, 1831–Feb. 14, 1877	July 1, 1814–Nov. 9, 1819; Feb. 4, 1821–Jan. 10, 1836; Feb. 9, 1847–Jan. 22, 1877		NLI	Pos. 2410

→

Map	Church	Baptisms	LIMERICK EAST Marriages	Burials	Location	Reference
32	St John's	1788–1900	1821–1900		LA	
		May 2, 1788–Dec. 30, 1797; Jan. 1, 1825–Jan. 26, 1829; Jan. 26, 1829–Oct. 31, 1841; Nov. 1, 1841–Dec. 31, 1849; Jan. 5, 1850–June 30, 1877	July 21, 1821–Dec. 15, 1850; Jan. 11, 1851–June 23, 1877		NLI	Pos.2411 to 1850; Remainder 2412
32	St Mary's	Jan. 2, 1745–Apr. 13, 1795; Mar. 2, 1795–Oct. 13, 1816; Nov. 1, 1816–Dec. 31, 1836; Jan. 6, 1837–June 24, 1862	Oct. 29, 1745–Apr. 13, 1795; Apr. 13, 1795–Oct. 3, 1816; Aug. 30, 1816–Nov. 30, 1836; Jan. 7, 1837–June 19, 1862		NLI	Pos. 2412 to 1816; remainder 2413
		1745–1900	1745–1900		LA	
32	St Michael's	Aug. 16, 1776–Oct. 18, 1801; Jan. 12, 1803–Feb. 23, 1807; Oct. 14, 1807–Apr. 12, 1813; Jan. 3, 1814–Sept. 13, 1819; Jan. 19, 1820–Mar. 28, 1824; May 13, 1824–Dec. 8, 1838; Feb. 14, 1825–Oct. 1, 1830; Dec. 9, 1838–Dec. 27, 1852; Dec. 27, 1852–Oct. 4, 1861; Oct. 9, 1861–Feb. 8, 1876	Feb. 3, 1772–Sept. 12, 1802; Mar. 28, 1803–July 28, 1804; Oct. 18, 1807–Aug. 21, 1808; June 3, 1810–May 6, 1813; May 6, 1821–Mar. 2, 1824; June 6, 1814–Nov. 26, 1819; May 13, 1824–Dec. 4, 1838; Feb. 6, 1826–Nov. 14, 1828; Dec. 26, 1838–Jan. 16, 1853; Jan. 18, 1853–Oct. 8, 1861; Jan. 18, 1863–June 30, 1877		NLI	Pos. 2415 to 1838; 2416 to 1861; remainder 2417
		1776–1900	1772–1900		LA	
32	St Munchin's	Nov. 1, 1764–Apr. 4, 1784; Apr. 8, 1784–June 30, 1792; Oct. 3, 1798–Aug. 30, 1819; Sept. 4, 1819–Oct. 31, 1835; Nov. 16, 1824–June 19, 1828; Feb. 15, 1836–Sept. 29, 1877	Nov. 4, 1764–Feb. 24, 1784; May 11, 1784–May 25, 1792; Oct. 2, 1798–May 12, 1819; Sept. 2, 1819–Nov. 10, 1835; Jan. 24, 1825–May 21, 1828; Dec. 3, 1837–Aug. 5, 1877		NLI	Pos. 2413 to 1819; remainder 2414
		1764–1900	1764–1900		LA	
32	St Patrick's	1805–1900	1806–1900		LA	
		Jan. 7, 1812–Apr. 30, 1844; May 8, 1844–Apr. 30, 1830; May 8, 1834–Dec. 27, 1875	Jan. 15, 1812–Sept. 17, 1740; Feb. 11, 1841–Oct. 24, 1880		NLI	Pos. 2410
33	Manister	See Fedamore				
34	Mungret	Nov. 3, 1844–Dec. 19, 1880	Nov. 27, 1844–Nov. 12, 1880		NLI	Pos. 2409/10
		1844–1900	1844–1900		LA	
35	Patrick's Well (Lurriga)	Oct. 2, 1801–Mar. 13, 1826; Mar. 16, 1826–Dec. 30, 1843; Jan. 5, 1844–Dec. 20, 1880	Apr. 26, 1802–Nov. 26, 1825; Jan. 10, 1826–Dec. 2, 1843; Jan. 20, 1844–Dec. 14, 1880		NLI	Pos. 2409
		1801–1900	1802–1900		LA	

LIMERICK WEST

LIMERICK DIOCESE
1 Abbeyfeale
2 Adare
3 Ardagh
4 Askeaton
5 Athea
6 Ballingarry & Granagh
7 Ballyagran &
   Colmanswell
8 Cappagh (see Kilcornan)
9 Castlemahon
   (Mahoonagh)
10 Croagh
11 Drumcollogher
12 Feenagh & Kilmeedy
13 Glin
14 Kilcolman & Coolcappa
15 Kilcornan (Stonehall)
16 Kildimo (Pallaskenry)
17 Killeedy (Raheenagh)
18 Knockaderry & Clouncagh
19 Loughill & Ballyhahill
20 Monagea

21 Newcastle West
22 Rathkeale
23 Shangolden & Foynes
24 Templeglantine (see
    Monagea)

25 Tournafulla &
    Mountcollins

CLOYNE DIOCESE
26 Freemount

			LIMERICK WEST			
Map	**Church**	**Baptisms**	**Marriages**	**Burials**	**Location**	**Reference**
1	Abbeyfeale	Feb. 11, 1829–Oct. 1843; Aug.. 4, 1856–Dec. 30, 1880	Nov. 5, 1856–Nov. 1880		NLI	B. 1829–43, Pos. 6779; remainder 2426
		1829–1900	1825–1900		LA	
2	Adare	July 7, 1832–Dec. 25, 1848; Jan. 4, 1849–May 29, 1865	Juy 4, 1832–Dec. 2, 1848; Feb. 17, 1849–Feb. 21, 1865		NLI	Pos. 2420
		1832–1900	1832–1900		LA	
3	Ardagh	Mar 24, 1845–Dec. 31, 1869	Oct. 25, 1841–Nov. 13, 1869		NLI	Pos. 2424
		1845–1900	1841–1900		LA	
4	Askeaton	1829–1900	1829–1900		LA	
		Jan. 9,1829–Sept. 1, 1861; Sept. 1, 1861–Dec. 26, 1880	Jan. 2, 1829–July 21, 1861; Oct. 3, 1861–July 18, 1880		NLI	Pos. 2419
5	Athea	1830–1900	1827–1900		LA	
		Apr. 16, 1830–July 20, 1856; Dec. 10, 1850–July 26, 1879	Nov. 1, 1827–Feb. 5, 1856; Feb. 23, 1851–July 19, 1879		NLI	Pos. 2424
6	Ballingarry	Jan. 21, 1825–May 29, 1828; Dec. 17, 1849–Dec. 18, 1880	Jan. 23, 1825–Feb. 16, 1836; Jan. 12, 1850–Oct. 16, 1880		NLI	Pos. 2421
		1825–1900	1825–1900		LA	
7	Ballyagran	Sept. 10, 1841–Nov. 17, 1844; Jan. 4, 1847–Aug. 30, 1847; Sept. 22, 1850–May 21, 1860; Sept. 14, 1860–Oct. 30, 1880; June 2, 1861–Nov. 8, 1880	Sept. 16, 1841–Sept. 21, 1844; Jan. 15, 1847–Oct. 1, 1847; Jan. 4, 1851–Nov. 4, 1859; June 19, 1860–Dec. 25, 1879; Jan. 15, 1861–Nov. 8, 1880		NLI	Pos. 2430
		1841–1900	1841–1900		LA	→

Map	Church	Baptisms	LIMERICK WEST Marriages	Burials	Location	Reference
8	Cappagh	Jan. 1, 1841–Nov. 3, 1880	Jan. 14, 1841–Apr. 20, 1880		NLI	Pos. 2421
		1841–1900	1841–1900		LA	
9	Castlemahon (Mahoonagh)	Mar. 24, 1812–Aug. 30, 1830; June 14, 1832–July 5, 1838; Nov. 14, 1839–June 19, 1869	Aug. 31, 1810–Feb. (?), 1826; Jan. 1826–May 1, 1839; Feb. 9, 1840– Aug. 10, 1869		NLI	Pos. 2424/25
		1812–1900	1810–1900		LA	
10	Croagh	1836–1900	1744 [?*sic*]–1900		LA	
		Aug. 10, 1836–June 11, 1843; Nov. 3, 1843–Oct. 31, 1859; Nov. 13, 1859–Dec. 15, 1880	Jan. 9, 1844–Oct. 16, 1880		NLI	Pos. 2420
11	Drumcollogher	Mar. 4, 1830–Sept. 30, 1850; Nov. 11, 1851–Nov. 10, 1864; Nov. 16, 1864–Dec. 27, 1880	Jan. 24, 1830–Sept. 14, 1850; Oct. 1, 1851– Oct. 17, 1864; May 26, 1866–Oct. 12, 1880		NLI	Pos. 2423
		1830–1900	1830–1900		LA	
12	Feenagh	1833–1900	1833–1900		LA	
		Aug. 29, 1854–Dec. 28, 1880	July 27, 1854– Dec. 18, 1880		NLI	Pos. 2424
13	Glin	Oct. 30, 1851–Dec. 31, 1880	Oct. 18, 1851–Oct. 4, 1881		NLI	Pos. 2426
		1851–1900	1851–1900		LA	
14	Kilcolman	1827–1900	1828–1900		LA	
		Oct. 28, 1827–Dec. 30, 1843; Jan. 8, 1844–Sept. 26, 1859; Oct. 22, 1859–Aug. 5, 1877	Jan. 13, 1828–Nov. 10, 1843; Jan. 13, 1844– Nov. 21, 1880		NLI	Pos. 2421
15	Kilcornan	1825–1900	1825–1900		LA	
		Apr. 9, 1825–1833; Jan. 26, 1834–July 26, 1848; July 30, 1848– May 27, 1883	Apr. 11, 1825–1833; Dec. 22, 1833–Mar. 7, 1848; Sept. 10, 1848–Feb. 6, 1883		NLI	Pos. 2420
16	Kildimo	Jan. 1, 1831–Nov. 21, 1845; Jan. 7, 1846–Dec. 31, 1880	Jan. 14, 1831–Nov. 30, 1845; Jan. 8, 1846– Aug. 1, 1880		NLI	Pos. 2419 (B. 1846–80); Pos. 2420
		1831–1900	1831–1900		LA	
17	Killeedy	1840–1900	1840–1900		LA	
		Aug. 11, 1840–Mar. 1, 1874	Dec. 13, 1840– Feb. 14, 1874		NLI	Pos. 2423
18	Knockaderry	1838–1900	1838–1900		LA	
		Feb. 24, 1838–Dec. 27, 1880	Feb. 24, 1838– Dec. 15, 1880		NLI	Pos. 2421
19	Loughill	Oct. 28, 1855–Dec. 26, 1880	Nov. 1, 1855–July 4, 1880		NLI	Pos. 2420
20	Monagea	1776–1900	1777–1900		LA	
		Jan. 11, 1809–July 21, 1813; Mar. 25, 1829–Dec. 19, 1831; Aug. 19, 1833–Nov. 30, 1841; Dec. 31, 1841–Nov. 3, 1880	Jan. 8, 1777–Feb. 29, 1792; Feb. 1, 1829– Dec. 27, 1880		NLI	Pos. 2423
21	Newcastle Union Workhouse	Nov. 14, 1852–July 4, 1869; June 17, 1869–Dec. 16, 1880			NLI	Pos. 2425

$\longrightarrow$

MAP	CHURCH	BAPTISMS	LIMERICK WEST MARRIAGES	BURIALS	LOCATION	REFERENCE
21	Newcastle West	May 28, 1815–Oct. 27, 1831; Nov. 3, 1831–Dec. 28, 1851; Jan. 2, 1852–Nov. 29, 1874	Apr. 20, 1815–Nov. 19, 1831; Nov. 3, 1831 –Dec. 28, 1851; Jan. 25, 1852–Feb. 2, 1871		NLI	Pos. 2425
		1815–1900	1815–1900		LA	
22	Rathkeale	Jan. 1, 1811–July 12, 1823; Sept. 23, 1831–May 12, 1839; June 1, 1839–Dec. 27, 1846; Jan. 4, 1847–Feb. 15, 1861; Feb. 20, 1861–Dec. 26, 1875	Jan. 1, 1811–Feb. 7, 1825; Jan. 7, 1811– May 7, 1839 (duplicates included); May 7, 1839– Feb. 12, 1861; Apr. 13, 1861–Jan. 1, 1876		NLI	Pos. 2422
		1811–1900	1811–1900		LA	
23	Shanagolden	Apr. 28, 1824–July 23, 1835; Aug. 3, 1835–Aug. 29, 1842; Sept. 3, 1842–Sept. 20, 1862; Oct. 2, 1862–Nov. 7, 1877	Apr. 27, 1824–Oct. 6, 1877		NLI	Pos. 2418/19
		1824–1900	1824–1900		LA	
24	Temple-glantine	Dec. 4, 1864–July 15, 1879	Jan. 14, 1865–June 8, 1879		NLI	Pos. 2426
		1864–1900	1864–1900		LA	
25	Tournafulla	1867–1900	1867–1900		LA	
		Jan. 13, 1867–Apr. 3, 1875	July 31, 1867–Aug. 31, 1880		NLI	Pos. 2424
26	Freemount	See Cork Northwest 12				

LONGFORD

ARDAGH & CLONMACNOISE DIOCESE

1 Abbeylara
2 Ardagh & Moydow
3 Cashel
4 Clonbroney
5 Clonguish
6 Columcille
7 Dromard
8 Drumlish
9 Granard
10 Kilcommuck
11 Kilglass (Legan)
12 Killashee
13 Killoe
14 Mostrim
15 Mohill-Manachain
16 Rathcline (Lanesboro)
17 Scrabby
18 Shrule (Ballymahon)
19 Streete
20 Templemichael & Ballymacormick
21 Taghshsiney, Taghsinod & Abbeyshrule

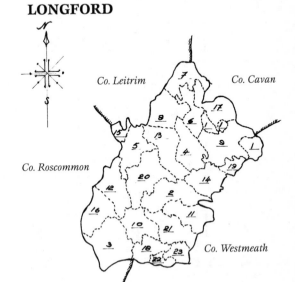

MEATH DIOCESE
22 Drumraney
23 Moyvore

			LONGFORD			
MAP	CHURCH	BAPTISMS	MARRIAGES	BURIALS	LOCATION	REFERENCE
1	Abbeylara	1822–1897	1855–1899	1854–1882	LGC	
		July 9, 1854–Dec. 28, 1880	July 12, 1854–Dec. 2, 1879	Aug. 9, 1854–Dec. 29, 1880	NLI	Pos. 4236
		1854–1984	1854–1984	1854–1984	LDS	BFA 1279229 items 3–5
2	Ardagh and Moydow	Feb. 12, 1793–Jan. 6, 1816; Oct. 6, 1822–Oct. 28, 1842; Nov. 1, 1842–Nov. 11, 1880	Feb. 12, 1793–Oct. 29, 1842; Nov. 10, 1842–Nov. 10, 1880	Nov. 26, 1822–Oct. 24, 1842; Nov. 1, 1842–Mar.13, 1876	NLI	Pos. 4235
		1793–1895	1792–1895	1822–1895	LGC	
		1793–1815; 1823–1977	1793–1984	1822–1984	LDS	BFA 1279220; 1279270
	Carrick-edmond	Apr. 8, 1835–Mar. 30, 1844; May 30, 1848–Dec. 3, 1880	Jan. 18, 1835–Aug. 19, 1842; May 31, 1848–June 14, 1880	Jan. 28, 1835–Nov. 17, 1842; May 26, 1848–Jan. 2, 1869	NLI	Pos. 4239
		1835–1901	1835–1887; 1890–1901	1835–1869	LDS	BFA 1279222 items 1–3
		1820–1887	1820–1888	1820–1899	LGC	
3	Cashel	1866–1899	1830–1899	1830–1880	LGC	
		1830–1910	1830–1910	1830–1831; 1839–1880;	LDS	BFA 1279221 items 3–4
		No registers received			NLI	
4	Clonbroney	Jan. 25, 1849–Mar. 2, 1862; Mar. 13, 1862–Nov. 9, 1880	Jan. 8, 1854–Feb. 27, 1862; Feb. 16, 1863–July 1880	Jan. 8 1854–Feb. 27, 1862 Mar. 5, 1862–Jan. 10, 1878	NLI	Pos. 4233
		1848–1911	1853–1911	1853–1892	LDS	BFA 1279229 items 11–13; 1279270 7–9
		1828–1901	1828–1899	1828–1892	LGC	
5	Clongish	1829–1887	1829–1879	1829–1881	LDS	BFA 1279219 items 11–12
		Oct. 25, 1829–Mar. 12, 1857; Aug. 3, 1829–Sept. 23, 1879; Mar. 15, 1857–Dec. 26, 1880	Aug. 3, 1829–Sept. 23, 1879;	Aug. 22, 1829–Dec. 15, 1880	NLI	Pos.4233
		1829–1888	1829–1880	1829–1879	LGC	
6	Colmcille	July 1845–Feb. 11, 1873	Aug. 3, 1845–May 22, 1871	July 22, 1845–Dec. 21, 1858	NLI	Pos. 4238
		1833–1984	1833–1871; 1876–1983	1932–1971	LDS	BFA 1279229 items 1–2, 14–15; 1279228
		1833–1899	1833–1858	1836–1858	LGC	
7	Dromard	1854–1910	1853–1885	1853–1881	LDS	BFA 1279229 items 8–9
		1840–1899	1853–1884	1853–1881	LGC	
		Jan. 14, 1838–July 15, 1845; Jan. 10, 1852–June 18, 1855; May 22, 1853–Dec. 26, 1880; Jan. 3, 1872–Dec. 26, 1880	Feb. 13, 1835–Apr. 15, 1855; Oct. 5, 1853–Nov. 2, 1868; Nov. 26, 1874–Nov. 22, 1880	Dec. 11, 1853–Oct. 15, 1868; July 26, 1874–Dec. 20, 1880	NLI	Pos. 4241
8	Drumlish	1834–1899	1834–1899	1834–1888	LGC	
		1834–1889	1834–1889	1834–1889	LDS	BFA 1279221 item 5
		Jan. 1, 1834–Mar. 13, 1868; Mar. 4, 1874–Dec. 30, 1880	Jan. 12, 1834–Feb. 25, 1868; Jan. 1, 1870–June 16, 1872; Jan. 15, 1877–Nov. 8, 1880	Jan. 2, 1834–Mar. 13, 1868; Feb. 16, 1870–July 10, 1872; Aug.13, 1876–Dec. 13, 1880	NLI	Pos. 4234

⟶

Map	Church	Baptisms	Longford Marriages	Burials	Location	Reference
9	Granard	Jan. 1, 1779–Apr. 2, 1811; 1812–1818 (fragments); Oct. 20, 1816–Feb. 26, 1832; Jan. 1832–June 2, 1869; Jan. 2, 1820–Dec. 26, 1880	Dec. 3, 1782–May 25, 1815; Sept. 10, 1816–July 14, 1836; July 18, 1836–May 6, 1869; June 30, 1869–Dec. 8, 1880	Dec. 18, 1782– Aug. 8, 1816; Apr. 29, 1818– Apr. 28, 1820; Sept. 16, 1816– Dec. 27, 1847; Jan. 3, 1848– May, 24, 1865	NLI	Pos. 4237
		1778–1894	1782–1869	1811–1865	LGC	
		1779–1928	1782–1900	1782–1862	LDS	BFA 12792298 items 1–6; 1279270, 13–
10	Kilcomoge	Sept. 7, 1859–Dec. 19, 1880	Sept. 13, 1859–Feb. 4, 1880	Nov. 13, 1859– Nov. 18, 1880	NLI	Pos. 4234
		1859–1880	1859–1880	1859–1880	LGC	
		1859–1984	1859–1981	1859–1880	LDS	BFA 12792222 items 5–7; 12879270 4–6
11	Kilglass (Legan)	Jan. 5, 1855–Dec. 29, 1880	Jan. 7, 1855–Dec. 11, 1880	Jan. 20, 1855– Dec. 25, 1880	NLI	Pos. 4234
		1855–1905	1855–1905	1855–1890	LDS	BFA 1279221 item 15
		1855–1899	1855–1896	1855–1890	LGC	
12	Killashee	Nov. 1, 1826–Nov. 4, 1843; Apr. 9, 1848–July 4, 1868; June 4, 1865–Nov. 24, 1880	Nov. 19, 1826–Oct. 23, 1843; June 18, 1848– Apr. 5, 1868; May 18, 1864–Oct. 9, 1880	Nov. 15, 1826– Aug. 3, 1843; Nov. 20, 1858– May 11, 1868	NLI	Pos. 4235
		1840–1898	1828–1898	1841–1865	LGC	
13	Killoe	1826–1917	1826–1868	1826–1868	LDS	BFA 1279221 items 6–14
		Jan. 1, 1826–July 21, 1832; Jan. 1, 1826–Aug, 31, 1852; Feb. 4, 1853–Oct. 7, 1868; Apr. 11, 1869–Dec. 18, 1880	May 29, 1826–July 18, 1832; Jan. 2, 1826–Oct. 21, 1852; Sept. 5, 1854– Dec. 16, 1868; Jan. 31, 1869–Nov. 1, 1880	Jan. 2, 1826– Aug. 23, 1853– Dec. 29, 1868; Jan. 20, 1869– Dec. 26, 1880	NLI	Pos. 4238
		1826–1917	1826–1917	1826–1844	LGC	
14	Mostrim	1838–1895	1838–1894	1838–1888	LDS	BFA 1279219 item 10
		1837–1895	1838–1891	1838–1888	LGC	
		June 8, 1838–Dec. 29, 1880	June 11, 1838–Oct. 29, 1880	May 23, 1838– Dec. 9, 1880	NLI	Pos. 4233
15	Mohill	See Leitrim 11				
16	Rathcline	1840–1889	1840–1903	1835–1869; 1839–1899	LDS	BFA 1279222 item 4
		1840–1899	1840–1899	1841–1899	LGC	
		No registers microfilmed			NLI	
17	Scrabby	1836–1899	1836–1899	1836–1899	CHGC	
		Feb. 12, 1833–Mar. 15, 1854; Mar. 4, 1855–Dec. 28, 1867; Apr. 29, 1870– Sept. 29, 1880	Feb. 17, 1833–Feb. 22, 1855; Apr. 15, 1855– June 29, 1871; June 11, 1877–Nov. 13, 1880	Sept. 9, 1835– Mar. 7, 1854; Apr. 7, 1856–Aug. 20, 1860	NLI	Pos. 4237
		1833–1920	1833–1871; 1877–1906	1833–1860	LDS	BFA 1279228 items 10–13
		1833–1899	1833–1867	1835–1860	LGC	⟶

Map	Church	Baptisms	LONGFORD Marriages	Burials	Location	Reference
18	Shrule	1820–1874; 1875–1902	1820–1874; 1875–1903	1830–1876	LDS	BFA 1279219 items 13–14; 1279221 1–2
		1820–1887	1820–1888	1820–1899	LGC	
		Mar. 26, 1820–Oct. 26, 1830; Nov. 1, 1830–Dec. 24, 1874	May 12, 1829–Oct. 25, 1830; Dec. 26, 1830–Nov. 8, 1874	Mar. 14, 1820–Sept. 12, 1830; Nov. 8, 1830–Aug. 17, 1876	NLI	Pos. 4235
19	Streete	July 6, 1820–July 14, 1827; Nov. 21, 1831–Dec. 20, 1831; Dec. 15, 1834–Dec. 29, 1880	Aug. 10, 1820–Jan. 22, 1828; Jan. 4, 1835–Nov. 19, 1880	Sept 27, 1823–Aug. 13, 1829; Dec. 14, 1834–Jan. 8, 1841; July 19, 1842–Dec. 29, 1880	NLI	Pos. 4236
		1820–1901	1820–1826; 1835–1881; 1887–1902	1834–1881 1887–1913	LDS	BFA 1279228 items 7–9
		1821–1863	1820–1900	1772–1995	DSHC	
20	Templemichael	1811–1885	1810–1897	1802–1829	LGC	
		1802–1920	1820–1900	1802–1869	LDS	BFA 1279219 items 1–9
		Jan. 5, 1802–Jan. 3, 1808; June 6, 1808–Jan. 28, 1829; Mar. 1, 1829–June 11, 1862; June 12, 1862–July 7, 1868; June 3, 1868–Dec. 31, 1880	Jan 20, 1802–Feb 26, 1829; Mar. 1, 1829–June 9, 1868; June 4, 1868–Dec. 13, 1880	Jan. 30, 1802–Feb. 19, 1829; Mar. 1, 1829–Oct. 4, 1865	NLI	Pos. 4232
22	Drumraney	See Westmeath 10				
22	Nougheval	See Westmeath 10				
23	Moyvore	See Westmeath 16				

LOUTH

ARMAGH DIOCESE
1 Ardee
2 Carlingford
3 Clogherhead
4 Collon
5 Cooley
6 Creggan Uppr
7 Darver
8 Dunleer
9 Dundalk
10 Faughart
11 Kilkerley
12 Kilsaran
13 Lordship
14 Louth
15 Mellifont
16 Monasterboice
17 St Peter's (Drogheda)
18 Tallanstown
19 Termonfeckin
20 Togher

CLOGHER DIOCESE
21 Carrickmacross
22 Inniskeen

MEATH DIOCESE
23 St Mary's (Drogheda)

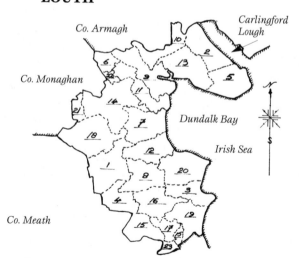

			LOUTH			
MAP	**CHURCH**	**BAPTISMS**	**MARRIAGES**	**BURIALS**	**LOCATION**	**REFERENCE**
1	Ardee	1763–1810;	1769–1800;	1765–1810;	PRONI	MIC.1D/52
		1821–1881	1821–1826	1821–1825		
		Apr. 10, 1763–June 24, 1802; July 20, 1802–Oct 25, 1810; Mar. 4, 1821–Dec. 11, 1880	Aug. 8, 1769–June 10, 1802; Aug. 10, 1802–Oct. 29, 1810; Mar. 5, 1821–Feb. 9, 1826	July 1, 1802–Oct. 31, 1810; Mar. 7, 1821–Feb 7, 1825	NLI	Pos. 5601
		1763–1900	1763–1900	1810–1921	AA	
2	Carlingford	1835–1900	1835–1900		AA	
		Apr. 2, 1835–Aug. 13, 1848; Aug. 13, 1848–Dec. 22, 1880	Apr. 23, 1838–Aug. 12, 1848; Sept. 13, 1848 –Dec. 30, 1880	Apr. 7, 1835– Aug. 12, 1848; Oct. 29, 1867– Dec. 30, 1880	NLI	Pos. 5594
		1835–1881	1835–1881	1835–1848; 1869–1882	PRONI	MIC.1D/45
3	Clogherhead (Clogher)	1744–1799; 1833–1900	1742–1799; 1833–1900	1742–1799	AA	
		1744–1777; 1780–1799; 1833–1881	1742–1771; 1780–1799; 1833–1881	1744–1772; 1780–1799 (gaps)	PRONI	MIC.1D/53
		Nov. 2, 1744–Oct. 17, 1777; Apr. 4, 1780–Dec. 30, 1799; Mar. 9, 1833–Oct. 23, 1836; Aug. 5, 1837–Dec. 21, 1880	Feb. 12, 1742–Aug. 25, 1771; Apr. 4, 1780–Sept. 18, 1799; Apr. 11, 1833–Oct. 27, 1836; Aug. 18, 1837–Nov. 21, 1880	Nov. 30, 1744–July 21, 1772; Mar. 20, 1780 –1799 (incomplete)	NLI	Pos. 5599
4	Collon	Apr. 2, 1789–Mar. 1807; Aug. 15, 1819–Dec. 29, 1836; Jan. 6, 1836–Dec. 14, 1880	Jan. 1789–Feb. 1807; Dec. 2, 1817–Dec. 21, 1835 (fragmented and disordered); Feb 7, 1836 –Sept. 19, 1845; Mar. 11, 1848–Nov. 27, 1880		NLI	Pos. 5597
		1789–1807; 1819–1881	1789–1807; 1817–1845; 1848–1881		PRONI	MIC.1D/48
5	Cooley (Carlingford South)	June 4, 1811–Aug. 13, 1838; Aug. 14, 1838–Dec. 29, 1880	Feb. 19, 1811–July 17, 1838; Sept. 19, 1838–Dec. 11, 1880		NLI	Pos. 5593
		1811–1881	1811–1882		PRONI	MIC.1D/44
		1811–1900	1811–1900	1811–1877	AA	
		See NLI			LDS	BFA 0926033
6	Creggan Upper	See Armagh 6				
7	Darver	See NLI			LDS	BFA 092603
		June 29, 1787–Oct. 26, 1819; Nov. 1819–Mar. 30, 1836; Nov. 23, 1833–1846; June 18, 1846–Dec. 31, 1880	July 27, 1787–June 23, 1836; May 3, 1837–Feb. 29, 1848; Feb. 4, 1847–Nov. 17, 1880		NLI	Pos. 5596
		1787–1880	1837–1883	1871–1879	PRONI	MIC.1D/47
		1787–1900	1787–1900	1871–1879	AA	
8	Dunleer	Oct. 29, 1847–Dec. 26, 1880	1772–98; 1848–80	1847–57; 1877–80	LDS	BFA 0926039
		Oct. 29, 1847–Dec. 26, 1880	Nov. 13, 1772–Feb. 21, 1798; Jan. 28, 1848–Nov. 24, 1880	Dec. 3, 1847–Dec. 7, 1858; Jan. 1, 1877–Dec. 6, 1880	NLI	Pos. 5602
		1798–1900	1772–1900	1832–1900	AA	

			LOUTH			
MAP	CHURCH	BAPTISMS	MARRIAGES	BURIALS	LOCATION	REFERENCE
8	Dunleer *(cont.)*	1847–1881	1772–1798; 1848–1882	1847–1858; 1877–1882	PRONI	MIC.1D/50
9	Dundalk	1790–1880 (gaps)	1790–1831 (gaps)	Aug. 17, 1790–Nov. 27, 1802	LDS	BFA 0979711 items 1–4
		1790–1802; 1814–1881	1790–1802; 1817–1831	1790–1802	PRONI	MIC.1D/46
		1790–1802; 1814–1900	1790–1802; 1817–1900	1790–1802	AA	
		Aug. 4, 1790–Sept. 30, 1802; May 25, 1814–Aug. 30, 1831; Aug. 29, 1831–Dec. 31, 1844; Jan. 25, 1845–Jan. 18, 1868; Jan. 21, 1868–Dec. 31, 1880	Aug. 15, 1790–Nov. 19, 1802; Oct. 27, 1817–Aug. 20, 1831	Aug. 17, 1790–Nov. 27, 1802	NLI	Pos. 5595
10	Faughart,	1851–1900	1851–1900		AA	
		Apr. 16, 1851–Dec. 23, 1880 (indexed)	Apr. 21, 1851–Nov. 24, 1880		NLI	Pos. 5596
		See NLI			LDS	BFA 0926040 items 1–5
		1861–1881 (indexed); 1851–1896	1851–1882; indexed 1851–1900		PRONI	MIC.1D/47
11	Kilkerley (Haggardstown)	Jan. 12, 1752–May 28, 1789; May 29, 1789–Aug. 21, 1838; July 5, 1838–Nov. 27, 1880	Jan. 21, 1752–Oct. 17, 1789; June 11, 1789–Aug. 27, 1838; Nov. 1, 1838–Nov. 25, 1880	Jan. 8, 1752–Sept. 12, 1789; Sept 4, 1789–Mar. 11, 1806; Sept. 9, 1831–Aug. 27. 1838	NLI	Pos. 5594
		1752–1880	1752–1880	1752–1806; 1831–1838	PRONI	MIC.1D/45
		1752–1900	1752–1900	1752–1838	AA	
12	Kilsaran	1809–1824; 1831–1836; 1853–1881	1809–1826; 1831–1836; 1853–1882		PRONI	53
		1809–1900	1809–1900		AA	
		Jan. 1, 1809–May 8, 1824; Aug. 3, 1831–June 28, 1836; June 19, 1853–Dec. 27, 1880	Jan. 23, 1809–Oct. 28, 1826; Aug. 30, 1831–Nov. 14, 1836; Sept. 11, 1853–Nov. 27, 1880		NLI	Pos. 5599
13	Lordship	1838–1881	1838–1880		PRONI	MIC.1D/46–47
		1833–1900	1833–1900		AA	
		See NLI			LDS	BFA 0926044/5
		Jan. 7, 1838–Aug. 27, 1864; Sept. 4, 1864–Dec. 30, 1880	Jan. 21, 1838–Aug. 28, 1864; Sept. 1, 1864–Nov. 25, 1880		NLI	Pos. 5595
14	Knockbridge	Nov. 3, 1858–1869	Sept. 19, 1858–1869		LDS	BFA 0926043
		Nov. 3, 1858–1869	Sept. 19, 1858–1869		NLI	Pos. 5594
		1858–1869	1858–1869		PRONI	MIC.1D/45
		1851; 1858–1869; 1881–1900	1858–1869; 1889–1900		AA	
14	Louth	Mar. 12, 1833–Sept. 25, 1871; Oct. 14, 1873–Dec. 4, 1880	Apr. 8, 1833–Dec. 18, 1873; Jan. 23, 1874–Dec. 7, 1880		NLI	Pos. 5593
		1833–1900	1835–1900		AA	
		1833–1871; 1873–1881	1873–1881		PRONI	MIC.1D/44
15	Mellifont	1821–1900	1821–1900		AA	
		1821–1881	1821–1882		PRONI	MIC.1D/53
		Dec. 2, 1821–Dec. 29, 1848	Dec. 14, 1821–Dec. 9, 1848		NLI	Pos. 5599

→

MAP	CHURCH	BAPTISMS	LOUTH MARRIAGES	BURIALS	LOCATION	REFERENCE
16	Monaster-boice	Nov. 1, 1814–Oct. 30, 1830; Jan. 9, 1834–Dec. 23, 1859; Jan. 6, 1860–Dec. 19, 1880	Nov. 2, 1814–Sept. 28, 1830; Oct. 21, 1830–Nov. 20, 1872; Jan. 20, 1870–Nov. 20, 1872	Nov. 5, 1814–Nov. 30, 1815; Jan. 4, 1820–Dec. 8, 1822; Sept. 12, 1830–Jan. 10, 1850	NLI	Pos. 5600
		1814–1830; 1834–1881	1814–1872	1814–1850 (gaps); 1857–1858; 1876–1877	PRONI	MIC.1D/51–52
		1814–1830; 1834–1900	1814–1872	1814–1822		AA
17	Drogheda: St Peter's	Jan. 9, 1744–May 2, 1757; Aug. 25, 1764–Oct. 27, 1771; Apr. 7, 1777–Feb. 26, 1778; June 14, 1781–Oct. 1, 1783; Nov. 28, 1783–Apr. 1795; Oct. 1803–Dec. 19, 1804; Nov. 1, 1815–July 24, 1842 (very poor); July 29, 1842 –Jan. 3, 1866; Jan. 1, 1866– Dec. 29, 1880	Nov. 1, 1815–July 24, 1842 (very poor); July 26, 1842–Jan. 4, 1866; Jan. 3, 1866–Dec. 26, 1880		NLI	Pos. 5597; From 1815 Pos. 5598
		1744–1757; 1764–1771; 1777–1778; 1781–1795; 1803–1804; 1815–1881	1815–1880		PRONI	MIC.1D/48–49
		1744–1880 (gaps)	1815–1880 (gaps)		LDS	BFA 0926036/7
		1744–1804; 1815–1899	1804; 1819–1900			AA
18	Tallanstown	Nov. 9, 1817–Apr. 13, 1825; Sept. 25, 1830–Nov. 6, 1835; Nov. 9, 1835–Sept. 28, 1875; Oct. 12, 1875–Dec. 27, 1880	Apr. 4, 1804–Mar. 16, 1816; Apr. 17, 1816–June 1, 1863; Aug. 31, 1867–Nov. 25, 1880		NLI	Pos. 5602
		See NLI			LDS	BFA 0979712 items 4–9
		1817–1825; 1835–1900	1804–1900			AA
		1817–1825; 1830–1881	1804–1863; 1867–1884		PRONI	MIC.1D/50
19	Termonfeckin	1823–1881	1823–1881	1827–1833	PRONI	MIC.1D/51
		1823–1900	1799–1900	1799–1833		AA
		Apr. 3, 1823–Feb. 3, 1853; Jan. 6, 1853–Dec. 17, 1880	Apr. 14, 1823–Nov. 27, 1852; Apr. 12, 1853 –Nov. 9, 1880	Jan. 1, 1827–Oct. 11, 1833	NLI	Pos. 5600
		See NLI			LDS	BFA 0926044/5
20	Togher	1791–1900	1791–1900	1791–1817		AA
		1791–1828; 1869–1881	1873–1881	1791–1817	PRONI	MIC.1D/48
		Nov. 1, 1791–Apr. 24, 1828; Aug. 8, 1869–Dec. 31, 1880	July 31, 1791–Mar. 17, 1828	June 3, 1791–May 8, 1817	NLI	Pos. 5597
21	Carrickmacross (Maghaire Rois)	See Monaghan 5				
22	Inniskeen	See Monaghan 10				
23	St Mary's Drogehda	See Meath 38				

MAYO

ACHONRY DIOCESE
1 Attymass
2 Bohola
3 Carracastle
4 Castlemore & Kilcolman
5 Foxford (Toomore)
6 Kilbeagh (Charlestown)
7 Kilconduff & Meelick
8 Kilgarvan
9 Killasser
10 Killedan (Kiltimagh)
11 Kilmovee
12 Kilshalvey, Kilturra, Cloonoghill
13 Templemore

GALWAY DIOCESE
14 Shrule

KILLALA DIOCESE
15 Addergoole
16 Ardagh
17 Backs
18 Ballycastle
19 Ballycroy
20 Ballysakeery
21 Belmullet
22 Crossmolina
23 Kilcommon-Erris
24 Kilfian
25 Killala
26 Kilmore-Erris
27 Kilmoremoy
28 Kiltane (Bangor)
29 Lackan
30 Moygownagh

TUAM DIOCESE
31 Achill
32 Aghagower
33 Aghamore
34 Aglish (Castlebar)
35 Annagh
36 Aughaval
37 Balla & Manulla
38 Ballinrobe
39 Ballyovey (Tourmakeady)
40 Bekan
41 Burrisacarra & Ballintubber
42 Burrishoole (Newport)
43 Clare Island
44 Cong & The Neale
45 Crosboyne & Tagheen
46 Inishbofin
47 Islandeady
48 Keelogues
49 Kilcolman (Claremorris)
50 Kilcommon & Robeen
51 Kilgeever
52 Kilmaine
53 Kilmeena
54 Kilvine
55 Knock
56 Mayo Abbey
57 Turlough

Killala Bay · *Co. Sligo* · *Lough Conn* · *Clew Bay* · *Co. Roscommon* · *Co. Galway*

MAP	CHURCH	BAPTISMS	MAYO MARRIAGES	BURIALS	LOCATION	REFERENCE
1	Attymass	See NLI			LDS	BFA 0926002 items 1–2
		1875–1900	1874–1897		MNFHRC	
		June 16, 1875–Aug. 22, 1880	Feb. 1, 1874–Oct. 15, 1880		NLI	Pos. 4224
2	Bohola	Oct. 1857–Dec. 26, 1880	Oct. 29, 1857–May 30, 1880		NLI	Pos. 4224
		1857–1900	1857–1900		MNFHRC	
3	Carracastle	1853–1900	1847–1900		MNFHRC	
		Jan. 17, 1853–Dec. 26, 1880	July 1, 1847–Nov. 21, 1880		NLI	Pos. 4223
		1853–1908	1847–1903		LDS	BFA 1279233 items 1–2

→

Map	Church	Baptisms	MAYO Marriages	Burials	Location	Reference
4	Castlemore and Kilcolman	1851–1900	1830–1900		RHGC	
		1851–1911	1830–1963		LDS	BFA 1279232 items 1–9
		1851–1900			SHGC	
		Nov. 1851–Nov. 17, 1861; Jan. 25, 1864–June 2, 1872; Jan. 5, 1860–Feb. 6, 1876; 1861; 1864–1872 (transcript); Feb. 13, 1876–Dec. 31, 1880	Aug. 10, 1830–Oct. 2, 1867; Feb. 4, 1868–Nov. 10, 1880		NLI	Pos. 4226
5	Foxford (Toomore)	Dec. 30, 1871–Jan. 6, 1880	Apr. 30, 1833–Mar. 17, 1840; Jan. 20, 1870–Dec. 22, 1880		NLI	Pos. 4223
		1871–1900	1872–1900		MNFHRC	
		1871–1893	1833–1911		LDS	BFA 12792031 items 18–19; 0926022
6	Kilbeagh	Jan. 1, 1855–Dec. 26, 1880	May 18, 1845–Mar. 13, 1866; Jan. 22, 1855–Sept 12, 1880		NLI	Pos. 4224
		1855–1924	1845–1902		LDS	BFA 1279230 items 1–6
		1847–1900	1844–1900		MNFHRC	
7	Kilconduff and Meelick	Mar. 19, 1822–June 26, 1826; May 12, 1841–Aug. 23, 1850 Sept 1, 1850–May 7, 1859; July 2, 1859–Sept. 29, 1875; Oct. 2, 1875–Dec. 31, 1900	June 7, 1808–July 3, 1846; July 3, 1846–Mar. 31, 1878; Apr. 24, 1878–Nov. 23, 1915		NLI	Pos. 4225
		1822–1826; 1841–1900	1808–1878		MNFHRC	
		1822–1915	1808–1915		LDS	BFA 1279233 items 5–9; 0926020
8	Kilgarvin	1870–1900	1897–1900		MNFHRC	
		Mar. 15, 1870–Dec. 31, 1880	Nov. 16, 1844–May 4, 1880		LDS	
		Mar. 15, 1870–Dec. 31, 1880	Nov. 16, 1844–May 4, 1880		NLI	Pos. 4224
9	Killasser	1848–1900	1847–1900		MNFHRC	
		1847–1902	1847–1921		LDS	BFA 1279232 items 16–17
		Nov. 1, 1847–Dec. 31, 1880	Dec. 13, 1847–June 5, 1880	Nov. 1, 1847–Apr. 3, 1862	NLI	Pos. 4223
10	Killedan	1861–1900	1855–1900		MSFRC	
		1860–1909	1834–1909		LDS	BFA 1279231 items 3–6
		Feb. 2, 1861–Dec. 29, 1880	May 22, 1834–Apr. 3, 1862; Nov. 6, 1861–Aug. 8, 1880		NLI	Pos. 4224
11	Kilmovee	Feb. 21, 1854–Dec. 21, 1880; June 18, 1854–Dec. 19, 1880	Nov. 3, 1824–Aug. 28, 1848; Oct. 12, 1854–Dec. 21, 1880		NLI	Pos. 4224
		1854–1900	1824–1900		MSFRC	
		1854–1913	1824–1848; 1855–1925		LDS	BFA 1279230 items 7–9; 0926017
12	Kilshalvey	See Sligo 11				→

MAP	CHURCH	BAPTISMS	MAYO MARRIAGES	BURIALS	LOCATION	REFERENCE
13	Templemore		May 20, 1872–Mar. 11, 1880		LDS	BFA 0926021
			May 20, 1872–Mar. 11, 1880		NLI	Pos. 4224
		1888–1900	1872–1900			MNFHRC
14	Shrule	1831–1900	1831–1900		MSFRC	
		July 7, 1831–Aug. 12, 1864	July 1, 1831–June 23, 1848; Oct. 26, 1855–May 10, 1864		NLI	Pos. 2438
15	Addergoole	Jan. 15, 1840–Mar. 2, 1866; Mar. 2, 1866–June 11, 1878; June 16, 1878–Dec. 26, 1880	Jan. 13, 1840–Mar. 10, 1878		NLI	Pos. 4229
		1840–1900	1840–1900		MNFHRC	
		1840–1880	1840–1878		LDS	BFA 1279205 items 9–11
16	Ardagh	Feb. 5, 1870–July 14, 1880			NLI	Pos. 4230
		1866–1900	1882–1900		MNFHRC	
			1870–1880		LDS	BFA 1279204 item 23
17	Backs	1829–1900	1815–1897		MNFHRC	
		1830–1851; 1854–1879; 1848–1879; 1865–1880	1829–1850; 1848–1864; 1865–1880		LDS	BFA 1279205 items 5–8
		Aug. 28, 1848–Dec. 11, 1859 (Rathduff); Jan. 2, 1861–Sept. 14, 1879 (Rathduff); Oct. 12, 1854–Oct. 2, 1856 (Knockmore); Mar. 4, 1858–Aug. 16, 1879 (Knockmore)	Dec. 1, 1848–Apr. 14, 1860 (Rathduff); Jan. 27, 1865–Dec. 2, 1869 (Rathduff); Feb. 24, 1874–Sept. 1879 (Rathduff); Sept. 25, 1860–Nov. 21, 1861 (Knockmore); Jan. 13, 1869–July 13, 1879 (Knockmore)		NLI	Pos. 4230
18	Ballycastle	Aug. 8, 1864–Dec. 15, 1880	Jan. 15, 1869–Sept. 3, 1880		NLI	Pos. 4229
		1853–1880	1869–1880		LDS	BFA 1279204 items 20–21
		1853–1900	1869–1900		MNFHRC	
19	Ballycroy	No records microfilmed			NLI	
		1885–1900	1869–1900		MNFHRC	
20	Ballysokeery (Cooneal)	c.1830–c.1870	c.1830–c.1870		LDS	BFA 1279204 item 24
		1844–1881	1843–1881		MNFHRC	
		Nov. 26, 1843–Dec. 19, 1880	Oct. 10, 1843–Dec. 21, 1880		NLI	Pos. 4230
21	Belmullet	1841–1900	1836–1900		MNFHRC	
		Feb. 15, 1841–Dec. 19, 1872; Dec. 21, 1872–Dec. 26, 1880	Jan. 8, 1836–May 11, 1845; Aug. 23 1857–Nov. 2, 1880		NLI	Pos. 4231
		1842–1880	1836–1880		LDS	BFA 1279205 items 13–15
22	Crossmolina	1831–1880	1832–1880		LDS	BFA 1279204 item 22
		1831–1900	1832–1900		MNFHRC	
		Aug. 27, 1831–Aug. 8, 1841; Apr. 23, 1845–Dec. 28, 1880	Nov. 18, 1832–Feb. 10, 1841; Mar. 10 1846–Dec. 27, 1880		NLI	Pos. 4230

Map	Church	Baptisms	MAYO Marriages	Burials	Location	Reference
23	Kilcommon Erris	No records microfilmed			NLI	
		1883–1910	1843–1848		MNFHRC	
24	Kilfian	Oct. 1, 1826–Apr. 7, 1836	July 2, 1826–Oct. 2, 1844	Oct. 6, 1826–Feb. 6, 1832	NLI	Pos. 4230
		1826–1836	1826–1836	1826–1836	MNFHRC	
		1826–1836	1826–1836; 1843–1844	1826–1832	LDS	BFA 1279205 item 2
25	Killala	Apr. 6, 1852–Aug. 25, 1873; Sept. 21, 18873–Dec. 23, 1880	Dec. 14, 1873–Nov. 3, 1880		NLI	Pos. 4231
		1852–1900	1873–1900		MNFHRC	
		1852–1880	1873–1880		LDS	BFA 1279204 items 17–19
26	Kilmore Erris	June 24, 1860–Dec. 27, 1880	Sept. 1, 1860–Nov. 4, 1880		NLI	Pos. 4231
		1860–1881	1860–1881		LDS	BFA 1279205 items 17–18
		1859–1900	1860–1900		MNFHRC	
27	Kilmoremoy	1823–1852; 1850–1867; 1868–1879	1823–1842; 1849–1868	1823–1842	LDS	BFA 1279205 items 15–16; 1279205, 3
		1823–1900	1823–1900	1823–1931	MNFHRC	
		May 15, 1823–Oct. 14, 1836; May 9, 1849–July 16, 1849; July 23, 1851–Sept. 8, 1867; Feb. 2, 1868–Dec. 31, 1880	May 15, 1823–Oct. 4, 1842; Oct. 22, 1850 –Feb. 4, 1868; Feb. 2, 1868–Dec. 31, 1880	Apr. 29, 1823 –Aug. 12, 1836; Sept. 12, 1840– May 3, 1844	NLI	Pos. 4231
28	Kiltane (Bangor Erris)	1860–1901	1860–1914		MNFHRC	
		1860–1881	1860–1881		LDS	BFA 1279205 items 12, 16
		Aug. 1, 1860–Dec. 26, 1880	Sept. 4, 1860–Mar. 28, 1880		NLI	Pos. 4231
29	Lacken	1852–1900	1854–1900		MNFHRC	
		Aug. 19, 1852–Nov. 24, 1874 (transcript–many gaps)	Mar. 29, 1854–Feb. 7, 1869 (transcript–many gaps)		NLI	Pos. 4230
		See NLI			LDS	BFA 1279205 item 4
30	Moygownagh	1877–1900	1881–1900		MNFHRC	
		No records microfilmed			NLI	
31	Achill	1868–1911	1867–1813		LDS	BFA 1279259 items 3–5
		1868–1900	1867–1900		MNFHRC	
		Dec. 29, 1867–Dec. 26, 1880	Oct. 18, 1867–June 25, 1880		NLI	Pos. 4222
32	Aghagower	Apr. 9, 1828–May 17, 1836; Mar. 17, 1842–Aug. 20, 1854; Sept. 24, 1854–Dec. 18, 1880	Nov. 16, 1854–Dec 7, 1880		NLI	Pos. 4210
		1828–1900	1828–1900		MSFRC	
		1828–1836; 1842–1854; 1854–1903	1854–1903		LDS	BFA 1279209 items 19–20; 1279210, 1–3
33	Aghamore	1864–1901	1864–1921		LDS	BFA 1279206 items 13–15

MAP	CHURCH	BAPTISMS	MAYO MARRIAGES	BURIALS	LOCATION	REFERENCE
33	Aghamore	1864–1900	1864–1900		MSFRC	
		Feb. 2, 1864–Dec. 26, 1880 (transcript)	Dec. 22, 1864–Sept. 22, 1880		NLI	Pos. 4217
34	Aglish (Castlebar)	Jan. 2, 1838–Apr. 17, 1855 (in disorder); Feb. 25, 1855–June 16, 1872; June 22, 1872–Dec. 28, 1880	June 16, 1824–Apr. 17, 1843; June 27, 1843–Dec. 9, 1880		NLI	Pos. 4214
		1838–1900	1824–1900		MSFRC	
		1838–1984	1824–1982		LDS	BFA 1279260/1
35	Annagh	Nov. 17, 1851–Dec. 30, 1870; Jan. 6, 1871–Dec. 26, 1880	June 14, 1852–June 30, 1870; Nov. 20, 1870–Dec. 1, 1880		NLI	Pos. 4217
		1854–1924	1852–1902		LDS	BFA 1279208 items 3–6
		1851–1900	1852–1900		MSFRC	
36	Aughaval	1845–1905	1823–1905		LDS	BFA 12792210/1 items 17–22, 1–4; More
		July 9, 1845–Nov. 14, 1858 (not precisely ordered); Jan. 18, 1859–Mar. 24, 1872; Jan. 19, 1862–Mar. 11, 1874; Apr. 7, 1872–Dec. 26, 1880; Mar. 15,1874–Dec. 29, 1880	Apr. 9, 1823–Oct. 6, 1837 (not precisely ordered); Aug. 10, 1834 –May 25, 1857 (not precisely ordered); Feb. 4, 1857–Feb. 1, 1861; Jan. 15, 1862–Dec. 20, 1880		NLI	Pos. 4210
		1845–1900	1823–1900		MSFRC	
37	Balla	1837–1900	1837–1900		MSFRC	
		1837–1905	1837–1905		LDS	BFA 1279209 items 2–3
		May 28, 1837–Dec. 27, 1880	July 3, 1837–Oct. 3, 1880		NLI	Pos. 4213
38	Ballinrobe	Aug. 20, 1843–Dec. 20, 1851 (inc. some marriages); Nov. 7, 1850–Apr. 17, 1856; Jan.18, 1861–Nov. 7, 1880; June 19, 1871–Dec. 29, 1880	Oct., 24, 1850–Apr. 30, 1856; Jan. 14, 1861–Nov. 7, 1880		NLI	Pos. 4215
		1843–1903	1850–1911		LDS	BFA 1279209 items 8–10; 0926219
		1843–1900	1850–1900		MSFRC	
39	Ballyovey (Tourma-keady)	Aug. 26, 1869–Dec. 26, 1880 (transcript)	1869–Sept. 5, 1880		NLI	Pos. 4216
		1862–1885	1870–1878; 1883–1903		LDS	BFA 1279206 item 16
		1869–1900	1847–1900		MSFRC	
39	Partry	Oct. 23, 1869–July 15, 1878.	Jan. 7, 1870–July 11, 1878		NLI	Pos. 4216
40	Bekan	Aug. 3, 1832–Feb. 2, 1844 (some missing); Dec. 15, 1844–May 20,1861 (some missing); Sept. 15, 1851 –May 7, 1871	May 7, 1832–Aug. 6, 1844 (some missing); Aug. 8, 1844–May 22, 1872 (some missing)		NLI	Pos. 4219
		1832–1900	1832–1900		MSFRC	→

Map	Church	Baptisms	MAYO Marriages	Burials	Location	Reference
41	Burriscarra	Sept. 1, 1839–Dec. 24, 1880	Sept. 29, 1839–Mar. 1, 1880		NLI	Pos. 4213
		1839–1900	1839–1900		MSFRC	
		1839–1895	1839–1903		LDS	BFA 1279210 items 15–16; 0979699 1–2
42	Burrishoole		Jan. 30, 1872–Nov. 27, 1880		NLI	Pos. 4222
		1872–1900	1872–1900		MNFHRC	
		1872–1920	1872–1911		LDS	BFA 1279207 items 9–11
43	Clare Island	Oct. 14, 1851–Nov. 21, 1880			NLI	Pos. 4211
		See NLI			LDS	BFA 0926220 item 3
44	Cong and The Neale	1870–1924	1870–1900		LDS	BFA 1279214 items 6–7
		1870–1900	1870–1900		MSFRC	
		Feb. 28, 1870–Dec. 20, 1880 (transcript)			NLI	Pos. 4214
45	Crossboyne and Tagheen	1825–1913	1791–1876		LDS	BFA 1279211 items 5–8
		1835–1900	1794–1900		MSFRC	
		July 7, 1862–Feb. 3, 1877; May 10,. 1877–Dec. 26, 1880	Jan. 9, 1877–July 29, 1880		NLI	Pos. 4217
46	Inishbofin	1867–1903	1877–1878		LDS	BFA 1279213 item 10
		1867–1900	1867–1900		GFHSW	
		Oct. 14, 1867–Dec. 15, 1880	Nov. 18, 1867–Oct. 25, 1880		NLI	Pos. 4219
47	Islandeady	1839–1913	1839–1898		LDS	BFA 1279213 items 11–14
		Sept. 7, 1839–Dec. 30, 1866; Jan. 6, 1867–May 14, 1876	Sept. 17, 1839–Sept. 2, 1880		NLI	Pos. 4212
		1839–1900	1839–1900		MSFRC	
48	Keelogues	Aug. 15, 1847–Dec. 24, 1880	Aug. 10, 1847–Sept. 4, 1880		NLI	Pos. 4215
		1847–1909	1872–1909		LDS	BFA 1279259 items 1–2
		1847–1909	1847–1909		MNFHRC	
49	Kilcolman	1835–1900	1805–1900		MSFRC	
		Apr. 7, 1835–Jan. 29, 1838; Mar. 26, 1839–May 16, 1858; May 16, 1858–May 28, 1873	June 8, 1806–Feb. 4, 1830; Jan. 7, 1835–Mar. 7, 1836; Dec. 29, 1838–June 25, 1871		NLI	Pos. 4217
		1835–1913	1806–1898		LDS	BFA 1279207 items 15–20
50	Kilcommon and Robeen	1857–1880; 1896–1924	1857–1880; 1865–1899; 1896–1924		LDS	BFA 1279209 items 11–12; 0926223
		1857–1900	1857–1900		MSFRC	
		Oct. 5, 1857–Dec. 24, 1880; Dec. 8, 1865–Dec. 24, 1880 (Roundfort)	Oct. 10, 1857–June 24, 1880; Nov. 25, 1865–Apr. 24, 1880 (Roundfort)		NLI	Pos. 4216

→

MAP	CHURCH	BAPTISMS	MAYO MARRIAGES	BURIALS	LOCATION	REFERENCE
51	Kilgeever	1850–1872; 1894–1922 1872–1880 Louisburgh	1844–1845; 1906–1922 1872–1880 Louisburgh		LDS	BFA 1279224 item 2; 0926224 1; & more
		1850–1900	1850–1900		MSFRC	
		Feb. 20, 1850–Mar. 7, 1869 (transcript); Aug. 1, 1872 –Dec. 12, 1880			NLI	Pos. 4212
52	Kilmaine	1854–1900	1854–1900		MSFRC	
		1854–1909	1855–1909		LDS	BFA 1279214 items 3–4; 0926225 2–4
		June 30, 1854–Dec. 31, 1877; Jan. 20, 1878–Dec. 24, 1880	May 19, 1855–Oct. 20, 1877		NLI	Pos. 4216
53	Kilmeena	1870–1900	1870–1900		MSFRC	
		1858 –	1858 –		LC	
		No records microfilmed			NLI	
54	Kilvine	1870–1900	1870–1900		MSFRC	
		1872–1911	1872–1908		LDS	BFA 1279206 item 10
		No records microfilmed			NLI	
55	Knock	Dec. 17, 1868–Dec. 29, 1880	Sept. 7, 1875–Dec. 5, 1880		NLI	Pos. 4218
		1868–1900	1874–1900		MSFRC	
		1868–1913	1875–1943		LDS	BFA 1279206 items 3–5
56	Mayo Abbey	1841–1899	1841–1906		LDS	BFA 1279209 items 6–7
		1841–1900	1841–1900		MSFRC	
		Apr. 4, 1841–Dec. 20, 1880	Sept. 10, 1841–June 5, 1880		NLI	Pos. 4215
57	Turlough	1847–1911	1847–1909		LDS	BFA 1279212 items 5–7
		1847–1900	1849–1900		MNFHRC	
		Aug. 1, 1847–Dec. 7, 1865; Dec. 8, 1865–Dec. 25, 1880	Aug. 8, 1847–June 8, 1880		NLI	Pos. 4213

MEATH

Co. Monaghan
Co. Cavan
Co. Louth
Irish Sea
Co. Westmeath
Co. Dublin
Co. Offaly
Co. Kildare

Map	Church	Baptisms	MEATH Marriages	Burials	Location	Reference
1	Collon	See Louth 4				
2	Moybologue	1867–1881	1868–1882		PRONI	MIC.1D/82
		Feb. 28, 1867–Dec. 18, 1880	May 12, 1868–Oct. 14, 1880		NLI	Pos. 5349
3	Ardcath	1795–1900	1797–1879		MHC	
		Oct. 25, 1795–June 29, 1879	June 18, 1797– June 30, 1879		NLI	Pos. 4180
4	Athboy	1794–1900	1794–1911	1794–1847	MHC	
		Apr. 18, 1794–Nov. 15, 1799; Mar. 3, 1807–May 16,1826 Jan. 14, 1827–Jan. 12, 1858; Jan. 1, 1858–Dec. 29, 1880	May 5, 1794–Nov. 7, 1799; Apr. 9, 1807 –Oct. 24, 1864; Feb. 6, 1865–Nov. 25, 1880	Apr. 23, 1794– Mar. 27, 1798; Mar. 18, 1807– Feb. 23, 1826; Jan. 2, 1865– Sept. 23, 1873	NLI	Pos. 4173
5	Ballinabrackey (Castlejordan)	Nov. 5, 1826–Aug. 28, 1870; Sept. 4, 1870–Dec. 29, 1880	Nov. 9, 1826–Aug. 21, 1870; Sept. 5, 1870–Oct. 8, 1880	Nov. 15, 1848– July 31, 1849	NLI	Pos. 4173
		1826–1900	1826–1870	1919–1993	DSHC	⟶

Map	Church	Baptisms	MEATH Marriages	Burials	Location	Reference
6	Balliver	1837–1901			MHC	
		See NLI			LDS	BFA 0926163 item 1
		Feb. 12, 1837–Dec. 9, 1880	Apr. 7, 1837–July 12, 1880	Feb. 12, 1837–Nov. 16, 1880	NLI	Pos. 4179
6	Kildalkey	No records microfilmed			NLI	
		1782–1901	1782–1901	1782–1901	MHC	
7	Batterstown (Kilcock)	Feb. 21, 1836–Dec. 12, 1880; Feb. 21, 1836–Dec. 12, 1880 (transcript)	Apr. 14, 1836–June 14, 1880; Apr. 14, 1836–June 14, 1880 (transcript)		NLI	Pos. 4177
		1836–1900	1836–1900		MHC	
8	Beauparc	1815–1900	1816–1900	1816–1839	MHC	
		Dec. 17, 1815–Sept. 8, 1880	Jan. 10, 1816–July 22, 1881		NLI	Pos. 4180
9	Bohermeen	1832–1900	1831–1900	1833–1868	MHC	
		June 2, 1832–Dec. 31, 1880	Apr. 22, 1831–May 30, 1881	Jan, 5, 1833–May 5, 1842; Jan. 15, 1865–Mar. 13, 1868	NLI	Pos. 4182
		See NLI			LDS	BFA 0926164
10	Carnaross	Aug. 25, 1806–Oct. 14, 1807; May 21, 1808–Sept. 28, 1815; June 2, 1827–Feb. 6, 1859; Feb. 27, 1859–Apr. 2, 1881	June 1805–Feb. 12, 1820; Feb. 16, 1823–Feb. 24, 1825; Jan. 27, 1828–Apr. 12, 1861; July 12, 1861–May 11, 1882	June 9. 1805–Sept. 13, 1856	NLI	Pos. 4184
		1806– 1900	1805–1900	1805–1856	MHC	
		See NLI			LDS	BFA 0926165 items 1–2
11	Carolanstown (Kilbeg)	Dec. 1817–Jan. 8, 1852; Mar. 17, 1858–Dec. 24, 1869	Jan. 15, 1810–June 16, 1813; Jan., 15, 1830–May 21, 1852; May 23, 1858–Oct. 10, 1869		NLI	Pos. 4184
		1815–1900	1829–1900	1830–1870	MHC	
		See NLI			LDS	BFA 0926173 item 4
12	Castletown–Kilpatrick	Dec. 18, 1805–Jan. 22, 1821; Apr. 12, 1821–May 28, 1822; Jan. 7, 1826–Sept. 26, 1832; Oct. 3, 1832–May 11, 1841; Apr. 1, 1841–Nov. 27, 1873; Nov. 27, 1873–Nov. 27, 1880	May 22, 1816–May 19, 1822; Jan. 24, 1824–Apr. 18, 1841; Nov. 10, 1842–Nov. 13, 1873; Nov. 13, 1873–Nov. 27, 1880		NLI	Pos. 4184
		1805–1900	1816–1900		MHC	
13	Clonmellon	1759–1901	1757–1901	1757–1993	DSHC	
		1759–1900	1757–1900	1759–1849	MHC	
		Jan. 6, 1759–Sept. 18, 1784 (some gaps); Feb. 3, 1785–Apr. 29, 1791; Jan. 3, 1815–Mar. 24, 1815; May 1, 1791–Mar. 10, 1809; Apr. 5, 1809–Nov. 2, 1809; June 18, 1819–July 10, 1845; July 11, 1845–Aug. 25, 1872	Jan. 17, 1757–Aug. 20, 1784 (some gaps); Aug. 16, 1784–Sept. 4, 1809; Jan. 19, 1815–Feb. 21, 1815; July 19, 1819 –July 29, 1845; Jan. 10, 1846–June 19, 1872	Jan. 30, 1757–Sept. 17, 1784 (some gaps); Dec. 25, 1878–Oct. 29, 1809; Nov. 7, 1819–July (15?), 1850	NLI	Pos. 4187

→

MAP	CHURCH	BAPTISMS	MEATH MARRIAGES	BURIALS	LOCATION	REFERENCE
14	Curraha (Donymore)	Apr. 30, 1802–June 23, 1823; Aug. 14, 1823–Nov. 16, 1880	June 17, 1802–June 7, 1823; July 23, 1823–Nov. 16, 1880	June 7, 1802–Apr. 14, 1823; Nov. 2, 1833–Apr. 11, 1863	NLI	Pos. 4179
15	Drumconrath	1811–1900	1811–1900	1861–1872	MHC	
		Oct. 1811–Aug.. 25, 1861; Sept. 15, 1861–Feb. 9, 1881	Sept. 31 [sic], 1811–Sept. 22, 1861; Oct. 4, 1861–Feb. 7, 1881	Aug. 11, 1861–Mar. 25, 1872	NLI	Pos. 4184
16	Duleek	See NLI			LDS	BFA 0926168
		1852–1901	1852–1911		MHC	
		Feb. 2, 1852–Mar. 7, 1880	Feb. 24, 1852–June 21, 1881		NLI	Pos. 4181
17	Dunboyne	1798–1900	1787–1900	1787–1877	MHC	
		Sept. 2, 1798–Apr. 19, 1823; May. 1, 1823–Aug. 11, 1844; Sept. 6, 1844–Dec. 16, 1877	June 31 [sic], 1787–Nov. 22, 1863; Feb. 2, 1834–Aug. 26, 1836; Jan. 12, 1864–Dec. 29, 1877	June 7, 1787–Oct. 31, 1877	NLI	Pos. 4176
18	Dunderry	1837–1900	1841–1901		MHC	
		Oct. 11, 1837–Oct. 24, 1857; Aug. 10, 1841–July 17, 1869; May 3, 1870–Mar. 20, 1881	Oct. 15, 1841–May 31, 1869; May 10, 1871–Oct. 7, 1883		NLI	Pos. 4187
19	Dunshaughlin	See NLI			LDS	BFA 0926166
		Jan. 1, 1789–Oct. 9, 1791; Jan. 8, 1849–Apr. 14, 1880	Oct. 25, 1800–July 26, 1801; Aug. 2, 1801–Feb. 11, 1834; Feb. 13, 1849–Apr. 1880	Oct. 9, 1791–Jan. 24, 1828; Jan. 7, 1863–Dec. 23, 1872	NLI	Pos. 4177
		1789–1880	1801–1880	1789–1872	MHC	
20	Enniskeen (Kingscourt)	See Cavan 6				
21	Johnstown	See NLI			LDS	BFA 0926170
		1839–1900	1839–1900		MHC	
		Jan. 12, 1839–Apr. 24, 1881	Jan. 2, 1839–Aug. 29, 1881		NLI	Pos. 4182
22	Kells	1791–1900	1791–1900	1784–1828	MHC	
		July 12, 1791–Dec. 2, 1827; July 17, 1828–Nov. 28, 1831; Jan. 27, 1832–Dec. 31, 1873 (some for 1830)	Aug. 1, 1791–Dec. 26, 1873	June 13, 1794–Mar. 30, 1824	NLI	Pos. 4185
23	Kilbride and Mountnugent	See Cavan 5				
24	Kilmessan (Killeen)	July 2, 1742–Aug. 26, 1750; Jan. 2, 1791–Mar. 25, 1832; Apr. 10, 1832–Dec. 30, 1864 (Kilmessan); Mar. 25, 1832 –Dec. 6, 1880 (Dunsany, Killeen); Jan. 21, 1865–Nov. 26, 1880 (Kilmessan)	Feb. 2, 1865–Aug. 26, 1880 (Kilmessan)	July 2, 1742–Aug. 26, 1750; Jan. 2, 1791–Mar. 25, 1832; Apr. 10, 1832–Oct. 24, 1871 (Kilmessan); Mar. 25, 1832–Dec. 6, 1880 (Dunsany, Killeen)	NLI	Pos. 4178
		1790–1896	1790–1896	1790–1896	MHC	
25	Kilskyre	1784–1901	1784–1900	1784–1921	MHC	
		See NLI			LDS	BFA 0926173 items 1–3

MAP	CHURCH	BAPTISMS	MEATH MARRIAGES	BURIALS	LOCATION	REFERENCE
25	Kilskyre (*cont.*)	Apr. 22, 1784–Dec. 30, 1838; Jan. 1, 1839–Oct. 19. 1841 (Ballinlough separately); Nov. 10, 1841–Mar. 4, 1873	Jan. 22, 1784–Nov. 2, 1790; June 12, 1808– July 31, 1841; Jan. 28, 1842–Feb. 16, 1874; Apr. 13, 1874– Oct. 30, 1880	Jan. 9, 1784– Aug. 29,1790; Nov. 29, 1859– Oct. 27, 1873	NLI	Pos. 4186
26	Lobinstown (Killine)	1823–1899	1823–1899		MHC	
		Oct. 8, 1823–Apr. 5, 1881	Sept. 28, 1823–May 19, 1881		NLI	Pos. 4183
27	Longwood (Killine)	1829–1877	1829–1877	1829–1855	MHC	
		Jan. 29, 1829–Jan. 15, 1833; Feb. 4, 1833–Mar. 4, 1878	Jan. 29, 1829–Jan. 15, 1833; Mar. 1833 –Nov. 29, 1877	Jan. 29, 1829– Jan. 15, 1833; Feb. 3, 1833– Feb. 9, 1855	NLI	Pos. 4179
28	Moynalty	July 25, 1830–Apr. 4, 1880	Dec. 1, 1829–Jan. 31, 1883	Mar. 2, 1830– Jan. 10, 1880	NLI	Pos. 4187
		1830–1900	1829–1900	1830–1879	MHC	
		See NLI			LDS	BFA 0926176 item 2
29	Moynalvey	Oct. 4, 1811–Oct. 5, 1828; Mar. 25, 1831–Dec. 24, 1877; Jan. 13, 1878–Dec. 26, 1880	Nov. 4, 1783–Nov. 6, 1786; Oct. 7, 1811– Sept. 29, 1828; Apr. 24, 1831–Nov. 1, 1880	Oct. 15, 1811– Sept. 29, 1828; Oct. 28, 1877– Dec. 18, 1880	NLI	Pos. 4178
		See NLI			LDS	BFA 0926177
		1811–1900	1783–1900	1811–1881	MHC	
30	Navan	Jan. 14, 1782–May 20, 1813; Sept. 7, 1842–Jan. 1881; Oct. 22, 1868–Dec. 29, 1880	Apr. 4, 1853–Oct. 21, 1868; Oct. 25, 1868– Nov. 19, 1881	June 18, 1868– July 4, 1880	NLI	Pos. 4181
		1782–1901	1853–1901		MHC	
31	Nobber,	July 22, 1754–Feb. 10, 1821; Jan. 6,1821–July 12, 1865	Jan. 17, 1757–Feb. 7, 1821; Mar. 5, 1821– May 11, 1865	Feb. 6, 1757– Jan. 23, 1821; Jan.23, 1821– Feb. 10, 1866	NLI	Pos. 4183
		1754–1900	1757–1900	1757–1856	MHC	
		See NLI			LDS	BFA 0926179
32	Oldcastle	Jan. 5, 1789–Feb. 9, 1807; Nov. 6, 1808–Mar (?) 28, 1834; Feb. 18, 1834–Nov. 14, 1877	Apr. 28, 1789–Feb. 10, 1807; Nov. 7, 1808– Nov. 28, 1840; Jan. 9, 1841–June 29, 1846; July 12, 1846–Nov. 17, 1877	Mar. 27, 1789– Feb. 4, 1807; Nov. 3, 1808– Jan. 2, 1809	NLI	Pos. 4188
		1789–1900	1789–1900		MHC	
		See NLI			LDS	BFA 0926180
33	Oristown	Dec. 25, 1757–July 25, 1784 (some gaps); 1774–1778 (various dates); Apr. 30, 1797– May 16, 1814 (some gaps); Feb. 14, 1831–Dec. 22, 1840 (some gaps); Nov. 14, 1847–Dec. 26, 1880	Nov. 1, 1763–May 27, 1780; Jan. 27, 1783– June 7, 1784; Apr. 24, 1797–Apr. 17, 1801; Sept. 15, 1801–Aug. 3, 1842; Mar. 7, 1848– Sept. 19, 1880		NLI	Pos. 4186
		1774–1900	1763–1900	1771–1831	MHC	
		See NLI			LDS	BFA 0926181
34	Rathcore and Rathmolyon	No records microfilmed			NLI	
		1878–1911	1879–1912		MHC	→

Map	Church	Baptisms	MEATH Marriages	Burials	Location	Reference
35	Rathkenny	1784–1900	1867–1900	1796–1816	MHC	
		Nov. 30, 1784–Dec. 6, 1815; July 12, 1818–Feb. 22, 1861; Aug. 5, 1866–Mar. 1, 1876	Nov. 27, 1784–Sept. 10, 1788; 1785–1816 (some entries only); Aug. 3, 1818–Dec. 5, 1844; May 21, 1846–Nov. 22, 1857; Oct. 1, 1866–Feb. 10, 1876		NLI	Pos. 4182
36	Ratoath	May 10, 1781–Jan. 23, 1818; Aug. 1, 1818–Dec. 29, 1880	Jan. 1780–May 7, 1818; Aug. 17, 1818–Dec. 13, 1880	June 26, 1789–Apr. 15, 1818	NLI	Pos. 4177
		See NLI			LDS	BFA 0926182
		1781–1900	1780–1900	1789–1814	MHC	
37	Rosnaree & Donore	Jan. 1, 1840–Feb. 5, 1881	Apr. 27, 1840–Sept. 7, 1881; (1841–1850 missing)		NLI	Pos. 4181
		1840–1900	1840–1900	1840–1841	MHC	
38	Drogheda: St Mary's	1835–1900	1870–1900	1870–1871	MHC	
		Apr. 30, 1835–June 9, 1867; June 9, 1867–Nov. 23, 1875; Jan. 2, 1872–Jan. 11, 1881	Apr. 24, 1870–Feb. 2, 1881		NLI	Pos. 4180
		See NLI			LDS	BFA 0926169
39	Skryne	Nov. 28, 1841–Dec. 12, 1880	Jan. 16, 1842–May 19, 1880		NLI	Pos. 4179
		1841–1900	1842–1900		MHC	
40	Slane	Jan. 1, 1851–May 29, 1881	Jan. 7, 1851–Nov. 26, 1881		NLI	Pos. 4187
		See NLI			LDS	BFA 0926183 item 1
		1851–1900	1851–1900		MHC	
41	Stamullen	1831–1901	1830–1901		MHC	
		Jan. 1, 1831–Dec. 22, 1879	May 3, 1830–Nov. 29, 1879	Jan. 3, 1834–Dec. 27, 1877	LDS	BFA 0926183 item 2
		See NLI			NLI	Pos. 4182
42	Summerhill	Apr. 13, 1812–Apr. 26, 1854; May 10, 1854–Dec. 12, 1880	Apr. 16, 1812–Feb. 26, 1854; July 13, 1854–Sept. 30, 1880	Apr. 14, 1812–Nov. 11, 1836	NLI	Pos. 4178
		See NLI			LDS	BFA 0926184
		1812–1900	1812–1900	1812–1836	MHC	
43	Trim	1829–1901	1829–1901	1831–1841	MHC	
		July 25, 1829–Dec. 29, 1880	July 30, 1829–Nov. 27, 1880	Jan. 7, 1831–Apr. 12, 1841	NLI	Pos. 4179
		See NLI			LDS	BFA 0926185 items 1–2

MONAGHAN

CLOGHER DIOCESE
1 Aghabog
2 Aughnamullan East
3 Aughnamullan West
4 Ballybay (Tullycorbet)
5 Carrickmacross (see also Magheracloone)
6 Castleblayney
7 Clones
8 Clontibret
9 Donagh (Glasslough)
10 Donaghmoyne
11 Drumully
12 Drumsnat & Kilmore
13 Ematris (Rockcorry)
14 Errigal Truagh
15 Killany
16 Killevan (Newbliss)
17 Mahgeracloone
18 Monaghan & Rockwallis
19 Tydavnet
20 Tyholland

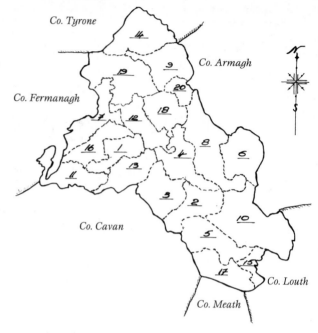

			MONAGHAN			
Map	Church	Baptisms	Marriages	Burials	Location	Reference
1	Aghabog (Killeevan)	1841–1842			MAR	
		1871–1881	1871–1881		PRONI	MIC.1D/20
		Jan. 29, 1871–Dec. 1880	Jan. 29, 1871–Aug. 25, 1880		NLI	Pos. 5577
2	Aughna-mullen East	1878–1900			MAR	
		See NLI			LDS	BFA 0979707 items 1–3
		1857–1881	1857–1881	1857–1881	PRONI	MIC.1D/19
		July 26, 1857–Oct. 26, 1876; Aug. 3, 1878–Dec. 9, 1880	July 26, 1857–Oct. 26, 1876; Aug. 20, 1878–Nov. 1, 1880	July 26, 1857 –Oct. 26, 1876;	NLI	Pos. 5576
3	Aughna-mullen West	1868–1880			MAR	
		1841–1881	1841–1881		PRONI	MIC.1D/18
		Feb. 14, 1841–Dec. 23, 1867; Jan. 3, 1868–Nov. 14, 1880	Feb. 2, 1841–Nov. 30, 1867; Jan. 9, 1868–Nov. 27, 1880		NLI	Pos. 5575
4	Ballybay (Tullycorbet)	Apr. 1862–July 22, 1876 (indexed); July 3, 1876–Dec. 13, 1880	May 27, 1862–June 15, 1876		NLI	Pos. 5573
		1862–1875; 1876–1900 (Ballybay)	1862–1876		MAR	
		1862–1881	1862–1876		PRONI	MIC.1D/16

			MONAGHAN			
MAP	**CHURCH**	**BAPTISMS**	**MARRIAGES**	**BURIALS**	**LOCATION**	**REFERENCE**
5	Carrick-macross (Maghaire Rois)	Jan. 6, 1858–Apr. 19, 1870; Jan. 1, 1878–Dec. 31, 1880	Feb. 21, 1838–Jan. 31, 1844; Jan. 17, 1858–Apr. 19, 1870		NLI	Pos. 5578
		See NLI			LDS	BFA 0926055 items 1–2
		1858–1870; 1878–1880	1838–1844; 1858–1881		PRONI	MIC.1D/21
6	Castleblayney (Muckno)	Nov. 1, 1835–Apr. 15, 1862; Apr. 21, 1862–Jan. 12, 1869; Dec. 4, 1868–Dec. 31, 1880	Oct. 31, 1835–Apr. 8, 1862; Apr. 28, 1862–Oct. 20, 1868; Nov. 15, 1868–Dec. 9, 1880		NLI	Pos. 5576; marriages from 1868 on Pos. 5577
		1835–1881	1835–1881		PRONI	MIC.1D/19–20
		See NLI			LDS	BFA 0979707 items 4–6
7	Clones	July 23, 1848–Apr. 30, 1854; Apr. 22, 1855–Feb. 18, 1866; Feb. 25, 1866–Dec. 29, 1880	May 30, 1821–Mar. 3, 1840; Oct. 1, 1840–Feb. 9, 1866; Apr. 17, 1866–Nov. 21, 1880		NLI	Pos. 5577; marriages from 1878 on Pos. 5578
		1848–1880	1821–1866		MAR	
		1848–1881	1821–1881		PRONI	MIC.1D/20–21
8	Clontibret	Feb. 12, 1861–July 4, 1874; Sept. 2, 1872–Dec. 24, 1880; July 4, 1874–Dec. 31, 1880	Aug. 27, 1861–Dec. 21, 1880		NLI	Pos. 5573
		1860–1881	1861–1881		PRONI	MIC.1D/16
		1861–1880			MAR	
9	Donagh	1835–1880	1836–1860		MAR	
		1836–1881	1836–1882		PRONI	MIC.1D/17; C.R.2/11
		May 2, 1836–Feb. 28, 1878 (illegible in many parts); Jan. 14, 1861–Dec. 30, 1880	May 2, 1836–Feb. 28, 1878 (illegible in many parts); Sept. 30, 1860–Nov. 25, 1880		NLI	Pos. 5574
10	Donaghmoyne	1863–1880	1872–1880		PRONI	MIC.1D/15
		1841–1900			MAR	
		Jan. 19, 1863–Jan. 28, 1878; Jan. 15, 1869–Dec. 10, 1880	Oct.. 11, 1872–Oct. 7, 1880		NLI	Pos. 5572
10	Inniskeen	1836–1848			MAR	
		July 3, 1837–Oct. 27, 1862; July 12, 1863–Dec. 29, 1880	Apr. 7, 1839–Nov. 26, 1850		NLI	Pos. 5575
		See NLI			LDS	BFA 0926053
		1837–1881	1839–1850		PRONI	MIC.1D/5; C.R.2/2
11	Drumully	Jan. 6, 1845–Apr. 2, 1866; July 7, 1864–Dec. 26, 1880	July 14, 1864–Oct. 31, 1880		NLI	Pos. 5572
		1845–1881	1864–1881		PRONI	MIC.1D/15
12	Drumsnat and Kilmore	1875–1881	1836–1872	1875–1883	PRONI	MIC.1D/18; C.R.2/13
		Feb. 16, 1836–June 13, 1872;	Feb. 16, 1836–June 13, 1872;	Feb. 16, 1836–June 13, 1872;	NLI	Pos. 5575
		1875–1880	1875–1880	1875–1880		
13	Ematris	1848–1876	1850–1861		PRONI	MIC.1D/21
		May 14, 1848–Mar. 22, 1860; Mar. 15, 1861–Mar. 9, 1876	Feb. 2, 1850–Nov. 2, 1861		NLI	Pos. 5578

→

MAP	CHURCH	BAPTISMS	MONAGHAN MARRIAGES	BURIALS	LOCATION	REFERENCE
14	Errigal Truagh	Nov. 1, 1835–June 20, 1852; Mar. 24, 1861–Dec. 29, 1880	Dec. 1, 1837–July 28, 1849; Jan. 28, 1862–May 27, 1880		NLI	Pos. 5576
		1835–1852; 1861–1881 1835–1880	1837–1849; 1862–1881		PRONI MAR	MIC.1D/19
		See NLI			LDS	BFA 0979706 items 1–3
15	Killanny	Jan. 9, 1857–Dec. 26, 1880	Jan. 20, 1862–Dec. 28,1880		NLI	Pos. 5574
		1857–1881	1862–1882		PRONI	MIC.1D/17
16	Kilskeery (Killeevan) See also Aghabog	1840–1881	1940–1882		PRONI	MIC.1D/11
		Oct. 3, 1840–June 15, 1862; June 19, 1862–Feb. 18, 1870; Jan. 27, 1870–Dec. 24, 1880	Aug. 30, 1840–May 27, 1862; July 17, 1862–Feb. 27, 1870; Feb. 3, 1870–Mar. 1, 1880		NLI	Pos. 5568
		See NLI			LDS	BFA 0926054 items 1–4
17	Maghera-cloone	1836–1863; 1865–1881	1826–1859; 1866–1880		PRONI	MIC.1D/17; C.R.2/17
		May 2, 1836–Nov. 8, 1863; Jan. 16, 1865–Dec. 10, 1880	Oct. 9, 1826–Mar. 8, 1859; Apr. 9, 1866–Nov. 21, 1880		NLI	Pos. 5574
18	Monaghan	Nov. 6, 1835–Dec. 21, 1847; June 12, 1849–Apr. 21, 1850 (indexed); Jan. 4, 1857–May 27, 1875; May 29, 1875–Dec. 26, 1880	Feb. 6, 1827–June 7, 1850; Jan. 12, 1857–Nov. 16, 1880		NLI	Pos. 5570
		1835–1847; 1849–1881 (indexed)	1827–1880		PRONI	MIC.1D/13; C.R.2/6
		1835–1900	1827–1850		MAR	
19	Tydavnet	Nov. 1, 1835–Dec. 12, 1862; Jan 1, 1863–Nov. 24, 1871; Nov. 22, 1871–Dec. 31, 1880	Apr. 18, 1825–Oct. 19, 1865; Jan. 9, 1876–Nov. 26, 1880		NLI	Pos. 5573; baptism from 1871, marriages from 1876 Pos. 5574
		1835–1881	1825–1865; 1876–1881		PRONI	MIC.1D/2, 16–17
		1835–1880			MAR	
20	Tyholland	1835–1881	1827–1882		PRONI	MIC.1D/3, 15
		May 1, 1835–Jan. 12, 1851; Jan. 19, 1851–Dec. 19, 1863; Dec. 18, 18865–Dec. 14, 1876; Dec. 12, 1877–Dec. 27, 1880	Jan 1, 1827–July 26, 1851; Jan. 19, 1851–Dec. 19, 1863; Feb 1, 1866–Nov. 28, 1872; Dec. 3, 1877–Nov. 5, 1880	Jan. 19, 1851–Dec. 19, 1863	NLI	Pos. 5572
		1835–1880			MAR	

OFFALY

ARDAGH &
CLONMACNOISE DIOCESE
1 Banagher (Gallen &
  Reynagh)
2 Clonmacnoise
3 Lemanaghan &
  Balnahown
4 Ferbane (Tisaran)

CLONFERT DIOCESE
5 Lusmagh

KILDARE & LEIGHLIN
  DIOCESE
6 Clonbulloge
7 Daingean
8 Edenderry
9 Killeigh
10 Portarlington
11 Rhode

KILLALOE DIOCESE
12 Birr
13 Bournea (Courageneen)
14 Dunkerrin
15 Kilcolman
16 Kinnitty

17 Roscrea
18 Shinrone

MEATH DIOCESE
19 Ballinabrackey
20 Clara & Horseleap
21 Eglish

22 Kilcormac
23 Rahan
24 Tubber
25 Tullamore

OSSORY DIOCESE
26 Seirkeiran

Co. Westmeath
Co. Meath
Co. Galway
Co. Kildare
Co. Tipperary
Co. Laois
Co. Tipperary

		OFFALY				
MAP	CHURCH	BAPTISMS	MARRIAGES	BURIALS	LOCATION	REFERENCE
1	Banagher (Gallen and Reynagh)	Nov. 16, 1811–Sept. 4, 1812; Sept 28, 1816–July 6, 1817; Oct. 2, 1816–Mar. 29, 1822; July 13, 1818–Sept. 12, 1827; Aug. 25, 1822–June 15, 1825; Mar. 6, 1829–Oct. 2, 1837; Feb. 18, 1838–Dec. 31, 1880	Oct. 16, 1797–July 23, 1837; Oct. 13, 1816–Apr. 20, 1822; Aug. 25, 1822–June 15, 1825; Feb. 18, 1838–Dec. 31, 1880	Nov. 15, 1803–Nov. 28, 1804; Nov. 13, 1819–Apr. 30, 1820; Aug. 25, 1822–June 15, 1825; Jan. 2, 1827–Sept. 7, 1827; Apr. 24, 1829–Sept. 27, 1831; 1807, 1809, 1811 (a few deaths recorded)	NLI	Pos. 4242
		1811–1899	1797–1899		IMA	
		1816–1973	1797–1983	1893–1980	LDS	BFA 1279226 items 10–18
2	Clonmacnois	1826–1908	1826–1899		IMA	
		1826–1908	1826–1908	1892–1906	LDS	BFA 1279227 items 7, 8
		Apr. 19, 1826–Feb. 28, 1846; Jan. 6, 1841–July 31, 1842; Feb. 1, 1848–Dec. 21, 1880; Jan. 16, 1876–Nov. 14, 1880	Apr. 24, 1826–Dec. 14, 1840; Feb. 2, 1841–Feb. 8, 1842; Feb. 21, 1848–Nov. 25, 1880; Feb. 17, 1876–Sept. 12, 1880	Jan. 2, 1841–Feb. 18, 1842; Feb. 3, 1848–Sept. 29, 1880	NLI	Pos. 4243
3	Lemanahan and Ballinahown	1821–1905 (some gaps)	1823–1974	1821–1828; 1829–1845; 1854–1881; 1882–1894	LDS	BFA 1279227 items 1–6

Map	Church	Baptisms	OFFALY Marriages	Burials	Location	Reference
3	Lemanahan and Balinahown (*cont.*)	Aug. 12, 1821–Dec. 21, 1824; Feb. 12, 1826–Feb. 25, 1839; Feb. 6, 1841– Sept. 21, 1845; July 23, 1854–Dec. 24, 1880	Jan. 7, 1830–Aug. 29, 1845; Oct. 15, 1854– Dec. 26, 1880	Nov. 21, 1829– Sept. 9, 1845; Sept. 2, 1854– Dec. 26, 1880	NLI	Pos. 4235
		1821–1899	1822–1899	1821–1846	IMA	
3	Moate	See Westmeath				
4	Ferbane (Tisaron and Galen)	Oct. 17, 1819–July 24, 1865; June 21, 1876– Apr. 28, 1877	Nov. 26, 1819–Nov. 26, 1833	Dec. 19, 1821– Aug. 9, 1835; Mar. 6, 1855– Jan. 24, 1876	NLI	Pos. 4243
		1819–1984	1819–1833; 1877–1984	1821–1877; 1883–1889; 1929–1984	LDS	BFA 1279226 items 4–9
		1819–1899	1819–1899		IMA	
5	Lusmagh	1833–1899	1832–1899	1837–1882	IMA	
		1833–1925	1832–1925	1833–1925	LDS	BFA 1279215 items 28–30
		Dec. 5, 1827–May 3, 1829; Apr. 22, 1833–Dec. 29, 1880	July 8, 1832–Nov, 25, 1880	Jan. 5, 1837– Dec. 15, 1880	NLI	Pos. 2433
6	Clonbulloge	1819–1899	1808–1899		IMA	
		Nov. 7, 1819–June 14, 1869; June 20, 1869–Dec. 26, 1880	Jan. 2, 1808–June 14, 1869; July 1, 1869–Oct. 30, 1880		NLI	Pos. 4202
7	Daingean (Philipstown)	Aug. 12, 1795–Sept. 23, 1798; Jan. 6, 1820–Feb. 18, 1855; Nov. 4, 1850– Dec. 30, 1866; Jan. 1, 1867–Dec. 26, 1880	Jan. 7, 1820–May 3, 1855; Jan. 27, 1851– Dec. 2, 1866; Feb. 1, 1867–Nov. 24, 1880		NLI	Pos. 4202
		1820–1899	1820–1899	1880–1919	IMA	
8	Edenderry	1820–1899	1820–1899	1935–1981	IMA	
		Jan. 2, 1820–Dec. 29, 1820–Nov. 20, 1838; Jan. 6, 1839–Jan. 2, 1880	Jan. 9, 1820–Nov. 20, 1837; Sept. 17, 1838– Jan. 7, 1880		NLI	Pos. 4207
		1844–1899			IMA	
9	Killeigh	1844–1899	1844–1899		IMA	
		Apr. 23, 1844–Dec. 11, 1875; Jan. 1, 1876–Nov. 19, 1880	1859–July 30, 1875; Feb. 17, 1876–Nov. 19, 1880		NLI	Pos. 4203
10	Portarlington	Jan. 1, 1820–Nov. 22, 1846 (indexed); Nov. 25, 1846–Feb. 27, 1876 (indexed); Mar. 5, 1876– Dec. 26, 1880 (indexed)	Nov. 24, 1822–July 16, 1845; July 21, 1845–June 21, 1876; Jan. 14, 1876 –Nov. 27, 1880		NLI	Pos. 4205
		1820–1899	1820–1899	1904–1960	IMA	
11	Rhode	Jan. 29, 1829–June 16, 1879; June 22, 1879–Dec. 14, 1880; Jan. 3, 1866– Dec. 14, 1880	Aug. 4, 1829–Feb. 23, 1878 (gaps)		NLI	Pos. 4205
		1829–1899	1829–1899		IMA	
12	Birr and Loughkeen	May 5, 1838–Jan. 6, 1847; Jan. 3, 1847–Dec, 30 1880	May 5, 1838–Nov, 28, 1846; Jan. 7, 1847–Nov. 27, 1880		NLI	Pos. 2478
		1838–1913	1838–1913		TNFHF	
		1838–1899	1838–1899		IMA	
		See NLI			LDS	BFA 0926091

			OFFALY			
MAP	CHURCH	BAPTISMS	MARRIAGES	BURIALS	LOCATION	REFERENCE
13	Bournea and Corbally	See Tipperary North 23				
14	Dunkerrin (Moneygall)	Jan. 8, 1820–Aug. 21, 1873	Jan. 24, 1820–June 14, 1873		NLI	Pos. 2479
		1820–1911	1820–1899		IMA	
		See NLI			LDS	BFA 0979695 item 1
15	Kilcolman	Mar. 7, 1830–Nov. 27, 1869	Apr. 29, 1830–Feb. 24, 1868		NLI	Pos. 2479
		Mar. 7, 1830–Nov. 27, 1869	Apr. 29, 1830–Feb. 24, 1868		LDS	BFA 0979695 item 2
15	Aghaucon	1830–1899	1830–1899		IMA	
		Nov. 5, 1870–Dec. 14, 1880	Jan. 27, 1870–Oct. 1, 1880		NLI	Pos. 2479
16	Kinnity (Roscumroe)	See NLI			LDS	BFA 0979695 items 4–5
		1833–1899	1833–1899	1936–1983	IMA	
		Feb. 13, 1833–Dec. 21, 1880	Jan. 9, 1833–Nov. 1, 1871; Jan. 28, 1872–June 26, 1880		NLI	Pos. 2479
17	Roscrea	See Tipperary North 34				
18	Shinrone	Feb. 21, 1842–Feb. 7, 1876; Jan. 4, 1875–Dec. 13, 1880 (most of 1875 missing)	Apr. 10, 1842–Feb. 7, 1876		NLI	Pos. 2480
		1842–1899	1842–1899		IMA	
19	Ballinabrackey (Castlejordan)	See Meath 5				
20	Clara and Horseleap	See Westmeath 6				
21	Eglish	1809–1899	1819–1899	1807–1899	IMA	
		Jan. 1, 1809–Dec. 23, 1810; Feb. 13, 1819–May 16, 1852; May 23, 1852–Dec. 18, 1880	Feb. 21, 1819–Mar. 3, 1829; June 4, 1829–Nov. 27, 1880	Feb. 26, 1819–Apr. 18, 1829; June 15, 1837–May 12, 1846; Jan. 8, 1848–Mar. 16, 1849; Jan. 1851	NLI	Pos. 4175
22	Kilcormac (Balliboy and Killoughy)	Jan. 5, 1821–Dec. 30, 1833; Jan. 5, 1834–Dec. 27, 1880	June 29, 1821–Dec. 5, 1833; Jan. 10, 1834–Oct. 28, 1880	Feb. 1, 1826–Dec. 30, 1880	NLI	Pos. 4175
		See NLI			LDS	BFA 0926171
		1821–1899	1821–1899		IMA	
23	Rahan and Lynallly	July 6, 1810–Apr. 28, 1816; Jan. 2, 1822–Dec. 27, 1835; Jan. 1, 1836–Mar. 31, 1845; Apr. 5, 1845–Feb. 7, 1880	July 31, 1810–Feb, 28, 1816; Jan. 9, 1822–Jan. 29, 1880		NLI	Pos. 4174
		1810–1899	1810–1899		IMA	
24	Tubber	See Westmeath 21				
25	Tullamore	June 14, 1809–Feb. 20, 1810; Nov. 1, 1820–Feb. 24, 1822; Feb. 1, 1827–Jan. 31, 1836; Mar. 1, 1836–Dec. 26, 1880	Apr. 26, 1801–Sept. 29, 1807; Apr. 9–10, 1809; Nov. 2, 1820–Feb. 19, 1822; Feb. 1, 1827–Dec. 29, 1880		NLI	Pos. 4174

Map	Church	Baptisms	OFFALY Marriages	Burials	Location	Reference
25	Tullamore (*cont.*)	1819–1899 See NLI	1801–1899		IMA LDS	BFA 0926186
26	Seirkieran	Apr. 11, 1830–May 3, 1857; June 19, 1857– Dec. 17, 1880	July 4, 1830–June 14, 1857; July 9, 1857– Nov. 27, 1880		NLI	Pos. 5013
		1830–1901	1830–1899	1877–1902	IMA	
		1870–1880	1870–1880		LDS	BFA 0979695 item 3

ROSCOMMON

ACHONRY DIOCESE
 1 Castlemore & Kilcolman

ARDAGH & CLONMACNOISE DIOCESE
 2 Kilronan (Arigna)

CLONFERT DIOCESE
 3 Creagh
 4 Taghmaconnell

ELPHIN DIOCESE
 5 Aganagh
 6 Ardcarne & Tumna (Cootehall)
 7 Athleague & Fuerty
 8 Ballintober & Ballymoe
 9 Boyle & Kilbryan
 10 Cloontuskert
 11 Dysart & Tisrara
 12 Elphin & Creeve
 13 Geevagh
 14 Kilbegnet & Glinsk
 15 Kilbride (Fourmilehouse)
 16 Kilcorkery & Frenchpark
 17 Kilgalss & Rooskey
 18 Kilkeevan (Castlerea)
 19 Killukin & Killumod (Croghan)
 20 Kilmore & Aughrim
 21 Kilnamanagh
 22 Kiltoom (Ballybay)
 23 Loughglynn (Lisacul)
 24 Ogulla & Baslick
 25 Oran (Cloverhill)
 26 Roscommon & Kilteevan
 27 St John's (Knockcroghery)

 28 St Peter's & Drum (Athlone)
 29 Strokestown
 30 Tarmonbarry
 31 Tibohine (Fairymount)

TUAM DIOCESE
 32 Kiltullagh
 33 Moore

MAP	CHURCH	BAPTISMS	ROSCOMMON MARRIAGES	BURIALS	LOCATION	REFERENCE
1	Castlemore and Kilcolman	See Mayo 4				
2	Kilronan	Jan. 1, 1824–July 27, 1829; Jan. 1, 1835–Mar. 25, 1876	Oct. 24, 1823–June 10, 1829; Jan. 7, 1835–Sept. 16, 1872	Jan. 16, 1835– July 18, 1872	NLI	Pos. 4242
		1824–1900	1823–1900	1835–1872	RHGC	
		1824–1829; 1835–1976	1823–1829; 1835–1872; 1877–1984	1835–1872	LDS	BFA 1279224 items 7–12
3	Creagh (Ballinasloe)	See East Galway 5				
4	Taughma-connell	July 31, 1842–Dec. 15, 1880	Jan. 13, 1863–Aug. 19, 1880		LDS	BFA 0926061
		1842–1900	1842 [*sic*]–1900		RHGC	
		July 31, 1842–Dec. 15, 1880	Jan. 13, 1863–Aug. 19, 1880		NLI	Pos. 2432
5	Aghanagh	See Sligo				
6	Ardcarne & Tumna (Cootehall)	Mar. 26, 1843–Mar. 25, 1861; Apr. 7, 1861–Aug. 4, 1869; Apr. 29, 1869–Dec. 24, 1880	Apr. 6, 1843–June 3, 1860; Apr. 14, 1861–Sept. 23, 1880		NLI	Pos. 4612
		See NLI			LDS	BFA 0989746
		1843–1900	1843–1900		RHGC	
7	Athleague	1842–1900	1863–1900		EGFHS	
		1808–1900	1808–1900	1808–1837	RHGC	
		Jan. 4, 1808–May 10, 1828; Aug. 20, 1834–Sept. 1835; Oct. 12, 1835–July 25, 1864; Jan. 8, 1865–Dec. 23, 1880	June 23, 1808–Feb. 11, 1834; Mar. 15, 1836–Aug. 25, 1865; Jan. 26, 1865–Mar. 5, 1878	Jan. 3, 1807–1837	NLI	Pos. 4613
8	Ballintubber and Ballymoe (Ballinakill and Kilcrone)	Dec. 21, 1831–Dec. 26, 1863 (poor condition); Feb. 18, 1840–Nov. 12, 1865; Feb. 26, 1864–Nov. 25, 1880	Aug. 7, 1831–Jan. 17, 1864; Feb. 15, 1840–Oct. 14, 1850; Apr. 23, 1855–Sept. 16, 1862; Jan. 12, 1863–Aug. 5, 1880		NLI	Pos. 4618
		1831–1900	1831–1900		RHGC	
9	Boyle	1793–1900 See NLI	1792–1900	1848–1864	RHGC LDS	BFA 0989743 items 1–3
		Feb. 13, 1793–May 13, 1796; Mar. 13, 1803–Mar. 1806; Jan. 4–Mar. 9, 1811; Apr. 18, 1814–Sept. 30, 1827; Sept. 2, 1827–June 27, 1848; July 1, 1848–Sept. 18, 1864; Sept. 30, 1864–Dec. 29, 1880	Nov. 13, 1792 –Jan. 23, 1797; July 1803–June 1804; July 4, 1808–Dec. 30, 1827; Sept. 24, 1828 –June 16, 1848; July 3, 1848–June 30, 1864; Oct. 6, 1864–Set. 25, 1880	July 2, 1848– Sept. 18, 1964	NLI	Pos. 4607, 4608
10	Clontuskert	See NLI			LDS	BFA 0989747
		Jan. 3, 1865–Nov. 7, 1880; Aug. 23, 1874–Nov. 16, 1878 (Kilgefin);	Feb. 9, 1865–Feb. 22, 1879; Jan. 18, 1875–Feb. 6, 1879		NLI	Pos. 4612
		1865–1900	1865–1900		RHGC	
11	Dysart	July 6, 1850–Oct. 26, 1862; Dec. 7, 1862–Dec. 30, 1880; Jan. 6, 1865–Dec. 18, 1871;	Dec. 23, 1862–Aug. 31, 1880; Feb. 2, 1865–July 9, 1870 (Tisara)		NLI	Pos. 4616

→

Map	Church	Baptisms	ROSCOMMON Marriages	Burials	Location	Reference
11	Dysart	1850–1900	1862–1900	1862–1865	RHGC	
		See NLI			LDS	BFA 0989755
12	Elphin	June 11, 1807–Dec. 23, 1808; Dec. 10, 1808–Feb. 16, 1810; Jan. 1, 1809–July 21, 1815; May 23, 1810–Apr. 29, 1818; Aug. 1, 1818–Sept. 26, 1825; Mar. 9, 1825–Oct. 13, 1843; Nov. 12, 1841–July 28, 1860; Jan. 13, 1866–Nov. 19, 1880	May 6, 1807–Sept. 11, 1808; Dec. 10, 1808–Dec. 21, 1824; May 3, 1824–Oct. 4, 1830; Mar. 31, 1864–Dec. 20, 1880		NLI	Pos. 4609, 4610
		1808–1900	1807–1900	1807–1838	RHGC	
13	Geevagh	See Sligo 16				
14	Kilbegnet	1836–1900	1836–1900	1836–1839	RHGC	
		Sept. 5, 1836–Jan. 28, 1846; Nov. 2, 1846 (?)–June 22, 1848; Mar. 15, 1849–Sept. 23, 1866; Oct. 6, 1866–Dec. 26, 1880	Nov. 1, 1836–Apr. 24, 1865; July 6, 1865–Nov. 1, 1880	Sept. 14, 1836–Sept. 20, 1839	NLI	Pos. 4620
15	Kilbride	See NLI			LDS	BFA 0989749 items 1–2
		July 12, 1835–Sept. 6, 1849; Apr. 12, 1868–Dec. 12, 1880	Sept. 10, 1838–Oct. 15, 1846		NLI	Pos. 4614
		1835–1900	1835–1900		RHGC	
16	Kilcorkery and Frenchpark (Belenagare)	Jan. 7, 1865–Dec. 27, 1880			NLI	Pos. 4618
		1865–1900	1865–1900		RHGC	
17	Kilglass	1865–1900	1865–1900		RHGC	
		Oct. 20, 1865–Dec. 24, 1880			NLI	Pos. 4611
18	Kilkeevin	1804–1900	1804–1900	1805–1855	RHGC	
		Nov. 15, 1804–May 15, 1809; Jan. 17, 1816–Aug. 31, 1819; Jan. 6, 1826–Jan. 23, 1840; Jan. 4, 1840–Jan. 28, 1860; Jan. 1, 1860–Dec. 31, 1864; Jan. 1, 1865–Jan. 27, 1878; Jan. 1878–Dec. 27, 1880	Nov. 17, 1804–July 31, 1809; Jan. 15, 1816–Apr. 27, 1820; Oct. 28, 1838–Dec. 29, 1839; May 20, 1839–Jan. 23, 1860; Jan. 11, 1860–Nov. 15, 1864; Feb. 20, 1805–May 6, 1809; Jan. 26, 1816–Oct. 4, 1819; Jan. 1, 1852–1855		NLI	Pos. 4619
19	Killucan	See NLI			LDS	BFA 0989741 items 1–4
		1811–1900	1825–1900	1820–1826	RHGC	
		June 24, 1811–June 27, 1833; July 4, 1833–June 24, 1850; June 24, 1850–Nov. 27, 1864; Dec. 4, 1864–Dec. 26, 1880	Apr. 7, 1825–June 17, 1833; July 11, 1833–Dec. 5, 1850; Jan.16, 1851–Oct. 9, 1864; Nov. 24, 1864–Nov. 13, 1880	Oct. 11, 1820–Mar. 4, 1826	NLI	Pos. 4606
20	Kilmore and Aughrim	Aug. 13, 1816–Dec. 23, 1837; Feb. 27, 1825–Feb. 2, 1860; Jan. 18, 1865–Dec. 27, 1880; Jan. 21, 1865–Dec. 31, 1880 (Kilmore and Clonaff);	Aug. 21, 1816–Dec. 9, 1837; Mar. 18, 1825–Nov. 19, 1859; Jan. 9, 1865–Sept. 13, 1880; Feb. 12, 1865–Oct. 4, 1880 (Kilmore)		NLI	Pos. 4610, 4611
		1816–1900	1816–1900		RHGC	→

MAP	CHURCH	BAPTISMS	ROSCOMMON MARRIAGES	BURIALS	LOCATION	REFERENCE
21	Kilnamanagh (& Estersnow) Ballinameen	Nov. 20, 1859–July 22, 1871; Sept. 3, 1871–Dec. 14, 1880	Feb. 5, 1860–Oct. 31, 1880		NLI	Pos. 4605
		1859–1900	1860–1900		RHGC	
		See NLI			LDS	BFA 0989738 items 1–3
22	Kiltomb	See NLI			LDS	BFA 0989751 items 3–5
		1835–1900	1835–1900	1837–1865	RHGC	
		Oct. 11, 1835–May 26, 1845; Apr. 1, 1848–Dec. 26, 1864	Oct. 20, 1835–July 2, 1846; Jan. 16, 1848–Dec. 27, 1864; Jan. 9, 1865–Nov. 19, 1880	June 24, 1837–Mar. 31, 1845; Jan. 15, 1857–May 17, 1862; Jan. 6–Nov. 23, 1865	NLI	Pos. 4617
23	Loughglynn	See NLI			LDS	BFA 0989753 items 1–3
		Mar. 10, 1817–Nov. 20, 1826; Dec. 15, 1829–July 30, 1835; July 6, 1835–Nov. 24, 1840; Dec. 17, 1849–Apr. 17, 1863; Jan. 1, 1865–Mar. 10, 1878; Jan. 10, 1865–May 19, 1867 (Lisacul and Erritt); Feb. 10, 1878–Dec. 19, 1880 (Lisacul and Erritt)	Apr. 10, 1817–Mar. 24, 1827; Feb. 10, 1836–Apr. 24, 1840; Dec. 23, 1849–Feb. 16, 1858; Jan. 11, 1865–Oct. 18, 1880; Jan. 30, 1865–May 5, 1867	Jan.14, 1850–June 18, 1854; 1868–1880	NLI	Pos. 4617, 4618
		1817–1900	1817–1900	1850–1880	RHGC	
24	Kilmurry (Tulsk)	1865–1900	1865–1900		RHGC	
		Jan. 15, 1865–Sept. 7, 1880	Feb. 8, 1869–Feb. 9, 1880 (?)		NLI	Pos. 4611
24	Ogulla	1865–1900	1864–1900		RHGC	
		Jan. 7, 1865–Dec. 26, 1880	Jan. 28, 1864–May 6, 1880		NLI	Pos. 4611
25	Oran	No registers microfilmed			NLI	
		1864–1900	1864–1900		RHGC	
26	Roscommon and Kilteevan	See NLI			LDS	BFA 0989748 items 4–6
		1837–1900	1820–1900	1821–1824	RHGC	
		Oct. 1, 1837–Sept. 22, 1864; Mar. 26, 1864–Dec. 30, 1880	Jan. 10, 1820–Aug. 27, 1864		NLI	Pos. 4614
27	St John's (Killinvoy)	July 26, 1841–July 7, 1859; Jan. 8– Feb. 19, 1860; May 25, 1854–Sept. 25, 1864; Oct. 1, 1864–Dec. 20, 1880	July 17, 1841–Feb. 15, 1858; Nov. 9, 1854–Sept. 24, 1864; Nov. 8, 1864–Nov. 7, 1880	1854–1880	NLI	Pos. 4617
		1841–1900	1841–1900	1854–1881	RHGC	
		See NLI			LDS	BFA 0989752 items 1–4
28	St Peter's & Drum (Athlone)	1789–1900	1789–1900	1789–1880	RHGC	
		See NLI			LDS	BFA 0989750
		Jan. 4, 1798–Feb. 24, 1810; Feb. 25, 1810–Jan. 31, 1845; Feb. 1, 1845–Sept. 30, 1864; Oct. 2, 1864–Aug. 12, 1877; Aug. 12, 1877–Dec. 31, 1880	Jan. 7, 1789–Jan. 12, 1817; Jan. 14, 1817–Feb. 4, 1845; Mar. 28, 1845–Sept. 18, 1864; Oct. 3, 1864–Nov. 22, 1880	Jan. 3, 1789–Dec. 15, 1816; Jan. 5, 1817–May 25, 1854; July 16, 1845–Oct. 26, 1880	NLI	Pos. 4603, 4604 items 1–3

Map	Church	Baptisms	Marriages	Burials	Location	Reference
			ROSCOMMON			
29	Strokestown	1830–1900	1830–1900		RHGC	
		See NLI			LDS	BFA 0989745 items 1–6
		Oct. 17, 1830–May 31, 1835; July 5, 1835–Jan. 12, 1846; Jan. 6, 1831– Feb. 16, 1833 (Lisonuffy and Cloonfinlough); June 24, 1842–Dec. 29, 1842; Dec. 14, 1851–Nov. 1, 1852; Nov. 20, 1853–Dec. 23, 1864; May 3, 1857– Nov. 30, 1862; Apr. 15, 1865–Nov. 18, 1866; Jan. 1, 1865–Dec. 30, 1880	Oct. 24, 1830–June 15, 1835; June 17, 1833– Oct. 30, 1864; Oct. 18, 1830–May 30, 1833 (Lisonuffy and Cloonfinlough); July 6, 1835–Sept. 27, 1849 (Lisonuffy and Cloonfinlough); Jan. 9, 1965–Nov. 11, 1880		NLI	Pos. 4608, 4609
30	Tarmonbarry	1865–1900	1865–1900		RHGC	
		Jan. 22, 1865–Dec. 23, 1880; Jan. 6, 1865–Dec. 19, 1880 (Lisonuffy and Bumlin)	Jan. 26, 1865–Dec. 31, 1880		NLI	Pos. 4611
31	Tibohine	1833–1900	1833–1900		RHGC	
		Jan. 1, 1833–Sept. 24, 1864; May 5, 1875–Dec. 18, 1880	Jan. 7, 1833–June 11, 1864; Feb. 7, 1865–Apr. 25, 1880		NLI	Pos. 4619. The microfilm of the earlier records is missing
32	Kiltulla	1839–1900	1839–1900		RHGC	
		See NLI			LDS	BFA 0926226
		Sept. 11, 1839–Oct. 27, 1860; Nov. 11, 1860–Nov. 21, 1880	Aug. 25, 1839–Oct. 7, 1860; Nov. 19, 1860– Apr. 16, 1874; Jan. 3, 1877–Dec. 26, 1880		NLI	Pos. 4212
33	Moore	1876–1938	1877–1907		LDS	BFA 1279214 items 9–10
		1876–1900	1876–1900		RHGC	
		Sept. 17, 1876–Dec. 26, 1880	Jan. 22, 1877–Nov. 19, 1880		NLI	Pos. 4220

SLIGO

ACHONRY DIOCESE
1. Achonry
2. Ballysadare & Kilvarnet
3. Castlemore & Kilcolman
4. Cloonacool
5. Curry
6. Drumrat
7. Emlafad & Kilmorgan
8. Kilfree & Killaraght
9. Killoran
10. Kilmacteigue
11. Kilshalvey, Kilturra, Cloonoghill

ARDAGH & CLONMACNOISE DIOCESE
12. Killenummery & Killery

ELPHIN DIOCESE
13. Aghanagh (Ballinafad)
14. Ahamlish
15. Drumcliffe
16. Geevagh
17. Riverstown
18. Sligo

KILLALA DIOCESE
19. Castleconnor
20. Easkey
21. Kilglass

22. Kilmacshalgan
23. Kilmoremoy
24. Skreen & Dromard
25. Templeboy

KILMORE DIOCESE
26. Glenade
27. Kinlough

Map	Church	Baptisms	SLIGO Marriages	Burials	Location	Reference
1	Achonry	1878–1899	1865–1905		SHGC	
		1878–Oct. 8, 1880	Aug. 3, 1865–Aug. 16, 1880		NLI	Pos. 4227
		1878–1908	1864–1942		LDS	BFA 1279231 items 20–21
2	Ballysodare and Kilvarnet	Apr. 25, 1842–Aug. 14, 1853; Feb. 28, 1858–Dec. 26, 1880	Jan. 14, 1858–Dec. 5, 1880		NLI	Pos. 4227
		1842–1899	1858–1899		SHGC	
		1842–1897	1858–1933		LDS	BFA 1279230 items 10–13
3	Castlemore and Kilcolman	See Mayo 4				
4	Cloonacool	1859–1908	1859–1921		LDS	BFA 1279230/1 item 18/1–2
		1859–1899	1859–1899		SHGC	
		Oct. 27, 1859–Nov. 9, 1880	Oct. 9, 1859–Nov. 9, 1880		NLI	Pos. 4227
5	Curry	1867–1923	1867–1903		LDS	BFA 1279231 items 14–15

→

MAP	CHURCH	BAPTISMS	SLIGO MARRIAGES	BURIALS	LOCATION	REFERENCE
5	Curry (*cont.*)	Oct. 6, 1867–Dec. 25, 1880	Nov. 3, 1867–Dec. 15, 1880		NLI	Pos. 4227
		1867–1899	1867–1899		SHGC	
6	Drumrat	1843–1899	1842–1899		SHGC	
		Nov. 12, 1843–June 24, 1847; Sept. 25, 1842–Mar. 6, 1855; Jan. 10, 1874–July 3, 1880	Jan. 12, 1842–May 5, 1851; Dec. 1872–May 15, 1881		NLI	Pos. 4228
7	Emlefad and Kilmorgan	July 4, 1856–Oct. 7, 1877; Nov. 27, 1874–Dec. 26, 1880	Aug. 12, 1824–Jan. 7, 1866; Feb. 11, 1866–Feb. 22, 1875		NLI	Pos. 4228
		1824–1899	1824–1899		SHGC	
8	Kilfree and Killaraght	May 4, 1873–Nov. 27, 1880	Feb. 19, 1844–Dec. 11, 1868; May 22, 1868–Nov. 20, 1880		NLI	Pos. 4227
		1873–1899	1844–1899		SHGC	
9	Killoran	1878–1899	1846–1899		SHGC	
		Apr. 19, 1878–Dec. 24, 1880	Apr. 22, 1846–Nov. 11, 1880		NLI	Pos. 4228
10	Kilmactigue	Apr. 8, 1845–Dec. 27, 1856; Jan. 5, 1857–June 18, 1864; July 1, 1864–July 24, 1880	Jan. 23, 1848–Sept. 4, 1880		NLI	Pos. 4226
		1845–1899	1848–1848		SHGC	
11	Kilshalvey	Jan. 3, 1842–Dec. 22, 1877; Mar. 31, 1860–Aug. 12, 1877	Apr. 30, 1833–Apr. 18, 1876		NLI	Pos. 4228
		1840–1908	1833–1930 (gaps)		LDS	BFA 1279233 items 10–11; 09260018
		1842–1899	1840–1899		SHGC	
12	Killenummery	See Leitrim 8				
13	Aghanagh	1803 –1900			RHGC	
		See NLI			LDS	BFA 0989739, 1–2; 0989740 items 1–4
		1803–1899	1860–1899		SHGC	
		May 9, 1803–Jan. 19, 1808 (trans.); Oct. 13, 1816– Dec. 22, 1818 (trans.); Jan. 3, 1821–Sept. 20, 1825 (trans.); Nov. 13, 1803–Nov. 12, 1807; 1817 –Nov. 1818; Jan. 1821–Nov. 1, 1841; Jan. 1844–1846; 1848–1852; 1856–1864; 1864–1880	Jan. 11, 1800–June 15, 1802; Apr. 7, 1829–Mar. 8, 1850; Nov. 1858–Feb. 27, 1863; Nov. 20, 1864 –Oct. 10, 1880	Mar. 3, 1800– Mar. 12, 1802; July 12–Sept. 16, 1816; Nov. 30, 1822–Sept. 20, 1846; Nov. 10, 1858–Oct. 17, 1874	NLI	Pos. 4606
14	Ahamlish	Nov. 27, 1796–May 28, 1829; Jan. 4, 1831–Nov. 29, 1835; Sept. 9, 1836–Nov. 25, 1845; Jan. 2, 1846–Dec. 31, 1863; Jan. 8, 1864–Mar. 19, 1879	Dec. 3, 1796–Dec. 27, 1830; Jan. 22, 1831–Sept. 22, 1857; Nov. 2, 1857–Dec. 29, 1863; Jan. 18, 1864–June 3, 1880	Nov. 26, 1796– Oct. 1822; Jan. 13, 1827–Sept. 24, 1830; Jan. 3, 1831–July 24, 1845	NLI	Pos. 4602
		1796–1899	1796–1899	1796–1845	SHGC	

			SLIGO			
MAP	CHURCH	BAPTISMS	MARRIAGES	BURIALS	LOCATION	REFERENCE
15	Drumcliff	1841–1899	1865–1899		SHGC	
		May 2, 1841–Dec. 31, 1864 (transcript); Jan. 1, 1865–May 2, 1880	Jan. 15, 1865–Nov. 28, 1880		LDS	BFA 0989735 items 1–3
		May 2, 1841–Dec. 31, 1864 (transcript); Jan. 1, 1865–May 2, 1880	Jan. 15, 1865–Nov. 28, 1880		NLI	Pos. 4603
16	Geevagh	1851–1899	1851–1899		SHGC	
		Feb. 25, 1873–May 20, 1880	Jan. 13, 1851–Nov. 25, 1880		NLI	Pos. 4607
17	Riverstown (Taunagh)	Nov. 1, 1803–Dec. 28, 1834; May 3, 1836–Dec. 27, 1864; Jan. 3, 1865–Dec. 29, 1880	Nov. 28, 1803–Jan. 25, 1809; May 12, 1836–Dec. 12, 1862; Jan. 29, 1865–Dec. 29, 1880	June 15, 1836–Jan. 21, 1843	NLI	Pos. 4604
		See NLI		June 15, 1836–Jan. 21, 1843	LDS	BFA 0989737 items 1–4
		1803–1899	1803–1899	1836–1843	SHGC	
18	Sligo: St John's	See NLI			LDS	BFA 0989736 items 1–4
		Oct. 3, 1858–Feb. 6, 1864; Feb. 7, 1864–May 24, 1870; June 23, 1870–Apr. 1, 1877	Oct. 7, 1858–Dec. 21, 1880		NLI	Pos. 4615, 4616
		1831–1899	1831–1899	1831–1848	SHGC	
19	Castleconnor	1835–1880	1835–1880	1855–1880	LDS	BFA 1279204 items 1–2
		1835–1899	1835–1899	1847–1880	SHGC	
		Jan. 14, 1855–Dec. 26, 1880	Oct. 26, 1854–Nov. 2, 1880		NLI	Pos. 4230
20	Easkey	1864–1899	1868–1899		SHGC	
		June 1864–Dec. 28, 1880			NLI	Pos. 4230
21	Kilglass	1825–1899	1825–1899	1825–1867	SHGC	
		Oct. 17, 1825–July 7, 1867; Aug. 15, 1867–Dec. 28, 1880	Nov. 2, 1825–May 2, 1867; Nov. 21, 1867–Dec. 22, 1880	Nov. 2, 1825–June 15, 1867	NLI	Pos. 4229
22	Kilmacshalgan	See Templeboy (25)				
23	Kilmoremoy	1823–1900	1823–1900	1823–1931	MNFHRC	
		May 15, 1823–Oct. 14, 1836; May 9, 1849–July 16, 1849; July 23, 1851–Sept. 8, 1867; Feb. 2, 1868–Dec. 31, 1880	May 15, 1823–Oct. 4, 1842; Oct. 22, 1850–Feb. 4, 1868; Feb. 2, 1868–Dec. 31, 1880	Apr. 29, 1823–Aug. 12, 1836; Sept. 12, 1840–May 3, 1844	NLI	Pos. 4231
		1823–1852; 1850–1867; 1868–1879	1823–1842; 1849–1868	1823–1842	LDS	BFA 1279205 items 15–16; 1279205, 3
24	Skreen and Dromard	Jan. 1, 1823–Aug. 9, 1859; July 17, 1848–Sept. 29, 1877; Sept. 27, 1877–Dec. 31, 1880	Nov. 13, 1817–Feb. 16, 1860; Feb. 12, 1878–Dec. 11, 1880; July 12, 1848–Aug. 18, 1869	Sept. 25, 1825–Feb. 29, 1828	NLI	Pos. 4229
		1823–1892	1817–1899	1825–1828	SHGC	
		1817–1892	1835–1880	1853–1880	LDS	BFA 1279204 items 6–11; 0926025 ⟶

MAP	CHURCH	BAPTISMS	SLIGO MARRIAGES	BURIALS	LOCATION	REFERENCE
25	Templeboy	1815–1838; 1875–1880	1815–1838		LDS	BFA 1279204 items 13, 14
		1815–1899; 1868–1903 (Kilmacshalgan)	1815–1899; 1868–1891 (Kilmacshalgan)	1815–1833	SHGC	
		Sept. 5, 1815–Nov. 26, 1816; May 30, 1826–Nov. 13, 1838; June 21, 1868–Dec. 26, 1880 (Kilmacshalgan) Nov. 1, 1875–Dec. 15, 1880 (Templeboy)	Oct. 22, 1815–Dec. 28, 1837; Jan. 20, 1868–Oct. 23, 1880 (Kilmacshalgan) Dec. 2, 1875–Sept. 5, 1880 (Templeboy)		NLI	Pos. 4230
26		Glenade	See Leitrim 19			
27		Kinlough	See Leitrim 23			

TIPPERARY SOUTH

CASHEL & EMLY DIOCESE
1 Anacarty (Donohill)
2 Ballingarry
3 Bansha & Kilmoyler
4 Boherlahan & Dualla
5 Cashel
6 Clerihan
7 Clonoulty
8 Drangan
9 Emly
10 Fethard & Killusty
11 Galbally & Aherlow
12 Golden
13 Killenaule
14 Knockavilla
15 Lattin & Cullen
16 Mullinahone
17 New Inn
18 Oola & Solohead
19 Tipperary

WATERFORD & LISMORE DIOCESE
20 Ardfinnan
21 Ballylooby
22 Ballyneale
23 Ballyporeen
24 Cahir
25 Carrick-on-Suir
26 Clogheen

27 Kilsheelan (Gambonsfield)
28 Newcastle
29 Powerstown
30 St Mary's, Clonmel
31 SS Peter & Paul, Clonmel

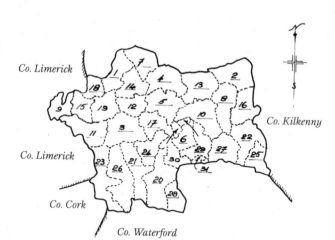

Map	Church	Baptisms	Marriages	Burials	Location	Reference
		TIPPERARY SOUTH				
1	Anacarty and Donohill	May 13, 1821–Oct. 1835; Oct. 2, 1835–Dec. 20, 1880	May, 13 1821–Feb. 11, 1839; Feb. 11, 1839–Oct. 28, 1880		NLI	Pos. 2496
		1804–1899	1805–1899		THU	
2	Ballingarry	1814–1900	1814–1900		THU	
		1842–1911	1842–1911		TNFHF	
		June 15, 1814–May 24, 1827; Aug. 30, 1827–Mar. 12, 1839; Mar. 12, 1839–Dec. 31, 1880	Apr. 19, 1814–Feb. 19, 1822; Jan. 8, 1826–July 16, 1837; Aug. 20, 1837 –Nov. 25, 1880		NLI	Pos. 2492
3	Bansha and Kilmoyler	Nov. 5, 1820–Jan. 13, 1855 (modern transcript); Jan. 15, 1855–Dec. 25, 1880	Jan. 22, 1822–Oct. 24, 1880 (modern transcript)		NLI	Pos. 2497
		1820–1899	1821–1899		THU	
4	Boherlahan and Dualla	Apr. 27, 1810–Dec. 20, 1823; Dec. 21, 1823–Dec. 28, 1839; Dec. 29, 1839–May 17, 1868	May 16, 1810–Jan. 21, 1824; Feb. 2, 1824–Jan. 30, 1840; Feb. 1, 1840–Feb. 24, 1868		NLI	Pos. 2504
		1736–1740; 1810–1900	1736–1740; 1810–1900		THU	
5	Cashel	Nov. 11, 1793–July 19, 1831; July 24, 1831–Dec. 23, 1839; Aug. 21, 1839–Mar. 31, 1866; Apr. 1, 1866–Dec. 16, 1880	Jan. 5, 1793–May 16, 1831; July 27, 1831–Nov. 22, 1880		NLI	Pos. 2501
		1793–1903	1793–1896		THU	
6	Clerihan	1852–1900	1852–1900		THU	
		Apr. 27, 1852–Dec. 25, 1880	Aug. 1, 1852–Aug. 7, 1880		NLI	Pos. 2501
7	Clonoulty	1804–1900	1804–1898		THU	
		Oct. 1, 1804–June 7, 1809; July 1809–June 10, 1821; June 20, 1821–Jan. 1, 1837; Jan. 9, 1856–Dec. 28, 1880	Oct. 7, 1804–June 7, 1809; Oct. 1, 1809–May 27, 1821; June 12, 1821–Nov. 4, 1836; Jan. 11, 1856 –Oct. 13, 1880	June 2, 1818–Apr. 25, 1821	NLI	Pos. 2502 to 1855; remainder on Pos. 2503
8	Drangan	1811–1898	1804–1898		THU	
		May 13, 1847–Dec. 28, 1880	Jan. 3, 1847–June 13, 1880		NLI	Pos. 2492 to 1846; remainder on Pos. 2493
9	Emly	July 31, 1810–May 4, 1839; May 10, 1839–Dec. 24, 1880	Apr. 27, 1809–Oct. 20, 1838; Jan. 26, 1839–Nov. 25, 1880		NLI	Pos. 2500
		1810–1899	1809–1898		THU	
10	Fethard and Killusty	Jan. 2, 1806–June 30, 1828; June 1, 1828–Feb. 27, 1835; Mar. 1, 1835–Jan. 30, 1847; Dec. 1, 1847–Dec. 25, 1880	Jan. 12, 1806–Apr. 27, 1820; Jan. 18, 1824–Jan. 9, 1838; Jan. 14, 1838–Nov. 11, 1880		NLI	Pos. 2504
		1806–1900	1806–1900		THU	
11	Galbally and Aherlow	Mar. 9, 1810–June 23, 1828 (July 1820–1821 missing); December 1828–June 1871	Oct. 1809–Aug. 34, 1880 (Mar. 1820–July 1821 missing)		NLI	Pos. 2499
		1810–1900	1809–1900		THU	
		1810–1900	1809–1900		LA	→

Map	Church	Baptisms	Marriages	Burials	Location	Reference
			TIPPERARY SOUTH			
12	Golden and Kilfeacle	May 20, 1833–Dec. 14, 1880	May 20, 1833–Nov. 7, 1880		NLI	Pos. 2503
		1833–1899	1833–1899		THU	
13	Killenaule and Moyglass	Dec. 25, 1742–Jan. 6, 1802; Jan. 2, 1814–Aug. 10, 1827; Aug. 10, 1827 –Feb. 29, 1852; Mar. 1, 1852–Dec. 28, 1880	Aug. 20, 1812–Sept. 19, 1827; Oct. 14, 1827– Nov. 29, 1851; Feb. 1, 1852–Nov. 25, 1880		NLI	Pos. 2494
		1742–1900	1741–1900		THU	
14	Knockavilla	May 10, 1834–Dec. 26, 1880	July 10, 1834–Nov. 15, 1880		NLI	Pos. 2503
		1834–1905	1834–1905		THU	
15	Latten and Cullen	1846–1899	1846–1899		THU	
		Dec. 4, 1846–Dec. 26, 1880	Sept. 10, 1846–Nov. 28, 1880		NLI	Pos. 2498
16	Mullinahone	July 3, 1809–Apr. 27, 1835; Apr. 30, 1835– Dec. 25, 1880	Feb. 26, 1810–Mar 3, 1835 (transcript); May 18, 1835–Sept. 23, 1880		NLI	Pos. 2488
		1810–1899	1810–1867		THU	
17	New Inn and Knockgraffon	Mar. 14, 1820– Mar. 31, 1847; Apr. 3, 1847 –Dec. 22, 1880	June 10, 1798–Nov. 26, 1834; Jan. 8, 1835– Oct. 2, 1880		NLI	Pos. 2502
		1820–1896	1798–1900		THU	
18	Oola and Sologhead	Oct. 18, 1809–Feb. 27, 1823; Mar. 2, 1823– Apr. 30, 1828; Feb. 25, 1837–Jan.23, 1854; Feb. 12, 1854–Dec. 31, 1880	Jan. 7, 1810–Nov. 24, 1828; Oct. 14, 1832– Jan. 30, 1854; Feb. 7, 1854–Nov. 27, 1880		NLI	Pos. 2498 to 1828; remainder on Pos. 2499
		1809–1880	1810–1880		LA	
		1809–1900	1810–1900		THU	
19	Tipperary	1780–1899	1793–1900		THU	
		Jan. 1, 1810–Sept. 30, 1822; Oct. 1, 1822; –Oct. 6, 1833; Jan. 1, 1833–Dec. 31, 1848 (transcript); Jan. 1849–Dec. 28, 1868; Jan. 11, 1869–Dec. 31, 1880	Feb. 11, 1793–May 20, 1809; Jan. 10, 1810– Nov. 30, 1844; Jan. 8, 1845–Nov. 25, 1880		NLI	Pos. 2495 to 1848; remainder on Pos. 2496
20	Ardfinnan	1810–1900	1817–1900		WH	
		Dec. 8, 1809–Nov. 30, 1826 (some pages missing); Jan. 24, 1827– June 26, 1845; Jan. 4, 1827–June 30, 1845; July 2, 1845–Dec. 31, 1880	Apr. 20. 1814 – Feb. 18, 1822; Aug. 3, 1845–Oct. 26, 1880		NLI	Pos. 2457
21	Ballylooby and Duhill	1828–1900	1828–1900		WH	
		May 25. 1828–Mar. 16, 1843; Mar. 18, 1843 –Jan. 14, 1862; Jan. 1, 1862–Dec. 27, 1880	May 25, 1828–July 14, 1880		NLI	Pos. 2457, 2458
22	Ballyneale and Grange-mockler	1839–1900	1839–1900		WH	
		Jan 2, 1839–Dec. 2, 1880			NLI	Pos. 2453

			TIPPERARY SOUTH			
MAP	CHURCH	BAPTISMS	MARRIAGES	BURIALS	LOCATION	REFERENCE
23	Ballyporeen (Temple-tenny)	Nov. 9, 1817–June 2, 1872; June 20, 1872 –Dec. 24, 1880	Jan. 25, 1818–Nov. 13, 1875; Feb. 7, 1876 –Nov. 28, 1880		NLI	Pos. 24
		1817–1900	1818–1900		WH	
24	Cahir	June 9, 1776–Mar. 10, 1793; Aug. 29, 1809 –Mar. 3, 1823; Mar. 9, 1823–Dec. 28, 1831; Jan. 25, 1832–Jan. 13, 1845; Jan. 1, 1845– Dec. 28, 1880	July 14, 1776–Nov. 28, 1835; Jan. 8, 1836–Oct. 1866; Nov. 3, 1864–Nov. 20, 1880		NLI	Pos. 2459, 2460
		1776–1900	1776–1900		WH	
25	Carrick–on –Suir	1788–1900	1788–1900		WH	
		Sept. 12, 1784–Sept. 30, 1787; Jan. 2, 1788–Apr. 24, 1803; May 31, 1805– Dec. 29, 1805; Jan. 3, 1806–July 2, 1819; Jan. 3, 1823–Oct. 10, 1826; Apr. 7, 1834–Apr. 6, 1845; Apr. 7, 1845–Dec. 23, 1864; Dec. 28, 1869– Dec. 26, 1880	Jan. 7, 1788 –Oct. 15, 1803; Jan. 10, 1806–Feb. 7, 1815; Jan. 7, 1823–Oct. 14, 1825; Jan. 8, 1826–Feb. 3, 1845; Jan. 30, 1845– Nov. 13, 1880		NLI	Pos. 2455, 2456, 2457
26	Clogheen	1778–1900	1814–1900		WH	
		Jan. 4, 1778–May 18, 1789 (some gaps); Mar. 17, 1809–June 5, 1814; June 1, 1815–July 20, 1851; Aug. 29, 1851– June, 4, 1868; Apr. 12, 1868–Dec. 27, 1880	July 11, 1814–Apr. 21, 1867		NLI	Pos. 2453, 2454
27	Gambons-field and Kilcash	1840–1900	1840–1900		WH	
		Jan. 1, 1840–Feb. 1, 1856; Feb. 16, 1856–Dec. 27, 1880	Jan. 11, 1840–Jan. 11, 1856; Jan. 14, 1856– Dec. 29, 1880		NLI	Pos. 2452, 2453
28	Newcastle	1814–1900	1822–1900		WH	
		July 1. 1814–Dec. 31, 1845; Jan. 1, 1846– Oct. 31, 1862; Nov. 2, 1862–Dec. 29, 1880	Jan. 7, 1822–Oct. 23, 1880		NLI	Pos. 2454
29	Powerstown	1808–1900	1808–1900		WH	
		Sept. 8, 1808–Oct. 18, 1845; Oct. 20, 1845 –Nov. 16, 1880	Aug. 11, 1808–Nov. 27, 1880		NLI	Pos. 2455
30	Clonmel: St Mary's	1790–1900	1798–1900		WH	
		Feb. 4, 1790–Dec. 26, 1790; Mar. 1, 1793–Dec. 31, 1793; Jan. 11, 1795– Mar. 28, 1797; Apr. 5, 1797– Aug. 5, 1823; Aug. 5, 1823– July 17, 1832; July 18, 1832–Dec. 28, 1842; Jan. 1, 1843–Jan. 7, 1874; Jan. 1, 1864–Sept. 20, 1878	Apr. 24, 1797–Feb. 10, 1836		NLI	Pos. 2460, 2461, 2462
31	Clonmel: SS Peter and Paul	1836–1900	1836–1900		WH	
		Feb. 11, 1836–Sept. 21, 1859; Sept. 21, 1859– Dec. 29, 1880	Feb. 11, 1836–Nov. 22, 1880		NLI	Pos. 2463

TIPPERARY NORTH

CASHEL & EMLY DIOCESE

1 Ballina
2 Ballinahinch
3 Borrisoleigh
4 Cappawhite
5 Doon
6 Drom & Inch
7 Gortnahoe
8 Holycross (Ballycahill)
9 Kilcommon
10 Loughmore
11 Moycarkey
12 Newport
13 Templemore
14 Templetuohy & Moyne
15 Thurles
16 Upperchurch

KILLALOE DIOCESE

17 Birr
18 Borrisokane
19 Castleconnell
20 Castletownarra

21 Cloughprior & Monsea
22 Cloughjordan
23 Couraganeen (Bournea)
24 Dunkerrin (Moneygall)
25 Kilbarron (Terryglass)
26 Kilnaneave & Templederry
27 Kyle & Knock

28 Lorrha & Dorrha
29 Nenagh
30 Shinrone
31 Silvermines (Kilmore)
32 Toomevara
33 Youghalarra
34 Roscrea

TIPPERARY NORTH

Map	Church	Baptisms	Marriages	Burials	Location	Reference
1	Ballina	Mar. 1832–Nov. 25, 1871	May, 1832–Feb.6, 1872		NLI	Pos. 2507
		1832–1911	1832–1872		THU	
		1832–1903	1832–1903		TNFHF	
2	Ballinahinch and Killoscully	1839–1899	1853–1899		TNFHF	
		July 7, 1839–Feb. 7, 1874	Jan. 26, 1853–Feb. 4, 1874		NLI	Pos. 2503
		1839–1899	1853–1899		THU	
3	Borrisoleigh	1814–1900	1814–1898		THU	
		Nov. 9, 1814–Dec. 31, 1826; Jan. 2, 1827–July 31, 1843; Aug. 1, 1843–Dec. 24, 1880	Nov. 24, 1814–Dec. 2, 1826; Jan. 17, 1827–July 31, 1843; Aug. 1843–Nov. 15, 1880		NLI	Pos. 2488 to 1826; remainder on Pos. 2489
4	Cappawhite	Oct. 5, 1815–Jan. 29, 1846; Feb. 4, 1846–Nov. 13, 1878	Feb. 13, 1804–Jan. 25, 1846; Feb. 3, 1846–Oct. 6, 1878		NLI	Pos. 2497
		1815–1900	1803–1900		THU	
5	Doon and Castletown	1824–1900	1839–1900		THU	
		1824–1900	1839–1900		LA	
		Mar. 25, 1824–Dec. 27, 1874	Jan. 20, 1839–Feb. 17, 1874		NLI	Pos. 2497
6	Drom and Inch	Mar, 25, 1827–Aug. 24, 1840; Aug. 18, 1840–Dec. 26, 1880	May 5, 1827–Oct. 16, 1880		NLI	Pos. 2491
		1809–1900	1807–1880		THU	
7	Gortnahoe	1805–1900	1805–1900		THU	
		Sept. 10, 1805–Dec. 20, 1830; Apr. 1, 1831–Nov. 28, 1843; Jan. 28, 1844–Aug. 27, 1878	Oct. 3, 1805–Nov. 27, 1830; Oct. 30, 1831–Dec. 31, 1843; Jan. 15, 1844–Oct. 7, 1880		NLI	Pos. 2493

Map	Church	Baptisms	Marriages	Burials	Location	Reference
		TIPPERARY NORTH				
8	Holycross and Ballycahill	Jan. 2, 1835–Oct. 16, 1878	Jan. 1, 1835–Dec, 29, 1878		NLI	Pos. 2493
		1835–1900	1835–1900		THU	
9	Kilcommon	Mar. 7, 1813–Jan. 30, 1840; Feb. 1, 1840–Apr. 23, 1847; May 1, 1847–Dec. 31, 1880	June 12, 1813–Jan. 26, 1840; May 30, 1840–Apr. 28, 1847; May 2, 1847–Nov. 25, 1880		NLI	Pos. 2506 to 1846; remainder on Pos. 2507
		1813–1895	1813–1899		THU	
		1813–1900	1813–1900		TNFHF	
10	Loughmore and Castleiny	1798–1899	1798–1899		THU	
		Mar. 25, 1798–July 28, 1840; Aug. 1, 1840–Dec. 29, 1880	Apr. 16, 1798–June 26, 1840; Sept. 6, 1840–Oct. 20, 1880		NLI	Pos. 2490
11	Moycarkey	1793–1900	1793–1900		THU	
		Oct. 13, 1793–Nov. 19, 1796; Jan. 1, 1800–Feb. 3, 1800; 1801 (a few entries); Jan. 2, 1801–Oct. 22, 1809; June 7, 1810–Nov. 22, 1810; Jan. 12, 1817–Apr. 11, 1818; Jan. 2, 1830–Jan. 24, 1833; Feb. 4, 1833–June 22, 1854; July 1, 1854–Dec. 30, 1880	Oct. 6, 1793–Oct. 16, 1796; Jan. 12, 1810–Nov. 8, 1817; Jan. 17, 1830–Feb. 3, 1822; Feb. 5, 1833–May 2, 1854; Sept. 13, 1854–Oct. 26, 1880		NLI	Pos. 2488
12	Newport	Oct. 18, 1795–Sept. 30, 1809; July 16, 1812–Mar. 18, 1830; Feb. 28, 1813–May 20, 1839; Mar. 20, 1830–May 25, 1847; May 27, 1847–July 17, 1859; Nov. 1, 1859–Dec. 31, 1880	Apr. 20, 1795–Feb. 8, 1809; July 26, 1812–Nov. 28, 1829; Feb. 28, 1813–May 20, 1839; Jan. 15, 1830–May 23, 1847; June 5, 1847–Feb. 24, 1859; Nov. 2, 1859–Dec. 9, 1880	Mar. 24, 1795–May 18, 1844; Feb. 28, 1813–May 20, 1839	NLI	Pos. 2505 to 1847; remainder on Pos. 3506
		1795–1900	1795–1900		THU	
13	Templemore	Aug. 16, 1807–Nov. 30, 1821; Aug. 16, 1807–Nov. 25, 1821 (transcript); Nov. 16, 1809–Jan. 31, 1829; Nov. 28, 1821–Nov. 19, 1835; Jan. 10, 1836–Oct. 28, 1849; Nov. 4, 1849–Dec. 27, 1880	Nov. 15, 1807–Apr. 10, 1825; Nov. 30, 1809–Jan. 13, 1820; Feb. 11, 1834–Oct. 23, 1849; Nov. 10, 1849–Sept. 12, 1880		NLI	Pos. 2491 baptism to 1835, marriages to 1825; remainder on Pos. 2492
		1809–1900	1809–1900		THU	
14	Templetuohy and Moyne	Jan. 4, 1809–Mar. 28, 1848; Apr. 2, 1848–Dec. 31, 1880	Feb. 1804–Nov. 8, 1880		NLI	Pos. 2491
		1809–1900	1804–1900		THU	
15	Thurles	1795–1924	1795–1924		THU	
		Mar. 9, 1795–Jan. 19, 1810; July 9, 1805–Nov. 17, 1821; Aug. 10, 1822–Dec. 29, 1833; Jan. 1, 1834–Apr. 28, 1870	Apr. 13, 1795–Nov. 18, 1804; Jan. 7, 1805–Feb. 15, 1820; Aug. 13, 1822–Dec. 30, 1833; Jan. 13, 1834–Feb. 14, 1870		NLI	Pos. 2489 to 1833; remainder on Pos. 2490
16	Upperchurch and Drombane	Oct. 27, 1829–Dec. 15, 1846; Dec. 8, 1846–Feb. 29, 1876	Feb. 12, 1829–Nov. 15, 1846; Jan. 24, 1847–Feb. 29, 1876		NLI	Pos. 2495
		1829–1900	1829–1900		THU	→

Map	Church	Baptisms	Marriages	Burials	Location	Reference
		TIPPERARY NORTH				
17	Birr and Loughkeen	May 5, 1838–Jan. 6, 1847; Jan. 3, 1847–Dec. 30, 1880	May 5, 1838–Nov. 28, 1846; Jan. 7, 1847–Nov. 27, 1880		NLI	Pos. 2478
		1838–1899	1838–1899		IMA	
		See NLI			LDS	BFA 0926091
		1838–1913	1838–1913		TNFHF	
18	Borrisokane	June 24, 1821–Dec. 29, 1835; Jan. 1, 1836–Sept. 3, 1844; Sept. 8, 1844–Dec. 30, 1880;	July 30, 1821–Nov. 28, 1835 (many pages illegible); Jan. 21, 1836–Jan., 21, 1844; Oct. 2, 1844–Nov. 16, 1880		NLI	Pos. 2483
		1821–1911	1821–1911		TNFHF	
19	Castleconnell	See Limerick				
20	Castletownarra (Portroe)	Nov. 11, 1849–Dec. 13, 1880 (transcript)	Nov. 18, 1849–Nov. 14, 1880 (transcript)		NLI	Pos. 2483
		1849–1911	1849–1911		TNFHF	
21	Cloughprior and Monsea	1834–1911	1834–1911		TNFHF	
		Feb. 1, 1834–Dec. 9, 1865	Feb. 2, 1834–Nov. 13, 1870		NLI	Pos. 2481
22	Cloughjordan	1833–1911	1833–1911		TNFHF	
		Aug. 25, 1833–Nov. 3, 1858; Nov. 8, 1858–Dec. 26, 1880	May 22, 1833–Nov. 17, 1858; Jan. 7, 1859–Nov. 25, 1880		NLI	To 1858, Pos. 2481; remainder 2482
23	Couraganeen (Bournea and Corbally)	July 10, 1836–Dec. 1, 1866; Jan. 27, 1867–Dec. 30, 1880 (1873 missing)	June 28, 1836–Dec. 1, 1866; Jan. 27, 1867–May 30, 1880 (1873 missing)		NLI	Pos. 2478
		1836–1866	1836–1866		TNFHF	
24	Dunkerrin (Moneygall)	See Offaly 14				
25	Kilbarron (Terryglass)	See NLI			LDS	BFA 0926102
		July 1, 1827–May 4, 1837 (transcript); May 6, 1837 –July 7, 1846 (transcript); July 12, 1846–Dec. 10, 1880 (transcript)	Sept. 11, 1827–Nov. 20, 1880		NLI	Pos. 2482
		1827–1911	1827–1911		TNFHF	
26	Kilnaneave and Templederry	Sept. 13, 1840–Feb. 13, 1850; 1842–Apr. 4, 1869; Mar. 25, 1869–Dec. 30, 1880	Feb. 11, 1839–Feb. 12, 1850; Dec. 13, 1846 (?) –Feb. 9, 1869	NLI	Pos. 2482	
		1840–1911	1839–1911		TNFHF	
27	Kyle and Knock	See Laois				
28	Lorrha and Dorrha	Oct. 4, 1829–Dec. 8, 1844; Jan. 1, 1845–Sept. 4, 1880	Oct. 18, 1829–Nov. 24, 1844; Jan. 20, 1845– Nov. 27, 1880		NLI	Pos. 2480
		1839–1911	1829–1903; 1908–1911		TNFHF	
29	Nenagh	1792–1797; 1830–1842; 1845 –1911	1792–1911		TNFHF	
		Jan. 1, 1792–Nov. 1809; Nov. 22, 1830–Nov. 1842; Jan. 1845–Apr. 19, 1858; Jan. 3, 1859–Dec. 27, 1880	Jan. 8, 1792–Feb. 26, 1797; Sept. 27, 1818–Sept. 28, 1840; Sept. 30, 1840–Mar. 4, 1851; July 7, 1850–Nov. 27, 1880		NLI	Pos. 2483 (B. to 1809); remainder, 2484

			TIPPERARY NORTH				
MAP	CHURCH	BAPTISMS	MARRIAGES	BURIALS		LOCATION	REFERENCE
30	Shinrone	See Offaly					
31	Silvermines	Nov. 29, 1840–Dec. 16, 1880	Jan. 28, 1841–Oct. 2, 1880			NLI	Pos. 2481
		Nov. 29, 1840–Dec. 16, 1880	Jan. 28, 1841–Oct. 2, 1880			LDS	BFA 0926098
		1840–1911	1841–1911			TNFHF	
32	Toomevara	1831–1911	1861–1911			TNFHF	
		Mar. 10, 1831–June 6, 1856; May 25, 1861 –Dec. 27, 1880	Aug. 31, 1830–Sept. 16, 1836; June 18, 1861– Nov. 12, 1880			NLI	Pos. 2481
		See NLI				LDS	BFA 0926103
33	Youghal Arra	1828–1911	1821–1911			TNFHF	
		Oct. 26, 1828–Dec. 31, 1846; Jan. 16, 1847 –Dec. 21, 1880	Oct. (?)1, 1820–May 16, 1880			NLI	Pos. 2483–4
34	Roscrea	1810–1832	1810–1832			LDS	BFA 0979696 item 1
		Jan. 1, 1810–June 13, 1822; June 17, 1822–July 31, 1832; Aug. 5, 1832 –Dec. 26, 1863; Jan. 1, 1864–Dec. 24, 1880	Feb. 10, 1810–Aug. 4, 1822; Apr. 30, 1823–Aug. 4, 1832; Aug. 14, 1832–Nov. 27, 1842; Jan. 20, 1842–Nov. 13, 1880			NLI	Pos. 2479 (B. & M. to 1832; remainder 2480
		1810–1880	1810–1880			TNFHF	

TYRONE

ARMAGH DIOCESE
1 Aghaloo
2 Ardboe
3 Artrea (Magherafelt)
4 Ballinderry
5 Ballintacker
6 Clonfeacle (Moy)
7 Clonoe
8 Coagh
9 Coalisland (see also Donaghenry)
10 Cookstown (Desertcreat & Derryloran)
11 Donaghenry (Coalisland)
12 Donaghmore (see Killeeshil)
13 Dungannon
14 Errigal Kieran
15 Kildress
16 Killeeshil
17 Lissan
18 Pomeroy
19 Termonmaguirk

CLOGHER DIOCESE
20 Aghalurcher
21 Clogher
22 Donaghcavey
23 Dromore
24 Errigal Truagh
25 Fivemiletown
26 Kilskeery

DERRY DIOCESE
27 Ardstraw East
28 Ardstraw West
29 Bodoney Lr
30 Badoney Uppr
31 Camus (Strabane)
32 Cappagh
33 Donaghedy (Dunamanagh)
34 Drumragh
35 Langfield
36 Learmount
37 Leckpatrick (Strabane)
38 Mourne (see also Camus)
39 Termonamongan
40 Urney

			TYRONE			
Map	**Church**	**Baptisms**	**Marriages**	**Burials**	**Location**	**Reference**
1	Aghaloo	1846–1900	1826–1900	1868–1900	HW	
		1846–1881	1832–1880		PRONI	MIC.1D/36
		Jan. 1, 1846–Dec. 31, 1880	Jan. 2, 1832–May 29, 1834; Oct. 2, 1837–Nov. 21, 1880		NLI	Pos. 5585
2	Ardboe	See Derry 1				
3	Artrea and Desertcreat	July 1, 1832–Mar. 28, 1834; Jan. 20, 1838–Feb. 16, 1843; Nov. 1, 1854–Feb. 21, 1869; Jan. 18, 1864–June 14, 1880	Apr. 14, 1830–July 12, 1843; Nov. 12, 1854–Feb. 6, 1869		NLI	Pos. 5584
		See NLI			LDS	BFA 0926030
		1832–1900	1830–1900		HW	
		1832–1834; 1838–19843; 1854–1939	1830–1843; 1854–1837 (gaps)		PRONI	MIC.1D/35
4	Ballinderry	Dec. 19, 1826–Oct. 30, 1838; Sept. 25, 1841–Dec. 18, 1880	Jan. 10, 1827–Nov. 7, 1880		NLI	Pos. 5581
		1826–1839; 1841–1881	1827–1880		PRONI	MIC.1D/32
		1826–1900	1826–1900		HW	
5	Ballintacker	1832–1881	1834–1882		PRONI	MIC.1D/35
		1832–1900	1834–1900		HW	
		Sept. 26, 1822–Dec. 26, 1880	July 11, 1834–Dec. 3, 1880		NLI	Pos. 5584
6	Clonfeacle	1814–1900	1814–1900		HW	
		See NLI			LDS	BFA 0979708 items 2–3
		1814–1900	1814–1900		AA	
		Oct. 16, 1814–Mar. 22, 1840; Aug. 25, 1840–Dec. 26, 1880	Nov. 9, 1814–Mar. 19, 1840; Apr. 23, 1840–Oct. 14, 1880		NLI	Pos. 5580
		1814–1881	1814–1881		PRONI	MIC.1D/31
7	Clonoe	1810–1816; 1822–1881	1806–1816; 1823–1881	1806–1816	PRONI	MIC.1D/30
		Feb. 15, 1810–May 23, 1816; July 21, 1810–Feb. 13, 1812; Oct. 2, 1822–Apr. 16, 1850; Apr. 14, 1850–Dec. 21, 1880	Dec. 3, 1806–June 25, 1816; Jan. 6, 1823–Jan. 11, 1850; Apr. 26, 1850–Nov. 27, 1880	Dec. 11, 1806–May 31, 1816	NLI	Pos. 5579
		1810–1900	1806–1816; 1823–1900		HW	
8	Coagh	1865–1882	1865–1881; 1884–1891		PRONI	MIC.1D/33
		1865–1900	1865–1900		HW	
		Dec. 21, 1865–Oct. 17, 1880	Dec. 25, 1865–Nov. 26, 1879		NLI	Pos. 5582
9	Coalisland and Stewartstown	1861–1880	1862–1879	1861–1868	PRONI	MIC.1D/34
		Dec. 24, 1861–Aug. 18, 1880	May 9, 1862–Feb. 6, 1879	Nov. 15, 1861–Mar. 4, 1868	NLI	Pos. 5583
		1822–1900	1822–1900		HW	
		1861–1877	1862–1877	1861–1868	LDS	BFA 0979709 item 3
10	Desertcreat	1814–1900	1811–1900		HW	

→

Map	Church	Baptisms	TYRONE Marriages	Burials	Location	Reference
10	Desertcreat (*cont.*)	Jan. 2, 1827–Dec. 28, 1851; Jan. 1, 1852–Sept. 10, 1858; Oct. 17, 1858–Dec. 19, 1880	Jan. 23., 1827–Sept. 8, 1858; Jan. 23, 1859–Dec. 4, 1880		NLI	Pos. 5585
		1827–1881	1827–1881		PRONI	MIC.1D/36
11	Donaghenry	See NLI			LDS	BFA 0979709 item 2
		1822–1840; 1849–1881	1822–1841; 1853–1880	1854–1869	PRONI	MIC.1D/8, 34
		Jan. 1, 1822–Dec. 22, 1840; Feb. 16, 1849–Dec. 23, 1880	Jan. 1, 1822–Dec. 26, 1840; May 28, 1853–Nov.16, 1880	Jan. 1, 1822–Jan. 27, 1839; Jan. 15, 1854–May 18, 1868	NLI	Pos. 5583
12	Donaghmore	1837–1880	1837–1860		PRONI	MIC.1D/33–34
		1837–1900	1837–1900		HW	
		1871–1880			LDS	BFA 0979709 item 1
		Feb. 24, 1837–Dec. 24, 1870; Jan. 11, 1871–Dec. 31, 1880	Mar. 7, 1837–July 30, 1868		NLI	Pos. 5582
13	Dungannon	1783–1790; 1821–1900	1783–1788; 1821–1881	1821–1900	HW	
		1821–1881	1821–1900	1821–1881	PRONI	MIC.1D/31–32
		Oct. 14, 1821–Oct. 30, 1826; Oct. 25, 1826–Dec. 2, 1829; Apr. 24, 1830–July 9, 1833; Aug. 11, 1833–June 10, 1834; Aug. 3, 1834–Dec. 30, 1851; Jan. 4, 1852–Dec. 31, 1880	Oct. 6, 1821–Oct. 30, 1826; Oct. 30, 1826–Dec. 10, 1829; May 2, 1831–May 26, 1833; Aug. 23, 1833–Nov. 12, 1834; June 16, 1834–Dec. 29, 1851; Jan. 3, 1854–Nov. 20, 1880	Oct. 11, 1821–June 7, 1826; Nov. 7, 1826–Nov. 24, 1829; Apr. 26, 1831–May 30, 1833; Aug. 13, 1833–June 1, 1834; July 3, 1834–Dec. 29, 1854; Jan. 4, 1852–Dec. 31, 1880	NLI	Pos. 5580 Baptisms and marriages from 1834, 5581
		See NLI			LDS	BFA 0926038 items 1–3
14	Errigal Kieran	Jan. 3, 1847–Dec. 28, 1880	Jan. 14, 1864–Dec. 16, 1880		NLI	Pos. 5584
		1847–1881 (Ballygawley); 1864–1881 (Ballymacelroy)			PRONI	MIC.1D/35
		1834–1897	1864–1900		HW	
15	Kildress	1835–1900	1835–1900	1835–1842	AA	
		1835–1900	1835–1900	1835–1842	HW	
		1835–1881 (gaps)		1835–1842	PRONI	MIC.1D/37
		Jan. 4, 1835–Dec. 6, 1852; Jan. 11, 1857–Aug. 10, 1859; Jan. 6, 1861–Feb. 17, 1865; Jan. 2, 1878–Dec. 6, 1880	Mar. 15, 1835–Jan. 29, 1876; Jan. 7, 1840–Feb. 19, 1851; Jan. 10, 1878–Dec. 4, 1880	Mar. 6, 1835–Dec. 24, 1842	NLI	Pos. 5586
16	Killeeshil	Aug. 10, 1845–Dec. 27, 1856; Jan. 14, 1857–Dec. 21, 1880	Sept. 3, 1845–Dec. 31, 1856; Jan. 14, 1857–Dec. 14, 1880	Aug. 13, 1845 –Dec. 16, 1856; Jan. 14, 1857–Jan. 27, 1875; Nov. 4 to Dec. 1880	NLI	Pos. 5582
16	Tullyallen	Jan. 1, 1816–Jan. 2, 1834; Mar. 2, 1837–Aug. 24, 1844; Jan. 14, 1849–Dec. 25, 1880	Jan 3, 1816–Jan. 2, 1834; Apr. 3, 1837–July 29, 1844; Jan. 9, 1849–Nov. 14, 1880	Jan. 2, 1816–May 29, 1834; Mar. 5, 1837–Aug. 22, 1844	NLI	Pos. 5582; from 1849. Pos. 5599

→

Map	Church	Baptisms	TYRONE Marriages	Burials	Location	Reference
16	Tullyallen (*cont.*)	1816–1880	1816–1883	1816–1875; 1880–1881	PRONI	MIC.1D/33
		1816–1900	1816–1900		HW	
17	Lissan	July 22, 1823–Dec. 30, 1880	Sept. 1, 1839–Nov. 20, 1880		NLI	Pos. 5585
		1822–1900	1822–1900		HW	
		1822–1830; 1839–1900			TGC	
		1839–1881	1839–1880		PRONI	MIC.1D/36
18	Pomeroy	1837–1852; 1857–1865; 1869–1882	1837–1865; 1869–1881	1837–1840; 1857–1861; 1871–1881	PRONI	MIC.1D/36
		1837–1900	1819–1900		HW	
		Feb. 26, 1837–Nov. 24, 1840; Dec. 5, 1841–May 2, 1852; Apr. 21, 1857–Aug. 3, 1865; Feb. 1, 1869–Dec. 9, 1880	Mar. 5, 1837–Dec.11, 1840; Dec. 5, 1841 –June 10, 1865; July 11, 1869–Dec. 25, 1880	Mar. 7, 1837–Dec. 5, 1840; Apr. 20, 1857–Apr. 12, 1861; July 27, 1871–Dec. 30, 1880	NLI	Pos. 5585
19	Carrickmore	No records microfilmed			PRONI	
		1881–1900	1881–1900		HW	
		No records microfilmed			NLI	
19	Termon-maguirk	1834–1857	1834–1857		HW	
		1834–1857	1834–1857		PRONI	MIC.1D/33
		Dec. 7, 1834–Feb. 9, 1857	Oct. 23, 1834–Dec. 31, 1857		NLI	Pos. 5582
20	Aghalurcher	Oct. 19, 1835–Dec. 28, 1880			LDS	BFA 979704 item 6
		1835–1883			PRONI	MIC.1D/12; CR.2/12
		Oct. 19, 1835–Dec. 28, 1880			NLI	Pos. 5569
21	Clogher	1856–1881	1825–1881		HW	
		1856–1881	1825–1835	1840–1881	PRONI	MIC.1D/10; C.R.2/14
		Apr. 12, 1856–Apr. 13, 1857; Apr. 18, 1857–Dec. 23, 1880	Sept. 28, 1825–Nov. 10, 1835; Mar. 1940–Feb. 19, 1857; Apr. 22, 1857–Oct. 21, 1880		NLI	Pos. 5567
22	Donagheavey	Nov. 24, 1857–Dec. 14, 1880	Oct. 26, 1857–Nov. 25, 1880		LDS	BFA 0926051 items 1–2
		Nov. 24, 1857–Dec. 14, 1880	Oct. 26, 1857–Nov. 25, 1880		NLI	Pos. 5571
		1857–1881	1857–1880		PRONI	MIC.1D/14
23	Dromore	Nov. 1, 1835–Dec. 30, 1864; Jan. 1, 1865–Dec. 19, 1880	Oct. 21, 1833–Nov. 23, 1864; Jan. 10, 1865–Nov. 23, 1880		LDS	BFA 0926052 items 1–2
		1835–1881	1833–1881		PRONI	MIC.1D/11
		Nov. 1, 1835–Dec. 30, 1864; Jan. 1, 1865 –Dec. 19, 1880	Oct. 21, 1833–Nov. 23, 1864; Jan. 10, 1865 –Nov. 23, 1880		NLI	Pos. 5568

→

MAP	CHURCH	BAPTISMS	TYRONE MARRIAGES	BURIALS	LOCATION	REFERENCE
24	Errigal Truagh	1835–1852; 1861–1881	1837–1849; 1862–1881		PRONI	MIC.1D/19
		1835–1880			MAR	
		Nov. 1, 1835–June 20, 1852; Mar. 24, 1861–Dec. 29, 1880	Dec. 1, 1837–July 28, 1849; Jan. 28, 1862–May 27, 1880		NLI	Pos. 5576
		See NLI			LDS	BFA 0979706 items 1–3
25	Fivemiletown (Aughintaine)	1870–1881	1870–1883		PRONI	MIC.1D/12
		Nov. 14, 1870–Dec. 28, 1880	Nov. 18, 1870–Jan. 13, 1880		LDS	BFA 0979704 items 1–2
		Nov. 14, 1870–Dec. 28, 1880	Nov. 18, 1870–Jan. 13, 1880		NLI	Pos. 5569
26	Kilskeery	See NLI			LDS	BFA 0926054 items 1–4
		1840–1881	1940–1882		PRONI	MIC.1D/11
		Oct. 3, 1840–June 15, 1862; June 19, 1862–Feb. 18, 1870; Jan. 27, 1870–Dec. 24, 1880	Aug. 30, 1840–May 27, 1862; July 17, 1862–Feb. 27, 1870; Feb. 3, 1870–Mar. 1, 1880		NLI	Pos. 5568
27	Ardstraw East	Dec. 18, 1861–Dec. 24, 1880	Dec.(?) 8, 1860–Oct. 13, 1880		NLI	Pos. 5765
		1860–1880	1860–1881		PRONI	MIC.1D/60
28	Ardstraw West	June 3, 1846–Mar. 10, 1850; Jan. 18, 1852–Jan. 30, 1877; Nov. 23, 1873–Dec. 19, 1880; Dec. 25, 1877–Dec. 26, 1880	May 15, 1843–Apr. 7, 1878; Feb. 10–Oct. 27, 1880		NLI	Pos. 5767
		1846–1881	1843–1878; 1880		PRONI	MIC.1D/62
29	Badoney Lower and Greencastle	1865–1881	1865–1880		PRONI	MIC.1D/60
		1865–1900	1865–1893		TGC	
		Oct. 31, 1866–Dec. 24, 1880			NLI	Pos. 5765
30	Badoney Upper	1866–1881			PRONI	MIC.1D/60
		1866–1881; 1865–1881 (Plumbridge)	1865–1881 (Plumbridge)		HW	
		Oct. 31, 1866–Dec. 24, 1880			NLI	Pos. 5765
31	Camus (Strabane/ Clonleigh)	Apr. 1, 1773–Feb 22, 1795; Jan. 10, 1836–May 18, 1837; Mar. 3, 1853–Sept. 7, 1879; Mar. 12, 1853–Mar. 25, 1870; May 1, 1864–Dec. 31, 1880	Aug. 1788–Sept. 14, 1781 [*sic*]; 1843–1879; Nov. 14, 1853–Apr. 20, 1870; Sept. 16, 1879–Nov. 13, 1880		NLI	Pos. 5766
		1773–1795; 1836–1837; 1853–1880	1778–1781; 1843–1881		PRONI	MIC.1D/61
		1773–1795; 1836–1837; 1853–1900	1778–1779; 1781; 1785; 1791; 1842–1900		TGC	
32	Cappagh	1843–1900	1843–1900	1843–1965	TGC	
		1843–1883	1843–1883	1843–1865	PRONI	MIC.1D/60–61
		July 16, 1843–Dec. 6, 1880; June 12, 1846–Oct. 1863 (1 page only)	July 24, 1843–Nov. 20, 1880	July 21, 1843–Jan. 13, 1865	NLI	Pos. 5766; baptisms from 1846 on Pos. 5765

Map	Church	Baptisms	TYRONE Marriages	Burials	Location	Reference
33	Donaghedy	1854–1880	1857–1859; 1862–1863	1857–1859	PRONI	MIC.1D/55–56
		1854–1900	1858–1859; 1862–1900		TGC	
		Apr. 1, 1854–June 28, 1863 (Dunamanagh); Sept. 1, 1853–Dec. 11, 1880	Nov. 11, 1857–July 11, 1859 (Dunamanagh); (Dec.?) 13, 1862–1 May 31, 1863	Dec. 4, 1857–July 15, 1859	NLI	Pos. 5761, 5466
34	Drumragh	May–Nov. 1846; Nov. 13, 1853–Dec. 22, 1880 indexed	June–Aug. 1946; Nov. 7, 1853–Dec. 26, 1880	May–Sept. 1846; Nov. 23, 1853 –Dec. 11, 1880	NLI	Pos. 5765
		1846; 1853–1881; Baptisms indexed 1846–1879	1846; 1853–1881	1846; 1853–1881	PRONI	MIC.1D/60; C.R.2/9
35	Langfield	1846–1880		1853–1856	PRONI	MIC.1D/60
		Sept. 6, 1846–Dec. 18, 1880	Sept. 17, 1846–Oct. 18, 1880	July 18, 1853–Feb. 2, 1856	NLI	Pos. 5765
36	Learmount (Cumber Upper)	May 18, 1863–Dec. 27, 1880	Sept. 20, 1863–Dec. 28, 1880		NLI	Pos. 5762
		1863–1881	1863–1882		PRONI	MIC.1D/57
		1853–1854; 1863–1900	1863–1900		TGC	
37	Leckpatrick	Sept. 13, 1863–Dec. 12, 1880	Oct. 25, 1863–Nov. 16, 1880		NLI	Pos. 5767
		1863–1881	1863–1884		PRONI	MIC.1D/62
		1863–1900	1863–1900		TGC	
38	Mourne	Jan. 6, 1866–Dec. 29, 1880	Apr. 1, 1866–Dec. 3, 1880 (transcript)		NLI	Pos. 5766
		1866–1881	1866–1883		PRONI	MIC.1D/62
39	Termona-mongan	1863–1881	1863–1880		PRONI	MIC.1D/60
		Mar. 28, 1863–Dec. 29, 1880	Sept. 12, 1863–Nov. 13, 1880		NLI	Pos. 5765
40	Urney	No records microfilmed			PRONI	
		From 1866	From 1866		LC	
		No records microfilmed			NLI	

WATERFORD

CLOYNE DIOCESE
1 Kilworth

OSSORY DIOCESE
2 Slieverue

WATERFORD & LISMORE DIOCESE
3 Abbeyside & Ring
4 Aglish
5 Ardmore & Grange
6 Ballyduff
7 Cappoquin
8 Carrickbeg
9 Clashmore & Kinsalebeg
10 Dungarvan
11 Dunhill & Fenor
12 Kilgobnet
13 Kill (Rossmore)
14 Kilrea (Dunmore East)
15 Kilrossanty
16 Kilsheelan (Gambonsfield)
17 Knockanore
18 Lismore
19 Modeligo
20 Newcastle (Fourmilewater)

Co. Tipperary South Riding

Co. Kilkenny

Co. Cork

21 Portlaw (Ballyduff)
22 Rathcormuch (Mothel)
23 Ring (Old Parish)
24 St Mary's, Clonmel
25 SS Peter & Paul, Clonmel
26 Stradbally (Ballylaneen)
27 Tallow
28 Touraneena
29 Tramore

Waterford city:
30 Ballybricken
31 Holy Trinity
32 St John's
31 St Michael's
31 St Patrick's
31 St Peter's
31 St Stephen's

Map	Church	Baptisms	Waterford Marriages	Burials	Location	Reference
1	Kilworth	See Cork East 18				
2	Slieverue	See Kilkenny 25				
3	Abbeyside and Ring	July 6, 1828–Dec. 26, 1842; May 21, 1842–Dec. 29, 1880	July 24, 1828–Feb. 8, 1842; May 26, 1842–Nov. 18, 1880		NLI	Pos. 2469
		1828–1900	1828–1900		WH	
4	Aglish	1831–1900	1833–1900		WH	
		May 17, 1838–Dec. 31, 1880	Jan. 25, 1877–Nov. 20, 1880		NLI	Pos. 2464
5	Ardmore and Grange	Oct. 17, 1823–Jan. 19, 1833; Jan. 1, 1857–Dec. 31, 1880	Nov. 24, 1857–Sept. 23, 1880	Jan. 8, 1826–Jan. 11, 1827	NLI	Pos. 2465
		1816–1900	1857–1900		WH	
6	Ballyduff	1849–1900	1853–1900		WH	
		June 23, 1849–Feb. 6, 1861; Apr. 14, 1861–June 4, 1878; Jan. 26, 1879–Dec. 21, 1880	Nov. 8, 1853–Feb. 12, 1861; June 8, 1861–Nov. 18, 1880		NLI	Pos. 2469, 2470
7	Cappoquin	1819–1900	1807–1900		WH	
		Apr. 14, 1810–June 16, 1870 (indexed transcript); June 19, 1870–Dec. 21, 1880	Jan. 7, 1807–Aug. 8, 1871; July 23, 1870–Oct. 2, 1880		NLI	Pos. 2467

→

Map	Church	Baptisms	WATERFORD Marriages	Burials	Location	Reference
8	Carrickbeg	1842–1900	1807–1900		WH	
		Jan. 1, 1842–Oct. 30, 1846; Feb. 27, 1847–Dec. 28, 1876	Jan. 11, 1807–Jan. 8, 1867; Nov. 23, 1866–Jan. 9, 1881		NLI	Pos. 2450
9	Clashmore and Kinsalebeg	Jan. 6, 1811–Oct. 1, 1845; Oct. 12, 1845–Aug. 23, 1879	Jan. 23, 1810–Aug. 23, 1879		NLI	Pos. 2462, 2464
		1811–1900	1810–1900		WH	
10	Dungarvan	Feb. 17, 1787–Apr. 27, 1787; Sept. 3, 1811–May 17, 1823; July 27, 1823–Apr. 30, 1830; May 1, 1830–July 13, 1839; Jan. 7, 1838–July 26, 1877; Sept. 1, 1877–Dec. 28, 1880	May 14, 1809–Nov. 29, 1828; Jan. 8, 1829–Dec. 2, 1838; Feb. 21, 1838–Sept. 1, 1877; Sept. 24, 1877–Nov. 12, 1880		NLI	Pos. 2468, 2469
		1787–1900	1809–1900		WH	
11	Dunhill and Fenor	Apr. 4, 1829–Nov. 18, 1843; Jan. 5, 1844–June 12, 1881; Nov. 16, 1852–Feb. 6, 1876	Nov. 26, 1836–Feb. 17, 1874; Jan. 14, 1853–Nov. 18, 1880 (Fenor)	Jan. 1, 1879–Nov. 24, 1881	NLI	Pos. 2448, 2449
		1829–1900	1837–1900		WH	
12	Kilgobnet	Ap. 7, 1848–Oct. 24, 1872; Mar. 14, 1873–Dec. 25, 1880	Oct. 10, 1848–Apr. 6, 1880		NLI	Pos. 2464
		1848–1900	1848–1900		WH	
13	Kill (Rossmore)	Mar. 27, 1797–Aug. 1830; Feb. 1831–Feb. 21, 1869	Apr. 27, 1797–Feb. 11, 1880		NLI	Pos. 2452
		1798–1900	1797–1900		WH	
14	Kilrea	May 7, 1815–July 20, 1820; Oct. 10, 1845–Dec. 13, 1863 (transcript); Feb. 17, 1874–Dec. 19, 1880 (transcript); Dec. 24, 1863–Mar. 17, 1881 (transcript)	Jan. 8, 1780–Oct. 9, 1791; Jan. 13, 1793–Feb. 18, 1798 (transcript); Apr. 3, 1815–July 20, 1820; Aug. 29, 1837–Aug. 3, 1838; Oct. 5, 1845–Apr. 27, 1882		NLI	Pos. 2450
		1809–1900	1780–1900		WH	
15	Kilrossanty	1822–1900	1859–1900		WH	
		July 4, 1822–Aug. 4, 1858; Jan. 9, 1859–Dec. 27, 1880	Jan. 16, 1859–Sept. 8, 1880		NLI	Pos. 2465
16	Kilsheelan (Gambonfsfield and Kilcash)	Jan. 1, 1840–Feb. 1, 1856; Feb. 16, 1856–Dec. 27, 1880	Jan. 11, 1840–Jan. 11, 1856; Jan. 14, 1856–Dec. 29, 1880		NLI	Pos. 2452, 2453
		1840–1900	1840–1900		WH	
17	Knockanore	May 4, 1816–Apr. 24, 1823; Sept. 1833–June 25, 1872; Jan. 17, 1872–Dec. 27, 1880	Feb. 7, 1854–June 12, 180		NLI	Pos. 2462
		1816–1900	1803–1900		WH	
18	Lismore	1820–1900	1822–1900		WH	
		Mar.13, 1820–Feb. 14, 1831; July 11, 1840–June 19, 1848; Feb. 21, 1849–Apr. 16, 1858; Aug. 27, 1866–Dec. 28, 1880	Nov. 24, 1822–Oct. 8, 1839; Feb. 27, 1840–Nov. 4, 1866; May, 1849–Feb. 20, 1857; Sept. 1866–Nov. 6, 1880		NLI	Pos. 2467, 2468

→

MAP	CHURCH	BAPTISMS	WATERFORD MARRIAGES	BURIALS	LOCATION	REFERENCE
19	Modeligo	1815–1900	1820–1900		WH	
		July 28, 1846–Dec. 22, 1880			NLI	Pos. 2470
20	Newcastle	1814–1900	1822–1900		WH	
		July 1, 1814–Dec. 31, 1845; Jan. 1, 1846–Oct. 31, 1862; Nov. 2, 1862–Dec. 29, 1880	Jan. 7, 1822–Oct. 23, 1880		NLI	Pos. 2454
21	Portlaw	1809–1900	1805–1900		WH	
		Jan. 26, 1809–Oct. 3, 1825; Dec. 16, 1825–Oct. 24, 1860; June 1, 1858–Jan. 23, 1881	Jan. 15, 1805–Feb. 27, 1881; Feb. 14, 1814–Nov. 19, 1862; Nov. 6, 1860–Feb. 21, 1882		NLI	Pos. 2449, 2450
22	Rathcormuch (Mothel)	1831–1900	1852–1900		WH	
		Mar. 23, 1831–June 17, 1852; June 20, 1852–Jan. 13, 1881	Mar. 4, 1845–Oct. 16, 1880		NLI	Pos. 2449
23	Ring and Old Parish	1813–1900	1813–1900		WH	
		Jan. 5, 1813–Apr. 24, 1840; Aug. 12, 1840–Aug. 15, 1859	Jan. 17, 1813–Feb. 13, 1840; Jan. 24, 1841–Mar. 8, 1859		NLI	Pos. 2465
24	St Mary's, Clonmel	See Tipperary South 30				
25	SS Peter and Paul, Clonmel	See Tipperary South 31				
26	Stradbally	Nov. 3, 1806–May 30, 1814; June 1, 1814–Sept. 22, 1828; Sept. 30, 1828–July 29, 1835; Aug. 1, 1835–Oct. 13, 1850; Oct. 19, 1850–Aug. 28, 1863; Aug. 20, 1863–Dec. 9, 1880	Aug. 4, 1805–Nov 28, 1840; Sept. 20, 1840–Aug. 2, 1863; Sept. 13, 1863–Oct. 13, 1880		NLI	Pos. 2465, 2466, 2467
		1797–1900	1805–1900		WH	
27	Tallow	1797–1900	1799–1900		WH	
		Apr. 19, 1797–Mar. 11, 1831; Apr. 9, 1831–Sept. 19, 1842; Jan. 19, 1856–Dec. 31, 1880	Apr. 20, 1798–Apr. 25, 1803; Oct. 11, 1808–Nov. 13, 1853		NLI	Pos. 24
28	Touraneena	1852–1900	1852–1900		WH	
		July 8, 1852–Dec. 11, 1880	June 20, 1852–Nov. 14, 1880		NLI	Pos. 24
29	Tramore	1798–1900	1785–1900		WH	
		Jan. 7, 1798–Oct. 24, 1831;	Jan. 29, 1786–July 29, 1840		NLI	Pos. 24
30	Waterford city: Ballybricken	Jan. 4, 1795–Oct. 13, 1816; Dec. 1, 1816–Apr. 30, 1832; May 1, 1832–Apr. 5, 1841; Apr. 6, 1841–Jan. 8, 1844; Jan. 8, 1844–Jan. 3, 1875; Jan. 3, 1875–Dec. 30, 1880	Jan. 7, 1797–Sept. 6, 1832; Sept. 10, 1832–Sept. 9, 1843; Jan. 8, 1843–Nov. 17, 1874; Jan. 7, 1875–Nov. 22, 1880		NLI	Pos. 2450, 2451 (B.); 2452 (M.)
		1797–1900	1797–1900		WH	→

Map	Church	Baptisms	WATERFORD		Location	Reference
			Marriages	Burials		
31	Waterford city: St Patrick's and St Olaf's	Apr. 11, 1731–Feb. 10, 1743; Feb. 13, 1743– Oct. 29, 1752; Oct. 30, 1752–June 3, 1772; June 6, 1772– May 22, 1783; June 18, 1783– Sept. 8, 1791; May 9, 1795–Mar. 27, 1798; Nov. 18, 1798–Mar. 2, 1801; Apr. 9, 1798–Jan. 8, 1799; Apr. 3, 1827–Oct. 11, 1839	May 24, 1743–Oct. 29, 1752; Oct. 30, 1752–June 3, 1772; Oct. 10, 1772–May 22, 1783; Nov. 23, 1783–May 8, 1791; Jan. 25, 1799–Dec. 9, 1800; Sept. 12, 1826–Sept. 19, 1839		NLI	Pos. 2447
		1706–1900	1706–1900		WH	
31	Waterford city: Holy Trinity	Jan. 15, 1729–July 15, 1752; Sept. 26, 1731–Mar. 5, 1749 (St Stephen's); Dec. 4, 1732–Jan. 6, 1787 (St Michael's); Apr. 13, 1795–June 4, 1796 (St Michael's); Nov. 1, 1737–Aug. 17, 1746 (St Peter's); July 22, 1752– Dec. 30, 1767; Jan. 2, 1768–July 4, 1775; Feb. 7, 1793–Dec. 29, 1805; Jan. 3, 1806–July 7, 1819; Dec. 3, 1809–Sept. 4, 1815; July 20, 1819–Sept. 16, 1838; Sept. 19, 1838– Dec. 31, 1863	Nov. 26, 1743–Jan. 8, 1787 (St Peter's); Sept. 5, 1747– Dec. 20 1756; Feb. 3, 1761– Aug. 30, 1777; Jan. 5, 1791 –June 28, 1795; June 26, 1796 –Nov. 24, 1796 (St Michael's); Jan. 9, 1797–Feb. 20, 1820; Aug. 2, 1819–Sept. 9, 1838; Sept. 25, 1838–Nov. 28, 1863		NLI	Pos. 2444, 2445
		1729–1900	1747–1900		WH	
31	Waterford city: SS Michael, Peter, Stephen	See Holy Trinity				
32	Waterford city: St John's	Apr. 7, 1706–Mar. 26, 1730; Mar. 5, 1759– Mar. 29, 1787; Oct. 1795– Aug. 10, 1807; Aug. 2, 1807 –Mar. 31, 1816; June 1, 1818–July 24, 1828; Aug. 17, 1828– July 17, 1837;	Apr. 7, 1706–Mar. 26, 1730; Feb. 10, 1760–Feb. 2, 1808; Feb. 2, 1808–June 1, 1817; Sept. 12, 1828–Nov. 28, 1856		NLI	Pos. 2446
		1759–1900	1760–1900		WH	

WESTMEATH

MEATH DIOCESE
1 Ballinacargy
2 Ballymore
3 Castlepollard
   (Lickblea)
4 Castletown-
   Geoghegan
5 Churchtown (Dysart)
6 Clara & Horseleap
7 Clonmellon
8 Collinstown
9 Delvin
10 Drumraney
11 Kilbeggan
12 Kilkenny West
13 Killucan
14 Kinnegad
15 Milltown
16 Moyvore
17 Mullingar
18 Multyfarnham
19 Rochfortbridge
20 Taghmon
21 Tubber
22 Tullamore
23 Turbotstown

ARDAGH & CLONMACNOISE DIOCESE
24 Lemmanaghan & Ballynahown

25 Moate (Kilcleagh & Ballyloughloe)
26 Rathaspick & Russagh
27 St Mary's, Athlone
28 Streete

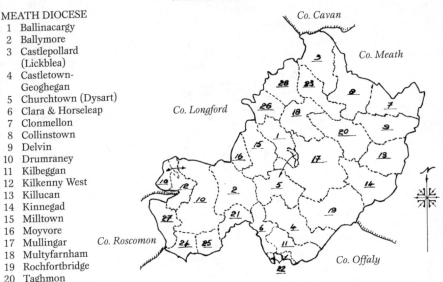

Map	Church	Baptisms	Westmeath Marriages	Burials	Location	Reference
1	Ballinacargy (Sonna)	Sept. 23, 1837–Dec. 31, 1880	Nov. 26, 1838–July 20, 1880		NLI	Pos. 4168
		1837–1900	1838–1900	1859–1993	DSHC	
2	Ballymore	1824–1900	1872–1900		DSHC	
		Sept. 22, 1824–Sept. 2, 1841; Mar. 18, 1839–Dec. 30, 1871 (some duplicates); Sept. 22, 1824–Sept. 2, 1841; Mar. 18, 1839–Dec. 30, 1871; Jan. 9, 1872–Dec. 31, 1880	April 1839–Sept.10, 1870; Feb. 4, 1872–Nov. 27, 1880		NLI	Pos. 4171
		See NLI			LDS	BFA 0926163 items 2–4
3	Castlepollard	Jan. 4, 1763–Mar. 25, 1765; Oct. 9, 1771–June 30, 1790;	1763–June 10, 1790;	Mar. 10, 1764– June 22, 1790;	NLI	Pos. 4164, 4165
		Jan. 4, 1795–Feb. 16, 1796; Feb. 21, 1796–Aug. 19, 1805; Aug. 23, 1805– June 24, 1825; Nov. 15, 1825–Mar. 20, 1837; Mar. 24, 1837–Oct. 17, 1875; Oct. 22, 1875–Dec. 22, 1880	Mar. 21, 1793–Aug. 15, 1793; Jan. 7, 1795–June 16, 1825; Nov. 21, 1825 –Sept. 14, 1875	Jan. 19, 1793– June 13, 1825		
3	Kilbride and Mountnugent	See Cavan 5				→

Map	Church	Baptisms	WESTMEATH		Location	Reference
			Marriages	Burials		
4	Castletown-Geoghegan	1829–1900	1829–1900	1829–1844	DSHC	
		Aug. 2, 1829–May 2, 1835; May 8, 1835–Mar. 29, 1850; Mar. 2, 1846–Dec. 12, 1880; June 23, 1861–Dec. 26, 1880	Feb. 8, 1829–Mar. 3, 1835; July 26, 1835–Feb. 10, 1850; Oct. 9, 1846–May 27, 1880; Jan. 7, 1862–Nov. 26, 1880		NLI	Pos. 4169
5	Churchtown (Dysart)	Aug. 10, 1836–Aug. 24, 1862; Apr. 28, 1861–Dec. 30, 1880	Feb. 5, 1825–Feb. 24, 1862		NLI	Pos. 4168
		1836–1900	1825–1900	1862–1900	DSHC	
6	Clara and Horseleap	1845–1910	1821–1899	1825–1865	IMA	
		Feb. 16, 1845–Dec. 26, 1880; Sept. 2, 1878–Dec. 14, 1880 (transcript)	Nov. 16, 1821–Nov. 25, 1880	Jan. 9, 1825–Feb. 23, 1854; Oct. 2, 1864–Oct. 4, 1868	NLI	Pos. 4174
7	Clonmellon	Jan. 6, 1759–Sept. 18, 1784 (some gaps); Feb. 3, 1785–Apr. 29, 1791; Jan. 3, 1815–Mar. 24, 1815; May 1, 1791–Mar. 10, 1809; Apr. 5, 1809–Nov. 2, 1809; Jun. 18, 1819–July 10, 1845; July 11, 1845–Aug. 25, 1872	Jan. 17, 1857–Aug. 20, 1784 (some gaps); Aug. 16, 1784–Sept. 4, 1809; Jan. 19, 1815–Feb. 21, 1815; July 19, 1819–July 29, 1845; Jan. 10, 1846–June 19, 1872	Jan. 30, 1757–Sept. 17, 1784 (some gaps); Dec. 25, 1878–Oct. 29, 1809; Nov. 7, 1819–July (15?), 1850	NLI	Pos. 4187
		1759–1901	1757–1901	1757–1993	DSHC	
		1759–1900	1757–1900	1759–1849	MHC	
8	Collinstown	Feb. 24, 1807–Apr. 29, 1815; Mar. 13, 1821–Nov. 18, 1843; Mar. 4, 1844–June 6, 1844; May 12, 1844–Dec. 24, 1880	June 21, 1784–June 6, 1837; June 15, 1837–Nov. 26, 1880	Apr. 24, 1784–Oct. 1949	NLI	Pos. 4168, 4169
		1807–1900	1784–1844	1809–1926	DSHC	
		1807–1901	1784–1901	1784–1849	MHC	
		See NLI			LDS	BFA 0926165 items 3–4
9	Delvin	Jan. 1, 1785–Mar. 17, 1789; July 23, 1792–July 20, 1812; July, 5 1830–Dec. 29, 1880	Feb. 7, 1785–Mar. 16, 1789; July 30, 1792–July 1812; Sept. 30, 1830–Oct. 4, 1880	Feb. 7, 1785–Mar. 5, 1789; July 7, 1792–July 26, 1812; Jan. 3, 1849–Apr. 1, 1855	NLI	Pos. 4172
		1783–1900	1785–1900	1785–1985	DSHC	
10	Drumraney	1834–1900	1834–1900		DSHC	
		See NLI			LDS	BFA 0926167 items 3–4
		Apr. 26, 1834–Dec. 22, 1880	May 2, 1834–Sept. 29, 1880		NLI	Pos. 4171
10	Nougheval	No records microfilmed			NLI	
		1857–1908	1857–1908	1920–1993	DSHC	
11	Kilbeggan	Nov. 4, 1818–Aug. 28, 1824; Apr. 24, 1825–Dec. 9, 1859; Jan. 8, 1860–Dec. 5, 1880	Oct. 23, 1818–Nov. 26, 1859; Jan. 7, 1860–Nov. 16, 1880	Sept. 28, 1818–Dec. 17, 1843	NLI	Pos. 4176
12	Kilkenny West	Aug. 5, 1829–Dec. 15, 1880			NLI	Pos. 417
		1829–1900	1829–1900	1829–1900	DSHC	

→

Map	Church	Baptisms	Westmeath Marriages	Burials	Location	Reference
13	Killucan	1866–1900	1821–1900		DSHC	
		May 7, 1821–July 28, 1838; July 26, 1838–Dec. 27, 1865; Jan. 6, 1866–Jan. 19, 1875; Jan. 20, 1875–Dec. 28, 1880	May 11, 1821–Sept. 30, 1847; Oct. 26, 1847–Nov. 27, 1874; Jan. 18, 1875–Nov. 26, 1880		NLI	Pos. 4166
		See NLI			LDS	BFA 0926172
14	Kinnegad	1827–1890	1844–1899	1833–1975	DSHC	
		June 22, 1827–Jan. 31, 1869; Jan. 29, 1869–Dec. 29, 1880	July 18, 1844–Jan. 25, 1869; Feb. 6, 1869–Sept. 8, 1880	Feb. 7, 1869–Dec. 23, 1880	NLI	Pos. 4170
15	Milltown	1791–1900	1781–1913	1781–1872	DSHC	
		Jan. 1, 1781–Sept. 12, 1808; Apr. 2, 1809–Oct. 3, 1825; Mar. 1, 1826–Nov. 15, 1849; Feb. 18, 1850–May 3, 1860; May 3, 1860–Oct. 16, 1869; Sept. 21, 1869–Nov. 18, 1872; Dec. 10, 1872–Dec. 22, 1880	Apr. 2, 1809–Oct. 3, 1825; Mar. 1, 1826–Nov. 15, 1849; Feb. 18, 1850–May 3, 1860; May 3, 1860–Oct. 16, 1869; Nov. 15, 1869–Nov. 3, 1872; Jan. 14, 1781–Feb. 11, 1805; Jan. 13, 1873–Oct. 16, 1880	Jan. 12, 1781–Nov. 17, 1808; Apr. 2, 1809–Oct. 3, 1825; Mar. 1, 1826–Nov. 15, 1849; Feb. 18, 1850–May 3, 1860; May 3, 1860–Oct. 16, 1869	NLI	Pos. 4167
16	Moyvore	1832–1900	1832–1900	1831–1865	DSHC	
		See NLI			LDS	BFA 0926167 items 1–2
		Sept. 5, 1831–Feb. 8, 1862; Feb. 18, 1862–Dec. 25, 1880	Feb. 12, 1832–Apr. 28, 1862; Mar. 2,1862–Dec. 25, 1880	Aug. 6, 1831–Apr. 1863; May 1863–Sept. 5, 1865	NLI	Pos. 4171
17	Mullingar	1742–1788	1737–1754; 1779–1782; 1783–1824; 1833–1859; 1860–1900	1830–1940	DSHC	
		See NLI			LDS	BFA 0926178
		1741/2 (a fragment); July 15, 1742–Dec. 29, 1763; Jan. 3, 1764–Sept. 30, 1775; Oct. 1, 1775–July 4, 1785; July 4, 1785–Nov. 24, 1793; Oct. 28, 1793–Dec. 19, 1796; Jan. 13, 1797–May 2, 1800; Jan. 1, 1800–Apr. 13, 1816; May 1, 1825–Dec. 2, 1832; Jan. 1, 1833–Nov. 23, 1842; Nov. 13, 1843–Jan. 24, 1863; Jan. 22, 1863–Mar. 12, 1872; Mar. 13, 1872–Dec. 31, 1880	Oct. 26, 1737–July 20, 1754; Jan. 10, 1779–Nov. 28, 1782; Dec. 1, 1782–July 12, 1792; July 15, 1792–Nov. 28, 1812; Nov. 29, 1812–Apr. 21, 1824; Jan. 8, 1833–Apr. 9, 1859; May 18, 1860–July 12, 1879; July 10, 1879–Nov. 27, 1880	May 6, 1757–Oct. 31, 1797; Jan. 4, 1833–May 26, 1838; Feb. 28, 1843–1880	NLI	Pos. 4161, 4162, 4163
18	Multyfarnham	Feb. 6, 1824–Dec. 28, 1841; Jan. 1, 1842–Dec. 26, 1880	Feb. 15, 1824–Dec. 9, 1841; Jan. 7, 1842–June 4, 1880	Jan. 28, 1831–July 16, 1844	NLI	Pos. 4168
		1824–1900	1824–1900	1830–1848	DSHC	
19	Rochfort-bridge	June 1, 1823–Apr. 9, 1847; Apr. 11, 1847–Dec. 28, 1856; Jan. 9, 1857–Dec. 27, 1880	Dec. 26, 1816–Dec. 1, 1855; Jan. 20, 1856–Nov. 26, 1880		NLI	Pos. 4172
20	Taghmon	Sept. 22, 1781–Mar. 7, 1790; June 8, 1800–June 30, 1800; Mar. 24, 1809–Dec. 28, 1840; Jan. 1, 1841–Dec. 29, 1850; Jan. 2, 1864–Dec. 30, 1880	Jan. 12, 1782–July 16, 1791; Aug. 7, 1809–May 14, 1848; Sept. 2, 1868–Nov. 3, 1880	Sept. 1, 1809–Feb. 25, 1848	NLI	Pos. 4165

Map	Church	Baptisms	WESTMEATH Marriages	Burials	Location	Reference
21	Tubber	Nov. 2, 1821–Dec. 25, 1880	Nov. 6, 1824–Dec. 13, 1880		NLI	Pos. 4176
		1820–1899	1820–1899	1832–1845	IMA	
		1820–1900	1824–1900	1824–1873	DSHC	
		Nov. 2, 1821–Dec. 25, 1880	Nov. 6, 1824–Dec. 13, 1880		LDS	BFA 0926185 item 2
22	Tullamore	June 14, 1809–Feb. 20, 1810; Nov. 1, 1820–Feb. 24, 1822; Feb. 1, 1827–Jan. 31, 1836; Mar. 1, 1836–Dec. 26, 1880	Apr. 26, 1801–Sept. 29, 1807; Apr. 9–10, 1809; Nov. 2, 1820–Feb. 19, 1822; Feb. 1, 1827–Dec. 29, 1880		NLI	Pos. 4174
		See NLI			LDS	BFA 0926186
		1819–1899	1801–1899		IMA	
23	Turbotstown (Mayne)	Aug. 1777–May 29, 1796; Jan. 22, 1798–Nov. 29, 1820; Apr. 2, 1824–Apr.; 5, 1835 Feb. 21, 1847–Aug. 22, 1863 (some pages missing)	Nov. 17, 1777–Apr. 24, 1796; Jan. 7, 1798–Dec. 1, 1820; May 9, 1824–July 4, 1843; Aug. 20, 1846–July 21, 1850; Nov. 2, 1864–Jul;y 19, 1880	Aug. 7, 1777–Nov. 27, 1796; Feb. 2, 1803–Sept. 9, 1820; Apr. 2, 1824–Aug. 9, 1844; Jan. 1864–Oct. 27, 1869; Jan. 4, 1846–July 31, 1850	NLI	Pos. 4167
		1777–1820; 1824–1835; 1847–1900	1777–1820; 1824–1843; 1864–1900	1777–1797; 1824–1869; 1919–1993	DSHC	
		See NLI			LDS	BFA 0926176 item 1
24	Lemmanaghan and Ballynahown	Aug. 12, 1821–Dec. 21, 1824; Feb. 12, 1826–Feb. 25, 1839; Feb. 6, 1841–Sept. 21, 1845; July 23, 1854–Dec. 24, 1880	Jan. 7, 1830–Aug. 29, 1845; Oct. 15, 1854–Dec. 26, 1880	Nov. 21, 1829–Sept. 9, 1845; Sept. 2, 1854–Dec. 26, 1880	NLI	Pos. 4235
		1821–1905 (some gaps)	1823–1974	1821–1828; 1829–1845; 1854–1881; 1882–1894	LDS	BFA 1279227 items 1–6
		1821–1899	1822–1899	1821–1846	IMA	
25	Moate	1820–1900; 1811–1900 (Ballyloughloe)	1830–1900 1824–1900 (Ballyloughloe)	1830–1900 1811–1900 (Ballyloughloe)	DSHC	
		No registers received			NLI	
		1830–1910	1830–1915	1830–1836; 1835–1916	LDS	BFA 1279227 items 9–11
26	Rathaspick and Russagh	Mar. 16, 1822–Sept. 9, 1826; July 24, 1832–Apr. 21, 1833; May 1, 1836–Dec. 9, 1843; Dec. 17, 1843–Oct. 18, 1846; Mar. 28, 1847–Dec. 30, 1880	Dec. 31, 1819–Feb. 7, 1826; Oct. 27, 1832–Oct. 4, 1833; Jan 11, 1838–Nov. 23, 1843; Jan. 7, 1844–Nov. 20, 1880	Mar 11, 1822–Feb. 20, 1826; Aug. 2, 1832–Nov. 1833; Aug. 15, 1837–Oct. 10, 1843; Feb. 8, 1844–Dec. 19, 1880	NLI	Pos. 4236
		1822–1984	1825–1983	1822–1909; 1928–1984	LDS	BFA 1279229 items 16–22
		1826–1900	1821–1842; 1844–1900	1828–1900	DSHC	
27	St Mary's, Athlone	1813–1900	1813–1900	1813–1900	DSHC	
		1813–1827; 1834–1984	1813–1827; 1834–1984	1813–1827	LDS	BFA 1279224 items 4–14; 1279226 1–3 ⟶

Map	Church	Baptisms	WESTMEATH Marriages	Burials	Location	Reference
27	St Mary's, Athlone (*cont.*)	Jan. 1, 1813–Sept. 24, 1826; Feb. 4, 1827–Mar. 17, 1827; May 3, 1839–Apr. 30, 1852; Feb. 1, 1853–Dec. 28, 1855; Jan. 1, 1856–Feb. 26, 1868	Jan. 1, 1813–Sept. 24, 1826; Feb. 4, 1827–Mar. 17, 1827; June 5, 1819–Apr. 17, 1827 (some deaths and baptisms included); Jan. 24, 1834–Dec. 26, 1851; Feb. 9, 1854–Feb. 5, 1863	Jan. 1, 1813–Sept. 24, 1826; Feb. 4, 1827–Mar. 17, 1827; June 4, 1819–Dec. 29, 1826 (some marriages and baptisms included)	NLI	Pos. 4242
28	Streete	1820–1901	1820–1826; 1835–1881; 1887–1902	1834–1881; 1887–1913	LDS	BFA 1279228 items 7–9
		1821–1863	1820–1900	1772–1995	DSHC	
		July 6, 1820–July 14, 1827; Nov. 21, 1831–Dec. 20, 1831; Dec. 15, 1834–Dec. 29, 1880	Aug. 10, 1820–Jan. 22, 1828; Jan. 4, 1835–Nov. 19, 1880	Sept 27, 1823–Aug. 13, 1829; Dec. 14, 1834–Jan. 8, 1841; July 19, 1842–Dec. 29, 1880	NLI	Pos. 4236

WEXFORD

DUBLIN DIOCESE
1 Arklow

FERNS DIOCESE
2 Adamstown
3 Ballagh (Oulart)
4 Ballycullane (Tintern)
5 Ballindaggin
6 Ballygarrett
7 Ballymore (Moyglass)
8 Ballyoughter
9 Blackwater (Killala)
10 Bree
11 Bunclody (Newtownbarry)
12 Camolin
13 Carrick-on-Bannow
14 Castlebridge (Screen)
15 Clongeen
16 Cloughbawn
17 Craanford & Ballymurrin
18 Crossabeg
19 Davidstown
20 Enniscorthy
21 Ferns
22 Glinn
23 Gorey
24 Kilanerin
25 Kilaveny & Annacorra
26 Kilmore
27 Kilrush & Askamore
28 Lady's Island
29 Litter
30 Marshalstown
31 Monageer (Boolavogue)
32 Monamolin

33 New Ross
34 Old Ross (Cushinstown)
35 Oylegate & Glenbrien
36 Piercetown & Murrinstown
37 Ramsgrange
38 Rathangan (Duncormuck)
39 Rathnure & Templeludigan
40 Suttons (Ballykelly)

41 Taghmon
42 Tagoat & Kilrane
43 Templetown
44 Tomacork (Carnew)
45 Wexford

KILDARE & LEIGHLIN DIOCESE
46 Borris
47 Clonegal
48 St Mullin's

Co. Wicklow

Co. Carlow

Irish Sea

Co. Kilkenny

Co. Waterford

Wexford Harbour

Map	Church	Baptisms	WEXFORD Marriages	Burials	Location	Reference
1	Arklow	See Wicklow 1				
2	Adamstown	Jan. 13, 1807–Dec. 30, 1836; Jan. 7, 1837–Oct. 7, 1848; Nov. 10, 1850– Sept. 11, 1864; Apr. 13, 1849–Mar. 27, 1861; Nov. 20, 1864–Oct. 30, 1880	Dec. 8, 1849–Feb. 13, 1865; Nov. 26, 1864–Oct. 19, 1880	Sept. 27, 1823– Jan. 30, 1832 (ages given)	NLI	Pos. 4258
		1849–1900	1892–1900		WGC	
3	The Ballagh	Oct. 29, 1837–Jan. 27, 1853; Feb. 25, 1875–Dec. 26, 1880; Oct. 1863– Dec. 17, 1880	Nov. 4, 1837–Nov. 26, 1852; Nov. 10, 1874– July 20, 1878		NLI	Pos. 4248
4	Ballycullane	1827–1900	1827–1896	1828–1832	WGC	
		Sept. 13, 1827–Sept. 3, 1880 (very poor condition)	Oct. 7, 1827–Sept. 12, 1880	Oct. 10, 1828– Jan. 31, 1832	NLI	Pos. 4259
5	Ballindaggin	July 18, 1871–Dec. 30, 1880	July 2, 1871–Nov. 11, 1880		NLI	Pos. 4251
6	Ballygarrett	Nov. 10, 1828–Feb. 19, 1863	Aug. 30, 1828–Nov. 13, 1865	Aug. 7, 1830– Apr. 18, 1857; Oct. 28, 1865– Apr. 19, 1867 (ages given)	NLI	Pos. 4255
		1828–1900	1830–1900	1830–1869	WGC	
7	Ballymore	May 22, 1840–Dec. 24, 1880	Feb. 13, 1840–Oct. 23, 1880		NLI	Pos. 4246
		1813–1900	1802–1899		WGC	
8	Ballyoughter	Sept. 30, 1810–Dec. 31, 1811; Aug. 5, 1815–Nov. 28, 1832; Aug. 18, 1844– Apr. 19, 1871; July 5, 1871–Dec. 27, 1880	Aug. 20, 1815–Feb. 10, 1868; July 13, 1871– Dec. 27, 1880		NLI	Pos. 4255
9	Blackwater	1825–1900	1815–1881	1840–1883	WGC	
		1815–Dec. 28, 1839 (early years barely legible); Jan. 4, 1840– Dec. 21, 1880	Jan. 8, 1815 –Dec. 10, 1839; Jan. 13, 1840– Nov. 27, 1880	Jan. 5, 1843– Dec. 20, 1880	NLI	Pos. 4245
10	Bree	Jan. 3, 1837–Dec. 26, 1880	Jan. 23, 1837–Nov. 27, 1880		NLI	Pos. 4251
11	Bunclody (Newtown- barry)	1834–Nov. 1, 1851; Apr. 26, 1857–Dec. 29, 1880	May 20, 1834–June 29, 1880	1834; 1857–8; 1872–3	NLI	Pos. 4251
12	Camolin	June 1, 1853–Dec. 10, 1880	Mar. 10, 1853–Nov. 7, 1880	Jan. 3, 1858– Feb. 7, 1879	NLI	Pos. 4257
13	Carrick-on– Bannow	1873–1900			WGC	
		Aug. 29, 1832–Nov. 9, 1873 (some missing); Aug. 10, 1873–Dec. 31, 1880	Sept. 11, 1830–Sept. 23, 1873; July 16, 1873– Nov. 27, 1880		NLI	Pos. 4244
14	Castlebridge	Oct. 30, 1832–Dec. 31, 1880; July 17, 1871– Dec. 24, 1880 (Screen)	Dec. 1, 1832–Oct. 27, 1880; Oct. 6, 1871–Oct. 20, 1880 (Screen)		NLI	Pos. 4247
		1832–1900	1832–1892		WGC	

→

| | | **WEXFORD** | | | | |
Map	Church	Baptisms	Marriages	Burials	Location	Reference
15	Clongeen	1847–1900	1847–1900		WGC	
		Jan. 29, 1847–Dec. 30, 1880	Apr. 25, 1847–Nov. 25, 1880	Jan, 30, 1856–Dec. 3, 1880 (ages given)	NLI	Pos. 4261
16	Cloughbawn (Killegney)	Mar. 17, 1816–Sept. 20, 1850 (part of 1824 missing); Jan. 20, 1853 –Oct. 24, 1880	Mar. 17, 1816–Sept. 20, 1850 (part of 1824 missing); Feb. 7, 1853– Dec. 2, 1880	Mar. 17, 1816 Sept. 20, 1850 (part of 1824 missing); Feb. 3, 1861–Sept. 12, 1880 (ages given)	NLI	Pos. 4250
		1816–1900	1816–1900	1816–1900	WGC	
17	Craanford	Jan. 8, 1856–Dec. 3, 1880; Aug. 26, 1871– Oct. 28, 1880	Nov. 30, 1871–Nov. 28, 1880		NLI	Pos. 4257
		1871–1900	1871–1900		WGC	
18	Crossabeg	Jan. 8, 1856–Dec. 3, 1880			NLI	Pos. 4251
		1794–1900	1794–1900	1899–1900	WGC	
19	Davidstown	1801–1900	1840–1900		WGC	
		1805–Dec. 24, 1880	June 1808–Nov. 27, 1880		NLI	Pos. 4251
20	Enniscorthy	1794–1900	1794–1900		WGC	
		May 16, 1794–June 10, 1804 (also in transcript); Mar. 1, 1806–May 23, 1816 (also in transcript); June 2, 1816–Dec. 31, 1835 (also in transcript); Jan. 1, 1836–Dec. 30, 1861; Jan. 1, 1836–Nov. 6, 1841; Jan. 2, 1862–Dec. 23, 1880	May 3, 1794–Sept. 25, 1805 (also in transcript); Sept. 17, 1805–May 12, 1816 (also in transcript); July 20, 1816–Nov. 28, 1835 (also in transcript); Jan. 1, 1836–Nov., 30, 1861; Mar. 6, 1821–Oct. 28, 1835;		NLI	Pos. 4249
21	Ferns	1819–1900	1840–1900	1840–1859	WGC	
		May 16, 1819–Feb. 14, 1840; Sept. 6, 1840– Dec. 24, 1880	May 14, 1819–Jan. 10, 1840; Nov. 2, 1840–Nov. 18, 1880		NLI	Pos. 4254
22	Glinn	Jan. 23, 1817–Feb 3, 1867; Feb. 7, 1867–Dec. 20, 1880	Jan. 26, 1817–Jan. 17, 1867; Feb. 5, 1867–Nov. 27, 1880	Jan. 6, 1823–Dec. 21, 1880 (ages given)	NLI	Pos. 4247
		1817–1900			WGC	
23	Gorey	May 26, 1845–Nov. 10, 1880	June 5, 1845–July 3, 1847; Aug. 4, 1847–May 2, 1880		NLI	Pos. 4256
24	Killanerin	Jan. 1, 1852–Oct. 31, 1880	Jan. 25, 1852–Oct. 14, 1880		NLI	Pos. 4255
25	Killaveny	1800–1835; 1875–1900	1800–1835; 1875–1900		WHC	
		Nov. 20, 1800–Dec. 20, 1836; Jan. 13, 1837–Apr. 29, 1875; Oct. 15, 1857– Apr. 10, 1864 (Anacorra)	Nov. 14, 1800–Sept. 10, 1836; Jan. 7, 1837–May 4, 1875; Aug. 5, 1860– Feb. 6, 1864 (Anacorra)	Oct. 19, 1862– Mar. 13, 1867 (Anacorra)	NLI	Pos. 4257
26	Kilmore	1768–1900	1768–1850	1768–1850	WGC	
		Apr. 6, 1752–Mar. 30, 1785; June 24, 1790–Nov. 3, 1794; Jan. 2, 1798– Mar. 12, 1826 (some pages missing); July 7, 1828–Sept. 29, 1854; Jan. 1,1850–Dec. 28, 1880	Apr. 6, 1752–Mar. 30, 1785; June 24, 1790– Nov. 3, 1794; Jan. 2, 1798–Mar. 12, 1826 (some pages missing) Nov. 4, 1827–Sept. 10, 1856; Jan. 26, 1850–Oct. 20, 1880	Apr. 6, 1752– Mar. 30, 1785; June 24, 1790– Nov. 3, 1794; Jan. 2, 1798– Mar. 12, 1826 (some pages missing)	NLI	Pos. 4246

Map	Church	Baptisms	WEXFORD Marriages	Burials	Location	Reference
27	Kilrush	May 29, 1841–Nov. 16, 1846; Mar. 6, 1855–Dec. 26, 1880			NLI	Pos. 4251
28	Lady's Island	1737–1900	1838–1900	1868–1900	WGC	
		Aug. 1737–May 24, 1740; May 16, 1752–Mar. 1763; Jan. 1766–Dec. 22, 1802; Jan. 18, 1807–Feb. 1, 1818; Apr. 26, 1838–Dec. 20, 1880	Feb. 17, 1753–Dec. 2, 1759; Feb. 16, 1754–May 1800 (1798/99 missing); Jan. 18, 1807 –Feb. 1, 1818;		NLI	Pos. 4244
29	Litter	Oct. 2, 1798–Sept. 8, 1816; Sept. 13, 1816–Dec. 18, 1853; Jan. 3, 1844–Dec. 11, 1880	Jan. 20, 1788–Apr. 14, 1798; Sept. 25, 1806–Oct. 3, 1880		NLI	Pos. 4255
		1818–1900	1876–1900		WGC	
30	Marshalstown	May 16, 1854–Dec. 22, 1880	Nov. 28, 1854–May 1, 1880	Oct. 10, 1854–Nov. 18, 1856; Feb. 15, 1860–Aug. 2, 1862; Oct. 28, 1876–Jan. 16, 1878	NLI	Pos. 4248
31	Monageer	Nov. 18, 1838–Dec. 13, 1880 (Monageer); May 12, 1842–Mar. 18, 1853; Oct. 26, 1869–Oct. 10, 1872; May 5, 1879–Dec. 13, 1880 (all Boolavogue)	Nov. 12, 1838 –Nov. 3, 1880 (Monageer); Jan. 16, 1847–Nov. 23, 1852; Oct. 7, 1869–Nov. 2, 1872; July 1879–Nov. 27, 1880 (all Boolavogue)	Aug. 1, 1838–Dec. 22, 1880 (ages given–Monageer); Oct. 25, 1847–Jan. 25, 1872 (Boolavogue)	NLI	Pos. 4248
32	Monamolin	Feb. 23, 1839–Sept. 24, 1856; Mar. 15, 1858–Oct. 13, 1880	Nov. 23, 1834–Apr. 1, 1856; Oct. 20, 1859–Aug. 13, 1880		NLI	Pos. 4255
33	New Ross	Nov. 22, 1789–Aug. 23, 1809; Aug. 27, 1809–Aug. 7, 1841; Aug. 1841–Apr. 6, 1870; Apr. 10, 1870–Dec. 12, 1880	Feb. 22, 1859–Nov. 30, 1880	May 14, 1794–July 22, 1809; Aug. 2, 1809–Nov. 17, 1814; Apr. 9, 1822–Feb. 15, 1859	NLI	Pos. 4259, 4260
		1789–1900	1817–1900		WGC	
34	Old Ross	Jan. 9 1759–Aug. 9, 1759; Jan. 27, 1778–Jan. 29, 1830; July 10, 1851–Mar. 8, 1863; Feb. 26, 1863–Dec. 19, 1880	Nov. 3, 1752–Feb. 27, 1759; Jan. 17, 1778–Feb. 29, 1824; Aug. 4, 1851 –Sept. 21, 1862; Apr. 15, 1863–Oct. 28, 1880	May 16. 1794–July 12, 1808 (ages given); May 1863–Dec. 27, 1880	NLI	Pos. 4259
35	Oylegate	Mar. 4, 1804–Dec. 3, 1820; Aug. 10, 1832–Nov. 30, 1853; Sept. 8, 1848–Dec. 23, 1880; Nov. 20, 1860–Dec. 24, 1880 (Glenbryan)	Apr. 18, 1803– Oct. 13, 1820; Oct. 14, 1832–Nov. 19, 1853; Sept. 28, 1848–Aug. 12, 1880; Nov. 18, 1860–Dec. 16, 1880 (Glenbryan)	Apr. 7, 1865–Dec. 6, 1870 (ages given); Oct. 27, 1860–Dec. 16, 1880 (Glenbrien–ages given)	NLI	Pos. 4254
		1804–1900	1803–1900	1865–1870	WGC	
36	Piercetown	Dec. 18, 1811–July 30, 1854; Jan. 18, 1839–July 28, 1854 (Murrintown); Aug. 8, 1854–Nov. 13, 1880	Jan. 10, 1812–July 26, 1854; Jan. 29, 1839–Nov. 27, 1852 (Murrintown); Aug. 12, 1854–Nov. 13, 1880		NLI	Pos. 4250
		1811–1900	1812 –1900		WGC	

→

Map	Church	Baptisms	Wexford Marriages	Burials	Location	Reference
37	Ramsgrange (St James and Hook)	Nov. 29, 1835–Aug. 10, 1840; Mar. 28, 1844–Sept. 17, 1873; Sept. 23, 1873–Dec. 29, 1880	Nov. 7, 1875–Nov. 29, 1880	Oct. 17, 1835–May 28, 1854 (ages given)	NLI	Pos. 4258
		1835–1873			WGC	
38	Rathangan	1803–1850; 1846–1854 (Cleariestown)	1805–1850; 1844–1854 (Cleariestown)		WGC	
		Jan. 27, 1803–Aug. 28, 1805; Jan. 19, 1813–Feb. 9, 1853; June 19, 1845–June 10, 1850; Mar. 30, 1844–Oct. 31, 1854; Apr. 2, 1853–Dec. 30, 1880	June 25, 1803–June 15, 1806; Jan. 7, 1813–Nov. 27, 1852; Nov. 26, 1846–July 29, 1854; Feb 15, 1854–Aug. 24, 1880		NLI	Pos. 4244
39	Rathnure and Templeudigan	Oct. 3, 1846–Jan. 25, 1853; Feb. 7, 1853–Jan. 23, 1878; June 17, 1877–Nov. 30, 1880; Mar. 18, 1878–Dec. 31, 1880	Oct. 17, 1846–Jan. 29, 1853; Feb. 7, 1853–Jan. 31, 1878; July 18, 1877–July 13, 1880; Mar. 4, 1878–Aug. 28, 1880	Oct. 18, 1846–Jan. 28, 1853 (ages given); Feb. 24, 1853–Feb. 9, 1878 (ages given); Feb. 18, 1878–Oct. 16, 1880 (ages given)	NLI	Pos. 4248
		1853–1878	1847–1853	1846–1853	WGC	
40	Suttons	Nov. 3, 1824–Nov. 7, 1879; Feb. 19, 1862–Dec. 15, 1880 (Ballykelly)	Feb. 12, 1825–Sept. 26, 1879; Feb. 22, 1862–Nov. 27, 1880 (Ballykelly)	May 17, 1827–Nov. 26, 1836; Jan. 13, 1858–Dec. 19, 1880	NLI	Pos. 4261
		1826–1900	1825–1894		WGC	
41	Taghmon	May 26, 1801–July 8, 1832; July 11, 1832–Dec. 21, 1865; Mar. 3, 1866–Dec. 19, 1880	May 29, 1801–Mar. 7, 1835; Apr. 6, 1866–Nov. 27, 1880	Jan. 3, 1828–Dec. 3, 1846 (ages given); Feb. 20, 1866–Dec. 23, 1880 (ages given)	NLI	Pos. 4247
		1801–1900			WGC	
42	Tagoat	1853–1881	1853–1881	1853–1881	WGC	
		Jan. 16, 1853–Dec. 8, 1875; Nov. 16, 1875–Dec. 30, 1880	Feb. 8, 1853–Nov. 27, 1875; Oct. 31, 1875–Nov. 21, 1880	Oct. 16, 1875–Aug. 3, 1880	NLI	Pos. 4245
43	St James and Templetown	1792–1900	1792–1900		WGC	
		Dec. 23, 1792–Oct. 27, 1793; Jan. 7, 1795–Nov. 8, 1798; Apr. 6, 1805–Mar. 28, 1815; Jan. 5, 1812–Dec. 22, 1815; Jan. 1816–Oct. 13, 1880; Mar. 6, 1870–Dec. 23, 1880	Nov. 18, 1792–June 11, 1815; Jan. 8, 1812–Nov. 26, 1842; Jan. 18, 1843–Nov. 30, 1860; Sept. 17, 1870–Nov. 24, 1880; Feb. 9, 1861–Nov. 1880; June 18, 1843–Nov. 3, 1880 (transcript)	Jan. 2, 1816–Apr. 21, 1879	NLI	Pos. 4245
44	Tomacork	1847–1900	1847–1900		WHC	
		Jan. 1785–May 20, 1786; Feb. 8, 1791–Nov. 24, 1797; Jan. 5, 1807–May 6, 1836; Nov. 15, 1832–May 27, 1847; May 31, 1847–Dec. 28, 1880	June 18, 1793–Feb. 23, 1797; Jan. 19, 1807–Mar. 1845; June 2, 1847–Sept. 12, 1880	May 12, 1794–Dec. 30, 1797; May 1, 1847–Nov. 13, 1856; May 18, 1864–Jan. 11, 1871; Apr. 20, 1873–Dec. 24, 1880	NLI	Pos. 4256

→

MAP	CHURCH	BAPTISMS	WEXFORD MARRIAGES	BURIALS	LOCATION	REFERENCE
45	Wexford	1686–1900	1671–1900		WGC	
		May 1671–1685 (poorly legible); Dec. 13, 1686–Jan. 29, 1698; Jan. 13, 1694–Mar. 19, 1710; Feb. 19, 1723–Aug. 7, 1787; June 2, 1815–June 26, 1838; June 27, 1838–Aug. 25, 1851; Aug. 28, 1851–Feb. 15, 1869; Mar. 1, 1869–Dec. 31, 1880	May 1671–1685 (poorly legible); Apr. 4, 1724–Dec. 10, 1822; Jan. 9, 1823–Nov. 25, 1867; Nov. 26, 1867–Nov. 27, 1880		NLI	Pos. 4252 (baptisms to 1851); 4253 (baptisms to 1880); 4254 (marriages)
46	Borris	See Carlow 3				
47	Clonegal	See Carlow 5			NLI	
48	St Mullin's	See Carlow 12			NLI	

WICKLOW

DUBLIN DIOCESE
1 Arklow
2 Ashford
3 Avoca
4 Ballymore Eustace
5 Blessington
6 Boystown (Valleymount)
7 Bray
8 Dunlavin
9 Enniskerry
10 Glendalough
11 Kilbride & Barnderrig
12 Kilquade & Kilmurray
13 Rathdrum
14 Wicklow

FERNS DIOCESE
15 Kilaveny & Annacorra
16 Tomacork (Carnew)

KILDARE & LEIGHLIN
DIOCESE
17 Baltinglass
18 Clonmore
19 Clonegal
20 Hacketstown
21 Rathvilly

Map	Church	Baptisms	Marriages	Burials	Location	Reference
			WICKLOW			
1	Arklow	1809–1843	1813–1843		WHC	
		May 25, 1809–June 4, 1809; Dec. 21, 1817–Dec. 31, 1843; Jan. 2, 1844–Oct. 27, 1856; Jan. 1, 1857–Oct. 2, 1868; Oct. 4, 1868–Dec. 29, 1880	Jan. 7, 1818–Nov. 27, 1843; Jan. 7, 1844–Oct. 27, 1856; Jan. 12, 1857–Nov. 26, 1880		NLI	Pos. 6474/75
2	Ashford	Sept. 18, 1864–Dec. 31, 1880	Oct. 6, 1864–Nov. 5, 1880		NLI	Pos. 6477/8
		1864–1900	1864–1900		WHC	
3	Avoca	1778–1900	1778–1900		WHC	
		June 15, 1791–Feb. 26, 1805; May 27, 1809–Dec. 21, 1825; Oct. 3, 1825–June 5, 1836; June 2, 1836–Apr. 23, 1867; Mar. 5, 1843–Apr. 18, 1867; Apr. 21, 1867–Dec. 25, 1880	June 15, 1791–Feb. 26, 1805; Oct. 23, 1778–Jan. 26, 1797; Nov. 6, 1812–Oct. 25, 1825; Oct. 10, 1825–Feb. 6, 1843; Apr. 22, 1844–Feb. 28, 1867; Apr. 15, 1844–Feb. 3, 1867; May 1, 1867–Nov. 2, 1880		NLI	Pos. 6476/77
4	Ballymore Eustace	Mar. 8, 1779–Apr. 27, 1792; Jan. 10, 1787–Mar. 1, 1790; May 3, 1792–Apr. 6, 1796; Jan. 5, 1797–Oct. 28, 1830; Apr. 23, 1826–Dec. 26, 1838; Jan. 1, 1839–Apr. 27, 1854; May 7, 1854–Dec. 31, 1880	Oct. 18, 1779–Nov. 27, 1794; Feb. 21, 1787–June 11, 1796; May 15, 1797 –July 19, 1830; Apr. 22, 1826–Dec. 1, 1838; Jan. 27, 1839–Nov. 26, 1863; Jan. 25, 1864–Oct. 25, 1880		NLI	Pos. 6481
		1779–1900	1779–1900		WHC	
		1779–1899	1779–1899		KHGS	
5	Blessington	Apr. 4, 1852–Nov. 14, 1880; 1852–1880 (Church of Kilbride)	Feb. 22, 1852–Dec. 4, 1880; 1877–1880 (Church of Kilbride)		NLI	Pos. 6483, 6615
		1821–1900	1834–1900		WHC	
6	Boystown (Blackditches, Valleymount)	June 9, 1810–Aug. 1825; May 4, 1830–June 10, 1830; June 9, 1826–Apr. 25, 1830; Feb. 15, 1833–Mar. 4, 1844; Mar. 10, 1844–May 8, 1862; 1860–1880	June 18, 1810–Aug. 1825; Aug. 6, 1826–June 7, 1833; Feb, 2, 1833–Jan. 25, 1845; Apr. 8, 1844–May 8, 1862; 1862–1880		NLI	Pos. 6483, 6615
		1810–1825; 1833–1898	1810–1900		WHC	
7	Bray	1792–1900	1792–1900		WHC	
		No registers microfilmed			NLI	
7	Little Bray	1863–1891	1863–1891		WHC	
		No registers microfilmed			NLI	
7	Rathdown Union Workhouse	No registers microfilmed			NLI	
		1841–1900	1876–1894		DLRHS	
8	Dunlavin	Oct. 1, 1815–Sept. 29, 1839; Oct.13, 1839–Sept. 8, 1857; 1857–Dec 15, 1880 (ink badly faded)	Feb. 14, 1831–Oct. 19, 1839 (ink badly faded); Nov. 12, 1839–Nov. 20, 1857 (ink badly faded); Feb. 12, 1857–Nov. 22, 1880		NLI	Pos. 6484
		1815–1900	1815–1900		WHC	

→

Map	Church	Baptisms	WICKLOW Marriages	Burials	Location	Reference
9	Enniskerry	1825–1900	1825–1900		WHC	
		Oct. 7, 1825–Sept. 22, 1861; Sept. 11, 1859–Dec. 5, 1880	Nov. 1, 1825–Sept. 29, 1861; Mar. 6, 1859–Nov. 18, 1880		NLI	Pos. 6478
10	Glendalough	June 20, 1807–Jan. 18, 1838; Aug. 24, 1839–May 1, 1866; Apr. 17, 1857–Dec. 24, 1880	Jan. 6, 1808–June 27, 1838; May 14, 1840–July 24, 1866; May 2, 1857–Oct. 6, 1880		NLI	Pos. 6474
		1807–1837; 1840–1881	1807–1837; 1840–1881		WHC	
10	Roundwood	No registers microfilmed 1857–1900	1881–1900		NLI WHC	
11	KIlbride	Jan. 1858–1880 1821–1835; 1858–1900	Feb. 1858–1880 1821–1827; 1858–1900		NLI WHC	Pos. 6615
12	Kilquade	1826–1900	1826–1900		WHC	
		Aug. 23, 1826–June 29, 1855; Dec. 17, 1861–Feb. 7, 1863	Aug. 12, 1826–Sept. 29, 1862; Nov. 4, 1862–Nov. 8, 1880		NLI	Pos. 6478
13	Rathdrum	Jan. 6, 1795–Jan. 29, 1799; Oct. 1, 1816–July 29, 1835; Aug. 2, 1835–Oct. 3, 1854; Sept. 27, 1854–June 12, 1875; June 12, 1875–Dec. 21, 1880	Nov. 7, 1816–Aug. 5, 1835; Aug. 3, 1835–Sept. 22, 1854; Nov. 14, 1854–Nov. 3, 1880		NLI	Pos. 6476
		1795–1797; 1816–1900	1810–1854		WHC	
14	Wicklow	1747–1791; 1829–1900	1747–1900		WHC	
		Jan. 7, 1747/8–Oct. 9, 1754; Sept. 9, 1753–Dec. 9, 1775; Sept. 27, 1761–Dec. 29, 1762; Jan. 1776–June 9, 1781; 1784/5 (4 entries only); May 15, 1796–Dec. 29, 1830; Nov. 29, 1829–Dec. 28, 1862; Oct. 17, 1861–June 7, 1874; July 29, 1874–Dec. 19, 1880	Jan. 7, 1747/8–Sept. 1, 1754; Jan. 19, 1753–Nov. 25, 1761; Dec. 19, 1761–May 13, 1777; Jan. 11, 1762–Feb. 22, 1778; Jan. 22, 1779–Oct. 2, 1780; Nov. 20, 1795–Feb. 15, 1874; June 23, 1874–Nov. 27, 1880		NLI	Pos. 6482
15	Killaveny	See Wexford 25				
16	Tomacork	See Wexford 44				
17	Baltinglass	May 31, 1807–Feb. 18, 1810; July 8, 1810–Apr. 4, 1811; Oct. 4, 1813 –Jan. 19, 1830; Mar. 7, 1830–July 12, 1857; May 12, 1857–Nov. 5, 1865; Nov. 12, 1865–Dec. 19, 1880	Feb. 2, 1810–Apr. 16, 1811; Nov. 20, 1813–Sept. 12, 1815; Apr. (?) 25, 1816–Apr. 25, 1831; Jan. 28, 1830–May 19, 1857; July 23, 1857–Feb. 12, 1866; May 3, 1866–Dec. 18, 1880	Aug. 12, 1824–Sept. 11, 1830	NLI	Pos. 4192
		See NLI			LDS	BFA 0926104 item 2
19	Clonegal	See Carlow 5				
18	Clonmore	See Carlow 6				
20	Hacketstown	See Carlow 8				
21	Rathvilly	See Carlow 11				

14. RESEARCH SERVICES, SOCIETIES AND REPOSITORIES

1. RESEARCH SERVICES

A. PROFESSIONAL ASSOCIATIONS

Two associations of professional researchers exist, the Association of Ulster Genealogists and Record Agents (AUGRA), based exclusively in Northern Ireland, and the Association of Professional Genealogists in Ireland (APGI), with members north and south. Both bodies are principally concerned with upholding research standards, rather than undertaking commercial research in their own right. The secretaries of both associations will supply a list of members on request:

The Secretary, AUGRA, Glen Cottage, Glenmachan Road, Belfast BT4 2NP, Northern Ireland.
The Secretary, APGI, c/o The Genealogical Office, 2 Kildare St, Dublin 2.

B. RESEARCH AGENCIES

The following are research agencies whose staff are members of the two professional associations:

Gorry Research, 12 Burrow Road, Sutton, Dublin 13. Tel. (01) 839 3942
Hibernian Research Co. Ltd, PO Box 3097, Dublin 6. Tel. (01) 4966 522 (24 hours); Fax 497 3011 (24 hours)
Research Ireland, Blue Rock, Killough, Kilmacanogue, Co. Wicklow. Tel. (01) 286 9645
Eireann Research, 96 Fisherman's Wharf, Dublin 4. Tel. (01) 668 8074

C. THE IRISH GENEALOGICAL PROJECT

In the early 1980s, as part of a series of government-sponsored youth employment and training schemes in the Republic of Ireland, local history and heritage societies and other interested bodies began to organise the indexing of local parish records. With some exceptions, at the outset little thought was given to the potential value of these records. In the mid-1980s, as the number of areas covered by the indexing projects grew, their efforts were co-ordinated by an umbrella body, the Irish Family History Council, later to become the Irish Family History Foundation. An ambitious plan was drawn up under the aegis of this body to transcribe and computerise not only all of the parish records of all denominations for the entire country, but also all other sources of major genealogical interest: the Tithe Books, Griffith's Valuation, the civil records of births, marriages and deaths, the 1901 and 1911 census returns, and local gravestone inscriptions. Expanded government funding was secured for this plan, known as the Irish Genealogical Project, and in 1990, with the adherence of four centres in Northern Ireland, the International Fund for Ireland also became involved.

The overall aim of the project was to realise the tourist potential of Irish genealogy by creating a single organisation which could combine the experience and expertise of professional genealogists with the speed and accuracy of the local databases to provide a comprehensive, affordable, Ireland-wide research service. Unfortunately, this aim is unlikely to be achieved in the foreseeable future. The very strengths which made the local centres possible — their voluntary ethos, diversity of funding and structure, and solid local roots — have made it virtually impossible to co-ordinate their activities into a single service.

This much said, the local centres continue to index and to provide research services, and some of these services are excellent. None of the centres allows direct access to its records — all research is carried out by the centre, for a fee. The list below also includes some centres which have not been directly involved in the IGP.

AREA	ADDRESS	COMMENT
Antrim/ Down / Belfast	Ulster Historical Foundation 12 College Square East Belfast BT1 6DD Northern Ireland Tel: (01232) 332288 Fax: (01232) 239885 email: enquiry@uhf.org.uk	Full commissioned research service. The UHF is a long-established, highly reputable research and publishing agency.
Armagh	Armagh Ancestry 42 English Street Armagh BT60 7BA Tel: (01861) 521802 Fax: (01861) 528329 email: ancestry@acdcnet.btinternet.com	Full commissioned research service, originally part of the archives of the Catholic Archdiocese of Armagh.
Carlow	Carlow Genealogy Project Old School College Street Carlow Tel: (0503) 30850	Partial commissioned research service. Not all church records are indexed as yet.
Cavan	Cavan Heritage and Genealogy Centre Cana House Main Street Cavan Co. Cavan Tel: (049) 61094 Fax: (049) 31384	Full commissioned research service. Extensive collection of indexed and comput-erised records.

AREA	ADDRESS	COMMENT
Clare	Clare Genealogy Centre Corofin Co. Clare Tel: (065) 37955	Full commissioned research service. One of the longest-established centres, this has completed indexing of all church records for the county, as well as virtually all the other major sources.
Cork city	Cork City Ancestral Project c/o Cork County Library Farranlea Road Cork Tel: (021) 46499 Fax: (021) 343254	Partial research service. Only some of the records for Cork city have been covered.
Cork North	Mallow Heritage Centre 27–28 Bank Place Mallow Co. Cork Tel: (022) 21778	Partial commissioned research service. Indexes for the Catholic records of North Cork and a substantial proportion of the Church of Ireland records. At the moment (1998) a centre to cover Cork South and West has yet to be designated
Derry	The Genealogy Centre 4–22 Burcher St Derry BT48 6HL Tel: (01504) 373177 Fax: (01504) 374818	Full commissioned research service. The centre, long established, has indexed virtually all the records for its area, which includes Inishowen in Donegal.
Donegal	Donegal Ancestry Heritage Centre Back Lane Ramelton Co. Donegal Tel: (074) 51266 email: donances@indigo.ie	Partial commissioned research service. Not all Catholic records are covered, though there is a substantial collection of non-Catholic records.
Down	See Antrim	
Dublin city	Dublin Heritage Group 2nd Floor, Cumberland House Fenian Street Dublin 2 Tel: (01) 459 1048 Fax: (01) 676 1628	Partial commissioned research service. The group has indexed church records for West Dublin, as well as some of the Dublin city records

AREA	ADDRESS	COMMENT
Dublin North	Fingal Heritage Project The Carnegie Library North Street Swords Co. Dublin Tel: (01) 840 3629	Partial commissioned research service. Virtually all church records for north Co. Dublin, including some of the north city records.
Dublin South	Dún Laoghaire Rathdown Heritage Society Moran Park House Dún Laoghaire Co. Dublin Tel: (01) 205 4700 ext. 4026 Fax: (01) 280 6969	Partial commissioned research service. A substantial proportion of the records for south Dublin.
Fermanagh/ Tyrone	Heritage World The Heritage Centre 26 Market Sq. Dungannon Co. Tyrone BT70 1AB Tel: 08–01868–724187 Fax: (01868) 752141	Full commissioned research service. A large collection of mainly non-church records.
Galway East	East Galway Family History Society Ltd Woodford Heritage Centre Main Street Woodford Co. Galway Tel: (0509) 49309 Fax: (0509) 49309 email: eastgalwayfhs@tinet.ie	Partial commissioned research service. A large proportion of the records of east Galway.
Galway West	Galway Family History Society West Ltd Unit 3, Venture Centre Liosbaun Estate Tuam Road Galway Tel: (091) 756737 (091)753590	Full commissioned research service. All church records and a large proportion of remaining records for the area.
Kerry	Killarney Genealogical Centre Cathedral Walk Killarney Co. Kerry (064) 35946	Partial commissioned research service. A large proportion of the Catholic records for the area.

AREA	ADDRESS	COMMENT
Kildare	Kildare Heritage & Genealogical Society Co. Ltd c/o Kildare County Library Newbridge Co. Kildare Tel: (045) 433602 Fax: (045) 436463 email: capinfo@iol.ie; http://www.iol.ie/ ~ infocap/khp.htm	Partial commissioned research service. Most of the church records for the county.
Kilkenny	Kilkenny Archaeological Society Rothe House Kilkenny Tel: (056) 22893 Fax: (056) 22893	Full commissioned research service. Not all church records are indexed.
Killarney	Killarney Genealogical Centre Bishop's House Killarney Co. Kerry Tel: (064) 35946	Full commissioned research service.
Laois/ Offaly	Irish Midlands Ancestry Bury Quay Tullamore Co. Offaly Tel: (0506) 21421 Fax: (0506) 21421 email: ohas@iol.ie	Full commissioned research service. Almost all church records, as well as a wide range of other sources.
Leitrim	Leitrim Heritage Centre c/o Leitrim County Library Ballinamore Co. Leitrim Tel: (078) 44012 Fax: (078) 44425	Full commissioned research service. Virtually all major records for the area.
Limerick	Limerick Archives The Granary Michael Street Limerick Tel: (061) 410777 Fax: (061) 415125	Full commissioned research service. All church records, and a wide range of other sources.
Longford	Longford Genealogical Centre 1 Church Street Longford Tel: (043) 41235 email: longroot@iol.ie	Partial commissioned research service. Not all church records completed.

AREA	ADDRESS	COMMENT
Mayo North	Mayo North Family History Research Centre Enniscoe Castlehill Ballina Co. Mayo Tel: (096) 31809 Fax: (096) 31885	Full commissioned research service. All church records, along with a wide range of other sources.
Mayo South	Mayo South Family Research Centre Town Hall Ballinrobe Co. Mayo Tel: (092) 41214 Fax: (092) 41214	Full commissioned research service. Virtually all major records for the area.
Meath	Meath Heritage Centre Trim Co. Meath Tel: (046) 36633	Partial commissioned research service. Almost all church records.
Monaghan	Monaghan Ancestral Research Monaghan County Council Cootehill Road Monaghan Tel: (047) 82304	Partial commissioned research service. Limited range of sources.
Offaly	See Laois	
Roscommon	Roscommon Heritage and Genealogy Centre Strokestown Co. Roscommon Tel: (078) 33380	Full commissioned research service. Almost all church records for the area.
Sligo	Áras Reddan, Temple Street Sligo Tel: (071) 43728	Full commissioned research service. Virtually all major sources for the area.
Tipperary	Tipperary Heritage Unit Family History Research Centre Marian Hall St Michael's Street Tipperary town Tel: (062) 52725 email: thu@iol.ie	Partial commissioned research service. Roman Catholic registers for Cashel and Emly diocese only.

AREA	ADDRESS	COMMENT
Tipperary North	Tipperary North Family History Foundation The Gate House Nenagh Co. Tipperary Tel: (067) 33850	Full commissioned research service. Catholic records for part of north Tipperary. A wide range of other sources.
Tipperary South	Brú Boru Heritage Centre Cashel Co. Tipperary Tel: (062) 61122 Fax: (062) 62700	Full commissioned research service. No church records. A wide range of other sources, including gravestone inscriptions and civil records.
Tyrone	See Fermanagh	
Waterford	Waterford Heritage Ltd Jenkin's Lane Waterford Tel: (051) 76123 Fax: (051) 50645 email: mnoc@iol.ie	Full commissioned research service. Almost all Catholic records for Waterford and Lismore diocese.
Westmeath	Dún na Sí Heritage Centre Moate Co. Westmeath Tel: (0902) 81183 (0902) 81661	Partial commissioned research service. A large proportion of church records for the area.
Wexford	Wexford Genealogy Centre Tagoat Community Development Tagoat Rosslare Co. Wexford Tel: (053) 31177 Fax: (053) 31177	Partial commissioned research service. Virtually all Catholic records for the area.
Wicklow	Wicklow Heritage Centre Court House Wicklow Tel:(0404) 67324	Full commissioned research service. Virtually all major sources for the area.

2. SOCIETIES

A. IRELAND

Ballinteer Family History Society, 29 The View, Woodpark, Ballinteer, Dundrum, Dublin 16. MEMBERS' FACILITIES ONLY

Cork Genealogical Society, 4 Evergreen Villas, Evergreen Road, Cork city. MEMBERS' FACILITIES ONLY

Dún Laoghaire Genealogical Society, 11 Desmond Avenue, Dun Laoghaire, Co. Dublin. MEMBERS' FACILITIES ONLY

Huguenot Society of Great Britain and Ireland, c/o Nora Fahie, 47 Ailesbury Road, Dublin 4.

Irish Family History Society, PO Box 36, Naas, Co. Kildare. Publishes *Irish Family History*

Irish Genealogical Research Society, 82 Eaton Square, London SW1W 9AJ. Publishes *The Irish Genealogist*

Irish Heritage Association, 162a Kingsway, Dunmurry, Belfast BT17 9AD. Publishes *Irish Family Links*

Kerry Genealogical Society, 119/120 Rock Street, Tralee, Co. Kerry.

North of Ireland Family History Society, c/o School of Education, Queen's University, 69 University Street, Belfast BT7 1HL. http://www.mni.co.uk/nifhs Publishes *North Irish Roots*

Raheny Heritage Society, 143 Howth Road, Dublin 13. MEMBERS' FACILITIES ONLY

Ulster Historical and Genealogical Guild, Ulster Historical Foundation, 12 College Square East, Belfast BT1 6DD, Northern Ireland. Publishes *Familia: Ulster Genealogical Review*

West Cork Heritage Centre, Bandon, Co. Cork.

Wexford Family History Society, 24 Parklands, Wexford. MEMBERS' FACILITIES ONLY

Wicklow County Genealogical Society, Summerhill, Wicklow Town, Co. Wicklow.

B. ABROAD

Family History Association of Canada, PO Box 91398, West Vancouver, BC V7V 3P1, Canada.

Federation of Family History Societies, 96 Beaumont Street, Mile House, Plymouth PL2 3AQ, England.

Irish Family Names Society, PO Box 2095, La Mesa, CA 92044, USA.

Irish Genealogical Society, PO Box 16585, St Paul MN 55116, USA. http://www.rootsweb.com/ ~ irish/ Publishes *Septs*

New Zealand Society of Genealogists, PO Box 8785, Auckland 3, New Zealand.

The Society of Australian Genealogists, Richmond Villa, 120 Kent St, Sydney, NSW 2000, Australia. Publishes *Descent*

3. REPOSITORIES

A. NORTHERN IRELAND

Area Libraries

North Eastern Education and Library Board, Library Service, Demesne Avenue, Ballymena BT43 7BG, Co. Antrim, Northern Ireland. Tel. (01266) 41531

Southern Education and Library Board, Library Service, 1 Markethill Road, Armagh BT60 1NR, Co. Armagh, Northern Ireland. Tel. (01861) 525353

Southeast Education and Library Board, Library Service, Windmill Hill, Ballynahinch BT24 8DH, Co. Down, Northern Ireland. Tel. (01238) 562639

Western Education and Library Board, Library Service, 1 Spillars Place, Omagh BT78 1HL, Co. Tyrone, Northern Ireland. Tel. (01662) 244821

Belfast Central Library, Royal Avenue, Belfast BT1 1EA. Tel. (0232) 243233 (Open 9.30 a.m.–8 p.m. Mon. & Thurs.; 9.30 a.m.–5.30 p.m. Tues., Wed., Fri.; 9.30 a.m.–1 p.m. Sat.)

Church of Jesus Christ of Latter-Day Saints Family History Centre, Hollywood Road, Belfast. Tel. (0232) 643998. (Open Wednesday evenings)

General Repositories

General Register Office, Oxford House, 49–55 Chichester St, Belfast BT1 4HL. Tel. (0232) 235211. Only the indexes are open for public research, and by appointment only.

Linen Hall Library, 17 Donegal Square North, Belfast BT1 5GD, Northern Ireland. Tel. (01232) 321707. (Open 9.30 a.m.–5.30 p.m. Mon.–Fri., 9.30 a.m.–4.00 p.m. Sat.)

Presbyterian Historical Society, Room 218, Church House, Fisherwick Place, Belfast BT1 6DW. Tel. (0232) 323936. (Open 10 a.m.–12.30 p.m. Mon.–Fri., 10 a.m.–12.30 p.m. and 2–4 p.m. Wed.)

Public Record Office of Northern Ireland, 66 Balmoral Avenue, Belfast BT9 6NY. Tel. (0232) 661621. (Open 9.15 a.m.–4.45 p.m. Mon.–Fri.)

Society of Friends Library, Meeting House, Railway Street, Lisburn, Co. Antrim. Postal queries only.

B. Republic of Ireland

County Libraries

Carlow: Dublin St, Carlow. Tel. (0503) 31126

Cavan: Farnham St, Cavan. Tel. (049) 31799

Clare: Mill Road, Ennis, Co. Clare. Tel. (065) 42461

Cork:
  (1) Farranlea Road, Cork. Tel. (021) 546499;
  (2) Cork City Library, Grand Parade, Cork. Tel. (021) 277110

Donegal: Oliver Plunkett Road, Letterkenny, Co. Donegal. Tel. (074) 21968

Dublin:
  (1) Gilbert Library, 138–142 Pearse St, Dublin 2. Tel. (01) 6777662;
  (2) Central Library, The ILAC Centre, Henry St, Dublin 1. Tel. (01) 8734333;
  (3) Dún Laoghaire-Rathdown Co. Library, 14 Carysfort Avenue, Blackrock, Co. Dublin. Tel. (01) 2781788;
  (4) Fingal County Library, 11 Parnell Square, Dublin 1. Tel. (01) 872777;
  (5) South Dublin County Library, Unit 1, Square Industrial Estate, Tallaght, Dublin 24. Tel. (01) 459 7834

Galway: Island House, Cathedral Square, Galway. Tel. (091) 562471

Kerry: Charles' Street, Listowel, Co. Kerry. Tel. (068) 23844

Kildare: Castledermot, Co. Kildare. Tel. (0504) 44483
Kilkenny: 6 John's Quay, Kilkenny. Tel. (056) 22021
Laois: County Hall, Portlaoise, Co. Laois. Tel. (0502) 22044
Leitrim: The Courthouse, Ballinamore, Co. Leitrim. Tel. (078) 44012
Limerick:
  (1) 58 O'Connell St, Limerick. Tel. (061) 318477;
  (2) Limerick Corporation Public Library, The Granary, Michael St, Limerick. Tel. (061) 314668
Longford: Annelly Car Park, Longford. Tel. (043) 41124
Louth: Roden Place, Dundalk, Co. Louth. Tel. (042) 35457
Mayo: Mountain View, Castlebar, Co. Mayo. Tel. (094) 24444
Meath: Railway St, Navan, Co. Meath. Tel. (046) 21134
Monaghan: The Diamond, Clones, Co. Monaghan. Tel. (047) 51143
Offaly: O'Connor Sq., Tullamore, Co, Offaly. Tel. (0506) 46800
Roscommon: Abbey St, Roscommon. Tel. (0903) 26100
Sligo: The Courthouse, Stephen St, Sligo. Tel. (071) 42212
Tipperary: Castle Avenue, Thurles, Co. Tipperary. Tel. (0504) 21556
Waterford: Lismore, Co. Waterford. Tel. (058) 54128
Westmeath: Dublin Road, Mullingar, Co. Westmeath. Tel. (044) 40781
Wexford: County Hall, Abbey St, Wexford. Tel. (053) 42211
Wicklow: Greystones, Co. Wicklow. Tel. (01) 287 3548

General Repositories

Church of Jesus Christ of Latter-Day Saints Family History Centre, The Willows, Finglas Road, Glasnevin, Dublin 11. Tel. (01) 830 6684. (Open evenings and Saturday morning)
Cork Archives Institute, Christ Church, South Main St, Cork. Tel. (021) 277809. (Open 10 a.m.–1 p.m., 2.30–5 p.m. Mon.–Fri.)
Dublin City Archives, South William Street, Dublin 2. Tel. (01) 475 9791
The Genealogical Office, 2 Kildare St, Dublin 2. Tel. (01) 661 8811. (Open 10 a.m.–4.30 p.m. Mon.–Fri.)
The General Register Office, Joyce House, 8–11 Lombard St E., Dublin 2. Tel. (01) 671 1000. (Open 9.30 a.m.–12.30 p.m., 2.15–4.30 p.m.)
Land Valuation Office, Irish Life Centre, Abbey Street, Dublin 1. Tel. (01) 676 3211. (Open 9.30 a.m.–12.30 p.m., 2–4.30 p.m. Mon.–Fri.)
National Archives, Bishop Street, Dublin 8. Tel. (01) 407 2300. http://147.252. 133.152/nat-arch/ (Open 10 a.m.–5 p.m. Mon.–Fri.)
National Library, Kildare St, Dublin 2. Tel. (01) 661 8811. (Open 10 a.m.–9 p.m. Mon.–Wed.; 10 a.m.–5 p.m. Thurs., Fri.; 10 a.m.–1 p.m. Sat.)
Registry of Deeds, Henrietta St, Dublin 1. Tel. (01) 670 7500. (Open 10 a.m.–4.30 p.m. Mon.–Fri.)
Society of Friends Library, Swanbrook House, Morehampton Road, Donnybrook, Dublin 4. Tel. (01) ?683684. (Open Thurs. 10.30 a.m.–1 p.m.)
Representative Church Body Library, Braemor Park, Rathgar, Dublin 14. Tel. (01) 497 8422. (Open 9 a.m.–1 p.m., 1.45–5 p.m. Mon.–Fri.)

4/00

GAYLORD S

ML